MANAGEMENT IN MARKETING CHANNELS

Louis W. Stern
John D. Gray Distinguished Professor of Marketing
Northwestern University

Adel I. El-Ansary
Professor and Chairman of Business Administration
The George Washington University

James R. Brown
Associate Professor of Marketing
Virginia Polytechnic Institute and State University

Prentice Hall, Englewood Cliffs, New Jersey 07632

Library of Congress Cataloging-in-Publication Data

Stern, Louis W., (date)
  Management in marketing channels.

  Includes index.
  1. Marketing channels—Management. I. Ansary,
Adel I. II. Brown, James R., (date). III. Title.
HF5415.129.S74 1988   658.8′4   87-32864
ISBN 0-13-547852-9

Editorial/production supervision and
  interior design: *Anne Kenney* and *Nancy Havas Farrell*
Cover design: *Marianne Frasco*
Manufacturing buyers: *Barbara Kittle* and *Margaret Rizzi*

 © 1989 by Prentice-Hall, Inc.
A Division of Simon & Schuster
Englewood Cliffs, New Jersey 07632

Printed in the United States of America

10 9 8 7 6 5 4 3 2

ISBN 0-13-547852-9

Prentice-Hall International (UK) Limited, *London*
Prentice-Hall of Australia Pty. Limited, *Sydney*
Prentice-Hall Canada Inc., *Toronto*
Prentice-Hall Hispanoamericana, S.A., *Mexico*
Prentice-Hall of India Private Limited, *New Delhi*
Prentice-Hall of Japan, Inc., *Tokyo*
Simon & Schuster Asia Pte. Ltd., *Singapore*
Editora Prentice-Hall do Brasil, Ltda., *Rio de Janeiro*

TO:
Rhona, Gladys, Beth, Debby, and Lisa
Nawal, Waleed, and Tarik
Donna, Corie, and Lacey

Contents

PART I: THE CONTEXT OF MARKETING CHANNELS

PREFACE   xi

1 MARKETING CHANNELS: AN OVERVIEW   1

Analyzing Marketing Channel Structures,   3
The Rationale for Marketing Channel Structures,   7
Composition of Marketing Channels,   12
Marketing Channels as a Network of Systems,   17
Channel Management and Competition,   19
Approach of the Text,   21
Organization of the Text,   22

2 UNDERSTANDING THE CHANNEL ENVIRONMENT   26

The Environment of Marketing Channels,   28
Demographic Environment,   29
Changing Consumer Resources,   34
Social and Cultural Environment,   35
Technological Environment,   38
Competitive Environment,   44
Legal and Political Environment,   52
Economic Environment,   55
Summary,   59

3 UNDERSTANDING CHANNEL PARTICIPANTS AND THEIR NEEDS: RETAILERS — 62

The Structure of Retailing, 63
Retail Marketing Strategy, 68
Customer Expectations, 70
Segmenting Retail Markets, 73
Retail Marketing Mix, 73
Summary, 93

4 UNDERSTANDING CHANNEL PARTICIPANTS AND THEIR NEEDS: WHOLESALERS — 96

Wholesaling Defined, 97
Rationale for the Emergence of Modern Wholesalers, 98
Types of Wholesalers, 99
The Structure of Wholesaling, 105
Selecting and Using Wholesalers, 108
The Strategic Management of Wholesaling Institutions, 120
Channel Management Issues in Using Wholesalers, 123
Summary, 124
Case Study: Gould, Inc.: Focus 800 Bat-tery, 125
Case Study: Quetzal Distributors, 127
Case Study: Mussleman Department Store, 129
Case Study: Carapace, Inc., 131

PART II: MARKETING CHANNEL MANAGEMENT AND THE MARKETING MIX

5 CHANNEL MANAGEMENT AND THE MARKETING MIX: PHYSICAL DISTRIBUTION AND PROMOTION STRATEGY — 140

Physical Distribution and Marketing Channel Management, 142
Promotion Strategy and Channel Management, 162
Summary, 173

6 CHANNEL MANAGEMENT AND THE MARKETING MIX: PRODUCT MANAGEMENT AND PRICING STRATEGY — 176

Product Strategy and Channel Management, 178
Pricing Strategy and Channel Management, 188
Marketing Channels and the Marketing Mix, 196
Summary, 198

7 MARKETING CHANNEL COMMUNICATION SYSTEMS 201

Elements of Marketing Channel Communication Systems, 203
Types and Sources of Communication Noise Within Marketing
Channels, 205
Methods for Overcoming Marketing Channel Communication
Noise, 209
Electronic Data Interchange Systems and Marketing Channels, 215
Summary, 220
Case Study: Universal Motors Parts Division, 221
Case Study: Scioto Company, 226
Case Study: Kelsey Manufacturing: Getting Middlemen to Promote the
Manufacturer's Products, 229
Case Study: Purex Industries, Inc., 232

PART III: ORGANIZING MARKETING CHANNEL ACTIVITIES

8 MARKETING CHANNEL STRUCTURE AND DESIGN 236

Understanding Customers' Needs for Channel Services, 238
Establishing Marketing Channel Objectives, 241
Setting Channel Strategy, 242
Selecting the Appropriate Channel Structure, 248
Choosing Specific Channel Partners, 261
Summary, 265

9 ADMINISTRATIVE PATTERNS IN MARKETING CHANNELS 269

Conventional Marketing Channels, 272
Administered Marketing Channel Systems, 274
Contractual Marketing Channel Systems, 277
Franchise Systems, 282
Corporate Vertical Marketing Systems, 293
Distinctive Advantages of Vertical Marketing Systems, 297
Legal Aspects of Vertical Marketing Systems, 299
Summary, 300
Case Study: Red Lion Knitwear Channel Design, 303
Case Study: Sta-Lube, Inc., 307
Case Study: Benson Ford, 316
Case Study: Westron Incorporated Administered Vertical Marketing
Systems, 318

Contents   vii

PART IV: COORDINATING AND CONTROLLING MARKETING CHANNEL ACTIVITIES

10 USING MARKETING CHANNEL POWER TO LEAD THE CHANNEL   320

Coordinating the Flows Within Marketing Channels, 323
Determining the Required Level of Marketing Channel
Services, 324
Identify the Necessary Tasks in the Marketing Channel, 324
Using Influence and Leadership Strategies to Specify Channel
Roles, 328
Who Should Lead the Marketing Channel?, 342
Channel Management by Wholesalers, 344
Channel Management by Retailers, 246
Channel Management by Physical Distribution Agencies, 349
So, Who Should Lead the Marketing Channel?, 351
Summary, 351

11 USING MARKETING CHANNEL POWER TO MANAGE CONFLICT   356

The Nature of Conflict in Marketing Channels, 358
The Causes of Marketing Channel Conflict, 361
The Consequences of Conflict in the Marketing Channel, 364
Effective Management of Conflict Within Marketing Channels, 369
Summary, 381

12 EVALUATING MARKETING CHANNEL EFFECTIVENESS   383

Channel System Effectiveness, 385
Channel System Equity, 388
Channel System Productivity, 391
Channel System Profitability, 401
Other Measures of Marketing Channel Performance, 415
Auditing Marketing Channel Performance, 416
Summary, 417
Case Study: Ace Brokerage Company, 422
Case Study: The Touch of Nature Company, 427
Case Study: Laramie Oil Company: Retail Gasoline Division, 428
Case Study: Bob Clayton's Sports Centers, 437
Case Study: Exxon Company, U.S.A.: ''Swing Store Program'', 443

PART V: MARKETING CHANNELS IN OTHER CONTEXTS

13 MARKETING CHANNEL MANAGEMENT IN OTHER CONTEXTS   453

International Marketing Channels,   454
Marketing Channels for Services,   473
Marketing Channels for Previously Used Materials and Products,   488
Summary,   497
Case Study: Levi Strauss: Developing a New Market in Japan,   500

INDEX   504

Preface

Channel members can achieve high yield performance primarily by ensuring that their activities are consistent with the needs and wants of their target markets. What is necessary to reach that consistency at one level of the marketing channel implies performance requirements and expectations at other levels. Retailers, for example, often measure a key aspect of their performance—productivity—as sales per square foot, sales per employee, and sales per transaction. To enable a retailer to achieve a high level of sales per square foot, manufacturers may have to incur heavy advertising expenditures, and wholesalers might be required to maintain high inventory levels. These large promotion and storage burdens may, in turn, reduce the return on investment available to manufacturers and wholesalers. Balancing the various performance requirements, policies, and practices at different levels of marketing channels dictates the need for systemwide communication and coordination.

As its title suggests, *Management in Marketing Channels* looks at the structure and behavior of marketing channels from a *managerial* frame of reference. Emphasis is on *planning* marketing channel activities, *organizing* institutions and agencies involved in the process of making products and services available to business and household consumers, *coordinating* the marketing efforts of those institutions and agencies, *evaluating* the performance of those organizations, and *controlling* marketing channel efforts. The end result of effective marketing channel management is to assure that all products and services which consumers need and want possess adequate levels of time, place, and possession utilities. Therefore, the focus of the text is on channel *performance*.

Part I of this text lays out the context of marketing channels. It explores the theories that describe why channels have emerged and introduces such concepts as marketing channel service levels and marketing flows. We rely heavily upon these concepts throughout the book. In addition, Part I discusses how the environment facing marketing channels affects both the demand for and supply of marketing channel services. The environment also impacts how institutions within the channels interact with each other. The structure and management of marketing channel intermediaries—retailers and wholesalers—are also addressed in Part I. We have not devoted a separate chapter to manufacturers because we assume that most readers have some knowledge of how manufacturers market their products, especially via previous course work or readings in marketing management.

Achieving effective performance within marketing channels requires skillful execution of an overall marketing strategy. Coordination among channel members is a must if this is to be achieved. Thus, Part II discusses the key elements of the marketing mix—physical distribution management, promotional strategy, product management, and pricing strategy—in terms of their interconnection with marketing channels management. Coordination within the channel is achieved through effective communication among marketing channel institutions. This topic, including a discussion of the communication process, communication noise, and electronic data interchange systems, are also discussed in Part II.

Parts III and IV comprise the "core" of the text. Organizing marketing channel activities is the subject of Part III. The two key elements of channel organization are channel structure and channel administration. A five-step procedure for developing marketing channel structures is described as is the theoretical basis of this procedure. Along with a description of the four key patterns for administering marketing channels—conventional, administered, contractual, and corporate channels—are some guidelines for choosing among them. Part IV deals with coordinating and controlling marketing channel activities. The use of power and dependence relations to coordinate marketing channel activities and to manage conflict among channel institutions is discussed. Determining which channel institution—manufacturers, wholesalers, retailers, or physical distribution agencies—should lead the channel is also explored. The nature of channel conflict, an inherent aspect of marketing channel arrangements, and techniques for managing it are presented. Evaluating the performance of marketing channels is explored along the four dimensions of equity, effectiveness, productivity, and profitability.

Part V of the text deals with marketing channels in other contexts (i.e., in the international arena, in service industries, and in the disposition of previously used materials and products). Exploring marketing channels in other countries enriches the analysis. It underscores the generalizability of channel management processes while recognizing the importance of cultural factors in specific applications. Although there are important subtleties in the marketing of services, the channel management processes discussed in the text are also applicable to the study of marketing channels for services. A final marketing channels context is the disposition of previously used materials and products. Recycling such materials as used bottles, cans, and paper is a significant social problem. The general marketing channels management processes discussed earlier in the text suggest potential solutions to that problem. Because they are not well-organized, we rarely think of marketing channels for used products. As concern about the earth's scarce resources grows, however, these extended channels will become prominent in our thinking. And once again, the channels management processes discussed earlier will help uncover solutions to the problem of how to squeeze longer economic lives from previously used products.

Because case analysis is frequently used as a pedagogical tool in courses dealing with marketing channels, we have included eighteen cases in the text. To meet different instructional needs, these cases are of different lengths; seven are short (1–2 pages), six are of medium-length (3–5 pages), and five are longer (8–10 pages). The objective of these cases is three-fold. First, they illustrate the concepts of marketing channels management discussed in the text. Second, they offer readers the opportunity to sharpen their analytical skills by making recommendations based upon the principles presented in the book. Finally, cases provide a good context for practicing effective communication skills—oral, written, or both.

The first edition of *Marketing Channels,* written by the first two authors of this text, was published in 1977. While the response to that text, now in its 3rd edition, continues to be extremely positive in terms of the breadth and depth of its coverage, the authors were approached (on more than one occasion) by a variety of individuals with requests to write a more down-to-earth text incorporating the same basic orientation. The new text, it was argued, might be more suitable for undergraduates and perhaps even for some executive education courses while the original text could continue to service advanced undergraduate and graduate level courses. In other words, we needed to re-write the original text from cover to cover to position it for a different market.

Management in Marketing Channels is our answer to these requests. To direct and fashion this important venture, we enlisted the help of a talented "brand manager" who had a wealth of experience teaching undergraduate channels courses and who, at the same time, was an accomplished and recognized marketing channels scholar. Professor James R. Brown was the ideal choice, as will be evidenced by anyone who reads this text and compares it with the original. He has kept the basic "guts" of the framework introduced in the original while generating a new and exciting version—one that is directly suited to its purpose. Jim Brown has done an outstanding job. We are very hopeful that the readers of this text will agree with us that *Management in Marketing Channels* should serve a significant role in marketing education. The first two authors are extremely grateful to Jim Brown for what he has been able to accomplish and are proud to have this text stand alongside the original.

ACKNOWLEDGMENTS

A variety of people have contributed, either directly or indirectly, to the third author's efforts in this book. He would like to thank his students who read early drafts of the manuscript and provided meaningful feedback used to refine the text. His appreciation also goes to Jean Stilwell and Jean Johnson for their editorial help as well as to Karen Griffin, Liesa McGill, and Ratna Prasad for their typing assistance and to Michelle Jacobs for her clerical support. Ralph L. Day, Edward F. Fern, Gary L. Frazier, Charles A. Ingene, Robert F. Lusch, Brian T. Ratchford, and Sherman A. Timmins deserve special thanks as their collaborative efforts in research have been instrumental in shaping his thinking about the field of marketing channels. Finally, words cannot adequately express his gratefulness for the love and patience of his two young daughters Corie and Lacey and his wife Donna.

Finally, all three authors owe a great deal of thanks to our editors at Prentice Hall. Although this project was the brainchild of Elizabeth Classon, Whitney Blake saw it through to its actual completion. Of course, we cannot forget their assistant, Gloria Schaffer, upon whom we relied more than once for advice, encouragement, and support. We also acknowledge the reviewers—John S. Berens (Indiana State University), Ernest R. Cadotte (University of Tennessee), David W. Glascoff (East Carolina University), Robert F. Lusch (University of Oklahoma), and Michael H. Morris (University of Central Florida)—whose helpful comments improved upon the original manuscript. We are especially indebted to the large number of authors whose work we cite throughout the text. Without their efforts, we could not have written this book.

L.W.S., A.I.E., and J.R.B.

1

Marketing Channels:
An Overview

LEARNING OBJECTIVES

Upon completing this chapter, you will be able to:

- *Explain that marketing channels have emerged because they reduce the number of times that goods change hands, reduce the basic differences that exist between how goods are produced and how they are consumed, make buying and selling easier, and reduce the amount of effort required to search for goods and services.*

- *Describe the basic composition of marketing channel structure.*

- *List the functions performed within every marketing channel.*

- *Recognize that consumers and industrial and organizational users perform some of the functions required in every marketing channel.*

- *See that the organizations that make up marketing channels act as interorganizational systems.*

- *Develop an appreciation of the marketing channel, rather than the firm, as a unit of competition.*

Example

One bright spring morning, Pamela Huntington walked into Reliable TV & Appliance looking for a new television set. Her Zenith was 12 years old and on the verge of conking out. The sales clerk gave Pamela a complete rundown on the features of the models that she was most interested in among the nearby 100 on display. Moreover, the clerk was able to answer Pamela's questions about brands not carried by the store.

The clerk made several points that impressed Pamela about why she ought to buy at Reliable. First, Reliable TV & Appliances had its own factory-authorized service staff in case Pamela should need it after the factory warranty expired. In addition, Reliable provided free loaner television sets while its customers' TVs were being repaired. The store also had a 90-day same-as-cash credit policy and a generous trade-in allowance for old TV sets.

Pamela decided on a brand-new 21-inch Sony color TV. Since the exact model she wanted was not in stock, it had to be ordered from the wholesaler. Furthermore, because she wanted to take advantage of Reliable's free delivery and installation service, Pamela had to wait three days for her new TV to arrive at home.

That same day Charlotte Jones went directly to the electronics section of her town's Target store. Like Pamela Huntington, Charlotte was looking for a new TV. And after doing some preliminary checking, she knew that Target had the best prices in town on the models she was interested in. Among the ten or so models displayed, Charlotte found a couple that she liked; Target even carried one of the models *Consumer Reports* had listed as a "good value."

After comparing the models she really liked, Charlotte decided on a General Electric and found a clerk to go to the stockroom to get it. Unfortunately, that Target store had no more of that model in stock and the clerk did not know when a new shipment would arrive. However, the clerk did offer to find the shipping carton for the floor model if Charlotte wanted to buy it. Charlotte was disappointed, but really needed a new TV as soon as possible. She rejected the idea of buying a floor model and finally decided on her second favorite model, a slightly smaller GE. After paying for her TV with a VISA debit card, Charlotte rushed home, uncrated her new purchase, and, after much difficulty in setting it up, tuned in *The Phil Donahue Show*. During a commercial break, she wondered if she could unload her old TV at the neighborhood's annual garage sale. She also wondered how difficult it would be to send her new set to the nearest GE repair service center, 75 miles away, in case it needed warranty service.

Of the two shoppers, Charlotte Jones paid the lower price for her TV. But who got the better deal? Did Pamela buy the same "product" that Charlotte did?

The answer to the second question is an emphatic *no*! The reason is that the two marketing channel systems patronized by these women provided different levels of service. For example, Charlotte had to rely on advertising, word of mouth, and *Consumer Reports* for information about the relative merits of different brands of televisions. Pamela, on the other hand, received product information from the store clerk. Through the float on her VISA debit card, Charlotte was able to finance her purchase for only a day or so; Pamela took advantage of Reliable's 90-day credit plan. The two stores also differed in delivery and installation services, repair services, and assortment of models. In addition, a short wait enabled Pamela to get exactly the TV she wanted. Thus, Charlotte paid a lower price but she received fewer services than Pamela did. Who, then, got the better deal? The answer to that question depends on a host of factors, including what "product" each woman intended to buy, what she expected that "product" to do, and what services she expected from the store.

The issues raised in this illustration are the stuff of marketing channels. What services make up the "total product"? How willing or able are consumers to perform some of these services themselves? What marketing institutions—manufacturers, wholesalers, retailers, banks, market research firms, advertising agencies, transportation companies, or warehousing concerns—should participate in the delivery of these services? How can these institutions be coordinated so that the "total products" are marketed at the least possible cost? These are just a few of the issues that will be addressed in this textbook.

This and the next three chapters provide the context within which marketing channels are constructed. Any attempt to manage a channel without at least a rudimentary understanding of this context would undoubtedly prove disastrous.

ANALYZING MARKETING CHANNEL STRUCTURES

An example might best illustrate what we mean by "channel structure." To reach its desired customers, IBM has chosen several different routes through which it markets its personal computers. A number of these routes are shown in Figure 1-1. Some of these distribution channels are company owned, while others are composed of independent dealers and distributors. Not all of these channels market to the same customer groups. For example, the direct sales force concentrates on medium and large business accounts, while IBM Direct specializes in small business and professional customers. Furthermore, many of these intermediaries, such as computer specialty stores like ComputerLand, carry other brands besides IBM.

Why would IBM, and other personal computer makers, choose these types of marketing channels? What roles do intermediaries in these and channels for

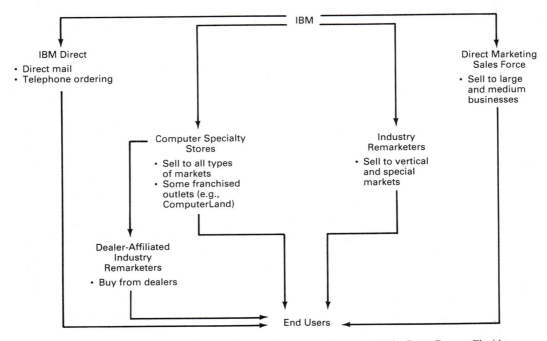

Figure 1-1 IBM manufactures its popular personal computers in Boca Raton, Florida. Finished products are shipped to one of several warehouses across the country, each servicing different distribution channels. For example, one warehouse stocks personal computers destined solely to independent dealers while another carries PC's distributed by the IBM-owned marketing channels. Major distributors, such as ComputerLand and Sears, receive their personal computer stocks directly from the Boca Raton factories.

The IBM-owned distributive mechanisms include the Direct Marketing Sales Force which reaches large- and medium sized corporate accounts as well as IBM Direct. IBM Direct enables small businesses and professionals to purchase computer hardware and software through the convenience of telephone and mail ordering.

Industry Remarketers are independent dealers which buy IBM PC's, add additional software and/or hardware to them, and resell them to specific markets, such as data processing companies, insurance companies, accounting firms, and oil companies. Computer Specialty Stores, either independently owned or operated by a vertical marketer, such as ComputerLand, Sears, or Valcom, are a major channel for IBM's personal computer products. Small volume industry remarketers are not profitable for IBM to service directly, so they buy their products from dealers. Appropriately enough, these are called Dealer-affiliated Industry Remarketers. *Source*: International Business Machines Corporation, January, 1988.

other products and services perform? Why don't marketers try to reach all markets through their own sales forces? Why is it important that the activities of the marketing institutions making up the channel be coordinated? Why do multiple channels such as those used by IBM pose problems from a management viewpoint? These are the kinds of questions that are addressed in this chapter.

Consumers are aware that literally thousands of goods and services are available through a very large number of diverse retail outlets. What they may not know is that the *channel structure*, or the set of institutions, agencies, and establishments through which the product must move to get to them, can be amazingly complex. To illustrate, the marketing channel structure for Clairol, Inc., a major marketer of personal-care items, is shown in Figure 1-2. Clairol's channel structure is fairly typical of its industry. It includes Clairol's own *internal marketing organization* (e.g., district sales managers) and independent *external organizations*, (e.g., distributors and retailers). Some of the members of the channel are large organizations, such as chain retail stores and wholesale distributors who carry a number of rival brands; others are small one or two-person operations.[1] To a large extent, Clairol's marketing success depends on how well it can coordinate the activities within its marketing channel structure. This structure includes Clairol's own internal and independent external marketing organizations.

Usually, combinations of manufacturers, wholesalers, retailers, and other institutions join forces in marketing channel arrangements to deliver goods to industrial users or customers and to final consumers. The same is true for the marketing of services. For example, hospitals, ambulance services, physicians, laboratories, insurance companies, and drugstores form an organized channel arrangement to ensure the delivery of critical health-care services. All these institutions depend on one another to cater effectively to consumer demand. Therefore, marketing channels can be viewed as *sets of interdependent organizations involved in the process of making a product or service available for use or consumption*. Not only do marketing channels *satisfy demand* by supplying goods and services at the right place, quantity, quality, and price, but they also *stimulate demand* through the promotional activities of the units (e.g., retailers, manufacturers' representatives, sales offices, wholesalers) composing them. Therefore, the channel should be viewed as an orchestrated network that produces value for the user or consumer by creating form, possession, time, and place utilities.[2]

To grasp this concept, consider how economic utilities are added to the Cheerios many people eat for breakfast. First of all, General Mills produces this cereal and ships it, via food wholesalers, to the local supermarket in larger quantities than any one family could possibly eat. The supermarket opens up the cases in which it receives the Cheerios and puts the individual packages on the proper shelf. Thus, the marketing channel enables consumers to get their Cheerios in the quantity (e.g., a simple 24-ounce package) or *form* they desire. Because Cheerios are distributed through many different retail outlets, some of which are open twenty-four hours a day, consumers can purchase this cereal *when* they want to and from *places* convenient to them. Because some stores selling Cheerios permit purchasers to write checks and offer bagging and carryout

[1] Benson P. Shapiro, "Improve Distribution with Your Promotional Mix," *Harvard Business Review*, March–April 1977, p. 116.

[2] Robert F. Lusch, "Erase Distribution Channel from Your Vocabulary and Add Marketing Channels," *Marketing News*, July 27, 1979, p. 12.

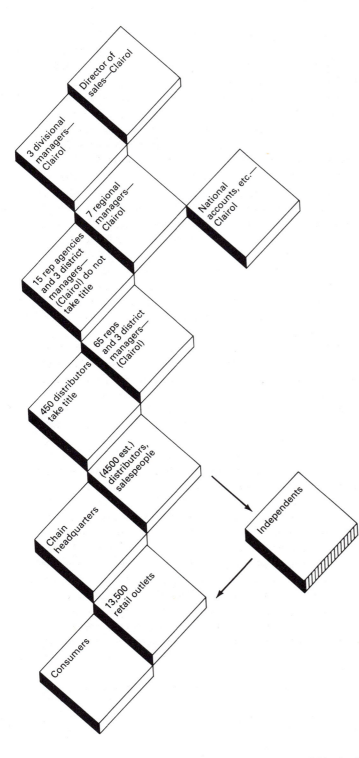

Figure 1-2 Clairol's appliance division distribution system. *Source*: Reprinted by permission of the *Harvard Business Review*. An exhibit from "Improve Distribution with Your Promotional Mix," by Benson P. Shapiro, (March/April 1977). Copyright © 1977 by the President and Fellows of Harvard College; all rights reserved.

services, they make it easy to *possess* this product. Thus, a "complete" product[3] must be comprised of all four types of utility.

THE RATIONALE FOR MARKETING CHANNEL STRUCTURES

Grasping the underlying reasons for the emergence of channel structures provides the basis for understanding marketing channels. Here the emphasis is on the economic rationale for the existence of channels, because economic reasons are the foremost determinants of channel structures. Later, key technological, political, and social factors, and how they influence the makeup of channel systems, will be examined.

The emergence and arrangement of the wide variety of distribution-oriented institutions and agencies, typically called *intermediaries* because they stand in between production on the one hand and consumption on the other, can be explained in terms of four logically related steps in an economic process:[4]

1. Intermediaries arise in the process of exchange because they can increase the efficiency of the process.
2. Channel intermediaries adjust the quantities and assortments produced with the quantities and assortments consumed.
3. Marketing agencies hang together in channel arrangements to make transactions routine.
4. Channels also facilitate the searching process.

Each of these steps is examined below.

Efficiency in Market Exchange

In primitive cultures, most household needs are *produced* within the household. However, at an early stage in the development of economic activities, *exchange* replaced production as a means of satisfying individual needs. Exchange occurs when there is a surplus in production over current household requirements and when this surplus cannot be held for future consumption, either because the products are perishable or because the household lacks storage facilities. Thus, if numerous households accumulate small surpluses of different products, a basis for exchange is developed.

As households find their needs satisfied by an increased quantity and variety of goods, the mechanism of exchange becomes more important. However, as the importance of exchange increases, so does the difficulty in maintaining *mutual* interactions between *all* households. For example, a small village of only five

[3] The term "product" is being used in its broadest sense to encompass all things of value, including objects, ideas, or services.

[4] The following discussion is based on Wroe Alderson, "Factors Governing the Development of Marketing Channels," in R. M. Clewett (ed.), *Marketing Channels for Manufactured Products* (Homewood, Ill.: Richard D. Irwin, 1954), pp. 5–22.

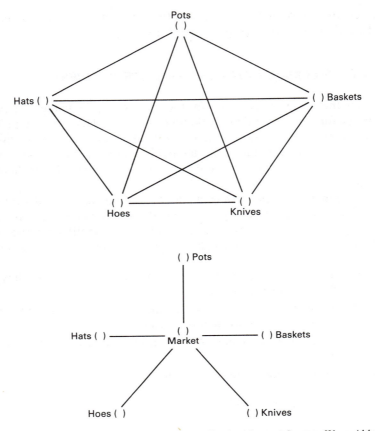

Figure 1-3 Decentralized versus centralized exchange. *Source*: Wroe Alderson, "Factors Governing the Development of Marketing Channels," in Richard M. Clewett (ed.), *Marketing Channels for Manufactured Products* (Homewood, Ill.: Richard D. Irwin, 1954), p. 7.

specialized households would require ten transactions to carry out *decentralized* exchanges (i.e., exchanges at each production point). To reduce the complexity of this exchange system and thus facilitate transactions, intermediaries appear in the process. By operating a central market, one dealer can considerably reduce the number of transactions. In the preceding example, only five transactions would be required to carry out a *centralized* exchange. This conception of decentralized versus centralized exchange is illustrated in Figure 1-3.

Implicit in the above example is the notion that a decentralized system of exchange is less efficient than a centralized network employing intermediaries. The same rationale can be applied to direct selling from manufacturers to retailers relative to selling through wholesalers. Figure 1-4 shows that, given four manufacturers and ten retailers who buy goods from each manufacturer, the number of contact lines amounts to 40. If the manufacturers sell to these retailers through one wholesaler, the number of necessary contacts is reduced to 14.

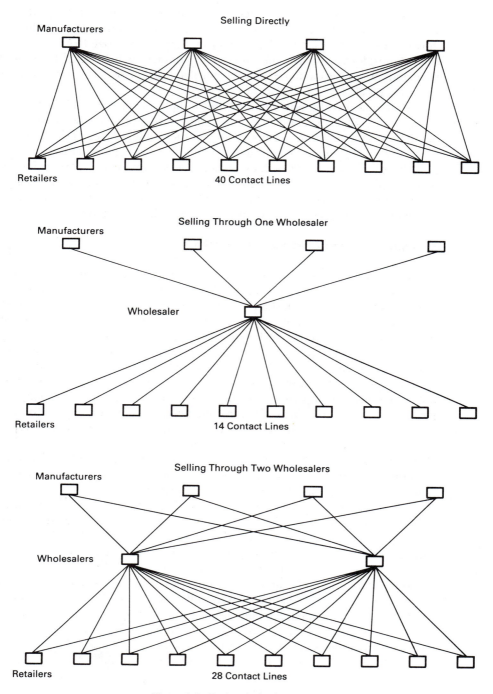

Figure 1-4 Rationale for intermediaries.

However, the number of necessary contacts increases dramatically as more wholesalers are added. For example, if the four manufacturers in the example above use two wholesalers, the number of contacts will rise from 14 to 28, and if four wholesalers are used, the number of contacts will be 64. Thus, employing more and more intermediaries is subject to diminishing returns in terms of market exchange efficiency.

It should also be noted that in this simple illustration the cost of any two contact lines of transaction—i.e., manufacturer-wholesaler, wholesaler-retailer, manufacturer-retailer—is assumed to be the same. Also, it is assumed that whenever more than one wholesaler is employed by a manufacturer, each retailer uses the services of each of these wholesalers. Obviously, accounting must be made for differences between direct and indirect communication costs, in the effectiveness and efficiency of the institutions involved in the transaction, and in the quality of the contact between the various channel members.

Breaking Bulk and Creating Assortments

In addition to increasing the efficiency of transactions, intermediaries smooth the flow of goods and services by creating possession, place, and time utilities. These utilities enhance the value of these goods and services to the consumer. One aspect of this "smoothing" process requires that intermediaries bridge the *discrepancy* of assortments. This discrepancy results from the fact that manufacturers typically produce a large quantity of a limited variety of goods, whereas consumers usually desire only a limited quantity of a wide variety of goods.

Breaking bulk is the process whereby marketing intermediaries break the large quantities produced by manufacturers down into the smaller quantities needed by their customers. Health and beauty aid wholesalers, for example, receive carloads of Dial soap from Armour and Company. They, in turn, sell this soap to supermarkets, grocery stores, and convenience markets in case lots. These retailers sell to their consumers individual packages of Dial. This process of breaking bulk generally coincides with the geographic movement of the goods from their points of origin to the end consumer.

Creating assortments is the process of building up a group of products used or bought in association with one another. Tennis clubs, for example, not only provide facilities in which consumers can play tennis, but also offer a variety of other goods and services tennis players might want in conjunction with playing tennis. Thus, a tennis club would sell tennis apparel and tennis equipment, including racquets, balls, and shoes; offer lessons from teaching professionals; suggest weight-training regimens to be followed in the club's weight rooms; and provide eating and drinking facilities for those wishing to relax after an invigorating workout. Or, to return to the Dial example, wholesalers wouldn't ship truckload quantities of Dial to individual supermarkets because the store wouldn't be able to sell a truckload in a year's time. Rather, the wholesaler creates an assortment of products sold by the supermarkets it serves and ships limited amounts of a variety of products at any one time.

Another example is provided by convenience stores, like 7-Eleven. The corner convenience store's stock-in-trade, in addition to its location and hours, is its assortment. Although the number of goods it carries is limited, this type of store must ensure that it has the right combination of products desired by its target market. Otherwise, it would not be fulfilling its role as a source for convenience goods (i.e., those products and services for which consumers are not willing to spend a great deal of effort to buy).

Making Transactions Routine

Each transaction involves buyers and sellers agreeing upon the quantity of goods or services to be purchased and sold, the transportation mode to be used and timing of delivery, the method and timing of payment, and other terms of exchange. If these terms of exchange could be made routine, bargaining over every transaction might be eliminated. This, of course, would make buying and selling more efficient.

Moreover, such routinization speeds the development of the exchange system. It leads to standardization of goods and services whose performance characteristics can be easily compared and assessed. It encourages production of items that are more highly valued. In fact, exchange relationships between buyers and sellers are standardized so that purchase quantities, frequency of delivery and payment, and communication become routine. Because of routinization, a sequence of marketing institutions is able to hang together in a channel arrangement or structure.

Automatic ordering is a prime illustration of how the marketing channel makes transactions routine. All of the details in this procedure are agreed upon in advance. As a result, many of the costs associated with placing orders are eliminated. For example, supplies of cereal and canned goods at Safeway and A&P supermarkets are automatically replenished from distribution warehouses. These distribution warehouses have direct on-line computers to communicate orders to manufacturers and other suppliers. Kellogg has direct on-line communication capabilities with the distribution warehouses of major retail supermarket chains. Similar ordering systems have been established in the marketing channels for medical supplies and industrial abrasives by American Hospital Supply and Norton, respectively. Thus, hospitals and manufacturing firms that deal with these companies are able to achieve high transaction efficiency in their purchasing of medical supplies and abrasives. Without routinization activities, the cost of distribution can increase dramatically.

Facilitating the Search Process

Buyers and sellers are engaged in a double information search process in the marketplace. The process of search involves gathering information to reduce the uncertainty of buying and selling. This uncertainty stems from producers not being sure of consumers' needs, and from consumers not knowing for certain that they will be able to find what they are looking for. Marketing channels can alleviate this uncertainty by facilitating the process of information search. For example:

- Wholesale and retail institutions are organized by separate lines of trade, such as drug, hardware, and grocery.
- Products such as over-the-counter drugs are widely available through thousands of drugstores, supermarkets, convenience stores, and even gasoline stations.
- Hundreds of thousands of parts are supplied to automotive repair facilities from local jobbers within hours after the orders are placed.

These examples have a common thread: all of the intermediaries described make market information available in one place. They provide market demand information to producers and product availability information to buyers. This is the essence of one-stop shopping—it facilitates the search process by making products and information available in one place. As a result, exchange becomes more efficient.

COMPOSITION OF MARKETING CHANNELS

A marketing or distribution channel is comprised of a set of interdependent institutions and agencies involved with the task of moving anything of value from its point of conception, extraction, or production to points of consumption. The institutions and agencies that make up marketing channels are manufacturers, wholesalers, retailers, and end users. As an example, some of the institutions and agencies involved in the distribution of air-conditioning equipment are portrayed in Figure 1-5. Note that Figure 1-5 depicts *nine* different channels of distribution for such equipment. Each of these channels may be designed to cater to the needs of different market segments and/or the operational requirements of the distributors, contractors, and/or dealers involved. For example, it is more efficient for large-volume dealers to deal directly with the manufacturer, while limited-volume dealers will have to order through distributors.

Functions and Flows in Marketing Channels

Manufacturers, wholesalers, and retailers, as well as other channel members, exist in channel arrangements to perform certain functions. For example, in the medical instrument industry, distributors perform four functions: (1) carrying inventory and physical distribution, (2) selling, (3) after-sale service, and (4) extending credit to their customers. If a manufacturer in the industry opts to sell directly to dealers and other customers, he will either have to assume all functions performed by his distributors or shift part of them to his dealers and other customers.[5]

This underscores three important principles in the structure of marketing channels:

[5] Shapiro, "Improve Distribution," pp. 116–117.

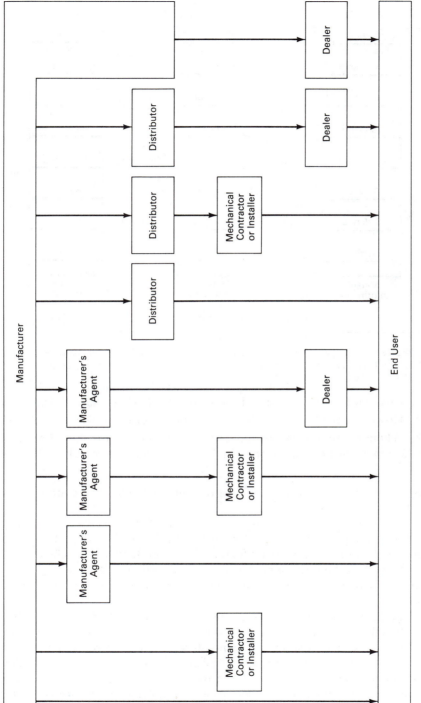

Figure 1-5 Marketing channels for air conditioning equipment.

13

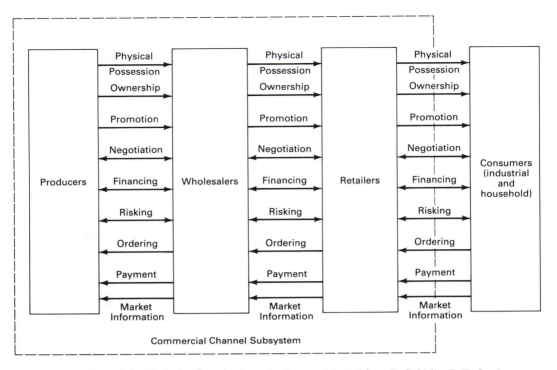

Figure 1-6 Marketing flows in channels. *Source*: Adapted from R. S. Vaile, E. T. Grether, and R. Cox, *Marketing in the American Economy* (New York: The Ronald Press, 1952), p. 133.

1. One can eliminate or substitute institutions in the channel arrangement.
2. However, the functions these institutions perform cannot be eliminated.
3. When institutions are eliminated, their functions are shifted either forward or backward in the channel, and therefore are assumed by other members.

It is a truism that "You can eliminate the middleman but you cannot eliminate his functions."

To the extent that the same function is performed at more than one level of the marketing channel, the work load for the function is shared by members at these levels. For example, manufacturers, wholesalers, and retailers may all carry inventory. This duplication may increase distribution cost. However, the increase in cost is justifiable if it enables customers to get their goods at the right quantity, quality, time, and place.

In this text, we will refer frequently to "flows" in channels. A flow is *identical* to a function. However, since the term *flow* is somewhat more descriptive of movement, we tend to prefer it. Figure 1-6 depicts nine universal flows or functions. Physical possession, ownership, and promotion are typically forward flows from producer to consumer. Each of these moves "down" the distribution channel—a manufacturer promotes his product to a wholesaler, who in turn promotes it to a

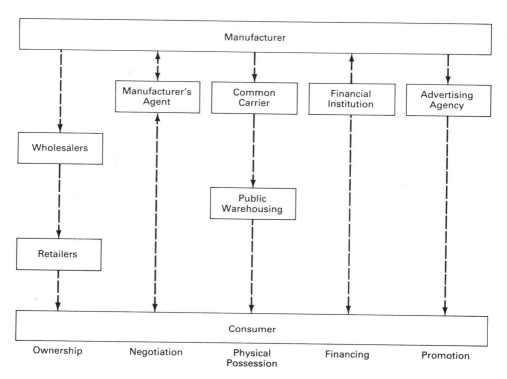

Figure 1-7 Marketing institutions particular to selected marketing flows.

retailer, and so on. The negotiation, financing, and risking flows move in both directions, whereas ordering, payment, and market information are backward flows.

Channel Member Specialization

All of the flows or functions are indispensable—at least one institution or agency within the system must assume responsibility for each of them if the channel is to operate at all. But it is not necessary that every institution participate in all of the flows. In fact, the channel of distribution is an example of a division of labor on a macro scale. Certain institutions and agencies specialize in one or more of the flows, as indicated in Figure 1-7. Some primarily participate in transferring the ownership and physical possession of the goods from the manufacturer to the consumer. Among these institutions are wholesalers, such as Fleming Foods and SuperValu, and retailers, such as Kroger and Safeway. Others *facilitate* the passage of title and the physical movement of the goods. Examples of these latter institutions are common carriers, such as the Burlington Northern Railroad; financial institutions, such as Citicorp and GMAC; advertising agencies, such as N. W. Ayer; and marketing research firms, such as Market Facts.[6]

[6] Philip Kotler, *Marketing Management: Analysis, Planning, and Control*, 5th ed. (Englewood Cliffs, N.J.: Prentice-Hall, 1984), pp. 541–542.

Which firms are used in the channel depends on how efficiently they can perform the marketing functions. As a result of their experience, their specialization, their contacts, and their size, marketing intermediaries can sometimes offer other channel members more than they could achieve by performing all of the marketing functions on their own.

Because channel members participate in different flows, they are in reality members of a number of different channels, i.e., an ownership or title channel, a negotiations channel, a physical distribution channel, a financing channel, and a promotional channel. The task of channel member coordination should be extended to the coordination of these different channels. Often, a manufacturer's new product introduction fails because he[7] has not synchronized the physical and promotional flows or channels. While national promotion may vigorously proceed on schedule, delays in transportation and lack of distribution warehouse space may delay the availability of the product at retail outlets.

Customers as Channel Participants

As stressed earlier, the marketing channel functions cannot be eliminated; however, they can be shifted either forward or backward in the channel. Many end users (either industrial or institutional users or household consumers) are often able and willing to participate in these flows. For example, some organizational buyers of personal computers have their own in-house service technicians who assemble the basic components when the product is first delivered and who perform routine maintenance and repair work over the computer's life. By participating in the service function, these buyers add form utility to their personal computers. For performing this function, the buyers are compensated in the form of lower purchase prices.

In early 1982, Atlantic Richfield quit accepting credit cards at its 7,000 domestic retail outlets.[8] In effect, ARCO was no longer performing the financing function for its retail customers. ARCO's customers had a choice between performing that function for themselves, and being compensated by lower prices, and switching to other gasoline retailers that did accept credit cards. Customers who use credit cards to buy gasoline are actually shifting the financing function backward in the channel to retailers and refiners. Of course, they pay, in the form of higher prices at the pump, for having someone else perform this function.

The key point is that customers often are able and willing to participate in the performance of marketing channel functions. To the extent that they can perform functions cheaper than someone else in the channel, customers will be receptive to the forward shifting of the marketing channel functions.

The success of no-frills airlines such as People Express attest to this fact. By flying these airlines, travelers save on airfare, but give up some of the amenities offered by the full-service carriers. For example, they

[7] We of course acknowledge the equal status of the female. However, we use the traditional "he" in this book to avoid unwieldy constructions.

[8] "Gas Credit Starts to Evaporate," *Business Week*, May 10, 1982, pp. 111, 114.

either must carry on their own luggage or pay a surcharge to have it checked. They receive no meals and beverages unless they are willing to fork over the additional cost for them.

Indeed, some market segments will actually seek out marketing channels that enable them to save money by performing some of the marketing flows. Thus, astute marketers recognize that the total marketing channel structure includes not only manufacturers, wholesalers, retailers, and other marketing institutions, but end users as well. The ability and willingness of some customers to participate in the marketing channel functions must be carefully considered in designing marketing channel structure and, as we shall see in Chapter 8, there are ways of doing precisely this.

MARKETING CHANNELS AS A NETWORK OF SYSTEMS

Perhaps the key to understanding marketing channel structure is the notion that channels consist of *interdependent* institutions and agencies. This interdependency stems from the fact that channel member firms rely upon each other to perform the marketing flows and functions. For example, McDonald's relies upon its suppliers to deliver hamburgers to its stores in the necessary quantities, with the right quality, and at the proper time. Unless the meat processors have these hamburgers ready for the suppliers to distribute to McDonald's, consumers will not be able to satisfy their Big Mac attacks. Thus, if one institution or agency in the marketing channel fails to perform its function, the entire system is jeopardized.

Because of this interdependency, marketing channels can be viewed as systems—sets of *interrelated* and *interdependent* components producing an output. A distribution channel is comprised of two major subsystems or sectors: *commercial* and *consumer*. The commercial subsystem (to which we will give major attention in this text) includes a set of vertically aligned marketing institutions and agencies such as manufacturers, wholesalers, and retailers. The final consumer and organizational buyer subsystem is incorporated into the *task environment* of the commercial channel.

Each channel member is dependent on other institutions for achieving its goals. The most dramatic example of channel member firms recognizing their interdependency might be the Toys 'R Us case.

Toys 'R Us, the major retailer of toys in the United States, was at one time threatened with bankruptcy because of the weak financial condition of its parent company, Interstate Stores, Inc. The Credit Committee of the Toy Manufacturers Association (TMA) worked directly with banks in devising a plan that not only kept Toys 'R Us healthy but also prevented the toy-producing industry from losing $80 million in sales. The banks' decision to grant credit to Toys 'R Us was largely based on the fact that six of the largest toy makers were willing to extend credit

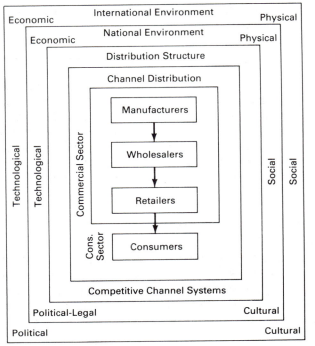

Figure 1-8 The channel as a processing subsystem within the environment.

to Toys 'R Us on their own.[9] Clearly, the six manufacturers and the members of the TMA Credit Committee realized the importance of adopting a systems perspective in the marketing channel for toys. As a result of these and other actions, Toys 'R Us has become an even more significant and successful force in toy retailing.

Although marketing channels may be conceived of as open systems with no boundaries, they are more easily studied if artificial boundaries are imposed. Some of these artificial boundaries are geographic (market area), economic (capability to handle a certain volume of goods of services), and human (capability to interact). Furthermore, a channel, like other systems, is part of a larger system that provides it with inputs and that imposes restrictions on its operation. A channel exists as part of an economy's distribution structure which encompasses other channels. The economy's distribution structure is a subsystem of the national environment, which, in turn, is a subsystem of the international environment. Both the national and international environments encompass physical, economic, social, cultural, and political subsystems that influence the development of and impose constraints on the focal channel system. The configuration of systems is portrayed in Figure 1-8. The impact of these environments on individual channel members and on channel organization and design is discussed in Chapter 2.

[9] "How the TMA Saves Toys "R" Us," *Toys*, May 1975, pp. 45–47.

It is important to recognize here that marketing channels evolve and function in dynamic environments. Channel structures are determined in part by the environment in which the channel operates. For example:

- As a result of high domestic labor cost, many U.S. footware manufacturers were displaced by international competitors from Brazil, Italy, and Spain.
- Direct "to consumer" marketing channels have become more popular in the 1980s as a result of the use of mass media, proliferation of toll-free telephone service, increased acceptance and popularity of bank credit cards, quick delivery through United Parcel Service, and the institution of trial periods, satisfaction guarantees, and return privileges.
- Changing consumer life styles, including the increased emphasis on leisure time, sports, and convenience, have resulted in the emergence and/or growth of specialty sporting goods, supermarkets, health spas, and 24-hour convenience grocery stores.
- Dramatic increases in transportation cost have led the brewing industry to establish more regional brewing plants closer to the points of consumption.

CHANNEL MANAGEMENT AND COMPETITION

Economic battles involving producers versus producers or middlemen versus middlemen will not, in the long run, determine the ultimate victors in the marketplace. Rather, the relevant unit of competition is an entire distribution system comprised of the entire network of interrelated institutions and agencies. For example, in the passenger tire industry, Firestone's system of distributors and dealers is in competition with Goodyear's entire system. The long-term standing of either company will depend in large measure on how well it manages relations among the institutions and agencies involved in the distribution task so as to best satisfy the needs of the end users of tires.

Exactly the same point applies to industrial goods. In the farm equipment and construction machinery markets, for instance, both Deere & Company and Caterpillar have achieved market dominance by fine-tuning their market channels so that farmers, contractors, and other customers are served in highly effective and efficient ways. In the case of Deere, it has been noted that

> Deere's marketing prowess . . . enhances the chances of succeeding with its strategy for thriving during a several-year stretch of slowing growth. Its vaunted marketing network—3,400 farm equipment dealers and a recently beefed-up corps of several hundred construction machinery vendors—is known for backing its products with extensive repair and parts-supply services, considered an important selling point for increasingly expensive and sophisticated equipment. One competitor observes: "The strength of Deere's dealer network is a very big influence in the success of that company."[10]

[10] "Deere: A Counter-Cyclical Expansion to Grab Market Share," *Business Week*, November 19, 1979, p. 80.

Viewing channels as competitive units is significant for all companies, including those that market their products through a number of different channels and those that develop assortments of goods and services by purchasing from a variety of suppliers. The way that the individual manufacturers coordinate their activities with the various intermediaries with whom they deal and vice versa will determine the viability of one type of channel structure versus other channel structures made up of different institutions and agencies handling similar or substitutable merchandise.

Sometimes, within a given marketing channel, an institution or agency does not coordinate effectively and efficiently with other members of the same network, but rather pursues its own goals in an independent self-serving manner. Eventually, such behavior will likely threaten the survival of the channel to which that firm belongs. Ideally, then, a channel member should attempt to coordinate his objectives, plans, and programs with other members so that the performance of the total distribution system to which he belongs is enhanced. However, such integrated action up and down a marketing channel is believed to be rare. The following comments by a consumer goods marketer are illustrative:

> If I could gain more help from my distribution channels, we could substantially increase volume and have even greater impact on profits. But when I press the button which says, "Get the distributors to increase sales of product A immediately," all too often I get a push on product C in three months. Our channels are so long and complex that we have little effect on them.[11]

Fortunately, there are exceptions to this attitude.

The virtually snowless winter in the Northeast and Midwest of the United States in 1979 left retailers loaded with 1979 models of ski equipment, snowmobiles, and snowblowers. Traditionally, manufacturers of ski equipment encouraged retailers to place large orders early in the first quarter of a calendar year by offering discounts of 15 percent or more. Deliveries were made in the late summer or early fall, and retailers were required to pay for the shipments by December 10, with extra discounts given for payments made a month or two earlier. However, because of the lessons learned during the winter of 1979, manufacturers revised their marketing methods. Salomon/North America, Inc., which holds about a 40 percent share of the ski bindings market, extended its early-order period—during which large discounts are available—until June 1. In addition, it now permits retailers to receive partial shipments throughout the winter, with payment due within 60 days of delivery. Another bindings manufacturer, Geze, Boster & Company, is now offering retailers "no-snow insurance," which extends the payment time according to a formula that compares each season's snowfall with the average over the last ten years.[12] In

[11] Shapiro, "Improve Distribution," p. 115.
[12] "Struggling to Cope Without Snow," *Business Week*, February 18, 1980, p. 66.

like manner, Toro, best known for its lawn mowers and snow throwers, has "improved its inventory-support program, giving independent dealers and distributors more protection from losses when their inventories exceed a 'normal year's' level."[13]

Channel participants are often not concerned with all the transactions that occur among the various links in the channel, however. Middlemen, in particular, are most concerned about the dealings that take place with those channel members immediately adjacent to them, from whom they buy and to whom they sell.[14] In this sense, channel intermediaries are not, in fact, functioning as components of an integrated distribution system, but rather are acting individually as *independent markets*, with each one choosing those products and suppliers that best help him serve the target groups for whom he acts as a purchasing agent. From this perspective, the middleman's method of operation—the functions he performs, the clients he serves, and the objectives, policies, and programs he adopts—is the result of his own independently made decisions.

This notion of each channel intermediary acting as an independent market must be qualified and analyzed with regard to total channel performance. Although an "independent" orientation on the part of any channel member may indeed be operational at times, it risks sacrificing the levels of coordination necessary for overall channel effectiveness, efficiency, growth, and long-run survival. Thus, a high degree of independent, suboptimizing behavior on the part of individual channel participants damages the viability of the total channel network. The problem for firms within any distribution network is, therefore, to cooperate in developing an interorganization system that will minimize suboptimization so that a high degree of channel coordination is still attainable.

APPROACH OF THE TEXT

The above discussion underscores the critical nature of channel member coordination in ensuring channel system viability. The *approach* of this text is *managerial*. It *focuses on planning*, *organizing*, *coordinating*, *directing*, and *controlling the efforts of channel members*.

The task of channel management is complex and taxing. Most businesses sell a number of products under different labels, and operate in a number of different markets. Products and services are marketed through several channels to a wide range of customers. Channel intermediaries differ in type, in volume purchased, in location, and many other operating characteristics. This "multimarketing"[15]

---

[13] "Toro: Coming to Life after Warm Weather Wilted Its Big Plans," *Business Week*, October 10, 1983, p. 118.

[14] Philip McVey, "Are Channels of Distribution What the Textbooks Say?" *Journal of Marketing*, Vol. 24 (January 1961), pp. 61–65.

[15] See Robert Weigand, "Fit Products to Your Markets," *Harvard Business Review*, January–February 1977, pp. 95–105.

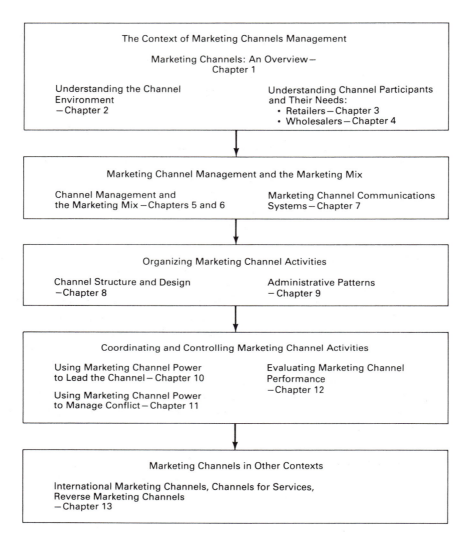

The Context of Marketing Channels Management

Marketing Channels: An Overview—
Chapter 1

Understanding the Channel
Environment
—Chapter 2

Understanding Channel Participants
and Their Needs:
• Retailers—Chapter 3
• Wholesalers—Chapter 4

Marketing Channel Management and the Marketing Mix

Channel Management and
the Marketing Mix—Chapters 5 and 6

Marketing Channel Communications
Systems—Chapter 7

Organizing Marketing Channel Activities

Channel Structure and Design
—Chapter 8

Administrative Patterns
—Chapter 9

Coordinating and Controlling Marketing Channel Activities

Using Marketing Channel Power
to Lead the Channel—Chapter 10

Using Marketing Channel Power
to Manage Conflict—Chapter 11

Evaluating Marketing Channel
Performance
—Chapter 12

Marketing Channels in Other Contexts

International Marketing Channels, Channels for Services,
Reverse Marketing Channels
—Chapter 13

Figure 1-9 Marketing channels: strategy and management.

phenomenon poses difficult channel management issues, which will be dealt with in the remainder of this text.

ORGANIZATION OF THE TEXT

The organization of this text emanates from the framework for understanding channel management that is shown in Figure 1-9. This framework specifies channel management systems in terms of interrelated sets of structural and managerial variables. The various chapters in the text relate to these sets of variables as denoted in Figure 1-9. The remainder of this section is devoted to an explanation of the organization of the text as outlined in the framework.

A necessary prerequisite to the effective management of marketing channels is a knowledge of why channels exist, the functions they perform, and the factors that account for the way they are structured. This first chapter has examined the key theoretical concepts that explain why specialized institutions and agencies have emerged to assist in the task of making goods and services available to industrial, institutional, and household consumers. The need for efficient exchange via sorting processes, routinization of marketing activities, and reasonably rapid search procedures is the reason there is a large variety of different types of intermediaries. The way in which these intermediaries are linked together depends on the services demanded by consumers. The more services demanded, the greater the number of institutions and agencies that will likely be required to bridge the gap between production and consumption. The means by which these services are generated is through the organization of the marketing functions or flows—physical possession, ownership, promotion, negotiation, financing, risking, ordering, and payment. The actual levels of performance of these functions depend, in turn, on the *economics* of distribution, which requires balancing channel members' needs to achieve profitability and manage risk and consumers' desire to receive the highest possible levels of service at the lowest possible price.

In addition to these considerations, a host of social, political, and cultural factors impinges on channel members. These factors influence, and sometimes dictate, how the channel will be structured. Because marketing channels do not operate in a vacuum, their levels of performance also depend on the strength of competing channels. Members of more successful channels view themselves as integral parts of entire marketing systems and understand the need to carefully coordinate all of their marketing activities.

As we noted above, elements in the environment other than economic ones affect how marketing channels are structured. Chapter 2 explores some of these trends—particularly the demographic, values and life-style, technological, economic, legal and political, and competitive changes—and explains how they affect the structure and operation of marketing channels. A good grasp of the context of marketing channels management is impossible without a working knowledge of the major distributive institutions. Therefore, Chapters 3 and 4 are devoted to a description of the structural and operational characteristics of retailing and wholesaling.

It should be noted at the outset that manufacturers and consumers are also significant components of marketing channels. However, specific chapters on manufacturer marketing strategy and on consumer behavior are not included in this text because these are extensively covered in almost all basic marketing and marketing management texts. In contrast, retailer, wholesaler, and physical distribution agency strategies are subjects of a special nature.

Part II of the text deals with the marketing flows that are the basic elements of marketing strategy. Chapters 5 and 6 explore the relationship of channel strategy to other elements of the marketing mix—pricing, advertising, personal selling, product, and physical distribution. The development of an appropriate network for the communication and exchange of vital information among channel members is essential for proper coordination of the channel. Chapter 7 examines channel communication systems and some of the problems that arise in communicating within marketing channels, as well as their solutions.

How marketing channels are organized is the central concern of Part III. The design of a marketing channel structure involves determining the institutions to be included in the channel structure, how intense the distribution coverage should be, the roles to be performed by each channel member, and the specific organizations to be included in the channel. Accordingly, Chapter 8 examines the design of marketing channels. Since marketing channels can also be organized administratively, Chapter 9 discusses the different administrative patterns that are used to reach similar or different market segments.

For a marketing channel system to compete effectively with other channel systems, the marketing activities of the organizations included in the channel must be properly coordinated and evaluated. Part IV examines the mechanisms for achieving this. Chapter 10 explores the use of power to lead marketing channels and discusses how either manufacturers, wholesalers, retailers, or other institutions may emerge as leaders of the channel. The interdependence of the institutions constituting marketing channels not only provides the basis for effective cooperation, it also underlies conflict among channel members. Chapter 11 discusses the causes and effects of this conflict and the methods used for managing conflict within marketing channels. A channel system cannot be managed without designing and implementing a performance control and audit system. Chapter 12 deals with the assessment of the performance of channel institutions and the channel system.

Part V, Chapter 13, examines marketing channel management in other contexts, namely, international marketing channels, channels for services, and channels for used products and materials.

DISCUSSION QUESTIONS

1. Ralph and Sarah Norman, wheat farmers in western Kansas, are sitting at their kitchen table late one fall afternoon, talking with the county extension agent about the dismal farm economy. Ralph is complaining about the low price he received on this year's wheat crop. He is also disgruntled about the high prices of bread at the local IGA. He can't understand why he receives less than 20 cents for each dollar consumers spend on bread, while the rest goes to the "greedy" food processors and other middlemen. Using the four economic utilities, explain to Ralph why he doesn't get a larger share of the consumer's food dollar.

2. The marketing channel that Hanes Corporation uses for its L'eggs pantyhose is a consignment channel. In these kinds of channels the retailer takes no title for the goods, makes no financial investment, and performs no delivery service or display maintenance, but receives only a certain percentage of the pantyhose sales for his allocation of space to the L'eggs display.

   What institutions and agencies might also participate in this marketing channel? To what extent would each participant perform the nine universal marketing flows?

3. Levitz' warehouse-showroom method of furniture distribution, which stocks large

quantities of furniture delivered to each warehouse-showroom at considerable savings, enables Levitz to pass lower prices on to the consumer.

What channel institutions likely participate in the physical possession, ownership, risking, and financing flows? How might these flows be shifted either among the members now in the channel or to different agencies or institutions not presently included in the system? What do you think the implications of such shifts are?

4. Lands' End is a mail-order marketer of traditional sportswear and luggage. It buys its merchandise from suppliers who produce to meet its specifications. Among other things, Lands' End offers its customers a ''no questions asked'' return policy, a 24-hour, seven-day-a-week toll-free number for ordering by credit card, and the United Parcel Service Blue Label option for speedy delivery, at extra cost.

What economic utilities is Lands' End adding to its suppliers' products? How extensively do consumers participate in the marketing functions of mail-order channels such as the ones Lands' End belongs to? How are consumers ''compensated'' for their participation? What functions might these marketers absorb for their consumers?

5. Some people have argued that routinization in marketing channels is really a way of limiting competition. Do you agree with this position? Why or why not? How are the concepts of routinization and search interrelated?

6. Many new forms of retailing have emerged as a result of channel members shifting the performance of marketing functions within the channel. Self-service gasoline stations and grocery warehouse stores are two examples of outlets whose consumers are performing some of the marketing functions. Name another retail institution that has developed as a result of shifting the market flows onto consumers. Which flows or functions were shifted? Speculate as to the target market served by this institution.

7. The chapter argues that marketing channels should be viewed as interorganizational systems, yet many distribution channels do not view themselves that way. Why do you suppose that is? What might be done to encourage a stronger systems view?

8. Figure 1-1 illustrated the marketing channels for IBM personal computers, while Figure 1-5 portrayed the marketing channels for air-conditioning equipment. In both cases, more than one channel is used to reach the end user. Why might this be the case?

9. Is it more useful, from a management perspective, to think of consumers (end users) as members of a channel or as elements in the task environment of the channel? Can consumers be ''manipulated'' and/or incorporated by channel management?

2

Understanding
the Channel Environment

LEARNING OBJECTIVES

   Upon completing this chapter, you will be able to:

- *List the major elements of the environment facing marketing channels and their member organizations.*

- *Discuss how these elements affect marketing channel structure and behavior.*

- *Identify the current trends in these environmental elements.*

- *Explain how these trends may be seen as either threats or opportunities facing the channel and its members.*

- *Outline the likely implications of these environmental trends.*

Electronic Shopping: Retailing of the Future?

Home shopping via the new electronic technology may someday be a large profitable business. Sears, J. C. Penney, Grand Union, Bank of America, Citicorp, General Mills, Johnson & Johnson, ITT, Federated Department Stores, and Dayton-Hudson are among the large retailers, financial institutions, and manufacturers that are beginning to dabble in "teleshopping" through videotex home-shopping experiments. Videotex allows consumers to receive news reports, make travel and entertainment reservations, bank, and shop through a computer-and-television hookup. So far, TV sets, stereo equipment, cameras, and appliances are the most popular items bought through such services, although supermarket products have done surprisingly well. Comp-U-Store, CompuServe, and a joint venture between Knight-Ridder Newspapers and AT&T are three videotex services that are in commercial operation.

Despite all of the optimism surrounding in-home electronic shopping, some industry observers are skeptical that such a revolution in shopping will ever take place: "The number of people who are going to change their behavior because of a technological change is small," says John Warwick, director of marketing for Times Mirror Company's videotex system. "To say that technology is going to make dinosaurs of retail stores is a little silly." For one thing, these systems do not offer the social interaction that many consumers enjoy by going to retail stores. For another, videotex makes comparison shopping extremely easy and marketers obviously do not want that to happen. Another damper on the enthusiasm over in-home electronic shopping is the current systems' lack of sophisticated graphics; many people feel that consumers will be leery of buying articles they cannot easily judge.

In any event, in-home electronic shopping services or videotex will continue to be studied and further developed. This technology is not likely to disappear and is a force with which marketing channels must reckon. *Source*: Based upon "Electronic Shopping Awaiting Consumer, Corporate Support," *The Wall Street Journal*, June 16, 1983, p. 23; and "Electronic Shopping Is Called Imminent, but Doubts Persist," *The Wall Street Journal*, June 23, 1983, p. 29.

The new technology has made in-home shopping, which was a vision in the 1960s,[1] a reality. These changes in technology will affect how products are marketed in the future. The implications for the structure and management of marketing channels are manifold.

By and large, major technological changes occur outside the marketing channel. They are not under the direct control of the channel, but are part of the environment facing the marketing channel and its member firms. Changes that *are* controlled by organizations within the channel, such as the elements of marketing

---

[1] Alton F. Doody and William R. Davidson, "Next Revolution in Retailing," *Harvard Business Review*, Vol. 45 (May–June 1967), pp. 4–16.

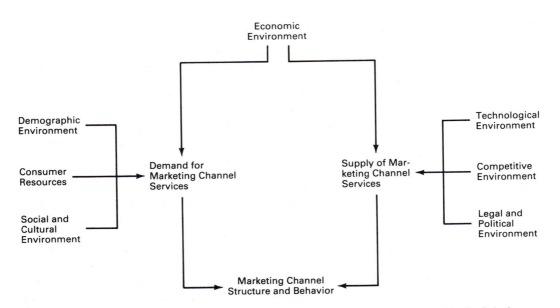

Figure 2-1 The environment of marketing channels. *Source*: Based upon an idea by Solveig Wikström, personal communication, November, 1983.

strategy, are not considered aspects of the channel environment. Thus, the *environment of marketing channels* is considered to be the totality of forces and institutions that are external and potentially relevant to those channels.[2]

Two goals of channel management are to ensure that the controllable changes are properly coordinated within the channel and to ensure that the uncontrollable or environmental changes do not adversely impact the channel. Therefore, understanding what makes up the environment and how it affects channel management is particularly important.

The Environment of Marketing Channels

The environment facing marketing channels is dynamic in that changes are occurring all the time. These changes can come from any aspect of the environment and affect both the supply of and the demand for marketing channel services. The supply and demand for these services, in turn, influences marketing channel structure and behavior (see Figure 2-1). The following sections discuss how the state of the economy, the basic social and cultural fabric of our society, the state of technological change, competitive structure, and the legal and political environment relating to marketing channels affect the management of marketing channels.

[2] Philip Kotler, *Marketing Management: Analysis, Planning, and Control*, 5th ed. (Englewood Cliffs, N.J.: Prentice-Hall, 1984), p. 77.

TABLE 2.1 Age Distribution of U.S. Population, 1960–2000 (percent)

Age	1960	1970	1980	Projected 1990	Projected 2000
Under 5 yrs.	11.3	8.4	7.2	7.7	6.6
5–13 yrs.	18.2	17.9	13.7	18.1	18.6
14–17 yrs.	6.2	7.8	7.1		
	24.4	25.7	20.8		
18–21 yrs.	5.3	7.2	7.7	10.3	9.2
22–24 yrs.	3.6	4.9	5.6		
25–34 yrs.	12.7	12.3	16.5	32.6	29.9
35–44 yrs.	13.4	11.3	11.4		
45–54 yrs.	11.4	11.4	10.0	18.6	22.7
55–64 yrs.	8.6	9.1	9.6		
65+	9.2	9.8	11.3	12.7	13.1

Source: U.S. Bureau of the Census, *Statistical Abstract of the United States: 1983*, 103rd ed. (Washington, D.C.: U.S. Government Printing Office, 1982), pp. 8, 25.

The Demographic Environment

The demographic environment is concerned with changes in the characteristics of the population. Several demographic trends affect marketing channels; these are the aging of the U.S. population, the changing character of the American household, geographic shifts in population, the education of the population, the occupational makeup of the population, and the ethnic mix of American society.[3]

The Aging U.S. Population

The "baby-boom" generation is made up of those persons born between 1945 and 1965. The oldest are entering their 40s, while the youngest are in their early 20s. Because this segment makes up the largest fraction of the population, is ever growing older, and is having fewer babies than its parents, the average age of the U.S. population is increasing (see Table 2-1). An aging population usually becomes more conservative in its political outlook and tastes. The implications of this for politicians are obvious, but perhaps not so for businesses. One company facing difficulties because its primary target market is growing older is Levi Strauss. Exhibit 2-1 describes how the graying of the population has affected Levi's sales and profitability as well as its distribution strategy.

The sheer size of the baby-boom generation makes it an appealing target market for many firms. As *Business Week* notes, "[T]he baby-boom generation is spurring the move toward mass-market segmentation, and its demand for specialized, premium goods and services is triggering a wave of new, small businesses catering to these tastes."[4] Such upscale retail outlets as premium ice cream parlors, running shops, cafés, discount stock brokers, and automated bank tellers

[3] Philip Kotler, *Principles of Marketing*, 2nd ed. (Englewood Cliffs, N.J.: Prentice-Hall, 1983).

[4] "Baby Boomers Push for Power," *Business Week*, July 2, 1984, p. 57.

EXHIBIT 2-1
Levi Strauss & Company

Two changes in the marketing environment have dramatically affected Levi Strauss & Company. First, the demographic character of the U.S. market for Levi's products has changed, and second, consumers' needs, wants, preferences, and tastes in clothing have shifted.

The graying of the U.S. population has had an impact on Levi Strauss. Its historical market has been the 3–13 and 14–17 age groups, as well as the 18–24 age group. As can be seen from Table 2-1, population growth in these groups is stagnant or even negative; thus, the size of Levi's traditional target markets has declined.

Coupled with the changing demographics is a shift in consumer tastes; people are dressier and more concerned about fashion today. (These trends might be due to a shift from blue-collar jobs, where jeans are not only socially acceptable but functional as well, to white-collar jobs, where work-related clothing is dressier.) As a result, not only is the size of the market for blue jeans and corduroys shrinking, but individual consumers buy fewer and fewer of these items, which represent over half of Levi's sales and profits. Although Levi's has attempted to reach the fashion-oriented markets, it has not been wholly successful in penetrating them.

Until the early 1980s, Levi's clothing could be found in "upscale" department stores, such as Macy's, Federated, and Dayton Hudson, and specialty jeans boutiques, such as The Gap and County Seat. To counter the changing age composition of its markets, Levi's expanded its distribution by 2,600 outlets, including mass merchandisers such as Sears and Penney's. By widening the availability of its jeans, Levi's attempted to capture that segment of the market that did not buy clothing through Levi's historical outlets.

Sources: David W. Cravens, Gerald E. Hills, and Robert B. Woodruff, *Marketing Decision Making: Concepts and Strategy*, rev. ed. Homewood, Ill.: Richard D. Irwin, 1980); Victor F. Zonana, "Levi Tries to Revive Sagging Jeans Business Amid Predictions of Denim Look's Demise," *The Wall Street Journal*, November 18, 1981, p. 25; Gary Putka, "Levi Strauss Falls to 52-Week Low as Doubts Rise over Plan to Use Mass Merchandisers," *The Wall Street Journal*, March 1, 1982, p. 39; "Levi Strauss: A Touch of Fashion—And a Dash of Humility," *Business Week*, October 24, 1983, pp. 85, 88; "A Kick in the Pants for Levi's," *Business Week*, June 11, 1984, pp. 47–48.

owe much of their success to the baby-boom market. Careful marketers recognize, however, that the baby-boom generation is not homogeneous. The affluent baby-boomers—the so-called yuppies—may stimulate the growth of specialty boutiques, given their numbers and the size of their discretionary incomes. But, because of the baby-boomers' tremendous demand for housing and the high interest rates of the early and mid-1980s, many blue-collar baby-boomers, who have fewer resources than yuppies, have been frustrated in their pursuit of the great American dream of a home in the suburbs with two cars in its garage. These

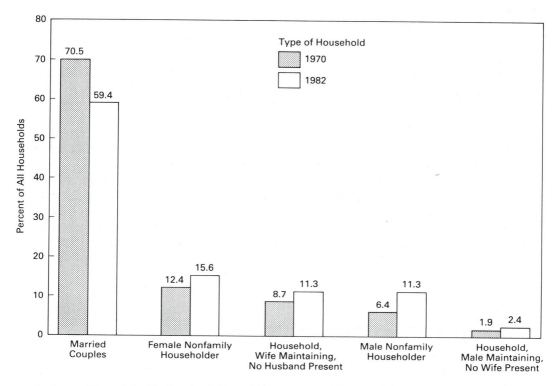

Figure 2-2 Changes in the American household. *Source*: U.S. Bureau of the Census, *Current Population Reports*, Series P-20, No. 381, Household and Family Characteristics: March 1982. (Washington, D.C.: U.S. Government Printing Office, 1983) p. 2.

baby-boomers would not likely be a good market for upscale ice cream, yogurt, running paraphernalia, bicycle equipment, and financial boutiques. They do, however, represent a challenging opportunity for marketers to come up with products and services that will enable them to fulfill their dreams at affordable prices.

The Changing American Household

From 1950 to 1980, the birth rate in the United States showed a significant decline. This trend, coupled with later marriages, an increased divorce rate, postponed childbearing, and more working women, has contributed to the overall decline in the size of the American household.[5] In addition to the declining size of U.S. households, the proportion of American households maintained by married couples dropped between 1970 and 1982, while the fraction of single-person households increased (see Figure 2-2).

[5] Leonard L. Berry, "The New Consumer," in Ronald W. Stampfl and Elizabeth Hirschman (eds.), *Competitive Structure in Retail Markets: The Department Store Perspective*, (Chicago: American Marketing Association, 1980), pp. 1–11.

The changing American household is a primary contributor to the increasing poverty of time. The smaller household size has given the traditional homemaker more discretionary time; by 1982, slightly under half of these women had entered the workforce. Indeed, by 1982, nearly half of all women of working age, either for economic reasons or to enhance their personal growth, had become employed.[6] Because husbands in traditional households have been slow to absorb some of their working wives' domestic duties,[7] these women are faced with increased demands upon their time. The growth of single-person households further adds to the number of people suffering from the "too much to do and too little time to do it in" syndrome, particularly when these people are single parents.

Time-poor consumers desire convenience in many household tasks, including shopping.[8] They are prime targets for ready-to-eat foods made available at either fast-food restaurants such as Roy Rogers Roast Beef, supermarkets such as Kroger, discount house snack counters such as K-mart, or convenience stores such as 7-Eleven. In addition, convenient store hours and locations, self-service merchandising, and broad merchandise variety enable the time-poor consumer to spend as little time as necessary shopping.[9] Marketers desiring to reach the time-poor consumer must ensure that their products are available at outlets offering convenience.

Geographic Shifts in the U.S. Population

Over the past few decades, the population has been moving from the Frostbelt region of the northeastern and north-central United States to the Sunbelt areas of Florida and the Southwest, and this trend is not likely to abate soon.[10] In addition, the population has been shifting from rural areas into metropolitan ones for the past century, and within these metropolitan areas, the shift has been from urban areas to the suburbs. Counter to this urban-to-suburban population move is a much smaller move into the central city by young professionals who desire to live closer to their place of employment. By renovating dwellings in older neighborhoods and thereby attracting upscale specialty shops, these people "gentrify" urban areas that were previously not very desirable either to live or to shop in.

Marketers located in areas from which the population is moving have two basic choices. First, they can follow their markets to the Sunbelt, the metropolitan areas, the suburbs, or the central city, depending upon where the markets are shifting. Or they can focus their efforts on those people remaining in the area. The key point is that markets rarely remain stagnant; they change in both size and

6 U.S. Bureau of the Census, *Statistical Abstract of the United States: 1984*, 104th ed. (Washington, D.C.: U.S. Government Printing Office, 1983), p. 414.

7 "The Shape of the American Family in the Year 2000," TAP 22, Trend Analysis Program, American Council of Life Insurance, Fall 1982.

8 See Berry, "The New Consumer," or Leonard L. Berry, "The Time Buying Consumer," *Journal of Retailing*, Vol. 55 (Winter 1979), pp. 58–69.

9 Michael Etgar, "Household Economics Approach to Change in Retailing," paper presented at the 7th Annual Macromarketing Seminar, Boulder, Colo., August 5–8, 1982.

10 John Naisbitt, *Megatrends: Ten New Directions Transforming Our Lives* (New York: Warner Books, 1982).

composition. A&P's failure to follow its market from urban areas into the suburbs is one of the major reasons for its decline. Careful manufacturers, wholesalers, and retailers monitor their markets so they can keep abreast of market changes. Sometimes the marketing channel must be adjusted to meet these market shifts.

Other Demographic Changes

Several other changes in the character of the American population affect marketing channel management and strategy. Among these are the increasing levels of education, the changing occupations of the U.S. workforce, and the changing ethnic composition of the U.S. population.

The fraction of the U.S. population with college degrees has increased from 7.7 percent in 1960 to 17.7 percent in 1982, and the proportion of the population with less than a high school education dropped from about 59 percent in 1960 to 29 percent in 1982.[11] Overall, Americans are becoming much better educated and, as a result, are growing more sophisticated in their shopping and buying. They are demanding higher-quality products and services, are scrutinizing the "total use" costs of products (that is, initial price, serviceable life, likely maintenance and repair costs, and energy costs), are less tolerant of poor service from high-service outlets, and are willing to use lesser-quality products such as generic and private-label brands where the difference in quality is insignificant compared to the difference in price.[12] They are also willing to substitute their own "labor" for overpriced labor (e.g., they pump their own gas).

The composition of the U.S. workforce is also changing. In addition to more women entering the workforce, there has been a shift out of farm and blue-collar work to white-collar and service occupations. As was seen in the Levi Strauss illustration (Exhibit 2-1), this trend may cause difficulties for manufacturers, wholesalers, and retailers whose traditional market is blue-collar and agricultural, particularly if they are unable to counterbalance it.

As a result of the immigration patterns of the late 1970s and early 1980s, the ethnic composition of the American population has changed, with dramatic increases in both the Hispanic and Asian populations. Because many of these groups are concentrated in specific geographic locations, they represent markets too sizable to ignore.[13]

Demographic Trends: A Caveat

This section has attempted to describe the major changes in the U.S. population as a whole. Manufacturers, wholesalers, and retailers must keep in mind that these trends may or may not apply equally to all segments of the market. For example, marketers may offer too much convenience in the mistaken belief that all consumers face a huge scarcity of time. Because the poverty of time varies over

[11] U.S. Bureau of the Census, *Statistical Abstract . . . 1984*, p. 144.
[12] See Berry, "The New Consumer," pp. 1–11.
[13] See Joel Garreau, *The Nine Nations of North America* (New York: Avon Books, 1981).

the family life cycle and according to socioeconomic status,[14] not all consumers are willing to pay a small premium to save time; in fact, some are quite willing to trade some of their time for a savings in out-of-pocket costs. The astute marketer understands these differences and develops the marketing mix accordingly. Another mistake is to assume that all ethnic markets are homogeneous. Hispanics located in Miami tend to be of Cuban extraction, for example, while those who live in Los Angeles are generally of Mexican origin. Although both markets are Hispanic, separate marketing programs, including marketing channels may be required to reach them adequately.[15]

These overall demographic trends reflect changes in the U.S. population in general. As such, they mask changes that are occurring at the regional and local levels. Moreover, not all segments of the population follow these trends. However, by keeping abreast of national trends and by understanding how these trends affect their markets, managers concerned with marketing channel strategy can more rapidly adapt their distribution systems to meet those demographic changes that do pertain to their markets.

Changing Consumer Resources

Changes in consumer resources can affect buying patterns and shopping habits, which, in turn, ultimately influence marketing channel structure. Among the major consumer resources are real income, education, and time. Other resources, such as home and automobile ownership, also affect consumer behavior.[16] The impact of the increasing poverty of time and rising levels of education on marketing channel structure, and retailing in particular, was discussed in the previous section and will not be addressed here. This section will focus on the effects of income and household durables ownership on marketing channel structure.

Throughout the mid-1970s and early 1980s, inflation coupled with recession had a drastic effect on consumers. From 1970 to 1982, real per-capita income rose 26.4 percent, while the Consumer Price Index, a widely used measure of inflation, increased by 148.6 percent.[17] Obviously, consumer purchasing power declined during this period. Recession compounded the problem for many families as unemployment rates hit levels unseen since the Great Depression of the 1930s.

Consumers adapted to this economic environment by (1) postponing purchases of housing, automobiles, household appliances, and other nonnecessities; (2) performing some routine home and automobile maintenance and repair themselves; (3) remodeling and expanding their current homes rather than buying new ones; (4) undertaking major repairs on other household durables rather than

---

[14] Michael Etgar, "The Household as a Production Unit," in Jagdish N. Sheth (ed.), *Research in Marketing*, Vol. 1 (Greenwich, Conn.: JAI Press, 1978), pp. 79–98.

[15] For additional insights on this point, see "Less Myth, More Research-Success in Minority Market," *Marketing News*, May 25, 1984, Sect. 1, p. 32.

[16] Robert C. Blattberg, Subrata K. Sen, Thomas Buesing, and Peter Peacock, "Identifying the Deal Prone Segment," *Journal of Marketing Research*, Vol. 15 (August 1978), pp. 369–377.

[17] U.S. Bureau of the Census, *Statistical Abstract . . . 1984*, pp. 457, 493; and authors' calculations.

buying new ones; and (5) stockpiling frequently used products, such as packaged foods, household cleaning supplies, and health and beauty aids.

To cope with their shrinking purchasing power, consumers also became more careful shoppers. They were more willing to comparison-shop, both within stores and across stores; they began to use coupons and to make purchases only during special sales—in other words, to buy on deal; they preplanned their shopping by using and sticking to lists; and they paid closer attention to the value of the products they bought.

Customers learned how to use their resources to shop more carefully. Those who owned automobiles and did not have to rely on public transportation shopped at geographically dispersed retail stores for the best buys. Home owners, who had more space than apartment dwellers, used it to stockpile frequently used items they bought on deal.[18]

Marketing channel members reacted to this environment in several ways. Those most directly affecting consumers will be addressed here; those indirectly affecting consumers will be discussed in the section on the economic environment. In general, retailers used a variety of purchasing strategies to retard the rapid increase in retail prices. Among these were buying on deal, stockpiling supplies, and "locking in" prices through long-term supply contracts. They also bought from diverters, which are wholesalers who buy large lots at heavy discounts from suppliers and then divert these shipments to other channel members. Some supermarket retailers offered the services of home economists to educate their customers as to how to shop more carefully and to prepare food in money-saving ways. Do-it-yourself retailers, such as home improvement centers, decorating centers, and craft stores, provided similar services for their customers. New retail institutions, such as self-service gasoline stations, off-price stores, and garages where do-it-yourselfers could rent service bays, sprang up to offer consumers ways of beating inflation.

Not all target markets were equally affected by these changes in consumer resources, nor are they likely to be in the future, so manufacturers, suppliers, wholesalers, distributors, and retailers must carefully monitor how such changes influence consumer behavior in their particular markets. Firms that learn to be perceptive to changes in consumer resources can gain a competitive advantage by altering their goods and services mix, their communications mix, and their distribution mix to better satisfy their target markets.

Social and Cultural Environment

Consumers gather information, select stores to patronize, and choose products and services partly on the basis of their general attitudes and life styles. These elements of consumer behavior, of course, affect the ways in which marketing channels are structured and managed. Two important aspects of the social and cultural environment that affect consumer behavior are overall consumer attitudes and consumer life styles.

[18] Blattberg et al., "Identifying the Deal Prone Segment."

Overall Consumer Attitudes: Some Examples

Several widely held consumer attitudes that have implications for marketing channels appear in Table 2-2. Two of these—the desire for instant gratification and time conservation—and their impact on marketing channel structure were discussed in earlier sections of this chapter. Here we will concentrate on the energy/ecological/environmental orientation and the blurring of male-female roles.

As consumers become increasingly concerned about resource conservation, they are demanding that the social and economic institutions about them do likewise. One way in which marketing channels are involved in this movement, and have been for quite some time, is recycling.[19] Soft-drink bottlers, dairies, brewers, and retailers carrying their products all participate in the recycling of returnable bottles. Scrap paper and metal dealers are key links in "reverse" channels for these recyclable materials.

Marketing channels also enable consumers, institutional and business users, and resellers to dispose of goods that are no longer valuable to them but may be of value to someone else. Automobile auctioneers, for example, are wholesalers of used cars. Through them, dealers are able to unload those used cars not suitable to their target markets and to find those that might be suitable. Other intermediaries, such as garage sales, used furniture stores, Goodwill stores, used machinery dealers, and used aircraft brokers, participate in these backward or extended channels for used products. Rather than simply scrapping used products, these channels provide a means for conserving the scarce resources needed to manufacture completely new products.

The blurring of male and female roles has resulted from the trends toward more single-person households and more working couples. These trends mean that household tasks that were previously done by males are now performed by females and vice versa. For example, a husband with a working wife might find himself sharing more in the preparation of the evening meal. Some housewares outlets, such as Friedman's Microwave Ovens specialty store, instruct both men and women in the art of microwave cooking. As a result, men become more comfortable using microwaves, may want more sophisticated models, and, at the very least, will buy additional microwave cooking accessories. Understanding how the target market looks at stereotypical male-female roles enables a store such as Friedman's to tap previously ignored markets.

Consumer Life Styles

Life style "is a powerful and convenient shorthand way of describing the main thrust of a person's way of life."[20] Often consumers purchase goods and services

---

[19] See, for example, Donald A. Fuller, "Recycling Consumer Solid Waste: A Commentary on Selected Channel Alternatives," *Journal of Business Research*, Vol. 6 (January 1978), pp. 17–31.

[20] Arnold Mitchell, *The Nine American Lifestyles: Who We Are and Where We're Going*, (New York: Warner Books, 1983), p. 28.

TABLE 2.2 Several Widely Held Consumer Attitudes and Their Implications for Marketing Channels

Consumer Attitudes	Examples of Implications for Channels	Examples of Channels Capitalizing on the Attitude
More casual life styles—a desire to live in a more relaxed, informal style with regard to dress, home environment, etc.	• Need to maintain a current assortment of life-style–oriented merchandise • Need to monitor changing tastes at the retail level	• Jeans West—casual apparel • Pier I—casual home furnishings
Instant gratification—desire for immediate access to goods and services	• Need for easier credit availability to facilitate purchasing • Reductions of in-store waiting time • Reductions of stockout levels	• Levitz—availability of furniture on an instant take-home basis • Caterpillar—worldwide availability of spare parts within 24 hours
Energy/ecological/environmental orientation—gradual spread of resource-conservation ethic	• Need for demonstrated energy/ecological/environmental concern	• Coors—aluminum can recycling program • Amoco—Premium gasoline blended with grain alcohol
Time conservation—growing recognition that time is a critical resource and constraint in many consumers' lives	• Need to develop products requiring a minimum of care and easy repair • Need to develop operating hours consistent with consumers' discretionary time	• General Electric—service contracts for major appliances • Citicorp—24-hour, 7-day-a-week 800-number transaction line
Naturalism—a revolt against the artificial, plastic, and "mass-produced" in favor of the more natural	• More natural product displays using wood, bricks, etc. • Adding a greater variety of products to the product line to satisfy consumers' individual tastes	• Perkins Pancakes—upgraded decor using natural wood fixtures and softer incandescent light • Wendy's—providing hamburgers with a couple of hundred different combinations
Blurring of male-female roles—men and women performing roles stereotypically reserved to the opposite sex	• Need to assist men and women in performing nontraditional roles	• Friedman's Microwave Ovens—offering microwave cooking classes to both men and women

Sources: Adapted from Albert D. Bates, *Retailing and Its Environment* (New York: Van Nostrand, 1979), p. 15; and James F. Engel and Roger D. Blackwell, *Consumer Behavior*, 4th ed. (Chicago: The Dryden Press, 1982), pp. 208–213.

more on the basis of their life styles than their demographics. For example, the living patterns and basic philosophy of a 30-year-old male steel worker is bound to be different from that of a 30-year-old male rock musician playing the Holiday Inn circuit, even though their incomes might be identical. Segmenting markets according to these life styles enables marketers to reach their markets more efficiently than they could if they relied solely on demographic characteristics.

Perhaps the most widely used typology for describing consumer life styles is the VALS (values and life styles) scheme developed by SRI International, a large research institute.[21] Figure 2-3 illustrates the VALS double hierarchy, which shows how a person might progress through the different life-styles categories. A brief description of these different categories, along with the buying patterns associated with each, is presented in Table 2-3.

Retailers in particular must pay careful attention to consumers' life styles if they want to create a distinct image in the marketplace. Different tastes in furniture are reflected by different VALS groups. Furniture stores cannot hope to attract customers from all of these VALS groups without offending at least one group. Therefore, understanding their customer's life styles will help these retailers to focus their images and, consequently, avoid confusing their customers.[22] Exhibit 2-2 portrays the different retail outlets and supplier arrangements for The Limited, Inc., a highly successful life-style retailer. Part of the reason for The Limited's success is that each of its outlets caters to a different life-style market by projecting a distinct image.

To satisfy the needs of their life-style market segments, retailers must choose suppliers who can provide the right products of the right quality at the right price. By the same token, manufacturers and wholesalers who segment their markets by life style must use retailers who cater to their target consumer groups. Although life styles are an important basis for segmenting markets, not all goods or services are bought according to them.[23] Demographics, for example, may be more useful method for describing some markets. The point is that effective marketers, in developing their marketing strategies, attempt to understand which bases of segmentation are most relevant for their goods and services.

Technological Environment

The technological environment has been undergoing rapid change in recent years. Much of this change has been caused by the revolution in telecommunications; other aspects of this transformation have been brought about by changes in marketing technology. This section concentrates on how these changes in the technological environment affect reaching target markets.

Reaching Target Markets

The videotex example at the beginning of the chapter illustrates how the new telecommunications technology can be used as a method of nonstore retailing. As more and more consumers come to own personal computers and subscribe to cable television, the capability for reaching large in-home markets will dramatically increase. Videotex services such as Comp-U-Store (Exhibit 2-3) and CompuServe may cease to be "gee-whiz" technology and become as commonplace as the local Sears store. By the mid-1980s, these services were already

[21] Ibid.; and James Atlas, "Beyond Demographics," *The Atlantic Monthly*, October 1984, pp. 49–58.

[22] Roger D. Blackwell and W. Wayne Talarzyk, "Life-Style Retailing: Competitive Strategies for the 1980s" *Journal of Retailing*, Vol. 59 (Winter 1983), pp. 7–27.

[23] Mitchell, *Nine American Lifestyles*.

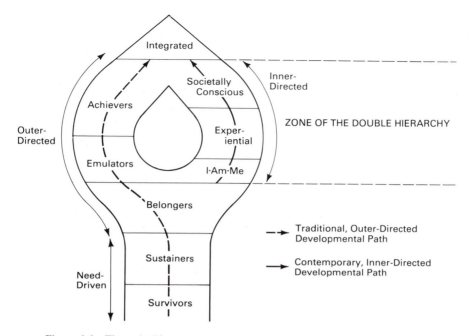

Figure 2-3 The vals life-styles double hierarchy. Reprinted by permission of Macmillan Publishing Company from *The Nine American Lifestyles: Who We Are and Where We're Going* by Arnold Mitchell. Copyright © 1983 by Arnold Mitchell.

available in southern Florida (Miami–Ft. Lauderdale), Chicago, and Orange County, California. If they prove successful, the following areas are scheduled to receive the services by the early 1990s: Phoenix; Atlanta; Columbus, Ohio; Oklahoma City; Durham, North Carolina; Minneapolis; San Francisco; Dallas; Denver; Hartford-Stamford-Greenwich, Connecticut; and Long Island, New York.[24]

Time-pinched consumers, especially those 25 to 44 and upscale (above average in income, job status, and education), tend to rely more heavily on convenient retail outlets. Because of this, they are likely to be among the first to purchase goods and services through electronic in-home shopping and information services.[25] Financial institutions, such as New York City's Chemical Bank and the small discount stock broker C. D. Anderson, have introduced in-home transactions services to reach consumers for whom convenience is important.[26] Comp-U-Mall even allows consumers to shop at many different outlets with just one "stop."

[24] "Times Mirror Opens Up Gateway," *Marketing News*, November 9, 1984, p. 5.

[25] Joel E. Urbany and W. Wayne Talarzyk, "Videotex: Implications for Retailing," *Journal of Retailing*, Vol. 59 (Fall 1983), pp. 76–92.

[26] See Stephen Koepp, "Armchair Banking and Investing," *Time*, November 14, 1983, pp. 90–101; Tim Carrington, "Stock Trading by Computer Enters Homes," *The Wall Street Journal*, October 6, 1983, p. 33; and "The Corner Bank Loses to High Tech," *Newsweek*, December 19, 1983, pp. 75–76.

TABLE 2.3 Characteristics of the VALS Life Styles

Life Style	Characteristics	Number (millions)	Age	% Female	Median Income	Education	Buying Patterns
Survivors	Old; intensely poor; fearful; depressed; despairing; far removed from the cultural mainstream; misfits	6	Most over 65	77	<$7500	8th–9th grade	Price dominant; buy for immediate needs; focused on basics
Sustainers	Living on the edge of poverty; angry and resentful; streetwise; involved in the underground economy	11	58% under 35	55	$11,000	11th grade	Price and warranty important; cautious buyers
Belongers	Aging; traditional and conventional; contented; intensely patriotic; sentimental; deeply stable	57	Median—52	68	$17,300	High school graduate	Buy for family and home; buy fads; middle and low mass markets
Emulators	Youthful and ambitious; macho; showoff; trying to break into the system, to make it big	16	Median—27	47	$18,000	High school graduate +	Conspicuous consumption; imitative; buy "in" items and popular fashions
Achievers	Middle-aged and prosperous; able leaders; self-assured; materialistic; builders of the American dream	37	Median—43	40	$31,400	32% at least college graduates	Give evidence of success; luxury and gift markets; buy "top of the line" and "new and improved" products

Group	Values and lifestyles	%			Median income	Education	Consumption patterns
I-Am-Me	Transition state; exhibitionist and narcissistic; young; impulsive; dramatic; experimental; active; inventive	8	91% under 25	36	$8,800	Some college	Display one's tastes; clique buying; experiment with fads; source of far-out fads
Experiential	Youthful; seek direct experience; person-centered; artistic; intensely oriented toward inner growth	11	27	55	$23,800	38% at least college graduates	Process over product; vigorous outdoor sports; introspective; crafts
Societally Conscious	Mission-oriented; leaders of single-issue groups; mature; successful; some live lives of voluntary simplicity	14	39	48	$27,200	58% college graduates; 39% some graduate school	Conservation emphasis; environmental concerns; frugality; simplicity
Integrated	Psychologically mature; large field of vision; tolerant and understanding; sense of fittingness	3.2					Varied self-expression; esthetically oriented; ecologically aware; one-of-a-kind items

Sources: Adapted from Arnold Mitchell, *Consumer Values: A Typology* (Menlo Park, Ca.: SRI International, 1978); and by permission of Macmillan Publishing Company from *The Nine American Lifestyles: Who We Are and Where We're Going* by Arnold Mitchell. Copyright © 1983 by Arnold Mitchell.

EXHIBIT 2-2
Life-Style Retailing: The Limited, Inc.

The Limited, Inc. is a growth company focused exclusively on women's apparel. The Company's primary business is to provide fashion, quality, and value to the American woman through multiple retail formats:

Limited Stores. There are 500 Limited stores in over 125 major markets throughout the United States. Limited stores sell medium-priced fashion apparel tailored to the tastes and lifestyles of fashion-conscious contemporary women 20 to 40 years of age. The majority of Limited stores are located in regional shopping centers with the remainder in key downtown locations.

Limited Express. Distinguished by a unique store design and merchandise selection, Limited Express stores offer an exciting assortment of popular-priced sportswear and accessories designed to appeal primarily to fashion-forward women 15 to 25 years of age. Currently there are 45 Limited Express stores located in regional shopping centers in California, Texas, and the Midwest.

Lane Bryant. Lane Bryant is the nation's leading retailer of women's special-size apparel. The 223 Lane Bryant stores specialize in the sale of medium-priced fashion, basic, and intimate apparel designed to appeal to the special-size woman, with particular emphasis on those over 25 years of age. The stores are located in regional shopping centers throughout the United States.

Brylane Mail Order. The nation's foremost catalogue retailer of women's special-size apparel and shoes. Brylane Mail Order published five catalogues, each directed to a specific special-size customer. The catalogues include *Lane Bryant, Roaman's, Tall Collection, Nancy's Choice,* and *LB For Short.*

Victoria's Secret. Through retail stores and a nationally distributed mail order catalogue, Victoria's Secret offers European and American designer lingerie for the fashionable contemporary woman 25 to 45 years of age. The 12 stores are located in the San Francisco, Boston, Columbus, Dallas, Chicago, and New York metropolitan areas.

Sizes Unlimited. This newly established division is an off-price retailer of women's special-size apparel. Composed of Sizes Unlimited and Smart Size stores, the division offers nationally known brand and private label merchandise designed to appeal primarily to women 25 to 50 years of age. The 77 stores are located in smaller shopping centers throughout the East and Midwest.

Mast Industries. Mast Industries is a large, international supplier of moderate-priced apparel for fashion-conscious women. The Commercial Division employs a worldwide network of 150 contract production facilities to produce merchandise against specific orders from retailers, wholesalers, and manufacturers. Through sales offices in New York and Los Angeles, as well as a field sales force, the Wholesale Division supplies a wide variety of apparel products to department and specialty stores throughout the United States.

Source: Roger D. Blackwell and W. Wayne Talarzyk, ''Life-Style Retailing: Competitive Strategies for the 1980s,'' *Journal of Retailing*, Vol. 59 (Winter 1983), p. 14

EXHIBIT 2-3

Comp-U-Store

Comp-U-Store, first commercialized in 1979, is one of several video-tex services that enables consumers to shop through their home computer terminals. Comp-U-Store provides products, billing, and delivery to the user. This service can be accessed either directly from the parent company, Comp-U-Card, or through various information services, such as The Source, CompuServe, Times Mirror Videotex Service, or Dow News/Retrieval Service.

Five services can be used by subscribers of Comp-U-Store:

1. *Direct product access* enables users to search for information about a specific product. They simply type in the product's name and model number and, in turn, receive product information along with a price quotation.

2. *Shopping and browsing* allows consumers to search for products in a product class they might not be familiar with. Users type in the product class name, brand name (if desired), price range, and/or product features, and Comp-U-Store lists all products meeting the shopper's requirements.

3. *Ordering* is the third service offered by Comp-U-Store. The user provides his address, the product desired, the quantity needed, and method of payment. Should any problems arise, Comp-U-Store provides a toll-free number to handle them.

4. Every month a special category of products, *bargains*, are deeply discounted and offered to subscribers of the videotex service.

5. Finally, Comp-U-Stakes is a *weekly auction* in which users may bid on certain items.

Source; Based upon Robert E. Widing II and W. Wayne Talarzyk, "Videotex Project Reviews II," Working Paper Series, College of Administrative Science, The Ohio State University, WPS 83-17, April 1983, pp. 16–18.

Comp-U-Mall, a service of Comp-U-Card, the parent company of Comp-U-Store, is aimed at young upscale professionals. This service enables these consumers to choose from among 80 different retail outlets, including Sears, Waldenbooks, RCA Record Clubs, Eastman Kodak, Hertz, American Express, American Airlines, Buick, E. F. Hutton, Neiman Marcus gifts, and *New York Times* Bookshops. In addition, Comp-U-Store will participate in this videotex system.[27] Thus, at any time of day, on any day of the week, Comp-U-Mall

[27] See Barbara Krasnoff, "Databases: Believe It or Not," *PC Magazine*, October 16, 1984, pp. 127–30; and "CompuServe Unveils 'The Electronic Mall,'" *Marketing News*, November 9, 1984, p. 3.

shoppers will be able to, among other things, make travel arrangements, conduct financial transactions, and buy gifts and have them sent anywhere in the world.

For consumers who do not possess the home electronics to tap into videotex systems, shopping convenience is possible through telephone and direct-mail ordering. In fact, mail-order merchandising is a $150 billion industry.[28]

Mary Stafford is a 35-year-old vice president of Fieldcrest Mills. Many a night she curls up in bed with her husband—a senior vice president at Chemical Bank—and relaxes with a pile of mail-order catalogs. The couple has lots of disposable income but not much free time. So they do their shopping, and plenty of it, in bed.

The couple defines upwardly mobile, affluent, educated young professionals. "In three months last year, we both got new jobs, and I had my second child," Stafford says. "So, at Christmas, I shopped for everyone by mail. Now, when I go to bed, I look at every catalog that comes in."[29]

To be successful, direct-to-consumer marketing channels require careful coordination among channel members. For example, the financing flow is becoming more integrated than ever with the other marketing flows. The consumer has to have, at the very least, a line of credit that is verifiable through data networks. Thus, suppliers are recognizing that banks and other financial institutions that provide consumer and commercial credit are indeed integral parts of the marketing channel. This example indicates why firms within these channels must operate more simultaneously than sequentially; production, data exchange, warehousing, and electronic payment are a few of the business functions that must be carefully orchestrated.[30]

COMPETITIVE ENVIRONMENT

The manufacturers, wholesalers, and retailers constituting marketing channels face competition on a variety of fronts. This section discusses changes in the competitive environment that affect marketing channels. Included in the discussion are the growth in intertype competition, the increasing importance of vertical marketing systems and free-form corporations, the accelerating retail life cycle, and the polarization of retail trade.

[28] Richard Greene, "A Boutique in Your Living Room," *Forbes*, May 7, 1984, pp. 86–94.

[29] Ibid., p. 86.

[30] For more about the implications of these forms of retailing, see Larry J. Rosenberg and Elizabeth C. Hirschman, "Retailing Without Stores," *Harvard Business Review*, Vol. 58 (July–August 1980), pp. 103–112.

TABLE 2.4 Competition Facing Marketing Channels

Type of Competition	Scope of Competition	Corporate Illustrations
Intratype competition	Competition between the *same* type of outlets	Thrifty vs. Walgreen
Intertype competition	Competition between *different* types of outlets	Kroger vs. K-Mart
Systems competition	Competition between *different* types of vertically integrated systems, including voluntary groups, cooperative groups, franchise networks, and corporate chains	A&P vs. IGA
Free-form competition	Competition between free-form corporations, each of which operates multiple types of outlets to serve multiple market segments	Carter, Hawley, Hale vs. Dayton-Hudson

Source: Bert C. McCammon, Jr., "Future Shock and the Practice of Management," paper presented at the Fifth Annual Attitude Research Conference of the American Marketing Association, Madrid, Spain, 1973, p. 8.

Increasing Intertype Competition

More and more products are being marketed through a variety of different types of outlets; this phenomenon is known as intertype competition (see Table 2-4). Consider the person who wants to save money by changing the oil in his car himself. He has a choice of several different stores from which to buy his favorite brand of oil. He can buy it at the corner Amoco station; the nearest K-mart or Target store; Osco Drug, which is featuring it as weekly special; or the neighborhood Kroger supermarket, which stays open 24 hours a day. These stores are all located within the same general shopping area. This example illustrates the essence of intertype competition: consumers have a choice of several different types of retail outlets when buying a certain good. No longer do gasoline stations compete just against other gasoline stations; now they compete against drugstores, supermarkets, convenience stores, and mass merchandisers as well. In fact, the largest gasoline retailer in the U.S. is 7-Eleven! No longer do supermarkets just compete against other supermarkets; they have added hot-food delicatessens to compete against fast-food outlets such as Kentucky Fried Chicken, McDonald's, and Long John Silvers.[31]

To meet intertype competition effectively, manufacturers and wholesalers must constantly monitor the relative importance their target markets attach to the various service outputs. Consumers change their valuation of these service outputs and these changes must be watched constantly. As noted earlier, convenience may become more important as people are faced with an increasing poverty of time. Oil refiners and jobbers that wish to reach the do-it-yourself market must understand how important convenience is to that market segment and adjust the number of outlets carrying motor oil accordingly.

[31] See Charles A. Ingene, "Intertype Competition: Restaurants versus Grocery Stores," *Journal of Retailing*, Vol. 59 (Fall 1983), pp. 49–75.

Growth of Vertical Marketing Systems

To deal with an increasingly complex and turbulent environment, many manufacturers, wholesalers, and retailers overtly coordinate their separate activities through such mechanisms as inventory control programs, total channel promotional campaigns, uniform accounting systems centralized buying, sophisticated store location analysis, common store layout, and extensive training programs. Coordination allows such firms as Sears, Ford, IBM, and SuperValu to react better to changes in the marketplace as well as to changes in other aspects of the environment. These firms, either through franchising or common ownership, compete as entire channel systems against other entire channel systems. Thus, when McDonald's competes with Wendy's, it is really McDonald's vertical marketing system competing with Wendy's vertical marketing system.

As vertical marketing systems become more dominant, small independent firms will be endangered to the extent that the vertical systems are better able to satisfy the market's needs and wants. To counter the market power of such systems, smaller firms may themselves align into vertical marketing systems. For example, voluntary chains such as IGA and Red and White Stores allow grocery retailers to remain independent, while at the same time achieving some of the advantages of franchise and vertically integrated systems. On the other hand, the smaller firms can use their smallness to their advantage by adapting to changes in their local markets more rapidly than the much larger vertical marketing systems.[32] For example, many local restaurants find market niches that the standardized menus and operating systems of McDonald's, Wendy's, and Burger King cannot satisfy.

Growth of Free-Form Corporations

Closely related to the growth of vertical marketing systems is the growth of free-form corporations, which may be thought of as both vertical and horizontal marketing systems. K-mart, Federated Department Stores, and Dayton-Hudson, for example, operate a number of distinct divisions aimed at reaching different target markets. Dayton's in Minneapolis and Hudson's in Detroit are traditional full-line department stores. Dayton-Hudson also operates Target discount stores as well as Mervyn's department stores. By reaching multiple target markets through multiple types of outlets, Dayton-Hudson is better able to cope with the accelerating retail life cycle and to combat intertype competition.[33] The growth of free-form corporations poses the same kind of threat to independent channel members as does the increase in vertical marketing systems. But though they are formidable competitors, these corporations may not be able to adapt to local market conditions as rapidly as smaller independent firms can.

[32] Joseph P. Guiltinan, ''Planned and Evolutionary Changes in Distribution Channels,'' *Journal of Retailing*, Vol. 50 (Summer 1970), pp. 79–91, 103.

[33] Louis W. Stern and Adel I. El-Ansary, *Marketing Channels*, 2nd ed. (Englewood Cliffs, N.J.: Prentice-Hall, 1982), p. 74.

Accelerating Institutional Life Cycles ✳ ✳

The evolution of retail institutions has been described by many theories, among them the wheel of retailing theory, the dialectic theory, the accordian theory, and the crisis-change model.[34] Another explanation for the evolution of retail institutions is the institutional life-cycle theory.[35] Like products, retail institutions progress through life cycles. The stages of the retail life cycle (illustrated in Figure 2-4) are innovation or early growth, accelerated development, maturity, and decline.[36]

Innovation or early growth occurs when a new retail institution emerges because it has some competitive advantage. This advantage may be a favorable cost structure, a distinctive product assortment, favorable locations, or different promotional methods. During this stage, sales increase rapidly as consumers begin to accept this new form of retailing. Profit growth usually lags because the new institution has incurred substantial start-up costs or has not yet produced significant economies of scale. As sales growth increases toward the end of this stage, profit growth begins catch up. Videotex is an example of a retail institution in the innovation or early growth stage of the retail life cycle.

Rapid rates of growth in both sales volume and profits are indicative of the *accelerated development* phase of the retail life cycle. In this stage, competitors start to enter the market and original innovators begin to expand geographically. Conventional outlets suffer as the new form of retailing picks up market share at their expense. Expanding sales volume allows the innovating firms to experience substantial economies of scale in the early phases of this life-cycle stage. As a result, profits steadily increase. Near the end of accelerated development, however, profits near their maximum levels because opportunities to achieve additional scale economies dwindle and maintaining control over expanding operations requires expending more resources. Home improvement centers and fast-food outlets are examples of retail institutions in the latter phases of the accelerated development stage of the life cycle.

In the *maturity* stage, market share stabilizes and profitability begins to decline. There are several reasons for this. First, innovating retail organizations are typically founded by entrepreneurs, and as they become more and more complex to manage, entrepreneurial styles must give way to more sophisticated management methods or the quality of operations will almost surely decline. Second, retailers often expand beyond levels justified by their markets, producing diseconomies of scale. Finally, newer retail institutions enter their life cycles at the innovation or early growth stages and begin to capture sales from more mature

---

[34] For an overview and critique of these theories, see Stanley C. Hollander, "Oddities, Nostalgia, Wheels, and Other Patterns of Retail Evolution," in Ronald W. Stampfl and Elizabeth Hirschman (eds.), *Competitive Structure in Retail Markets: The Department Store Perspective* (Chicago: American Marketing Association, 1980), pp. 78–87.

[35] See William R. Davidson, Albert D. Bates, and Stephen J. Bass, "The Retail Life Cycle," *Harvard Business Review*, Vol. 54 (November–December 1976), pp. 89–96, and William R. Davidson and John E. Smallwood, "An Overview of the Retail Life Cycle," in Stampfl and Hirschman (eds.), *Competitive Structure in Retail Markets*, pp. 53–62.

[36] This section draws heavily from Davidson, Bates, and Bass, "The Retail Life Cycle."

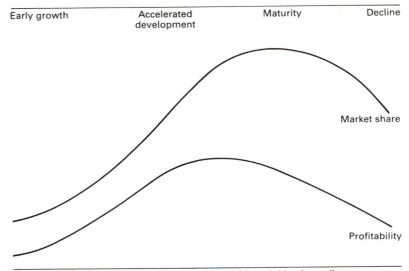

| Early growth | Accelerated development | Maturity | Decline |

Market share

Profitability

Note: The duration of the stages (horizontal scale) is variable, depending on many circumstances. The four stages are portrayed equally on the time scale for schematic purposes only.

Figure 2-4 Stages in the retail life cycle. *Source*: Reprinted by permission of the *Harvard Business Review*. An exhibit from "The Retail Life Cycle" by William R. Davidson, Albert D. Bates, and Stephen J. Bass. (November/December 1976). Copyright © 1976 by the President and Fellows of Harvard College; all rights reserved.

retail forms. Diseconomies of scale due to management inefficiencies and overexpansion cause costs to rise at a time when demand is being sapped by newer retail institutions. On balance, then, profitability will decrease. Examples of retail institutions in the maturity stage are convenience stores, mail-order houses, and gasoline stations.

The final stage of the retail life cycle is *decline*. At this stage, market share losses are large, profits are marginal, and firms find themselves unable to compete effectively. This stage can be avoided or postponed by revamping the marketing mix in many cases, but not necessarily in all. General stores are one institution in the decline phase of the retail life cycle; variety stores are another.

Just as with many facets of American society, the pace of the retail life cycle is accelerating. As Table 2-5 illustrates, the time between the introduction of a new retailing institution and when it reaches maturity is becoming progressively shorter.

An understanding of the retail life cycle has several implications for marketing channels (see Table 2-6). First, suppliers should maintain flexible distribution systems. As new forms of retailing evolve, suppliers must position themselves to take advantage of these new ways of reaching their target markets. To be locked into a particular retailing form is to invite obsolescence, particularly as the life cycle's pace accelerates. Second, retailers in the latter stages of the life cycle require closer coordination with their suppliers. If they provide unique

TABLE 2.5 Illustrations of the Stages of the Retail Life Cycle

Institutional type	Period of Fastest Growth	Period from Inception to Maturity (years)	Stage of Life Cycle	Representative Firms*
General store	1800–40	100	Declining	A local institution
Single-line store	1820–40	100	Mature	Hickory Farms
Department store	1860–1940	80	Mature	Marshall Field's
Variety store	1870–1930	50	Declining	Morgan-Lindsay
Mail-order house	1915–50	50	Mature	Speigel
Corporate chain	1920–30	50	Mature	Sears
Discount store	1955–75	20	Mature	K-Mart
Supermarket	1935–65	35	Mature/declining	A&P
Shopping center	1950–65	40	Mature	Paramus
Cooperative	1930–50	40	Mature	Ace Hardware
Gasoline station	1930–50	45	Mature	Texaco
Convenience store	1965–75	20	Mature	7-Eleven
Fast-food outlet	1960–75	15	Late growth	Shoney's
Home improvement center	1965–80	15	Late growth	Lowes
Super specialists	1975–85	10	Late growth	The Limited
Warehouse retailing	1970–80	10	Maturity	Levitz
Videotex	1983–?	?	Early growth	South Florida videotex

*These firms are representative of institutional types and are not necessarily in the stage of life cycle specified for the institutional group as a whole.

Source: Adapted from Joseph Barry Mason and Morris Lehman Mayer, *Modern Retailing: Theory and Practice*, rev. ed. (Plano, Tx.: Business Publications, Inc., 1981), p. 93.

merchandising programs, adapt to changes in the retailers' target markets, and assist in inventory and store fixture financing, suppliers should be able to protect these retailers from newer forms of distribution.

The key point is that both retailers and suppliers must remain flexible. Suppliers should consider alternative forms of distributing their products, as Jos. A. Bank, direct-mail clothes is doing by opening retail stores. Retailers might consider adopting these newer retailing institutions themselves, as Associated Dry Goods did by buying Caldor, a discount store chain, and Loehran's, an off-price clothing chain. In addition, retailers and suppliers must work together to develop new methods of satisfying the changing needs of their target markets if both members of the channel are to remain viable.

Increasing Polarization in Retailing

A final aspect of the competitive environment is the trend toward the polarization of retail trade (Figure 2-5). At one pole are *high-tech* retail outlets that emphasize self-service and, to a lesser extent, lower prices. SuperValu's Cub warehouse food stores, Zayre's T. J. Maxx off-price stores, McDonald's restaurants, and Southland's 7-Eleven convenience stores cater to consumers who are willing to

TABLE 2.6 Management Activities in the Retail Life Cycle

		Stage of Life-Cycle Development			
	Area or Subject of Concern	1 Innovation	2 Accelerated development	3 Maturity	4 Decline
Market characteristics	Number of competitors	Very few	Moderate	• Many direct competitors • Moderate indirect competition	• Moderate direct competition • Many indirect competitors
	Rate of sales growth	Very rapid	Rapid	Moderate to slow	Slow or negative
	Level of profitability	Low to moderate	High	Moderate	Very low
	Duration of new innovations	3–5 years	5–6 years	Indefinite	Indefinite
Appropriate retailer actions	Investment/growth/risk decisions	Investment minimization—high risks accepted	High levels of investment to sustain growth	Tightly controlled growth in untapped markets	Minimal capital expenditures and only when essential

	Stage 1	Stage 2	Stage 3	Stage 4
Central management concerns	Concept refinement throught adjustment and experimentation	Establishing a preemptive market position	• Excess capacity and "overstoring" • Prolonging maturity and revising the retail concept	Engaging in a "run-out" strategy
Use of management control techniques	Minimal	Moderate	Extensive	Moderate
Most successful management style	Entrepreneurial	Centralized	"Professional"	Caretaker
Appropriate supplier actions — Channel strategy	Develop a preemptive market position	Hold market position	Maintain profitable sales	Avoid excessive costs
Channel problems	Possible antagonism of other accounts	Possible antagonism of other accounts	Dealing with more scientific retailers	Servicing accounts at a profit
Channel research	Identification of key innovations	Identification of other retailers adopting the innovation	Initial screening of new innovation opportunities	Active search for new innovation opportunities
Trade incentives	Direct financial support	Price concessions	New price incentives	None

Source: Reprinted by permission of the *Harvard Business Review*. An exhibit from "The Retail Life Cycle" by William R. Davidson, Albert Bates, and Stephen Bass (November/December 1976). Copyright© 1976 by the President and Fellows of Harvard College; all rights reserved.

forgo a great deal of personalized service and sales assistance or who want to complete their shopping tasks quickly.

At the other pole are *high-touch* retail outlets, those that offer high levels of personalized service, greater prestige, knowledgeable salespeople, and a variety of specialized services such as delivery, installation, credit, and special ordering. Consumers who are highly ego involved in their purchases are likely to patronize these types of retail institutions. For example, a customer desiring gourmet food items, either for personal consumption or for gift giving, might shop at such prestige food retailers as Macy's Cellar, Byerly's, Food Emporium, and Hickory Farms of Ohio to obtain the personalized attention they need.

In essence, then, the poles of retailing institutions may be described as high-tech mass merchandisers and convenience stores at the one end, and high-touch specialty stores and boutiques at the other. In the middle are traditional supermarkets, department stores, and variety stores, whose customers are being pulled toward either end. Besides the pressure from high-tech store retailers, these traditional outlets are facing increased competition from nonstore marketers, including Lands' End, Avon, and Tupperware, which are able to provide high-touch services without having to invest in retail facilities. Other direct marketers, such as L. L. Bean and videotex, would be categorized as more high tech. Unless the traditional outlets shift their merchandising strategies more toward either high tech or high touch, consumers will see them as neither offering extensive personalized services nor providing quick shopping with minimum hassle.[37] If they fail to project a strong image in either direction, these retailers will continue to lose customers and will cease to be viable members of the marketing channel.

The increasing polarity of retail trade will not only affect the types of retail institutions through which suppliers can market their goods, but also the types of marketing channels used. As direct marketers increase their share of retail sales, promotion, delivery, and creating assortments will be shifted from the retail store level to the supplier level in the channel. To coordinate the activities of the channel more carefully, direct marketers will develop vertical marketing systems.[38]

LEGAL AND POLITICAL ENVIRONMENT

The legal and political environment directly influences marketing channel structure and behavior, as shown in Figure 2-1. In this section, we will highlight federal legislation, labor unions, and deregulation, and discuss how these elements of the legal and political environment affect marketing channel management.

[37] For a variety of perspectives on the polarity of retail trade, see Stephen P. Arbeit, "Confronting the Crisis in Mass Marketing," *Viewpoint*, Vol. 2 (1982), pp. 2–10; William R. Davidson, "Changes in Distributive Institutions," *Journal of Marketing*, Vol. 34 (January 1970), pp. 7–10; and Malcolm P. McNair and Eleanor G. May, "The Next Revolution of the Retailing Wheel," *Harvard Business Review*, Vol. 56 (September–October 1978), pp. 81–91.

[38] For further implications of these trends for channels, see McNair and May, "The Next Revolution"; and Rosenberg and Hirschman, "Retailing Without Stores."

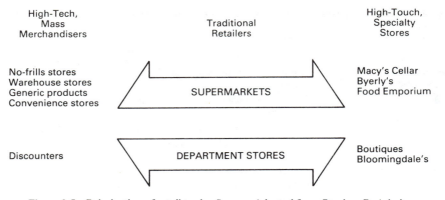

Figure 2-5 Polarization of retail trade. *Source*: Adapted from Stephen P. Arbeit, "Confronting the Crisis in Mass Marketing," Olgivy and Mather's *Viewpoint*, Vol. 2 (1982), p. 5.

Among the more important *federal laws* regulating marketing channel activities are the Sherman Act, the Clayton Act, the Celler-Kefauver Act, the Federal Trade Commission Act, and the Robinson-Patman Act (see Table 2-7 for the key provisions of these laws). To manage effective interorganizational programs that will not conflict with federal legislation, the marketing manager should be aware of how these laws constrain the coordination of marketing channel activities, including markets served, products carried, prices charged, promotional support undertaken, and ownership of channel institutions (i.e., vertical integration). A specific discussion of how legislation affects these activities will be postponed to Chapters 5 and 6, the chapters explicitly dealing with these marketing mix issues.

One important aspect of the legal and political environment is the impact of *labor unions* on the operation of the marketing channel. Unions affect marketing institutions and agencies in several basic ways. First, they try to provide their members with decent wages, job security, and a safe workplace. Certain of these union objectives directly increase the costs of performing the marketing flows; as long as all institutions at a particular channel level are unionized, these costs can be passed along to others in the channel and, eventually, to the ultimate consumer. However, when some firms are unionized and others are not, management is under intense pressure to lower total costs, including labor costs. As a result, unions may gain higher wages at the expense of job security.[39]

Next, certain provisions in labor contracts prohibit "the shifting of defined [retail] store functions, such as display arrangement and stocking of shelves, to wholesale route service personnel, manufacturer's representatives, or others not covered by the contract[s]."[40] In effect, these prohibitions restrict flexibility in designing marketing channel structure.

[39] "Slim Pickings for Supermarket Workers," *Business Week*, August 27, 1984, p. 26.

[40] William R. Davidson, Daniel J. Sweeny, and Ronald W. Stampfl, *Retailing Management*, 5th ed. (New York: John Wiley & Sons, 1984), p. 470.

TABLE 2.7 Principal Federal Laws Affecting the Interorganization Management of Marketing Channels

Act	Key Provisions
Sherman Antitrust Act, 1890	1. Prohibits contracts or combinations in restraint of interstate and foreign commerce. 2. Makes monopoly or attempt at monopoly a crime in interstate or foreign commerce.
Clayton Antitrust Act, 1914	Where competition is substantially lessened, it prohibits: 1. Price discrimination in sales or leasing 2. Exclusive dealing 3. Tying contracts 4. Interlocking directorates among competitors 5. Intercorporate stockholding
Celler-Kefauver Act, 1950	Prohibits purchase of assets of another firm if competition is lessened:
FTC Act, 1914	1. Prohibits unfair trade practices injurious to competition or a competitor. 2. Sets up FTC to determine unfairness.
Robinson-Patman Act, 1936	1. Discriminatory prices are prohibited if they reduce competition at any point in the channel. 2. Discriminatory prices can be given in good faith to meet competition. 3. Brokerage allowances are allowed only if earned by an independent broker. 4. Sellers must give all services and promotional allowances to all buyers equally if the buyers are in competition. Alternatives must be offered. 5. Buyers are prohibited from knowingly inducing price discrimination. 6. Price discrimination can be legal if it results from real cost differences in serving different customers. 7. Prohibits agreement with competitors to change unreasonably low prices to destroy competition.
FTC Trade Practice Rules	1. Enforced by FTC. Define unfair competition for individual industries. These practices are prohibited by FTC. 2. Define rules of sound practice. These rules are not enforced by the FTC, but are recommended.

Other contract provisions may prohibit employees from being transferred from department to department within the store to utilize their time more effectively. Moreover, unions often oppose technological changes aimed at increasing labor productivity, particularly when the effect of these changes will be to reduce the size of the workforce.

Thus, flexibility in managing marketing channels is often restricted by labor agreements. If they understand how labor contracts affect the structure and behavior of marketing channels, member firms can either avoid painful and costly labor strife by not implementing policies that violate the agreements, or attempt to negotiate changes in the most restrictive contract provisions.[41]

[41] For additional insight into the effects of unionization on the functioning channel institutions,

Another important aspect of the political environment is the federal government's policy of *deregulation,* which was begun in the Ford administration and continued through the Carter and Reagan administrations. Three basic industries have been most affected by this policy: financial services, telecommunications, and transportation.[42] Deregulation has had a dramatic effect on their marketing channels.

Deregulation has resulted in several changes in the financial industry. First, many financial services, previously only available from separate firms, can now be obtained from a single outlet. The Sears Financial Network, comprised of Coldwell Banker real estate, Allstate Savings and Loan, Allstate Insurance, and Dean Witter stock brokerage, is a prime example of this kind of consolidation. Second, many firms have unbundled their services, which means that customers are charged only for the services they use. Discount brokerage firms appeal to those investors who do their own research or obtain it independently of their stock brokers. Third, suppliers of financial services have enhanced their productivity by installing automatic teller machines. ATMs enable these firms to deliver convenience in ways that are not possible with "bricks and mortar" branch locations. The final effect of deregulation on the financial services industry is intensified competition. Local banks compete against brokerage houses, large regional and national banks, mass merchandisers like Sears, and savings and loans, among others. Deregulation has blurred the distinction among these various institutions. With interstate banking on the horizon, competition will become even more ferocious.[43]

Deregulation has had the same sorts of effects on the transportation and telecommunications industries. Productivity has been raised through the adoption of new technology, customers are being charged only for those services they actually use, the availability of goods and services has increased, competition has intensified, and prices have declined.[44]

Economic Environment[45]

The economic bonanza of the post-World War II years demonstrated a remarkable degree of continuity between 1947 and 1973, when it was replaced by a more sobering set of realities. The mid-1970s to the mid-1980s were characterized by high unemployment and underemployment, high inflation, higher energy costs, lower real growth in gross national product, erosion of consumer confidence, growing entanglement of resource availabilities with international politics, uncer-

and retailing in particular, see Davidson et al., *Retailing Management,* p. 470; and Ronald D. Michman, "Union Impact on Retail Management," *Business Horizons 10* (Spring 1967), pp. 79–84.

[42] "Deregulating America," *Business Week* November 28, 1983, pp. 80–82.

[43] "The Revolution in Financial Services," *Business Week,* November 11, 1983, pp. 88–89.

[44] See "Deregulating America"; "The Revolution in Financial Services"; and "The Big—and Bruising—Business of Selling Telephones," *Business Week,* March 12, 1983, pp. 103–104, 106.

[45] Except where noted, this section is largely based on Albert D. Bates, *Retailing and Its Environment* (New York: D. Van Nostrand, 1979), pp. 14–20 and Chap. 2.

tain capital availability, and a growing ethic of resource conservation and environmental protection. Although many of these difficulties had somewhat subsided by the mid-1980s, memories of them were still fresh enough to affect marketing channel planning and operations. This section discusses these lingering effects, particularly those related to inflation and deflation, recession, capital costs, labor productivity, construction costs, and merchandise availability.

Inflation and Deflation

Hardly any industries were spared the ravaging effects of high inflation, high interest rates, and high unemployment in the late 1970s and early 1980s. The distributive trades were certainly no exception. As noted earlier in the chapter, many manufacturers, wholesalers, and retailers locked in prices through long-term supply contracts and shifted more of the marketing functions to the consumer in order to offset the effects of rising prices; many wholesalers and retailers bought only heavily discounted merchandise. These tactics gave rise to several new retail institutions, including off-price stores, do-it-yourself stores, self-service gasoline stations, and warehouse grocery stores. These were the survivors; other retailers were not as fortunate.

In automobile retailing, for example, rapid increases in prices and high interest rates caused new car demand to plunge during the late 1970s and early 1980s. In addition, manufacturers reduced their dealer margins, which restricted the dealers' ability to discount their prices to consumers.[46] The result was that 4,400 new car dealerships folded during that period.[47] This high number of failures meant that many geographic markets were no longer being served by the distribution systems for new automobiles. From a competitive standpoint, manufacturers whose dealerships closed lost market representation, and hence were likely to lose their customers permanently.

Ironically, the lower inflation rates of the mid-1980s had exactly the same effect on the supermarket business. Given the high inflation rates of the late 1970s and early 1980s, supermarkets, in their strategic planning, assumed a sales growth rate of 8–12 percent; most of it due to inflation. However, lower inflation and lower population growth rates have meant that a supermarket's growth has had to come at its competitors' expense. Thus, vigorous and sometimes unprofitable price-cutting has occurred in some markets. In 1983, Grand Union sold or closed stores in the District of Columbia, Houston, and Florida because it was unable to achieve profitability by expanding its share of the market.[48] Its suppliers, unless they could find other outlets, also suffered a lack of representation in those markets.

[46] "Auto Dealers Try to Hang On," *Business Week*, May 4, 1981, pp. 128, 130.

[47] "Dealers Rediscover the Consumer," *Business Week*, February 21, 1983, pp. 32–34.

[48] "How Inflations Stings the Supermarkets," *Business Week*, March 19, 1984, p. 34.

Recession

The general economic recession of the early 1980s affected the farm economy well into the mid-1980s. Low farm prices coupled with high interest rates drove many farmers and the companies supplying them out of business. Farm implement dealers particularly felt the squeeze.

Low farm prices, high interest rates, and the payment-in-kind (PIK) program of 1983, which idled nearly 50 percent of American cropland, contributed to reduced farm implement sales. Moreover, because farmers were afraid of adding to their heavy debt loads, they were holding on to their old equipment three to four years longer than usual. As with automobile dealers, the recession caused many farm implement dealers to fold. By the spring of 1984, these factors forced the remaining farm equipment dealers to carry a 12-month supply of inventory, nearly double the normal amount.[49] "Even the equipment service business, which usually flourishes in recessions when farmers try to make do with old farm implements, [was] in shambles."[50]

As the above example illustrates, many manufacturers and wholesalers attempt to shift inventory through the channel during recessions. Farm implement dealers, new car dealers, and retailers of other high-ticket items are usually caught between suppliers forcing goods through the channel and customers postponing purchases. Without assistance in performing the financial flow from other channel participants, many of these retailers could not have survived. Careful coordination of marketing channel activities is especially important during times of economic crisis, particularly if the channel is to survive as a competitive entity.

Capital Costs

The ability to raise capital is an extremely critical function of channel member firms. Since many channel participants operate on relatively thin profit margins, even a small increase in interest rates can disastrously affect their bottom lines. As a result, firms in the distributive trades are not considered very desirable investments and must pay somewhat higher interest rates than manufacturers.[51] In the early 1980s, the interest rate situation was so desperate that one New York merchant commented, "We'd rather run out of goods and miss a few sales than have to finance overstocks."[52]

[49] See "Farm Suppliers Face Another Bad Year," *Business Week*, March 21, 1983, pp. 114, 116; and "The Drought in Farm Equipment Isn't Over Yet," *Business Week*, April 23, 1984, p. 36.

[50] "Farm Suppliers Face Another Bad Year," p. 116.

[51] Bates, *Retailing and Its Environment*, p. 16.

[52] "The Customer Returns—Warily," *Business Week*, October 29, 1980, p. 37.

Labor Productivity

Retailing and wholesaling suffer from a strange paradox. Historically, these industries have had the lowest wage rates while simultaneously being among the most sensitive to wage increases. Although retail wages average $1.10 per hour below those in manufacturing, retailing is one of the few remaining labor-intensive industries. Even in self-service operations, payroll is over half the expense account, and for conventional department stores, payroll is almost two-thirds of it.[53]

Construction Costs

"Rentals" account for the second largest chunk of retailing operating expenses. For example, sharply rising construction costs pushed rental charges in new regional shopping malls from $5 per square foot in 1970 to over $15 per square foot in 1980. Indeed, many retailers, like K-Mart, prefer to use freestanding locations rather than shopping centers and malls. Another resulting trend has been to recycle existing facilities, such as abandoned supermarkets, variety stores, discount department stores, warehouses, and even train stations. Others are experimenting with new low-cost construction techniques, as well as with less elaborate interior designs and modular construction, which allows rapid dismantling and rearrangement of display spaces. Given the pressures they face, retailers can increasingly be expected to turn to their suppliers for more direct investment assistance. In particular, the financing of inventory and fixtures could become integral parts of some suppliers' marketing programs.

Merchandise Availability

Peacetime product shortages were phenomena largely unknown to U.S. channels until the 1970s. The oil embargos of the 1970s had a widespread impact on marketing institutions and agencies far beyond the effect they had on retail service stations. Petroleum-based industries, particularly plastics, and energy-dependent industries witnessed acute supply problems and rapidly escalating prices. Other shortages, such as the coffee shortage of 1976–1977, affected profits in other industries.[54] While these specific instances are things of the past, the availability of raw material resources remains highly uncertain and is more and more entangled with international politics. Retailers may have to increase the length of their contracts with suppliers or even reduce the number of suppliers with whom they deal so as to assure themselves of access to needed goods. Clearly, this will increase their dependency on their suppliers and thus alter relationships within the marketing channel. The importance of such dependencies within the channel is examined in detail in Chapter 10.

[53] Bates, *Retailing and Its Environment*, p. 17. Labor productivity is discussed more fully in Chapter 12 where attention is turned to the performance of retailing institutions.

[54] See for example, "Fast Food Chains Take a Beating on Breakfast," *Business Week*, February 21, 1977, p. 30.

SUMMARY

Marketing channels are affected by environmental forces beyond the control of the channel as a whole as well as of its individual participants. Changes in the demographic environment, in consumer resources, and in consumers' basic values affect consumer knowledge of, attitudes toward, and behavior within the marketing system. These factors, in turn, influence consumer demand for the services provided by the marketing channel. Changes in the demographic, social/cultural, technological, competitive, legal/political, and economic environments affect the supply of services offered by the marketing channel. Thus, the channel structure and the behavior of marketing institutions and agencies within the channel are influenced by a host of environmental factors.

The environmental factors influencing the demand for marketing channel services seem to point to the *increasing importance of convenience* for a large segment of the market. Convenient store hours and locations are a must for retailers wishing to reach these time-poor consumers. Advances in telecommunications provide the ultimate in convenience—24-hour shopping within the home. Marketers who ignore these channels (direct mail and videotex) run the risk of yielding an ever-increasing portion of the market to their competitors. That consumers are demanding *more value for their money* should come as no surprise; marketers must ensure that the value of the channel services supplied is at least equal to the price charged. Another trend is *customers' increasing willingness to perform some of the marketing functions themselves*. Retailers and industrial suppliers can offer lower prices to those buyers who participate more heavily in the marketing flows.

Environmental factors influencing the supply of marketing channel services are manifold. Among the most prominent are: (1) the technological advances in direct channel systems, including videotex and catalog shopping; (2) the competitive trends, such as increasing intertype competition, growth of vertical marketing systems, growth of free-form corporations, accelerating institutional life cycles, and increasing polarization in retailing; (3) federal legislation aimed at restricting marketing channel activities that substantially restrain competition, are unfair competitive practices, or may lead to monopolization; and (4) such trends in the economic environment as inflation and deflation, recession, capital costs, labor productivity, construction costs, and merchandise availability.

DISCUSSION QUESTIONS

1. A growing proportion of American households have personal computers. How might this trend impact the demand for marketing channel services in the marketing research industry? How might it affect the supply of marketing channel services in this industry? Hint: Trace this trend through the model of the environment of marketing channels depicted in Figure 2-1.

2. Marsh Williams operates Buckeye Distributing Company, a northeastern Ohio wholesaler of insulation material. In addition to supplying several insulating contractors, Buckeye insulates buildings and homes itself. Competition for insulating jobs has

become increasingly intense as fewer new homes are being built and as owners of older homes have added more insulation. Marsh believes that he should investigate the possibility of going into other businesses before both his wholesaling and his insulating operations become unprofitable.

Does Marsh Williams view the changing competitive environment as a threat or an opportunity? Explain your answer. Given the environmental trends discussed in this chapter, provide Marsh with some new business opportunities to explore, assuming that (1) he wants to stay in the home improvement business, and (2) he would like to remain both an industrial user and a wholesaler.

3. Describe the demographic characteristics of the target market for one of the goods or services listed below. Using U.S. Census data, determine the current size of that market and its projected size by the year 1995. How might the growth, decline, or stability of that market influence the marketing channels for that good or service by 1995?
   a. Classical music—format FM radio stations
   b. Undergraduate business majors in state universities
   c. Mortuary services
   d. Home videocassette recorders
   e. Private telephone services
   f. Dental chairs, instruments, and other equipment

4. John Martin has decided that he wants to market his Waterbed Wonderland specialty retail outlet to baby-boomers. He knows that baby-boomers are not as homogeneous as the media sometimes portray them. Therefore, he thinks age is only of limited value in segmenting his market, but is unsure how else to proceed. Because of your expertise in marketing, he comes to you for assistance. How would you describe John's target market? Be specific in your answer.

5. Jane Phillips has hit upon a new franchising concept, Vito's for Veggies, a vegetarian sit-down restaurant. Given the discussion in this chapter, describe Janet's likely target market. What marketing channel services might these target markets want delivered? What channel institutions and agencies might deliver these services? Diagram the marketing channel for Vito's for Veggies.

6. As noted at the beginning of the chapter, videotex might not become as widespread as quickly as some observers now believe. A major reason for this is that consumers are reluctant to shop from an outlet where they cannot touch, smell, listen to, taste, try on, or see the exact merchandise they are buying. The same problem confronts other direct marketers. Chester's Cheddar Cheese Castle of Chilton, Wisconsin, is considering buying space on the Keyfax videotex system operating in Chicago. Chester Charles, owner of Chester's Cheddar Cheese Castle of Chilton, has never before used direct-to-consumer marketing channels. He is concerned that consumers might not patronize his outlet since they cannot use their senses to evaluate the quality of his gift cheeses. On the other hand, Chester wants to preempt other gift cheese emporiums on the Chicagoland videotex. Explain how Chester's Cheddar Cheese Castle of Chilton can assist consumers in overcoming their reluctance to order gift cheese through videotex.

7. Choose two of the following goods or services and describe how the various aspects of the competitive environment impact their marketing channels.
   a. Soft drinks
   b. Hospital services
   c. Automobiles

d. Financial services

e. Beer

f. Photocopying services

8. BULLETIN! THE REAGAN ADMINISTRATION HAS JUST ANNOUNCED THAT IT WILL RECOMMEND TO CONGRESS THAT THE POSTAL SERVICE BE DISBANDED AS OF JANUARY 1, 1995. ALL MAIL AFTER THAT DATE WILL BE HANDLED BY PRIVATE MAIL CARRIERS.

First, diagram the marketing channel for mail services, using Figures 1-1, 1-5, and 1-7 as models. Next, explain how the (obviously bogus) Reagan administration proposal will affect this channel structure. In your answers be sure to discuss the various marketing flows and what channel institutions and agencies, including the customer, participate in their performance.

9. Walnut Computer, Inc., a large maker of personal computers, has recently refused to sell its computers to dealers and distributors who market its popular IIId computer through telephone or mail order. Walnut argues that personal service, including training and warranty and repair service, cannot be provided by such outlets. Main Street Electronics, which operates a huge mail-order division in addition to its 33 nationwide retail stores, has sued Walnut on the grounds that its refusal to deal constitutes a restraint of trade. Main Street Electronics maintains that Walnut's policy was instituted to placate full-service dealers who complained about price-cutting on the IIId by the mail- and telephone-order houses. What are the major legal issues of this case? Explain. How legal do you think Walnut's action was? Why?

10. A well-known student of marketing channels once remarked that new channel institutions and agencies arise to respond to environmental crises. This person went on to say that these new channel member firms really do not perform any new marketing functions or flows; they simply perform them in new combinations or shift them to others in the channel.

What new marketing channel instititutions and agencies were developed as a result of the economic downturn of the late 1970s and early 1980s? What marketing flows or functions were either performed in new combinations or shifted to others participating in the channel? Describe these new channel member organizations.

3

Understanding Channel Participants and Their Needs: Retailers

LEARNING OBJECTIVES

Upon completing this chapter, you will be able to:

- *Describe trends in retail sales for store retailing, services retailing, and nonstore retailing.*

- *Characterize the major types of retail outlets.*

- *Understand that the major components of retailing strategy are consumer expectations and the retail marketing mix.*

- *Discuss what consumers specifically expect from retail outlets.*

- *Review the main factors to be considered in segmenting retail markets and understand what is meant by positioning a retail outlet.*

- *Describe the key elements of the retail marketing mix and how they work together in forming consumer images of retail outlets.*

Modern retailing has become fiercely competitive and innovative. It is characterized by an ever-growing variety of institutions and, as noted in Chapter 2, faces a highly fluid environment. The objective of this chapter is to describe the structure and strategy at the retail end of the marketing channel so that managers can adapt channel structures and processes to accommodate developments at the "front line" of distribution.

THE STRUCTURE OF RETAILING

Retailing deals with the activities involved in selling goods and services to ultimate consumers. Thus, a retail sale is one in which the buyer is an ultimate consumer, as opposed to a business or institutional purchaser. The buying motive for a retail sale is always personal or family satisfaction stemming from the final consumption of the item being purchased.[1]

Retailing is one of the major industries in the United States. It consists of over 1.5 million single-unit and over 330,000 multiunit establishments and accounts for approximately 18 percent of all business in the country.[2] Transacted sales were $1,174 billion in 1983.[3]

While the business of retailing is usually thought of as being conducted in stores, through the mail, by telephone, by house-to-house salespersons, and from automatic vending machines, it actually encompass all "outlets" that seek to serve ultimate consumers. These include service establishments such as motels and hotels, as shown in Table 3-1. Under the broadened concept of marketing, such "outlets" as hospitals, day-care centers, churches, and perhaps even public schools might also be included. These latter institutions, as well as banks and financial institutions (the "retailers" of money), have been omitted from Table 3-1 for a simple reason—it is difficult to quantify their output in terms of dollar sales volume.

Over the past 50 years, retail sales have grown approximately nine times as fast as population and at about the same rate as income. Contrasted to the phenomenal growth in sales, the total number of retail outlets has increased only marginally from about 1.5 million to 2 million during this time period. This discrepancy reflects the increased importance of large-scale, high-volume operations in all fields of retailing and the use of more sophisticated management to foster that expansion.

Of the various categories of retailing institutions listed in Table 3-1, store retailing is by far the most significant, accounting for 85 percent of total retail sales volume. Within the store retailing category, food stores obtain the greatest share,

[1] Theodore N. Beckman, William R. Davidson, and W. Wayne Talarzyk, *Marketing*, 9th ed. (New York: Ronald Press, 1973), p. 234.

[2] The 330,000 multiunit establishments (defined as having two or more units) were owned by 43,700 firms in 1977. U.S. Bureau of Census, *1977 Census of Retail Trade, Establishment and Firm Size*, RC77-S-1 (March 1980), pp. 1–62.

[3] U.S. Bureau of Census, *Current Business Reports: 1983 Retail Trade*, BR-83-13 (September 1984), p. 4. The $1,174 billion figure excludes sales of the service institutions shown in Table 3-1, but does include nonstore retailing.

TABLE 3.1 Retail Sales of Store, Nonstore, and Service Institutions

Institution	1972 Sales $ billions	1972 Sales % of total	1981 Sales[a] $ billions	1981 Sales[a] % of total	Average Annual Percent Increase (1972–1981)
Store Retailing	414.2	88.1	946.1	85.3	14.3
Food stores	99.0	22.0	237.9	21.4	15.6
Automobile dealers	88.5	19.7	187.3	16.9	12.4
General merchandise group stores[b]	62.7	14.0	126.6	11.4	11.3
Eating and drinking places	36.2	8.1	95.0	8.6	18.0
Gasoline service stations	33.4	7.4	102.8	9.3	23.1
Apparel stores	24.1	5.4	47.8	4.3	10.9
Lumber and building material stores	23.3	5.2	51.3	4.6	13.4
Drugstores	15.3	3.4	34.5	3.1	13.9
Furniture and home furnishing stores	22.0	4.9	46.2	4.2	12.2
Liquor stores	9.7	2.2	16.7	1.5	8.0
Nonstore Retailing[c]	NA	NA	25.2	2.3	NA
Services	55.7	11.9	137.8	12.5	16.4
Hotels, motels, tourist courts, camps	10.6	2.2	27.9	2.5	18.1
Personal services (laundry, dry cleaning, beauty shops, barber shops, photographic, shoe repair, funeral, alterations, etc.)	13.9	2.9	25.3	2.3	9.1
Automobile repair and other automotive services	12.0	2.6	34.0	3.1	20.4
Miscellaneous repair services (electrical, watch, jewelry, furniture, etc.)	5.8	1.2	18.9	1.7	25.1
Amusement, recreation services, motion pictures (dance halls, theatrical presentations, bowling, billiards, commercial sports, etc.)	13.4	2.9	31.7	2.9	15.2

[a]Unadjusted for inflation. The total for store and nonstore retailing does not add up to $1174 billion, the figure cited in the text, because the sales of certain kinds of retailers, such as fuel oil dealers and used merchandise stores, are included in the total but are not included in any of the classifications shown in the table.

[b]Includes department stores, discount department stores, miscellaneous general merchandise stores, variety stores, and jewelry stores.

[c]Includes sales made by mail-order catalog desks located within department stores of some mail-order firms, sales of automatic merchandising machine operators (vending machines), and sales of direct-selling establishments (house-to-house canvass, party plan, telephone selling, etc.).

Sources: U.S. Bureau of the Census, *Current Business Reports, BR-13-81S, Revised Monthly Retail Sales and Inventories: January 1972–December 1981* (April 1982), p. 15; U.S. Bureau of the Census, *Current Business Reports, BS-13-77S, Monthly Selected Services Receipts; January 1972–August 1977* (November 1977), p.11; U.S. Bureau of the Census, *Current Business Reports, BR-81-12, Monthly Retail Trade: December 1981* (February 1982), p. 4; and U.S. Bureau of the Census, *Current Business Reports, BS-81-12, Monthly Selected Services Receipts: December 1981* (February 1982), p. 2.

accounting for 23 percent of total retail sales in 1981. If one adds eating and drinking place receipts to the food store sales, then food-oriented purchases would consume almost one-third of all retail expenditures, giving some notion of the emphasis Americans place on eating and drinking. The automotive group (auto dealers, gas stations) transacted about 28 percent of all sales, while general merchandise stores accounted for approximately 12 percent.[4]

To a significant extent, however, statistics do not reveal the underlying dynamics of the exciting developments that have occurred over the past century. There has been a veritable revolution in retailing, even though small shopkeepers are still local "landmarks" in every community. In this chapter, however, the focus is on the current status of retailing structure and strategy.[5]

A clear grasp of the retailing structure in the United States cannot be gotten without understanding the major types of retailing institutions and forms of organization. Figure 3-1 illustrates the many ways in which retail institutions are classified. The following paragraphs describe some of the more common of these classifications.[6]

Department stores are retail organizations such as Marshall Field, Macy's, Jordan Marsh, Burdine's, and Bullock's. These stores typically

- Sell a wide variety of merchandise, including clothing and accessories, home furnishings, and furniture
- Are organized by department
- Have large sales
- Sell mainly to women
- Are most often located in downtown shopping districts or in shopping malls or centers
- Frequently establish branch operations
- Usually offer a large amount of customer service

Specialty stores market a broad selection of a restricted class of goods. While some large specialty stores departmentalize their operations (e.g., Filene's and I. Magnin), the term *specialty store* is most commonly applied to small- and medium-sized establishments or boutiques handling lines of soft (clothing, linens, etc.) or hard (housewares) goods.

Kroger, Safeway, and Sears are prime examples of *chain store systems*. These systems are characterized by

- Central ownership or control

---

[4] It is important to note that there are significant problems in using and analyzing Census of Business data to portray movements and shifts over time. Scrambled merchandising, changes in Census classifications from one enumeration to another, and reclassification of establishments to reflect changes in the character of their operations are prominent difficulties in using Census data. Another problem is that the Census defines a retail establishment as one that makes at least 51 percent of its sales to retail customers. As a result, up to 49 percent of a store's sales could be misclassified.

[5] For a historical perspective on the changes in retail trade, see Louis P. Bucklin, *Competition and Evolution in the Distributive Trades* (Englewood Cliffs, N.J.: Prentice-Hall: 1972); and Malcolm P. McNair and Eleanor G. May, *The Evolution of Retail Institutions in the United States* (Cambridge, Mass.: Marketing Science Institute, 1976).

[6] For a complete description of the different types of retailing institutions, see Beckman et al., *Marketing*, pp. 237–250.

A. By *Ownership of Establishment*
  1. Single-unit independent stores
  2. Multiunit retail organizations:
     a) chain stores
     b) branch stores
  3. Manufacturer-owned retail outlets
  4. Consumers' cooperative stores
  5. Farmer-owned establishments
  6. Company-owned stores (industrial stores) or commissaries
  7. Government-operated stores (post exchanges, state liquor stores)
  8. Public utility company stores (for sale of major appliances)

B. By *Kind of Business (Merchandise Handled)*
  1. General merchandise group:
     a) department stores
     b) dry goods, general merchandise stores
     c) general stores
     d) variety stores
  2. Single-line stores (e.g., grocery, apparel, furniture)
  3. Specialty stores (e.g., meat markets, lingerie shops, floor coverings stores)

C. By *Size of Establishment*
  1. By number of employees
  2. By annual sales volume

D. By Degree of *Vertical Integration*
  1. Nonintegrated (retailing functions only)
  2. Integrated with wholesaling functions
  3. Integrated with manufacturing or other form-utility creation

E. By Type of *Relationship with Other Business Organizations*
  1. Unaffiliated
  2. Voluntarily affiliated with other retailers:
     a) through wholesaler-sponsored voluntary chains
     b) through retailer cooperation
  3. Affiliated with manufacturers by dealer franchises

F. By Method of *Consumer Contact*
  1. Regular store:
     a) leased department
  2. Mail order:
     a) by catalog selling
     b) by advertising in regular media
     c) by membership club plans
  3. Household contacts:
     a) by house-to-house canvassing
     b) by regular delivery route service
     c) by party plan selling

G. By Type of *Location*
  1. Urban:
     a) central business district
     b) secondary business district
     c) string street location
     d) neighborhood location
     e) controlled (planned) shopping center
     f) public market stalls
  2. Small city:
     a) downtown
     b) neighborhood
  3. Rural stores
  4. Roadside stands

H. By Type of *Service Rendered*
  1. Full service
  2. Limited service (cash-and-carry)
  3. Self-service

I. By *Legal Form of Organization*
  1. Proprietorship
  2. Partnership
  3. Corporation
  4. Special types

J. By *Management Organization or Operational Technique*
  1. Undifferentiated
  2. Departmentized

Figure 3-1 Alternative ways of classifying retail establishments. *Source:* Theodore N. Beckman, William R. Davidson, and Wayne Talarzyk, *Marketing*, 9th ed. (New York: Ronald Press, 1973), p. 239.

- Central management
- Similarity of store merchandise, layout, and design
- Eleven or more different locations (according to the Bureau of Census classification scheme)

Effective chain store systems are able to obtain efficiencies by buying in large quantities, spreading their advertising expenditures over a greater number of stores, and using their managerial staffs more intensively.

Supermarkets are generally low-margin, high-turnover retail organizations operated on a self-service basis. In the food industry, a supermarket can be defined as a large departmentalized retail establishment offering a relatively broad and complete stock of dry groceries, fresh meat, perishable produce, and dairy products. Supermarkets also offer a variety of convenience goods, including nonfood items. The supermarket concept has been applied to several lines of trade other than food retailing. Among them are furniture (Levitz), sporting goods (Herman's), toys (Toys 'R Us), and hardware and building materials (Payless Cashways).

Planned shopping centers are integrated real estate developments under single ownership, with coordinated and complete shopping facilities and with adequate parking space. The stores in the centers are leased to various retailers. Frequently, center stores engage in joint advertising, promotional, and public relations programs.

Discount houses, such as K-mart, Target, and Wal-Mart, are retail establishments that generally have the following features:

- A broad merchandise assortment, including both hard and soft goods
- Price as the main sales appeal
- Relatively low operating costs as a percentage of sales volume
- Relatively inexpensive buildings, equipment, and fixtures
- An emphasis on self-service operations
- Limited customer services
- Emphasis on rapid merchandise turnover
- Large stores and parking areas
- Carnival-like atmospheres
- Frequent use of leased departments

Nonstore retailing takes place in a variety of arenas. Among the nonstore retailing institutions are the following general types of organizations:

- *Automatic vending machines* offer limited assortments of low-priced products with stable demand—in other words, convenience goods. The costs of operating these machines are usually high because of their high initial costs as well as the costs of restocking and repairing them. Accordingly, the prices charged and margins earned tend to be relatively high.

- *Mail-order houses* are establishments that receive their orders by mail, telephone, or other electronic media. The merchandise is delivered by mail, parcel post, express courier, truck, etc. Retail mail-order houses are of three main types: (1) department store merchandise houses (e.g., Alden's; Montgomery Ward; Sears, Roebuck; and Speigel); (2) smaller general merchandise firms that carry narrower lines than would be found in department stores (e.g., L. L. Bean, Lands' End); and (3) specialty houses (e.g., Franklin Mint, Time-Life Books). Generally, installment credit is used extensively. Other commonly offered services are acceptance of bank cards, convenient pickup depots, catalog stores, strong guarantees, and liberal return policies. Prices are supposedly lower than at conventional retailers' outlets, although postal and delivery charges tend to bring the prices closer to those found in stores.

- *House-to-house* selling is typified by organizations, such as Avon and Tupperware, that make direct sales to consumers in their homes. Demonstration and return after trial are among the various services offered by house-to-house sellers. Cash, rather than credit, is the usual mode of transaction. In general, overhead costs are relatively low for these organizations, with the major expenses being travel costs and salesperson turnover.

These types of retailing institutions exist because they offer different combinations of channel services to the ultimate consumer. Thus, the marketing strategy used by a retailer will determine what type of institution that retailer is and which firms it is likely to find as direct competitors.

In the previous chapter, several recent environmental trends affecting retailing were discussed. In this chapter, the focus is on how retailers develop their marketing strategies to cope with these trends. Unless they have such knowledge, people concerned with the marketing of consumer goods are likely to be shortsighted and ineffective in managing their marketing channels.

RETAIL MARKETING STRATEGY

Lucy Cousins hates to go shopping, but especially at Darrell's Discount Den. She has to drive too far to get there and she can never spot where the products she wants are on Darrell's shelves. Once she found pickles stocked with paint in the building supplies department ("Makes as much sense as anything else in this store since both products begin with the letter P," Lucy reasoned). Even if she does manage to locate the proper shelf, Lucy never seems to find the product she wants in stock and she cannot stand the long lines at the checkout. In short, Lucy hates to shop and Darrell's always seems to reinforce her attitude.

Lucy's husband, Carl Levine, on the other hand, loves to shop, and he enjoys going to Darrell's Discount Den. He likes the excitement of mingling with other people in crowded shopping malls and stores; he finds haggling with salespeople stimulating; he enjoys exploring stores like Darrell's to find the products he wants to buy; he meets interesting people in the checkout lines. For Carl, shopping is an adventure.

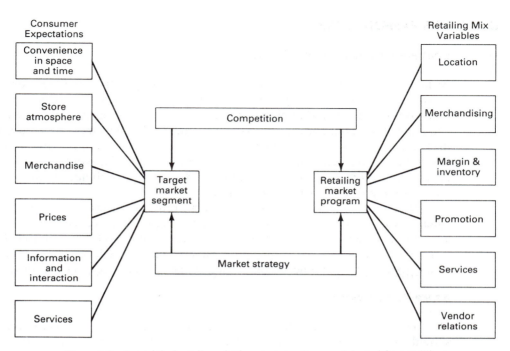

Figure 3-2 A model of retail marketing strategy. *Source*: Adapted from William R. Davidson, Daniel J. Sweeney, and Ronald W. Stampfl, *Retailing Management*, 5th ed. (New York: John Wiley & Sons, 1984), p. 77.

Both Lucy and Carl enter retail stores with expectations about how well their needs and wants will be satisfied by the shopping experience. Not all consumers, and certainly not all households, have the same set of expectations about the levels of channel services retail stores can and do deliver.

Retail stores develop retail marketing mixes to deliver channel services that will satisfy consumers' needs and wants. Since not all segments of the market have similar sets of expectations, retailers select those market segments whose needs and wants they can best satisfy. In other words, they choose target markets. A retail marketing strategy is developed when retailers formulate marketing mixes expressly to satisfy the needs and wants of their target customers. If a store is successful at doing this, it develops a unique position within the market compared to its competition.

The essence of retail marketing strategy is illustrated in Figure 3-2. The following sections present in further detail the two basic aspects of retail marketing strategy: consumer expectations (i.e., what channel services consumers expect from retail outlets) and the retail marketing mix (i.e., what elements of the marketing mix retailers use to deliver those services).

CUSTOMER EXPECTATIONS[7]

Convenient Location and Hours

As noted in Chapter 2, many consumers face a poverty of time and therefore want to spend as little time as possible on mundane activities. For many of these time-poor consumers, shopping is one such activity. To reach these consumers and others for whom convenience is important, retail outlets must be located near their homes or workplaces and must operate at hours convenient to them. Locational convenience should be considered in terms of travel time rather than distance; traveling five miles in a major metropolitan area obviously takes longer than traveling five miles in the countryside.

Other consumers have excess time (e.g., retirees, vacationers, stay-at-home spouses with older children). Because their ''opportunity costs'' are relatively low, these consumers are willing to expend more travel time, during hours inconvenient to other people, to shop at outlets that offer reduced prices. They are willing to devote more time to comparison shopping than time-poor consumers are.

Store Atmosphere

Shoppers like to feel comfortable in the stores they patronize. Thus, retailers should ''provide an atmosphere in which customers 'feel at home,' with which they can identify, and which is consistent with their life style.''[8] Store atmosphere comprises such things as how the merchandise is presented, how lighting is used, how the store is decorated, how traffic patterns within the store are structured, what kind of music is piped into the store, and how odors and other appeals to the senses are used.[9] Some apparel shoppers, for example, are not bothered by untidy shelves and merchandise strewn over sale tables; others are so highly offended that these stores show such little care for their merchandise that they refuse to shop in them.

Merchandise

Merchandise is essentially the goods the retail outlet offers for sale. Consumers may view this merchandise as either convenience goods, shopping goods, or specialty goods. Convenience goods are those for which the consumer is unwilling to put forth much effort to buy; bread, milk, candy bars, cigarettes, gasoline, and soft drinks are examples of convenience goods. Goods the consumer is willing to expend much effort to buy are called specialty goods; Rolex watches, Rolls-Royce automobiles, and Ralph Lauren sport shirts are illustrative of specialty goods.

[7] This section is loosely based on William R. Davidson, Daniel J. Sweeney, and Ronald W. Stampfl, *Retailing Management*, 5th ed. Copyright © 1984 by John Wiley & Sons, Inc. Reprinted by permission from John Wiley & Sons, Inc.

[8] Ibid., p. 86.

[9] For further discussion, see Philip Kotler, ''Atmospherics as a Marketing Tool,'' *Journal of Retailing*, Vol. 49 (Winter 1973–1974), pp. 48–64; ''Sight, Smell, Sound: They're All Arms in Retailers' Arsenal,'' *The Wall Street Journal*, April 19, 1979, pp. 1, 17.

TABLE 3.2 Classification of Consumer Goods
(Based on Degree of Consumer Prepurchase Planning)

	Classification of Goods		
	Convenience Goods	Shopping Goods	Specialty Goods
Degree of prepurchase planning made by consumer	Little	Some	Considerable
Degree of brand preference	Little	Makes brand comparison	Insists on specific brand
Amount of shopping effort used by consumer	Minimum	Moderate	Maximum

Source: Raymond A. Marquardt, James C. Makens, and Robert G. Roe, *Retail Management: Satisfaction of Consumer Needs*, 3rd ed. (Chicago: The Dryden Press, 1983), p. 105.

Consumers are willing to expend a moderate amount of effort—especially to compare prices—when they are buying shopping goods. For many consumers, furniture, automobiles, and clothing are examples of shopping goods (see Table 3-2).

If Sue Beatty hurriedly dashes into a drugstore to buy a roll of Velamints and the store does not carry them, she is not likely to return to that drugstore for convenience goods because it did not meet her expectations. Likewise, Sue believes that because Calvin Klein jeans are sold "everywhere," "Calvin" must feel that people don't really want to put much effort into buying them. She reasons that if "Calvin" feels that way, she does, too; accordingly, she puts zero effort into buying his jeans and buys Guess jeans (a big, expensive brand) instead.

Price

Consumers often patronize retail outlets according to their expectations about price. They have beliefs about the general range of prices each store charges for its merchandise. For example, Bloomingdale's Department Store may have a reputation for being very high priced compared with other outlets in the market. Shoppers also often have general expectations about prices for specific products or product lines. Bloomingdale's may be high-priced for children's apparel but competitively priced for women's accessories, for example. Because people avoid stores for which their price expectations are negative, those stores have little opportunity to positively change consumers' expectations.

Although price expectations are an important factor in a consumer's store choice, value expectations may be more critical. Strictly speaking, *value* is the ratio of perceived product or service quality to its perceived total cost.[10] The price paid for the product or service is only part of its perceived total cost. Also

[10] Kent Monroe, *Pricing: Making Profitable Decisions* (New York: McGraw Hill, 1979), p. 38.

included are such hidden costs as the "opportunity cost" of time (if much travel or waiting time is involved), the risk that the product or service will not perform as it is supposed to, and the cost of gathering purchase information.

Recall the example of the two television buyers at the beginning of Chapter 1. One paid a lower price, did not get exactly what she wanted, and received few services; the other paid a higher price, got exactly what she wanted after a short wait, and received many services. The value that each buyer received depended on her perceptions of the quality she got versus her perceptions of the TV's total price. Thus, shoppers' perceptions of the value offered by retail outlets can be more crucial in determining where they patronize than their perceptions of price.

Information and Personal Interaction

Many consumers patronize retail outlets to gather information they may use in making either an immediate purchase or a later one. At a minimum, a retail outlet provides information about what brands are available at that store. Stores with qualified sales personnel can offer *product information* about alternative brands as well as *information about the store's services*. For example, Donald Johnson is considering two different brands of clothes washers at ABC Appliances. Minerva Floyd, one of ABC's salespeople, gives him technical information about the capacities, prices, extra features, warranties, and serviceable lives of the two machines. She also describes for Donald, ABC's delivery, installation, credit, and store warranty policies. Thus, as a part of their purchase decision processes, consumers look to retail outlets as sources of both store and product information.

In addition to gathering information about products and stores, many people *shop to satisfy a variety of social needs.*[11] For example, a camera buff may visit his neighborhood photography shop to discuss the latest equipment or new techniques with the store's personnel or other knowledgeable shoppers. The photography shop, then, serves as a focal point for people with similar interests. Some such stores sponsor clubs to formalize these social interactions. Other consumers like to shop because they enjoy the feeling of being waited upon; still others find bargaining with salespeople pleasurable.

Services

Consumers also form expectations about the number and nature of the services offered by the retail outlet. These services may include credit, delivery and installation, warranties or guarantees, sales assistance, repair, and shopping services. Such expectations often determine whether a particular consumer will patronize a certain store. For example, some consumers require delivery services for refrigerators and stoves. Stores that do not offer free home delivery are not considered viable outlets by these shoppers.

[11] This discussion is largely based on Edward M. Tauber, "Why Do People Shop?" *Journal of Marketing*, Vol. 36 (October 1972), pp. 46–49.

Young Single Professionals	Middle-Income Household with Children at Home	Low-Income Older Shopper with Limited Education	Customer Segments / Offering
X			24-hour opening
	X	X	Generics
X	X		Check cashing
X	X		In-store bakery
X			Delicatessen department
	X	X	Frequent sales or specials
	X	X	Unit pricing
		X	Helpful personnel
X			Strong nonfood department

Figure 3-3 Market expectations for the offerings of a new supermarket. *Source*: Adapted from J. Barry Mason and Morris L. Mayer, *Modern Retailing: Theory and Practice*. (Plano, TX: Business Publications, 1984), p. 378.

SEGMENTING RETAIL MARKETS

Consumers differ in terms of what they expect from retail outlets. Some people expect large amounts of sales assistance; others do not want to be "hounded" by retail sales clerks. Some people want lots of attendant services (e.g., credit, delivery, installation), while others regard these as needless frills and prefer lower prices instead. The key point is that markets are composed of segments, and retailers must understand which segment or segments they are aiming at to compete successfully in today's marketplace. For example, the management of a new supermarket has identified three demographic market segments (see Figure 3-3). In addition, it has specified nine different services that could be offered. Although the services desired by each segment somewhat overlap, the segments are, by and large, distinct. Therefore, the supermarket management would stress different services to different market segments.

RETAIL MARKETING MIX

The nature of almost all retail institutions is determined by the choices management makes in light of pressures from the marketplace. These choices constitute the elements of the retail marketing mix and include location decisions, assortments of merchandise to be carried, margin and inventory goals, promotional activities, customer services to be offered, and vendor relations. Thus, as discussed earlier, department stores, specialty stores, chain stores, supermarkets, planned shopping centers, discount houses, and nonstore retailers differ from one another according to the elements of the retail marketing mix chosen by their managements. The retail marketing mix ultimately adopted by management is the result of two major forces: (1) consumer demand for marketing channel services and (2) the organization's internal financial requirements.

The following sections give an overview of each of the elements of the retail marketing mix listed above.

Location Decisions

Management faces two distinct retail location decisions: where to geographically locate the store and where to locate the merchandise within the store. The former are termed *store location decisions* and the latter are called *store layout decisions*.

Store Location.   As discussed earlier, products can be classified on the basis of consumer purchasing patterns. That is, they are thought of as being convenience, shopping, or specialty goods (see Table 3-2). Because of consumer purchasing patterns, store location decisions affect the other elements of the retail marketing mix. As noted in Chapter 2, population movements in and out of certain geographic locations also affect store location decisions.

Retail stores can also be classified according to whether they are convenience, shopping, or specialty stores.[12] Table 3-3 illustrates how the three product types can be cross-classified with the three store types. Retailers first select target markets and then develop locational strategies to reach those segments. For example, 7-Eleven convenience stores carry convenience goods for their target markets. These stores are highly accessible to residential areas, located in heavy traffic areas, and often removed from other convenience stores and supermarkets.

The amount of consumer shopping effort varies between consumer segments as well as between product categories. It also varies over time as life-style changes occur across market segments. For example, the tendency in recent times has been toward decreased shopping. Both working and nonworking women make fewer than two food shopping trips during the typical week.[13] As noted in Chapter 2, saving time is becoming as important to people as saving money. This trend, coupled with widespread access and exposure to mass media, reduces both shopping frequency and the necessity for an information "search" outside the home.

These changes mean that location decisions are becoming even more critical to the survival of retail outlets. Once a retailer has selected a specific geographic market segment that he wishes to enter (e.g., the Southwest) and a specific metropolitan or rural market within that region that he wishes to serve (e.g.,

[12] Louis P. Bucklin, "Retail Strategy and the Classification of Consumer Goods," *Journal of Marketing*, Vol. 27 (January 1963), pp. 50–55. For an extension of Bucklin's scheme, see Morris L. Mayer, J. Barry Mason, and Morris Gee, "A Reconceptualization of Store Classification as Related to Retail Strategy Formulation," *Journal of Retailing*, Vol. 47 (Fall 1971), p. 35.

[13] Effie H. Hacklander, "Do Working Wives Shop Differently for Food?" *National Food Review*, April 1978, pp. 20–23.

TABLE 3.3 Suitable Locations for Various Store and Merchandise Types

Store Classification	Type of Merchandise Sold	Consumer Purchasing Behavior	Most Suitable Type of Location
Convenience store	Convenience goods	Consumer buys most readily available brand at most accessible store	Neighborhood business district near target market population, away from competition, and in heavy pedestrian traffic areas
Convenience store	Shopping goods	Consumer selects purchase from assortment carried by most accessible store	Neighborhood business district near target market population and away from competition
Convenience store	Specialty goods	Consumer purchases favorite brand from most accessible store carrying the item in stock	Planned neighborhood shopping center or downtown central business district
Shopping store	Convenience goods	Consumer is indifferent to the brand of product but shops different stores to secure better buy	Neighborhood business district near target market population
Shopping store	Shopping goods	Consumer makes comparisons among both outlet and brand	Planned shopping center or downtown central business district near similar outlets
Shopping store	Specialty goods	Consumer has strong brand preference but shops a number of stores	Planned shopping center or downtown central business district near similar outlets
Specialty store	Convenience goods	Consumer prefers a specific store but is indifferent to the brand	Freestanding site—consumer preference for outlet is stronger than brand preference
Specialty store	Shopping goods	Consumer prefers a specific store but is uncertain as to which product he will buy	Freestanding site—consumers will search for outlet
Specialty store	Specialty goods	Consumer has preference for a particular store and for a specific brand	Highway, freestanding site—consumers will search for outlet

Source: Raymond A. Marquardt, James C. Makens, and Robert G. Roe, *Retail Management: Satisfaction of Consumer Needs*, 3rd ed. (Chicago: The Dryden Press, 1983), p. 162.

Austin), he must determine the relevant trading area for the type of retailing establishment he wishes to build. Then he must pick a specific site within the trading area on which to locate the store. Because these decisions are so crucial, we now turn to a brief discussion of the major factors involved with each.

Trading Area Measurement and Evaluation. A trading area is the geographic area from which a retailer draws or expects to draw the vast majority of his customers. Since retailing is a localized activity, the bulk of any establishment's sales come from people within the immediately surrounding area. Basically, the extent of a trading area is determined by the nature of the products or services being offered, including assortment, price, availability from other sources, and the extent to which the merchandise or service reflects the user's taste. It is also influenced by consumers' perception of the shopping task or their attitude toward the buying process. The more a store's market is made up of consumers who consider shopping a pleasure, the larger that store's trading area is likely to be.

In operational terms, a *trading area* can be defined from a buyer's, a seller's, or a sales volume standpoint:

- From a *buyer's standpoint*, a trading area is the region inside which the buyer may reasonably expect to find goods and services at competitive and prevailing prices.
- From a *seller's perspective*, a trading area is the region inside which it is economical, in terms of volume and cost, to sell and/or deliver a good or service.
- From a *sales volume point of view*, a trading area is the region from which a retailer attracts approximately 90 percent of his customers for a representative group of merchandise and services. Sometimes the trading area is classified in terms of primary and secondary areas. The primary area includes 75 percent of the customers, while the secondary area includes 15 percent. The remaining 10 percent represents the fringe or tertiary trading area.

Determining a store's trading area is a complex process since it depends on the individual store's character and mode of operation as well as on the cluster of stores surrounding the individual store. For example, if the store sells unique and exclusive merchandise, its trading area definitely becomes larger. Because of its novel assortments, Neiman-Marcus in Dallas has a trading area that encompasses cities well beyond Dallas. Furthermore, because Neiman-Marcus uses mail order extensively for some items during Christmas, its trading area is considerably broader than that of other department stores. In fact, with the increased popularity of mail-order selling and in-home purchasing, trading areas for a wide variety of organizations have increased markedly in recent years.

Trading areas result from the collective trade-offs the market makes in balancing the attractiveness of near and distant retail outlets against the time, cost, and energy customers must expend in overcoming distance.[14] For example, consumers are more willing to travel and search for style and fashion goods than for low-value bulky items such as lumber or convenience goods such as food.[15] The size of trading areas for existing stores and shopping centers can be established through the use of automobile license checks, charge account records, mail-order lists, check clearings, automobile traffic flow, and newspaper circulation. For example, Sears uses an optical scanner to read customer addresses from credit records; the addresses are then plotted by the computer on maps.[16] An analysis of the customer's demographic characteristics can be obtained from these same records to develop a profile of each store's trading area within the Sears organization.

Selecting a Specific Site. Once potential trading areas are defined, several sites within each are proposed and described in terms of such factors as accessibility and traffic flow, extent of trading area population and its distribution, income, economic stability, and competition.[17] The value of a site can be approximated by (1) consumer preference for an existing store or cluster of stores, and (2) natural or man-made barriers prohibiting customers from moving freely in the direction of the proposed site. Exhibit 3-1 highlights a few of the factors that were considered by personal computer retailers in choosing some of their early sites.

Even though retail site location analysis is still more an art than a science, it is possible to go well beyond this first approximation in assessing a potential site. For example, Victory Markets, a chain that comprises nearly 100 supermarkets operating out of Norwich, New York, uses a computerized evaluation model to predict the weekly retail sales of a potential site. The predictions generated by Victory have been within 2 percent of the actual sales generated.[18]

Over the years a number of approaches to the problem of retail site selection have been developed.[19] Because most of these methods suffer from theoretical,

[14] Douglas J. Dalrymple and Donald L. Thompson, *Retailing: An Economic View* (New York: The Free Press, 1969), p. 98.

[15] Ibid.

[16] Computer graphics are becoming extremely useful in trading area and site location analysis. See "The Spurt in Computer Graphics," *Business Week,* June 16, 1980, pp. 104–106.

[17] See Saul B. Cohen and William Applebaum, "Evaluating Store Sites and Determining Store Rents," *Economic Geography,* Vol. 36 (January 1960), pp. 1–35.

[18] "Site Selection by Computer Model," *Chain Store Age—Executive Edition,* Vol. 47 (September 1971), p. E77. For another example of computerized site selection, see the approach the Rayco Company has employed with considerable success in "Can a Computer Tell You Where to Locate Stores?" *Chain Store Age—Executive Edition,* December 1964, p. E28.

[19] Among the more prominent of these methods are the analog methods (see William Applebaum, "Methods for Determining Store Trade Areas, Market Penetration and Potential Sales," *Journal of Marketing Research,* Vol. 3 (May 1966) pp. 127–141); the Huff model (see David L. Huff, "Defining and Estimating a Trading Area," *Journal of Marketing,* Vol. 28 [July 1964], pp. 34–38; and the Multiplicative Competitive Interaction (MCI) model (see Arun K. Jain, and Vijan Mahajan, "Evaluating the Competitive Environment of Retailing Using Multiplicative Competitive Interaction Model," in Jagdish N. Sheth, (ed.) *Research in Marketing.* Vol. 2, [(Greenwich, Conn.: JAI Press, 1979] (pp. 217–235).

operational, or practical difficulties, the retailer must use qualitative judgment in making a final decision. One method that has long endured enables retailers to codify these qualitative judgments. This technique, known as the *checklist method*, is illustrated in Table 3-4.

Retail site location decisions are relatively permanent, given the costs of selecting a new site, readying the facility, and physically moving merchandise, fixtures, and personnel. Because location is so critical for reaching the target customer, this decision requires careful thought and thorough planning.

Store Layout.[20]   Store layout is the physical arrangement and location of merchandise, fixtures, and departments within a store. "The purposes of store layout are to provide for customer movement, present merchandise or services

[20] This section is largely based on Davidson et al., *Retailing Management*, pp. 197–206, 420–424.

TABLE 3.4 A Site Evaluation Checklist

Rating: E G F P[a]

I. Trading area potential
   A. Public utility connections (residential)
   B. Residential building permits issued
   C. School enrollment
   D. New bank accounts opened
   E. Advertising linage in local newspapers
   F. Retail sales volume
   G. Sales tax receipts
   H. Employment-specific
   I. Employment-general

II. Accessibility
   A. Public transportation (serving site)
   B. Private transportation (serving site)
   C. Parking facilities
   D. Long-range trends (transportation facilities)

III. Growth potential
   A. Zoning pattern
   B. Zoning changes
   C. Zoning potential
   D. Utilities trend
   E. Vacant-land market (land zoned for residential use)
   F. Land use pattern (in areas zoned for other than residential)
   G. Retail business land use trend
   H. Retail building trend (building permits issued for new retail business construction)
   I. Retail improvement trend (permits issued for remodeling expansion, etc., in existing properties)
   J. Retail location trend (changes in occupancy of retail business locations)
   K. Income trend for average family unit
   L. Plant and equipment expenditure trend
   M. Payroll trend

IV. Business interception
   A. Location pattern—competitive businesses between site and trade area
   B. Location pattern—competitive businesses between site and trade area (served by and sharing traffic arteries with site)

V. Cumulative attraction potential
   A. Neighboring business survey

VI. Compatability
   A. Compatibility factors

VII. Competitive hazard survey
   A. Competitive pattern—competitors within 1 mile of site (nonintercepting)
   B. Competitive pattern—potential competitive sites

VIII. Site economics
   A. Cost and return analysis
   B. Site efficiency
   C. Natural description
   D. Adjacent amenities (for both vacant-land and existing building sites)

[a]Excellent, Good, Fair, Poor.

Source: Richard Nelson, *The Selection of Retail Locations* (New York: McGraw-Hill, 1958), p. 66.

attractively, and to generally maximize sales.''[21] Store layout includes several decisions: (1) classifying merchandise into related groups or departments; (2) deciding upon the general layout arrangement; (3) determining the amount of space to be allocated to each department or merchandise group; (4) selecting merchandise locations within the store; and (5) planning the most advantageous arrangement of items within merchandise groupings.

Two basic store layouts are the grid and free-flow arrangements (see Figure 3-4). The grid arrangement is designed for efficiency, while the free-flow layout is designed to expose consumers to the merchandise.[22] Table 3-5 lists the advantages and disadvantages of each of these alternatives.

Once the basic layout has been selected and departments or merchandise groups have been assigned locations within the store, the next decision is to allocate selling space within a department. Many retailers are turning to computer models to assist them at this. Exhibit 3-2 describes how one small supermarket chain has benefited from using such a model.

Merchandising Decisions

Traditionally, retail stores were described as ''general,'' ''variety,'' or ''specialty'' stores. These descriptions reflected the *extent* of the merchandise they carried, (i.e., the extent of consumer selection they offered). However, while the specialty store has demonstrated a remarkable upswing in the last two decades, general and variety stores have so drastically changed that these terms have little meaning in the world of U.S. retailing today.

The strategic problem for variety chains is that supermarkets and drugstore chains are selling more and more variety-store-type merchandise. Traditional trade distinctions are rapidly evaporating in a very fluid market. Therefore, rather than cling to old-hat definitions, it is better to use the term *variety* to describe generically different classes of goods making up the product offer, i.e., the *breadth* of product lines. The term *assortment*, on the other hand, refers to the *depth* of product brands or models offered within each generic product category.

Typically, a discount department store like K-mart would have a limited assortment of fast-moving, low-priced items across a wide variety of household goods, ready-to-wear, cosmetics, sporting goods, electric appliances, auto accessories, and the like. In contrast, a specialty store dealing only, or primarily, in home audio-visual electronic goods, such as Radio Shack or Palmer Electronics, would have a very large and complete line of radios, tape recorders, and high fidelity equipment, offering the deepest selection of models, styles, sizes, prices, etc.

Two concepts related to variety and assortment strategies are creaming and scrambling. The *creaming approach* incorporates largely presold, fast-moving items picked out from some other line of retailing. For example, a specialty store adding some lines of impulse goods, such as candy bars, would typically offer only a small number of the fastest-selling brands out of the scores of brands available

---

[21] J. Barry Mason and Morris L. Mayer, *Modern Retailing: Theory and Practice*, 3rd ed. (Plano, Tex: Business Publications, 1984), p. 680.

[22] For further discussion, see ibid., pp. 680–684.

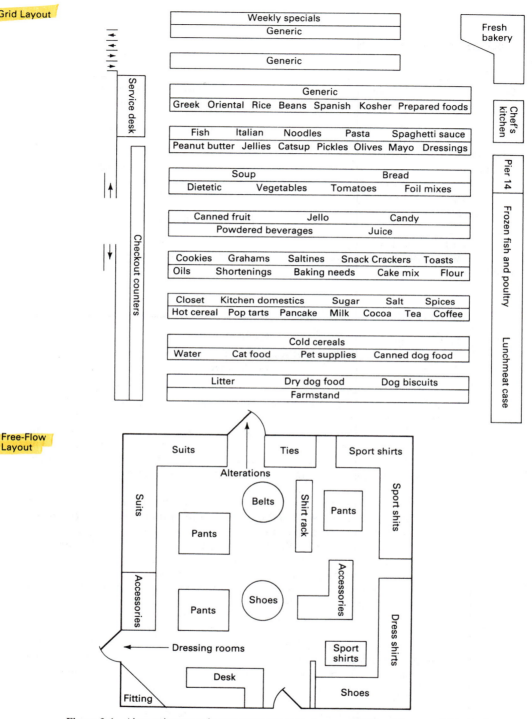

Figure 3-4 Alternative store layout arrangements. *Source*: J. Barry Mason and Morris L. Mayer, *Modern Retailing: Theory and Practice*. (Plano, TX: Business Publications, 1984), p. 680.

Chap. 3   Understanding Channel Participants and Their Needs: Retailers   **81**

TABLE 3.5 Advantages and Disadvantages of Grid and Free-Flow Layouts

Type	Advantages	Disadvantages
Grid	1. Low cost 2. Customer familiarity 3. Merchandise exposure 4. Ease of cleaning 5. Simplified security 6. Possibility of self-service	1. Plain and uninteresting 2. Limited browsing 3. Stimulation of rushed shopping behavior 4. Limited creativity in decor
Free-flow	1. Allowance for browsing and wandering freely 2. Increased impulse purchases 3. Visual appeal 4. Flexibility	1. Loitering encouraged 2. Possible confusion 3. Waste of floor space 4. Cost 5. Difficulty of cleaning

From Robert F. Lusch, *Management of Retail Enterprises*, (Boston: Kent Publishing Company, 1982), p. 471. © by Wadsworth, Inc. Reprinted by permission of PWS-KENT Publishing Company, a division of Wadsworth, Inc.

EXHIBIT 3-2
A New Method of Evaluating Supermarket Shelf Space

Dick's Supermarkets, a chain of five stores headquarted in Platteville, Wisconsin, uses point-of-sale scanner data to measure shelf space and return on investment.

For example, weekly data on unit sales, dollar sales, gross profit dollars, gross profit dollar per cubic foot of shelf space, estimated shelf inventory, return on inventory investment (ROII), and an ROII index were gathered for peanut butter, and jams, jellies, and honey.

"Two stores moved some larger sizes up from the bottom shelf to eye level, but we judged ours to be doing their fair share of profits where they were. . . . One of the values of considering gross profit dollars rather than the traditional percentages or unit sales was brought home by results in our specialty jams and jellies," [Darlene Meyers, manager of one of the Dick's Supermarkets] adds. "They appeared to be slow movers but actually were generating more profit than some of the fast movers with low margins. Needless to say, they have more facings than they used to." (p. 59)

Thus, by using advanced computer modeling techniques, Dick's Supermarkets can keep closer tabs on the space productivity of individual products within a merchandise line as well as on the space productivity of entire product lines.

Source: Adapted from Robert E. O'Neill, "A Competitive Weapon with a Future," *Progressive Grocer*, June 1984, pp. 53, 55, 57, 59.

for display. Creaming is a low-risk ("small but sure") profits tactic, because brands with strong consumer preferences typically allow only small retail margins.[23] Supermarkets and drug chains appear to be creaming when compared to the more systematic departmentalization of discounter product mixes. Drugstores are carrying *selected* cameras, auto accessories, and even camping equipment and lawn furniture, but they certainly are not setting up whole departments in these lines.

Retailers with an eye to larger profit contributions tend to turn to *scrambling*. Scrambling typically involves a much more diverse and unrelated mix of product lines. The brands carried offer higher margins, are slower moving, and do not generate as strong consumer preferences. Scrambling is a "large but unsure" profit tactic with a greater measure of risk. It is likely to involve the retailer in promotional activity to support the line. Scrambling is a widely practiced growth and profit strategy of mass retailers. Nonprescription drugs and watches were among the first products to fall prey to scrambling by high-volume retailers.

Scrambling and creaming illustrate the fact that many modern retailing institutions have diversified their traditional lines of merchandise. Thus, a discussion of general merchandising strategies applicable to a variety of retail operations is more useful here than a discussion of specific merchandising strategies appropriate for a limited set of retailers, since the latter would be quickly outdated.

One such general strategy considers the major trade-off between providing one-stop shopping convenience and offering locational convenience. The size of operation required to carry the wide variety of products that permit one-stop shopping works against building stores at very many locations. On the other hand, an operation that offers locational convenience finds it prohibitively expensive to carry in each store the wide variety of products necessary to satisfy all but the most common market needs.

Another general merchandise strategy involves substantial integration of whole lines of trade. The objective is to enhance one-stop shopping convenience and, as a spillover, to increase consumers' exposure to the store's entire merchandise line. Mass merchandisers such as Sears, K-Mart, and Target are successful examples of this kind of strategy.

A third general merchandising strategy is to offer private-label brands. Private-label goods are those that carry the wholesaler's, retailer's, or buying group's brand name rather than the manufacturer's or national brand name. Sears' Kenmore appliances, Topco's Top Frost frozen foods, A&P's Ann Page peanut butter, and 7-Eleven's Big Gulp fountain soft drinks are prominent examples of private-label merchandise carried by major retailers. Retailers may also consider making generic products available to their target markets.

The reasons retailers offer private-label brands are to gain more control over the promotion and pricing of their merchandise, to build store loyalty, to help introduce new products under the private-label umbrella, to compete against off-price retailers that sell national brands at deep discounts, and to generate high

[23] Ronald R. Gist, *Retailing: Concepts and Decisions* (New York: John Wiley & Sons, 1968), p. 102.

TABLE 3.6 Characteristics of Low-Margin/High-Turnover Retailing Strategies vs. High-Margin/Low-Turnover Strategies

Low Margin, High Turnover	High Margin, Low Turnover
National advertised "presold" or "self-sold" merchandise—customers "buy," as distinct from being "sold" by store personnel	Merchandise "sold" in-store
Assumes low prices are the most important patronage determinant	Assumes service, distinctive merchandise, and sales skill are the most important patronage determinants
Few, if any, "free" services are offered: a separate or "optional" charge may be involved for these	Many services—besides sales help, credit, delivery, many subsidiary services also; e.g., baby-sitting, cooking classes, amusement rooms for children
Tends toward isolated or "low rent" locations	Downtown or shopping center "cluster" locations
Simplified organizational structures—few staff specialists, supervisory and administrative positions	Complex organization, relatively large number of specialists, supervisors, and administrators

Source: Adapted from Ronald R. Gist, *Retailing Concepts and Decisions* (New York: John Wiley & Sons, 1968), pp. 39–40.

unit margins.[24] Private-label brands, then, allow retailers to attract price-conscious consumers who feel that a trade-off in quality, if any, is worth the reduced price.

Margin and Turnover Decisions

Traditional and modern retailing institutions can be characterized by high margin, low turnover, and numerous personal services on the one hand, and low margin, high turnover, and minimum services on the other. Both sets of institutions continue to exist, but in the twentieth century, the spotlight has focused on the efficiencies of the latter style of operation.

Essentially, the low-margin/high-turnover model is aimed at lowering operating costs and passing on the savings to the customer. However, many of the savings "passed on to the customer" must be seen as involving a *transfer* of cost rather than a clear elimination of it. Thus, reductions in the level of store-provided channel services, such as product assortment, convenience of location, atmosphere, personal services, and financial and delivery services, are typical of low-margin/high-turnover retailers. In essence, this operating philosophy capitalizes on the willingness of certain consumer segments to absorb marketing functions or flows in particular purchasing situations.

Table 3-6 characterizes these two operating strategies, and Figure 3-5 illustrates how specific stores may be positioned along the margin and turnover dimensions. Clearly, retailing organizations can fall anywhere in the space

[24] Douglas J. Dalrymple and Leonard J. Parsons, *Marketing Management: Strategy and Cases,* 3rd ed. (New York: John Wiley & Sons, 1983), p. 364.

Figure 3-5 The margin-turnover classification. *Source*: Joseph B. Mason and Morris L. Mayer, *Modern Retailing: Theory and Practice* (Dallas: Business Publications, Inc., 1978), p. 27.

described by the two axes. This is shown by the similarities and contrasts among the three types of grocery retailing institutions depicted in Table 3-7. Sometimes an outlet has been forced by price competition to maintain low margins. Because of a poor location, incompetent management, or undercapitalization, it is unable to generate a sufficient volume of business.[25] Such an outlet might be described as operating in the low-margin/low-turnover quadrant of Figure 3-5. Obviously, this quadrant does not represent an institutional type that is likely to be successful over the long run.

Margin and turnover decisions are particularly crucial for an emerging retail institution, off-price retailing. Off-price retailers, typically in the apparel line of trade, offer well-known brands at 30 to 50 percent below department and specialty store prices.[26] These firms are able to discount their merchandise so heavily because they buy manufacturer close-outs or overruns and operate a no-frills retail atmosphere. Off-price retailers cater to those market segments that desire high-quality merchandise and, to get it at low prices, are willing to sacrifice locational convenience, up-to-date styling, and credit availability. Exhibit 3-3 presents a brief portrayal of one off-price retail organization.

Promotion Decisions

One way in which retailers communicate their store offerings to their target markets is through their promotional strategies. A variety of means for promoting a store are available. These include advertising, personal selling, sales promotion, and publicity. The purpose of this section is to briefly review these elements of retail promotional strategy. Before proceeding, however, we should note that the amount and relative emphasis of each of these promotional elements depends upon the retailer's objectives for promotion. These objectives may be either short-term or longer-run (see Figure 3-6).

[25] Mason and Mayer, *Modern Retailing*, p. 29.

[26] Davidson et al., *Retailing Management*, p. 99.

TABLE 3.7 Different Grocery Retailing Institutions

Convenience Store Characteristics	Combination Store Characteristics	Warehouse Store Characteristics
Normally less than 1,000 items	Generally range from 35,000 to 60,000 square feet	Reduced gross margins, running as low as 11–12%
Limited number of national brands and sporadic brand/item availability	Full food mix, including perishables	Reduced labor costs, usually under 4% of sales or one half to one third that of a conventional supermarket
Generally one brand and one size per item	Features a pharmacy, health and beauty aids, toiletries, and all general merchandise normally carried by a super-drugstore	High unit sales; individual store tapes run as high as five times the supermarket average
Store hours limited		
Items displayed in cut cartons	Ratio of food to drug usually 60–40	Limited item selection; brands, sizes, and varieties carried by warehouse markets vary, but range from 1,000 to 8,000 items
No individual item pricing		
Little or no perishables	Average annual volume $13 million, with some reaching $20 million or more	Erratic brand/item availability
Customers do their own bagging		
Generally 5,000–14,000 square feet of selling area	25% to 30% of sales attributed to general merchandise	Special deal items; different brands will appear and disappear as manufacturer deals come and go
No check cashing	Common checkout area for food, drug, and general merchandise items	Limited perishables; some warehouse markets carry fresh meat and push big cuts or large orders. Many carry frozen meat only— or none at all. Produce may be limited or in bulk only if available at all
Little advertising	Average 13 checkouts with average weekly sales of $19,000 per checkout	
		Varied locations; warehouse stores emerged in fringe market areas drawing blue-collar workers, but many are now opening in large cities and drawing a cross section of the population
		Low construction costs; preexisting buildings or simple concrete block construction with minimum decor are generally preferred

Source: Adapted from "Continuing Evolution in Grocery Retailing." *The Nielsen Researcher*, No. 2 (1980), pp. 4, 5, and 8.

Advertising. Retail advertising decisions involve a host of interrelated factors. Among them are the size of the advertising budget, the media to be used, and the timing of advertising.

Size of the Budget. The size of the advertising budget varies from retail firm to retail firm. Some retailers allocate a certain percentage of sales to advertising; others allocate what they can "afford." Still other retail organizations determine the size of their advertising on the basis of the promotional objectives

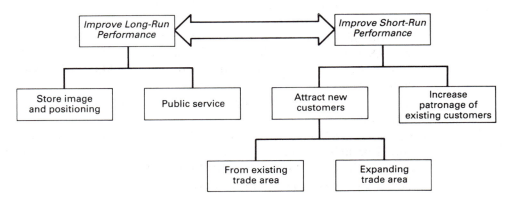

Figure 3-6 Possible promotion objectives in retailing. From Robert F. Lusch, *Management of Retail Enterprises*, (Boston: Kent Publishing Company, 1982), p. 519. © by Wadsworth, Inc. Reprinted by permission of PWS-KENT Publishing Company, a division of Wadsworth, Inc.

TABLE 3.8 Factors in Allocating Advertising Dollars

High Advertising Allocation	Low Advertising Allocation
High gross margin percentage	Low gross margin percentage
High advertising elasticity of demand	Low advertising elasticity of demand
Dominant or potentially dominant market share in department or merchandise line	Low market share and limited potential for being dominant market share department or line
Good backup resources (space, inventory, accounts receivable, people)	Poor backup resources (space, inventory, accounts receivable, people)
Willingness to allocate enough to achieve "critical mass"	Unwillingness to allocate enough to achieve "critical mass"

From Robert F. Lusch, *Management of Retail Enterprises*, (Boston: Kent Publishing, 1982), p. 530. © by Wadsworth, Inc. Reprinted by permission of PWS-KENT Publishing Company, a division of Wadsworth, Inc.

to be reached and the tasks to be performed to achieve them.[27] Table 3-8 details some of the factors to be considered in setting either high or low retail advertising budgets.

Media for Retail Advertising. The major media available to retail advertisers are the same as those for other advertisers: newspapers, radio, television, magazines, billboards, and direct mail. Other advertising media the advertiser might consider are the Yellow Pages, transit advertising, and shopping newspapers. The Yellow Pages and transit advertising are primarily used to promote the store itself, while shopping newspaper advertising is largely used for price promotions.[28] The advantages and disadvantages of the different advertising media for retailers are presented in Table 3-9.

Timing.[29] The time of day, day of the week, week of the month, and month of the year in which the consumer receives the advertising are the essence of the timing decision. The following are some conventional pieces of wisdom to be considered in choosing the timing of retail advertising:

- Ads should appear on, or slightly precede, the days when customers are most likely to purchase. Thus, grocery ads should appear on Wednesday and Thursday if most customers do their grocery shopping on Thursday, Friday or Saturday.
- Advertising should be concentrated around the times when customers receive their paychecks.
- Retailers with limited advertising funds should concentrate their advertising during periods of highest seasonal demand. Thus, small toy stores should advertise heaviest during the Christmas season.
- Because poor weather keeps shoppers indoors and few sales are attractive

[27] For further discussion of how retail advertising budgets are determined, see Robert F. Lusch. *Management of Retail Enterprises* (Boston: Kent Publishing, 1982), pp. 526–530.

[28] Ibid., p. 533.

[29] This section is based heavily on ibid., pp. 534–535.

TABLE 3.9 Advantages and Disadvantages of Different Advertising Media for Retailers

Medium	Advantages	Disadvantages
Newspapers	• Wide circulation • Permanence • Low cost • Short advertisement preparation time	• Overuse by all retailers • Lack of suburban coverage
Television	• Visual impact • Total market coverage	• High cost • Technical difficulties • Temporary nature of message
Radio	• Low cost • Demographic targeting possible • Quick response time • High creativity possible	• No visual impact • Radio does not command listener attention
Magazines (Regional editions)	• High prestige • Strong fashion appeal possible	• High cost • Demographic waste
Billboards	• Wide coverage • Low cost per viewer • Geographic selectivity	• Limited message length
Direct Mail	• Precise market targeting	• Very high costs • Potential overuse

Source: Albert D. Bates, *Retailing and Its Environment* (New York: Van Nostrand, 1979), p. 209.

enough to entice them outside, retailers should minimize advertising during periods of bad weather.

- The retailer should time ads to appear during the time of day or day of the week when an ad is most likely to reach its target audience.
- The higher the degree to which purchases within a product class are made out of habit, the more the advertising should precede the habitual time of purchase.
- The greater the carryover effects (i.e., the more likely the ad is remembered and influences sales in the future), the more the advertising should precede the time of purchase.

Personal Selling. Too many retail organizations have become also-rans because they underestimated the importance of personal selling in creating a pleasant and helpful atmosphere for the customer. That personal selling is a critical element of retail promotional strategy is obvious in stores that emphasize personal service and assistance. However, even in self-service operations, retail personnel have face-to-face contact with the store's customers and, in effect, are involved in personal selling, although they (and the store's management) may not be aware of it. Obvious inexperience, poor aptitude for selling, indifference toward customers, improper use of high-pressure sales tactics, distasteful dress and unclean or slovenly appearance, breaches of social etiquette, inadequate knowledge of the merchandise, and failure to work hard enough to make the sale or close the sale are serious weaknesses in retail personnel that should be overcome whether the organization uses self-service or personalized service.[30]

The key point is that personal selling is pervasive in retail organizations and that retail management should ensure that each employee understands that he or she is an integral part of the retail marketing program.[31]

Sales Promotion. Sales promotion techniques are those promotional devices, other than personal selling, advertising, and publicity, that are used to generate demand.[32] Among the more frequently used sales promotion tools are special sales events, store displays, consumer premiums, games, and product demonstrations.

Special Sales Events.[33] Special sales events may be held for the entire store or for one or more departments simultaneously, and may last anywhere from a single day to an entire month. Special sales events are conducted to (1) stimulate sales of regular merchandise by temporary markdowns; (2) sell promotional merchandise bought especially for the event; or (3) reduce inventories of seasonal, slow-moving, or broken assortments of merchandise. Among the disadvantages of this form of sales promotion are potential legal problems stemming from the use of price advertising, the risk of not increasing permanent store traffic, possible declines in sales volume immediately before the event because consumers anticipate reduced prices, a potential overemphasis on special sales events, and an increase in ill-will if the quality of customer service suffers because of increased store traffic. On the other hand, special sales events may be quite effective when integrated with a long-term plan of retail marketing communications that includes advertising, personal selling, and publicity.

Store Displays. Store displays comprise window displays and interior displays and signs. The objective is either to sell the featured merchandise or to draw customers into the store. Effective displays reinforce the store's advertising campaigns by supplementing them with in-store information.

Consumer Premiums and Games of Chance. Consumer premiums are gifts or discounts on merchandise if the shopper buys a particular product or a particular quantity of merchandise. A home appliance store, for example, may offer a free stand for every microwave oven purchased. Or a supermarket may offer so many trading stamps for each dollar of purchase. Or a savings and loan may give away blankets, cookware, or brass decorative items for various sizes of deposits.

The chance to win a gift is the inducement offered by games. The difference between premiums and games is that with a premium, anyone satisfying the

---

[30] Davidson et al., *Retailing Management*, p. 227.

[31] For a discussion of the major elements in managing the retail personal sales staff, see Lusch, *Management of Retail Enterprises*, pp. 544–561.

[32] Except where noted, this section is largely based on ibid., pp. 536–541.

[33] This section is based heavily on Davidson et al., *Retailing Management*, pp. 241–244.

requirements is eligible for the gift, while with a game, only one or a few buyers will receive the gift.

Both premiums and games can be effective short-term adjuncts to personal selling, advertising, publicity, and other forms of sales promotion if they are carefully planned and integrated with the retail store's total communication effort. Sometimes, however, competitors allow themselves to get sucked into premium and games "wars," with each outlet trying to capture the other's customers. The results are that no retailer gains any permanent new customers and all must bear the expense of the premium or game merchandise. In these wars, the costs of premiums and games dramatically exceed their benefits.

Product Demonstrations. Using in-store demonstrations can sometimes help retailers increase short-term sales for some of their merchandise. For example, midwestern supermarkets occasionally offer free samples of Wilson's fresh country sausage as an inducement to consumers to try or to buy more of that product. State fairs, home shows, and other exhibitions often provide retail stores with the opportunity to demonstrate their merchandise. Friedman's Microwave Ovens specialty store, for example, conducts free microwave cooking demonstrations four times daily during the state fair. The objective, of course, is to show the benefits of microwave cooking, to demonstrate how easy it is to become an accomplished microwave cook, and to point out how simply one can buy a microwave oven at Friedman's.

Publicity. Publicity is any form of nonpaid promotion received by the retail store; it usually takes the form of news about the store. News stories about a J. C. Penney store relocating within a metropolitan area would be an illustration of publicity. Examples of non-news retail publicity are Macy's Thanksgiving Day parade in New York City; Ethel's 76 service stations' sponsorship of a Little League baseball team; and Ronald McDonald Houses, which are lodging facilities for parents and relatives who are visiting hospitalized children. The advantages of publicity are that it is considered objective and credible because it is seen as news, and that it reaches a mass audience. The primary disadvantages are that publicity is difficult to control and to time properly. To make publicity as effective as possible, it should be treated as a retail promotional technique and should be integrated, as far as practicable, with the advertising, personal selling, and sales promotional strategies.

Services

The services offered by a retail store often distinguish it from its competitors as well as from other retail institutions carrying the same physical merchandise. The more common services retailers provide to their customers are listed in Table 3-10.

Because customers and products differ in their service requirements, successful retail operations can be designed around different levels of service. Thus, self-service outlets, such as warehouse retailers, supermarkets, and discount stores, perform very few services, emphasize price appeals, and generally

TABLE 3.10 Sales Support Services Used Frequently by Retailers

Free (or reduced-rate) parking	Public restrooms
Free (or reduced-rate) bus service	Birthday (anniversary) reminders
Product delivery	Extended product warranties
Telephone shopping	Use of *Consumer Reports* or other consumer journals
Mail-order (catalog) shopping	Special orders for items not stocked
Lay-away	Free coffee (or champagne) while shopping
C.O.D. payment	Information desks
Bridal registry	Party counseling
Fashion shows	Baby strollers
Gift wrapping	Gift certificates
Alterations	Trade-ins
Liberal returned goods policies	Children's playrooms
Check cashing	Product locator (checking with other stores on product availability)
On-sight [sic] product usage (such as pools for testing fly casting equipment)	Product repair
Demonstration models (for at-home use)	In-store banking
Parcel pickup service	Free telephone calls
Baggage/parcel lockers	Personal shopping
After-hours shopping (for preferred customers)	Lost and found
Stag nights (male shopping only)	Bill payment (in-store)
Shopping consultants	
Home economists	

Source: Albert D. Bates, *Retailing and Its Environment* (New York: D. Van Nostrand Company, 1979), p. 290.

focus on staple goods. Full-service outlets, such as specialty and department stores, provide a wide variety of services and tend to be oriented toward merchandising fashion or specialty goods.

The most dramatic innovations in retailing over the past 45 years have hinged on reducing customer services. However, competitive pressures have made many of these innovators (e.g., discount houses, warehouse stores, and catalog showrooms) reinstate certain services (check-writing privileges and credit cards, for example). Many full-service retailing institutions, on the other hand, have also experienced robust growth during the same period. Mail-order selling (e.g., L. L. Bean, Lands' End, J. C. Whitney), numerous specialty stores (e.g., The Limited, The Gap, Crate & Barrel), and vending machine retailing have either maintained or increased their services to consumers.[34]

Vendor Relations

Vendor relations refers to the relationship a retail institution maintains with its suppliers. The growth in vertical marketing systems noted in Chapter 2 has dictated that members of the marketing channel cooperate to a greater degree than

[34] Despite the fact that vending machines rely on self-service, they are not low in service. Except for in-home shopping, "automatic" retailers offer the highest delivery and convenience service of all retailing institutions.

ever before if they wish to be competitive. In addition, the other environmental pressures discussed in Chapter 2 impact the marketing channel as a whole. These factors also push channel members to increase their cooperation. Essentially, this cooperation entails coordinating the firms' marketing mix elements more carefully, assuring steady sources of supply, and providing a desirable pool of customers.

The primary focus of this book is on relationships among members of the marketing channel, including those between retailers and their suppliers. Thus, such issues as buying direct from manufacturers versus buying through wholesalers, evaluating prospective vendors, power and dependence relations with vendors, conflict with suppliers, and coordinating the retailer's marketing mix elements with those of other channel members are topics that will unfold as the book progresses.

SUMMARY

The structure and strategy of retailing during the past century has been extremely dynamic. Older institutions have faded away as newer ones have evolved to fill market needs better. Differences in retailing institutions can be described by differences in their marketing strategies. This chapter explored the structure of retailing and the basic elements of retailing strategy.

Retailing deals with the selling of goods and services to ultimate consumers. The business of retailing is conducted in stores, in homes, over the telephone, through the mail, and by vending machines. Some of the more common retailing institutions—department stores, chain stores, supermarkets, planned shopping centers, discount houses, automatic vending machines, mail-order houses, and house-to-house selling—were described. It was also noted that over the past 50 years or so the number of retail institutions has grown only marginally compared to the growth in retail sales. This means the retailing industry is now characterized by larger firms.

Retailing marketing strategy comprises customer expectations, retail market segmentation, and the retail marketing mix. Customers of retail outlets form many expectations about what they believe the stores should and actually do offer. Expectations about locational convenience and store hours, store atmosphere, merchandise, prices, information and interaction, and services dictate which stores consumers will patronize and which ones they will avoid.

Because customers have varying sets of expectations, retailers can segment their markets and focus on those customers whose expectations they are best equipped to meet. By targeting key sets of customers and by developing marketing mixes to serve these markets, retailers can position their firms to be both attractive to their targets and distinct from their competitors' stores.

The key factors for developing an effective retail marketing mix are store location and layout, merchandise strategies, margin and inventory turnover considerations, promotional strategy, services, and vendor relations. As with nonretail firms, the elements of the marketing mix must be carefully coordinated to ensure consistency within the mix, as well as with the market target's expectations and the overall corporate goals and objectives.

In addition to customer expectations, retail market segmentation, and the retail marketing mix, effective retail marketing strategy must consider the key elements of the environment of marketing channels discussed in Chapter 2. Retailers must pay particular attention to the facets of the environment that affect the demand for marketing channel services, but must not overlook facets that influence their supply.

DISCUSSION QUESTIONS

1. How would you describe competition in retailing (perfect competition, monopolist competition, oligopolistic competition, pure monopoly) for the following lines of trade?
   a. Exotic motor cars (e.g., Ferraris, Rolls-Royces, Lamborghinis)
   b. Unprepared food (i.e., perhaps processed, but not cooked)
   c. Prepared food (i.e., ready-to-eat, either on premises or to take out)
   d. Home computers
   e. Athletic shoes
   f. Women's cosmetics

2. Table 3-1 shows how the composition of retail sales changed between 1972 and 1981. What do you think the composition will be in 1995? Explain the rationale for your answer.

3. The chapter discussed six different types of expectations that consumers form about retail outlets. Describe the assumptions each of the following retail institutions makes about each of the six types of expectations. (For example, a 7-Eleven store assumes that consumers have high expectations for locational and temporal convenience.)
   a. Conventional supermarkets
   b. Off-price stores
   c. Department stores
   d. Mail-order apparel outlets
   e. Specialty shops
   f. Catalog showrooms

4. Cal O'Rie is planning to open a new restaurant in a medium-sized midwestern college town. Before he settles on a concept, a menu, and price ranges for his venture, Cal wants to determine the type of clientele he should be trying to reach. Identify four possible market segments for prepared food. What kinds of information should Cal gather before he chooses one of these segments as his target market? Explain.

5. The text suggests that a poor retail location can be offset by unique merchandise, good prices, and effective use of the other elements of the retail marketing mix. Find examples of stores in your city or region that fit this situation. Discuss how these stores have overcome their poor locations.

6. Using the retail site checklist in Table 3-4, evaluate the retail locations of two competing stores in any one of the following lines of trade:
   a. Fast food
   b. Automatic teller machines
   c. Personal computers

d. Hardware

e. Dry cleaners

f. Ice cream (on-premise consumption only)

7. Felix Schwartzkatz had just opened his first videogame parlor and was considering how to best promote his new venture. Specifically, he wondered how large his advertising budget should be, what media he should use, and when he should advertise. Advise Felix, keeping in mind the his target market consists primarily of students 10 to 25 years old.

8. If personal selling is such an important aspect of retail promotional strategy, why do so many retailers seemingly ignore it? Or do they really ignore it? Use examples from your city or region to support your arguments.

9. As noted in the text, new retailing institutions develop by offering unique combinations of location, merchandise assortments, margin and turnover elements, promotional strategy, services, and vendor relations. For one of the following lines of trade, describe the major retailing institutions that carry these goods or offer these services. Develop a new retailing institution that might successfully compete against these existing ones. Explain your innovation.

a. Gasoline

b. Motion pictures

c. Books and magazines

d. Pastries

e. Camping equipment

f. Stationery and office supplies

4

Understanding Channel Participants And Their Needs: Wholesalers

LEARNING OBJECTIVES

Upon completing this chapter, you will be able to:

- *Understand how wholesalers contribute to the functioning of the marketing channel.*

- *Characterize the three basic institutions constituting wholesale trade—merchant wholesalers, agents and brokers, and manufacturers' sales branches and offices.*

- *Describe the basic trends in the structure of wholesaling.*

- *Discuss how wholesalers can serve suppliers, retailers, and business users.*

- *Understand the major threats to the viability of wholesalers serving both consumer and business markets.*

- *Describe some of the key elements of wholesale marketing strategy.*

WHOLESALING DEFINED

One of the most confusing aspects of marketing channels is determining exactly what wholesaling is. The nomenclature of the distributive trades adds to this confusion. Wholesalers are called jobbers, distributors, and middlemen. Manufacturers' agents, rack jobbers, food brokers, commission merchants, and a host of other functionaries are also members of the wholesaling "industry." Therefore, any attempt to define just what a wholesaler is is bound to apply in some situations but miss the mark in others.

Nevertheless, to avoid semantic debates, we can adopt the U.S. Bureau of the Census's definition for starters:

> Wholesaling is concerned with the activities of those persons or establishments which sell to retailers and other merchants, and/or to industrial, institutional, and commercial users, but who do not sell in significant amounts to ultimate consumers.

Of course, accepting this definition as the gospel truth means that every sale made by every organization to anyone but an ultimate consumer is a "wholesale sale." This would include every sale by a manufacturing firm (with the exception of the small amount of sales made through factory outlets to household consumers) as well as sales made by such diverse organizations as hotels, insurance companies, and accounting firms when they deal with "industrial, institutional, and commercial" users in booking rooms, arranging pension plans, or preparing annual reports.

In actuality, then, almost all organizations (except those dealing solely with ultimate consumers) are engaged in wholesale transactions. Taking such a broad perspective in this chapter would force us to consider every form of marketing at every level in a channel other than retailing. Our intention is not to provide a global view of marketing practices, but to take a brief look at some of the structural and strategic dimensions of wholesale trade. For our purposes, then, wholesale trade is defined narrowly to encompass only the operations of specialized independently owned and operated wholesaling institutions and establishments engaged primarily in domestic marketing. About 50 percent of the total output marketed "at wholesale" passes through such institutions and establishments. In addition, this chapter focuses largely on so-called merchant wholesalers—independently owned firms that purchase goods from suppliers for their own account, operate one or more warehouses in which they receive and take title to goods, store them, and later reship them.[1]

Such a narrow focus permits a fuller exposure to and a more thorough examination of those channel members normally referred to as "wholesalers." Thus, when specific approaches to channel management are discussed in later chapters, account may be taken of the unique contributions, characteristics, and orientations of these institutions in forming the most beneficial systemwide strategies for the channel.

[1] Richard S. Lopata, "Faster Pace in Wholesaling," *Harvard Business Review*, Vol. 47 (July–August 1969), p. 131.

RATIONALE FOR THE EMERGENCE OF MODERN WHOLESALERS

The wholesaler's functions are shaped by the vast economic task of coordinating production and consumption.[2] Thus, wholesalers aid in bridging the time and space gap between periods and places in which goods are produced and those in which they are consumed or used.

This matching process of wholesalers is the key to their economic viability. As noted in Chapter 1, the quantities in which goods are produced or the characteristics of those goods frequently do not match either the quantities in which they are demanded or the characteristics desired by those who use or consume them. In other words, manufacturers usually produce a large quantity of a limited number of products, whereas industrial and household consumers purchase only a few items of a large number of diverse products. Middlemen (e.g., wholesalers and retailers) reduce this *discrepancy of assortments*, thereby enabling consumers to avoid dealing directly with individual manufacturers in order to satisfy their needs.

A wholesaler exists because of the functions he performs for the suppliers and customers he serves, be they retailers, other wholesalers, institutions (e.g., hospitals, schools, restaurants), manufacturers, or any other type of business enterprise. For example, with respect to his customers, a wholesaler can often provide the following services:

- *Physical possession.* A wholesaler can store goods in anticipation of customer needs and provide quick delivery when the goods are desired because he is usually located closer to customers than more centralized manufacturing facilities.
- *Ownership.* Many wholesalers take title to the goods they store; therefore, they absorb inventory carrying costs for their customers. Customers can purchase from wholesalers in small lots; whereas, if they purchase directly, they generally must assume a larger inventory burden.
- *Financing.* A wholesaler finances the exchange process by investing in inventory and by extending credit to customers.
- *Risk-taking.* A wholesaler assumes risk when he takes possession and ownership of products that can deteriorate or become obsolete. He can also assist his customers in reducing risk by providing information about technical features, appropriate usage, availability, product quality, competitive conditions, and so on.
- *Negotiating.* Wholesalers generally bring together an *assortment* of merchandise, usually of related items, by negotiating with a number of different sources.
- *Ordering.* A wholesaler can anticipate his customers' needs and thereby simplify their buying tasks. Rather than having to negotiate and purchase

---

[2] Wroe Alderson, "Factors Governing the Development of Marketing Channels," in William G. Moller, Jr., and David L. Wilemon (eds.), *Marketing Channels: A Systems Viewpoint* (Homewood, Ill.: Richard D. Irwin, 1971), p. 20.

from a large number of sources, a customer can order from one source—the wholesaler—the assortment of products required. In addition, a wholesaler may inspect, test, or judge the products he receives for quality, thereby assuming an even greater role in the ordering process for his customers.

Thus, for example, where integrated circuits are components in security alarm systems, it may be less costly for the security alarm producer to place the burden of handling, owning, storing, delivering, and ordering the goods on a wholesaler than to order in very large lots directly from the integrated circuit manufacturer. This is especially true if the goods will have to be held a considerable period of time before they are fully used up in the production process. Similar economies are available to purchasers of certain consumer goods, such as toys. For instance, almost 80 percent of all retail toy sales are made during November and December. Although thousands of toys are marketed every Christmas season, probably less than a hundred are best sellers. Because the demand for toys tends to be faddish, retailers cannot accurately predict their needed inventory too far in advance. Therefore, they place numerous reorders of popular toys during the peak selling season. Wholesalers maintain large speculative inventories close to retail markets, thus permitting speedy delivery of toys on short notice.

TYPES OF WHOLESALERS

Because of the varying needs of different target markets for the services described in the previous section, a variety of wholesaling institutions have emerged and evolved. Figure 4-1 illustrates a number of these different types of wholesale institutions. Such a variety of wholesale alternatives offers buyers and sellers many choices for structuring their marketing channels. The reason this variety is such an advantage is that it makes possible a high degree of shifting of the marketing functions or flows. All of the wholesaling functions might be shifted or only a part of them might be transferred, depending upon the number and type of wholesalers used.

There are three basic types of wholesale institutions—merchant wholesalers, agent wholesalers, and manufacturers' sales branches and offices. Each is discussed below.

Merchant Wholesalers

Merchant wholesalers take ownership of goods in which they deal. Merchant wholesalers are independently owned from suppliers, on the one hand, and from retailers, on the other. They are compensated for their services on a profit margin basis. Merchant wholesalers are of two general classes: full-function or service wholesalers and limited-function wholesalers.

Full-Function or Service Wholesalers. These merchant wholesalers perform all or most of the marketing functions normally associated with wholesaling. They

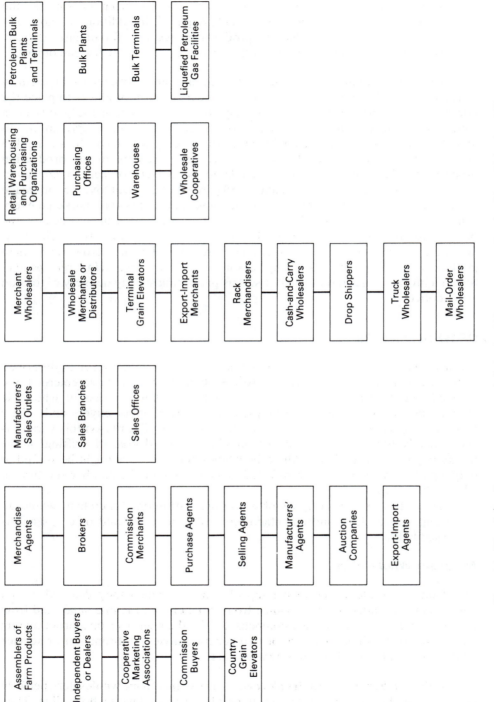

Figure 4-1 The wholesaling structure—types of wholesale middlemen. *Source:* Reprinted from Richard M. Hill, *Wholesaling Management* (Homewood, Ill.: Richard D. Irwin, 1963).

may carry a broad variety of goods. A full-function food wholesaler such as Fleming, for example, might carry meats, produce, groceries (i.e., packaged food items), dairy products, and nonfood items such as health and beauty aids. Full-function wholesalers such as Mass Merchandisers carry a more limited line of supermarket items; they handle nonfood items such as health and beauty aids, light bulbs, and hardware. Service wholesalers may even specialize in a very narrow range of goods such as health foods or fresh produce. The extent of product-line specialization depends upon the particular needs and wants of the wholesaler's target markets.

By taking ownership of the products they carry, service wholesalers assume the risks of selling these goods at a profit. Full-function wholesalers, through the physical possession flow, maintain inventories of their product lines. From these stocks, customer orders are filled and delivered. Personal selling, advertising, and sales promotion (especially through extensive catalogs) are some of the ways in which these wholesalers perform the promotion function in the marketing channel. Negotiating with buyers and sellers over the prices of the goods, their quality, the order quantity, and other terms of sale along with extending credit to buyers are other tasks undertaken by full-function wholesalers. Of course, these wholesalers order stocks for their inventories, make up special orders for their customers, pass along market information to their suppliers, and accept payment for their customers' purchases. All in all, then, service or full-function wholesalers participate in most of the marketing channel flows or tasks.

Limited-Function Wholesalers. These merchant wholesalers perform only some of the functions typically associated with wholesaling. Among the more common limited-function wholesalers are cash-and-carry wholesalers, drop shippers, truck wholesalers, mail-order wholesalers, producers' and retail cooperatives, and rack jobbers.[3] The functions which these intermediaries perform are outlined in Table 4-1.

Cash-and-carry wholesalers offer their small business customers no credit or delivery. Nor do they provide their customers with much in the way of managerial assistances. Although they do sell to the ultimate consumer, warehouse clubs such as Sam's Place and Price Club are prominent examples of cash and carry wholesalers, since they emphasize the small business market.

Drop shippers do not take possession of the goods they handle; therefore, they do not store inventory nor provide delivery for their customers. By taking ownership of the goods they carry, however, drop shippers do absorb risk for both their suppliers and their customers. Commodities and natural resources such as grain, lumber, and coal are typically marketed through drop shippers.

Truck wholesalers or wagon jobbers provide most of the functions listed in Table 4-1. Because their inventories are carried right on their trucks, these limited-function wholesalers provide their customers with a high degree of locational convenience. Snap-On Tools which markets its high-quality tools

---

[3] For further discussion, see E. Jerome McCarthy and William D. Perreault, Jr., *Basic Marketing: A Managerial Approach*, 9th ed. (Homewood, Ill.: Richard D. Irwin, 1987), pp. 330–337.

TABLE 4.1 Functions Provided by Limited-Function Merchant Wholesalers

Functions	Cash-and-Carry	Drop Shipper	Truck	Mail-Order	Cooperatives	Rack Jobbers
For Customers:						
Anticipates needs	X		X	X	X	X
"Regroups" goods (one or more of four steps). . .	X		X	X	X	X
Carries stocks.	X		X	X	X	X
Delivers goods			X		X	X
Grants credit.		X	Maybe	Maybe	Maybe	Consignment (in some cases)
Provides information and advisory services		X	Some	Some	X	
Provides buying function . .		X	X	X	Some	X
Owns and transfer title to goods	X	X	X	X	X	X
For Producers:						
Provides producers' selling function.	X	X	X	X	X	X
Stores inventory	X		X	X	X	X
Helps finance by owning stocks.	X		X	X	X	X
Reduces credit risk	X	X	X	X	X	X
Provides market information	X	X	Some	X	X	Some

Source: E. Jerome McCarthy and William D. Perreault, Jr., *Basic Marketing: A Managerial Approach*, 9th ed. (Homewood, Ill.: Richard D. Irwin, 1987), p. 331.

directly to all types of mechanics and service stations is a prominent example of a truck wholesaler.

Mail-order wholesalers operate similar to mail-order retailers; the primary difference is that wholesalers serve the business, governmental, and institutional markets.

Independent farm producers often band together to market their output jointly and to buy farm implements and supplies at quantity discounts; associations of independent retailers are sometimes formed to gain the advantages of quantity buying and joint advertising. These associations are called *producer cooperatives* and *retail cooperatives*, respectively. Examples of the former are Sunkist Growers, Land O'Lakes, and Farmland Industries. Among the most notable of the retail cooperatives are Ace Hardware, Cotter & Company (True-Value Hardware), and Topco Associates, a private-label food wholesaler owned by a group of supermarket chains and grocery wholesalers. More about both types of cooperatives will be discussed in Chapter 9.

Marketing nonfood items to smaller grocery stores, usually in smaller geographic areas, is the stock-in-trade of *rack jobbers*. In some cases, these wholesalers sell their goods on a consignment basis. Among the products carried

TABLE 4.2 Functions Provided by Agent Wholesalers

Functions	Manufacturers' Agents	Brokers	Commission Merchants	Selling Agents	Auction Companies
For Customers:					
Anticipates needs..........	Sometimes	Some			
"Regroups" goods (one or more of four steps).......	Some		X		X
Carries stocks	Sometimes		X		Sometimes
Delivers goods............	Sometimes		X		
Grants credit			Sometimes	X	Some
Provides information and advisory services	X	X	X	X	
Provides buying function	X	Some	X	X	X
Owns and transfers title to goods................			Transfers only		Transfers only
For Producer:					
Provides selling function.....	X	Some	X	X	X
Stores inventory	Sometimes		X		X
Helps finance by owning stocks					
Reduces credit risk........				X	Some
Provides market information..	X	X	X	X	

Source: E. Jerome McCarthy and William D. Perreault, Jr., *Basic Marketing: A Managerial Approach*, 9th ed. (Homewood, Ill.: Richard D. Irwin, 1987), pp. 335.

by rack jobbers are toys and games, inexpensive jewelry, pet food, a very few lines of clothing, and so forth.

Agent Wholesalers

Unlike merchant wholesalers, agent wholesalers do not take ownership, and rarely take possession, of the products they market. These intermediaries are primarily involved in the buying and selling of goods and services. The main marketing tasks they participate in are negotiation, market information, promotion, and ordering (see Table 4-2). Agents receive a commission for performing these functions.

Among the different types of agents are manufacturers' agents, brokers, commission merchants, selling agents, and auction companies. Each is briefly discussed below.[4] While these agent wholesalers are largely involved in domestic trade, agent wholesalers also play an integral role in international trade. The discussion of international wholesalers will be deferred to Chapter 13.

Manufacturers' agents are independent firms which typically handle noncompeting lines of a variety of manufacturers and are often used in place of a manufacturer's own sales force. New companies use manufacturers agents when they have neither the expertise nor the resources to develop their own sales force. Established firms rely upon manufacturers agents when they wish to concentrate

[4] For further discussion, see ibid.

upon manufacturing and prefer to subcontract their distribution activities or when they wish to enter new markets. In this latter instance, manufacturers' agents are generally more familiar with the market and can provide more immediate representation than the producer could by developing his own sales force.

Brokers unite buyers and sellers by dealing in market information including what products particular suppliers have available, what products specific buyers demand, and what both the general and specific price levels are. Brokers are commonly used in the real estate industry where they negotiate the buying and selling of property as well as negotiate its rental and leasing. Brokers play a key role in the distribution of food products as well. In fact, many small food producers and small food wholesalers rely heavily upon food brokers to provide them with outlets for their products and sources of supply, respectively.

Commission merchants sometimes called ''factors,'' receive goods on consignment and then sell them on a commission basis. Except for not owning the goods they handle, these agent wholesalers operate much like full-service merchant wholesalers. That is, they often participate in the physical possession, promotion, negotiation, financing, risking, ordering, payment, and market information flows.

Selling agents differ from manufacturers' agents and brokers in that they normally carry a supplier's entire product line. Unlike manufacturers' agents and brokers, they usually set prices, terms of sale, and the promotional activities to be undertaken. Thus, selling agents, in effect, act as the manufacturer's sales force. Note that as with other agent wholesalers, selling agents do not take title nor possession of the goods they handle.

Unlike other agent wholesalers, *auction companies* unite buyers and sellers in a single physical location, either at the seller's location or at the auction company's site. In addition to bringing buyers and sellers together, auction firms promote the goods they handle and actively negotiate the sale of those goods. These wholesalers participate to a lesser degree in the other marketing flows, except for ownership. Auctioneers are often used in marketing channels for such products as real estate, household goods, used automobiles, and equipment and machinery of all kinds. These firms also play a key role in the marketing of some commodities such as tobacco.

Manufacturers' Sales Branches and Offices

Branches, sometimes called *captive distributors*, are wholesaling operations owned and operated by a manufacturer. Branch operations are common, for example, in electrical supplies (e.g., Westinghouse Electric Supply Company) and in plumbing (e.g., Crane Supply Company and the Amstan Division of American Standard). Captive branch operations are also employed heavily by truck manufacturers, full-line farm equipment manufacturers, and large producers of major appliances.[5] A large proportion of captive distributors' sales are typically to other wholesalers, especially merchant wholesalers.

[5] Lopata, ''Faster Pace in Wholesaling,'' p. 131.

Producers use sales branches and offices for a variety of reasons, particularly when (1) independent wholesalers are unable to provide the technical expertise customers require; (2) these intermediaries cannot handle the quantities involved; (3) the manufacturer wishes to achieve more control over the promotion and physical possession activities of marketing the product; and (4) the wholesaling operations provide the manufacturer with additional profit opportunities.

THE STRUCTURE OF WHOLESALING

As noted above, full-function merchant wholesalers participate in all of the marketing flows, while brokers and manufacturers' agents participate in only a few of them. Commensurate with the functions they perform in the channel, the former incur operating expenses of approximately 13 percent of sales, while the latter's operating expenses range, on average, from 2.9 percent of sales for merchandise brokers to 6.6 percent of sales for manufacturers' agents.[6] Therefore, if a manufacturer "employs" full-function merchant wholesalers, the discount granted to these wholesalers is considerably more than the commission he would have to pay to manufacturer's agents or brokers for selling his products to end users. But when a manufacturer does not use a full-function wholesaler, he does not "save" the full 13 percent because he must assume all of the services that the wholesaler would have provided.

Several salient facts can be gleaned about the structure of wholesaling, in general, and about specific types, in particular, from Tables 4-3 and 4-4 and from computations based on the data contained in them. First, the volume of wholesale trade in *constant dollars* was almost half again as large in 1982 as in 1967. Second, merchant wholesalers continue to hold the largest share of wholesale trade and their share appears to be growing. Third, between 1967 and 1982, the number of wholesale establishments increased substantially (i.e., over 33 percent). Over the same period, the number of retail establishments remained relatively constant, while retail sales grew at a rate comparable to that for wholesaling. Logically extrapolated, this means that the differential in size between the typical wholesale and retail establishment has been continually declining. If size can be taken as an indicator of vertical market power, such a change may have vast implications for channel leadership, as will be discussed in more depth in Chapter 10. However, despite any of the trends apparent in the data, wholesaling, like retailing, is predominately an industry of small businesses; the average wholesaling establishment had only 12 employees in 1982.

Because of their obvious importance in the wholesaling structure, some additional developments within merchant wholesaling, among manufacturers' sales branches and offices, and among agents and brokers are mentioned below.

---

[6] Figures are based on U.S. Bureau of the Census, *1982 Census of Wholesale Trade*, Geographic Area Series, Report No. WC82-A-52 (December 1984), pp. 3–18, and authors' calculations.

TABLE 4.3 Trends in the Share of Wholesaling Establishments and Sales[a]

	Establishments (number)					Sales ($ billions)				
	1963	1967	1972	1977	1982	1963	1967	1972	1977	1982
Total	308,177	311,464	369,791	382,837	415,829	$358.4	$459.5	$728.5	$1258.4	$1997.9
	(percentage of total)					(percentage of total)				
Merchant Wholesalers	72.4%	72.0%	73.4%	80.3%	81.3%	49.3%	49.5%	50.8%	56.8%	58.0%
Manufacturer Sales Branches and Offices	9.4	9.9	11.9	10.6	9.2	34.5	36.0	36.8	37.9	31.4
Sales branches (with stock)	5.3	5.4	8.4	7.0	5.3	16.2	15.4	18.0	18.6	15.7
Sales offices (without stock)	4.1	4.5	3.5	3.6	3.9	18.2	20.7	18.8	19.3	15.7
Agents and Brokers	8.2	8.5	8.4	9.1	9.5	15.8	14.0	10.9	11.0	10.6

[a]Some of the percentages do not add up to 100 percent either because figures have been rounded or because some data are absent.

Source: U.S. Bureau of the Census, *Census of Wholesale Trade*, various years; and authors' calculations.

TABLE 4.4 Sales of Selected Durable and Nondurable Goods by U.S. Merchant Wholesale Groups

	Sales ($ billions)		% Growth 1977–1982
Durable Goods	1977	1982	
Total	$296.0	$ 476.8	61.1
Motor vehicles and automotive parts and supplies	55.1	91.4	65.9
Furniture and home furnishings	11.1	17.7	54.1
Lumber and other construction materials	27.6	33.1	19.1
Sporting, recreational, photographic, and hobby goods, toys, and supplies	8.1	13.7	69.1
Metals and minerals, except petroleum	32.8	49.0	49.4
Electrical goods	30.4	55.8	83.6
Hardware and plumbing and heating equipment and supplies	19.9	29.3	47.2
Machinery, equipment, and supplies	85.7	140.9	64.4
Nondurable Goods			
Total	380.1	682.5	79.6
Paper and paper products	15.1	25.9	71.5
Drugs, drug properties, and druggists' sundries	10.1	18.6	84.2
Apparel, piece goods, and notions	17.9	29.6	65.4
Groceries and related products	111.6	174.7	56.5
Chemicals and allied products	9.9	19.5	97.0
Petroleum and petroleum products	59.5	167.1	180.8
Beer, wines, and distilled alcoholic beverages	22.4	36.5	62.9
Tobacco and tobacco products	9.6	12.7	32.3
All Lines of Trade			
Total	676.1	1159.3	71.5

Sources: U.S. Bureau of the Census, *1977 Census of Wholesale Trade*, Vol. II, Geographic Area Statistics, Part I, U.S. Summary (February 1981); U.S. Department of Commerce, Bureau of the Census, *1982 Census of Wholesale Trade*, WC 82-A-52, Geographic Area Series (December 1984); and authors' calculations.

Merchant Wholesalers

The sales of merchant wholesalers have increased significantly over the time period covered in Table 4-3. In addition, the proportion of merchant wholesaler establishments grew rather dramatically relative to the increase in the number of establishments of other wholesaler types. However, while overall growth—in sales and establishments—has been strongly positive, the success of merchant wholesalers has varied widely from the standpoint of individual product class groupings. (The sales growth of selected nondurable and durable goods by merchant wholesale groups is shown in Table 4-4.)

In addition, some merchant wholesalers have found considerable success by restricting their activities to a limited range of products within a product grouping. In groceries, drugs, hardware, and jewelry, specialty wholesalers have been able to aid retail chains in expanding their product lines in directions unfamiliar to chain buyers and merchandisers (e.g., nonfood items in grocery stores).

TABLE 4.5 Sales by Agent Wholesalers, 1977 and 1982 ($ millions)

Type of Operation	1977		1982	
	Volume of Trade	Percentage of Total	Volume of Trade	Percentage of Total
Auction companies	10,826	8.3	15,781	7.5
Brokers	30,585	23.4	71,750	33.9
Commission merchants	27,996	21.4	34,995	16.5
Import agents	3,920	3.0	11,860	5.6
Export agents	8,822	6.8	9,957	4.7
Manufacturers' agents[a]	48,369	37.1	67,232	31.8
Total	130,488	100.0	211,575	100.0

[a]Includes selling agents.

Source: U.S. Census of Business, *Wholesale Trade, Summary Statistics*, 1977 and 1982.

Manufacturers' Sales Branches and Offices

As can be seen from Table 4-3, the number of manufacturers' sales branches and offices began to decline between 1967 and 1982, after a period of steady growth. The proportion of wholesale sales accounted for by these operations shows a similar pattern during the same time period. Thus, the relative importance of manufacturers' sales branches and offices in wholesale distribution is slipping slightly as compared to merchant wholesalers.

Agents and Brokers

The final aspect of the structure of wholesaling pertains to the overall decline in the relative sales volume coming from agents and brokers during the 1967–1982 period. Compounding the decline in their proportion of sales, the relative number of agent and broker wholesale establishments increased during the same period. Table 4-5, however, indicates that certain categories of agents and brokers, such as brokers and import agents, accounted for an increasing share of sales by this general wholesale type at the expense of others, most notably manufacturers' agents and commission merchants.

Manufacturers in a few industries have tended to move away from relying on any type of agent wholesaling organization. The reason is that they view such firms as not being service-oriented, controllable, innovative, efficient, or reliable.[7] The result of this trend is that the average size of agent and brokerage firms, in terms of sales, is declining relative to other forms of wholesaling.

SELECTING AND USING WHOLESALERS

It is an old axiom of marketing that it is possible to eliminate the wholesaler (or any middleman, for that matter), but it is impossible to eliminate his functions.

[7] James R. Moore and Kendall A. Adams, *"Functional Wholesaler Sales: Trends and Analysis,"* in Edward M. Mazze (ed.), *1975 Combined Proceedings* (Chicago: American Marketing Association, 1976), pp. 403–404.

The major question facing a manufacturer is whether, by vertically integrating (that is, by establishing his own sales branches and warehouse facilities), he can perform the functions more effectively and efficiently than a wholesaler can.

In general, the cost of marketing through wholesalers is not likely to be *vastly* different from the cost of performing the same marketing functions in-house. However, the fact that a given type of wholesaling firm participates in a number of marketing flows enables it to be more effective in reaching the desired target market. In deciding whether or not to use wholesalers, it is important to understand, first, what wholesalers do. The following sections outline how wholesalers theoretically serve their suppliers, their retail customers, and business users. In addition, a hard-nosed estimate of their actual performance is presented.

How Can Wholesalers Serve Suppliers?

Ideally, wholesalers have a great deal of potential as channel partners for suppliers. From an operational perspective, suppliers of both industrial and consumer goods may rely on wholesalers for several key reasons.[8]

1. Wholesalers are located in and understand local markets. Being close to customers, they initiate the sale of any product by identifying prospective users and determining the extent of their needs.
2. Wholesalers make possible local availability of stocks and thereby relieve suppliers of their oft-unprofitable small-order business.
3. Within their territories, wholesalers can provide suppliers with a sales force that is in close touch with the needs of customers and prospects. Also, because a wholesaler represents a number of suppliers, he can often cover a given territory at a lower cost than the manufacturer's own sales force could.
4. By taking ownership of the goods and providing payment for them, wholesalers perform financial services for suppliers by allowing them to recover capital that would otherwise be invested in inventories.

From the point of view of the manufacturer, the several criteria listed in Table 4-6 must be evaluated in determining the type of wholesaling establishment to use; these factors must always be considered in light of the ultimate market for the goods in question.

How Can Wholesalers Serve Retailers?

Manufacturers are interested in encouraging retailers to promote and sell their particular lines of products. On the other hand, wholesalers have a strong vested interest in building up their retail customers as merchants. Particularly in the case of smaller retail establishments, an individual wholesaler is able to supply a large part of the retailer's requirements for merchandise. It is in the wholesaler's

---

[8] Many of these same points have been made in more detail by Richard M. Hill, *Wholesaling Management* (Homewood, Ill.: Richard D. Irwin, 1963), pp. 10–14. See also Frederick E. Webster, Jr., *Industrial Marketing Strategy* (New York: John Wiley & Sons, 1979), pp. 161–168.

TABLE 4.6 Criteria of Choice in the Decision of What Type of Wholesaling Establishment to Use—Point of View of the Manufacturer

1. Evaluation of sales efforts of wholesaler
   a. Extent and activity of sales force of wholesaler
   b. Does sales force *sell*, or does it just take orders?
   c. Extent to which manufacturer must supplement wholesaler's sales efforts with own promotion, salesmen, and/or detail men
   d. Number of lines handled by wholesaler
      (1) Does wholesaler handle too many lines to give sufficient attention to manufacturer's line?
          (a) Use of heavy advertising, good margins, realistic pricing to stimulate attention on part of wholesaler
          (b) Preference, sometimes, for more attention to individual line by use of specialty or limited-line wholesalers
      (2) Does wholesaler handle competing lines?
          (a) Use of sales or manufacturers' agents sometimes indicated
          (b) May necessitate creation of exclusive distributorships
2. Evaluation of relationship of wholesaler to channel of distribution for the product
   a. Type of wholesaler that can give widest distribution and assurance of sufficient retail outlets for line
   b. When particular types of retail outlets are desired, what type of wholesaler can best handle them?
   c. Quality and continuity of relationships maintained between wholesaling and retailing firms
   d. Degree to which wholesaler cooperates in promotion, pricing, financing, and other marketing activities
   e. Willingness of wholesaler to maintain continuous relationships with manufacturer

Source: Department of Marketing, University of Pennsylvania, Wharton School of Finance and Commerce.

self-interest to spend considerable effort and resources training, stimulating, and aiding retailers to become better managers. That is why wholesalers become directly involved in retail merchandise management. In this respect, the benefits to the retailer derived from relying on wholesalers may be described as follows:[9]

1. Wholesalers can give their retail customers a great deal of direct selling aid in the form of price concessions on featured items, point-of-sale material, and cooperative advertising.

2. Wholesalers often can provide expert assistance in planning store layout, building design, and material specifications.

3. Wholesalers generally offer retailers guidance and counsel in public relations, housekeeping and accounting methods, administrative procedures, and the like.

In the toy industry, for instance, many retailers prefer to make some or all of their total annual toy purchases from wholesalers rather than from manufacturers, because, as one retail executive has indicated:

[9] See Hill, *Wholesaling Management*, pp. 16–21, for more explanation and details.

1. In many instances reorders are filled more quickly.
2. Wholesalers guarantee the sale (any items that are not sold can be returned for full credit).
3. Defective products are replaced promptly.
4. The wholesaler extends long-term credit.
5. The percentage of markup due to working through a wholesaler is more than offset by decreased inventory costs and improved service.[10]

Obviously, the foremost advantage for many retailers in relying on wholesalers is the fact that the latter buy in large quantities, break bulk to suit the convenience of their customers, and then pass along the savings. Thus, by using wholesalers, independent retailers can avoid diluting the energies of their often overtaxed executive staffs. Furthermore, wholesalers give these retailers access to a large group of products of small manufacturers that they might not otherwise be able to obtain. Even large establishments in certain product lines gain an advantage by using wholesalers because they can then convert storage space into profit-making selling or customer service space.[11] For example, although supermarket and discount chains can buy at the same price as a rack jobber or service merchandiser, the latter's hold on the market comes from knowing precisely what to buy and minimizing the handling and inventory costs of a variety of nonfood products, such as health and beauty aids, phonograph records, hardware, and sporting goods.

Some of the significant criteria used in evaluating, from the perspective of the retailer, whether and what type of wholesaler to "employ" are listed in Table 4-7. As in the case of the manufacturer or supplier, these criteria should be considered in light of the products that the retailer carries and the market he serves.

How Can Wholesalers Serve the Business User?

Merchant wholesaler sales are divided about equally between retailers and business or industrial users. Although many of the advantages to the business user from relying on wholesalers are exactly the same as those mentioned above relative to retailers, there are some additional factors, which are briefly discussed here.

The short lead time on deliveries made available through wholesalers is especially important to industrial users. Flexibility in production scheduling can generally be achieved if production planners know that speedy local deliveries are forthcoming. This factor is why industrial distributors, perhaps more than most types of wholesale firms, are plagued by the problem of small orders. One steel warehouse reported that 31.7 percent of the orders it received averaged $7.50, created 32 percent of its administration cost, and contributed only 6 percent to its total sales.[12]

[10] Richard N. Cardozo and James E. Haefner, *Note on the Toy Industry* (Boston, Mass.:Intercollegiate Case Clearinghouse, No. ICH 14M60, 1970), p. 9.

[11] Paul L. Courtney, "The Wholesaler as a Link in the Distribution Channel," in Moller and Wilemon, *Marketing Channels*, p. 178.

[12] Richard M. Hill, Ralph S. Alexander, and James S. Cross, *Industrial Marketing* 4th ed. (Homewood, Ill: Richard D. Irwin, 1975). p. 231.

TABLE 4.7 Criteria of Choice in the Decision of What Type of Wholesaling Establishment to Use—Point of View of the Retailer

1. Lines
   a. Does wholesaler supply all or most of the lines needed by the retailer?
   b. Does wholesaler supply all or most of the brands required by the retailer for each of his lines?
   c. Does the wholesaler stock an assortment of varieties, styles, sizes, and colors sufficient to meet retailer's needs?
2. Services
   a. Can wholesaler assure a continuous and regular supply of merchandise without excessive out-of-stocks or back orders?
   b. What is the extent of aid given to retailer by wholesaler (e.g., promotion, pricing, inventory maintenance)?
   c. Extension of credit by wholesaler?
   d. Delivery by wholesaler?
   e. Do types of wholesalers used result in too-frequent and time-consuming calls by salesmen?
   f. What kind of help is given by salesmen?
   g. Does wholesaler's cost structure permit a low enough selling price to retailer to allow sufficient retail margins?

Source: Department of Marketing, University of Pennsylvania, Wharton School of Finance and Commerce.

In addition, many types of wholesalers provide unique forms of technical assistance. For example, machine tool and accessories wholesalers often have specialists on their staffs who are available to help customers with technical problems pertaining to the use of tools and parts. Indeed, it is not unusual to find such technically trained persons as metallurgists, chemists, draftsmen, and mechanical and civil engineers employed by wholesalers to assist customers with the problems involved in buying and using products.[13] Even managerial assistance is being increasingly provided to business users by wholesalers. For example:

> An electronics distributor in Ann Arbor analyzed the stockkeeping methods of one of his industrial customers and recommended revised delivery schedules, prearranged items, packs suitable for assembly line use, and standardized item identification. The customer was able to reduce the possession costs of his stock by 15% of its value.[14]

Business users and retailers alike must be concerned with the overall or *ultimate cost* of the good that they purchase, handle, and store–not merely with the price at which such goods are obtained. Often the *ultimate cost* of dealing with wholesalers is less than the ultimate cost of dealing directly with manufacturers, even in spite of the latter's quantity discounts. This *ultimate cost concept* can sometimes justify using wholesalers in situations where they might not otherwise appear to be economical.[15]

Recognition of the ultimate cost concept by both wholesalers and their customers has led to "systems selling."

[13] Hill, *Wholesaling Management*, pp. 22–23.

[14] Lopata, "Faster Pace in Wholesaling," p. 140.

[15] The term *ultimate cost concept* was introduced to the authors by Richard S. Lopata and Richard E. Peterson, principals, SAM Associates, Inc., Chicago, Illinois.

Systems selling is a broad, inconclusive term that may be used to describe any form of cooperative contracting relationship between an industrial distributor and his customer for the ordering and distribution of low-value, repetitively used items for maintenance, repair, or operating (MRO) purposes, or for the use in manufacturing original equipment.[16]

Wholesalers offer such purchasing systems to reduce the high cost and paperwork facing firms seeking to acquire a wide variety of items, ranging from power tools and welding supplies to lamps, electronic equipment, and hardware. Wholesalers' system selling arrangements generally include (1) shifting the bulk of the customer's on-premises MRO inventory back to the stocking wholesaler, (2) providing for automatic and semiautomatic ordering of these items on an as-needed basis, and (3) one-day delivery of the ordered items.[17] Customers benefit from these arrangements because they (1) reduce the time spent in purchasing low-value items; (2) reduce the paperwork in purchasing; (3) simplify requisitioning; (4) free more in-plant storage space; and (5) foster greater harmony and closer ties with the wholesaler.

Indeed, the notion of systems selling ranges far beyond applications to items used to support or maintain manufacturing processes. For example, a major discount chain has a system selling arrangement with a Columbus, Ohio, drug wholesaler for its health, beauty, and pharmaceutical merchandise. The chain retains very little warehouse or backroom stocks of the items; rather, the wholesaling firm provides all of the services required to maintain an adequate assortment of the items on the shelves of each of the chain's stores within its assigned territory. Similar kinds of arrangements exist between medical supply companies such as American Hospital Supply Company and a number of hospitals. Hospital inventories are generally not well managed, thereby increasing the need to shift such functions back onto wholesalers.[18]

Systems purchasing is not always an appropriate arrangement for a wholesaler's customers. But it illustrates in a specific way the potential scope of a wholesaler's functions and it demonstrates the ultimate cost concept. Wholesalers will rarely offer the lowest prices. However, using them as channel partners may provide *total cost* savings through reductions in paperwork, vendor analysis, requisitioning, inefficient inventory operations, and the like.

A Hard-Nosed Assessment

Most of the above discussion describes what a wholesaler can do for suppliers, retailers, and business users; however, the channel analyst should be cautious in selecting wholesalers as channel partners. Since wholesalers can spread the costs

---

[16] William J. Hannaford, "Systems Selling: Problems and Benefits for Buyers and Sellers," *Industrial Marketing Management*, Vol. 5 (June 1976), p. 139.

[17] Ibid. pp. 140-141: see also Marsha A. Scheidt, I. Frederick Trawick, and John E. Swan, "Impact of Purchasing Systems Contracts on Distributors and Producers," *Industrial Marketing Management*, Vol. 11 (October 1982), pp. 283–289.

[18] P. Ronald Stephenson, "Strategic Analysis of Wholesaler Distribution: A Study of the Medical Supply Industry," *Industrial Marketing Management*, Vol. 5 (March 1976), p. 39.

of participating in the marketing flows over an entire commodity line (e.g., groceries, electrical supplies, plumbing and heating equipment) they have the potential for reducing the overall cost of distribution. Despite this, most are not aggressive marketers because of their size, their managerial limitations, and their traditional orientations. In fact, wholesaling firms are generally much more preoccupied with logistics functions than with penetrating markets. Because of this preoccupation, they have been unable to respond to major changes occurring within certain industries and have had to scramble to maintain viability within them.

While there are significant and numerous exceptions to this generalization, merchant wholesalers—the dominant group among wholesalers both in numbers and in dollar volume—are, for the most part, very small family-owned companies ($1 million to $5 million in sales and fewer than 20 employees) who rely on their contacts with other small companies, either suppliers or clients, for survival. These companies frequently lack management expertise and organizations capable of putting into practice sophisticated marketing methods. They exist by virtue of the fact that the suppliers and/or customers with whom they are linked simply cannot afford to integrate the wholesaling functions and therefore must rely on such intermediaries to reach markets or obtain supply. Often the link between wholesalers and their clientele is more personal (e.g., family ties) than economic.

Over the past 30 years, the position of wholesalers has been significantly threatened with regard to the marketing of consumer goods. Relatively few wholesalers have been successful in meeting the challenges head-on. Although there have been changes in the marketing of industrial goods, industrial distributors appear to have shown greater adaptability and innovativeness in their approaches to suppliers and markets than their consumer goods counterparts have. In order to obtain a realistic perspective of wholesaling, an understanding of developments in both sectors of the economy as they have affected wholesalers is important.

Consumer Goods Wholesalers. Retailers have been particularly active in revolutionizing physical distribution practices. They have taken advantage of large-volume purchasing, warehousing, and delivery operations through the formation of mass merchandising chain organizations, as discussed in Chapter 2. To a large extent, as the chains grew and prospered, numerous wholesalers selling consumer goods continued to be order takers rather than developing expertise in marketing strategy and tactics. They relied on manufacturers to stimulate demand for brand-name products among ultimate consumers via advertising, and then waited for the generated demand to pull the brands through the channel. Indeed, many wholesalers were easily replaceable by retailers because they no longer offered an economical or effective alternative to achieving sales or logistical services. What mass retailers could not obtain from the manufacturers directly, they could produce themselves; thus, many wholesalers were quickly relegated to serving small business. Because tens of thousands of small manufacturers and retailers still exist, these wholesalers of consumer goods have continued to serve an economic purpose, but for a shrinking portion of the market.

On the other hand, a few wholesalers acted purposively to counter the market impact of large-scale retail chain operations. They formed voluntary (wholesaler-sponsored) chains (e.g., Super Valu Stores, Fleming, and Malone & Hyde in groceries), franchised systems (e.g., Midas International and Western Auto in the automotive aftermarket), and administered systems (e.g., Genuine Parts' automotive jobber NAPA network); they also permitted themselves to become part of retailer-sponsored cooperatives (e.g., Cotter's True Value and Ace Hardware), which account for nearly 40 percent of total full-line hardware wholesale sales.[19] Through each of these forms of distribution, the locally owned individual retail units are able to achieve the marketing and physical distribution advantages of the large retail chains.

The return on investment of many of these various kinds of systems that are organized around wholesalers is frequently above 20 percent.[20] Given that the average return for wholesaling corporations for which public data are available is around 14 percent, as shown in Chapter 12, the performance of these wholesalers is significantly above the norm. In fact, their effect on marketing channels is so important that separate discussion of their activities is saved for Chapter 9, where we examine a number of vertical marketing systems, including those centered around wholesalers, in which purposive interorganization management is being practiced.

Beyond those consumer goods wholesalers who have formed vertical marketing systems, there are others who have been successful without changing their corporate organization. Some have restricted their activities to a limited range of products and have sought out market niches that do not require high sales volume to be competitive. In groceries, drugs, hardware, and jewelry, specialty wholesalers have been able to develop a substantial volume of business. For example, in the grocery trade, these firms supply such products as frozen food, dairy products, fancy or gourmet foods, bread and baked goods, and beverages.

> They exist only to the extent that the inventory, handling, and transport require-
> ments are so specialized that they cannot be duplicated by the chain (or general-line
> wholesaler) or that their product line is such that these competing organizations
> cannot attain sufficient volume to offset the costs of handling desirable assortments.[21]

Service merchandisers or rack jobbers have been particularly effective. The more successful specialty wholesalers, like rack jobbers, have been able to serve both

[19] "Dealer-Owned Wholesalers' Growth Leveling Out," *Hardware Age*, (April 1982), p. 54.

[20] See Bert C. McCammon, Jr., and James M. Kenderdine, "High Performance Wholesaling," *Hardlines Wholesaling*, Vol. 9 (September 1975), pp. 17–51.

[21] Louis P. Bucklin, *Competition and Evolution in the Distributive Trades* (Englewood Cliffs, N.J.: Prentice-Hall, 1972), pp. 233–234.

large suppliers and large buyers, thus severing the wholesalers' traditional dependence on small-scale retailing.[22]

On the other hand, there have also been a number of general- or full-line consumer goods wholesalers who have achieved viability. Their route to success has been to improve their management and marketing practices in line with strict adherence to stated marketing channel objectives. The practice of one of these wholesalers, United Stationers, is illustrated in Exhibit 4-1. Unfortunately, United Stationers is atypical of wholesaling firms that sell items for resale. Very few wholesalers engage in profit planning; analyzing long-run trends, threats, and opportunities; studying customer types and market segment differences; and developing strong systems for market analysis, planning, and control.

EXHIBIT 4-1

United Stationers: A Marketing-Oriented Wholesaler

Over 70 percent of the sales of United Stationers, a Maywood, Illinois–based office products wholesaler, come from retail stationers. These retail customers resell to ultimate consumers and, through their sales forces, to commercial accounts. United competes head-on with such manufacturer-integrated wholesaling operations as those run by Boise-Cascade, Champion International, and Zellerbach Paper Company. It has been able to generate over $150 million in sales by adopting a marketing strategy containing the following elements:

1. A stated commitment to lower the cost of distribution for its suppliers and its customers.
2. A series of syndicated catalogs made available to its customers which the customers use, under their own names, to sell to their clients.
3. A complete set of pricing services, utilizing microfiche and other media, which permits the continuous updating of prices—especially important during inflationary periods.
4. An on-line order entry system, an on-line inventory system, and an on-line inventory forecasting system.
5. Four regional distribution centers (Forest Park, Illinois, Pennsauken, New Jersey, Livonia, Michigan, and Dallas, Texas) each stocking over 20,000 office products. (The Forest Park facility is over 200,000 square feet.)
6. Customer service representatives assigned to every distribution center who place regularly scheduled WATS telephone calls to retailers within their geographic area at a frequency determined by the retailers individually.

---

[22] Ibid., p. 235. For an excellent example in the magazine and paperback book industry, see Paul Doebler, ''Charles Levy-Spawned Company Computerizes the Problems Out of Distribution and Sales,'' *Publishers Weekly*, Vol. 205 (February 4, 1974).

7. A network of ten satellite distribution centers. (Each day, every distribution center ships orders taken over the phone during that day by the customer service representatives. These shipments travel directly to retailers or their customers, or to the satellite distribution centers. If shipped to the satellites, the orders are available to dealers on a will-call, local delivery, or drop shipment basis.)

8. Quarterly reviews of retailers' purchases via company account executives and specific retailer-oriented printout of purchase records.

9. An automated rebuying procedure.

10. A computerized automatic reorder system for retailers.

Industrial Distributors. Manufacturers of many types of industrial goods tend to be more engineering-oriented than marketing-oriented. They prefer to allocate resources to research and production rather than to distribution, which they know has historically delivered a much lower return on investment. Given this orientation, it is not surprising that they frequently turn "troublesome" marketing problems over to distribution specialists. This is why, as contrasted with consumer goods, industrial distribution has been a particularly viable sector of wholesaling over the years.

An industrial distributor typically

sells primarily to manufacturers. He stocks the products he sells, has at least one outside salesperson as well as an inside telephone and/or counter salesperson, and performs a broad variety of marketing channel functions. . . . The products stocked include: *maintenance, repair, and operating supplies* (MRO items); *original equipment* (OEM) supplies, such as fasteners, power transmission components, fluid power equipment, and small rubber parts, which become part of the manufacturer's finished product; *equipment* used in the operation of a business, such as hand tools, power tools, and conveyors; and *machinery* used to make raw materials and semi-finished goods into finished products.[23]

On average, industrial distributors are as small as the wholesalers serving retailers, but the median size is increasing as the number of distributors declines and as the market expands. The increase in size means that more firms are able to adopt electronic data processing for inventory control, order processing, and other administrative controls. (However, it is estimated that only 60 percent of such firms use computers,[24] which means that nearly half are still operating manual, relatively archaic systems.)

The distributor's importance in the marketing channel for industrial goods is growing for a variety of reasons. Among these are manufacturers' desire to shift more physical distribution responsibilities to distributors because of the pressures

[23] Frederick E. Webster, Jr., "The Role of the Industrial Distributor in Marketing Strategy," *Journal of Marketing*, Vol. 40 (July 1976), p. 11.

[24] "38th Annual Survey of Distributor Operations," *Industrial Distribution*, Vol. 73 (July 1984), p. 50.

of interest costs; the tendency of a number of products to become commodities (e.g., bearings), which permits distributors to gain more control over the relationship with the customer; and the increased value that distributors are adding to products by performing special services, such as assembly and submanufacturing, for their customers.[25] For example, estimates by Joseph T. Ryerson & Son, Inc., a major metal distributor, indicate that the marketing of processed steels (i.e., steel that is cut or fabricated by the distributor) could go as high as 90 percent of its sales in the near future. The metals "service center" is no longer a "warehouse" where a buyer may go for small lots; it now adds value to the generic products it carries by performing such operations as welding, bending, shearing, and stamping.

Industrial distributors have become more capable at fulfilling their major responsibility in the channel from the supplier's perspective. That is, their job has been primarily to contact present and potential customers and to make the product available—with the necessary supporting services such as delivery, credit, and technical advice—as quickly as economically feasible.[26] In this respect, they may have discouraged the kind of integration of wholesaling functions so prevalent in consumer goods channels. In fact, it is much easier for the industrial goods manufacturer to go "direct" than it is for the consumer goods manufacturer. This point will be expanded upon in Chapter 8. It would, for example, be virtually impossible for General Foods Corporation to sell its products directly to millions of consumers, but it is feasible for Monsanto to sell its products directly to hundreds of industrial end users. Thus, in consumer goods, the major problem for wholesalers is the backward vertical integration of retailers into wholesaling. In industrial goods, the problem is one of manufacturers integrating forward. While such integration is occurring, the problem for wholesalers appears to be more acute relative to consumer goods.

One of the ways in which industrial distributors have maintained and even increased their importance in the marketing channel is by specializing their operations. While specialists carry fewer product lines than the general-line distributor, their inventory is usually deeper. For example, more than 90 percent of Semiconductor Specialists' $20 million sales come from semiconductors and microprocessors alone. A. M. Castle, a metals distributor, sells more nickel, alloys, and specialty metals than its competitors. And Premier Industrial has 14 completely separate divisions, each with its own sales force to serve a distinct market. These divisions range from J. L. Holcomb Manufacturing, which sells cleaning agents, brushes, insecticides, and the like, to Certanium Alloys & Research Company, which sells welding electrodes, brazing alloys, solders, and other welding aids. In addition to specializing their product lines, a number of distributors have hired technical experts.

Another way in which industrial distributors have enhanced their role in the marketing channel is by forming distributor chains, either by acquisition or by internal expansion. As a result, they have been able to secure significant

[25] Webster, *Industrial Marketing Strategy*, p. 169.
[26] Webster, "The Role of the Industrial Distributor," p. 13.

economies of scale by establishing one highly sophisticated central inventory, purchasing, and distribution system.[27] The merger trend is particularly strong among bearing and power transmission distributors. Some of the advantages that distributor chains have over small, privately owned single-warehouse firms are:[28]

1. *Inventory power*. Chain inventories are not only deeper and cheaper, but also broader and more diversified.
2. *Central warehouses*. Such warehouses permit adding highly sophisticated computerized systems, purchasing in quantity, and stocking in depth. The result is lower warehousing costs per outlet.
3. *Quantity discounts*.
4. *Multiple brand coverage*.
5. *Private labeling*. This movement is particularly strong for such product lines as bearings, electrical motors and equipment, and MRO supplies. (For example, private labels account for almost 100 percent of Associated Spring's sales, 75 percent of W. W. Grainger's sales, and 90 percent of Lawson Products' sales.)

Clearly, these chains pose a threat for small, single-warehouse distributors. To counter the chains' enormous inventory power, some independents are setting up swapping arrangements on some products. These inventory exchange agreements are aimed at reducing warehousing costs and enhancing the assortments of each member.[29]

From a potential customer's perspective, the chains are better able to keep delivery promises, offer better discount structures, maintain efficient phone order systems, provide stock breadth and depth, offer technical services, enact appropriate sales procedures (e.g., regular sales calls), maintain strong assortments of brand names, offer quick delivery time and provide quality assurance. Indeed, because of their capabilities, manufacturers seeking to employ *both* independent and chain distributors in their channels are faced with managing competition between the two different channels.

Despite the significant changes in industrial distribution that were cataloged above, manufacturers frequently remain frustrated by the low level of management competence among distributors and their lack of management depth, as well as by distributors' inadequate financial management and the frequent lack of provision for management succession.[30] In fact, industrial goods distributors, like their counterparts in consumer goods wholesaling, are viewed as basically noninnovative and unsophisticated, especially from a marketing perspective. Their salesmen are seen more as order takers than as creative individuals who are interested in finding new accounts and aggressively promoting new products.

[27] "The Chain of Events in Industrial Distribution," *Marketing News* , January 30, 1976, p. 7. (This article was reprinted from *Management Practice*, 1976, a quarterly publication.)

[28] Ibid.

[29] Ibid., p. 7.

[30] Webster, *Industrial Marketing Strategy*, p. 7.

They are perceived by manufacturers as having little interest in market research and as an inadequate source of information about the markets in which they operate. Though there have been important improvements, industrial distributors, on average, appear to have a long way to go before they can be counted on to perform in accordance with the modern marketing concept.

THE STRATEGIC MANAGEMENT OF WHOLESALING INSTITUTIONS

The success of wholesale firms can be defined in at least two major ways. The first way is effectiveness—how well wholesalers satisfy their customers' market needs and wants. The second is profitability—how well wholesalers achieve target rates of return on assets or on investment.

Effectiveness

Effective wholesale marketing management centers around (1) identifying target market needs, (2) developing a product and service mix to satisfy those needs, and (3) adjusting that product and service mix to meet changes in the target markets' needs.

Understanding target market needs is central to the success of any marketing institution. Without a clear understanding of the services and products required by the market, wholesaling (and other marketing institutions, for that matter) have no idea how best to approach their customers or how to maintain long-term supplier-customer relationships with them.

Earlier in the chapter, we discussed various ways in which wholesalers can serve suppliers, retailers, and business users. Among the services offered to these marketing institutions are (1) market information, (2) local inventories, (3) quick delivery, (4) selling assistance, (5) technical assistance, and (6) various management assistances. Not every potential customer or supplier will need all of these services; the key is to determine which services are required by which target market.

In Chapter 2, we discussed many of the environmental trends affecting marketing channels and their institutions. These trends impact not only the supply of marketing channel services, but their demand as well. Astute wholesalers will, if possible, anticipate, and at minimum keep abreast of, these trends and their likely influence upon their customers. They will then adjust their product and service offerings to make them consistent with changing customer needs. For example, many general-line industrial distributors are paring their product lines to focus on the specific needs of particular customers; in effect, they are moving from general-line distribution to specialty wholesaling.

Profitability

Profitable wholesale marketing strategy centers around (1) managing net profit margins and (2) achieving high rates of asset turnover.

Margin Management. Net profit margin is a function of gross margin achieved and operating expenses incurred. Net profit is extremely sensitive to the level of gross margin. In wholesaling, a small change in gross margin will carry directly through to net profit, producing a disproportionately large change. As a result, gross margin is widely used as a critical decision variable at the wholesale level of distribution. Likewise, net profits are extremely sensitive to expense changes.

The margins that wholesalers receive are highly dependent upon the prices they are able to negotiate with suppliers, the prices they charge their customers, the mix of products they carry (i.e., their assortments), the market segments they choose to serve, and their desired growth rates. In the long run, strategic decisions surrounding these critical variables commit individual firms to specific gross margin and operating cost characteristics. For example, in the medical supply industry:

> A high growth strategy . . . involves commitment (on the part of wholesalers) to the hospital market with relatively low gross margins and the need for highly streamlined operating characteristics producing low average operating costs. On the other hand, emphasis on the physician segment means relatively high available gross margins, but commitment to a high operating cost strategy—high sales/service requirements, increased logistical demands, and relatively small average transaction size.[31]

Margins vary widely by line of trade served, depending, of course, on the needs and requirements of customers served. Thus, gross margins of electrical supply distributors vary from over 25 percent for MRO items sold to industrial accounts to less than 10 percent for household appliances sold to retailers.

Asset Management. In addition, wholesalers can generate high rates of asset turnover through intense asset management. Typically, a very high proportion (nearly two-thirds, as shown in Table 4-8) of total assets are invested in the current category, primarily in accounts receivable and inventory. Unlike the manufacturer, who has heavy investments in fixed plant and equipment, the wholesaler basically must exercise strong short-term credit and inventory controls in an effort to achieve desirable asset turnover levels. The overall liquidity of wholesaling operations means that it is very difficult for a wholesaler to go bankrupt. Three factors seem to account for the average wholesaler's buoyancy, irrespective of his marketing failings. First, the typical wholesaler has many suppliers and customers; therefore, he is not dependent on any one source of supply or sales. Second, many wholesalers are able to turn over their inventories about six times a year, on average, which means that they are a minimum of 120 days away from a cash position. Third, they are generally only 90 days away from cash relative to accounts receivable. The question, then, is not usually how to achieve appropriate asset management for survival purposes, but rather how to generate a high rate of return.

Accounts Receivable. Often 90 percent or more of a wholesaler's sales are made on a credit basis. Proper use of credit in building sales, as well as effective

[31] Stephenson, "Strategic Analysis of Wholesaler Distribution," p. 41.

TABLE 4.8 Composition of Assets for Wholesaling Corporations

Assets	Percent
Current Assets	
Cash or its equivalent	8.3%
Accounts receivable	25.3
Inventory	27.6
All other	3.7
Total	64.9%
Fixed Assets	
Property, plant, and equipment	21.5%
All other	13.6
Total	35.1%
Total Assets	100.0%

Source: Federal Trade Commission, *Quarterly Financial Report for Manufacturing, Mining, and Trade Corporations, Fourth Quarter 1984, Series QFR 84-4* (Washington, D.C.: U.S. Government Printing Office, March 1985), p. 83; and authors' calculations.

employment of the capital invested, therefore requires careful attention to credit management.

Achieving an adequate cash flow is critical to a wholesaler's operation and demands careful evaluation and selection of credit risks, collection of accounts, and overall control of credit. For example, the average collection period varies considerably among different kinds of wholesale business, depending in part on the customary terms of sale. (The average collection period for certain grocery wholesalers is only 14 days, compared with between 45 and 50 days in dry goods, footwear, and floor coverings.)

Inventory. In wholesaling as well as in retailing, achieving a reasonably high inventory turnover rate is the key to obtaining an adequate rate of return on invested capital. As turnover increases, the costs of possession—interest on capital invested in inventory, insurance, property taxes, and warehousing space—decline. Increased inventory turnover, along with advantageous supplier credit terms and careful inventory control, can also reduce the amount of capital invested in inventory.

Various surveys and trade conferences suggest that the merchant wholesaler's major problem is inventory control and management.[32] Such a heavy investment in inventory is made necessary by the large number of items that wholesalers must carry in order to serve the needs of their clients. Compounding the problem is the fact that suppliers generate enormous quantities of new products. For example, the automotive distributor carries over 70,000 identifiable items, compared with 40,000 ten years ago. Furthermore, many of the items that wholesalers must carry are slow-moving articles that are required infrequently but, when needed, are vital to the operations of the wholesaler's customer.

Some of the wholesaler's reactions to his inventory problems have been (1) to demand that suppliers reduce the size and variety of the lines they offer, (2) to

[32] Lopata, "Faster Pace in Wholesaling," p. 138.

select only popular items from among a supplier's line (called, by the trade, *cherry picking*), and (3) to select items and set stock levels according to item demand and item movement.[33] In the last case, wholesalers drop many slow-moving and/or low-revenue-producing supply items from their assortments; they then place stronger sales efforts behind higher-priced product lines with larger dollar volumes. At the same time, these wholesalers retrain their salespeople to become equipment demonstrators and discourage them from merely taking small orders.

Clearly, improved management practices are a prerequisite to improved inventory control. Such practices must not only encompass the setting of minimum-order policies but must also include the broader aspect of developing effective management information systems. Indeed, the discussion on inventory control in Chapter 5 is exceedingly pertinent to wholesaling; without appropriate management of the marketing flows of ownership and physical possession, the wholesaler will not only derive lower rates of return, but will also forfeit a significant amount of his value to the channel as a whole.

CHANNEL MANAGEMENT ISSUES IN USING WHOLESALERS

Large, professionally managed wholesaling firms—such as Genuine Parts Company in the automotive industry; Bergen Brunswig Corporation in the drug industry; Foremost-McKesson Company in the drug, grocery, liquor, and health and beauty aid industries; Graybar Electric Company in electrical supply; Fleming Companies, Inc., in groceries; American Hospital Supply Corporation in medical supplies; and Earl M. Jorgensen Company in metals[34]—tend to be the exception rather than the rule. Most wholesaling firms can, as noted previously, be categorized as small, entrepreneurially oriented, relatively unsophisticated, and generally risk-averse businesses. Therefore, when a manufacturer turns to a wholesaler for assistance in making his products available for sale and for stimulating demand among industrial, institutional, or commercial end users or among retailers, he cannot relinquish responsibility for effective marketing, nor can he expect the wholesaler to respond to all of his suggestions. Rather, the manufacturer must assume a new responsibility—that of making the wholesaler more effective through programs of product development, careful pricing, promotional support, technical assistance, order servicing, and training for wholesaler salesmen and management.[35] In the long run, the manufacturer can expect to deal with a larger and stronger wholesaling organization that he has helped to create. The development of mutual dependencies will produce a more cohesive channel system.

[33] Ibid.

[34] For a comprehensive listing, see McCammon and Kenderdine, "High-Performance Wholesaling", pp. 17–51.

[35] Webster, *Industrial Marketing Strategy*, op. cit., p. 178.

SUMMARY

The significance of the wholesaler's role in a channel of distribution is defined by how well he helps match the heterogeneous output of suppliers with the diverse needs of retailers, other wholesalers, and business users. The major types of wholesalers vary in their abilities to perform the marketing functions necessary for this matching process. Manufacturers' sales offices and branches tend to participate in most of these marketing functions, while agents and brokers are typically involved in only a few of them. Some merchant wholesalers (full-function wholesalers) can perform most of the marketing channel services, while others (limited-service wholesalers) perform fewer of them.

Many suppliers use wholesalers to reach their customers because they prefer to turn troublesome, supposedly lower-return distribution activities over to specialists. The benefits available to suppliers (manufacturers, growers, etc.) from wholesalers are continuity in and intimacy with local markets, local availability of stocks, coverage of small-order business, lower costs because wholesalers can spread overhead over many suppliers' products, and relief from the burden of holding inventory.

Often the wholesaler's perceived self-interest is more directly involved with the well-being of retailers than with that of manufacturers; therefore, many wholesalers do, in fact, offer retailers direct selling aid, expert assistance in all aspects of retail operations, local and speedy delivery, relief from inventory burdens, quick adjustments, credit extension, and, in some cases, guaranteed sales. Business users can receive many of the same benefits, which may be especially important when it comes to production scheduling and technical assistance.

It was noted that the average wholesaler has significant weaknesses as a marketing institution. These findings make wholesaling firms vulnerable to elimination from the marketing channel. Before that can be accomplished, however, some other institution that is capable of performing the tasks done by wholesalers must be put in place. Dropping wholesalers from the channel is valid *only* if the tasks they perform can be either partially eliminated or performed more efficiently by some other marketing channel institution.

DISCUSSION QUESTIONS

1. Darrell McClain recently bought a new audio system for his home at Wholesale Electronics Distributors. Of course, he bragged to nearly everyone who would bother to listen about what a good deal he had received on his sound system. Darrell claimed that because Wholesale Electronics Distributors was a wholesale outfit, he was able to get "wholesale prices." Karen Jones, a marketing channels honor student, wasn't as sure as Darrell that Wholesale Electronics Distributors was really a wholesaler. She believed that the firm might be simply a retailer using its store name to project a low-price image to people like Darrell. Who is likely correct, Darrell or Karen? Explain your answer.

2. Consider the following statement:
   A wholesaling firm can be eliminated from the marketing channel but someone must

perform the wholesaling tasks and absorb the costs formerly borne by the eliminated firm. The underlying assumption, of course, is that the wholesaling tasks are necessary. Take a position, either pro or con, on this statement and support your reasoning.

3. Ellen Daltry is a sales representative for The Klein Tobacco Company, a candy and tobacco wholesaler located in Broken Cactus, Arizona. Ellen calls upon each of her small grocery store and gas station customers about once every two weeks, rotating and replenishing their stock and periodically introducing new products. What kind of wholesaling institution is The Klein Tobacco Company? Explain your answer.

4. Using some of the environmental trends discussed in Chapter 2, explain why the percentage growth in merchant wholesale sales of some of lines of trade in Table 4-4 did not keep up with the total growth rate for all lines of trade.

5. Pick a supermarket and a convenience store with which you are familiar. Which one of these retail institutions is more dependent on its wholesale suppliers for performing the marketing channel functions? Why?

6. Gravas' Old World Cookie Company bakes gourmet cookies for restaurants and delicatessens. Gravas' purchases its key ingredients, flour and sugar, on long-term contracts with food supply wholesalers. Other items used in the baking and distribution of the cookies, such as boxes, waxed paper, and point-of-purchase display placards, are bought periodically from a variety of paper goods wholesalers. The Weston Paper Company, one of these wholesale intermediaries, is trying to persuade Gravas' to allow Weston to install a systems purchasing arrangement. Describe the advantages to the Gravas' Old World Cookie Company of agreeing to such an arrangement. Explain some of the disadvantages of systems purchasing to Gravas'.

7. This chapter seems to paint a dismal portrait of wholesaling management. If these intermediaries are so poorly managed, why did they account for nearly $2 trillion in sales in 1982? Why are wholesale sales nearly double retail sales for the same period?

8. Pick some specific industries, such as steel, groceries, hardware, fluid power equipment, power tools, drugs, electronics, and describe what changes, if any, are needed over the next ten years if wholesalers in those industries are to remain competitive.

9. Interview a local wholesaler, retailer, or business user who buys some of his products through wholesalers. Describe the services the firm obtains from its wholesalers. Determine which services the wholesalers do very well and which they do poorly. Ascertain exactly why the firm uses wholesalers instead of performing those services for itself.

Gould, Inc.: Focus 800 Bat-tery

Gould, Inc., a diversified manufacturer of electrical equipment, is launching a major test of an innovative plan for direct consumer sales to help it gain a larger share of the sagging $2.5 billion replacement automobile battery market. Gould invented the maintenance-free battery and makes about one out of seven car batteries made in the United States, but almost all of its batteries are sold under private labels, mostly through oil companies and mass-merchandisers. The new direct marketing plan will bring the company into competition with some of its own biggest private-label customers, such as J. C. Penney, K Mart, and Mobil's Montgomery Ward. The plan is now being tested in the seven-county Chicago area.

The 800 BAT-TERY plan calls for the establishment of a roadside service for standard motorists by maintaining a fleet of leased "Rover" vans in the Chicago area and equipping them with a stock of fresh batteries. A motorist unable to start his car can dial the 800 BAT-TERY number toll free between 6 A.M. and 10 P.M. seven days a week. If the dispatcher, after a diagnostic dialogue with the caller, believes it is a battery problem, a van is dispatched and will usually arrive within an hour. If roadside tests show a battery is needed, one is sold and installed by the van driver at a price ranging from $49.50 to $69.50. If the battery is not faulty and the car can be started the charge is $15 payable to the van driver by cash, check, or credit card (credit risk is verified by the dispatcher when the call is first received). If the car cannot be started, there is no charge. The plan is believed to be quite attractive to consumers because it offers greater convenience at no higher cost compared with batteries purchased in traditional outlets.

Most replacement batteries are purchased at a national retail chain (such as Sears, K Mart, and Penney's) or through a gasoline station. Gould supplies both types of retailers as well as some vehicle manufacturers, but its batteries are always sold under their brand name rather than the Gould name. Consequently, a dissatisfied retailer can easily switch to another supplier without affecting consumer demand. Since there is overcapacity in the industry, all manufacturers are anxious to supply retailers. This puts the battery manufacturers in a difficult bargaining position, which has resulted in battery sales being more profitable for the retailers than the manufacturers.

Gould could have decided to develop a chain of retail outlets, as has been done by the big tire manufacturers, e.g., Goodyear, Firestone, and General. However, it was unlikely that batteries would draw as well as tires because they are usually purchased on an emergency basis and less frequently. To attract motorists, other merchandise or services would have to be offered. Even then, the stores would have little to distinguish them from competing stores. Moreover, if the capital investment in each store were $200,000 and the interest rate 15% per year, the interest charge alone would be $30,000 per year per store. Considering the number of stores necessary to service adequately the seven-county Chicago area (not to mention the entire country!), the retail store option requires a substantial capital investment.

An examination of the experience of Federal Express revealed that a leased van fleet could be operated for much less money and more time and space flexibility than retail stores. In fact, the cost of leasing 24 vans in the Chicago area was estimated to be $7,000 a month (*Business Week*, June 15, 1981, p. 82). There are other costs associated with entering the retail battery market such as advertising to establish consumer awareness, but these costs would be approximately the same for the van or store plan.

Before establishing this system, Gould undertook consumer research to determine the demand. There are approximately 47 million replacement battery sales per year with the possibility of even more as new-car price increases encourage drivers to keep and maintain their existing cars. Replacement sales can be categorized as *anticipatory* or *distress*. Anticipatory sales are those in which serviceable batteries are replaced because the owner feels that the battery may fail under tough starting conditions. Anticipatory sales are about 20% of total replacement sales but are highly seasonal. They represent 50% of replacement sales in September. Distress sales make up 80% of replacement sales and are also highly seasonal. Automobiles require extra starting power in cold weather and batteries deliver less power as the temperatures drop. Peak demand is experienced on extremely cold mornings.

Gould tested the new approach in Wilkes-Barre, Pa., and raised its market share by five percentage points. That area was used because it could be serviced by one of the company's nearby battery plants. If the Chicago area test is successful, Gould will eventually extend it to 42 markets.

What opportunities and threats does the plan face and how should the management deal with them?

This case was prepared by Professor Richard Yalch. Gould no longer manufactures and markets batteries.

Quetzal Distributors

Quetzal Distributors is an importer and distributor of a wide variety of South American and African artifacts. It is also a major source of southwestern Indian—especially Hopi and Navajo—jewelry and pottery. While the firm's headquarters is located in Phoenix, Arizona, there are branch offices currently in Los Angeles, Miami, and Boston.

Quetzal (named after the national bird of Guatemala) originated as a trading post operation near Tucson, Arizona, in the early 1900s. Through a series of judicious decisions, the firm established itself as one of the more reputable dealers in authentic southwestern jewelry and pottery. Over the years, Quetzal gradually expanded its product line to include pre-Columbian artifacts from Peru and Venezuela and tribal and burial artifacts from Africa. For example, the company was among the first to offer African trade beads, sometimes called slave beads, in the United States. By careful inspection of these South American and African artifacts in terms of their authenticity, Quetzal Distributors developed a national reputation as one of the most respected importers of these types of artifacts.

In the early 1970s, Quetzal expanded its product line even further to include "natural" jewelry—jewelry handcrafted from semiprecious stones, seashells, wood, and the like. This expansion was undertaken only after considerable prodding by the firm's clients desiring more modernistic jewelry items.

Gross sales in 1975 were approximately $12.3 million, with a gross margin of 43.7 percent. In 1974 gross sales were $9.9 million. Myron Rangard, the firm's national sales manager, attributed the sales increase to the recent popularity of its product line, especially natural jewelry, and the expanded distribution of southwestern jewelry and South American and African artifacts:

> Indian jewelry became popular among the general population four years ago. Prior to that time, Quetzal served a very select clientele who knew our jewelry as a collectable item and an investment. The same was true for our pottery. At about the same time, natural jewelry caught on like wildfire. The day that Elizabeth Taylor first wore that puka shell necklace marked the beginning of the craze for naturalistic jewelry.
>
> For some reason, our South American and African artifacts have been gaining greater acceptance. Two of our department store customers featured examples of our African line in their Christmas catalogs last year. I personally think consumer tastes are changing from the modern and abstract to the more concrete, like our products.

Quetzal distributes its products exclusively through specialty shops (including interior decorators), firm-sponsored "showings," and a few exclusive department stores. Often, the company is the sole supplier to its clients. The reasons for this limited distribution were recently expressed by Mr. Rangard:

> Our limited distribution has been dictated to us because of the nature of our product line. As acceptance grew, we expanded our distribution to specialty shops and some department stores. Previously, we had to push our products through our own showings.
>
> Furthermore, we just didn't have the product. These South American artifacts aren't always easy to get and the political situation in Africa is limiting our supply. Even some of the Indian art has been hard to come by. We have begun to distribute some contemporary Indian jewelry and pottery, but it has had to meet our authenticity standard of being done in the traditional manner—which takes time. We don't distribute the items produced in assembly-line fashion, like much of the current jewelry and pottery.
>
> Our perennial supply problem has become even more critical in recent years for several reasons. Not only must we search harder for new products, but the competition for authentic artifacts has increased tenfold. On top of this, we must now contend with governments not allowing exportation of certain artifacts because of their "national significance." Take even a fairly common natural jewelry component such as coral; Italy is sitting on its supply as a natural resource. I personally think the government is just waiting for the price to go up.

The problem of supply has forced Quetzal to add three new buyers in the last two years. Whereas Quetzal identified five major competitors in 1973, by mid-1976, there were eleven. "Our bargaining position has eroded," noted David Olsen, director of procurement. "We have watched our gross margin slip in recent years due to aggressive competitive bidding by others."

"And competition at the retail level has increased also," injected Rangard. "Not only are some of our larger specialty and department store customers sending out their own buyers to deal directly with some of our Indian suppliers, but we are often faced with amateurs or fly-by-night competitors. These people move into a city, and either dump a bunch of jewelry at low prices or foist some inauthentic jewelry on the public at exorbitant prices. In either case they give all the industry a bad name."

By early 1975 several mass merchandise department store chains and a number of upper-scale discount operations began selling merchandise similar to that offered by Quetzal. Even though product quality was often mixed, occasionally an authentic group of items was found in these stores, according to company sales representatives. Subsequent inquiries by both Rangard and Olsen revealed that other competing distributors had signed purchase contracts with these outlets. Moreover, the items were typically being sold at retail prices below those charged by Quetzal.

In late 1976, Mr. Rangard was contacted by a mass-merchandise department store concerning the possibility of carrying a complete line of Quetzal products. The chain was currently selling a competitor's items, but wished to add a more exclusive product line. A tentative contract submitted by the chain stated that it would buy at 10 percent below Quetzal's existing prices, and that the initial purchase would be for not less than $150,000. Depending on consumer acceptance, purchases were estimated to be at least $1 million annually.

Thus, in January 1977, Rangard and Olsen scheduled a meeting to decide whether Quetzal should accept the department store offer. Included in this meeting was to be a discussion of the fast fashion cycle of Quetzal's natural jewelry line, currently running about six months ("much of what is being worn in Milwaukee today is out of date in Los Angeles by eighteen months").

This case was prepared by Professors Robert Peterson, The University of Texas, Austin, and Roger Kerin, Southern Methodist University, Dallas, as a basis for class discussion; it is not designed to illustrate effective or ineffective handling of an administrative situation.

Source: Roger A. Kerin and Robert A. Peterson, *Strategic Marketing Problems: Cases and Comments*, 3rd ed. (Boston: Allyn and Bacon, 1984), pp. 54–56.

Mussleman Department Store

(*In the Musselman Department Store—located in Milltown and catering to the low- to middle-income group—David Dirkson, salesman for the Zenith Drug Company, a wholesale drug firm, is calling on Beatrice Bishop, the buyer for the Cosmetics and Drug Sundries Department.*)

SALESMAN. Miss Bishop, I represent the Zenith Drug Company. We're expanding our services to offer a wholesale prescription service, which I'm sure your customers would find attractive.

BUYER. A wholesale prescription service? I've never heard of that.

SALESMAN.

It *is* novel, isn't it?—and that's why it should mean some new, plus business for you.

BUYER. But what is it? How does it work?

SALESMAN. When your customers are here in the store, shopping for other items, no doubt right here in your department, they leave their prescriptions with you, and we pick them up at 5:00 P.M., fill them overnight, and have the medicine all neatly put up in bottles and labeled—with the store's name, Musselman Department Store Prescription Service—back at 9:00 A.M. the next morning, ready for delivery.

BUYER. But where is the advantage?

SALESMAN. Your customers save 25 percent of the retail price, 25 percent off what they'd pay in a drugstore. There is a lot of talk these days about the high price of drugs; 25 percent—that's a lot of money on some of the new miracle drugs that cost $10 or $15 a prescription.

BUYER. That does sound interesting. Tell me more about your firm.

SALESMAN. Oh, we've been in business in Exeter County for over 75 years, and now we're operating here in Monroe County—have been for several months now. As a matter of fact, we've chosen Monroe County as the scene for this new prescription service.

BUYER. Why?

SALESMAN. Well, partly because we don't have as many retail drugstore accounts here; they might not welcome this particular kind of competition. We think Monroe is a good county. And Milltown, particularly, is a real shopping center.

BUYER. What kind of markup would we get?

SALESMAN. If you want to give your customers the full 25 percent saving, you'd still get the traditional department store figure of 40 percent of the selling price; or you could fatten your share by given them a saving of only 15 or 20 percent.

BUYER. Do you think it would fit in with cosmetics, vitamins, bathing caps and so on? We don't carry any medicines now, you know.

SALESMAN. Of course it would. And it might be the entering wedge for a full-scale drug business. The regular drugstores carry enough department store merchandise, Lord knows!

QUESTIONS

1. What is the problem underlying the decision Miss Bishop must make?

2. What are the questions she must ask herself—and answer?

3. Should she take on the new service?

4. Why would Musselman gain competitively by this move?
5. Why would Zenith Drug gain?

Source: Edward C. Bursk and Stephen A. Greyser, *Cases in Marketing Management*, 2nd ed. (Englewood Cliffs, N.J.: Prentice-Hall, 1975), pp. 71–72.

Carapace, Inc.

Carapace, Incorporated, is a Tulsa, Oklahoma–based firm specializing in plaster bandages used in making casts for broken bones. Carapace was established in 1973, when Bill Klintworth, his father, and Jeff Nooleen, an orthopedic supplies dealer in Tulsa, Oklahoma, purchased a plaster company from its founder. Prior to 1973, the firm had prospered as a sole proprietorship by satisfying the bandage needs of a geographically limited market. In 1974, Carapace had gross sales of $100,000 with a pre-tax profit of $20,000. Carapace serviced the west south-central United States through Nooleen's dealership and the efforts of one salesman in 1975. "Market acceptance was particularly high in Texas and Oklahoma due to the previous owner's reputation for high quality bandages. This reputation got our foot in the door, and by maintaining our quality, we have established potentially long-term relationships with our existing customers," remarked Klintworth.

By mid-1975, Carapace had expanded its production capacity to produce $1.8 million in bandage sales. After discussing future growth plans with his father and Nooleen, Klintworth realized that the geographical market served by Carapace had to be expanded. In late 1975, Klintworth stated that Carapace's objectives for 1976 were to (1) expand the firm's market coverage from the west south-central region (Texas, Oklahoma, Arkansas, Louisiana, and Mississippi) to a national level, and (2) capture 3 percent of the United States plaster bandage market within two years.

In November 1975, Klintworth was contacted by two major distributors of orthopedic supplies concerning the possibility of selling the Carapace plaster bandage. Both sought exclusive rights to Carapace's plaster bandages. Klintworth believed that he should first review his marketing program before deciding which distributor's proposal should be accepted.

THE CAST MATERIAL MARKET

Plaster has been used in medicine as an immobilizer since the sixteenth century. Until several decades ago, casts were made by doctors through a process whereby they prepared a solution of plaster, then dipped strips of gauze bandages into it, and wrapped them around the limb until they hardened into a cast. Eventually, a method was developed that allowed plaster to be impregnated onto gauze, and then dried and rolled, thus making it possible for plaster bandages to be mass-produced and distributed.

Plaster's Competition

Recently, synthetic materials have emerged as contenders for a portion of the estimated $15 million cast material market. For example, in 1973, Merck & Company introduced a cast called Lightcast II. This cast is made of polypropylene, glass fiber, and resin which can be as much as 50 percent lighter in weight and three times stronger than plaster. Also, because it can be immersed in water, Lightcast II enables bathing and permits hydrotherapy. This type of cast presents a formidable rival to the heavier plaster cast that is still not completely waterproof.

Market Dominance

In spite of plaster's apparent drawbacks, 99.3 percent of the cast material market volume is still in plaster. The main reason for the popularity of plaster is its price. Synthetic casts are seven to ten times more expensive than plaster casts. Many doctors find it hard to pass this added expense onto their patients when other medical costs are rising. Furthermore, patients seem to prefer plaster since synthetics often make the "cast-signing" ritual difficult due to the uneven surface of synthetics. In addition to these attributes, chemical additives are constantly improving the quality of plaster casts. Resins help strengthen plaster casts and improve their water resistance. Whiteners are added to improve the cosmetic appearance. Depending on the amount of potassium sulfate that is used in the original plaster mixture, setting times can be varied to meet the particular needs of the user. Finally, some types of casts require the use of plaster due to its superior conforming qualities. Because of these various attributes, plaster is expected to continue to dominate the cast materials market in the foreseeable future.

Consumer Use

About 6,000 tons of plaster were used for medical purposes in 1974. Of the four million casts applied in the United States that year, 75 percent were for setting fractures, while the remainder was used for the support of sprained limbs and for orthopedic immobilization.

Although figures are not available for total cast material sales, hospitals account for an estimated 50 percent of market sales volume. Remaining sales are

EXHIBIT 1

**Average Annual Dollar Expenditures for
Casts for Hospitals by Geographical Region,
1975**

Region	No. of Hospitals in Region	Average Expenditure	Sample Size
New England	432	$1,287	26
Middle Atlantic	927	1,523	87
East N. Central	1,201	1,229	90
West N. Central	947	615	48
South Atlantic	1,022	986	63
East S. Central	593	957	32
West S. Central	1,016	505	48
Mountain	426	769	19
Pacific	887	1,081	37

Source: Company Records. Data obtained from marketing research report prepared by an independent research firm.

to medical schools, orthopedic clinics, doctors' offices, veterinarians, and others. In general, a company's share of the hospital cast material market is believed to equal its share of the national market.

Hospital sales in 1975 are estimated to be about 29 million units. (A unit may be anything from a 5-inch by 30-inch splint to an 8-inch by 5-yard roll). This represents a 14.7 percent increase in volume from the previous year. Total cast material sales in dollars have grown to an estimated $7.3 million in sales to the nation's 7,451 hospitals. Exhibit 1 shows estimated average annual cast material dollar purchases for hospitals within the nation's nine geographic regions. Exhibit 2 shows hospital sales by region and market share by firm for the first six months of 1975. It suggests that the East North Central, the South Atlantic, and the Middle Atlantic are the three largest areas for cast material sales. Exhibit 3 shows sales by hospital size according to the number of beds, and the market shares for major marketers for the various size hospitals.

The three bandage sizes that are most popular with doctors are the 4" × 5" bandage (30 percent of unit sales), 6" × 5 yd. bandage (30 percent of unit sales) and the 3" × 5 yd. bandage (20 percent of unit sales). When setting a large arm cast, doctors use three of these rolls in varying combinations.

Competition

Johnson & Johnson is the recognized leader in cast material sales. Due to their dominance as a supplier of hospital materials, their name alone is often enough to generate sales of cast material,'' according to Klintworth. Johnson & Johnson

EXHIBIT 2

Hospital Cast Material Dollar Sales by Geographical Area and Market Share by Firm

(January–June, 1975)

		East			Central		
	Total	Total	New Eng.	Middle Atl.	Total	E.N. Cent.	W.N. Cent.
Region volume ($000s)	3696	983	278	705	1026	737	290
Mkt. share by firm							
Johnson & Johnson	74.5	62.1	70.9	58.6	74.8	75.9	71.5
Parke-Davis	10.2	14.8	14.2	15.0	12.5	9.1	20.4
Solar	10.0	16.6	12.8	18.2	7.6	8.4	3.3
Kendall	2.7	4.4	2.0	5.3	3.5	3.3	3.9
Acme Cotton	1.8	1.6	.0	2.2	2.5	3.1	1.0
All others	.8	.5	.1	.7	.1	.1	.0

		South			West		
	Total	South Atl.	E.S. Cent.	W.S. Cent.	Total	Mountain	Pacif.
Region volume ($000s)	1043	504	284	256	644	164	479
Mkt. share by firm							
Johnson & Johnson	83.9	86.0	64.2	87.7	78.0	81.8	76.7
Parke-Davis	3.8	5.4	4.3	.0	10.0	14.2	8.6
Solar	6.7	3.0	19.2	.0	10.3	.0	13.8
Kendall	2.0	1.0	5.7	.0	.1	.0	.2
Acme Cotton	2.3	1.7	3.4	2.3	.3	1.3	.0
All others	1.3	.9	3.2	10.0	1.3	2.7	.8

Source: Company Records. Data obtained from marketing research report prepared by an independent research firm.

alone accounted for an estimated 81.1 percent of the hospital cast material volume in 1975. Parke-Davis was the next largest with 12.4 percent volume (see Exhibit 4). Parke-Davis distributes plaster bandages for Anchor Continental. Klintworth believed that in three or four years, Anchor Continental will distribute cast material on its own.

Several months ago Kendall decided to exit the cast material market. Owned by Colgate Palmolive, Kendall had tried to compete directly with Johnson & Johnson by modeling their packaging, product, and prices after Johnson & Johnson. Klintworth believed that Carapace should orient its product to fill the void created by Kendall's exit from the market. He noted, "With the departure of Kendall, about 3 percent of the market should be available to us, or about $450,000."

EXHIBIT 3
Cast Material Dollar Sales by Hospital Size
and Market Share by Firm

(January–June, 1975)

	Total	500 & over	300– 499	200– 299	100– 199	Under 100
Dollar volume (000s)	3,696	737	917	662	682	698
Market share by firm:						
Johnson & Johnson	74.5%	71.3%	74.0%	66.0%	83.6%	77.6%
Parke-Davis	10.2	11.6	13.0	15.7	5.6	4.1
Solar	10.0	8.9	7.1	16.1	3.4	15.9
Kendall	2.7	4.6	4.2	.8	3.4	0.0
Acme Cotton	1.8	2.3	1.1	1.3	4.0	.7
Others	.8	1.3	.5	.1	.1	1.8
	100.0%	100.0%	100.0%	100.0%	100.0%	100.0%

Source: Company Records. Data obtained from marketing research report prepared by an independent research firm.

CARAPACE PRELIMINARY MARKETING STRATEGY

Product Positioning

Klintworth believed Carapace should stress quality, service, and its specialization in plaster bandages. The last point was especially important since an estimated 90 percent of the market was controlled by Johnson & Johnson, Parke-Davis, and

EXHIBIT 4
Cast Material Market Shares Among
Hospitals, 1975 Estimated

Firm	Unit Shares		Dollar Shares	
	Volume (000s)	Percent	Volume (000s)	Percent
Johnson & Johnson	23,855.6	81.1	5,339	73.0
Parke-Davis	3,661.3	12.4	733	10.2
Solar	209.6	0.7	651	9.0
Kendall	1,128.7	3.8	263	3.6
Acme Cotton	567.9	1.9	173	2.4
Others	29.4	0.1	62	.9
Total	29,451.5	100.0%	7,221	100.0%

Source: Company Records. Data obtained from marketing research report prepared by an independent research firm.

EXHIBIT 5

Carapace Price List

		Bandages	
	Single Case Quantity Per Case Price	Price Per Dozen	Price Per Unit
2" x 3 yds.—6 dozen to a case	$23.40	$ 4.75	$.325
3" x 3 yds.—6 dozen to a case	27.30	5.60	.387
3" x 5 yds.—6 dozen to a case	39.30	7.90	.545
4" x 5 yds.—6 dozen to a case	40.20	8.25	.558
5" x 5 yds.—4 dozen to a case	32.60	9.85	.679
6" x 5 yds.—4 dozen to a case	37.20	11.45	.775

Source: Company Records.

Kendall; also, all three market hundreds of other medical supplies. The advantage of specialization was emphasized in Carapace's advertising brochure:

> Just as there are specialists in the medical profession, CARAPACE is a specialist in the making of a superior plaster bandage. Other competing manufacturers consider the plaster bandage as only one of a long line of products. At CARAPACE we make only one product and we are the best at what we do.

Pricing and Cost Structure

Carapace's prices on its plaster products were established to reflect the high quality of its offering, according to Klintworth. Manufacturing and material costs are estimated to be 20 percent of the retail price. Overhead costs were approximately $50,000. Present suggested retail prices on Carapace products are shown in Exhibit 5.

Promotion

At this point, $1,000 has been spent to develop a brochure for Carapace. This brochure emphasizes quality, service, product attributes, and the importance of remaining small:

> As a statement of business philosophy, it is our desire never to mass produce our CARAPACE bandage—to remain small enough so that we can continue to produce the best and the most inexpensive bandage available and still offer personal, fast service to our customers. Sure, we're small; but that is why we are so good.

Klintworth outlined Carapace's important selling points which could be selected for future promotional efforts:

- "Wetting out" is faster with Carapace bandages. That is, they absorb water faster when preparing the bandages for wrapping.

- Plaster loss is low. The use of adhesives in Carapace plaster reduces the amount of plaster melting off the gauze during application.
- It is the "Cadillac of bandages" due to the high quality of chemicals used in the mixture.
- The initial setting time is faster—three to four minutes, as opposed to five to eight minutes.
- Eventual hardening time is faster than others. With Carapace, a foot cast can be walked on the next day, while other products require forty-eight hours to harden completely.
- Packaging: it is easier to remove the Carapace bandage from its plastic bag as opposed to rival products that are heat-sealed in plastic.
- Carapace has an indefinite shelf life.
- Carapace doesn't delaminate in water.
- It's "organic," unlike Johnson & Johnson's whose bandage contains formaldehyde as a preservative. Therefore, Carapace plaster smells better and causes no skin irritation.
- It finishes out prettier, whiter, and smoother than other plaster casts.
- Carapace gives off less exothermic heat during the cast-hardening process.
- The delivery time is faster than Johnson & Johnson's.
- There is a 5 percent discount if payment is in by the tenth of the month.
- Carapace won't "telescope," that is, slide down the patient's limb.

Distribution

Klintworth was unsure of how to reach the cast material market with his plaster bandage. He had ruled out using his own sales group due to sales administration, recruiting, and training costs. Accordingly, he welcomed the interest of two nationally recognized orthopedic supply distributors.

On succeeding days in November, 1975, Klintworth was contacted by Miller Medical Associates and Continental, Incorporated.[1] Both described their organizations and presented him proposals including exclusive rights to represent Carapace in the United States.

Miller Medical Associates (MMA). MMA has sixty-two salespersons located throughout the United States except for the west south-central and east north-central regions (see Exhibit 6). In addition, MMA also services twenty-two established orthopedic dealers situated in major metropolitan areas in territories serviced by salespersons. MMA does not compete with its dealers for accounts.

For its sales effort, MMA would receive a 5 percent commission on retail sales below $500,000; 4 percent on retail sales up to $1 million; and 3 percent on retail sales over $1 million. This commission is obtained both from sales by MMA to final users (e.g., doctors, hospitals, etc.), and from retail sales through dealers. MMA dealers also receive a 20 percent commission on their own sales. According

[1]Disguised names.

```
                    EXHIBIT 6
        Miller Medical Associates Sales Personnel

    Region                         Number of Sales Personnel

    New England                              5
    Middle Atlantic                          9
    East N. Central                          0
    West N. Central                         11
    South Atlantic                          11
    E. S. Central                            7
    West S. Central                          0
    Mountain                                 8
    Pacific                                 11
                                            ——
         Total                              62

    Source: Company Records.
```

to the MMA representative, sales volume of Carapace bandage would be split 70–30 percent between dealers and salespersons, respectively.

During the previous three months, MMA had been selling a new synthetic cast called Hexcalite. Since this cast could only be used for certain kinds of injuries, MMA sought out Carapace to complement this product. In addition to bandages, MMA is a distributor of hundreds of orthopedic products and related products. Its product mix contains a wide variety of items ranging from medical equipment priced in five figures to much smaller items such as bandages.

Continental, Incorporated. Continental is a smaller distributor of orthopedic supplies than MMA. Continental has 50 salespersons operating in the United States in addition to fifteen established dealers in territories serviced by salespersons. Continental does not compete with dealers for accounts. Its sales organization has representatives in every region (see Exhibit 7). Continental's commission schedule indicates that it receives a 6 percent commission on sales less than $1 million and a 4 percent commission on sales of $1 million or more. This commission is obtained from both sales by Continental to final users and from sales through dealers. Dealers receive a 20 percent commission on their own sales and would account for 40 percent of Carapace bandage sales.

Continental, which does not currently handle a line of plaster bandages, sought out Carapace to fill a gap in its assortment, according to its representative. Continental carries a more limited product assortment than MMA and does not represent manufacturers of medical equipment.

"Having two proposals is a mixed blessing," remarked Klintworth. "While it confirms our confidence in our product, we now have to figure out which one will most likely help us reach our objectives." Nooleen noted that MMA was the older more established distributor, but he wasn't sure about the attention MMA

EXHIBIT 7
Continental, Inc. Sales Personnel

Region	Number of Sales Personnel
New England	4
Middle Atlantic	6
East N. Central	3
West N. Central	9
South Atlantic	9
East S. Central	3
West S. Central	3
Mountain	4
Pacific	9
Total	50

Source: Company Records.

would give Carapace. Continental was more aggressive, but "it is spread pretty thin nationally," commented Nooleen.

This case was written by Mr. Gregory Grimshaw, The University of Texas, Austin, and Roger Kerin, Southern Methodist University, Dallas, as a basis for class discussion rather than to illustrate appropriate or inappropriate handling of administrative situations. The authors wish to thank Carapace, Incorporated, for its cooperation in the preparation of this case.

Source: Roger A. Kerin and Robert A. Peterson, *Strategic Marketing Problems: Cases and Comments* (Boston: Allyn and Bacon, 1978), pp. 298–305.

5

Channel Management and the Marketing Mix: Physical Distribution Management and Promotion Strategy

LEARNING OBJECTIVES

> *Upon completing this chapter, you will be able to:*

- *Explain that the physical distribution concept refers to minimizing the total costs of the physical flow given a particular level of customer service.*

- *Outline a procedure for determining the level of customer service desired by the target market.*

- *Describe the major components of physical distribution—warehousing, inventory, and transportation—used in delivering the appropriate levels of customer service.*

- *Distinguish among the major types of warehouses and discuss the factors that determine the number and location of warehousing facilities.*

- *Calculate key elements of inventory decisions—how much to reorder and when to reorder.*

- *Compare the advantages and disadvantages of the five major transportation modes—rail, truck, air, water, and pipeline—used to deliver goods to marketing channel intermediaries.*

- *Describe symptoms of "maldistribution."*

- *Explain the differences between "push" and "pull" promotional strategies.*

- *Describe the major promotional activities undertaken by manufacturers, wholesalers, and retailers within marketing channels.*

- *Discuss when using cooperative advertising would be advantageous to both manufacturers and retailers.*

- *Understand the reasons intermediaries may not undertake some of the promotional activities within the marketing channel.*

- *Outline the legal aspects of promotional strategy within the marketing channel.*

Caterpillar Tractor Company: An Integrated Marketing Strategy

Caterpillar is known throughout the world for its high-quality earth-moving equipment, diesel engines, and materials-handling machinery. Until the mid-1980s, the primary markets for Cat's heavy equipment included energy-related projects and construction in OPEC and Third World countries. Much of Caterpillar's success arose from its careful coordination of the pricing, distribution, promotion, and quality of its product lines.

One reason that Caterpillar traditionally prices 10 percent above its nearest competitor is its reputation for high-quality products and reliable service. In fact, Caterpillar backs up this reputation by offering extended product warranties on certain models and by its famous parts availability policy. If a customer doesn't receive replacement parts for any Caterpillar machine within 48 hours of ordering, that customer will get the parts free.

To be able to deliver on such a promise, Caterpillar operates a huge warehouse carrying a 60-day inventory of more than 200,000 parts in Morton, Illinois. In addition, a vast computerized information network tracks inventories of parts at dealers and warehouses throughout the world. This inventory and information system also enables Caterpillar to provide next-day delivery to dealers ordering any part through the Morton facility.

Many observers believe that the dealership network is Caterpillar's greatest competitive weapon. These dealers are all independently owned and are managed by sophisticated business people who pride themselves on understanding and responding to their customers' needs. To assist their dealers in doing this, Caterpillar offers sales and support programs such as deferred payment programs, lease and rental programs, personal selling assistance, seminars, and parts buy-back programs. Without a strong dealership network, many of Caterpillar's customers would buy from its competitors.

Integrating its own customer service policies with a strong dealer network, high-quality product lines, and plenty of dealer selling support has enabled Caterpillar to capture a commanding market share and to charge premium prices. Without such a *total* marketing program, Caterpillar would not be nearly as successful as it is, even in the face of strongly declining demand as the result of softening construction markets and a stronger U.S. dollar.

Sources: "Caterpillar: Sticking to Basics to Stay Competitive," *Business Week*, May 4, 1981, pp. 74–80; "Caterpillar's Backbone: A Long Dealer Network," *Business Week*, May 4, 1981, p. 77; Harlan S. Byrne, "Caterpillar's Business Slides Sharply as Its Markets Slump World-Wide," *The Wall Street Journal*, March 2, 1983, p. 25; and "A Shaken Caterpillar Retools to Take on a More Competitive World," *Business Week*, November 5, 1984, pp. 91, 94.

As the Caterpillar example illustrates, a marketing channel is only as strong as the other elements of the marketing mix surrounding it. Note that many of the marketing channel functions or flows discussed in Chapter 1—physical possession, promotion, negotiation, financing, risking, ordering, payment, and market information—correspond directly to the traditional elements of the marketing mix—price, promotion, distribution, and product. This chapter and the next focus on how the other aspects of the marketing mix—physical distribution, promotion, product strategy, and pricing—can be fitted together with marketing channel strategy to form an effective total marketing strategy. The final chapter of Part II—Chapter 7—addresses communication systems which are used in coordinating marketing channel strategy.

PHYSICAL DISTRIBUTION AND MARKETING CHANNEL MANAGEMENT

For marketing channels to serve the industrial user or ultimate consumer effectively, the product must be moved in the right quantity at a specific time to a specific place. As shown in Figure 5-1, the physical possession flow in marketing channels refers to the task of moving materials and products from their points of extraction or production to their points of final consumption. This task is generally performed by the "logistics systems"; *physical distribution* usually refers to the delivery of final products. In this text, however, we use the term to refer the general task of moving material and products, regardless of their destination.[1]

Several basic aspects of physical distribution are discussed in this chapter. The *physical distribution concept* is the philosophy that underlies current physical distribution management. The output of the logistics system is *customer service*, and how efficiently it is delivered is the standard against which physical distribu-

[1] For alternative definitions and explorations of the concept, see John F. Magee, *Industrial Logistics* (New York: McGraw-Hill, 1968), p. 2; Ronald H. Ballou, *Business Logistics Management*, 2nd ed. (Englewood Cliffs, N.J.: Prentice-Hall, 1985), pp. 5–7; Douglas M. Lambert and James R. Stock, *Strategic Physical Distribution Management* (Homewood, Ill.: Richard D. Irwin, 1982), pp. 8–20; Roy D. Shapiro and James L. Heskett, *Logistics Strategy* (St. Paul, Minn.: West, 1985), p. 1; and Donald J. Bowersox, *Logistical Management* (New York: Macmillan, 1978), pp. 3–23.

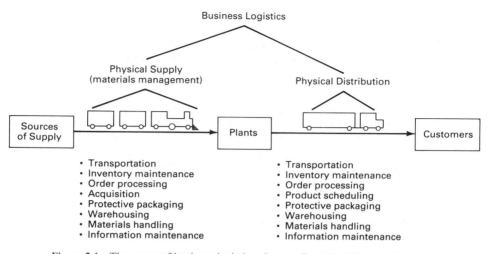

Figure 5-1 The scope of business logistics: *Source*: Ronald H. Ballou, *Business Logistics Management: Planning and Control*, 2nd ed. © 1985, p. 7. Reprinted by permission of Printice-Hall, Englewood Cliffs, N. J.

tion systems are measured.[2] To provide the appropriate level of customer service, physical distribution managers must make decisions concerning *warehousing*, *inventory management and control*, and *transportation systems*.[3]

The Physical Distribution Concept

As noted above, the physical distribution (PD) concept is a philosophy of logistics management. Specifically, the PD concept is a *cost-service* orientation, backed by an integrated physical distribution network, which is aimed at *minimizing* the total costs of distribution at a *given level of customer service*.

Recall from the Caterpillar illustration that Cat guarantees that its customers will receive repair parts within 48 hours of placing an order. For Caterpillar, the given level of customer service is its 48-hour policy. Warehouses, inventories, and transportation systems must be coordinated to achieve that level of customer service at the lowest possible total cost. Thus, Cat balances the higher transportation costs of airfreight against the lower inventory costs of the centralized Morton, Illinois, parts warehouse. Exhibit 5-1 shows how Gillette and Montgomery Ward have also balanced the individual costs of providing customer service to minimize the total cost of PD.

[2] Lambert and Stock, *Strategic Physical Distribution Management*, p. 65.

[3] Because these components of physical distribution are more generalizable to various types of channel members than, say, materials handling or protective packaging, they are the focus of the discussion in this section.

EXHIBIT 5-1
Balancing Cost Trade-offs in Physical Distribution: The Gillette and Montgomery Ward Experiences

The Gillette Company, the world's largest producer of safety razors, was faced with an ever-expanding assortment of products because it had expanded into a broad range of toiletry products. To give good customer service the company started using airfreight, an expensive form of distribution. Upon studying their distribution system, they discovered that their problem was in the slowness with which orders were processed. By simplifying paperwork they were able to reduce the time required to process orders. Gillette was able to return to lower-cost surface transportation and still be able to meet delivery schedules. The cost trade-off was between order-processing costs that *increased* and transportation costs that *decreased;* and the net result was that total distribution costs *decreased.*

The Montgomery Ward Company found that significant inventory reductions could be achieved by consolidating all their slower-moving products into one central warehouse. This facility is located only seven miles from Chicago's O'Hare Airport. When a slow-moving product or part is needed, the Chicago warehouse is notified and the requirement is often sent via airfreight to the requesting party. While this procedure greatly increases the transportation charges involved in sending a product or part to a customer, the inventory holding cost reduction more than offsets the increased per-unit transportation charges.

Source: James C. Johnson and Donald F. Wood, *Contemporary Physical Distribution and Logistics* (New York: Macmillan, 1984), pp. 10–11.

Customer Service Standards

It is continually emphasized throughout this text that the process of formulating marketing strategy and policy starts with determining customer needs and desires. This adage applies with equal force to the setting of physical distribution policies. In fact, certain studies indicate that many industrial buyers consider physical distribution service to be one of the most important factors in selecting their suppliers.[4]

The key PD service level measures used by manufacturing and merchandising, i.e., retailing and wholesaling, firms are shown in Table 5-1. The critical question confronting the distribution manager is which of these customer service elements are of major importance to his clientele. The importance given to each

---

[4] See, for example, Harvey Shycon and Christopher R. Sprague, "Put a Price Tag on Your Customer Servicing Levels," *Harvard Business Review*, Vol. 53 (July–August 1975), pp. 71–78; Donald R. Lehmann and John O'Shaughnessy, "Difference in Attribute Importance for Different Industrial Products," *Journal of Marketing*, Vol. 38 (April 1974), pp. 36–42; and Richard H. Evans, "Choice Criteria Revisited," *Journal of Marketing*, Vol. 44 (Winter 1980), pp. 55–56.

TABLE 5.1 Selected Service Level Measurements Used by Manufacturing and Merchandising Firms

Major Category	Subcategory
Product availability	Line item availability Product group availability Invoice fill Cases/units
Order cycle time	Order entry Order processing Total cycle time
Consistency	In order cycle time In shipment dispatch In transit time In arrival time In warehouse handling
Response time	Order status Order tracing Backorder status Order confirmation Product substitution Order shortages Product information requests
Error rates	Shipment delays Order errors Picking and packing errors Shipping and labeling errors Paperwork errors
Product/shipment-related malfunction	Damaged merchandise Merchandise refusals Claims Returned goods Customer complaints
Special handling	Transshipment Expedited orders Expedited transportation Special packaging Customer backhauls

Source: B. J. LaLonde and P. H. Zinszer, *Customer Service; Its Meaning and Measurement* (Chicago: National Council of Physical Distribution Management, 1976), p. 184.

of these various elements varies according to different product/market and purchasing contexts. For example, for some retail buyers, faster average order cycle time (i.e., shorter elapsed time from order placement to order delivery) is not as important as a less variable order cycle. These buyers would accept longer delivery times if the variability of order cycle times were reduced or if price concessions are offered. This situation does not hold, however, for retailers of drug sundries; the latter place a greater emphasis on actual delivery speed.

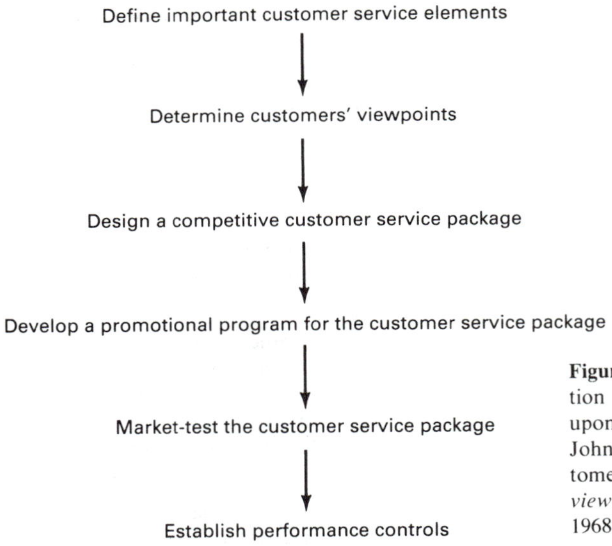

Define important customer service elements

↓

Determine customers' viewpoints

↓

Design a competitive customer service package

↓

Develop a promotional program for the customer service package

↓

Market-test the customer service package

↓

Establish performance controls

Figure 5-2 Managing physical distribution customer service. *Source*: Based upon William M. Hutchinson, Jr., and John F. Stolle, "How to Manage Customer Service," *Harvard Business Review*, Vol. 46 (November–December, 1968), pp. 85–96.

Several steps are necessary to arrive at an appropriate customer standard. Figure 5-2 presents a schematic overview of this process.[5]

Define Important Customer Service Elements.   Market research, using in-house cost data and informal questioning of the sales force and customers, can reveal the current levels of customer service and their costs. Additional research can identify which elements of customer service are most critical to which market segments.

Determine Customers' Viewpoints.   This step attempts to identify which additional elements of physical distribution service are most critical to which market segments. In addition, research should uncover how each element of PD service affects the customers' costs and sales effectiveness. For example, rapid delivery times may enable a retail buyer to stock fewer staple items. This level of service not only reduces the retailer's inventory costs but also limits the retailer's costs due to stockouts. Customers' perceptions of competitors' PD service levels should be gathered in preparation for the next step in developing effective customer service standards.

Design a Competitive Customer Service Package.   Once the important elements of customer service are established, the next step is to specify possible changes in these elements and identify the costs associated with these alternatives. For example, market research may suggest that the firm's present in-stock level of 95 percent (indicating that when a customer wants a product, it is

[5] The following sections are based heavily on William M. Hutchinson, Jr., and John F. Stolle, "How to Manage Customer Service," *Harvard Business Review*, Vol. 46 (November–December 1968), pp. 85–96.

immediately available 95 percent of the time) should be increased to 96 percent; however, this would require 6 percent more safety stock.[6] Moreover, even when the service level is raised to 96 percent, the product or service will be unavailable 4 percent of the time. Whether or not this is significant depends on such factors as how brand-loyal the firm's ultimate customers are, how sensitive purchasers (e.g., marketing intermediaries) are to customer service failures, how effective competitors' service levels are relative to one another, and so on. For certain frequently purchased consumer and industrial goods, though, stockouts are likely to be costly. Therefore, the stockout factor should be explicitly considered in evaluating alternative customer service packages.

Should the customer service levels need to be increased, an additional question is whether potential or actual purchasers are willing to pay for this improved service. Through market research of the firm's customers, alternative customer service packages (including their cost to the buyer) can be evaluated.[7] Among those alternative packages evaluated, of course, should be competitors' customer service levels. The ultimate result of the market research undertaken in this step should be a customer service package that is competitive with similar offerings to the firm's target market.

Develop a Promotional Program to Sell the Customer Service Package. Once the "best" customer service package is identified, distribution management can plan to reinforce or adjust existing customer service standards so that PD service may become a competitive weapon for the company. The most competitive PD package could very well be the one that offers a lower level of service accompanied by a lower price. In any event, new PD service programs must be introduced as new products would be; customers should be given enough advance warning so that they can adjust their customer service levels accordingly.

Market-Test the Customer Service Package and Promotional Program. As with any aspect of the marketing mix, the customer service levels and the program to promote them should be tested to ensure that the firm's customers will respond to them as anticipated. This step in the design process allows physical distribution management to make any necessary last-minute adjustments before the package is implemented on a larger scale.

Establish Performance Controls. Once the "optimal" customer service package is decided upon, management can determine the appropriate warehousing, inventory, and transportation policies that will assure the proper implementation of the desired customer service standards. In addition, necessary checks must be developed to make sure that the desired level of customer service is actually being delivered.

[6] This is one of several distribution rules of thumb; see Shycon and Spraque, "Customer Servicing Levels," p. 75.

[7] Several methods of eliciting these evaluations from purchasers are discussed in William D. Perreault, Jr., and Frederick A. Russ, "Physical Distribution Service: A Neglected Aspect of Marketing Management," *MSU Business Topics*, Vol. 22 (Summer 1974), pp. 37–45.

Warehousing represents perhaps the first vital link in the logistics system for carrying out the customer service standards established by the firm. The following section discusses several of the key managerial issues in the warehousing component of physical distribution strategy.

Warehousing Decisions

Efficient production requires that manufacturing operations be conducted as continually as possible at relatively few locations. Thus, warehouses maintained by marketing intermediaries or by manufacturers themselves are needed to store finished goods inventories. In turn, these warehouses can be strategically located in or near centers of demand to facilitate delivery of the desired levels of customer service. Furthermore, because production is usually not perfectly synchronized with market demand, the inventories held at warehouses act as buffers to variations between production and sales.

The two key functions of warehousing are movement and storage.[8] The *movement* function refers to the "efficient movement of large quantities into the warehouse and customized orders out of the warehouse."[9] Thus, breaking bulk and creating assortments are central aspects of the movement function.

Goods entering some warehouses may be stored for awhile rather than moved quickly through the facility. The *storage* function occurs as distribution managers add goods to the basic stock, store seasonally produced items such as canned tomato paste, counter erratic demand such as for snow throwers before the onset of winter, or condition perishable products such as ripening bananas before they reach the final link in their distribution.

The basic decisions a physical distribution manager must make about warehousing are (1) which type of warehouse facility to use, (2) how many warehouses to use to achieve desired customer service levels, and (3) where these warehouse facilities should be located.

Types of Warehouse Facilities. Two basic types of warehouse facilities are available to channel members. These are *privately* owned by the firm and *public* facilities, in which space is leased by the firm. Table 5-2 summarizes and compares many of the basic trade-offs involved in choosing between public and private warehousing arrangements.

Public Warehousing. Whereas private warehouses are often built to suit the owner's specialized needs, public warehouses come in a number of types and offer a wide range of services. Some specialization takes place in public warehousing, but only within broad product categories. In general, public warehouses are classified into five basic types:

1. *Commodity warehouses.* These are warehouses that limit their services to certain commodity groupings. The warehouses may specialize in storing and handling such commodities as lumber, cotton, tobacco, and grain.

[8] Bowersox, *Logistical Management*, pp. 212–214.
[9] Ibid., p. 212.

TABLE 5.2 Decision Variables in choosing Among Types of Warehouses

	Types of Warehousing Arrangements		
	Private		
Decisions Variables	Owned	Leased	Public
1. Fixed investment	Very high	Moderate, depends on the lease's terms	No fixed investment is involved
2. Unit cost	High, if volume is low	High, if volume is low	Low, since facilities are on "for hire as needed" and fixed costs are widely distributed among users
3. Control	High	High	Low managerial control
4. Adequacy to product line	Highly adequate	Moderately adequate	May not be convenient
5. Flexibility	Low	Low	High; termination of usage can be easily arranged

2. *Bulk-storage warehouses.* Some warehouses offer storage and handling of products in bulk, such as liquid chemicals, oil, highway salts, and syrups. Mixing products and breaking bulk may also be part of the service.

3. *Cold-storage warehouses.* These are controlled, low-temperature warehouses. Perishables, such as fruits, vegetables, and frozen foods, as well as some chemicals and drugs, require this type of storage for preservation.

4. *Household goods warehouses.* Storage and handling of household articles and furniture are the specialty of these warehouses. Although furniture manufacturers may use these warehouses, the major users are the household goods moving companies.

5. *General merchandise warehouses.* These warehouses handle a broad range of merchandise, which usually does not require the special facilities or the special handling noted for the four previous types of warehouses.[10]

In practice, hybrids of these basic types exist. For example, a general merchandise warehouse handling food products may have to operate a refrigerated section to satisfy the needs of food grocers. By the same token, bulk storage warehouses may handle general merchandise.

Lately, the public warehousing industry has been experiencing a steady rate of growth. One reason for the increased use of public warehousing is the ability of such organizations to provide services to companies with varied distribution needs. Exhibit 5-2 illustrates how several companies have been able to take advantage of the services of public warehousing firms.

Private Warehousing. A major development in private warehousing is the emergence of *distribution centers.* Distribution centers are distinguished from

[10] Creed H. Jenkins, *Modern Warehouse Management* (New York: Mc Graw-Hill, 1968), p. 29, as quoted in Ballou, *Business Logistics Management,* p. 251.

EXHIBIT 5-2

**Public Warehousing: Part of the Total
Physical Distribution Picture**

Balanced Foods, Inc., a small health-food supplier, shifted much of its participation in the physical possession flow to General Warehouse Corporation when it expanded during the late 1960s. By doing so, it was able to realize multiple benefits, including a greater amount of warehouse space allocated to its products, the use of expensive high-efficiency equipment that the firm itself could not have afforded, a reduction in distribution costs by 15 percent, and a reduction in order cycle time to 24 hours. These benefits permitted the company to concentrate heavily on its other marketing operations, with the result that it sales volume grew from $3 million to $11 million in five years.

Large companies are also making increased use of public warehouses for a variety of reasons. Mead Johnson & Company has always relied predominantly on public warehousing because of its space flexibility; Tonka Corporation finds public warehousing useful because its space needs fluctuate widely owing to the seasonality of the toy business; Alcoa has turned to public warehouses in some areas to speed up its deliveries to customers; Kresge uses public warehouses for a month or two before each of its new store openings to ensure that initial inventories are on hand when needed; Owens-Corning Fiberglas Corporation and Johns-Mansville Corporation have begun to use public warehouses to supplement their own network of private warehouses.

Source: Walter F. Friedman, "Physical Distribution: The Concept of Shared Services," *Harvard Business Review,* Vol. 53 (March–April 1975), p. 26.

---

conventional private warehousing operations by the fact that they are major centralized warehousing operations that are primarily established for the movement of goods rather than their storage.[11] As one marketing executive observed regarding his company's distribution center, "Our terminal is in constant motion. At no time is merchandise warehoused here . . . we're strictly a distribution terminal."[12] Thus, the rationale underlying the development of distribution centers is to maintain the company's product in a constant and efficient flow from the moment it leaves production until the day it arrives at its destination. Many of the world's foremost corporations now operate distribution centers as an integral part of their physical distribution systems. Exhibit 5-3 provides some illustrations.

Storage in Transit. Storage in transit—the time that goods remain in transportation equipment during delivery—reduces the need for and cost of warehousing. For example:

[11] Marjorie Person and Diane Mitchell, "Distribution Centers: The Fort Wayne Experience," *Business Horizons*, Vol. 19 (August 1975), pp. 89–95.

[12] "Meeting Those Distribution Center Needs," *Handling and Shipping*, July 1975, p. 37.

EXHIBIT 5-3

Distribution Centers: Some Illustrations

IBM's "World Trade Distribution Center" (WTDC) is one of the largest and most sophisticated of its kind in the world. From its location in New York, the WTDC uses a complex communications network to control the annual movement of more than 23 million pounds of equipment, parts, and supplies. Similarly, Levi Strauss, Inc., operates a huge distribution center in Little Rock, Arkansas, responsible for the rapid movement of its 48,000 product line items from its ten U.S. manufacturing plants to distributors in 70 foreign lands and more than 17,000 stores domestically. Further, from a single distribution center covering 28 acres and more than 1¼ million square feet, the Anchor Hocking Corporation ships 1¼ million pounds of housewares products daily, one of the highest tonnage-shipped-per-day figures in the United States.

Sources: Janet Bosworth Dower, "How IBM Distributes—Worldwide," *Distribution Worldwide*, (now DISTRIBUTION) October 1973, pp. 51–54, 58–60; and Jim Dixon, "Streamlining Storage and Distribution," *Distribution Worldwide*, (now DISTRIBUTION) May 1975, pp. 28–29, 32.

The United Processors Company harvests and processes a variety of fruits and vegetables in southern and western farming regions of the country. For certain of these products such as strawberries and watermelon, there tends to be strong demand in the East and Midwest just ahead of the local growing season. Because United must harvest earlier than the northern climates, supply builds before demand peaks. Inventories normally build in the growing areas before truck shipments are made to the demand areas. By switching to rail service and the longer delivery times associated with it, the company could, in many cases, ship immediately after harvesting and have the products arrive in the marketplace just as strong demand develops. The railroad serves the warehousing function. The result is a substantial reduction in warehousing costs and transportation costs as well.[13]

Therefore, transportation equipment should be viewed as *moving warehouses*.

Determining the Number and Location of Warehousing Facilities. Whether a channel member chooses to employ public or private warehousing operations in his physical distribution system, questions still remain as to how many warehouses should be established and where they should be located. Determining the number of warehouses to be used directly depends upon the customer service levels established by the firm. A channel member faced with high customer service requirements will often establish a series of warehouses. Care must be taken, however, that the number of warehouses employed to ensure customer service is not so great as to raise costs inordinately for other PD functions (inventory management, transportation, etc.). For example, the number of locations a firm establishes has a cost relationship to several other logistical

[13] Ballou, *Business Logistics Management*, pp. 257–258.

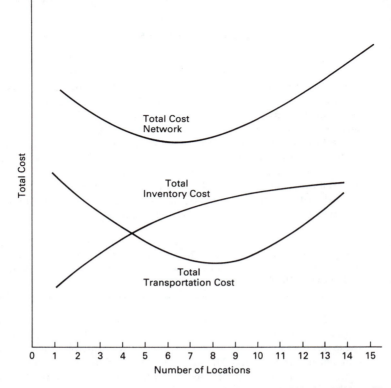

Figure 5-3 Total cost logistical network. Reprinted with permission of Macmillan Publishing Company from *Logistical Management* 2nd ed., by Donald J. Bowersox. Copyright © 1978 by Macmillan Publishing Company.

variables. Thus, the *total costs* associated with the number of warehouses employed must be taken into account. Although the least-cost solution to this problem is unique for each firm because of differences in customer service standards and the costs of meeting those standards, the total cost related to the logistical network can be generalized in a manner similar to that shown in Figure 5-3. The low point on the total *transportation* cost curve in Figure 5-3 is at eight warehouse locations. However, total cost related to average *inventory* commitment clearly increases with each additional location. Thus, once the cost trade-offs have been accounted for, the lowest *total* cost for the overall logistical structure is shown in Figure 5-3 to be a network consisting of six warehouse locations.

Just as the number of warehouses established directly affects the ability of the organization and its marketing channel to serve its customers at a reasonable cost, so, too, does the selection of appropriate warehouse locations. A number of warehousing facility location models and solution techniques developed over the past two decades have been important in aiding management to make better decisions.[14] Critical to each are estimates of sales lost because of customer distance from warehouses, the cost of operating warehouses, and transportation cost (both inbound and outbound).

Inventory Decisions

Were it not for the presence of and need for inventories, there would be no purpose in discussing warehousing decisions. In fact, although the decisions involving ownership, type, number, and location of warehouses are obviously important, inventory decisions are crucial to the viability of all commercial channel members, irrespective of the decisions made about warehousing.

The objective of inventory management is to minimize total inventory costs subject to demand and service constraints. The primary cost functions that must be balanced are those associated with holding inventory, ordering inventory, and risking stockouts. Figure 5-4 shows the trade-offs among the relevant cost functions and their respective components. Because the fundamental purpose of any inventory control system is to tell a firm (1) how much to reorder, (2) when to reorder, and (3) how to control stockouts at the lowest cost, the discussion below focuses directly on these three key problem areas. It also underscores the importance of sales forecasting to effective inventory control systems.

How Much to Reorder. The quantity to order can be arrived at using an "economic lot size" or "economic order quantity" (EOQ) formula. One of the oldest and most widely accepted economic lot size formulas is stated as follows:

$$Q^* = \sqrt{\frac{2DS}{IC}}$$

Quantity to reorder in inventory.

where

Q^* = the order quantity in units
D = annual demand in units
S = the order processing cost (cost per order in dollars)
I = annual inventory carrying cost as a percentage of C
C = value of a unit held in inventory (unit price in dollars). An illustration of how EOQ is calculated appears in Exhibit 5-4.

Although this classical EOQ formula is straightforward and used widely by many manufacturers and merchant wholesalers, it is likely to be of little help to retailers in carrying out their ordering policies. The most serious problem in applying the classical EOQ equation is the problem of determining costs. In practice, the actual ordering costs are not fixed, as required by the classical EOQ equation. Inventory carrying cost can vary, for example, with management's changing estimates of the cost of capital. Both inventory carrying cost and ordering cost, when applied to retail situations, include elements of fixed and variable costs that would be very difficult to separate. Moreover, determining the

[14] For an overview of these models, see ibid., pp. 300–355.

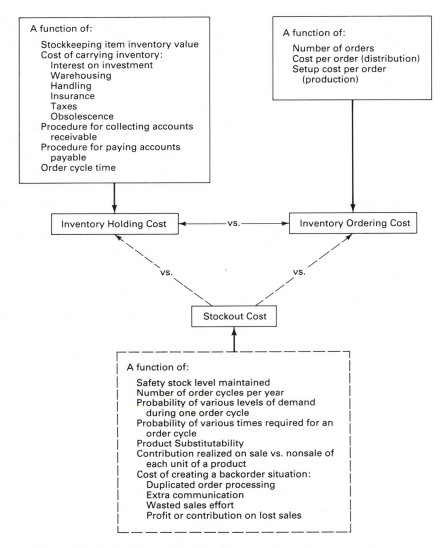

Figure 5-4 Trade–offs typically found in managing and controlling inventory levels. *Source*: James L. Heskett, Nicholas A. Glaskowsky, Jr., and Robert M. Ivie, *Business Logistics*, 2nd ed. (New York: The Ronald Press, 1973), p. 313.

real costs involves extensive, time-consuming cost studies. Thus, in many cases, the cost estimates are merely subjective ones. Because of this problem, the classical EOQ formula must be modified before it can be used to solve retail inventory problems.[15]

[15] *Retail IMPACT—Inventory Management Program and Control Techniques Application Description*, 6th ed. (White Plains, N.Y.: IBM Technical Publications Department, March 1970), p. 73.

When to Reorder. [16] To determine when to reorder, the projected demand or sales forecast as well as the delivery lead time and the length of the review period must be known. Delivery lead time is usually expressed as the number of days it takes to receive stock in available inventory after an order has been placed. The main components of lead time are order processing time, order picking and handling time, transit time, and unloading and stocking time. On the other hand, the *length of the review period* is usually expressed as the number of days between forecasts, or the number of days between possible reorder decisions. In retailing, the review period is often very short (e.g., a week) because retail demand is highly seasonal and fluctuates constantly over time, necessitating frequent review. In manufacturing and wholesaling, the review period is typically longer and frequently coincides more closely with estimates derived from EOQ considerations. Exhibit 5-5 illustrates how the length of the review period can be approximated from the classical EOQ formula.

To compute a reorder point, the projected demand of a product during the review period is added to the projected demand for the product during the delivery lead time. The result is then compared to the quantity of the product available in inventory. The reorder point is reached when the overall projected demand (i.e., the overall forecasted sales) is greater than the amount available in inventory. (An example of how this is done appears in Exhibit 5-6.) Thus, the rules for deciding whether to reorder an item held in inventory are the following:

[16] Adapted with permission from *Handling & Shipping Management*, July, 1966 issue. Copyright © 1966, Penton Publishing, Cleveland, OH. Also drawn from ibid.

EXHIBIT 5-5
Estimating Length of Review Period from the EOQ Model

A good approximation of the length of the review period can sometimes be obtained from the basic EOQ model. If the economic order quantity is Q*, then the number of orders that should be placed in a year is obtained by dividing projected demand for the year by Q*. Dividing the number of orders that should be placed in a year into the number of weeks or days in a year will tell how frequently the stock level should be reviewed.

Using the data from Exhibit 5-4 and letting N* stand for the optimum order interval, the length of the review period can be estimated:

$$N* = D/Q*$$
$$N* = 52,000/2404$$
$$N* = 21.63 \text{ orders per year}$$

(52 weeks/year)/(21.63 orders/year) = 2.404

Therefore, IDI will place about 22 orders each year, which means that it should reorder about every two and a half weeks.

EXHIBIT 5-6
Determining Reorder Point: An Illustration

Rodgers' Office Products, Inc., an office supply retailer, wants to know the reorder point for its two-drawer file cabinets. Assume that Rodgers' has a review period of 7 days, a lead time of 10 days, and an available inventory of 110 units. Also assume that the sales forecast for the next 17 days projects that 102 units of these cabinets will be sold. The projected average daily sales for the 17-day period is, therefore, 6 units (102/17). Because the next review period is 7 days away, an estimated 42 units will be sold in that time leaving 68 units (110 − 42) in available inventory. If Rodgers' waits until the next review period to reorder, the order will arrive when available inventory is down to 8 units {68 [units in stock at the end of the next review period] *less* 6 [estimated average daily sales] *times* 10 [number of days lead time}.

Suppose, however, that the forecast showed that expected sales during the next 17 days were 119 units. If Rodgers' waited until the next review period to replenish its inventory, it would be out of stock the day before the new stock arrives. Selling 7 units a day (119/17), Rodgers' would need 49 units to cover the period before the next review point. This would leave it with only 61 units (110 − 49) to cover the 10-day lead time during which it will need 70 units in stock.

Source: Adapted with permission from *Handling & Shipping Management*, July, 1966 issue. Copyright © 1966, Penton Publishing, Cleveland, OH.

1. If net on hand (available inventory) is greater than the forecasted sales, take no action.

2. If net on hand (available inventory) is less than the sales forecast, place a reorder.

Forecasting.   In determining how much to reorder and when to reorder, the sales forecast is the most critical variable affecting the final outcome. In fact, the short-term sales forecast is the heart of any system designed to solve these problems. For any channel member, the type of forecasting method to be used depends upon the pattern of customer demand.

For most types of customer demand patterns, a short-term computer forecast is the most efficient and consistent way of obtaining future sales projections. It assumes that the historical sales patterns of a product can be used to predict its future sales, and therefore relies on such historical data-based forecasting methods as moving averages, weighted moving averages, regression, and exponential smoothing.[17]

Lack of a sales forecast, inaccurate sales forecasting, and/or failure to share sales forecast information among retailers, wholesalers, and manufacturers can create inventory problems throughout the marketing channel. First, a sudden increase in sales volume at the retail level creates a ripple effect back through the channel because of time lags of order processing and flows of goods. Second, unpredicted sales increases result in stockouts, and frequent stockouts may result in substantial lost sales and in widespread customer ill-will.

Controlling Stockouts.   Up to this point in the discussion of inventory control techniques, attention has been focused on the maintenance of "base stocks." If sales forecasting were perfectly accurate, carrying only base stock in inventory would always provide "perfect" inventories; the problem of stockouts would never occur. However, since each forecast will have some error in it, action must be taken to ensure that this error does not seriously weaken customer service. Estimates of this error can be used to determine how much extra "safety" stock is needed to cushion against customer demand larger than the sales forecast.[18]

It is important to note that, for inventory control purposes, safety stocks should not be counted with base stocks. When reorder points are computed, for example, the required safety stocks should be subtracted from available inventory before it is compared to the forecast, because safety stocks are only insurance against forecast errors. If they are counted as available inventory, the result is a low forecast that will, in turn, lead to a stockout.

As indicated earlier, every channel member must determine the customer

[17] For an excellent discussion of various forecasting techniques, see Spyros Makridakis and Steven Wheelwright, *Forecasting: Methods and Applications* (New York: John Wiley & Sons, 1978).

[18] For insight into the use of forecasting error to estimate safety stocks, see Edward W. Smykay and Allan D. Dale, "Inventory Control: What Price Service? Part 2," *Handling and Shipping*, July 1966, pp. 60–63.

TABLE 5.3 Relative Operating Characteristics of Five Basic Transportation Modes

Operating Characteristic	Transportation Mode				
	Rail	Truck	Water	Pipeline	Air
Speed	3	2	4	5	1
Availability	2	1	4	5	3
Dependability	3	2	4	1	5
Capability	2	3	1	5	4
Frequency	4	2	5	1	3

Source: Reprinted with permission of Macmillan Publishing Company from *Logistical Management*, 2nd ed. by Donald J. Bowersox. Copyright © 1978 by Macmillan Publishing Company.

service level best suited to it by balancing the cost of holding additional safety stock versus the costs of stockouts.

Although not discussed in detail here, it should be noted that order processing is as critical to customer service as carrying adequate inventory at appropriate locations and selection of the right transportation mode. Delays in order processing can severely hamper customer service. Many manufacturers, wholesalers, and other suppliers resort to the use of toll-free numbers and electronic data processing to speed the receipt and processing of orders.

Transportation Decisions

Inadequate transportation service and uncertain delivery times can cause a company to hold several days' more inventory than needed. These problems add to the cost of carrying inventory, not to mention the undesirable effects they have on customer service and product promotions. Consequently, selecting the appropriate transportation modes is critical to accomplishing distribution objectives. This section describes various transportation modes and the functions they can perform in moving goods through the marketing channel.

In the United States, the bulk of freight is handled by five basic modes of transportation—rail, truck, waterways, pipeline, and air. In selecting transportation modes, distribution managers in the marketing channel must consider the speed, availability, dependability, capability, and frequency of each mode. The relative operating characteristics of rail, truck, water, pipeline, and air are examined in Table 5-3. These modes are ranked from 1 (the top ranking) to 5 (the lowest) for each operating characteristic.

Rail. Although the dominant trend over the past several decades has been a decrease in the share of freight carried by rail, railroads are still the major long-haul mover of bulk commodities such as coal, lumber, canned foods, and grain. There are two major reasons for this. First, railroads often provide important services to their customers such as expedited handling (to guarantee arrival within a certain number of hours) and pickup and delivery. Second, rail generally has cheaper freight rates relative to air and motor carriers, and compares favorably in terms of loss and damage costs.[19]

Truck.   Truck carriers have some inherent advantages over rail. Among these are door-to-door service, frequently scheduled routes, wide availability of service, and dependability. For these reasons, trucking lines carry the largest proportion of small shipments (i.e., those less than 10,000 pounds) and account for the highest tonnage of most consumer goods shipped, including meat, bakery products, beverages, cigars, toys, sporting goods, and clothing.

Water.   Water transportation played a key role in the early economic history of the United States because it was then the only means for moving large volumes of goods. Although water transportation is relatively slower, less dependable, and limited to bulk cargo service along waterway systems, it has competitively lower cost than other transportation modes. But restrictions on automation on the waterfront, escalating fuel prices, large wage increases, and selective rate-cutting by competing modes of transportation have led to a decline in the share of freight business handled by water transportation in recent decades.

Pipeline.   Pipeline carriers have significantly increased their share of total ton-miles in the past several years. Natural gas, crude oil, chemicals, and slurry products (e.g., coal dust suspended in water) are shipped via this transportation mode. The growth in the number and capacity of pipelines is due mainly to the increasing need for moving these products cheaply and in large volumes. Pipeline transportation provides a very limited range of services and capability because only a few products can be moved through pipelines. However, it is the most dependable of all transportation modes and has the lowest rates of loss and damage to the product.

Air.   Air handles a very small fraction of all freight shipped when compared with the other modes of transportation. Because of its high cost, air transportation is viewed by most shippers as a "premium, emergency service."[20] The chief advantage of air transportation is its unmatched origin-destination speed; however, this speed does not include pickup and delivery times or ground handling time. Thus, a well-managed and coordinated truck-rail operation can often match the schedule of the air transport system.

Various combinations of transportation modes are often used to offset a single mode's weaknesses. For example, a combination of truck and rail services is called *piggyback* or TOFC (trailer on flat car) service. This *intermodal combination* enables the shipper to obtain lower rates than he could by using truck alone, while achieving the availability of service in locations not normally served by rail.[21]

---

[19] Lambert and Stock, *Strategic Physical Distribution Management*, p. 110.

[20] Ibid., p. 104.

[21] For further discussion of intermodal combinations, see ibid., pp. 113–118.

Although they are not transportation modes, *freight forwarders* play a critical role in delivering customer service. Freight forwarders

> act much in the same capacity as wholesalers in the marketing channel. They purchase transport services from any one or more of the five modes and consolidate small shipments from a number of shippers into large shipments that move at lower rates.[22]

Thus, for many small shippers, using freight forwarders rather than dealing directly with a transportation carrier is a cheaper way of moving the product to marketing channel intermediaries. In addition, freight forwarders sometimes provide more extensive services and faster delivery for their customers than carriers can.[23]

The Problem of "Maldistribution"

Many channel members are not effective in managing the physical possession flow. In fact, research shows that companies with comparatively high distribution costs frequently provide *poorer* service than some of their competitors who have lower distribution costs, even though they are supplying essentially the same products to identical markets.[24] This problem—termed *maldistribution*—occurs repeatedly in companies of varying sizes across a wide variety of industries.

Exhibit 5-7 lists four signs of maldistribution. If any of these signs appears, a channel member should undertake a careful study of his PD system.

Furthermore, management is well advised to adopt periodic audits of PD functions, activities, and strategy. The audit may incorporate questions such as the following:[25]

1. What levels of service (a) do our customers expect? (b) do our competitors provide?
2. How do competitors achieve the service levels that we think they achieve?
3. Through how many outlets should we distribute our products? of what type? where?
4. Are our plants located and focused properly to support corporate strategy?
5. Where is our company on the logistics life cycle for all or a portion of its business?
6. Have we taken advantage of the full potential for postponement and speculation, standardization, consolidation, and differentiation in our logistics programs?

[22] Ibid., p. 113.

[23] Ibid.

[24] Stephen B. Oresman and Charles D. Scudder, "A Remedy for Maldistribution," *Business Horizons*, Vol. 19 (June 1974), p. 63.

[25] Direct quote from James L. Heskett, "Logistics Essential to Strategy," *Harvard Business Review*, November–December 1977, pp. 90–94.

EXHIBIT 5-7
Signs of Maldistribution

1. *Inventories That Turn Slowly.* Distribution inventories should turn between 6 and 12 times per year in most companies, except in unusual product situations; distribution inventories that turn less than 6 times per year are a frequent sign of control problems.

2. *Poor Customer Service.* Inventory investment equal to about two months of sales should provide about 99 percent service. Investment of about half this amount should provide about 90 percent service. Failure to achieve these levels of results can mean that the inventory is in the wrong products, the wrong location, or both.

3. *Interwarehouse Shipments.* Because stock transfers require double handling, distribution managers rarely transship except in emergencies. A significant amount of interwarehouse transfers is a sign of a system in continual trouble.

4. *Premium Freight Charges.* A distribution system that relies on premium freight is in trouble for the same reasons. Cost savings are usually significant when the problem is corrected.

Source: Stephen B. Oresman and Charles D. Scudder, "A Remedy for Maldistribution," *Business Horizons*, Vol. 19 (June 1974), p. 72.

7. To what extent have we assured ourselves that our strategy meets desired levels of costs and services where it counts most, to the enduser?

8. To what extent have we employed "channel vision" in determining who should do what, when, where, and how in our channels of distribution? Have we taken steps to ensure that all parties carry out their functions as planned?

9. What implications do technological trends have for our company?

10. What implications do regulatory trends have for us?

11. Does our logistics strategy support our corporate strategy? To what extent should our strategy be logistics-oriented?

Physical Distribution Management: Conclusions

Physical distribution management is a critical factor in the successful marketing of all products. Underlying effective and efficient physical distribution management is the physical distribution (PD) concept. This concept takes a cost-service orientation that is aimed at minimizing the distribution costs for delivering a given level of customer service through a coordinated PD network.

Developing a PD system should begin with determining customer service standards. The system must balance the costs of providing desired customer service levels against the cost of lost sales from not delivering those levels of service. A critical aspect of this "balancing act" is selecting warehousing, inventory, and transportation policies that ensure that the desired customer service levels are met.

Effective channel management will periodically evaluate the PD function to make certain that customers are receiving their desired degree of PD service, that the costs of delivering that service are being kept as low as possible, and that environmental trends (competitive and technological, in particular) are being monitored.

PROMOTION STRATEGY AND CHANNEL MANAGEMENT

Promotion to and through the marketing channel is another key aspect of marketing strategy. In fact, consumer packaged-goods manufacturers spent 41.2 percent of their marketing budgets on trade promotion—discounts and allowances taken by wholesalers and retailers for the promotional functions they perform—in 1982; that compares with 35.4 percent spent on media advertising, the bulk of which was aimed at final consumers.[26] Thus, as with the other marketing functions, the promotional task can be divided among manufacturers, wholesalers, and retailers.

This section explores some of the promotional activities undertaken within the distribution channel by marketing institutions. The discussion starts with "push" and "pull" promotional strategies. Intermediaries' promotional activities are presented next, followed by a discussion of manufacturers' promotional activities within the marketing channel. The willingness of intermediaries to perform aspects of the promotional flow is also investigated. Finally, the legal aspects of promotion within marketing channels are discussed.

Push versus Pull Promotion

Manufacturers have two basic promotional strategies available to them—pull and push (see Figure 5-5). Arrow, for example, advertises its shirts to consumers during professional football telecasts to develop brand awareness and preference. The objective is to get the consumer to ask for the Arrow brand at his favorite department store or men's specialty shop. If the store does not carry Arrow shirts and enough consumers request them, Arrow hopes that the retailer will order them through the marketing channel. This strategy is called *pull*—manufacturers advertise to the ultimate customer, these customers request the product from their suppliers, and eventually, the manufacturer receives orders from its marketing channel intermediaries. In short, the product is pulled through the channel by the demand from the ultimate customers.

Some manufacturers promote their products and services to their intermediaries who, in turn, promote them to the ultimate customers. This promotional strategy is termed *push*. Rather than using consumer advertising, producers following a push strategy employ personal selling, cooperative advertising, point-of-purchase displays, intermediary sales force training programs, and so forth. For example, Palm Beach, a men's suit manufacturer, utilized a "pure" push promotional strategy for many years. Mitsubishi, on the other hand, uses a mixed form of push by promoting its consumer electronics, such as televisions and videocassette recorders, to both distributors and retail dealers. Mitsubishi engages in very little consumer advertising.

[26] "'Pull' Promotions Gaining on 'Push,'" *Marketing News*, June 7, 1985, p. 16.

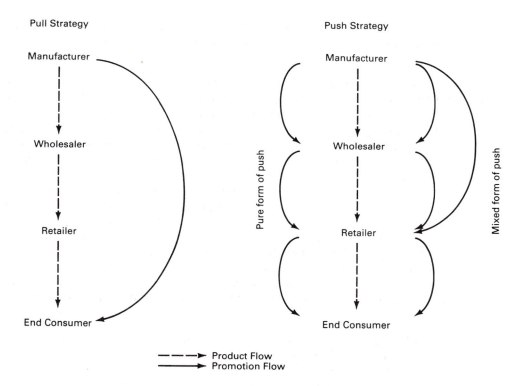

Figure 5-5 Push vs. pull promotional strategies. *Source*: From *Principles of Marketing* by Thomas C. Kinnear and Kenneth L. Bernhardt. Copyright © 1983 by Scott, Foresman and Company. Reprinted by permission.

Note that Figure 5-5 depicts pull and push strategies as entirely separate. In practice, many manufacturers use a combination of pull and push. Procter and Gamble, for example, uses advertising and sales promotion (e.g., coupons) to reach ultimate consumers and employs its sales force to reach wholesalers and retailers. The relative emphasis between push and pull promotion depends upon a variety of market conditions, as we shall see in the discussion of cooperative advertising.

Since our focus here is on the marketing channel and the functions performed within it, the following sections discuss both intermediary and manufacturer promotional activities within the marketing channel. In other words, our emphasis is on push strategies. An in-depth presentation of pull strategies is more appropriately covered in promotional strategy and advertising texts.

Intermediaries' Promotional Activities[27]

A key task for manufacturers is to gain the cooperation of their intermediaries in performing a part of the promotional function within the channel. Wholesalers and

[27] This section is based on James F. Engel, Martin R. Warshaw, and Thomas C. Kinnear, *Promotional Strategy*, 5th ed. (Homewood, Ill.: Richard D. Irwin, 1983), pp. 467–469, 481–483.

retailers alike can undertake many promotional activities on behalf of the manufacturer. This section describes some of those activities.

Personal Selling. Both wholesalers and retailers perform a variety of promotional functions within the distribution channel. Wholesale personal selling staffs check their customers' inventory levels; assist them in placing advertising and developing merchandise displays; provide them with advertising material, catalog information, and other promotional assistance; handle their complaints; suggest seasonal merchandise and advise on stock needs; and offer technical advice and service.

Retail personal selling, on the other hand, basically consists of providing product and store information and taking orders. The extent to which the retail sales force provides information varies according to the focus of the store. Self-service retail operations assume that consumers are willing to perform the information-gathering function themselves. They also assume that manufacturers will perform the information-providing function. Thus, self-service stores offer very little product information to their target consumers. As we noted in Chapter 3, however, the value of personal selling in these retail outlets should not be overlooked.

Advertising. Advertising is another function undertaken by both wholesalers and retailers. Wholesale advertising takes two basic forms. First, it is generally used to pave the way for the wholesaler's sales force, to inform customers about new products, and to promote the wholesale establishment in general rather than particular product lines. Mass media, such as trade magazines, are often used, as is direct mail. The second important form of wholesale advertising is wholesale catalogs. They present the product lines and describe the key features of each product. Because many wholesalers like to maintain price flexibility, price lists are usually not included in catalogs, but distributed separately.

Retail advertising is used to communicate information about (1) the particular retail store and (2) a particular manufacturer's product. In general, retailers are more interested in the former than the latter. Under certain circumstances, to be discussed in a later section, retail advertising often contains both product and store appeals. (For a review of some of the major decisions concerning retail advertising, see Chapter 3.)

Samples and Displays. To make the wholesaler's sales force more effective, samples are often provided to assist in the selling process. Samples may be the actual product, models or photographs of it, or visual aids. They are particularly crucial when the product attributes are difficult to assess and product quality is important in the buying process.

As noted in Chapter 3, the goals of retail display are to present featured merchandise or to draw customers into the store. In-store merchandise displays can often be made more effective with promotional material provided by manufacturers and wholesalers. Point-of-purchase assistance might include shelf signs, dump bins, ceiling hangars, seasonal theme banners, and preconstructed, ready-to-use displays.[28]

Effective point-of-purchase displays are those that balance the needs of the retailer with those of the manufacturer. Manufacturers would like retailers to display their products in prominent positions, while retailers are chiefly interested in displaying those products that enhance their profitability and store image. Where that balance is achieved, the chances are higher that retailers will use the displays. Where it is not achieved, some retailers will take the display allowance without using the displays (see Exhibit 5-8), often illegally. As implied in Exhibit 5-8, effective supervision of display promotions can limit abuses within the channel. Needless to say, disagreements over point-of-purchases displays are a common source of conflict within the marketing channel.

[28] For retail grocers' reactions to manufacturers' point-of-sale assistances, see "Time Is Right for Merchandisers to Help Grocers with Promotional Efforts: Walzer," *Marketing News*, October 29, 1982, p. 3.

TABLE 5.4 Examples of Manufacturers' Promotional Activities Within Marketing Channels

Cooperative advertising	Salesperson incentives
Point-of-purchase display material and assistance	Contests for buyers and salespeople
Demonstrators	Missionary sales force
Coupon-handling allowance	Retail sales force training
Promotional allowances	Deals of all types
Retailer tag lines in manufacturer advertising	Store fixtures

Source: Reprinted with permission from *Advertising Age* (July 21, 1958), Copyright Crain Communications, Inc. All rights reserved.

Manufacturers' Promotional Activities Within the Marketing Channel

Nearly all aspects of manufacturers' promotional strategies directly affect marketing channel institutions. Table 5-4 presents a fairly comprehensive list of these promotional elements. The discussion will focus on cooperative advertising, missionary selling, and coupon handling in some depth because of their specific importance in marketing channels.

Cooperative Advertising

In a marketing channels context, cooperative advertising refers to "advertising initiated and implemented by retailers and partially paid for by a single or several manufacturers."[29] Whirlpool Corporation, for example, provides its dealers with materials for developing local advertising, publicity, and store displays (see Exhibit 5-9). Typically, Whirlpool reimburses its dealers up to 50 percent for the cost of advertising and allows them to receive up to 3 percent of their purchases in cooperative advertising allowances. Since its dealers place the ads and initially pay for them, they receive the lower local advertising rates for which Whirlpool, as a national advertiser, cannot qualify. Thus, cooperative advertising enables Whirlpool to enjoy lower advertising rates and to share its advertising costs with its dealers.

The following sections discuss some major considerations in the management of cooperative advertising. First, the conditions favorable to cooperative advertising are explored. Then, some problems that arise in implementing and controlling this form of promotion are addressed.

When Cooperative Advertising Should Be Used. Cooperative advertising is used in a variety of conditions. It is an essential element in push promotional strategies, where manufacturers rely heavily on marketing intermediaries to perform the promotional functions. Shopping goods and ego-involving purchases are examples of two situations where in-store merchandising and personal selling are critical to a producer's overall promotional campaign. Table 5-5 lists several other conditions that affect the relative importance of cooperative advertising.

[29] Robert F. Young and Stephen A. Greyser, *Managing Cooperative Advertising: A Strategic Approach* (Lexington, Mass.: Lexington Books, 1983), p. 3.

Exhibit 5-9 Local advertising mats: Whirlpool Corporation. *Source*: Whirlpool Corporation.

TABLE 5.5 Conditions Defining the Relative Importance of Cooperative Advertising

Cooperative Advertising Plays a Significant Role in the Marketing Mix: Retailer-Dependent Marketing	Cooperative Advertising Plays a Lesser Role in the Marketing Mix: Manufacturer-Dominated Marketing
Shopping goods	Convenience goods
Infrequently purchased goods	Frequently purchased goods
Relatively expensive	Relatively inexpensive
Considered purchase	Impulse purchase
Purchase for ego enhancement	Utilitarian purchase
Hidden attributes	Easily observed product attributes
Brand loyalty low	Brand loyalty high
Personal service retailing	Self-service retailing
Selective distribution	Broad distribution

Source: Robert F. Young and Stephen A. Greyser, *Managing Cooperative Advertising: A Strategic Approach* (Lexington, Mass: Lexington Books, 1983), p. 22.

The left-hand side of the table might be illustrated by the purchases of large household appliances, apparel, and linens. For these high-involvement situations, the role of cooperative advertising in conjunction with manufacturer-sponsored (i.e., national) advertising is presented in Figure 5-6.

This "hierarchy of effects" model indicates that national advertising is important in the formation of customer attitudes. Awareness of the brand and knowledge of its benefits and features are developed through national advertising. These stages of the hierarchy are aimed at getting the consumer to consider the brand when a purchase occasion arises. When that occasion does arise, local advertising, of which cooperative advertising is an important part, is instrumental in communicating where the product is available and at what price (see Figure

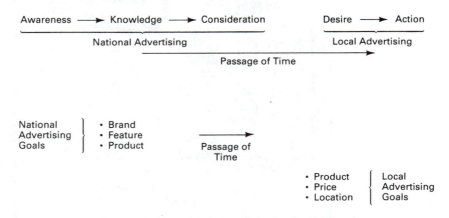

Figure 5-6 Hierarchal models of consumer behavior for high-involvement purchases. *Source*: Robert F. Young and Stephen A. Greyser, *Managing Cooperative Advertising: A Strategic Approach.* (Lexington, Mass.: Lexington Books, 1983), pp. 30, 31.

5-6). This information is crucial in moving the customer to the "action" or purchase phase of the hierarchy of effects.[30]

Problems with Cooperative Advertising. The fact that both manufacturers and retailers have a financial stake in cooperative advertising sometimes strains marketing channel relations. Retailers want their advertising to stress patronage appeals; they want to create images for their stores and to increase traffic in them. Manufacturers, on the other hand, want to stress brand appeals. These conflicting goals manifest themselves in how the advertisements are laid out, the kind of copy that is used, the particular merchandise that is displayed, and the number of competing brands that are advertised.

For manufacturers, the problem is how to restrict the content of cooperative advertisements and, at the same time, enlist retailers to participate in the cooperative advertising program without wasting money. For retailers, the issue is how to control the content of the cooperative advertisements and, at the same time, qualify for cooperative advertising allowances. When push promotion is critical to marketing the product or service, manufacturers allow retailers more discretion in the content of the cooperative advertising. Where pull is more effective, manufacturers wield more control over these advertisements.

A second problem, which comes from a variety of sources, is the increasing pressure to raise cooperative advertising budgets. First, because newspaper advertising is an effective way of bolstering short-term sales, manufacturers come under pressure to raise their cooperative advertising budgets. In addition, since part of their promotional budget is funded by manufacturers, retailers demand higher levels of cooperative advertising from their suppliers. These demands become greater as competitors boost their levels of cooperative advertising support. Moreover, since manufacturers' special promotions (i.e., those beyond the usual promotional programs) have a way of becoming the industry norm, they further the pressure for higher cooperative budgets.

In spite of these difficulties, cooperative advertising is an important element of promotional strategy within the marketing channel. Manufacturers rely on it to obtain retailers' support for their products. Retailers rely on it to defray some of their advertising expenses.

Missionary Selling[31]

Manufacturers often supplement their intermediaries' personal selling efforts through a "missionary sales force." These are salespersons who call upon retail or wholesale accounts to ensure that adequate inventory is being held, who introduce new products, who assist in setting up merchandise displays, and who provide selling advice (in some cases, actual sales training). A missionary salesperson may even assist wholesalers' salespeople by accompanying them on some of their sales calls. The central function of the missionary sales force is to build goodwill for the manufacturer.

---

[30] For more information about the hierarchy of effects and related models of marketing communications, see Engel et al., *Promotional Strategy*, pp. 164–168.

[31] This section is based on ibid., pp. 503–505.

In many instances, however, the missionary sales force may actually damage goodwill.

A cereal producer distributed its products through wholesalers to retail grocery stores. This manufacturer had a regular salesforce which called upon wholesale accounts and a missionary salesforce which called upon retailers to solicit orders. These orders were then handled by the wholesalers who received the same gross margin regardless of whose salesforce obtained the order.

The primary duty of this missionary salesforce was to expand the market coverage. By pulling the product through the channel, the cereal maker was able to "force" distribution by getting the wholesalers to increase their stocks or to carry new products. Wholesalers feared that the manufacturer, through its "pull" promotion efforts, would eventually establish its own wholesale branches and no longer use them. Needless to say, this manufacturer severely tested the goodwill built up within the channel through this use of the missionary salesforce.[32]

A missionary sales force works best when it *supplements* rather than supplants the wholesalers' and retailers' personal selling efforts. Too much missionary selling creates resentment by intermediaries for two reasons. First, wholesalers and retailers may feel the manufacturer will eventually integrate their functions, leaving them without the manufacturer's product to carry. Second, the missionary sales force can get in the way of the intermediaries' selling efforts. Oftentimes, missionary salespersons attempt to change displays for their brands at the expense of their competitors' brands. This may conflict with how retailers wish to feature their private labels. Imagine what would happen if, for example, the missionary salespersons for both Procter and Gamble and General Foods attempted to rearrange a supermarket's coffee shelf display at the same time, without considering the store's own brand.

Excessive missionary selling might also indicate problems in the manufacturer's promotional mix. For example, wholesalers may not be providing the promotional support that their margins require of them. On the other hand, perhaps the wholesalers' personnel are not adequately trained in how to sell the manufacturer's product and the missionary sales force is needed to close sales. This situation indicates that additional sales training is in order.

Consumer Coupon Promotions

Manufacturers' consumer promotions often involve other marketing channel members. For example, retailers redeem consumer coupons that may be distributed through newspapers and direct mail or on the product packages.

[32] Ibid., p. 504.

Coupon redemption, however, can become a source of friction within the marketing channel. For example, expiration dates, odd-shaped coupons, coupons requiring multiple purchases, and coupons with more than one face amount (i.e., those with coin ruboff markings) require more point-of-sale handling, thus reducing the efficiency with which retailers process coupons. Extra handling cuts into the retailers' compensation for redeeming coupons (in 1984, this amounted to 8 cents per coupon handled). Manufacturers, on the other hand, view these coupon features as enhancing the effectiveness of the coupon promotion. Thus, there is a conflict between the manufacturer's desire for effective promotion and the retailer's desire to handle coupons efficiently.[33] Methods for resolving such conflict within marketing channels is the topic of Chapter 11.

Intermediaries' Willingness to Undertake Promotional Activities Within the Marketing Channel[34]

A common perspective of marketing channels is that manufacturers control the channel and that wholesalers and retailers are at their "beck and call." This view may hold in some channels, but certainly not in all. As will be discussed in Chapter 9, retailers and wholesalers may hold veto power over manufacturers' marketing plans. In addition, these intermediaries may themselves attempt to coordinate the activities of other intermediaries and manufacturers. The point is that the willingness of intermediaries to cooperate will affect the success of manufacturers' cooperative advertising, missionary selling, consumer couponing, and other promotional activities within the marketing channel.

Assuming that the intermediaries are capable of performing some of the promotional functions within the marketing channel, several factors affect their desire to undertake these activities.

First, the promotional programs must be consistent with the intermediaries' objectives. Wholesalers and retailers first attempt to market their own establishment, and only then try to market particular suppliers' products and services. If a particular manufacturer's promotional program excludes patronage appeals, intermediaries are unlikely to participate in it.

Second, many, though not all, retailers and wholesalers carry hundreds or thousands of products and must allocate their promotional efforts across these items. One way they do this is by balancing the costs of undertaking these functions against the gains. In addition to the margins provided by suppliers, intermediaries weigh the extent to which manufacturers agree to assist them. The greater the assistance—such as pull promotion, point-of-purchase displays, advertising layouts, cooperative advertising programs, demonstrators and samples, and training programs—the less effort the wholesalers and retailers must expend to achieve sales and profitability goals for the product. Accordingly, channel intermediaries are more willing to promote products whose manufacturers offer support in the form of promotional programs.

[33] P. Rajan Varadarajan, "Issue of Efficient Coupon Handling and Processing Pits Manufacturers Against Retailers, Coupon Clearinghouses," *Marketing News*, September 28, 1984, p. 13.

[34] This section is based on Engel *Promotional Strategy*, pp. 474–478, 484–486.

The third factor affecting the willingness of intermediaries to participate in the promotional function within the channel is the extent of the competition they face. For example, the higher the degree of channel intensity (i.e., the number of firms at the same channel level carrying the manufacturer's product), the less likely the intermediary will expend much effort promoting the product. Intensive distribution increases the likelihood of price competition. In this situation, any additional promotional effort in behalf of the manufacturer will place even more pressure on already-squeezed margins.

Dual distribution, where the manufacturer distributes through several different channels, is another example of a competitive situation that will make intermediaries reluctant to promote the product.

> It is very difficult for a . . . [jeweler] to understand why a watch manufacturer asks for its personal selling support and then distributes through the local discount store, which sells watches on a price basis.[35]

Finally, the higher the margin manufacturers offer to their intermediaries, the more willing retailers and wholesalers will be to perform the promotion function within the channel. (There will be more about this point later in the next chapter.)

Legal Aspects of Promotional Strategies in Marketing Channels

Cooperative advertising—in fact, all trade promotion—is a source of many legal headaches for manufacturers. The chief legal requirement is that promotional allowances be made available to all customers on a proportionately equal basis. In addition, the manufacturer must ensure that the promotional activities were actually undertaken and that reimbursements to intermediaries reflect their actual costs. Furthermore, the Robinson-Patman Act limits promotional practices within the marketing channel.

All these legal requirements compound the problems of administering promotional programs with the trade. To prevent fraud, the provisions and restrictions of these programs (especially cooperative advertising and point-of-purchase displays) must be enforced, and this obviously strains manufacturer-retailer relations. Also, the mechanics of reimbursing dealers and distributors are a complicated task that can cause conflict within the channel if not handled effectively.

In addition, suppliers sometimes offer free merchandise, vacations, or direct monetary payments to retail or wholesale employees as special incentives to promote their products. While these bonuses are generally permitted, the Robinson-Patman Act and the FTC may limit them if they substantially injure competition.

[35] Ibid., p. 486.

Promotion Strategy Management: Conclusions

Communicating to the target market is a key element in the marketing mix for the marketing channel. Effective marketing channel systems are those that balance the market communication needs of each channel member. Manufacturers are primarily interested in developing brand awareness, preference, and purchase; wholesalers and retailers, on the other hand, are chiefly concerned with increasing patronage of their establishments.

In conjunction with their advertising to target customers, manufacturers use a variety of techniques involving wholesalers and retailers to promote their products. Among these are cooperative advertising, missionary selling, and consumer coupons. Marketing intermediaries also perform a variety of promotional activities within the marketing channel, including personal selling, advertising, sampling, and in-store displays.

The extent to which manufacturers, wholesalers, and retailers successfully mesh these promotional activities depends on several factors. The margins offered, the extent of competition the product being promoted faces, the amount of promotional materials and assistance the supplier provides, and the channel members' own promotional objectives determine how well the marketing channel will coordinate its promotional tasks.

As with the other aspects of the marketing mix within distribution channels, a manufacturer's promotional policies are limited by antitrust legislation. In general, promotional allowances of any kind must be offered to all intermediaries of the same type (i.e., all wholesalers, all retailers) on a proportionately equal basis.

The physical distribution and promotion functions represent only two of the elements of the marketing mix in which channel members participate. Marketing channel functions related to product and pricing strategies are also crucial and will be discussed in the next chapter.

SUMMARY

In this chapter we have examined two key elements of the marketing mix—physical distribution management and promotion strategy—in the context of the marketing channel. As indicated throughout the chapter, these marketing functions may be performed anywhere within the channel.

Physical distribution refers to the physical flow of goods through the marketing channel. Among the major decisions that must be addressed in this element of the marketing mix are: (1) the levels of customer service desired by the target markets; (2) the ownership, type, number, and location of warehouses; (3) the amount and timing of inventory holdings; and (4) the modes of transportation. The last three decisions are necessary to ensure that the desired levels of customer service are delivered.

The *promotional flow* within the marketing channel primarily involves how the marketing communications function is to be divided among channel members. The promotional activities undertaken within the channel include personal selling, advertising, and sales promotion. Particularly critical to manufacturers' overall promotional programs are point-of-purchase displays, cooperative advertising, missionary selling, and consumer coupon programs; each of these activities involves, to one degree or another, marketing intermediaries. The extent to which they are involved depends partially upon their willingness to perform these functions; in other words, wholesalers and retailers are not necessarily at the sole beck and call of their suppliers.

DISCUSSION QUESTIONS

1. Herbie Clanton is the physical distribution manager for Tilley Manufacturing Company, a small but successful men's apparel maker. Herbie has recently been barraged by complaints from his retail customers about late deliveries, improperly filled orders, and damaged merchandise. He doesn't quite understand all the fuss. After all, Tilley has one of the lowest freight costs in the industry and prides itself on passing the savings along to its retailers. Explain to Herbie the importance of the physical distribution concept and how implementing it might mitigate the retailers' complaints.

2. At a local meeting of professional physical distribution managers, Herbie Clanton (see Question 1) is discussing some of his retailers' complaints with you, an internationally known logistics consultant. He tells you, "I can't understand their whining. We start processing the orders as soon as they arrive in the morning mail; those people expect us to read their minds and have the merchandise at their unloading docks as soon as they make the mental commitment to buy. . . . Some of those buyers must have taken penmanship in medical school; no wonder the orders get fouled up!" You reply, "Well, Herbie, I usually charge a large fee for what I'm about to tell you, but since you're such a nice, but misguided, guy, I'll give you some free advice. What you should do is ———.''

3. Montrose Cristwell—"Monte" to his friends—owns a vineyard operated on some reclaimed strip-mining land in the hills of southeastern Ohio. After several years of experimenting with a couple of varieties of grapes, Monte began preparing for wine production. One of the decisions he had to make was the type of warehouse to use. Should he use a warehouse, a distribution center, or storage-in-transit? Explain your answer. If you think Monte should use a warehouse, what type should it be—public or private? Why?

4. Barbara Clayton-Smythe is a branch manager of the 1st National Bank of Clampett (Iowa). One of the services Barbara's branch offers is the sale of travelers' checks. Barbara is particularly concerned that she keeps too much of the branch's funds tied up in travelers' checks. As a test, she decides to use the economic order quantity model to assist her in deciding how many travelers' checks to inventory. Calculate the EOQ for her using the following assumptions.

   Forecasts show that the demand for the checks during the three-month summer test period is reasonably stable. They also indicate that during this period the demand for travelers' checks is $60,000 and that the branch should stock only the $50 denomination. Barbara estimates that it costs her branch $15 each time she orders an additional supply of these checks from the main office. She also believes that the annual inventory carrying costs are 16 percent.

5. Assume that Barbara Clayton-Smythe (see Question 4) computed the economic order quantity for travelers' checks to be 150 $50 checks, or $7,500 worth. The lead time between when Barbara orders additional checks from the main office and when they are ready for sale is usually three days. How often should Barbara reorder additional travelers' checks for her branch's inventory?

6. On June 9, Barbara Clayton-Smythe (see Questions 4 and 5) is deciding whether to order additional travelers' checks. Assume that she must make this decision every eight days and that, on average, 12 checks are sold daily. A quick peek at her current inventory reveals 120 $50 travelers' checks on hand. Should she reorder now or wait until June 17 to do it?

7. Recall the Caterpillar vignette at the beginning of this chapter. What modes of transportation must Cat use to achieve its customer service standards for spare parts? Why would it use these modes?

8. The Palmer Pharmaceutical Company, a large ethical drug manufacturer, uses its own sales force to attempt to persuade physicians to prescribe its drugs for their patients. Palmer also uses its sales force to call upon wholesale channels that serve pharmacies.
   a. Diagram how Palmer's pharmaceutical products physically flow through the marketing channel.
   b. Diagram the promotional flow Palmer uses.
   c. Does Palmer follow a push or a pull strategy? Explain. Why does Palmer use such a promotional strategy?

9. For each of the following types of products, explain whether or not cooperative advertising would be an appropriate promotional tool.
   a. Fresh eggs
   b. Cigarettes
   c. Furniture
   d. Best-selling books
   e. Personal computer software
   f. Soda pop

10. As indicated in the text, several of the promotional tools manufacturers use can cause friction within the marketing channel. What should manufacturers do to avoid such conflict, while at the same time achieving their promotional goals?

6

Channel Management and the Marketing Mix: Product Management and Pricing Strategy

LEARNING OBJECTIVES:

> *Upon completing this chapter, you will be able to:*

- *explain how the intensity of distribution and the extent of vertical integration vary across the different stages of the product life cycle;*

- *describe the reasons intermediaries develop private label products;*

- *discuss the importance of store and product positioning to retailers and wholesalers, respectively;*

- *outline the legal elements of product strategy within the marketing channel;*

- *calculate, from pricing information, gross margins available to marketing channel intermediaries;*

- *list various discounts and allowances manufacturers grant to wholesalers and retailers;*

- *distinguish between interbrand and intrabrand competition and describe their relationship to pricing within the marketing channel;*

- *explain the steps manufacturers must undertake to gain the support of channel intermediaries;*

- *pose questions to evaluate the effects of price changes upon the channel of distribution;*

- *outline the legal elements of pricing strategy within the marketing channel; and*

- *appreciate the importance of coordinating the entire marketing efforts of all members in the channel.*

Caterpillar Tractor Company: Effects of Pricing upon Marketing Channels

Caterpillar Tractor Co., as we saw at the beginning of Chapter 5, is a worldwide producer and marketer of excavation and loading equipment. In the mid-1980s, Cat faced, as did many firms, the problem of gray market competition.

The gray market occurs when popular, branded products are imported outside of the manufacturer's authorized distribution network. When dramatic price differences exist between countries for the same or similar products, gray market or parallel importers can save their customers substantial amounts over what authorized distributors would charge. Although the gray market is widespread for consumer goods such as Seiko watches, Charles of the Ritz fragrances, Mercedes-Benz automobiles, and Minolta cameras, industrial goods producers such as Caterpillar are also not immune to this problem.

Caterpillar's Model 215B hydraulic excavator is built in Peoria, IL and lists in the U.S. for $120,000. A nearly identical machine, built in Cat's Belgian plant, can be bought overseas for about $74,000. This huge $46,000 disparity in prices permits unauthorized distributors to import Belgian-made Cat excavators, resell them to Cat dealers for about $85,000 each (15% under what Cat charges them for the U.S.-made version) or to contractors for nearly $95,000 (about 20% off the list price), and still make a profit.

What the gray market importers of Cat equipment do not do, however, is provide warranties, service agreements, guarantees of parts availability, and often, financing. For contractors and dealers willing to perform these marketing functions for themselves, the gray market is a highly attractive source of supply.

What can Cat do about the unauthorized importation and sales of its construction equipment? First, it could drop its U.S. prices to eliminate the price disparity between countries. This would erode any price advantage the gray marketers would have over the authorized dealers and would, therefore, drive the parallel importers out of business. Second, Cat could shift more of its production overseas to take advantage of the dollar's strength, thereby lowering its production costs. As of mid-1985, this second approach is what Caterpillar planned to do.

Source: Adapted by permission of *Forbes* magazine, May 6, 1985, p. 31 © Forbes, Inc., 1985.

In the previous chapter, we discussed two aspects of the marketing mix—physical distribution management and promotion strategy—and their link to overall marketing channel strategy. As shown in this chapter's Caterpillar example, an organization's pricing strategy directly affects its marketing channels—be they authorized or unauthorized channels. A firm's product strategy is also intertwined with its channels strategy. This chapter addresses how two other aspects of the marketing mix—product management and pricing strategy—relate to marketing channels management.

PRODUCT STRATEGY AND CHANNEL MANAGEMENT

In addition to physical distribution and promotional strategies, members of the marketing channel must consider product strategy. For example, manufacturers must contemplate changes in distribution strategy as the product progresses through the product life cycle. Each stage of the life cycle requires different strategies if the product is to be successful. How the product is positioned and serviced will also affect marketing channel strategy. Finally, suppliers must understand and address the legal implications of their product strategies within the marketing channel.

The product life cycle, product positioning, technical and warranty service, and the legality of certain product line policies—and how these all affect marketing channel strategy—are discussed in the following sections.

The Product Life Cycle and Marketing Channel Strategy

The product life cycle illustrates how the sales and profits of a good or service vary over time (see Figure 6-1). The shapes of the sales and profits curves depend upon several factors. First, the product life cycle will vary according to how general the product is. For example, automobiles as a product category have had a long life cycle, while the brand Chevrolet has had a shorter one; the car model Vega had an even shorter life cycle. Second, the curves depend upon the degree of competition—how many competitors there are and how strongly they compete. For example, widespread competition may propel the product through the growth stage much faster than would happen if only one or two firms controlled the market. Next, how quickly the market accepts the product will affect the shapes of the curves. For example, the curves for fads, such as Davy Crockett coonskin caps, hoola hoops, Nehru jackets, pet rocks, mood rings, CB radios, leisure suits, video games, and Cabbage Patch dolls, tend to peak and decline quite rapidly as

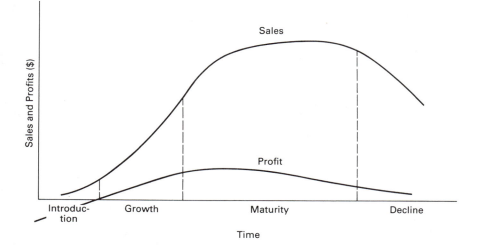

Figure 6-1 The product life cycle: sales and profit curves. *Source*: Philip Kotler, *Marketing Management: Analysis, Planning, & Control* 5e. © 1984, pp. 354, 605. Reprinted by permission of Prentice-Hall, Inc., Englewood Cliffs, New Jersey.

the products catch on swiftly and fall into disfavor just as quickly. Finally, the regulatory environment can alter the product life cycle for goods and services. For example, deregulation in the airline industry stimulated widespread price competition in the mid-1980s. As a result, many people who previously found air travel too costly became airline customers. On the other hand, the life cycle of a product can come to an abrupt end if it is banned (e.g., pesticides with toxic ingredients) or if it receives unfavorable publicity as a result of government investigations (e.g., Ford Pinto).

As noted earlier, the marketing strategy of a good or service must be adapted if the product is to be successful over the long run. Table 6-1 illustrates how the key elements of marketing strategy change over the stages of the product life cycle.

Marketing channel strategy varies over the product life cycle. The number of intermediaries used at a particular channel level in a given market (i.e., the intensity of distribution), the extent to which a marketing institution participates in the marketing flows (i.e., the degree of vertical integration), and the type of promotional strategy used by manufacturers (i.e., push versus pull) all vary over the product life cycle.[1]

The Intensity of Distribution. As noted in Table 6-1, the intensity of distribution varies over the product life cycle. New products are initially marketed through selective distribution for two reasons. First, marketers may want to control to whom the product will be marketed.

[1] Hans B. Thorelli and Stephen C. Burnett, "The Nature of Product Life Cycles for Industrial Goods Business," *Journal of Marketing*, Vol. 45 (Fall 1981), pp. 97–108.

TABLE 6.1 Implications of the Product Life Cycle for Marketing Action

Effects and Responses	Stages of the PLC			
	Introduction	Growth	Maturity	Decline
Competition	None of importance	Some emulators	Many rivals competing for a small piece of the pie	Few in number with a rapid shakeout of weak members
Overall strategy	Market establishment; persuade early adopters to try the product	Market penetration; persuade mass market to prefer the brand	Defense of brand position; check the inroads of competition	Preparations for removal; milk the brand dry of all possible benefits
Profits	Negligible because of high production and marketing costs	Reach peak levels as a result of high prices and growing demand	Increasing competition cuts into profit margins and ultimately into total profits	Declining volume pushes costs up to levels that eliminate profits entirely
Retail prices	High, to recover some of the excessive costs of launching	High, to take advantage of heavy consumer demand	What the traffic will bear; need to avoid price wars	Low enough to permit quick liquidation of inventory
Distribution	Selective, as distribution is slowly built up	Intensive; employ small trade discounts since dealers are eager to store	Intensive; heavy trade allowances to retain shelf space	Selective; unprofitable outlets slowly phased out
Advertising strategy	Aim at the needs of early adopters	Make the mass market aware of brand benefits	Use advertising as a vehicle for differentiation among otherwise similar brands	Emphasize low price to reduce stock
Advertising emphasis	High, to generate awareness and interest among early adopters and persuade dealers to stock the brand	Moderate, to let sales rise on the sheer momentum of word-of-mouth recommendations	Moderate, since most buyers are aware of brand characteristics	Minimum expenditures required to phase out the product
Consumer sales and promotion expenditures	Heavy, to entice target groups with samples, coupons, and other inducements to try the brand	Moderate, to create brand preference (advertising is better suited to do this job)	Heavy, to encourage brand switching, hoping to convert some buyers into loyal users	Minimal, to let the brand coast by itself

Source: Reprinted by permission of the *Harvard Business Review.* An exhibit from "Forget the Product Life Cycle Concept!" by Nariman K. Dhalla and Sonia

When home computers first appeared on the market, they were sold through computer stores and toy and hobby shops. Those innovators and early adopters most likely to buy these products could be most efficiently reached through these outlets. At this life cycle stage, marketing through mass merchandisers would not have been very efficient nor very effective, since word-of-mouth is necessary for the later adopters to begin buying these kinds of products.

Second, marketers may have difficulty in getting wholesalers and retailers to carry the product. This is particularly true in cases where demand is uncertain.

In the growth phase of the product life cycle, distribution is broadened to reach new markets beginning to adopt the product. The key task in this stage is to place the product in those outlets most likely to be patronized by the target market. Foreclosing these outlets to the competition is another distribution goal in this phase.

When home computers reached this stage of the product life cycle, they were distributed more intensively; in addition to computer stores and toy and hobby shops, these products were marketed through mass merchandisers such as Target and K-Mart. At one time, Commodore was even testing supermarkets as a possible outlet for its home computers.

Maintaining the intensity of distribution is the prime channel objective of the *maturity phase* of the product life cycle. Generous trade allowances and heavy dealer support through liberal return allowances, cooperative advertising programs, and strong manufacturer advertising are crucial in keeping dealers interested in carrying and promoting the product.

Procter and Gamble, in the early 1980s, suffered a lack of sales growth in several of its maturing product lines—laundry detergents, liquid detergents, paper towels, toilet tissue, and toothpaste. To counter stagnant sales growth, P&G began to soften some of its strict policies toward the trade (i.e., wholesalers and retailers carrying P&G's products). For example, it permitted customers to deduct promotional allowances directly from merchandise invoices. The old policy was to force retailers and wholesalers to wait 45 to 60 days to receive reimbursement for special instore displays, retail price reductions, and cooperative advertising. These changes made P&G's policies consistent with the trade norms, thus enabling it to compete with other established brands as well as with generic products in these maturing markets.[2]

[2] This example is based on "Why P&G Wants a Mellower Image," *Business Week*, June 7, 1982, pp. 60, 64.

To forestall the decline phase or to extend the growth phase, manufacturers sometimes use new forms of distribution to reach new target markets. For example, watches were traditionally sold as expensive gift items through jewelry and department stores. In the 1950s, U.S. Time changed all of that by distributing its Timex watches through drugstores. By selling its L'eggs panty hose through supermarkets, Hanes expanded the distribution of women's hosiery beyond women's specialty shops and department stores. Both U.S. Time and Hanes were able to extend their own product life cycles by using radically new forms of distribution. In addition, these new marketing channels for watches and hosiery enabled the two industries to extend their life cycles.

In the *decline phase* of the product life cycle, the intensity of distribution decreases. Dealers drop unprofitable products and manufacturers drop unprofitable dealers. In this stage, dealer support programs and heavy trade discounts are drastically reduced, though large product allowances may be granted to dispose of unwanted inventories.

Vertical Integration.[3]   When a marketing channel participant vertically integrates, it performs more and more of the marketing tasks itself. The more of these functions performed in-house, the more vertically integrated the firm. For example, Hartmarx, a major manufacturer of men's tailored suits, uses its Kuppenheimer Direct stores as retail outlets for its Kupperheimer line of suits. In contrast, it markets its Johnny Carson line of clothing through independent outlets, including Sears. Thus, Hartmarx has vertically integrated the retail marketing functions for its Kuppenheimer line, but not for its Johnny Carson line.

Some channel members attempt to integrate most of the marketing functions, while others only perform a few for themselves. The extent of vertical integration varies according to the stage of the product life cycle, among other things.

In the *introductory phase* of the product life cycle, firms may not vertically integrate the marketing functions because they lack the economies of scale to perform them efficiently. For example, a small, new electronics wholesaler may find it cheaper to contract for repair services rather than to perform them itself. As the demand for repair services expands, the wholesaler may hire service personnel to handle the repairs "in-house."

On the other hand, many firms find themselves forced to vertically integrate in the introductory phase of the product life cycle "in order to prove the worth of new products to ultimate consumers.[4] The classic example is the new entrepreneur who cannot persuade wholesalers or retailers to distribute his new product; the entrepreneur must therefore promote it directly to the ultimate consumer. When a producer cannot rely on others to perform the marketing functions, particularly promotion, he must perform these tasks himself.

In the *growth phase* of the product life cycle, more competitors enter the market, overall market demand increases, and firms begin to focus on particular

[3] This section is based, in part, on Kathryn Rudie Harrigan, *Strategies for Vertical Integration* (Lexington, Mass.: Lexington Books, 1983), pp. 23–27.

[4] Ibid., p. 23.

market segments. Because the market expands rapidly in this phase, firms begin to experience economies of scale in performing many of the marketing functions and vertical integration becomes attractive. For example, in the early growth phase of the personal computer industry, Apple Computer Company changed its distribution system in 1980 "when [it] terminated independent distributors and established company-owned, regional support centers."[5] The chief reasons for this change were to provide better support to Apple's dealers and to help Apple better reach the business and professional markets.

In the *maturity phase* of the product life cycle, competition becomes heavy and causes marginal firms to drop out of the industry. Sales volume begins to stabilize, as does membership in marketing channels. Firms entering the market during this stage may be forced to integrate in order to acquire sources of supply, to obtain distribution outlets for their products and services, and to gain control over how their products and services are marketed. For example, because the dissemination of product information to physicians is so critical to successful marketing in the mature ethical pharmaceuticals industry, all producers use their own "sales forces to educate physicians and promote their firms' products."[6] On the other hand, control over the promotion function is not as critical to reach the pharmacy market; thus, some companies, such as Upjohn and Merck, sell directly to pharmacies, while others, such as Lilly and American Hoescht, rely heavily on independent wholesalers. Moreover, because of their computerized pharmaceutical inventory systems, many wholesalers can hold inventories more cheaply than some manufacturers can. For these producers, vertically integrating the wholesaling function is not a viable strategy.

Sales volume and profitability show chronic decreases in the product life cycle's *decline phase*. As demand declines, firms that are vertically integrated may be strapped with excess capacity for performing the marketing functions. These firms then become vulnerable to low-cost competitors or to suppliers and customers who can perform the marketing functions more cheaply.

Gasoline is an example of a product in the decline phase of the product life cycle. The gasoline crises of the 1970s made motorists more price-conscious and less brand-loyal. By 1981, Getty, Mobil, Union, and Texaco, among other refiners, pulled out of weak market areas or stopped marketing their products under branded names. By 1982, other refiners, such as ARCO and Pennzoil, dropped their consumer credit card programs, while still others, such as Amoco and Texaco, instituted charges for credit card transactions. Thus, many refiners have disintegrated their promotional functions by no longer supporting their branded gasolines, and their financing functions by either dropping or charging for credit card transactions.[7]

---

[5] Ibid, p. 261.

[6] Ibid., p. 186.

[7] Ibid., pp. 100–103.

Product Positioning Within the Marketing Channel

Product Branding Decisions. All intermediaries within the marketing channel must decide how to brand the products they carry. Some manufacturers, such as General Motors, IBM, and Wilson Sporting Goods, produce and market goods under their own labels. Others, such as Whirlpool, Warwick Electronics, and Mobil Refining, produce some of their goods under private labels (brands sponsored by wholesalers or retailers). A further option for channel members is to produce and carry generic-label goods; for example, in the late 1970s and early 1980s, Falstaff supplied generic beer for several midwestern supermarket chains.

Manufacturers use their own brands for several reasons.[8] Developing and supporting their own labels permits them to more easily segment their markets, create brand loyalty, and build their corporate images. In short, manufacturers can control how their goods are marketed through the channel to the extent that they are able to generate a strong customer franchise for their products.

Carrying manufacturers' brands has several benefits for distributors. Manufacturers' brands make it easier to handle products, identify suppliers, enforce product quality standards, and develop buyer preferences and store loyalty. In short, manufacturers' brands are often "presold" via pull strategies, and therefore require little distributor participation in the promotional flow. Many car buyers, for example, make up their minds as to the make and model of car they will buy *before* they enter the showroom.

Although manufacturers' brands offer channel intermediaries many advantages, private labels are a profitable alternative. To use excess capacity, manufacturers may be willing to produce private-label merchandise for wholesalers and retailers. These distributors participate much more heavily in the promotion of these goods than the producer does. Accordingly, they pay the producer a lower price—that is, they get a higher compensation for performing this function. Because some intermediaries simply use the store or wholesale name as the brand name, any promotion for the store automatically carries over to the brand; thus, minimal brand advertising is needed in many instances for private-label goods. For these reasons, private- and generic-label goods are often sold at much lower prices than their manufacturers' branded competitors.

Because of these advantages, private label and generic brands account for substantial sales volumes in many lines of trade. In 1985, for example, annual sales of these brands in the retail food industry amounted to about $15 billion or roughly 15 percent of grocery store sales of products shipped from the warehouse (excluding soft drinks, snack foods, and bakery products).[9]

Other intermediaries use their own labels to develop certain images, to build store traffic, and to expand vertically. Sears with its Kenmore appliances, Craftsman tools, and Diehard batteries is a prime example of a channel member following this strategy. Midas International, originally an automotive wholesaler,

---

[8] Much of this discussion comes from Philip Kotler, *Marketing Management: Analysis, Planning, and Control* (Englewood Cliffs, N.J.: Prentice-Hall, 1984), pp. 484–485.

[9] Derived from authors' calculations and "No-Frills Products: 'An Idea Whose Time Has Gone,'" *Business Week*, June 17, 1985, p. 64.

capitalized on its private labels to develop a franchise system of muffler and brake shops.

The major issue the branding decision poses for distribution management is the extent to which individual channel members participate in the promotion function. Where either manufacturers or distributors take the primary responsibility for developing and promoting their own labels, the degree of conflict among channel members is much lower than where both manufacturers' and private labels vie for the distributors' scarce shelf space. Power struggles among channel members over shelf space has particularly heated up in the packaged foods industry.[10] The basis for these struggles will be the topic of Chapter 10; resolving such conflicts will be discussed in detail in Chapter 11.

Store and Product Positioning. As noted in Chapter 3, retailers attempt to position their stores so that they are differentiated from their competitors', yet at the same time are attractive to their target customers. To achieve effective store positioning, retailers must understand their target markets very well, develop an integrated retail marketing mix, and constantly monitor the marketplace to keep pace with changes in competition and consumer tastes. Accordingly, Sears and Penney's attempt to vary their retail positions periodically to respond to K-mart's changes in its retail mix or to accommodate changes in the emphasis consumers place on quality.

A key element in effective retail positioning is choosing the appropriate suppliers. Retailers want to ensure that the merchandise they buy is consistent with the images they are trying to create in terms of quality and price.

Manufacturers are no different; they want to be sure that their products are attractive to target customers, yet differentiated from their competitors' goods and services. Choosing the appropriate marketing channel is a key aspect of effective product positioning.

As mentioned earlier, "Hartmarx . . . [distributes] its lower-priced Johnny Carson line of men's clothing to Sears while saving its prestigious Hickey-Freeman label for more-exclusive markets."[11] Such an agreement benefits both Sears and Hartmarx. Sears gets to carry a well-known national brand of men's apparel, while Hartmarx gains access to Sears' highly valued target market; Sears upgrades its men's clothing image without damaging Hartmarx's Hickey-Freeman image. Thus, from a channel systems point of view, the supplier's product positioning efforts and the retailer's store positioning strategies must be congruent if either is to be successful.

Not all channels operate as systems, however. Many retailers circumvent normal channels to get the merchandise they wish to carry. For example, in the early and mid-1980s, the Japanese found that cameras they produced for the European market were entering the United States through the "gray market." Because of favorable exchange rates, U.S. retailers could buy cameras through

[10] See, for example, "No-Frills Food: New Power for the Supermarkets," *Business Week,* March 23, 1981, pp. 70ff.

[11] "Caught in a Cross Fire, Brand-Apparel Makers Design Their Defenses," *Wall Street Journal,* January 24, 1984, p. 12.

European distributors for considerably less than they could them for through the "official" U.S. distributors. This put pressure on the U.S. distributors to cut prices, resulting in an erosion of image for many camera brands.

Technical and Warranty Service

For many products, technical and warranty service must performed by some institution within the marketing channels. Some manufacturers perform their own technical and warranty service (e.g., IBM mainframe computers); others delegate this function to wholesalers or retailers (e.g., Caterpillar heavy equipment, General Motors automobiles, Sears Kenmore appliances); still others contract with specialty repair shops to undertake this function (e.g., Whirlpool appliances); and some manufacturers even encourage their customers to perform their own repair service (General Electric major appliances).

Product service is an important aspect of a manufacturer's overall product strategy. It is no less important to a retailer's overall marketing strategy. As with the other marketing functions, the amount of product service offered and where it is performed in the channel depends on the expectations of the target customers. Some expect to perform their own service; some want service performed within the channel. In addition, market segments vary on the degrees of temporal and locational convenience they expect for product service. All of these factors, then, must be considered in deciding on the channel structure for technical and warranty service. The specific approaches to be used in developing channel structures for product service and the other marketing functions will be explored in Chapter 8.

Legal Aspects of Product Strategy Within the Marketing Channel

One element of product strategy that manufacturers attempt to control is the product line of their distributors and dealers. This section describes some of the policies manufacturers use to gain such control.

Exclusive Dealing. Oftentimes, a manufacturer, wholesaler, or distributor will require that its customers sell only its products, or at least none of its direct competitors. This policy is termed *exclusive dealing* and is used for several key reasons. First, it makes reseller demand more predictable. Next, it enables the supplier to operate more effectively against entrenched competitors. Finally, exclusive dealing ensures resellers of a source of supply.[12] Suppliers must use exclusive dealing policies carefully. Although they are not illegal per se, they may be deemed illegal if their effect is to substantially foreclose resellers to competition.[13]

[12] Louis W. Stern and Thomas L. Eovaldi, *Legal Aspects of Marketing Strategy: Antitrust and Consumer Protection Issues* (Englewood Cliffs, N.J.: Prentice-Hall, 1984), p. 304.

[13] Ibid., p. 302.

Tying Contracts. Suppliers, typically manufacturers, sometimes use tying contracts in the marketing of product lines. A tying contract exists

> when a seller, having a product or service that buyers want (the *tying product*), refuses to sell it unless a second (*tied*) product or service is also purchased, or at least is not purchased from anyone other than the seller of the tying product.[14]

For example, Eastern Digital, a large computer manufacturer, requires that retailers who wish to carry its popular personal computer must also handle its rather mediocre dot-matrix printer; thus, Eastern Digital uses a tying contract to market its line of personal computers and peripherals. If Eastern required its dealers to carry its entire product line, it would be using a policy of *full-line forcing,* a special type of tying arrangement.

The legality of tying arrangements is nebulous at best. In franchising, for example, where "the tying product is the franchise itself, and the tied products are the supplies that the franchisee must purchase to operate his business,"[15] tying contracts are legal under certain circumstances. Where the franchisor attempts to maintain quality control through the tied products (e.g., the Colonel's secret herbs and spices), attempts to enter a new market or industry, or tries to preserve its market identity, tying contracts may be deemed legal.[16] In situations other than franchising, tying arrangements may sometimes be legally used. One instance might be where the products are made to be used jointly so that the tying product will not work properly without the tied one. Another instance is "if a company's goodwill depends on proper operation of equipment, a service contract may be tied to the sale or lease of the machine.[17]

In general, however, tying arrangements are not looked upon very favorably by the courts. Suppliers would therefore be wise to avoid them.

Refusals to Deal. Manufacturers, distributors, and wholesalers generally have the legal right to choose to whom they will sell their goods and services. Terminating or cutting off existing dealers, on the other hand, has increasingly led to legal difficulties, particularly in those instances where suppliers have refused to deal without showing just cause.[18]

Managing Product Strategy: Conclusions

This section of the chapter has examined product strategy and its relationship to marketing channel strategy. As we have seen, these two elements of marketing strategy are closely intertwined. The intensity of distribution as well as the degree of vertical integration were shown to vary over the product life cycle. Product branding strategies were found to be interlinked with the decision as to which

[14] Ibid., p. 307.
[15] Ibid., p. 312.
[16] Ibid., p. 314.
[17] Ibid., p. 317.
[18] Ibid., pp. 331–334.

channel members participate most heavily in the promotional function of the channel. Store and product positioning were both found to affect the images retailers and manufacturers attempt to project to their target markets. Determining the appropriate channel structure for product service was pointed out as a key aspect of product strategy. Finally, the legality of exclusive dealing, tying contracts, and other policies manufacturers use to control the product lines of their dealers and distributors was noted to be questionable under certain circumstances.

Up to this point in the chapter, the emphasis has been on the marketing functions performed within the channel. The next section addresses how marketing channel institutions are compensated for their participation in these tasks. In other words, we now turn to the pricing element of the marketing mix.

PRICING STRATEGY AND CHANNEL MANAGEMENT

Pricing decisions within the marketing channel, like the other elements of the marketing mix, are essential to creating the correct product image for both ultimate consumers and the marketing institutions within the channel. This section discusses pricing within the context of the marketing channel. The major aspects to be considered in determining prices within the channel are (1) the marketing functions to be performed, (2) the competitive environment, and (3) the legal implications of pricing.[19] Accordingly, the topics addressed in this section are list prices, discounts and allowances from list, competitive aspects of pricing, pricing to secure marketing channel support, assessing the effects of price changes on the channel, and key legal issues of pricing in the marketing channel. First, however, the concept of price will be explored.

The Concept of Price

Klein's Department Store recently received a shipment of blue jeans from TexTiles, Ltd., an El Paso–based garment manufacturer. The price Klein's paid TexTiles was $10.00 per pair, with terms of 2/15/net 60. Klein's expects to make a 60 percent margin on these goods that, by the way, carry Klein's private label, Our Jeans. For Klein's, the price paid is $10.00 per pair ($9.80 if the cash discount is earned). In return, TexTiles provides Klein's with a pair of blue jeans, labeled with the Our Jeans brand and delivered to the store's receiving docks. (Those not familiar with the pricing terminology used in this illustration should refer to Exhibit 6-1, which presents a glossary and application of the terms used here.) Since Klein's has up to 60 days to pay the invoice, TexTiles performs part of the financing function in the channel by providing credit to the store. The point of this illustration is to demonstrate that price is more than simply the amount that is shown on the sales invoice. In fact, "price is the amount of money and services (or goods) the buyer exchanges for an assortment of products and services provided by the seller."[20]

---

[19] See Martin R. Warshaw, "Pricing to Gain Wholesalers' Selling Support," *Journal of Marketing*, Vol. 26 (July 1962), pp. 50–54.

[20] Kent B. Monroe, *Pricing: Making Profitable Decisions* (New York: McGraw-Hill, 1979), p. 6.

EXHIBIT 6-1
A Glossary and Application of Pricing Terms
Used in the Marketing Channel

Net sales: The final selling price of the merchandise.

Total cost of goods sold: The invoice cost of merchandise less any applicable trade or quantity discounts plus any in-bound transportation costs, if paid by the buyer. Cash discounts are usually deducted from the total cost of goods sold for all merchandise at the end of an accounting period.

Gross margin of profit: The dollar difference between the total cost of goods sold and net sales.

Gross margin percentage: The gross margin of profit divided by net sales.

Application to Klein's Department Store Illustration

A pair of Our Jeans sells for $25.00. Since Klein's cost of goods sold is $10.00 per pair, the store's gross margin of profit is $15.00 per pair ($25.00 less $10.00). The gross margin percentage is then 60 percent ($15.00/$25.00), which is Klein's goal for Our Jeans.

If Klein's takes the cash discount and deducts it from the invoice cost of merchandise, the gross margin of profit becomes $15.20 ($25.00 less $9.80). The gross margin percentage increases to 61 percent ($15.20/$25.00).

As noted in Chapter 1, the prices marketing institutions receive for their goods and services reflect how extensively they participate in the marketing functions or flows. Many manufacturers publish *list prices*, which may be either wholesale or retail prices. Rarely do marketing intermediaries pay these list prices, however. Discounts and allowances from list prices are given as incentives to channel members' to perform certain marketing tasks and to compensate them for doing so. For example, allowances may be made to defray advertising, to obtain preferred shelf or floor space, or to compensate for unsold merchandise. In addition, discounts may be granted to compensate for the performance of channel functions, to encourage prompt payment, to stimulate quantity purchases, to cover shipping costs, and so forth. The following section discusses some of the more commonly used discounts and allowances in more detail.

Discounts and Allowances Offered to Marketing Channel Members

Cash Discounts. Cash discounts are offered to resellers to encourage early or prompt payment on account. A typical cash discount is 2/10/net 30, meaning the buyer may take a 2 percent discount from the invoice price if he makes payment before or on the tenth day after the invoice date. If the buyer does not pay by that date, the full invoice amount is due 30 days after the invoice date.

The 2 percent cash discount translates into an effective annual interest rate of 36 percent (2 percent times 360 days/20 days). Thus, passing up cash discounts can be very costly. Unless their merchandise turns over very rapidly, some intermediaries that operate on slim margins simply cannot realize a profit on a merchandise shipment unless they take advantage of the cash discount. By maintaining a line of credit at low interest rates, these channel members use short-term loans to pay their invoices within the cash discount period.

Trade Discounts. Trade discounts are offered to marketing channel institutions according to their position within the channel. They are usually quoted in a series of percentages, such as list price less 33%–15%–5%, for different channel intermediaries. Thus, if the list price is $100, trade discounts are granted as follows for different channel members:

List price	$100.00	
Less 33%	33.00	Retailer's discount
	67.00	Price to retailer
Less 15%	10.05	Wholesaler's discount
	56.95	Price to wholesaler
Less 5%	2.85	Broker's commission
	$54.10	Net revenue to manufacturer

Presumably, these discounts reflect the marketing tasks each of these intermediaries performs. In practice, however, the discounts are often offered simply because of the buyer's position in the channel, since it is difficult to isolate the functions each channel intermediary performs.[21]

In the Klein's Department Store illustration, Klein's must sell Our Jeans at $25 a pair to realize a 60 percent gross margin percentage. Since the wholesale price—the price that Klein's pays—is $10, the gross margin of profit is $15. This margin compensates Klein's for developing the brand image for Our Jeans, keeping the product in stock, offering retail credit to its customers, employing salespeople to help customers select the proper sizes and to provide them with product information, displaying the blue jeans prominently, and providing the physical location for marketing the product. After Klein's has deducted the cost of performing these tasks from the gross margin, the amount remaining is the net profit Klein's realizes. Naturally, the lower the functional costs, the higher Klein's net profit; however, the tasks must be performed effectively if Klein's is to satisfy its target market's needs.

Promotional Allowances.[22] Promotional allowances compensate channel members for participating in the promotional flow. These allowances are typically deducted from the manufacturer's invoice price of the goods. *Case allowances* are discounts on each case of merchandise ordered during a particular time period.

[21] Ibid., p. 169.

[22] This section draws heavily from Paul W. Farris and John A. Quelch, *Advertising & Promotion Management* (Radnor, Pa.: Chilton, 1983), pp. 198–200.

For example, retailers may qualify for a 50-cent case allowance for goods normally wholesaling at $5 per case if they buy at least one dozen cases during a six-week promotional period. *Merchandising allowances* compensate retailers for extra in-store displays or for featuring the product in their store advertising. Allowances offered to encourage retailers to stock new products are called *listing allowances;* manufacturers use these to stimulate rapid distribution of new products. Since retailers may allow their inventories of a product to deplete in anticipation of a manufacturer promotion period, *floor stock protection* allowances are given to retailers to maintain their inventories. Manufacturers sometimes offer *rebates* to retailers to (1) encourage them to increase their purchases and (2) reduce their prices to consumers in order to stimulate demand.

Quantity Discounts.[23]   Quantity discounts are given to marketing channel intermediaries to stimulate larger purchases of goods. For example, *carload and truckload prices* may reflect lower freight costs when the product is purchased by the rail carload or truckload. *Annual volume rebates* are based on total purchases over the year; the larger the total purchases, the larger the rebate percentage. *Base contract allowances* are off-invoice allowances offered on each order over some minimum quantity or dollar volume.

Seasonal Discounts.   These are discounts given to marketing channel members who order products and services before a certain date. The objective is to smooth production more evenly over the course of the year.

Product Allowances.   Product allowances are offered to intermediaries who buy damaged goods, second-quality merchandise, odd-size goods, or obsolete products. Demand is somewhat uncertain for these types of merchandise, and product allowances enable the manufacturer to unload them to channel members who better understand the market for this merchandise.

Competitive Aspects of Pricing in the Channel

Basically, two forms of competition face marketing intermediaries of a manufacturer's product. First, *interbrand* competition occurs when one manufacturer's product competes against another manufacturer's brand. Coca-Cola faces interbrand competition from Pepsi-Cola, for example. Second, *intrabrand* competition occurs when two marketing channel members at the same level (e.g., two retailers) compete against each other with the same brand. For example, Osco Drug is engaged in intrabrand competition with IGA supermarkets since both stores carry Coke and Coca-Cola Classic.

The extent of interbrand competition depends on how substitutable the competing products are in consumers' eyes. For instance, if consumers view Coke and Pepsi as very similar products, the extent of interbrand competition would be quite high. On the other hand, if consumers are very brand loyal (as many cola drinkers are) and Coke and Pepsi are seen as very different cola

[23] Ibid., p. 198.

beverages, the extent of interbrand competition would be much lower. Obviously, the manufacturer, in setting wholesale prices, must provide the marketing channel members with enough margin to compete with rival brands. In addition, the manufacturer must consider the competing brands' prices and the competitors' likely reactions to its price.[24] The greater the degree of interbrand competition, the more carefully this must be done.

Intrabrand competition stems from having several different types of marketing channels handle the same brand. For example, Bic pens are marketed through drugstores, supermarkets, convenience stores, book and stationery stores, and discount stores, among others. The larger of these retailers buy directly from the factory, bypassing office supply wholesalers. By purchasing direct, they receive lower prices than they would by purchasing through wholesalers, but they do not benefit from the functions provided by the wholesalers. This bypassing becomes a problem whenever the large-scale retailers can perform the marketing functions more cheaply than the wholesalers who sell to smaller retailers. These larger retailers can then undercut the prices of the smaller stores because of their greater efficiency.

Pricing to Secure Marketing Channel Support

Pricing within the marketing channel is a twofold problem. First, the prices set must make the product or service attractive to the ultimate consumer. Second, the price must encourage marketing channel intermediaries to carry the product or offer the service and provide the necessary marketing functions to ensure that the entire product package is attractive to ultimate consumers. The former problem lies in the domain of consumer behavior, and therefore is outside the scope of this text. The latter is discussed in the following paragraphs.

One step in securing marketing channel support through pricing is to ensure that the margin will attract enough channel members to provide adequate market coverage. If too few outlets want to carry the product, that should be a tip-off to the manufacturer or wholesaler that something in the marketing mix is wrong. The reseller margin might be the culprit.

Adequate coverage is only one element of securing marketing channel support through pricing. The margins should be large enough to enable an *efficient* reseller to realize a reasonable profit while performing the necessary marketing functions, such as carrying adequate inventory, featuring the product in reseller promotions, and undertaking delivery and repair service. Obviously, not all marketing channel members will be able to make a profit since not all are efficient enough. If most cannot make a profit on the margins offered, some adjustments must be made. Either the marketing functions required of the intermediaries should be reduced or the margins paid to them should be increased. Thus, "each class of reseller margins [e.g., full-function versus limited-function wholesalers, full-service versus self-service retailers] should vary in rough proportion to the cost of the functions the reseller performs."[25]

[24] Alfred R. Oxenfeldt, *Pricing Strategies* (New York: Amacom, 1975), p. 143.
[25] Ibid., p. 140.

Closely related to this is the fact that marketing channel intermediaries expect to realize margins that are typical for carrying similar products or performing similar services. If they don't, these channel members will probably resent the supplier and fail to give the necessary support to the product.[26]

"[O]nce traditional prices for a specified distribution channel have been determined, the margins may be wider or narrower at any particular level, depending on the market power of the interacting institutions."[27] As will be discussed in further detail in Chapter 10, the market power of channel institutions depends on their size, access to information, reputation, and differential advantage, as well as on their access to alternative sources of supply or alternative channel outlets. For example, Sears is able to secure favorable prices from its suppliers because of the quantities it buys, its understanding of its target market, its reputation with consumers, its effectiveness as a mass merchandiser, and its access to literally thousands of suppliers. On the other hand, a small camera shop handling Nikon equipment may have to take lower margins on Nikon items than it does on brands of less popular cameras because of Nikon's market power.[28]

In addition to securing their support, manufacturers often wish to influence marketing channel members' resellers' prices. There are two primary reasons for this; (1) manufacturers want to protect other intermediaries within the channel from price-cutters and (2) they believe that their quality image would be damaged by heavy price-cutting to consumers.

As will be discussed below, suppliers are prohibited by law from setting reseller prices. However, they can, legally try to influence those prices by a number of means. First, manufacturers and wholesalers often publish price lists with suggested prices included. Next, some suppliers directly advertise their prices to consumers; many fast-food franchisors, for example, do this periodically. Third, suppliers may price-mark their goods at their warehouses; channel intermediaries are free to either re-mark the merchandise or leave the suppliers' price unchanged. Another method to influence reseller prices is to grant channel members exclusive territorial rights for the product or service. In effect, exclusive territories eliminate intrabrand competition, and thus price-cutting resellers. A fifth method of influencing the prices of marketing channel members is to refuse to sell to price-cutting intermediaries. Finally, by offering their resellers operating and marketing assistance, suppliers provide ways other than price-cutting for those firms to enhance their profitability.[29]

Assessing the Effects of Price Changes on the Marketing Channel

Price is viewed by many as the easiest element of the marketing mix to change. This may be an oversimplification, however, since the effects on the marketing

[26] Ibid., p. 144.

[27] Mark I. Alpert, *Pricing Decisions* (Glenview, Ill.: Scott, Foresman and Company, 1971), p. 23.

[28] These examples are adapted from ibid.

[29] Oxenfeldt, *Pricing Strategies*, pp. 135–136.

channel of manufacturers or wholesalers changing prices cannot be ignored. Before instituting price changes—and hence margin changes—for any particular type of marketing channel intermediary, the manufacturer or wholesaler should evaluate the impact of these changes. Among the questions to be asked are:[30]

- How would [the] actual price charged by that reseller and others be affected by the change in margin? (Suggested prices are not to be confused with actual prices.)
- How would the number of resellers who carry the brand be altered?
- What kinds of resellers would be attracted by the change? What kinds would be lost as a result of the change?
- What amount of sales effort would be given the brand by the different types of reseller[s] as a result of different levels of margin?

Answers to these questions should guide the channel member in evaluating the appropriateness of the proposed price or margin changes.

Legal Implications of Pricing Within the Marketing Channel

A variety of pricing approaches within the marketing channel have legal implications. In this section, the legality of three of the most commonly encountered approaches—resale price maintenance, price discrimination, and brokerage allowances—are discussed.

Resale Price Maintenance. In this approach, suppliers, usually manufacturers, set the prices that marketing channel intermediaries can charge to their customers. As noted above, manufacturers desire to control their resellers' prices in order to protect their channel intermediaries from price-cutting and to preserve their products' quality images from being damaged by price-cutting.

Resale price maintenance has been ruled to be illegal under all circumstances by federal courts. Thus, suppliers would do well to avoid specifying reseller prices.

> It should be noted, however, that there is nothing inherently illegal about suppliers suggesting or recommending resale prices. What has been held to be illegal is any attempt to enforce them, such as by threatening to terminate dealers who do not comply with them.[31]

Manufacturers can, however, take several steps to minimize the legal difficulties associated with resale price maintenance.[32] For established distribution networks,

[30] Direct quote from ibid., p. 152.

[31] Stern and Eovaldi, *Legal Aspects of Marketing Strategy,* p. 330.

[32] The following steps are from Mary Jane Sheffet and Debra L. Scammon, "Resale Price Maintenance: Is It Safe to Suggest Retail Prices?" *Journal of Marketing,* Vol. 49 (Fall 1985), pp. 89–91.

manufacturers are advised to: (1) act unilaterally in announcing price changes or in refusing to sell to price-cutting dealers and (2) avoid coercing price-cutting dealers to maintain recommended prices. For new distribution networks, manufacturers: (1) should avoid known discounters and (2) establish resale prices at the time distribution arrangements are made. Of course, a third option, if economically feasible, exists—vertical integration.

Price Discrimination. Sellers engage in price discrimination when they charge different prices to different resellers for the same or similar merchandise. Price discrimination can also occur when a buyer demands a price lower than the seller charges the buyer's competition for the same or similar merchandise. The following example illustrates price discrimination:

General Foods sells 50 cases of Jello to A&P Supermarkets for $5 a case. General Foods has just signed a new Jello contract with A&P's major competitor, Kroger Stores. For 50 cases of Jello, Kroger pays General Foods $4.75 a case. The quantities are the same, as is the merchandise.

Unlike resale price maintenance, price discrimination is not illegal, under all circumstances but the legal issues are so complicated that an astute marketer would be wise to avoid the practice if it fails to meet the requirements listed below. In general, *price discrimination is illegal* when the effect is to substantially lessen competition or to tend to create a monopoly. Exceptions to this may occur, in general: (1) if price discrimination is used to sell "unsellable" goods, such as obsolete, damaged, or second-quality merchandise; (2) if a marketer simply passes along the savings from lower-cost methods of manufacture, selling, or delivery when different methods of selling or delivery are used or different quantities are sold; or (3) if price discrimination is used in "good faith" to meet a competitor's equally low price.[33]

Brokerage Allowances. Brokerage allowances are payments to channel intermediaries who use a company-owned sales force or buying office. In this sense, they are functional discounts. As long as these allowances are granted to independent third parties for actual marketing functions performed, they are permissible. However, under the following circumstances brokerage allowances are illegal: (1) when buyers do not perform any of the brokerage functions; (2) when they demand that sellers grant them brokerage allowances anyway; and (3) when buyers use these allowances as a method of getting lower prices from suppliers.[34]

In addition to resale price maintenance, price discrimination, and brokerage allowances, other marketing channel pricing policies, such as discounts and allowances, should be scrutinized to ensure that they are legal.

[33] Stern and Eovaldi, *Legal Aspects of Marketing Strategy*, pp. 263–276.
[34] Ibid., pp. 453–455.

Managing Pricing Strategy: Conclusions

This section of the chapter addressed the major aspects of pricing within the marketing channel. The first consideration in setting prices within the channel, of course, is their impact on either organizational demand (e.g., shoemakers' demand for leather) or final consumer demand (e.g., consumers' demand for shoes). From these demand factors, the price setter must determine what the list price should be. How discounts and allowances from list price can be used to gain market coverage and to stimulate the performance of the necessary marketing functions must then be evaluated. The relative bargaining positions of the various channel intermediaries will also affect the discounts and allowances each receives. In addition, the degree of interbrand and intrabrand competition influences the amount of control over reseller prices the supplier attempts to wield. The effects of any changes in the prices within the channel should be carefully monitored. Finally, the legality of pricing policies must be carefully examined to make certain that federal, state, and local laws are not violated.

We have stressed here the fact that the functions to be performed by the marketing channel intermediaries affect the margins each receives, and hence the ultimate price charged to consumers. As noted in Chapter 5, the higher the physical distribution service standards are, the more costly the physical flow of goods from their points of origin to their points of consumption will be. Cash, trade, quantity, and seasonal discounts are used to compensate channel members for extensive participation in the physical distribution activities of the marketing channel. Product and promotional allowances compensate them for participating in the risk-taking and promotional activities of the channel.

MARKETING CHANNELS AND THE MARKETING MIX

Delivering the target market's desired levels of service outputs is the key task to be performed by marketing channels. Because, as noted in Chapter 1, marketing institutions are interdependent, manufacturers, wholesalers, and retailers must consider one another's marketing strategies in developing their own. Thus, for example, the marketing flows wholesalers participate in are partly determined by the functions manufacturers and retailers decide to perform. Moreover, the specific strategies selected must be congruent with those of the other channel members if the service outputs desired by the target markets are to be delivered effectively. Exhibit 6-2 illustrates why a supplier's distribution, promotion, and product strategies must mesh with the product strategies of producers using the "just-in-time" inventory method.

As will be discussed in Chapter 9, some channel participants have attempted to develop fully integrated marketing programs for the entire marketing channel. Retailers such as Sears, wholesalers such as Ace Hardware, manufacturers such as Hartmarx, and franchisors such as McDonald's are prime examples. Other channel members have focused on only a few of the channel functions in developing their marketing programs. Rather than involving the entire channel,

EXHIBIT 6-2
Just-in-Time Supply Systems

By the mid-1980s, the Japanese "just-in-time," *kanban,* ticket, or stockless inventory system was beginning to be implemented in the United States, particularly in the automotive and appliance industries. The focus of this system is on the flow of material and components rather than on their storage. For example, in "Japanese firms, trucks with side-loading/unloading capability often deliver the materials directly to the production line, bypassing the incoming inspection process." Thus, the *kanban* system enables producers to reduce their inventories at all stages of production, and hence to substantially increase their inventory turnover levels.

To make *kanban* systems effective, suppliers must adapt their marketing strategies to reach their target customers. Indeed, the just-in-time (JIT) system requires careful coordination between suppliers and producers in a variety of areas. Among them are the following:

1. *Production quality.* Suppliers must provide products of consistently high quality because no backup inventories are available to substitute for poor-quality materials and components. Producers provide suppliers with considerable design leeway to enable them to arrive at the needed quality levels. This obviously requires close coordination between suppliers and their customers.

2. *Supplier location.* Because of the short lead times necessary in JIT systems, suppliers must locate production or warehouse facilities near their customers' plants.

3. *Supplier delivery schedules.* "The JIT concept requires frequent deliveries with small lot sizes synchronized with production schedules. This often means multiple deliveries daily."

Kanban inventory systems necessitate long-term buyer-seller relationships between suppliers and their customers. A supplier's promotional strategy thus must emphasize communication among a variety of supplier and customer personnel. The goal is to ensure that the customer's demands for service outputs are met.

By carefully coordinating the key elements of their marketing strategies with the needs of their customers, the logistics channel for such goods as motorcycles, bicycles, and automobiles becomes more efficient. Ultimately, this enables producers to deliver the service outputs demanded by their customers better; the entire supplier → producer → consumer channel benefits from better coordination in the supplier-producer link.

Source: Based on an article from *Marketing News*, published by the American Marketing Association, "Devise New Marketing Strategies to Serve 'JIT' Producers," by Charles R. O'Neal, September 14, 1984, pp. 20–21.

TABLE 6.2 Extent of Retail Services Offered by Full-Line Hardware Wholesalers

Accounting Services		Buying Services	
Accounts payable	19%	Private-label merchandise	41%
Accounts receivable	28%	Dealer shows	50%
Balance sheets	19%	Drop-ship programs	80%
Payroll	6%	Pool order programs	60%
General ledger	9%	Catalog service	56%
Merchandising Services		Telephone ordering	52%
Store planning	42%	Microfiche	22%
Store identification	38%	**Advertising Services**	
Management Services		Radio	51%
Preprinted bin and price tickets	91%	Television	39%
Gross margin by merchandise		Newspapers	54%
line reports	81%	Circulars	56%
Purchase summaries	75%		

Source: Adapted from *Hardware Age* Survey of Hardware Wholesalers, 1984, cited in "Distribution Update VI," *Hardware Age*, June 1984, p. 41.

many of these programs deal with a limited number of marketing institutions. Typical of these marketing programs are those developed by full-line hardware wholesalers for their retail store customers (see Table 6-2).

SUMMARY

Chapters 5 and 6 described how the marketing mix elements of manufacturers, wholesalers, and retailers are closely interrelated. In addition, we provided some guidelines for managing the marketing mix element within distribution channels.

We examined two key elements of the marketing mix—product and pricing strategies—in the context of the marketing channel. As indicated throughout the chapter, these marketing functions may be performed anywhere within the channel.

Product strategy within the marketing channel has several facets. First, the product life cycle concept stresses the fact that distribution strategy (i.e., distribution intensity and vertical integration) changes as the product evolves. Second, manufacturers, wholesalers, and retailers may all develop branding strategies within the channel; therefore, manufacturers often find themselves competing with other channel members for the favor of their common target markets. Other aspects of product strategy within the channel include store and product positioning and technical and warranty service.

The extent to which marketing institutions are compensated for the functions they perform is the essence of *pricing* within marketing channels. Various discounts and allowances are offered to accomplish this task. Pricing within the channel also has its competitive aspects. Channel members must understand how others within the channel as well as competitors react to prices and price changes.

Federal regulations limit how the marketing mix can be implemented within distributive channels. In this chapter, we addressed specific product and pricing activities that are either explicitly or potentially illegal. In general, activities that are unfair methods of competition, that limit or injure competition, or that tend to create monopolies are deemed illegal.

PROBLEMS

1. Brookwood Technologies has developed a revolutionary process for magnetizing fabrics and sees limitless possibilities for this dramatic innovation. Brookwood recently bought a fabric mill in North Carolina and has been producing a line of outdoor wear. These garments substitute small strips of magnetized fabric for buttons, snaps, zippers, and Velcro. Brookwood has been having difficulty acquiring distribution for this merchandise.
   a. What should Brookwood do to make marketing intermediaries more enthusiastic about these garments?
   b. How intensively should Brookwood distribute its outdoor wear at this point? Explain.
   c. Discuss the likelihood that Brookwood will have to integrate further forward to market its garments.

2. Medical Food Services, Ltd., is a medium-sized food wholesaler whose market primarily consists of nursing homes, hospitals, and convalescent centers. Medical Food Services has developed an excellent reputation and, as a result, is quite successful in the markets it has entered. Its line of food products has historically been made up of manufacturers' brands; however, the company has been considering adding a small number of private labels to capitalize on its reputation and to earn a larger profit margin. Discuss the conditions under which Medical Food Services would be successful in introducing merchandise under its own label.

3. Midwest Foods, Inc., is a producer of frozen foods and is best noted for its Señora Gonzàles line of Mexican dinners and entrees. Midwest uses a traditional food broker → food wholesaler → grocery store marketing channel. Its trade discount structure is list less 20-15-5 percent.
   a. If the list price is $60 per case of Señora Gonzales' enchilada frozen dinners, how much does the retailer pay the wholesaler per case? How much does the wholesaler pay for a case of these dinners? What is the broker's commission?
   b. What is Midwest Foods' gross margin on a case of these frozen dinners?
   c. Suppose Midwest wants grocery stores to feature its Señora Gonzales line and offers retailers a $3 case allowance on a minimum order of a dozen cases during the four-week promotional period. How much would the retailer then pay for a case of enchilada dinners?
   d. If Midwest offers a cash discount of 2/10/net 60, how much does it receive for a case of the frozen enchilada dinners?
   e. Consider both the cash discount and the case allowance. Now how much is Midwest paid per case?

4. One possible difficulty facing Brookwood Technologies (see Question 1) in obtaining distribution for its innovative outdoor wear is its pricing policy. Brookwood did very little advertising and aimed most of its promotional effort at securing distribution. Retailers were asked to take deliveries on their orders four months in advance of the

selling seasons. No unsold or damaged merchandise returns were allowed. Cash discounts of 2/30/net 60 were offered; the industry norm was 2/10/net 30. Consistent with the industry norm, a 45 percent gross margin on the suggested retail prices was offered. How might Brookwood revise its concept of price to encourage retail support of its new garments?

5. The Frederick Manufacturing Company is an old, very well established maker of high-quality firearms. To protect its image, Frederick has a policy of exclusive distribution whereby only a single dealer is allowed to serve a particular geographic area. Lately, the company has been concerned about the activities of some of its dealers. These retailers have drastically cut their prices and begun selling directly through national publications. Naturally, the other dealers are screaming about these practices. What should Frederick do to protect its retail price structure? Discuss the legality of your suggestions.

7

Marketing Channel Communication Systems

LEARNING OBJECTIVES

Upon completing this chapter, you will be able to:

- *Describe the process by which marketing channel members communicate with one another.*

- *List the different media by which marketing channel members communicate with one another.*

- *Discuss and provide examples of the two different types of communication noise within marketing channels.*

- *Describe the four primary sources or causes of noise in marketing channel communications.*

- *Discuss several mechanisms for reducing or preventing communication noise within marketing channels.*

- *Specify the steps for developing an effective marketing channel information system.*
- *Describe electronic data interchange (EDI) networks and how they improve marketing channel communications.*
- *List the advantages and disadvantages, to both suppliers and buyers, of EDI systems.*

Example

Karen Lyons, a pharmacist at General Hospital, complained one day to Gene Johnson, president of a drug wholesaling firm, "Pharmaceutical houses just don't bother introducing their new products to me. I have to find out what's new on the market by talking to the pharmacists at the other hospitals here in the city. Why don't salespeople let me know about the new drugs? Why don't I get any product information sheets anymore?"

Gene agreed that the manufacturers were "falling down on their job," but when he interviewed the detail people (sales personnel) for several manufacturers, he found that they, too, were frustrated. They had more than adequate information—written and oral—to give out. To them, the pharmacist herself was the villain. They were fed up with waiting as much as four hours to conduct a detail call. "That pharmacist thinks she is God," one salesman said. "She couldn't care less about how long she makes us detail people wait." Gene took the initiative, told Karen what the real problem was, and made appointments for her to see the detail people at given hours.

In this situation it was really the manufacturers' communication lines that broke down, not the wholesaler's. The manufacturers relied upon detail people to tell the potential pharmacist buyer about their products, which were then sold and delivered by the wholesaler to the buyer. The wholesaler's responsibility in communication was only to tell prospective buyers that they had the manufacturers' products available. Obviously, the manufacturers' feedback was inadequate in that it took a wholesaler to straighten out the communication problem.

Source: Based upon *Combined Proceedings 1971 Spring and Fall Conferences*, published by the American Marketing Association (Chicago, 1972), "Towards the Measurement of Trade Channel Perception," by Reavis Cox, Thomas F. Schutte, and Kendrick S. Few, Fred C. Allvine (ed.). pp. 190–191.

Communication among marketing institutions provides the mechanism for coordinating activities within the distribution channel. Poor or ineffective communications can be a major roadblock to implementing successful marketing programs. Ideally, problems of this nature would be avoided; in reality, omission and distortion of messages frequently occur within marketing channels. In fact, inadequate communication or miscommunication may contribute to or result from deep-rooted channel conflict.

This chapter focuses on problems arising from the lack of effective communication within channels. Specifically, an overall model of marketing channel communication is presented. As will be noted in the model, "static," "interference," or "noise" may hamper the effectiveness of communications within the channel. The types and causes of this noise are identified and methods for overcoming it are suggested. A preliminary model for designing marketing channel information systems is then presented, and the chapter concludes with a discussion of an emerging marketing channel communication system—electronic data interchange networks.

ELEMENTS OF MARKETING CHANNEL COMMUNICATION SYSTEMS

The successful development and operation of a channel communication system is frequently limited by the legality, availability, cost, and confidentiality of the information flow. A distortion-free communication system is an unrealistic goal because of the different perceptions of the individuals employed by manufacturing, wholesaling, retailing, and logistics organizations. Nevertheless, constructing a moderately successful system is necessary to achieve reasonably coordinated marketing channels.[1] However:

> The adequacy of the vertical channel communication systems that have evolved within various firms and industries varies considerably. Two reasons appear fundamentally to account for a weak system: (1) the profitability potential of providing certain data to associated firms in the channel may not have been analyzed, or (2) if the profitability is recognized, a *standard* procedure for such data communication has not been established.[2]

Developing an effective information system generally results in a higher degree of loyalty and commitment on the part of the channel members to a particular channel arrangement. Furthermore, the firm that originates and maintains the system may acquire more power within the channel as the other members become more dependent on the data transmitted. Hence, there are several incentives for firms to play an active role in formulating and maintaining a channel communication system.

To grasp the problems that arise when marketing channel members attempt to communicate with one another, it is important to understand the overall communication process within marketing channels. Figure 7-1 is a diagram of this process.

Assume that the sender is a retailer wishing to relay demand information about a new product to its supplier. The retailer encodes its message about demand into the appropriate symbols for transmission to the supplier. These

[1] Walter Gross, "Profitable Listening for Manufacturers and Dealers: How to Use a Communication System," in William G. Moller, Jr., and David L. Wilemon (eds.), *Marketing Channels: A Systems Viewpoint* (Homewood, Ill.: Richard D. Irwin, 1971), p. 351.

[2] Ibid., p. 352.

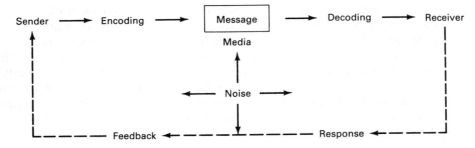

Figure 7-1 Elements in the communication process. *Source*: Philip Kotler, *Marketing Management: Analysis, Planning, and Control*, 5th ed. (Englewood Cliffs, N.J.: Prentice-Hall, 1984), p. 605.

symbols may be words, pictures, images, stock numbers, industry jargon, and so forth. The message is then sent through communications media to the supplier. Figure 7-2 illustrates some of the media that channel members use to communicate with one another. The supplier next decodes the message by assigning meaning to the words, pictures, and so on sent by the retailer. The supplier may act, in one way or another, on the market information relayed by the retailer. Or

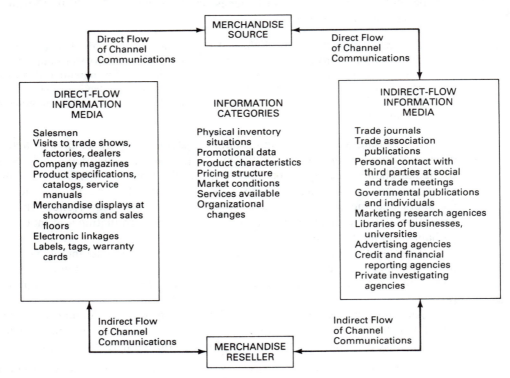

Figure 7-2 Direct and indirect communications media available to merchandise sources and resellers. *Source*: Gross, *Business Horizons*, December 1968, p. 39; used with permission.

the supplier may ask the retailer to clarify the message received. In either instance, the retailer receives feedback as to how well the original message was communicated.

As shown in Figure 7-1, noise can arise anywhere in the communication process, preventing the retailer's message from being received as intended. The next section explores the major types of communication noise or interference and how they arise.

TYPES AND SOURCES OF COMMUNICATION NOISE WITHIN MARKETING CHANNELS

Accurate communication within a marketing channel occurs when a channel member's message is received by another as it was originally intended. However, between the time a message is transmitted and when it is received, many things can occur to change the message from what was intended. These changes to the message are called *noise* and the "things" that occur are the sources or causes of noise.

Types of Communication Noise

There are two general types of communication noise within the marketing channel—omission and distortion.

> *Omission* [emphasis added] occurs when a complete message is transmitted but not received, or when the symbols are technically received but their meaning is ignored.[3]

For example, a well-known tire manufacturer prided itself on its dealer point-of-purchase promotional pieces. After conducting a research study on its in-store displays, the company learned that the dealers did not want the promotional materials and discarded them almost immediately upon receipt.[4] Since the manufacturer really did not know what the dealers needed and had not made an effort to find out, the dealers were simply ignoring the tire maker's message.

Distortion, on the other hand,

> occurs when the message is received but some change has taken place in the signal between the transmitter and the receiver, or a change in content meaning occurs between what the sender intended and that which the [receiver] attaches to it.[5]

---

[3] John R. Grabner, Paul H. Zinszer, and Larry J. Rosenberg, "Communication in the Distribution Channel," in Arch G. Woodside, J. Taylor Sims, Dale M. Lewison, and Ian F. Wilkinson (eds.), *Foundations of Marketing Channels* (Austin, Tex.: Austin Press, 1978), p. 229.

[4] This example was drawn from Reavis Cox, Thomas F. Schutte, and Kendrick S. Few, "Towards the Measurement of Trade Channel Perception," in Fred C. Allvine (ed.), *Combined Proceedings 1971 Spring and Fall Conferences* (Chicago: American Marketing Association, 1972), pp. 190–191.

[5] Grabner, et al., "Communication in the Distribution Channel," p. 229.

For example, Midwest Foods, a well-known food manufacturer offered a special listing allowance to encourage grocery retailers to stock and promote its new brand of ready-to-eat cereal. In one region, however, supermarkets stocked the new food product but failed to feature it in their promotions. Midwest Foods ultimately discovered that retailers in that region presumed that listing allowances were simply to encourage their stocking new products and that additional allowances would be offered to them to promote the new cereal. Thus, distortion in communication often arises as marketing channel members use similar words, terms, and phrases to mean different things.

Sources of Communication Noise [6]

Omission and distortion within marketing channel communications stem from a variety of causes. Among them are communication overload, secrecy, poor timing in communications, and perceptual differences among channel members.

Communication Overload. Because channel member organizations have limited abilities to handle communication messages, there is a potential for overload. Communication overload occurs when the channel member receives too many messages to process adequately. As a result, messages may be ignored (omission) or may be so carelessly attended to that their meanings change (distortion). Exhibit 7-1 provides an illustration of communication overload in marketing channels for pharmaceuticals.

Secrecy. Secrecy within marketing channels often accounts for a significant degree of communication noise. Marketing institutions will withhold information from one another for a variety of reasons. One reason a firm might not want to reveal its plans to other channel members is that marketing intermediaries are frequently excellent sources of competitive information. Too much competitive secrecy, however, can cause communication problems and perhaps conflict within the marketing channel.

A major producer of electric appliances hired a well-known actress to introduce new products on a television program. When she announced a new electric frankfurter cooker, it was not only news to the consumer; it was also news to retailers, and even to the manager of a wholesale subsidiary owned by this manufacturer. Imagine the dismay of consumers trying to buy the product from retailers who had never heard of the product. Imagine the reaction of those retailers! [7]

---

[6] This section draws heavily on John R. Grabner, Jr. and L. J. Rosenberg, et al., "Communication in Distribution Channel Systems," in *Distribution Channels: Behavioral Dimensions*, Louis W. Stern, (ed.), (Boston: Houghton Mifflin, 1969), pp. 239–242.

[7] This example was drawn from Gross, "Profitable Listening for Manufacturers and Dealers," p. 348.

As we shall see in Chapter 10, channel members often withhold information from one another to gain power. A retailer, for example, might want to develop a bargaining advantage over a supplier by not revealing demand forecasts or information about competitors' marketing plans. Moreover, wholesalers often do not divulge their customer lists to their suppliers for fear that suppliers will sell directly to those customers.

Poor Timing in Communications. Noise may occur when messages are transmitted or received at inopportune times.

> If it arrives too soon, the message may either be ignored because the receiver may fail to see its relevance or the meaning attached to a message may differ significantly from that which would have been placed on it had it been received when similar messages were being received from other channel members.[8]

For example:

Ford Motor Company's Supplier Online Management Information System enables some 3,000 suppliers to communicate shipping infor-

---

[8] Grabner et al., "Communication in the Distribution Channel," p. 231.

mation electronically. This system allows suppliers to notify Ford as soon as parts are shipped. Under the old communication system, "the truck carrying the parts would sometimes arrive before we received the shipping notice," says Norman Lewis, Ford's director of information systems.[9]

Messages received too late are not very valuable, either. For example, if a food wholesaler gets an announcement from a food manufacturer about a special promotional campaign only days before the event is to begin, he will have little time to order additional stock to support the campaign-generated increase in demand.

Perceptual Differences Among Channel Members.   For a variety of reasons, marketing channel institutions interpret information quite differently. First, the language used to communicate is imprecise, particularly for nonstandardized and intangible products. For example, technical jargon, which is incomprehensible to most laypeople, enables manufacturers, wholesalers, and retailers to communicate efficiently with one another; a particular word or two of jargon may convey as much information as a layperson's 200-word statement. But technical terminology can be a source of communication problems when the sender and receiver do not completely agree on what the terms mean.

Second, different frames of reference can limit the effectiveness of communication within the channel. Different channel members having different goals commonly creates communication noise within the channel. In the automobile industry, for example, car makers depend upon a certain amount of sales volume to maintain economical production levels. A high sales volume, they believe, leads to greater profitability. Dealers, on the other hand, are more directly interested in achieving profitability, either through selling or servicing cars. They may not be concerned about selling a particular model as long as the overall product line generates reasonable profits. However, to avoid the costly shutdown of their plants, manufacturers want dealers to emphasize particular models, especially those that are not very popular. These different frames of reference may, therefore, cause messages to be improperly encoded or inappropriately decoded (see Figure 7-1).

Third, source credibility and legitimacy may bear on the effectiveness of communication within the channel. Retailers, for instance, often resent it when manufacturers intrude on what they believe are legitimately their decisions. Or if a retailer consistently fails to keep promises or to tell the truth, suppliers may interpret that retailer's messages differently from what is intended.

Exhibit 7-2 provides some illustrations of how perceptual differences can cause difficulties within the marketing channel.

[9] This example was drawn from Gary Stix, "Ending the Supplier Paper Chase," *Computer Decisions*, July 30, 1985, p. 69.

EXHIBIT 7-2

Illustrations of Perceptual Differences as Causes of Communication Noise Within Marketing Channels

- A manufacturer's research indicated that consumers wanted a package that would be easier to open. Accordingly, the product (bubble gum balls) was packaged in a redesigned box with a simple tear-open feature. Retailers were highly upset with the new package because it led to free sampling by children as well as display floor cleanup problems.[a]

- An appliance manufacturer provided its distributors and dealers with promotional incentives, including travel prizes and free merchandise for their outstanding salespeople. Difficulties arose when the travel prizes contributed to the intermediaries' personnel shortages during peak sales periods. Additional problems occurred when the middlemen learned that their salespeople were selling the free merchandise to customers on company time.[b]

- An advertising agency recommended that one of its clients—a national food manufacturer—use odd-shaped cents-off coupons (e.g., poodle-shaped for dog food). The manufacturer enthusiastically endorsed the recommendation, but found retailers up in arms about the promotional scheme. If enacted, retailers would have found it extremely difficult to stack, sort, and store the coupons.[c]

[a] This example was drawn from Walter Gross, "Profitable Listening for Manufacturers and Dealers: How to Use a Communication System," in *Marketing Channels: A Systems Viewpoint*, William G. Moller, Jr. and David L. Wilemon (eds.), (Homewood, Ill.: Richard D. Irwin, 1971), p. 341.

[b] This example was drawn from ibid., p. 342.

[c] This example was drawn from Stephen Baker, "Wild Shapes, Sizes Are Today's Look in Coupons," *Advertising Age*, August 4, 1969, as paraphrased in *1969 Full Conference Proceedings*, published by the American Marketing Association (Chicago, 1970), Philip A. McDonald (ed.), "A Look at Channel Management" by Reavis Cox and Thomas F. Schutte, p. 102.

METHODS FOR OVERCOMING MARKETING CHANNEL COMMUNICATION NOISE[10]

Several methods are available for either reducing or preventing communication noise within marketing channels. Predominant are (1) instituting feedback; (2) using specialized languages; (3) altering technologies; (4) queuing and sequencing; (5) employing redundancy or repetition; and (6) predetermining information needs.

[10] This section draws heavily on Grabner and Rosenberg, "Communication in Distribution Channel Systems," pp. 242–247.

Instituting Feedback

One of the simplest methods for reducing communication noise within marketing channels is to develop feedback mechanisms to ensure that the intended message was what was received. Consider how the Norton Company—a large manufacturer of industrial grinding wheels and abrasives—uncovered valuable information about its promotional programs through feedback from its distributors.

Several years ago, the Norton Company used a series of promotional programs that involved prizes for its distributors' salesmen. These programs were quite successful and the sales goals were achieved. Feedback from the distributors, however, was surprising: they wanted Norton to limit programs of this type because their salespeople were spending too much time on the Norton line. They also resented the fact that *Norton* was directing their sales force rather than *they*.

Norton found, from its distributors' feedback, that (1) it could direct its distributors' sales forces more effectively than it realized and (2) distributor management resented too much of that type of interference from its suppliers.[11]

Several methods can be used for obtaining feedback from the channel. Reports from the sales force calling upon marketing channel institutions is the simplest way to ensure that communications within the channel are effective. Routine information gathered by the organization (e.g., sales volume, order size) can provide insight into the effectiveness of a firm's marketing program. Marketing research, using customer surveys, store audits, or dealer surveys, is a third method of instituting feedback within the channel. A fourth feedback technique that manufacturers sometimes use is dealer advisory councils made up of a small number of dealers (e.g., 12 to 25) who are either chosen by the manufacturer or elected by the other dealers. Council members relate dealer concerns about the channel relationship to the manufacturer. Attending conferences or conventions is the fifth way in which marketing institutions can obtain feedback about activities within the channel. Another method of gathering feedback is through personal visits of channel member management with personnel of other channel member organizations.

Because the Norton Company relies so heavily upon its distributors to reach its wide and varied markets, Norton deems it very important to listen to its distributors since they are close to the market. In addition to other feedback mechanisms, Norton's marketing management be-

---

[11] Adapted from Robert N. Hamilton, "Listening More Attentively to Your Distributors," remarks before a panel on "Are You Really Listening?" The 1981 Marketing Conference, The Conference Board, October 28–29, 1981, New York, pp. 4–5.

lieves that their personal visits to distributors uncover a wealth of information, including ideas for new products, physical distribution customer service problems, suggestions for promotional programs, and insight into the distributor's business.[12]

Specialized Languages

Specialized languages (e.g., technical jargon, governmental "bureaucratese") enable senders and receivers to exchange large amounts of information while using relatively few symbols. Stock, part, invoice, and account numbers are examples of such specialized languages.

A commonly used specialized language in the food marketing industry is the *universal product code* or UPC. The UPC symbol is a unique 12-digit identification number assigned to a particular product. It consists of both decimal characters and a bar code that can be read by an optical scanner (see Figure 7-3). Note from Figure 7-3 that the UPC does not contain price information. Those data are maintained in the store's computer system and accessed whenever the scanner reads the code at the checkout counter. Since each manufacturer and each product item has a unique code, the UPC represents a common language with which food manufacturers, brokers, wholesalers, and grocery retailers can more accurately communicate with one another. Coupled with electronic data networks (to be discussed later in this chapter), the UPC enables channel members to communicate not only more accurately but also more rapidly.

Guard bars to assure readability of UPC and symbols

0 = Grocery item
(3 = drug item
5 = coupon)

Manufacturer's 5-digit number coded into symbols

Product identification size, flavor, color, etc.

Figure 7-3 The universal product code and symbols.

Altering Technologies

By changing the form in which messages are sent and received, firms can reduce the amount of noise occurring in marketing channels. In general, using different technologies improves the quality and speed of communications. It also forces channel members to consider the sequencing and timing of their messages in

[12] Ibid., pp. 5–7.

developing communications systems. One company that has benefited enormously from altering its method of communicating with its customers is the McKesson Drug Company (see Exhibit 7-3).

EXHIBIT 7-3

**McKesson Drug Company: Benefits of
Altering Communication Technologies**

McKesson is a wholesaler of chemicals, pharmaceuticals, health and beauty aids, and sundries with sales of approximately $2 billion. Its major customers are retail drugstores, mass merchandisers, and hospitals.

One of McKesson's electronic communications systems, Economost, links it with its retail customers. Economost processes about 95 percent, in dollar value, of all orders McKesson receives. The Economost system uses an electronic device to enter bar code scan information from shelf labels for items that need to be restocked. The clerk in the retail store transmits an order automatically over telephone lines at a speed of 600 items per minute. The order is received in McKesson's Data Center, transmitted to the McKesson distribution center nearest the customer, filled, and delivered the following day.

By using such *inter*organizational communication systems coupled with advanced *intra*organizational communication technologies, McKesson has been able to improve its physical distribution activities. For example, the company realized an increase of more than 50 percent in stock turns as a result of its improved communication systems. It has reduced the number of its distribution centers (stocking points) from 92 in 1975 to 56 in 1983, without any deterioration in delivery performance. A cadre of 250 telephone sales clerks who took orders and typed up purchase forms eight years ago has been virtually eliminated. In addition, 13 buyers at a central location have replaced the 160 located at the 92 distribution centers in 1975. Further, McKesson Drug's order fulfillment ratio stands at a remarkable 96 percent; that is, only 4 percent of the dollar value of orders received is out of stock. Finally, because of its ability to provide overnight delivery and thereby lower its customers' inventory levels, McKesson Drug has been able to reduce customer payment terms from the conventional 30 days to 15. The result has been a marked reduction in the company's working capital requirements.

Not only has the speed with which McKesson communicates with its customers increased, but the accuracy of these communications has improved as well. Thus, altering communications technology has enhanced McKesson's ability to perform the physical distribution flow within the marketing channel for ethical pharmaceuticals.

Source: Adapted from E. Raymond Corey, ''The Role of Information and Communications Technology in Industrial Distribution,'' in Robert D. Buzzell (ed.), *Marketing in an Electronic Age* (Boston: Harvard Business School Press, 1985), pp. 29–51, 32, 36–37.

Queuing and Sequencing

As noted earlier, noise in marketing channel communications often occurs simply because receivers attempt to process too many messages at one time. This overload happens when messages arrive at the receiver in batches. One way of reducing communication noise is to place messages in a queue so that the receiver has adequate time to process the messages properly.

Channel communication noise also occurs when messages arrive out of sequence. Another aspect of queuing, then, is to ensure that the messages are placed in the proper order for processing. Exhibit 7-4 illustrates how essential queuing and sequencing are for General Mills to monitor the shipment of its products via railroad.

Redundancy

When senders repeat a message several times, possibly through different communications media, they are using redundancy to reduce the amount of omission and distortion in channel communications. This noise-reduction mechanism operates

---

EXHIBIT 7-4

Queuing and Sequencing in the Marketing Channel: An Illustration

General Mills has developed a "Shipment Status System" (called S-3 by the company) to ensure on-time delivery of its railroad shipments. In consultation with railroad management, General Mills established standard times for reaching various checkpoints along every route relative to the number of days or hours required for a shipment to go from a company plant or distribution center to its destination. Under S-3, General Mills' computer communicates with railroad computer terminals on a daily basis to determine if particular freight cars have arrived at designated checkpoints. If a car fails to arrive at a designated checkpoint within a one-day grace period, General Mills reports this fact on computer "exception" sheets to railroad personnel, who then track down the car and correct the situation. Because of the S-3 system, the company has achieved the highest rate of on-time delivery service (76 percent) in its history.

Without assigning specific times for the two computer systems to communicate, General Mills would waste much time awaiting access to the railroad's computers. In addition, the standard route times are critical for determining the sequence of messages to be sent from the railroad to General Mills. Without this sequence, General Mills would not be able to determine the status of its deliveries.

Source: Adapted from a personal correspondence from Professor James C. Johnson, St. Cloud State University.

---

in two ways. First, by using different communications media, the sender can overcome any biases the receiver might have toward any one of them. For example, an advertisement in a trade publication, widely viewed as disreputable, might be considered much differently than the same message communicated by a trusted salesperson. Second, repetition ensures that any bits and pieces of the message lost during the original transmission will be received. This is one reason for using saturation advertising campaigns.

Predetermining Information Needs

By now it should be apparent that meaningful communication about all of the marketing flows is essential if marketing channels are to perform successfully as interorganizational systems. An important step in developing a channel information or communication system is understanding *which* marketing institutions need *what* information so that they can effectively perform their marketing functions. Such an understanding improves the likelihood that only useful messages will be sent through the communication system, and that only those channel members who really need the information will receive it; others will be bypassed. This kind of advance planning reduces the amount of irrelevant information transmitted and received in the marketing channel.

Uncertainty absorption—the process of one channel member gathering, interpreting, and transmitting valuable information, such as market demand information, to other channel members[13]—is another technique that can be used to reduce the amount of information flowing through channel communication systems. This process eliminates unnecessary information, so that only the inferences drawn from the original data are transmitted.

Figure 7-4 outlines a step-by-step procedure for determining information needs before developing a marketing channel communication system.

Problems Arising from Attempting to Reduce Noise

Attempts to reduce marketing channel communication noise sometimes have unfortunate side effects. That is, the effort to get rid of some noise can result in introducing additional noise into the system.

For example, repetition and feedback increase the amount of information being transmitted and received; the result may be communication overload. In addition, feedback itself is subject to communication noise, thus compounding the problem. Moreover, fitting a message to specialized languages may cause a sender to omit valuable information about the context of the message. Uncertainty absorption suffers from a similar drawback: the perceptual biases of the channel member making inferences from the raw data can cause message distortions or omissions. Finally, altering technologies tends to increase the speed of communications, which reduces the amount of information "float" (i.e., the time between a message's transmission and its receipt). With this reduction in slack,

[13] See James G. March and Herbert A. Simon, *Organizations* (New York: John Wiley & Sons, 1958), p. 165.

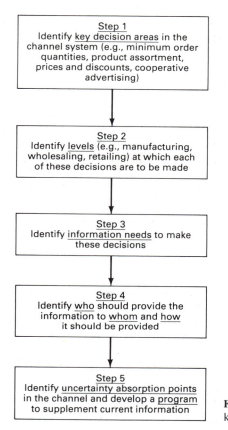

Step 1
Identify <u>key decision areas</u> in the channel system (e.g., minimum order quantities, product assortment, prices and discounts, cooperative advertising)

Step 2
Identify <u>levels</u> (e.g., manufacturing, wholesaling, retailing) at which each of these decisions are to be made

Step 3
Identify <u>information needs</u> to make these decisions

Step 4
Identify <u>who</u> should provide the information to <u>whom</u> and <u>how</u> it should be provided

Step 5
Identify <u>uncertainty absorption points</u> in the channel and develop a <u>program</u> to supplement current information

Figure 7-4 Steps in designing a marketing channel information system.

managers in marketing channels have less room for error; and in the case of some channels (such as McKesson Drug and its customers; see Exhibit 7-3), new communication technologies can reduce the amount of financial float as well.

Obviously, then, any attempt at reducing marketing channel communication noise should balance the costs of implementing the noise-reduction mechanism against the gains. In addition to the monetary costs and benefits, the net amount of noise reduction should be evaluated.

One of the new methods of communication within marketing channels is electronic data interchange systems. The following section discusses this emerging communication technique.

ELECTRONIC DATA INTERCHANGE SYSTEMS AND MARKETING CHANNELS

Electronic data interchange (EDI) systems permit marketing channel institutions to communicate rapidly and accurately with one another. In many instances, EDI networks enable channel members to reduce their operating costs—directly through more accurate communications, and indirectly through faster communications. An example of the former is the EDI program General Foods uses with its freight carriers, which has produced substantial direct savings in the clerical and paper costs required to process transactions.[14] An example of the latter is ethical drug wholesalers who, by ordering electronically, reduce their delivery lead times by as much as four days. This time savings translates into a potential annual cost savings of $1 million for some wholesalers.[15]

One strategic benefit that accrues to the earliest developers of EDI systems in an industry is a distinct competitive advantage. Not only do EDI systems make it more difficult for current competitors but they also provide entry barriers to potential new competitors. American Airlines' EDI system, for example, enabled it to strengthen its competitive edge (see Exhibit 7-5).

EXHIBIT 7-5
American Airlines' Sabre Reservations System

In the airline industry, travel agents act as intermediaries between air carriers and their markets—passengers. American Airlines has developed an EDI network, the Sabre reservation system, linking the carrier with its marketing channel intermediaries.

American provides its Sabre reservation system, which lists the flight schedules of every major airline in the world, to 48% of the approximately 24,000 automated travel agents in the U.S. They pay American $1.75 for every reservation made via Sabre for other carriers.[a] . . . Travel agents can [also] use it to get visas and book hotels. American gets a cut on all the services the agents sell.[b]

The number of travel agents connected to the Sabre system as well as the comprehensiveness of the information it handles has given American a distinct competitive advantage. In fact, Sabre has enabled the carrier to increase its share of the air travel market.

[a] Catherine L. Harris, "Information Power: How Companies Are Using New Technologies to Gain a Competitive Edge," *Business Week*, October 14, 1985, p. 109.
[b] ibid., p. 111.

Other actual and potential benefits of EDI to both manufacturers and distributors are:[16]

[14] Stix, "Ending the Supplier Paper Chase," p. 67.

[15] Ibid.

[16] Benefits quoted from Louis W. Stern and Patrick J. Kaufmann, "Electronic Data Interchange in Selected Consumer Goods Industries: An Interorganizational Perspective," in Robert D. Buzzell (ed.), *Marketing in an Electronic Age* (Boston: Harvard Business School Press, 1985), p. 56.

1. Reduced order lead time.
2. Higher service levels.
3. Fewer out-of-stock situations.
4. Improved communication about deals, promotions, price changes, and product availability.
5. Lower inventory costs.
6. Greater accuracy in ordering, shipping, and receiving.
7. A reduction in labor costs.

The disadvantages, actual and potential, of EDI systems to both manufacturers and distributors include the following:[17]

1. Inflexibility in changing orders since they are transmitted, processed, and shipped so rapidly.
2. Reduced slack time for performing logistics functions.
3. The need for two communications systems (paper and EDI) to accommodate customers and suppliers without EDI capabilities.
4. Concern about a lack of security and control over information transmitted, particularly when third-party computer service bureaus are used.
5. Difficulties in arriving at message and communications standards.
6. Extensive coordination between manufacturers' and distributors' computer systems, legal, accounting, financial, buying, sales, and logistics departments.
7. Unclear contract law and antitrust implications of EDI networks.

EDI systems can either be computer-to-computer links or terminal-to-computer links between channel members. Terminal-to-computer linkages connect one channel member's computer terminal with another's computer. The reservations systems operated by American, United, TWA, and Eastern airlines are examples of this type of EDI system; they tie travel agents' terminals to the carriers' computers. Computer-to-computer systems connect one channel member's computer with another's computer. These linkages are more problematic in that messages and communications protocols (i.e., computer languages) must be standardized so that the messages are received as intended. Several industries have taken the lead in standardizing computer-to-computer communications within their marketing channels.

"[T]he grocery industry, under the stewardship of the National-American Wholesale Grocers Association, Falls Church, VA, developed a system of sending electronic purchase orders and invoices to complement another industry foray into automation: the barcodes, or Uniform Product Codes, now routinely placed on food products for

[17] Gleaned from ibid., pp. 52–73.

inventory tracking.''[18] This system—Uniform Communication Standard (UCS)—standardizes both messages and communications protocols, enabling manufacturers, brokers, and wholesalers to communicate electronically with one another more readily. Given the 15 million purchase orders, bills of lading, invoices routed among 2,000 distributors, 5,000 manufacturers, and 2,000 brokers during 1984,[19] the potential savings from UCS is substantial.

"Ralphs Grocery, a 126-store Compton, CA–based chain and subsidiary of Federated Department Stores (Cincinnati), trades purchase orders and invoices using EDI for about 25 percent to 30 percent of the merchandise moving through its warehouse. Ralphs saves .1 percent of its annual sales, about $1.6 million annually, says Kenneth Hite, director of supermarket systems.''[20]

In addition to marketing channel institutions operating EDI systems, other organizations specialize in providing these communications services to channel members. The following section describes how these information intermediaries assist in the performance of the marketing flows.

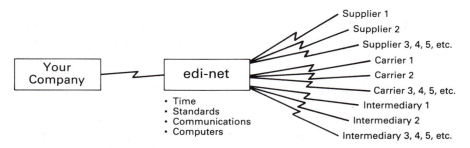

Figure 7-5 McDonnell Douglas electronic interchange systems. *Source*: McDonnell Douglas Electronic Interchange Systems Company.

Role of Third Parties in EDI

A third-party service bureau is an independent organization that acts as an intermediary by receiving information from and transmitting it to marketing channel members. "A service bureau may translate messages sent in the format of the sender into a format recognizable by the addressee as well as provide a communications interface between two or more companies.''[21] Figure 7-5 diagrams how a service bureau can fit into the ordering and market information flows of the marketing channel.

[18] Stix, "Ending the Supplier Paper Chase," p. 67.
[19] Ibid., p. 68.
[20] Ibid.
[21] Stern and Kaufmann, "Electronic Data Interchange," p. 61.

EDI-Net, a subsidiary of McDonnell Douglas Corporation, is a third-party service bureau. EDI-Net enables suppliers, intermediaries, or transportation carriers to overcome discrepancies they face in communicating electronically with one another. For example, EDI-Net (1) buffers time differences due to different domestic and international time zones and different operating schedules; (2) operates under five different communication standards, including UCS; (3) communicates with a variety of different communications protocol; and (4) can handle linkages with eight different computer systems.[22]

Thus, third-party service bureaus offer several advantages to marketing channel members. First, by acting as information intermediaries, they reduce the number of communication contacts among channel members. They also absorb the risk of operating under a variety of time discrepancies, communications standards, communications protocols, and computer systems. Service bureaus free manufacturers, wholesalers, retailers, and logistics companies from being concerned with these discrepancies. Finally, by specializing in the performance of one of the marketing flows, these information intermediaries may undertake these functions more economically than channel members could.

Third-party service bureaus also have some distinct disadvantages. For one thing, they may be more expensive than some proprietary or in-house communication systems. For another, they are an additional link in the communication network between suppliers and distributors, and it is a rule of thumb that the more links there are in a communication system, the more opportunities there are for noise to occur. A third disadvantage is the startup costs marketing channel members incur when they must learn another communications system in addition to their own proprietary system. Security is yet another key issue in using information intermediaries. Besides the danger that competitors will be able to access proprietary information, there is the possibility that "hackers" will break into computer systems via telephone lines and vandalize important data files. Finally, a service bureau may gain power within the marketing channel as it uses its expertise and knowledge to its advantage and to the detriment of other channel members.

Currently, most EDI systems serve as electronic mailboxes. As these systems become more sophisticated, however, channel members will be connected by direct access (i.e., they will be on-line) and processing will be done on a real-time basis rather than batch. One potential development is the merger of EDI systems with electronic funds transfer (EFT) systems. This would make possible the simultaneous transfer of paperwork and funds, which would greatly speed up the transaction process. The information communicated through EDI systems eventually will be used in marketing research. The sizes of orders and their frequency, products purchased and when, deals taken, and so forth can be

[22] Based upon promotional materials of McDonnell Douglas Electronic Data Interchange Systems Company.

analyzed by customer to enable channel members to better serve their markets. Finally, the promotion function will be partially transferred to EDI systems by shifting catalogs from paper to electronic media.[23]

SUMMARY

If the diverse activities of marketing channel members are to be coordinated successfully, communication among marketing institutions must be effective. To ensure this, channel members must understand the basic elements of the communication process within marketing channels.

One critical aspect of this process is eliminating noise that interferes with the meaning of the message being communicated. The two major types of noise are omission and distortion. Omission occurs when the complete message is either ignored or not received; distortion occurs when the meaning somehow changes between the sending of the message and its reception.

Communication noise in marketing channels is caused by several factors. Communication overload, secrecy, poor timing, and perceptual differences among channel members are the chief reasons omission and distortion occur within marketing channels.

By instituting feedback, adopting specialized languages, altering the communication technologies, queuing and sequencing messages, repeating messages, and predetermining information needs, communication noise can be reduced. These noise-reduction methods must be carefully implemented, however, since a possible side effect is the introduction of even more noise into the communication system.

An emerging method of communication within marketing channels is electronic data interchange (EDI). EDI systems enable channel members to communicate much more rapidly and accurately with one another. Specialized intermediaries (third-party service bureaus) have emerged to mediate communications among marketing channel members more economically.

DISCUSSION QUESTIONS

1. Using the communication process shown in Figure 7-1, describe the ordering and payment flows for each of the following marketing channel situations.
   a. New cars   d. Toys and games
   b. Sporting goods   e. Office supplies
   c. Lubricating oils   f. Earth-moving equipment
2. a. What type of communication noise is occurring between Cookie and the food supply unit? Explain.
   b. What are the likely causes or sources of noise in this situation? Explain.
   c. Discuss what might be done to eliminate, or at least reduce, the amount of noise in the Cookie–food supply distribution channel. The following questions pertain to Camp Swampy's food supply channels, as depicted in the Beetle Bailey cartoon on the next page.

[23] Stern and Kaufmann, "Electronic Data, Interchange," pp. 67–69; and Stix, "Ending the Supplier Paper Chase," p. 72.

BEETLE BAILEY

by Mort Walker

Source: Reprinted by permission of King Features Syndicate.

3. The chapter explained that EDI systems offer great potential for improving communications within marketing channels. Discuss the implications of such systems for personal selling. How are EDI systems likely to affect the ways marketing institutions buy goods and services? Explain.

4. Visit a drugstore and find out from the store manager (or a department manager) how the store communicates orders to its major supplier. Ask about any feedback mechanisms that exist. Then write a short report on your findings, making sure to integrate what the store does with the concepts discussed in the chapter.

5. Electronic Data Interchange (EDI) systems are used in several industries, among them the automotive supply, ethical drug, grocery, freight, hardware and housewares, and service merchandising industries. Visit a wholesaler, supplier, or transportation carrier in one of the industries that uses an EDI system and find out how the system works, which marketing functions are coordinated through it, and what future plans exist for it. Then write a short report on your findings, making sure to integrate what the EDI system does with the concepts discussed in the chapter. In the report, be sure to diagram the marketing flows through the channel, including third-party service bureaus if they are used.

Universal Motors Parts Division

Six months ago, William Frank, general manager of the parts division of Universal Motors Corporation began to feel uneasy about certain trends that had been developing in the automotive parts aftermarket. Products in this market fall into two major categories, service parts and accessories. Service parts are those used in repair and replacement, including mechanical, body/frame, and chassis components. Accessories, either appearance or functional items used to improve performance or dress up the car, include fog lights, outside rearview mirrors, or interior floor mats.

Over the past ten years, total aftermarket parts sales in the United States had stabilized in the $70 billion to $80 billion range after growing steadily along with new car sales since World War II. In the last two years, the total number of outlets selling aftermarket parts had declined dramatically, and it was predicted by industry analysts that in five years there would be 20 percent fewer outlets than there are today. Last year the average U.S. car owner spent $405 per vehicle on tires, batteries, accessories, and service parts. In the last three years, service parts sales had increased from $19 billion to $23 billion nationwide.

Like many firms, Universal Motors had also seen its sales patterns shift to follow population trends. Sales in the South and West were expanding at a faster rate than in the North and East.

The major types of outlets for aftermarket parts are service stations, garages, new vehicle dealers, specialized repair shops (for example, muffler shops), mass merchandisers, and jobbers. Exhibit 1 shows how market shares of these types of outlets have changed over the last five years.

Fifty-three years ago, the Parts Division of Universal Motors was established by consolidating the aftermarket service parts warehousing and distribution activities of three marketing divisions. Twelve years ago, the Parts Division of Universal Motors Corporation became a separate operating division with aftermarket parts responsibility for all six of the North American marketing divisions. This had been done to provide one centralized service parts organization which was devoted entirely to the nationwide distribution of replacement parts to UM dealers. Sales and marketing activities continued to be performed by the marketing divisions, whereas the Parts Division concentrated on improving service, warehousing, and distribution.

EXHIBIT 1
Percentage Market Shares by Type of Retail Outlet

Number of Years Ago	Type of Outlet						
	Service Stations	Garages	New Car Dealers	Specialized Repair Shops	Mass Merchandisers	Jobbers	Total
5	25	12	30	18	10	5	100
4	24	11	31	17	11	6	100
3	23	10	30	20	14	5	100
2	18	11	29	24	13	5	100
1	21	9	27	22	17	4	100

Then, six years ago, sales and marketing functions were also assigned to the Parts Division, thus giving it total responsibility for marketing and distribution of parts to UM dealers. This move was soon followed by incorporation of all truck division service parts into the Parts Division system, and finally, two years ago operations were expanded from North American to include all aftermarket parts marketing and distribution activities to UM dealers worldwide. This remains its current status today.

Universal Motors Parts Division (UMPD) and Allied Division are UM's marketing and distribution arms that service the automotive aftermarket. UMPD distributes only to UM dealers, whereas Allied serves independent distributors. Each division maintains its own sales force and network of distribution centers. Many of the parts inventoried are identical; yet, for sales and merchandising reasons, the two divisions operate independently of each other. Also, many of the accessory items sold by both UMPD and Allied are contract manufactured for UM by independent manufacturers.

In an indirect way UMPD and Allied actually compete because independent jobbers are free to sell to UM dealers, as is shown in Figure 7-6.

William Frank realized that the sales trends he had observed, if continued, would call for adjustments in the distribution system. He called in his director of operations, Dave Hert.

"Dave, I want to reevaluate our entire operational network. This division needs to operate even better and more efficiently than it has in the past. I know there is no fat to cut, but we have to trim someplace, and I'm depending on you to come up with some answers. Let's get together in 30 days and you show me what you've got."

Hert knew from past experience that such requests from the boss were not to be taken lightly and that completing an entire operational review in 30 days would be no easy task. He worked late that night and the next two deciding what information would be required. On the fourth day after his meeting with Frank, he drafted a memo to each of his 23 regional distribution center managers, requesting a selected audit of the previous 12 months' operations.

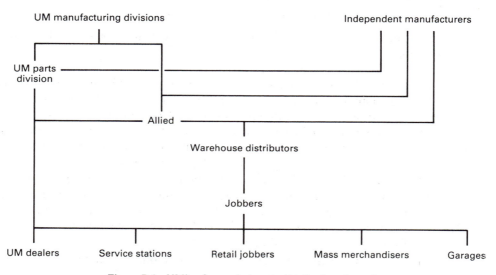

Figure 7-6 UM's aftermarket parts distribution channels.

EXHIBIT 2

Distribution Center Operating Review
[for average 30-day period]

	Midwest		South	
	Toledo	Indianapolis	Atlanta	Memphis
Inbound Freight				
LTL				
Volume (tons)	125	260	152	171
Distance (miles)	77	86	380	275
Cost (thousands)	157.85	366.70	901.05	733.59
TL				
Volume	195	196	228	114
Distance	91	88	410	320
Cost	230.68	224.22	1,112.41	434.11
Inventory Carrying				
High turnover				
Amount (tons)	174	319	180	130
Cost (thousands)	22.45	37.64	19.44	11.96
Low turnover				
Amount	146	137	200	155
Cost	24.82	25.35	26.80	20.30
Outbound Freight				
LTL				
Volume	170	237	304	200
Distance	55	68	40	75
Cost	153.34	264.30	189.70	234.00
TL				
Volume	150	219	76	85
Distance	31	42	62	90
Cost	20.15	119.57	56.07	91.04

Specifically, he wanted monthly average figures in each of the following categories.

1. Inbound freight volume in tons, broken down by shipment size. That is, what amount was received in less than truckload (LTL) shipments and what amount was received in full truckload (TL) quantities. For both the LTL and TL inbound freight he wanted to know average distance traveled and total freight charges billed. All of this information could be obtained directly from trucking company invoices and internal records.

2. Inventory handled in tons, again in two categories, high-versus low-turnover items. High-turnover items include routine service parts such as spark plugs, oil filters, and shock absorbers. Low-turnover parts include sheet metal and frame parts such as door panels and bumpers. Total inventory carrying costs for each category would also be needed.

3. Outbound freight volumes in tons, reported in the same manner as inbound freight.

EXHIBIT 3
Inventory Carrying Cost Factors

	Midwest		South	
	Toledo	Indianapolis	Atlanta	Memphis
Number of Employees	20	26	17	14
Total Average Monthly Wage (thousands)	30.60	39.78	18.79	15.47
Cubic Feet of Storage Space (thousands)	200	275	220	140
Utilization (%)	78	84	87	88
Building Age (years)	12	19	14	6

Hert asked that the information be in his hands in two weeks. This was pressing things, but he wanted the remaining two weeks to absorb the information and do follow-up if needed.

After one week reports from the field began to come in. Soon 20 of the 23 distribution center managers' figures were in hand. Two had not been received because key people were on vacation, and in one location a newly installed minicomputer was experiencing start-up problems. Nevertheless, Hert was satisfied that he would be able to present an accurate picture of the current state of affairs when he met with Frank. Deciding to group the distribution center data by sales region, he displayed the highest- and lowest-cost operation in each region. The data for two of these regions appear in Exhibit 2.

Looking at these figures, it was obvious to Hert which operations were most and least costly; yet he still was unsure that the figures clearly pointed to any particular course of action. To get a clearer picture, Hert went back to the original reports and zeroed in on the sources of the inventory carrying costs. He believed these were the most directly controllable and therefore deserved the greatest attention. For each distribution center, he reviewed the figures on number of employees, total monthly wages, number of cubic feet of storage space in the building, percentage of space utilized, and building age. These figures for the Toledo, Indianapolis, Atlanta, and Memphis distribution centers are shown in Exhibit 3.

In the meeting, Frank mentioned that the sales figures continued to be unencouraging and that something would have to be done to reduce operational costs fairly quickly. Hert had been in the industry many years and he knew that it was highly cyclical. Sales often expanded dramatically during the early stages of a business cycle upturn, and he did not want to jeopardize the overall ability of the distribution network to respond. The ability to serve customers reliably and on time was still most important in the long run.

After an hour and a half of going over the figures in some detail, Frank turned to Hert and said, "What do you think we should do?"

Advise Universal Motors Parts Division.

Scioto Company

The Scioto Company manufactures and distributes a rather innovative product called Coloring Rolls. These coloring books in scroll form are 30 feet long when unrolled and are printed the full length without repetition of pictures by means of the firm's unique presses. Coloring Rolls once enjoyed annual sales in excess of 1 million units. In 1972, however, annual sales were only about 200,000 rolls. Management is obviously interested in developing marketing strategy that will return this product's sales to the successful level it once held.

COMPANY BACKGROUND

The Scioto Company was founded in 1969 through the purchase of the assets of a printing company. The firm manufactures educational devices, such as rapid reading pacers and "teaching machines," and the home game derived from the television show "Concentration." All of these items, however, are marketed by their own firms, and Scioto merely bids on the contracts to produce them. The company is, therefore, quite anxious to increase the sale of its own product, Coloring Rolls, in order to reduce its dependence upon contractual and bid items. Total sales for the company in 1972 amounted to about $250,000, with Coloring Rolls accounting for approximately 20 percent of the total.

PRODUCT INFORMATION

Coloring Rolls are printed on specially built rotary presses that produce large intermediate rolls 36 inches in diameter. These are then placed on a rewind machine that wraps the Coloring Rolls on a spiral-wound paper core, resulting in a finished roll $10\frac{1}{2}$ inches wide and 30 feet long. The product is then placed by hand into a polyethylene printed bag and packed in cartons for distribution.

Rolls are printed on one side only, and each tells a complete story with no repetitive pictures. The product allows more than one child to color simultaneously on the same roll. The finished product can be displayed as a wall mural in total or in part. A brief description of the nine available rolls is given in Exhibit 1. "Noah's Ark" and "Circus" are the best sellers by a wide margin.

CHANNELS OF DISTRIBUTION

Past Methods of Distribution

Coloring Rolls were first marketed by the printing company by means of toy brokers. These brokers, who served as manufacturers' representatives, received

EXHIBIT 1
Brief Story Lines for the Product Offering

- Circus Parade—This story is geared toward the younger children (of Scioto's 4-to-9 market). There are over 200 pictures of circus clowns and animals to color. There is a great deal of free white space on which the child can create.
- Adventures in Space—This Roll puts the child in the driver's seat of his own space capsule. Each picture is in an individual frame with a sentence describing the scene.
- Daniel Boone—This Roll tells the story of Daniel Boone from boyhood to manhood. Each picture is in a separately drawn frame with a sentence describing the picture.
- Our American Heritage—This Roll gives a brief survey of American history from Plymouth Rock to the Sea of Tranquility. Each picture is in a separate frame and has an accompanying explanation.
- Favorite Bible Stories—This includes pictures of both the Old and New Testaments. Each picture is in a separate frame with a sentence describing the scene. There is an intermittent "connect-the-dots" type picture.
- Adventures of Hattie the Hare—This Roll is geared toward the younger child. It is a continuous story with occasional frame break. There are no words.
- Around the World with Loco—This is a story of a trip around the world with Loco, the burro. The pictures and story that go with it are of educational value in that they describe key points of interest like the Taj Mahal in India.
- Headin' West—This is a continuous picture about the pony express and the problems arising in delivering the mail. There are no words.
- Noah's Ark—This depicts the story of Noah in separate picture frames with words describing each scene.

a 5 percent commission of sales for their services. Their principal customers were the large chains of variety stores, such as G. C. Murphy, Woolworth, and Kress. Sales were more than a million units per year for the first two years.

Several of the chains carried Coloring Rolls with varying degrees of success. The toy jobbers had little difficulty selling the Coloring Rolls to the purchasing agent of the chain store, but reorders were spotty. Several stores would report a big sale, whereas the majority would never reorder.

The toy broker for the printing company then conducted a survey of some of the stores that were selling the product successfully and compared them to a few that were not. The survey showed that sales were excellent in stores that still had sales clerks who could (or would) explain the product, but the majority of the stores were self-service and the Coloring Rolls just sat in the bins and failed to attract customers' attention, or motivate them to buy. It was concluded that the product was too unusual for the average customer to recognize, and since all the stores were fast converting to self-service, no further attempt was made to promote the product through the toy jobbers.

A few faithful customers continued to buy regular quantities of the product, and two of these, Walter Drake & Son of Colorado and David C. Cook, religious publisher of Chicago, Illinois, offered Coloring Rolls for sale in their mail-order catalogs. During this time period sales declined to around 40,000 units per year.

Present Method of Distribution

When Scioto assumed manufacture and distribution of the Coloring Rolls, the new company renewed promotional efforts. Noting that the items seemed to sell in catalogs, it made a mailing to all known catalog houses. The response was quite favorable, and a number—notably Breck's, Sunset House, and Spencer Gifts— added the Coloring Rolls to their catalog line. A total of seven mail-order catalogs, with a combined circulation of over 10 million, offered Coloring Rolls.

Each catalog features a photograph or drawing of the product and a short paragraph of copy. When contracts are signed with the catalog houses, Scioto usually pays an "advertising allowance" of $25 to $50 to cover the cost of photographing the item and including it in the catalog.

The price each catalog house charges depends upon its estimate of the mailing cost for the item, but in every case the price is considerably above the original variety store price. Customers of mail-order houses apparently expect to pay more because of the postage. Sales from these sources amounted to about 140,000 in 1972. The remaining sales were generated by direct orders from retail stores and some unsolicited individual requests from consumers who had evidently previously purchased from catalog houses.

PRICING INFORMATION

At an annual volume of 200,000 units, the basic cost of producing a Coloring Roll is around 18.6 cents, about half of which represents allocation of fixed manufacturing costs. An additional average of 2.0 cents per roll is required if Scioto pays shipping expenses.

In reviewing its pricing and distribution strategy, management gathered the following information on the toy industry:

All industries have trade practices that are difficult for the small firm to ignore, and the toy industry is no exception. In determining the price for Coloring Rolls, one of the most important of these practices is the policy of pricing all items in multiples ending in the digit nine (9). For example, a product may be priced at 39 cents or 49 cents for retail sale, but never at, say, 43 cents. Therefore, if a product cannot be made to sell (with all discounts) for 39 cents, it jumps to 49 cents.

The most common discount in the trade is 50 percent off list price. If the suggested price is 49 cents, the retailer pays the manufacturer 24½ cents and earns 24½ cents upon selling the product. If a wholesaler is used he receives approximately 30 percent of the manufacturer's selling price; therefore, it pays the manufacturer to circumvent the wholesaler if possible and go directly to the retailer.

Also of vital importance is the matter of freight allowances which has come to the front in recent years due to the rapidly rising cost of postage and freight rates. Most large buyers expect, even demand, some consideration on freight, and this may take the form of straight cash allowances, usually 5 percent, or a policy of allowing the customer to deduct the freight from the invoice when he pays. Depending upon the mode and distance shipped, this can amount to as much as 15 percent of the selling price.

Last is the cash discount policy that the firm employs. If it is short of cash, a 2 percent discount is usually offered, but with increasing interest rates, many firms have discontinued cash discount policies. Toy purchasers, on the other hand, often insist upon a trade practice known as "datings" where, in return for an early order in slow months, they will not pay for the goods until a later predetermined date.

FOCAL TOPICS

1. What channels of distribution would offer the greatest opportunities for the marketing of Coloring Rolls?
2. What type of a pricing strategy should the firm adopt for Coloring Rolls?
3. Are there other segments or marketing opportunities open to this product? How can they best be served?
4. Do you feel that the firm should initiate any marketing research at this time? What type and scope of research should be involved if any is undertaken?

Source: W. Wayne Talarzyk, *Contemporary Cases in Marketing*, 2nd ed. (Hinsdale, Ill.: The Dryden Press, 1979), pp. 23–28.

Kelsey Manufacturing Company: Getting Middlemen to Promote the Manufacturer's Products

The Kelsey Manufacturing Company is one of the largest manufacturers of repair materials for automobile tires and tubes in the United States. One of the major objectives set by management was for the company to show a continuous growth in sales and profits at a rate of 10 percent a year. In view of this goal, management was greatly concerned by the fact that Kelsey's annual sales volume had remained at about the same level for eight years. Some executives labeled the sales volume as "stable," while others referred to it as "stagnant." Whatever description was given to this sales situation, management believes it would be improved considerably if the company's wholesalers and retailers could be persuaded to promote Kelsey's products more aggressively. Consequently, management was trying to figure out how to "spread the word"—i.e., disseminate its product and promotional messages—through the company's rather lengthy channels-of-distribution system, so that the ultimate customer—the retail service station operator—effectively received these messages.

The Kelsey Company was founded in the early 1920s as a small, family-owned company to manufacture cold patches for repairing inner tubes. Within a few years hot-patch material was introduced, marking the beginning of a period of great growth. Tire repair was a service in much demand during the Depression years and World War II. During that war the government took about 90 percent of the production. In 1972 the Kelsey Company was acquired by a large, diversified chemical corporation and was operated as a division of one of that corporation's subsidiary firms.

One key official said, "Once we were just a nice-size family. Now we're really in the mainstream of corporate life. We used to be able to communicate with each other and with our customers on an informal party-line basis. Now we have to pay close attention to the proper channels. As the prison warden said in the movie *Cool Hand Luke*, 'What we've got here is a problem in communication!'"

Kelsey manufactured tire and tube repair materials under three brand names: Lion, which accounted for 54 percent of the sales; Topps, 10 percent of sales; and Air Float, 36 percent. Under the Lion brand the company produced the following products: Chembond patches (a chemical application), rubber cement, liquid buffer and cleaner, Perma Strip patches (outside tire repair), hot vulcanizing patches, clamps, repair gum, cold patches, unitized patches, boot cement, tubeless sealant, tire talc, and rattle stops. In addition, a number of other items were purchased for resale under the Lion name. As a result of the merger with the chemical corporation, Kelsey Manufacturing Company added a new product line consisting of some 280 items in the category of tire valves and accessories.

As the number of products increased, the problem of communicating with the customers was intensified. The sales manager, Ralph Knott, summed up the problem by saying, "In the old days our sales representatives could carry the entire line in a small briefcase. Now, we'd be hard pressed to get everything in a station wagon. We just aren't able to let the customers know what we really can do for them."

Top executives in the Kelsey Company believed that the firm held about 15 percent of the total tire and tube repair market. The major competitors were H. B. Egan Company, Bowes Seal Fast Company, Monkey Grip Sales Company, Remaco, Inc., and Kex Products Company. Kelsey, however, marketed the most complete line of products in their field.

Kelsey's annual net sales for the years 1965–1973 were as follows:

1965	$4,589,000
1966	4,136,000
1967	4,028,000
1968	4,284,000
1969	4,208,000
1970	4,058,000
1971	4,151,000
1972	4,205,000
1973	3,998,000

During the above period there were no significant fluctuations in the company's gross margin (30 to 40 percent of sales) or the net profit before taxes (10 percent of sales). While most of Kelsey's sales were to wholesalers who in turn sold to retail service stations, the company also sold in the export market and under private brands to major oil companies and to chain stores such as Western Auto, Goodrich Tire stores, and Sears.

In recent years there was an increasing demand for the chemical (Chembond) patch, at the expense of hot patches. This change in product popularity had enabled competition to make some inroads in the market, since the Kelsey company did not have the advantages productionwise in chemical patches that it had in hot patches.

Looking to the future, Kelsey's management recognized that it faced two problems, which were created by technological improvements in other areas: (1) tires are continually being improved, mainly through creation of better rubber and fabric, and (2) the highway system is continually being upgraded. These factors tend to produce less tire trouble per mile traveled with less use of repair materials per mile traveled.

However, these points may be offset by the increase in the number of vehicles on the road and the number of miles traveled per vehicle. Also, the two-ply tire, which is standard on most new cars, is more susceptible to punctures than is the four-ply tire. Still another positive factor in this repair-products industry is the large increase in the number of motorbikes, pneumatic industrial tires, and other inflatable rubber and/or plastic items.

The Kelsey Company, like most of its competitors in the industry, distributed its products through manufacturers' representatives (agents) who sold to automotive-parts warehouse distributors. These distributors sold to smaller automotive-parts jobbers who, in turn, sold to service stations. In a sense, the service station sells the product to the individual automobile owner, but by the very nature of the tire repair business, the ultimate consumer seldom knows what kind of products have been used to repair his or her tire or tube.

Because of this lengthy channel of distribution, the Kelsey Company was having trouble getting its product story down to the service station. Obviously, no *real* sale occurred until the service station bought the product. Unless the retailers bought, the jobbers and warehouse distributors, in turn, would not reorder.

In the past, most of Kelsey's manufacturers' agents had handled Kelsey products exclusively. With the increasing difficulty in realizing growth in sales, however, all the representatives now handled other automotive lines, thus dividing their loyalty and decreasing the time available to communicate to the customer about the Kelsey products. Part of the reasoning behind the addition of the new product line of tire valves and accessories was the hope of rebuilding the agents' loyalty to Kelsey.

As Charles Bronson, the Kelsey vice-president, said: "Our real problem right now is getting our story told. We've got to have better contacts with the customers. In the past our reps had to tell the story effectively or they didn't eat. Now, they're handling so many other customers that our story gets lost in the shuffle. As we have traveled across the country and talked with service station operators, we find that they have very little knowledge about the benefits or use of our tire repair materials."

On the other hand, Ray Levine, the manufacturers' representative covering Texas, Oklahoma, and Louisiana, saw the problem this way: "The product line is now so large that you can't possibly do justice to the Kelsey products. I'd have to spend a week with each customer to tell him what the company wants told about each product. There just isn't enough time or money to do what they want."

DISCUSSION QUESTION

1. What should the Kelsey Company do to get its middlemen to promote the company's products more informatively and aggressively?

   Source: Bert Rosenbloom, *Marketing Channels: A Management View*, 3rd ed. (Chicago: The Dryden Press, 1987), pp. 506–508.

Purex Industries, Inc.

Purex is a manufacturer and marketer of industrial and consumer products, primarily price-promoted items in both the branded and nonbranded categories. The company is the fourth-largest maker of household cleaning products and the largest producer and distributor of private-label household cleaning products. Purex claims a 25 percent share of the home liquid-bleach market, second only to Clorox; and it claims a substantial share of the clothes-dryer fabric-softener market, second only to Procter & Gamble.

The following internal and external developments have recently brought about a new competitive situation that may call for changes in Purex's consumer products' marketing efforts, especially those relating to the household cleaning products:

1. Private label and generic products now represent a significant and growing share of industry sales, particularly in the paper goods and household cleaning categories. Consumers are showing greater acceptance as a result of economic conditions and other influences, but acceptance varies by product, retail outlet, and area.

2. Retailers, eager to attract price-conscious consumers and improve their profits, are moving toward nonbranded products and "no-frill" retailing in conventional supermarkets. New types of "no-frill" retail food stores, such as Aldi, A&P's Plus, and Jewel's T Box, as well as warehouse stores, placing great emphasis on value, are becoming more numerous. Some outlets have reduced the number of categories of goods stocked, while others carry only the two or three leading brands in each category.

3. Nationally advertised brand manufacturers, suffering from the inroads made by generics and private labels, are bringing out more price-oriented brands. Scott Paper Company, the leading producer of toilet paper, has products at both ends of the price spectrum. Procter & Gamble has launched an economy-priced unadvertised line of paper products under the name Summit. P&G has also introduced an economy-priced Ivory shampoo, but in its test markets did not stress price as a selling point. It is not clear how much advertising support is planned.

4. Purex itself has taken several steps toward adjusting to changing conditions:

    a. Purchased the Decatur, Illinois–based A. E. Staley Company's assets and business in household products and retail food products, which gave Purex additional laundry products, fabric softeners, corn starch and syrup products, and four manufacturing facilities in the United States.

    b. Purchased the New York–based Witco Chemical Company's two strategically located low-cost spray-drying detergent manufacturing plants, thus increasing Purex's capacity to five such units.

    c. Sold some of its losing or marginal industrial and agricultural businesses and shifted, on a royalty basis, the manufacture and sale of its drugstore products to Jeffrey Martin Inc., an international marketing firm, which scored a great success with its Porcelana skin spot fade cream. The brands shifted include Ayds appetite suppressant products, Doan's pills, and Cuticura medicated skin-care products. These actions have increased Purex's available cash, allowing reallocation of assets.

    d. Realigned its operations to give separate worldwide organizations to consumer and industrial products and services.

Historically, Purex's first product was household liquid bleach, and its principal competition was, and is, Clorox. Each company sought to differentiate in the minds of consumers its brand of this commodity-type product through advertising, packaging, and product labels. The product itself was and is chemically the same. Over the years Purex acquired a number of well-known brand products, sometimes after they had passed their peak. Among them were Old Dutch Scouring Cleanser, Bo-Peep Ammonia, LaFrance Bluing, Cameo Copper

Cleanser, Fels Naptha Laundry Bar Soap, Sweetheart soap products, Dobie Cleaning Pads, Brillo Soap Pads, Ellio's Pizza, Pope brand tomatoes, and other Italian products. The company also developed products to give it a full line of household cleaning items.

Purex's management has attributed much of the company's success with its branded products to (1) its "key account" selling plan aimed at retailers and (2) its "price/value" concept aimed at consumers and retailers.

The "key account" concept involves working effectively with a limited number of large retail chains, which account for a disproportionately large share of Purex's consumer product sales. By working closely with these "key accounts," learning their needs, coordinating activities, and fulfilling these needs, the company's key account representatives have been highly successful with the retailers. This successful Purex approach—i.e., cultivating mutually beneficial relationships with selected large retailers—has become more widely accepted by competitors, thereby decreasing one of Purex's earlier advantages.

The Purex "price/value" marketing concept elements are: competitive quality at lower prices, relatively light advertising support, and heavy retailer incentives. Purex has claimed that the retailers' gross profit margin on Purex products is significantly higher than on competitors'. The company's "Symbol of Value" logo, consisting of a circle around an outstretched hand holding a bar of Purex soap above the words "Symbol of Value," appears in almost all advertisements and on product packages. Such value is somewhat difficult to demonstrate. Procter & Gamble, on the other hand, has claimed that its products provide superior product performance that can be perceived by consumers. This can be demonstrated.

Purex sold price-promoted products under the "price/value" concept through the 1960s, but in the 1970s it pushed the concept more aggressively by adjusting the price downward even more sharply. Purex-branded bleaches and detergents were priced at 30 percent below top-selling brands. Trade observers now believe that competition will become even more severe for Purex if generics become more accepted and economy-priced branded products are proliferated by major premium-branded-goods manufacturers. The success of the "price/value" concept depends upon whether consumers believe they are getting a good value at a low price.

Household liquid bleach, a commodity-type product, is a case in point. The active ingredient in all liquid bleaches sold for household use in the United States is sodium hypochlorite in the amount of 5.25 percent. The remaining 94.75 percent is water. Yet the following prices for various branded and nonbranded bleaches have been observed in a large chain supermarket:

	National	Regional	Private Label	Generic
1 qt.	$ .52			
2 qts.	.88		$ .59	
4 qts.	1.05	$ .79	.79	$ .61
6 qts.	1.57			

Price differences of this type exist in most outlets where liquid bleach is sold even though all the bottles contain essentially the same bleach solution. Whether these price differences continue will depend on whether sellers are able to make meaningful differentiations in the minds of consumers. At one time Purex tried to differentiate its product by increasing the active ingredient to 5.75 percent, thus allowing it to claim a stronger, more effective product. Later the 5.25 percent formulation was restored and has continued. Clorox has developed a convenient nondrip bottle.

It is estimated that nonbranded products, including the private label and generics, now account for almost 35 percent of Purex's household cleaning product sales. Some observers consider this a potential problem because this price-sensitive business comes in large orders with no consumer loyalty. Purex and other nonbranded product suppliers recognize the strong bargaining power of large retail chain buyers, especially when a supplier becomes overly dependent on one or a few buyers.

For many years Purex has enjoyed the advantage of its "value/price" marketing concept. In view of the new competitive situation, the question is whether the concept and marketing plans based on it will be sufficient for Purex to maintain its reasonably good growth and earnings record.

What recommendations would you make to the Purex management?

Source: Philip Kotler, *Principles of Marketing*, 2nd ed. (Englewood Cliffs, N.J.: Prentice-Hall, 1983), pp. 505–507.

Part III ORGANIZING MARKETING CHANNEL ACTIVITIES

8

Marketing Channel Structure and Design

LEARNING OBJECTIVES

Upon completing this chapter, you will be able to:

- *Describe how the target market's needs and wants for marketing channel services are the linchpin of marketing channel structure and design.*
- *Define four key marketing channel services—locational convenience, lot size, waiting time, and product variety.*
- *Explain how an organization's goals are important in shaping its marketing channel structure.*
- *Outline the factors that influence how intensive the channel's market coverage is.*
- *Discuss how consumer patronage behavior determines the extent of market coverage.*
- *Describe why channel coverage and channel ownership are important elements of marketing channel strategy.*

- *Use the theories of postponement-speculation and functional spin-off and the checklist method to explain and construct different marketing channel structures.*

- *Explain the major constraints in developing marketing channel structure.*

- *Determine from a set of alternatives the best channel structure, using two different evaluative process models.*

- *Outline the key factors used in selecting individual organizations to be members of marketing channels.*

Changes in Marketing Channel Structure in the Apparel Industry

Esprit de Corp, a San Francisco–based sportswear manufacturer, has traditionally marketed their ". . . breezy, colorful fashions . . ."[a] through department stores.

Esprit, however, is

. . . among the growing number of clothing manufacturers that are opening retail outlets to deliver their sales pitch directly to consumers. Taking a cue from fashion designers such as Yves Saint Laurent and Giorgio Armani, these makers of less pricy garments think they can build sales—both in their own shops and in department stores. 'We want to show how our goods can be displayed and prove we can move more fashion merchandise than the chains believe we can,' says Roger Kase, president of Esprit's retail division.[b]

These manufacturers desire to take greater control over the marketing of their products because of their dissatisfaction with how department stores have handled their lines.

Apparel makers . . . complain that department stores have cut back on sales help in an effort to boost margins. 'It's hard to do well in a store where there is no sales staff and little money for visual presentation,' says an executive of one leading designer's company. To get the attention of the chains and to build the right image with consumers, 'we have to become a self-promoting resource,' one manufacturer says. That often means opening new stores.[c]

A variety of challenges face these manufacturers as they open their new stores. "One problem for would-be retailers is finding a broad enough line of merchandise to fill a store [with customers]."[d] Another difficulty is that retailing is a totally different industry from manufacturing. It requires different management skills as well as additional financial resources to become established. "Perhaps the biggest danger in the move into retailing

---

[a] "Clothing Makers Go Straight to the Consumer," *Business Week*, (April 29, 1985), p. 114.

[b] ibid.

[c] ibid.

[d] ibid., p. 115.

is that manufacturers risk alienating their traditional outlet—the department store."[e]

Part III of this text examines how marketing channels are organized. Channel organization comprises two basic decisions.

The first is choosing the *channel structure or design.* Marketing channel structure refers to "the specific type, number, and [organization] of institutions that make up the channel."[1] When firms such as Esprit de Corp choose outlets to carry their merchandise, they are actually making decisions about marketing channel structure and design. Arriving at these decisions requires asking several questions about the distribution element of the marketing mix: What kinds of channel services do consumers need and desire in purchasing these products? What kinds of institutions should be involved in the marketing of these products? How many of any one type of institution should be used? What kinds of marketing functions will these institutions perform? What specific organizations should be included in the marketing channel? Understanding how to address these and similar issues is the subject of this chapter.

The second basic decision concerning channel organization is determining *administrative patterns* for coordinating the channel's activities. In essence, this decision deals with how extensively channel members participate in the marketing flows—in other words, how much they vertically integrate. The administrative patterns of marketing channels will be covered in Chapter 9.

As noted in the earlier chapters, marketing channels are structured according to the availability and willingness of channel institutions to perform the marketing functions necessary to satisfy the target market's desire for channel services. This chapter takes a systematic look at how marketing channel structures are developed. Figure 8-1 presents an overview of this process.

UNDERSTANDING CUSTOMERS' NEEDS FOR CHANNEL SERVICES

The starting point in planning marketing channels is targeting an industrial, consumer, institutional, household, or specific ultimate consumer market. Channel design and selection of channel partners cannot be meaningful unless they take place in the context of the target markets that the channel designer (which can be a manufacturer, a wholesaler, or a retailer) wishes to serve. Knowledge of what buyers need, where they buy, why they buy from certain outlets, when they buy, and how they buy is critical. To plan a marketing channel, sellers must determine the most profitable and effective ways to reach these customers. Such a determination is possible only from an understanding of buyer behavior, irrespective of whether the buyers are purchasing for personal consumption or for organizational purposes.

The design of marketing channel structures depends upon what services the target market desires and what services the channel institutions are willing to

[e] ibid., p. 115.

[1] Louis P. Bucklin, *A Theory of Distribution Channel Structure* (Berkely, Cal.: IBER Special Publications, 1966), p. 107.

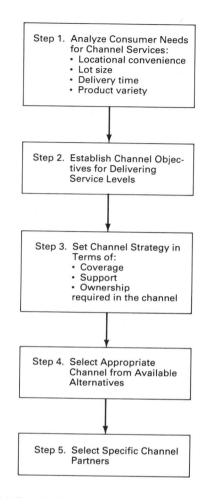

Figure 8-1 Steps in the channel structure and design process.

offer. The services marketing channels can deliver to their target customers include the provision of credit, maintenance of product quality, availability of information, stability and accessibility of supply, availability of personal service and attention, and risk reduction. Our discussion will focus on four key services offered by marketing channels: (1) locational convenience (sometimes called *market decentralization*), (2) lot size, (3) waiting or delivery time, and (4) product variety (also termed *assortment breadth*).[2]

Locational convenience provided by market decentralization of wholesale and/or retail outlets increases target customers' satisfaction by reducing the distance they must travel and decreasing their search costs. Community shopping centers, neighborhood supermarkets, convenience stores, vending machines,

[2] Ibid., pp. 7–10.

auto parts jobbers, and gas stations are but a few examples of outlets that satisfy customers' desire for locational convenience.

Similarly, the *lot size* or number of units purchased during a transaction can obviously affect the organizational or household consumer's welfare. When the marketing channel system allows buyers to purchase in small units, goods purchased may be consumed more quickly. If, as noted in Chapter 1, consumers are required to purchase in larger lots, discrepancies between purchasing and consumption patterns emerge. These discrepancies cause consumers to perform more of the product storage and maintenance activities.

When food prices increase dramatically, many price-conscious consumers shop at wholesale food terminals. These outlets price their merchandise 20 to 40 percent less than supermarkets do. However, to receive these lower prices, consumers must buy in the larger lot sizes (e.g., cases or crates) that are typically required for purchasing at food terminals.

Waiting time is defined as the period between ordering and receiving goods. Again, the longer the waiting time, the more inconvenient it is for consumers, since they must plan their consumption farther into the future. For example, the reason fast-food restaurants and automatic teller machines have been so successful is that they reduce the amount of consumer waiting time. On the other hand, consumers who are willing to wait are compensated through lower prices; an example is ordering through the Sears catalog.

Finally, a wide *product variety* or breadth and depth of assortment provides organizational and household consumers with higher levels of channel service. Less information search is necessary because alternative goods are stocked in one location. One-stop shopping also allows for lower transportation costs. The success of mass merchandisers like K-Mart, Target, and Wal-Mart is partially due to their ability to satisfy their target markets' demand for assortment breadth.

Organizational or household consumers can provide these services themselves, or they can buy them from commercial channel members. The higher the service levels required by consumers, the more likely it is that intermediaries will be included in the channel structure. Thus, if consumers wish to purchase in small lot sizes, numerous wholesalers and retailers will be needed to perform the necessary sorting operations between manufacturers and the final users. If waiting time is to be reduced, more convenient outlets are necessary, and therefore more intermediaries will be included in the channel structure. The same type of reasoning can be applied to all of the different channel services.

As channel service levels increase, costs also increase. When these higher costs are reflected in higher prices, some customers are spurred to perform more of the marketing channel services for themselves. On the other hand, when all other things are equal—especially price—customers prefer to deal with a marketing channel that provides a higher level of services.

Construction machinery manufacturers, such as Caterpillar or J. I. Case, purchase brake parts in carload quantities from firms like Gould or Bendix. Because they are willing to wait several months for delivery from distant plants, they can expect to pay lower prices than if they were to order the same parts from a local warehouse distributor who can ship in smaller quantities and deliver the parts much more quickly.

As noted in Chapter 2, the tastes and preferences of target markets are dynamic. Therefore, customers' needs for channel services must be periodically monitored through marketing research to determine whether and how these needs have changed. Marketing research can also indicate how willing customers are to perform these services for themselves. With this information, adjustments to channel structure can be made to ensure that the target market receives the desired level of channel services.

ESTABLISHING MARKETING CHANNEL OBJECTIVES

From the perspective of the marketing channel institutions, channel structure must be derived from channel objectives. These objectives, in turn, result from a careful analysis of the service levels desired by consumers and from management's long-run overall goals for the organization (e.g., return on investment, market share, sales and growth, absolute profit levels). Global goals are important in that the design and selection of a channel are long-term decisions relative to many other marketing decisions. In addition, they can be costly, complex, and not easily reversible. In fact, changes in a channel may affect the entire character of the organization and the way in which it is perceived. Thus, altering channel structure is done very infrequently and often proves highly risky. Clearly, a firm may make modifications once in a while, but radical alteration of the channel usually requires the approval of highest-level management.

The specific (as opposed to global) objectives for the channel must be couched in terms of the service levels that are needed to meet the demands of the channel's target market. To be effective, these goals must be, at a minimum, related to the global objectives and stated in quantitative terms.

A well-known food processor recently developed a high-quality prepared frozen entree to be sold in supermarkets and convenience stores. The channel objectives for this manufacturer were clearly stated. "We want this product to be no more than a ten-minute drive from 75 percent of the full-time working women in the United States. We plan to reach this goal within 12 months of our product roll-out."

Such a statement of channel objectives is directly related to the service levels desired by the target market (i.e., rapid delivery time and locational convenience).

In addition, the firm's growth goals require that the new product be widely distributed as soon as possible.

If several market segments are targeted, different sets of service outputs may be demanded by the different targets. The organization will then have to use multiple channels to reach these targets. In fact, the use of a single channel is becoming rare in today's marketplace.

Converse has long been known for its basketball shoes, the best-selling brand in its category. This product line is primarily distributed through department and discount stores. In the mid-1980s, it emphasized running and tennis shoes to catch up with Nike, the market leader in branded athletic footwear. To do this, Converse developed shoes that match its competitors' in technical sophistication. The company poured millions of dollars into media advertising and increased distribution in specialty shoe stores. In addition, Converse's entrenched position in department and discount stores enhanced the trade's acceptance of the company's newer product lines. Thus, the advertising campaigns and specialty store distribution provided the basis for obtaining market acceptance by influential consumers, while discount and department store distribution enabled Converse to expand to the mass markets.[3]

Multiple distribution channels are used by industrial goods marketers as well as by consumer goods organizations (see Exhibit 8-1).

Once channel objectives have been stated in terms of service levels, the next step in the channel structure and design process is to develop marketing channel strategy.

SETTING CHANNEL STRATEGY

One of the key elements of marketing channel strategy, evident in the Illinois Tool Works, Converse, and apparel industry examples, is the degree of marketing channel coverage and support necessary to achieve corporate objectives. In other words, how many sales outlets should be established in a given geographic area and what channel services should be required from each of the outlets must be known in order to serve existing, potential, and past customers adequately. If the correct amount of coverage and support cannot be achieved from independent marketing channel institutions, marketers must either perform those functions themselves or somehow induce their target markets to perform them. Thus, the ownership of channel institutions is the third important aspect of marketing channel strategy.

[3] This example is based on "Converse: Trying a Full Court Press in Athletic Shoes," *Business Week*, May 7, 1984, pp. 52, 56.

Channel Coverage

As implied above, market coverage (or distribution intensity) refers to the number
of outlets of a particular intermediary type established in a given geographic area.
Three basic choices are available: intensive distribution, selective distribution,
and exclusive distribution.

Intensive distribution occurs when a product, brand, or service is located in
as many outlets as possible. This strategy is often used for goods and services that
organizational and household consumers wish to purchase frequently and with a
minimum of effort. Examples are tobacco products, soap, newspapers, chewing
gum, candy bars, gasoline, aspirin, office supplies, lubricating oils, and cleaning
supplies.

When a product, brand, or service is made available at only one outlet in a
given geographic market, it is distributed *exclusively*. This form of distribution is
used for two reasons. First, customers are willing to put forth much effort to
search for the product or service; in other words, locational convenience is not an
important channel service for these buyers. For example, a well–heeled Nebraska
cattle baron may be more than willing to drive 350 miles to Denver to buy a new
Rolls Royce. Second, exclusive distribution eliminates intrabrand competition
(see Chapter 6), enabling suppliers and resellers to form greater partnerships to
compete more effectively on an interbrand basis. New automobiles, some major
appliances, commercial air-conditioning equipment, some brands of apparel,
high-priced furniture, and construction and farm machinery are commonly
distributed through exclusive territories.

Selective distribution falls somewhere between intensive and exclusive coverage. This distributive arrangement is best suited for goods and services that consumers are willing to put forth some effort to find, though they are not willing to overextend themselves. Certain brands of television sets (e.g., Zenith, RCA), mattresses (e.g., Simmons), cosmetics (e.g., Esteé Lauder), industrial supplies (e.g., Norton abrasives), and clothing (e.g., Arrow shirts) are examples of products distributed selectively.

The choice of a market coverage strategy is related to a number of factors, among them: (1) customer patronage motives; (2) distribution saturation; and (3) a channel member's desire for control over the marketing functions within the channel.

Customer Patronage Motives. A central determinant of market coverage is customer patronage motives—how both existing and potential consumers view stores and how they perceive products. Table 8-1 presents a useful scheme for seeing how consumer perceptions of products and stores interact to determine marketing channel intensity.

In addition to the type of store and type of product, the extent of market coverage depends upon how saturated distribution is.

Distribution Saturation. A key consideration in deciding on distribution intensity is whether there are too many or too few outlets within the market area. When an organization has too few outlets, sales and market share growth are difficult to achieve. On the other hand, with too many outlets, each outlet steals from the others' demand.

Crazy Carol's Copies is a regional photocopy shop franchisor. In one of its medium-sized markets, Crazy Carol's Copies is considering granting its franchisee an additional location, giving that franchisee a total of six Crazy Carol's Copies shops in this market. Since all copy centers in this city offer about the same services and charge about the same prices, competition is based primarily on location and hours. With the new location, Crazy Carol's Copies will have twice as many outlets as its nearest competitor.

When there are too many outlets in a market, new stores are located so close to existing stores that their sales and market share growth come at the expense of the latter. The new Crazy Carol's Copies shop would, in this case, cannibalize the sales of the five current locations. To prevent cannibalization, each new outlet must attract the competitors' hard-core customers. This might be difficult to do if those customers are loyal because of locational convenience, special services, and so forth. Therefore, adding outlets could increase intrabrand competition if the market area is nearly saturated. This can cause increased conflict within the channel, and ultimately result in the stores' providing reduced support for the product line or dropping the line altogether.

TABLE 8.1 Selection of Suitable Distribution Policies Based on the Relationship Between Type of Product and Type of Store

Classification	Consumer Behavior	Most Likely Form of Distribution
Convenience store/ convenience good	The consumer prefers to buy the most readily available brand of product at the most accessible store	Intensive
Convenience store/ shopping good	The consumer selects his purchase from among the assortment carried by the most accessible store	Intensive
Convenience store/ specialty good	The consumer purchases his favorite brand from the most accessible store carrying the item in stock	Selective/exclusive
Shopping store/ convenience good	The consumer is indifferent to the brand of product he buys but shops different stores to secure better retail service and/or retail price	Intensive
Shopping store/ shopping good	The consumer makes comparisons among both retail-controlled factors and factors associated with the product (brand)	Selective/exclusive
Shopping store/ specialty good	The consumer has a strong preference as to product brand but shops a number of stores to secure the best retail service and/or price for this brand	Selective/exclusive
Specialty store/ convenience good	The consumer prefers to trade at a specific store but is indifferent to the brand of product purchased	Selective/exclusive
Specialty store/ shopping good	The consumer prefers to trade at a certain store but is uncertain as to which product he wishes to buy and examines the store's assortment for the best purchase	Selective/exclusive
Specialty store/ specialty good	The consumer has both a preference for a particular store and for a specific brand	Selective/exclusive

Source: Reprinted from *Journal of Marketing*, published by the American Marketing Association, "Retail Strategy and the Classification of Consumer Goods" by Louis P. Bucklin, Vol. 27 (January 1963) pp. 50–55. The specific table was developed by and appears in Burton Marcus et al., *Modern Marketing* (New York: Random House, Inc., 1975), p. 550.

With too few outlets, the retailer cannot enjoy economies of advertising and promotion. If, for example, Crazy Carol's Copies adds the sixth shop, it can spread the costs of a single radio commercial over six stores instead of five. On a per-store basis, this amounts to nearly a 17 percent decrease in radio advertising costs. In addition, with too few outlets, customers will notice outlets only infrequently and will tend to forget them. Thus, the promotional effect of a large number of outlets will not be realized.

Figure 8-2 illustrates the relationship of distribution intensity to market share.[4] Note that share of outlets refers to a firm's intensity of distribution relative to that of its competitors.

[4] For mathematical approaches to this problem, see Gary L. Lilien and Philip Kotler, *Marketing Decision Making: A Model Building Approach* (New York: Harper & Row, 1983), pp. 449–454.

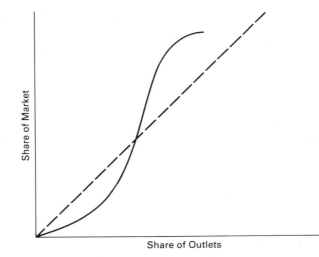

Figure 8-2 Relationship of market coverage to market share. *Source*: John J. Cardwell, "Marketing and Management Science - a Marriage of the Rocks?" *California Management Review*, Summer 1968, p. 8.

Channel Member Desire for Control. The degree to which a marketing channel member wishes to control the marketing functions within the channel will partially determine the distribution intensity strategy used. For example, when channel members adopt an intensive market coverage strategy, they generally relinquish a significant amount of control over how the product is marketed. The only way they can reestablish control is to assume greater participation in each of the marketing flows. An example of a firm able to do this is O. M. Scott (see Exhibit 8-2).

On the other hand, as channel members move toward exclusive distribution, control over the marketing functions becomes more clearly delineated. In fact, agreements, both formal and informal, among channel members are used to specify which channel members will perform which functions. Issues that are typically covered in such agreements are products to be carried, target markets to be served, territories to be covered, inventories to be held, installation and repair services to be performed, sales quotas to be achieved, and advertising and promotional activities to be conducted.

The whole issue of control within the marketing channel is so critical to effective channel management, regardless of the extent of market coverage, that three chapters—Chapters 9, 10, and 11—deal directly with that topic.

Channel Support

In addition to market coverage, support of the marketing functions from channel members is a key element of marketing channel strategy. Essentially, channel support refers to the ability and willingness of channel members to perform the necessary marketing functions so that the good or service can be marketed successfully to the target market. As the O. M. Scott example illustrates, the issues of channel support and control over the marketing functions are closely intertwined.

When certain channel members are unable or unwilling to perform certain marketing functions, other channel members, or even customers themselves, must pick up the slack.

When a well-known producer of small electrical appliances decided to adopt a more intensive distribution strategy a few years ago, it found that it could not obtain adequate service from its expanded retail network. The company had to institute a nationwide, company-owned chain of service outlets in order to satisfy the needs of its target markets.

Thus, when other channel members cannot provide adequate coverage and support, and more control over the marketing functions is desired, a firm may have no alternative other than owning the institutions necessary to perform the channel tasks.

Channel Ownership

As noted above, one of the key elements of marketing channel strategy is determining how the channel flows or functions can be divided among other marketing institutions to assure that the target market receives the channel services it desires. A basic strategic choice involves associating with intermediaries or suppliers versus vertically integrating manufacturing, wholesaling, or retailing functions. With a vertically integrated system, control of the marketing tasks is accomplished through internal planning and monitoring. Vertical integration or outright ownership is an effective means of securing increased coordination, integration of effort, and heightened channel commitment. However, as will be pointed out in Chapter 9 in the discussion of vertical marketing systems, vertical integration is often an extremely costly undertaking and involves a number of trade-offs, not the least of which is bureaucratic inflexibility. Therefore, it may not be justified in a wide variety of circumstances.

On the other hand, associating with independent organizations as channel partners is more difficult, from a managerial point of view, than owning one's own system. Divergent goals and expectations can result in control and coordination problems. However, a nonvertically integrated management allows the producer and the intermediary to concentrate on activities within their specific areas of expertise. Thus, channel functions that can be performed more effectively and efficiently by specialized institutions are assigned to various channel members. In certain circumstances and for certain kinds of products, this division of labor may result in lower overall distribution costs than a vertically integrated system.

In a number of cases, marketing channels have the characteristics of vertically integrated systems without actual ownership. Chapter 9 is devoted to a discussion of a variety of such channels. One of the channel systems discussed there is franchising, which is employed by such companies as McDonald's and Southland Corporation (7-Eleven Convenience Food Stores). Through franchising, McDonald's and Southland maintain tight control over the performance of the marketing flows within their channels without assuming the enormous capital and other resource obligations of outright ownership.

SELECTING THE APPROPRIATE CHANNEL STRUCTURE

Since various channel institutions specialize in undertaking particular marketing tasks, and since all of the marketing functions *must* be performed by each marketing channel, which marketing institutions are included in a channel depends on which institutions perform which functions. Decisions concerning the service levels to be delivered by channel members are dictated by the amount of service desired by consumers. Thus, the interplay of channel member specialization and consumer demand for channel services results in a channel structure or arrangement that is capable of satisfying the needs of both groups.

Several approaches have been developed over the years to assist decision makers in structuring marketing channels. Among these approaches are the theory of postponement-speculation, the theory of functional spin-off, and the checklist method. In the following sections, each of these approaches is discussed separately, followed by an attempt to tie them all into a meaningful understanding of how marketing channel structure is developed. Also explored are some of the forces that prevent the channel structures actually developed from being optimal. Finally, models that assist in making marketing channel structure and design decisions are briefly discussed.

Postponement-Speculation and Channel Structure

Channel structure is frequently determined by where inventories should be held in order to provide appropriate service levels, fulfill the required sorting processes, and still deliver an adequate return to channel members. One explanation of the processes involved in determining inventory locations is the principle of postponement-speculation.[5] Efficiency in marketing channels is promoted by the *postponement* of changes in (1) the form and identity of a product to the latest possible point in the marketing process and (2) inventory location to the latest possible point in time. Risk and uncertainty costs increase as the product becomes more differentiated. Postponement promotes efficiency by moving differentiation nearer to the time of purchase, when demand is more certain, thus reducing risk and uncertainty costs. Also, the cost of physical distribution of goods is reduced by sorting products in large lots and in relatively undifferentiated states.

Postponement is a tool used by a channel member to shift the risk of owning goods to another channel member. For example:

- Manufacturers of special industrial machinery postpone by refusing to produce except upon receipt of orders.
- Intermediaries postpone by buying from sellers who offer faster delivery, thus shifting inventory backward.
- Consumers postpone by buying from retail outlets where goods are available directly from the store shelf.

Speculation is the *opposite* of postponement. This concept holds that "changes in form, and the movement of goods to forward inventories, should be made at the earliest possible time in the marketing process in order to reduce the costs of the marketing system."[6] Thus risk is shifted to, or assumed by, a channel institution rather than shifted away from it. Speculation allows for cost reductions through (1) economies of large-scale production, which are the result of changing

[5] Louis P. Bucklin, "Postponement, Speculation, and the Structure of Distribution Channels," *Journal of Marketing Research*, Vol. 2 (February 1965), pp. 26–31.

[6] Ibid., p. 27.

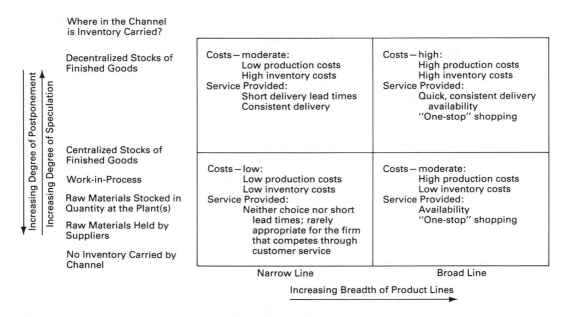

Where in the Channel
is Inventory Carried?

Increasing Degree of Postponement
Increasing Degree of Speculation

Decentralized Stocks of
Finished Goods

	Narrow Line	Broad Line

	Costs — moderate:
	   Low production costs
	   High inventory costs
	Service Provided:
	   Short delivery lead times
	   Consistent delivery
		Costs — high:
		   High production costs
		   High inventory costs
		Service Provided:
		   Quick, consistent delivery
		      availability
		   "One-stop" shopping

	Costs — low:
	   Low production costs
	   Low inventory costs
	Service Provided:
	   Neither choice nor short
	      lead times; rarely
	      appropriate for the firm
	      that competes through
	      customer service
		Costs — moderate:
		   High production costs
		   Low inventory costs
		Service Provided:
		   Availability
		   "One-stop" shopping

Centralized Stocks of
Finished Goods

Work-in-Process

Raw Materials Stocked in
Quantity at the Plant(s)

Raw Materials Held by
Suppliers

No Inventory Carried by
Channel

Increasing Breadth of Product Lines

Figure 8-3 Degrees of postponement-speculation: differing levels of costs and services. *Source*: Reprinted by permission from *Logistics Strategy: Cases and Concepts* by Roy D. Shapiro and James L. Heskett. Copyright © 1985 by West Publishing Company, p. 53. All rights reserved.

form at the earliest point; (2) the elimination of frequent orders, which increase the costs of order processing and transportation; and (3) the reduction of stockouts and their attendant cost in the form of consumer dissatisfaction and potential brand switching. An accurate sales forecast is essential in marketing channels for consumer goods, most of which are dominated by speculation.

Strategies of postponement and speculation result in different levels of costs and service. Figure 8-3 illustrates the trade-offs involved in costs and service levels for different degrees of postponement-speculation within a marketing channel.

The theory of postponement-speculation is a useful basis for understanding channel structure. For example, speculative inventories create the opportunity for new institutions to hold title in the channel. The existence of speculative inventories leads to the use of indirect or short channels; that is, those with one or more intermediaries between the producer and the consumer. These intermediaries may be capable of reducing the cost of inventory risk-taking (i.e., the costs associated with participating in the flows of physical possession and ownership). On the other hand, postponement creates an opportunity for different types of institutions in the channel. The latter are freight forwarders, drop shippers, and agent wholesalers who do not take title to merchandise but who, in the absence of speculative inventories, facilitate the use of more direct channels of distribution.

The principle of postponement-speculation can assist in understanding the differences between household and industrial buying. Much household buying is fragmented, involves small lots, and is undertaken frequently, especially with

---

EXHIBIT 8-3

Postponement-Speculation in the Automobile Industry

Accuracy in sales forecasting is a critical feature of speculation. This fact was underscored during 1979 by the troubles that plagued Chrysler Corporation. In order to achieve economies of scale in production, Chrysler amassed enormous speculative inventories of large, gas-guzzling cars. It had forecast that U.S. consumers were wedded to large cars, and therefore would continue to demand them, even though sales of foreign imports of smaller cars were increasing. Its forecast was dead wrong, and the corporation was left with thousands of automobiles that it could not sell. General Motors, on the other hand, has always followed the postponement principle; GM produces an automobile only when it has received a specific order from its dealers. Thus, in accordance with its policy of postponement, it makes changes in the form and identity of the automobiles it produces only at the latest possible point in time in the marketing process.

---

regard to convenience and some shopping goods. The costs of holding large household inventories tend to be relatively high. Thus, longer and more indirect channels often exist for convenience goods. Speculation is an important determinant of the channel structure for such goods because there are more points in the channel where inventory may be held. In industrial purchasing, however, the opposite factors generally operate, and thus the desire to postpone has led to the development of a different type of institutional arrangement where there are more direct, shorter channels.

How postponement-speculation works in the automobile industry is illustrated in Exhibit 8-3.

Functional Spin-off and Channel Structure

Another approach to examining marketing channel structure is the theory of functional spin-off.[7] The essence of this theory is that a marketing channel institution will delegate those functions that other firms can perform more cheaply and will undertake only those tasks for which it has cost advantages. By knowing the relative costs of performing each of the marketing flows, functional spin-off theory can be used to structure marketing channels.

Assume, for example, that a manufacturer must choose between two marketing channel structures. In Alternative 1, the producer employs its own sales force and maintains a system of wholly owned warehouses. In Alternative 2, the manufacturer sells through manufacturers' representatives and rents space in public warehouses. In Alternative 1, the producer performs the personal selling and product storage functions itself, while in Alternative 2, it spins off the

---

[7] Bruce E. Mallen, "Functional Spin-off: A Key to Anticipating Change in Distribution Structure," *Journal of Marketing*, Vol. 37 (July 1973), pp. 18–25.

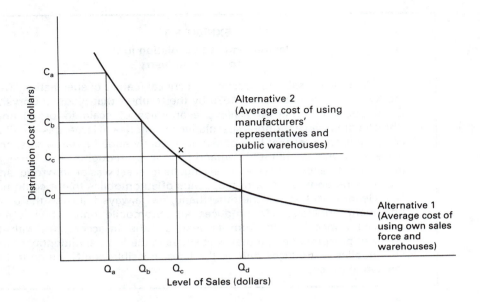

Figure 8-4 Functional Spin-off: an illustration.

personal selling function to specialized agent wholesalers (i.e., manufacturers' representatives) and the storage function to a specialized logistics firm (i.e., public warehouse).

Figure 8-4 portrays the average costs associated with these two alternatives. The average cost of Alternative 2 to the producer (i.e., spinning off both functions) is constant over the range of sales, while the per-unit cost of Alternative 1 (i.e., employing its own sales force and owning its own warehouses) declines as the level of sales increases. (Note that average costs in Alternative 1 only decline if the sales force is paid on a straight salary basis and the warehouses are bought outright and not leased back.)

In this highly simplified example, the point where the two alternatives have equal costs is at X. Thus, at sales less than Q_c, the manufacturer should choose Alternative 2; that is, the producer should spinoff the personal selling and storage functions to the manufacturer's reps and public warehouses, respectively. At sales greater than Q_c, the manufacturer should perform these functions itself.

Chapter 6 described how channel ownership or vertical integration changes over the life of the organization. The theory of functional spin-off is useful in explaining why this occurs.[8] New firms with limited resources in a competitive industry may delegate certain marketing functions to independent organizations that specialize in them. For example, a small electronics manufacturer might choose to use less costly manufacturers' agents instead of employing its own sales force. As firms grow, however, they may decide to reintegrate some of these functions because they have gained the wherewithal to perform them more

[8] George J. Stigler, "The Division of Labor Is Limited by the Extent of the Market," *Journal of Political Economy*, Vol. 59 (June 1951), pp. 185–193.

cheaply than other marketing institutions. This evolution is not restricted to producers.

Sears started as a mail-order retailer and expanded horizontally. As its operations grew larger and larger, Sears integrated backward by operating its own warehousing and other wholesaling facilities. It integrated even further backward by owning or controlling some of its own manufacturing facilities.

Thus, when a firm's output and its market are limited, it will likely shift flows onto others in its channel, or it may attempt to convince others to accept responsibility for these tasks. This is not always the case, however. Very small firms often have difficulty in securing needed services from agent wholesalers, advertising agencies, and financial institutions, often because they are viewed as credit risks. Such firms must integrate these functions, even though it would be more economical to pass them along to another marketing institution. In Figure 8-4, for example, when sales are at Q_a, the manufacturer may be forced to integrate the personal selling and storage functions even though spinning them off would be cheaper. The reason is that sales of Q_a may not be high enough to attract independent marketing institutions. At Q_b, however, the sales volume may be high enough to induce other channel members to perform the manufacturer's personal selling and warehousing tasks.

Not only do commercial channel members engage in functional spin-off or shifting, but, as noted in Chapter 1, organizational and household consumers do so as well. The success of warehouse food markets, for example, is directly attributable to consumers' willingness to bag their own groceries, provide their own carry-out service, cash in their returnable bottles elsewhere, mark their own prices, and so forth. Thus, functional shifting to consumers plays an important role in the development of new forms of retail institutions.

Implementing the functional shifting concept, however, is not an easy task. First of all, separating the joint costs associated with the performance of many marketing flows (e.g., physical possession and ownership) may be exceedingly difficult. Furthermore, most companies deal with multiple products and services for which costs are shared. Nevertheless, the concept of shifting marketing flows is a useful one and, like so many other management decisions, demands appropriate accounting procedures to be implemented correctly.

Checklist Methods for Determining Channel Structure

The checklist methods provide a list of factors that affect the number of intermediaries used in the channel. Table 8-2 enumerates several of these factors affecting the length or directness of marketing channel structure. They are (1) market factors, (2) product factors, (3) organizational factors, and (4) channel member factors. As noted in Chapter 2, a fifth factor—environmental considerations—also influences channel design and structure; since an entire chapter was

TABLE 8.2 Factors Considered in the Checklist Methods of Determining Channel Structure

Factor	Long Channels	Short Channels
Market Factors		
Market size	Small	Large
Geographical concentration	Dispersed	Dense
Purchase frequency	Infrequently	Frequently
Average order size	Small	Large
Product Factors		
Bulk and weight	Light, compact	Heavy, bulky
Perishability and rapid obsolescence	Low	High
Unit value	Low	High
Product standardization	High	Low
Width of product line	Narrow	Wide
Depth of product line	Shallow	Deep
Technical complexity	Low	High
Company Factors		
Size	Small	Large
Financial strength	Weak	Strong
Managerial expertise	Low	High
Desire for control	Low	High
Channel Member Factors		
Availability	Available	Unavailable
Willingness	High	Low
Number of services performed	Many	Few
Quality of services performed	High	Low
Relative cost	Low	High

Source: Partially based on material in James R. Brown, "Factors Influencing the Organization of Effective Distribution Channels," unpublished manuscript, 1975; and Bert Rosenbloom, *Marketing Channels: A Management View*, 2nd ed. (Hinsdale, Ill.: The Dryden Press, 1983), pp. 151–157.

devoted to this factor, it will not be discussed here. The following sections provide a brief overview of the other four factors.

Market Factors. The characteristics of the target market shape the design and structure of marketing channels. For example, the fewer the customers, the larger the size of the target market, and the more geographically concentrated the market, the more likely it is that direct channels will be used, all other factors held constant. If the opposite conditions occur, managing the channel will be more cumbersome and intermediaries will be used to reduce the burden.

Product Factors. Product factors will directly influence channel design, assuming market, company, and channel member factors remain the same. Perishable products require direct marketing, or at least the use of intermediaries who can assure rapid turnover of merchandise. Bulky products require channels that minimize shipping distance and excessive handling. Complex products that call for technical expertise in selling may require direct channels to ensure that buyers receive accurate product information. The costs of using a direct channel can be allocated across more items when the firm has wide product lines.

Organizational Factors. Obviously, companies vary in their financial strength, their experience with certain types of resellers or suppliers, their ability to perform many of the marketing functions themselves, and their desire to control how their products are marketed. Financially strong organizations, able to perform many of the marketing functions for themselves and desiring much control over the marketing flows, will use direct channels, if all of the other factors are assumed to be the same.

Channel Member Factors. In structuring distributive channels, the characteristics of the marketing institutions potentially making up the channel must be examined. Among these factors are the availability of channel members, in a particular market area, to perform the necessary marketing functions; their willingness to perform these functions; the number of channel services a particular institution performs; the quality of those services; and the relative costs of different channel members performing the same task.

The choice of outlets, in the case of manufacturers, and of suppliers, in the case of resellers, is frequently highly restricted. In other words, channel institutions are either unavailable or unwilling to perform the marketing functions for a particular supplier or intermediary. Consider the market for personal computers.

In early 1983, over 150 different personal computer makers were vying for scarce shelf space in 2,100 computer stores. Many of the smaller, newer firms were not at all successful in getting their products into retail outlets. First, IBM and Apple dominated this market and were able to command prime shelf space in the best dealerships. Second, retailers wanted to see evidence that these smaller computer makers could generate consumer demand. Since most concentrated on trade shows, press articles, and word of mouth and ignored consumer advertising, their products were not very attractive to computer dealers. As a consequence, most of these firms did not get retail distribution and, by the mid-1980s, had fallen by the wayside.[9]

Suppliers can also be unavailable or unwilling to participate in marketing channel flows. For example, wholesalers are obviously restricted from many channels in which manufacturers distribute their products through relatively short channels (e.g., automobiles, mainframe computers). Some retailers may similarly be prohibited from carrying certain brands because of suppliers' policies of dealing with only particular types of outlets. Some manufacturers—e.g., Schwinn with its bicycles, Stiffel with its lamps, and Cuisinart with its food processors—do not sell their products to discount houses.

The number and quality of channel services performed by various types of retail and wholesale institutions were discussed in Chapters 3 and 4, respectively,

[9] "Newcomers in Personal Computers Have Trouble Breaking into Market," *The Wall Street Journal*, February 18, 1983, p. 21.

and the fact that manufacturers can perform many or few of these tasks has been noted throughout the text. The relative costs of marketing channel institutions largely depend on their relative economies of scale. Large-scale retailers like Sears, Penney's, and Ward's can more efficiently advertise and personally sell women's gloves and purses, for example, than can small manufacturer-suppliers.

It should be clear by now that these market, product, organizational, and channel member characteristics imply different channel structures for different marketing functions or flows. Grain, for example, is a very bulky product, indicating that a relatively direct channel for the physical flow is needed. The ownership channel for grain, however, can be quite indirect, since commodity traders buy and sell the grain stored at a particular elevator (i.e., grain wholesaler) many times over before the product is actually transported to be milled, or even planted, for that matter!

Understanding the Relationship Among the Methods for Determining Channel Structure

The concepts of postponement-speculation and functional spin-off both directly pertain to the economic aspects of marketing channel structure. Postponement-speculation basically deals with where inventories should be held and where changes in product form should take place. Functional spin-off is more general in that it can be applied to all of the marketing flows or functions. The result of both theories is the same, however. Whichever marketing channel participant, including the organizational or household consumer, can perform the marketing flow more economically will be included in the channel structure. Less efficient marketing institutions will be excluded from it.

On the surface, the checklist method for evaluating marketing channel structure (Table 8-2) seems quite different from either postponement-speculation or functional spin-off. This method appears to be more comprehensive in that it examines more than just the economics of alternative channel structures. A closer look, however, reveals that the factors included in the checklist are actually the components underlying the cost curves for each of the marketing functions.

As noted earlier, direct or short channels are recommended for perishable items, such as fresh Maine lobster going to Kansas City. The reason is that for these products the cost of inventory losses due to spoilage in indirect channels more than offsets the cost of using airfreight in direct ones.

Direct channels are also advised for geographically concentrated markets (e.g., metropolitan Chicago), while longer ones are suggested for dispersed markets (e.g., Wyoming, Montana).

Kellogg's salespeople call directly on the Jewel supermarket account in Chicago. Because of Jewel's intensive distribution in that market, the costs of these sales calls can be spread over a large number of stores and boxes of cereal. The costs of having Kellogg's sales force reach a similar number of supermarkets in the more geographically dispersed

Rocky Mountain states is much greater. For this reason, Kellogg's uses food brokers and wholesalers to reach these outlets.

Thus, the costs of serving geographically dispersed markets are higher than those for reaching concentrated ones. Because channel intermediaries typically carry broader product lines than suppliers, their costs of reaching dispersed markets, on a per-unit basis, are lower.

In addition, the more a channel member desires control over the performance of the marketing functions, the shorter or more direct the channel should be. One reason for this rule of thumb is that, under certain conditions, the costs of controlling independent organizations are much higher than those of monitoring internal operations.[10]

Superficially, the three methods of determining marketing channel structure—the theory of postponement-speculation, the theory of functional spin-off, and the checklist method—are different approaches. In reality, however, they are very similar in that they all relate to the costs of performing the marketing functions. And those marketing channel participants—manufacturers, wholesalers, retailers, organizational buyers, and household consumers—that can more economically undertake the marketing flows will make up the structure of the channel.

Impediments to Designing Marketing Channel Structure

After considering all of the factors discussed above and finally choosing a marketing channel structure, it might not be possible to implement it for several reasons. The most important of these are environmental factors, individual channel member factors, reseller solidarity, and organizational rigidity.

Environmental Factors. As noted in Chapter 2, the legal and political, technological, competitive, and economic climates all affect both marketing channel structure and behavior. These environmental considerations can constrain the choice of a marketing channel structure.

Decision makers must be particularly careful not to select channel structures that violate federal, state, or local laws, nor to run afoul of the prevailing political climate. The legality of elements of marketing channel structure such as exclusive territories, resale restrictions, refusals to deal, and consignment selling must be examined.

Sellers often grant geographical monopolies or *exclusive territories* to a buyer reselling their product or brand. Such arrangements are legal, for example, when new manufacturers or manufacturers entering new markets try to persuade resellers to carry their products. They are also legal when they are used to induce resellers to provide necessary service and repair facilities, or when manufacturers

[10] For much more depth, see Oliver E. Williamson, *The Economic Institutions of Capitalism* (New York: The Free Press, 1985), pp. 85–130.

need to protect the safety and quality of their products. For these reasons, Coca-Cola can legally grant its franchised wholesaler-bottlers exclusive territories. Exclusive territories are not illegal in all situations; each litigated case is decided on its merits (i.e., on a rule-of-reason basis). The relevant laws are the Sherman Anti-Trust Act and Section 5 of the Federal Trade Commission Act.[11]

Resale restrictions require customers to resell their products only to specified clientele. This type of restriction often occurs when manufacturers wish to serve larger accounts themselves and to confine resellers to smaller ones. They are also used to prevent authorized resellers from putting the product in the hands of unauthorized dealers. Since the legality of such restrictions is uncertain, marketers must be careful in setting such guidelines.[12]

Refusal to deal is the right of sellers to choose their own customers or to stop serving a given customer according to their own criteria and judgment. Under most circumstances, its use is permitted under Section 2(a) of the Robinson-Patman Act and under the Colgate doctrine precedent. However, certain types of franchises, such as automobile franchises, cannot be terminated arbitrarily. Refusals to deal are forbidden if they foster restraint of trade or substantially lessen competition.[13]

Consignment selling occurs when a channel intermediary markets the seller's goods but does not take ownership of them. For example, L'eggs panty hose is sold on consignment; supermarkets provide floor space and take payment for the hose sold. These stores do not own the merchandise nor the racks on which it is displayed. This practice is legal in many circumstances, except where its effect is similar to that of vertical (retail) price-fixing. Price-fixing or resale price maintenance, of course, is strictly prohibited by the Sherman Act.[14]

Channel Member Factors. As noted in the discussion above and in Table 8-2, channel members may not always be available in particular market areas, nor capable of performing the desired marketing functions, nor willing to carry them out even if they are available and capable. Thus, the absence of certain marketing channel members may impede the development of the "best" channel structure.

Reseller Solidarity.[15] Channel participants often organize and function as groups that tend to support traditional trade practices and long-established institutional relationships. Trade associations sometimes attempt to prevent changes in marketing channel structure. For example, in the 1930's, independent

[11] Louis W. Stern and Thomas L. Eovaldi, *Legal Aspects of Marketing Strategy: Antitrust and Consumer Protection Issues* (Englewood Cliffs, N.J.: Prentice-Hall, 1984), pp. 319–324.

[12] Ibid., pp. 324–325.

[13] Ibid., pp. 331–334.

[14] William L. Trombetta, "Distribution Practices Meet a Revitalized Sherman Act," in Robert F. Lusch and Paul H. Zinszer (eds.), *Contemporary Issues in Marketing Channels* (Norman: University Printing Services, The University of Oklahoma, 1979), pp. 113–119.

[15] Bert C. McCammon, Jr., "Alternative Explanations of Institutional Change and Channel Evolution," in Stephen A. Greyser (ed.), *Toward Scientific Marketing* (Chicago: American Marketing Association, 1963), pp. 477–490, reprinted in Bruce J. Walker and Joel B. Haynes (eds.), *Marketing Channels and Institutions: Selected Readings* (Columbus, Ohio: Grid Publishing, 1973), p. 82.

retailers tried to outlaw chain stores, and in the 1950s, department store operators tried to block discount stores from opening. In more recent years, the National Automobile Dealers Association has impeded the development of new channels in the industry, such as with Porsche. Also, pharmacy associations insist that pharmacies can be open only if a registered pharmacist is on duty.

Organizational Rigidity.[16]   For any organization, changing established ways of doing business causes uncertainty and, for some employees, perhaps a loss of status. Since, as noted earlier, decisions about marketing channel structure are long-term and may affect the character of the organization, changing channel structure can be a slow and painful process. Many firms would prefer to avoid doing so, and they often do!

Marketing Channel Structure Decision Models

Several decision models have been developed to assist in evaluating alternative channel structures. These models very widely in sophistication from evaluation process models (e.g., weighted factor models, conjunctive models[17] to computer simulation methods[18] to mathematical programming techniques (e.g., linear programming, geometric programming).[19] Because of their sophistication, the computer simulation and mathematical programming models are beyond the scope of this text.

Evaluation process models, on the other hand, are relatively easy to use and allow the decision maker to combine both economic criteria and qualitative criteria, which are often evaluated on the basis of experience, intuition, and subjective judgment. In addition, the constraints in the channel design decision can be incorporated into this basic approach. Exhibit 8-4 illustrates how two of these models (i.e., the weighted factor and sequential elimination methods) can be used to select among alternative marketing channel structures.

Once the appropriate marketing channel structure has been selected, the next step in designing the channel is to choose the specific organizations to fit into that structure. For example, if the Commodity Chemical Company (the fictional firm of Exhibit 8-4) decides to use new distributors already selling to the swimming pool market, it must determine exactly which distributors to use. The next section explores how this decision might be undertaken.

[16] Ibid., pp. 83–84.

[17] For a review of these models and their application in a retail buying context, see Louis W. Stern and Adel I. El-Ansary, *Marketing Channels*, 2nd ed. (Englewood Cliffs, N.J.: Prentice-Hall, 1982), pp. 92–97.

[18] For example, see Mary A. Higby, *An Evaluation of Alternative Channels of Distribution: An Efficiency Model*, East Lansing: Division of Research, Graduate School of Business Administration, Michigan State University, 1977); and Michael Levy and Michael Van Breda, "A Financial Perspective on the Shift of Marketing Functions," *Journal of Retailing*, Vol. 60 (Winter 1984), pp. 23–42.

[19] For example, see Marcel Corstjens and Peter Doyle, "Channel Optimization in Complex Marketing Systems," *Management Science*, Vol. 25 (October 1979), pp. 1014–1025; and V. Kasturi Rangan, Andris A. Zoltners, and Robert J. Becker, "The Channel Intermediary Selection Decision: A Model and An Application," *Management Science*, Vol. 32 (September 1986), pp. 1114–1122.

EXHIBIT 8-4

**Methods for Choosing the Appropriate
Channel Design:
The Commodity Chemical Company**

The Commodity Chemical Company (CCC) is an old-line maker of chemicals that is seeking new products and new markets to extend the growth phase of its product life cycle. One new product CCC has developed is a swimming pool germicide that it believes is superior to existing swimming pool chemicals. Since CCC has had no previous experience in marketing to consumers, its new products marketing team had to design new marketing channels to reach potential customers for the swimming pool germicide.

The central question was how to reach swimming pool owners. CCC considered marketing through five different types of retailing institutions: (1) conventional retail outlets, such as hardware stores and drugstores; (2) specialized swimming pool supply and equipment dealers; (3) swimming pool service companies; (4) mass merchandisers, such as supermarkets, department stores, and discount houses; and (5) direct-mail supply houses.

To reach these retailers, however, CCC had to decide on a wholesaling structure. Five alternative arrangements were considered: (1) marketing through present distributors, (2) marketing through new distributors already selling to the swimming pool trade, (3) buying a small company already in this market to utilize its distributors, (4) producing the chemical in bulk for companies already in this market to sell under their own labels; and (5) packaging and selling the chemical through direct-mail campaigns aimed at swimming pool owners.

In evaluating the five wholesaling structures, CCC developed a list of the factors it deemed most important. Each factor was assigned an importance weight according to the following rules: Each factor weight could only range between 0 and 1 and all summed together must equal 1.0. Each alternative was then rated according to how well it met each of the five criteria. The ratings ranged from 0 to 1.0, with the larger numbers indicating higher performance on the factor.

The accompanying table presents the ratings for each of the five alternative wholesaling structures. Note that the table also includes the weighted ratings—the factor weight multiplied by the factor rating. In the *weighted factor method*, these weighted ratings are summed and the alternative with the highest score is the chosen wholesaling structure. In this case, CCC would select alternative five—packaging and selling through direct-mail campaigns aimed at swimming pool owners.

Another procedure CCC could use for choosing the wholesaling structure for its swimming pool germicide is the *sequential elimination method*. With this method, management sets minimum acceptable ratings for each criterion. (See the last column in the accompanying table.) All alternatives are then evaluated against each factor in order of importance. Alternatives that do not reach the minimum acceptable rating for that factor are then eliminated from further consideration. For example, the most important criterion is the amount of investment involved. Only the third alternative, buying a small company, does not meet the minimum level. This alternative is therefore dropped from further analysis. The next most important factor is the amount of profit; the private label alternative fails to meet this minimum cutoff value, and so is no longer considered. And so the process goes, until only the third alternative—marketing through new distributors already selling to the swimming pool trade—remains.

CHOOSING SPECIFIC CHANNEL PARTNERS

The final decision in channel design is choosing the specific marketing organizations to be included in the channel. Manufacturers must decide which types of intermediaries are best suited for delivering the marketing channel services desired by the target market. Intermediaries, in turn, must decide which products best suit the needs of their target markets and how much support they should give them. One particularly useful approach to choosing channel members is the following six-step procedure.[20]

1. Establish a short list of *must* requirements for each type of marketing institution. For example, in the case of Commodity Chemical Company, this list would include the functions that absolutely must be performed by the chosen distributor.
2. Develop a list of *desirable* qualities. These are "nice to have" characteristics, but not absolutely necessary ones.
3. Compile a list of the marketing organizations performing the desired functions for each target market, in order of preference, including competitors' channel members.
4. Evaluate each potential channel member (from Step 3) on the basis of each of the *must* requirements (from Step 1). Any of the channel structure decision models discussed in the previous section can be adapted for this step.
5. Assess the most attractive alternatives identified in Step 4 according to the *desirable* characteristics (from Step 2).
6. Select, on the basis of the evaluation in Step 5, the appropriate channel members.

A multitude of criteria are suitable for Steps 1 and 2; these criteria may be used by manufacturers assessing channel intermediaries or by resellers evaluating suppliers. A general list of these factors appears in Table 8-3.

Manufacturers most frequently use credit rating and financial position to

---

[20] These steps are based on the discussion in John M. Brion, *Marketing Through the Wholesaler/Distributor Channel* (Chicago: American Marketing Association, 1965), p. 34.

		Alternative										
	Factor Weight	Current Distributors		New Distributors		Buy Small Company		Private Label		Direct Mail		Minimum Cut off
Factor		Raw	Wtd.	Raw	Wtd.	Raw	Wtd.	Raw	Wtd.	Raw	Wtd.	
Effectiveness in reaching swimming pool owners	0.15	0.1 Fail	.015	0.3 Pass	.045	0.8 —	.120	0.8 —	.120	0.8 —	.120	0.3
Amount of profit if this alternative works well	0.25	0.5 Pass	.125	0.5 Pass	.125	0.9 —	.225	0.2 Fail	.050	0.9 Pass	.225	0.5
Experience CCC will gain in consumer marketing	0.10	0.1	.010	0.2	.020	0.8	.080	0.1	.010	0.9	.090	0.4
Amount of investment required (high score for low investment)	0.30	0.8 Pass	.240	0.8 Pass	.240	0.1 Fail	.030	0.8 Pass	.240	0.3 Pass	.090	0.3
Ability of CCC to cut short its losses	0.20	0.7 Pass	.140	0.7 Pass	.140	0.1 —	.020	0.7 —	.140	0.3 Fail	.060	0.5
	1.00		.530		.570		.475		.560		.585	

Source: Based upon Philip Kotler, *Marketing Decision Making: A Model Building Approach* (New York: Holt, Rinehart and Winston, 1971), pp. 290–296.

TABLE 8.3 Criteria for Selecting a Channel Member

1. Size of Prospective Channel Member
   Sales
   Financial strength
2. Sales Strength
   Number of salespersons
   Sales and technical competence
3. Product Lines
   Competitive products
   Compatible products
   Complementary products
4. Reputation
   Leadership
   Well-established
5. Market Coverage
   Geographic coverage—outlets per market area
   Industry coverage
   Call frequency or intensity of coverage
6. Sales Performance
   Performance of related lines
   General sales performance
   Growth prospects
7. Management
8. Advertising and Sales Promotion
9. Sales Compensation
10. Acceptance of Training Assistance
11. Transportation Savings
12. Inventory
    Kind and size
    Inventory Minimums—safety stocks $\left.\begin{array}{l}\text{Extent of}\\ \text{postponement}\\ \text{speculation}\end{array}\right.$
    Reductions in manufacturer inventories
13. Warehousing
    Supplied in field
    Ability to handle shipments efficiently
14. Lot quantity costs
    Willingness to accept ordering policies

Source: Douglas M. Lambert, *The Distribution Channels Decision* (New York: National Association of Accountants, 1978), p. 37.

assess potential wholesalers and retailers because they want to be sure that their resellers will pay their bills. In addition, manufacturers examine the number, quality, and technical competence of the prospective channel member's sales force. This is crucial for manufacturers that rely heavily on push promotion strategies. Producers are also concerned about their product images; they do not want them used as a point of direct comparison by the competition. Thus, producers prefer resellers whose merchandise lines do not include products in direct competition with theirs, but rather contain compatible and complementary products. Finally, manufacturers want the quality of their resellers' lines to be equal to or greater than their own.[21] As stressed throughout this chapter, the

[21] This discussion is based partly on Bert Rosenbloom, *Marketing Channels: A Management View* (Chicago: The Dryden Press, 1983), pp. 185–187.

TABLE 8.4 Factors Retailers Use in Selecting Suppliers[a]

1. Accepts damaged merchandise returns	13. Makes new products available
2. Has quick and easy ordering procedures	14. Has understanding sales representatives
3. Accepts unsold merchandise returns	15. Provides adequate margins on suggested list prices
4. Provides prompt delivery	
5. Maintains adequate supply	16. Offers quantity discounts
6. Handles complaints promptly	17. Extends credit beyond 30 days
7. Is known as being honest	18. Employs well-trained sales representatives
8. Has good reputation	19. Offers adequate overall promotional support
9. Carries large product breadth	20. Offers cooperative advertising
10. Provides small-lot delivery	21. Provides store displays
11. Offers frequent promotional allowances	22. Has low sales representative turnover
12. Requires no minimum order size	23. Offers promotional advice for specific products

[a]Listed in order of importance.

Source: Adapted from *Marketing in the 80's: Changes and Challenges*, published by the American Marketing Association (Chicago, 1980), Richard P. Bagozzi et al. (eds.), ''A Crosschannel Comparison of Retail Supplier Selection Factors,'' by James R. Brown and Prem C. Purwar, pp. 217–220.

wholesaler's or retailer's target market should overlap with the manufacturer's. In most cases, the overlap will not be perfect; but in order to efficiently distribute the product, it should be as great as possible.

Retailers and wholesalers use a different set of criteria. Table 8-4 lists some of the factors they consider in selecting their suppliers.

Once Step 6 has been completed (i.e., the desired channel members have been selected), they must be approached about carrying the product line or supplying the desired products. This may not be an easy task because specific manufacturers, wholesalers, retailers, or other marketing institutions are sometimes unwilling to participate in the marketing channel.

With over 12,000 items in the typical supermarket and with limited shelf space in which to stock those items, many suppliers find themselves locked out of particular supermarkets

During the 1970s, Sears requested Levi Strauss & Company many times to supply its blue jeans to Sears' retail outlets. Levi's steadfastly refused Sears' proposal on the grounds that the loss in sales from specialty shops' and department stores' dropping the line would exceed the increase in business from Sears. However, as noted in Chapter 2, by 1982, Levi's market situation had changed, and by 1983, Levi's had full distribution through Sears.

Thus, a channel member's willingness is a key factor both in deciding on channel structure and in selecting specific channel partners. As a practical matter then, channel member selection is very closely intertwined with determining channel structure. The dealer selection process for the Colt automobile marketing channel in the United Kingdom illustrates how the market coverage decision (i.e., channel structure) was closely interwoven with the choice of dealers (see Exhibit 8-5).

The Colt marketing channel selection process drives home a another important point about channel structure and design, one that we cannot overstress. That is, channel member selection is *always* a two-way process—suppliers select resellers and, *at the same time*, resellers choose suppliers. Neither suppliers nor resellers may always be able to select the exact channel partners they wish. Certainly, the extent of financial or market power held by a channel member seeking to enter or enlarge a distribution network will strongly affect the amount of choice available. How channel organizations obtain power over other channel members and use it to influence them is the subject of Chapter 10.

SUMMARY

Marketing channel structure and design are central to developing effective marketing channels. The keystone of designing channel structure is understanding the needs and wants of the target market for the services provided by the marketing channel. Without this, most attempts at designing successful marketing channels are doomed to failure over the long run although luck and inept competitors sometimes allow ineffective channels to succeed.

Once the target market's demand for marketing channel services is known, channel objectives can be developed. To be effective, they must include the organization's overall or global goals and should also be as specific as possible. Ideally, they should be stated in terms of channel service levels. If this is done, the channel objectives serve as standards against which the performance of the channel can be assessed. Evaluating marketing channel performance will be covered in Chapter 11.

From channel objectives, marketing channel strategy in terms of market coverage, support, and ownership can be developed. *Channel coverage* or intensity ranges from intensive to selective to exclusive distribution, and is determined by customer patronage patterns, channel length, distribution saturation, and channel member control. *Channel support* refers to the ability and willingness of channel members to perform the necessary marketing functions. Where channel support cannot be found, organizations must decide whether or not to own the channel institutions performing the needed functions. This ownership may come either through acquisition or through internal expansion. The topic of channel ownership will be discussed in more detail in Chapter 9.

Selection of the appropriate channel structure builds upon the previous steps: understanding the target market's demand for channel services, setting objectives for the channel, and developing marketing channel strategy. The theory of postponement-speculation, functional spin-off theory, and checklist methods are alternative, but very similar, methods for developing marketing channel structure. Environmental factors such as legal restrictions, channel member willingness and availability, reseller solidarity, and organizational rigidity constrain the choice of channel structures.

EXHIBIT 8-5
The Colt Car Company Ltd.:
Developing a Dealer Network

The Colt line of automobiles is manufactured in Japan by Mitsubishi and imported into Britain by the Colt Car Company Ltd., a joint venture of Mitsubishi (49 percent ownership) and Colt Automotive Ltd. (51 percent ownership). This car make was introduced into the British market in January 1975.

Before forming the Colt Car Company Ltd., the principals visited a substantial number of automobile dealers to see if the market was large enough for another line of cars. A reasonable number of dealers were looking for another line to handle, yet in many areas none was available. On the basis of these results, the principals concluded that the market could support another car line, and therefore began the Colt Car Company Ltd.

The marketing channel structure for Colt automobiles was basically producer→importer→franchised dealer. To complete the final link in the channel structure, Colt had to evaluate and select dealers to handle its product line.

The importing company had initially hoped to sell through 100 dealers nationwide, and had planned to recruit more dealers as the brand established itself. The company did not want to accept poor existing dealers, since it believed that it was easier to start with relatively high standards and maintain them than to try to elevate standards at some later date. The distribution intensity of Colt dealers was largely based on population statistics and the location of other manufacturers' dealers. Thus, for example, a town with 20 dealerships became one in which the company felt it needed to be represented whereas, say, a town with 5 dealerships could possibly be tackled at some later date.

A good number of dealers survived the evaluation process and expressed an interest in the Colt franchise. However, when the time arrived for firm commitments, nearly 50 percent of these dealers were no longer interested. By the time the Colt line was launched—January 1975—79 retailers, covering England, Scotland, Northern Ireland, and Wales constituted the dealer network. The accompanying table lists the factors those dealers used in choosing to carry the Colt line.

Dealer Decision Factors[a]

1. Competitive prices
2. Accessibility of Colt management
3. Model Range
4. Colt forecast of spares and delivery service
5. Quality of Colt management
6. Lack of local Colt competition
7. Colt success overseas
8. Japanese success in U.K.
9. Trade discount offered
10. Good sales incentives
11. Few demands made of dealer
12. Business advice service

[a]Listed in order of importance.

Source: Philip Rosson, "Dealer Adoption of a New Car Franchise: An Exploratory Study," *Journal of Management Studies*, Vol. 14 (October 1977), pp. 331, 336.

The final step in marketing channel structure and design is selecting specific organizations to be included in the channel. A variety of criteria are used by manufacturers to select resellers and by wholesalers and retailers to choose suppliers. Channel selection is basically a mutual process; while channel members are chosen to join channels, they concurrently choose to join them. In not all cases do channel members get their first choices as channel partners. Thus, without this mutual agreement, channel relationships do not take place.

DISCUSSION QUESTIONS

1. In early 1983, Apple Computer introduced its Lisa personal computer. With an initial $10,000 price tag, Lisa was clearly aimed at large corporations. At this time, Apple primarily distributed its personal computers through independent computer dealers and a very small sales force. Was this marketing channel structure likely to provide Lisa's target market with the channel services it desired? Explain.

2. For each of the following products, discuss whether intensive, selective, or exclusive distribution should be used.
   a. Panty hose   d. Drill presses
   b. Tractors   e. Toasters
   c. Lottery tickets   f. Ambulance services

3. Describe an example of each of the following product and store combinations. How intensively is that product or service distributed?
   a. Specialty store/specialty good
   b. Shopping store/convenience good
   c. Specialty store/convenience good
   d. Convenience store/specialty good
   e. Convenience store/shopping good
   f. Shopping store/specialty good

4. Marketing channel participants (including organizational and household consumers) extensively engage in postponement-speculation. Describe how each of the following channel institutions uses either postponement or speculation.
   a. Supermarkets   d. Automobile dealers
   b. Grain brokers   e. Soft-drink bottlers
   c. Plumbing supply houses   f. Building supply centers

5. Given the checklist in Table 7-2, predict the marketing channel structure for each of the following products. Explain your predictions.
   a. Soy beans   d. Rock music concerts
   b. Earth-moving machinery   e. Architectural services
   c. High-lift fork trucks   f. Candy bars
   Using the resources at your disposal (either from personal experience, the library, or interviews with knowledgeable people), describe how well the actual channel structures match your predictions.

6. The Carleton Electric Company is a well-known manufacturer of home appliances, including refrigerators, stoves, microwave ovens, and dishwashers. Carleton has decided to enter the Clarence, New York, market with an exclusive dealership and has narrowed down its potential dealers to Ray's Appliances, Empire State Appliances, and

Genesee Furniture. Given the following information, use the weighted factor method to help Carleton decide which channel member to select.

	Factor Weight	Ray's Appliances	Empire State Appliances	Genesee Furniture
Credit and financial position	0.25	7	3	6
Target market overlap	0.30	6	4	8
Reputation	0.25	8	5	7
Ability to provide after-sale service	0.20	3	6	1

7. The Saturn Corporation, a wholly-owned subsidiary of General Motors, has been charged with producing and marketing a small automobile to be competitive with Japanese small cars. Saturn has been given free reign to radically rethink the way in which U.S. car makers do business, ranging from corporate administration to production to distribution. Thus, Saturn will develop its own marketing channel system. The major objectives of this system are twofold. First, GM wants to increase its control over retail sales and service. Second, it wants to deliver better and more consistent service to its customers.
Develop a marketing channel structure that will enable Saturn Corporation to achieve its objectives.

9

Administrative Patterns in Marketing Channels

LEARNING OBJECTIVES

Upon completing this chapter, you will be able to:

- *Describe what vertical marketing systems are.*
- *Discuss the differences between conventional marketing channels and vertical marketing systems.*
- *Explain what administered marketing channel systems are and how they compare to conventional channels.*
- *Give examples of some of the marketing activities that are programmed in administered marketing channels.*
- *List the three principal forms of contractual marketing channel systems and distinguish among them.*
- *Explain the advantages and disadvantages of wholesaler-sponsored voluntary chains, retailer-sponsored cooperative groups, and franchise systems.*

- *Describe what corporate vertical marketing channel systems are and give examples of them.*

- *Discuss the advantages and disadvantages of corporate marketing channels.*

- *Explain, in general terms, the legality of vertical integration.*

- *Compare and contrast the different types of vertical marketing systems with one another and with conventional marketing channels.*

The Fleming Companies: Administering the Retail Channel for Food

The Fleming Companies, based in Oklahoma City, is one of the nation's largest food wholesaler with sales of $5.5 billion and a return on investment of 11.6 percent in 1984.

Fleming's success is partially due to its ability to administer the marketing channel for food products, particularly at the wholesale and retail levels. As a part of its overall marketing program, Fleming provides its customers with a variety of retail services, among them shelf management programs, retail accounting programs, and pricing assistance. In addition, the company helps its retailers to plan, buy, and maintain scanning systems. Its private-label program, including the Rainbow and Good Value brands, is another facet of its services to retailers.

In addition to these services, Fleming, through its store development program, assists retailers in planning and opening new supermarkets. Under this program, Fleming provides market information, site selection services, lease negotiation assistance, store layout planning, store financing arrangements, help in buying store fixtures, and insurance plans.

Even after a new store is opened, Fleming's sales service representatives counsel the supermarket operator on such retail marketing mix activities as promotion and advertising, merchandise display, store layout, and shelf-space management.

By making its supermarkets stronger competitors, Fleming's wholesaler-to-retailer channels are better able to compete effectively against integrated chain store operations such as Safeway and Kroger.

Source: Scoreboard Special Issue, *Business Week*, March 22, 1985, pp. 56–57, 130; and personal interviews with Jim Clark and Ann Bornholdt, The Fleming Companies, November, 1985.

Firms such as Fleming actually face two basic decisions in organizing their marketing channels. The first, the marketing channel structure or design decision, involves choosing which institutions should perform which marketing functions within the channel. Fleming has decided to concentrate on the wholesaling functions, and thus remains independent of both food manufacturers and retailers. The second decision involves determining which administrative patterns (i.e., the degree of vertical control or ownership) should be used to coordinate channel activities. Although Fleming's customers are independent food retailers, they rely heavily on Fleming for assistance in performing the retailing functions. Thus, the decision about administrative patterns deals with how extensively a channel member will be involved in performing the marketing functions. While Chapter 8 focused on the channel structure decision, this chapter emphasizes the administrative pattern decision within the marketing channel.

The basic administrative patterns available to decision makers within marketing channels range from those with low degrees of vertical control (i.e., conventional channels) to those with moderate or high degrees of vertical control (i.e., vertical marketing systems). Manufacturers, such as Ford (automobiles), IBM (computers), M&M/Mars (candy), Kraft (dairy products), Hartmann (luggage), and Cessna (aircraft); wholesalers, such as Greenman Bros. (toys), Fleming (food), Cotter & Company (hardware), Ryerson (steel); and retailers, such as Sears, Child World, Walgreen's, and ComputerLand, all must exert some control in managing their marketing channels. When channel institutions hold little market power or few resources, they have little discretion over the administrative patterns used. On the other hand, nearly all the firms mentioned above have been able to develop either backward (i.e., from retailers toward their sources of supply) or forward (i.e., from producers toward their customers) vertical marketing systems.

A *traditional* or *conventional* marketing channel can frequently be described as a coalition of independently owned and managed institutions that evolves over time. Each of the channel member firms is motivated by profit and has little concern about what goes on above or below it in the distributive sequence. Such coalitions have no systemwide goals; decision making and authority take place exclusively at the individual channel member level. Conventional channels have no formally structured division of labor, and member firms are not strongly committed to the distribution "system."[1]

In contrast to the conventional channel, vertical marketing systems

> are professionally managed and centrally programmed networks . . . [and are] designed to achieve technological, managerial, and promotional economies through the integration, coordination, and synchronization of the marketing flows from points of production to points of ultimate use.[2]

Thus, vertical marketing systems are characterized by centralized power within the system, which provides for channel leadership, division of labor, coordination, conflict management, and control.

In this chapter, the organization and design of such systems are explained in some detail. Conventional marketing channels and the various types of vertical marketing systems (i.e., administered, contractual, and corporate channels) are

[1] The basis for this perspective can be found in Roland L. Warren, "The Interorganizational Field as a Focus for Investigation," in M. B. Brinkerhiff and P. R. Kunz (eds.), *Complex Organizations and Their Environments* (Dubuque, Iowa: Wm. C. Brown Company, 1972), p. 316.

[2] Bert C. McCammon, Jr. "Perspectives for Distribution Programming," in Louis P. Bucklin (ed.), *Vertical Marketing Systems* (Glenview, Ill.: Scott, Foresman and Company, 1970), p. 43.

compared and contrasted. Before the different administrative patterns can be evaluated, however, exactly what these channels are must be understood.

CONVENTIONAL MARKETING CHANNELS

Conventional marketing channels generally consist of isolated and independent institutions. Each organization performs a traditionally defined set of marketing functions, with little concern or awareness of other firms in the channel. Conventional channels tend to evolve over time, as relationships develop among manufacturers, intermediaries, and end consumers. These channels

> are coordinated through the operation of prices and the related modes of market mechanisms; the types and variety of products to be handled, levels of promotion, and location of retail outlets are determined by the interaction of manufacturers and distributors as buyers and sellers in intermediary markets.[3]

Thus, coordination among channel members is primarily achieved through bargaining and negotiation rather than by detailed or purposeful planning.

Because of the nature of conventional channels, there is a significant lack of loyalty among channel members; they have few, if any, common goals. Decisions within such channels are often based on tradition. These loose ties between channel members, however, make it easy for firms to enter and exit conventional channels. The conventional channel network, then, is relatively unstable.

Although conventional channels seldom achieve either the efficiency or the effectiveness of vertical marketing systems, they do have the ability to meet rapidly changing needs in the marketplace, and this is their primary strength. In addition, they are effective in marketing nonstandardized goods and services.[4] Many brands of ready-to-wear clothing, housewares, processed foods, office supplies, furniture, property and casualty insurance, life insurance, health care, and used automobiles are distributed through conventional channels. The marketing channel for motion pictures offers an illustration of some of the problems encountered in using conventional channels (see Exhibit 9-1).

As Exhibit 9-1 illustrates, individual channel members, such as theater owners, can sometimes be exploited by their suppliers or by customers who do not understand the benefits to be derived from a channel system orientation. Moreover, conventional channels run into difficulty when a need for systemwide strength and coordination arises. Despite these weaknesses, the conventional marketing channel is the most common form of distribution in capitalistic societies.

In an effort to manage the challenges facing entire marketing channels more effectively and efficiently, several significant methods of administering channels have emerged. We discuss each of these methods in turn, starting with the least

---

[3] Michael Etgar, "Effects of Administrative Control on Efficiency of Vertical Marketing Systems," *Journal of Marketing Research*, Vol. 13 (February 1976), p. 12.

[4] For further elaboration, see Joseph P. Guiltinan, "Planned and Evolutionary Changes in Distribution Channels," *Journal of Retailing*, Vol. 50 (Summer 1974), pp. 79–91, 103.

EXHIBIT 9-1
Marketing Channels for Motion Pictures: ⚹
Conventional Channels Run Amok

The distribution channels for motion pictures provide an excellent example of the negative aspects of conventional marketing channels.[a] The commercial channel for movies comprises producers (companies that actually make the movies), distributors, and exhibitors (theater owners). Prior to 1948, the channel was almost totally integrated—the companies that made the movies also owned the theaters that played them. In 1948, the U.S. Supreme Court ordered the five major film production-distribution companies to divest themselves of their movie theaters.[b] During the years since 1948,

> the new, independent theatre chains were able to bully producers and distributors suddenly bedeviled by television. In recent years, however, the distributors have gained the upper hand. With fewer and fewer pictures being made, the movie world has become a seller's market. The distributors have a limited number of films to rent, and the theatre owners are competing furiously with each other to land the few prize attractions. . . .

> "[T]here has never been any love lost between the major distributors (companies like Universal, Twentieth Century–Fox, and United Artists) and the theatre owners. For example, one Chicago representative of a distribution company has been quoted as telling a theatre owner, 'If you make any money on this deal, I'm not doing my job right.' "[c]

While the representative's remark is obviously facetious, the actions taken by distributors show that there is considerable truth behind it. Theater owners must bid against one another for the right to show a distributor's movie. Often these channel members must bid in a process called *blind bidding*, without ever having seen the films. In addition, distributors may require *block booking*, whereby bidding is for a package or block of films. A typical block includes not only a "surefire hit" but some obvious "duds" as well. Distributors may also ask exhibitors to give them advances or guaranteed revenue before a picture even opens.[d]

Distributors argue that such practices are necessary. First, they believe that exhibitors should share the movie-making risks and the higher costs of producing successful box office draws. Second, the distributors claim that without the advances from the theater owners, fewer films would be made.[e]

In any event, the movie-going public suffers as a result of these practices. First, because only the large downtown movie houses and a few shopping center theaters can afford the large, first-run, advance guarantee costs, smaller theaters are squeezed. Particularly disadvantaged are people who live near the small theaters typically located between downtown and the suburbs or in rural areas. Second, blind bidding can cause unseen "bombs" such as *Heaven's Gate* to be booked during the prime movie-going summer and Christmas holiday periods. After dropping these "duds," exhibitors must then scramble to find box office replacements, which are usually not as attractive as the first-run movies showing at their competitors' theaters. In addition to losing box office draw, these theater owners lose their advance money for such "bombs." Finally, block booking results in the spring and fall movie "deserts" when consumers must suffer through the duds that exhibitors take to get the hits they show during prime time. Thus, a lack of a systemwide orientation within the marketing channel for movies severely impairs the output of the channel from the consumer's perspective.

Certainly, distributors could use their power more constructively to compete more effectively against television, particularly the hated HBO. However, until they begin to see the theater owners as key partners in the distribution of motion pictures, the channel for movies will retain all of the negative attributes of many other conventional marketing channels.

[a]Gene Siskel, "Five Powerful Pieces Set into Place," *Chicago Tribune*, Sect. 6, February 23, 1975, pp. 2, 3, and 8.

[b]*United States v. Paramount Pictures, Inc.*, 334 U.S. 131 (1948); see also *Theatre Enterprises, Inc. v. Paramount Film Distributing Corp.*, 346 U.S. 537 (1954).

[c]Siskel, "Five Powerful Pieces," p. 2.

[d]"Heaven's Gate Leaves Theater Owners Fuming," *Business Week*, December 8, 1980, pp. 29, 31.

[e]Ibid.

integrated (in a formal ownership sense) and moving to the most highly integrated form. Note that as channel members move closer to formal vertical integration, there is a trade-off between the amount of control they achieve and the amount of investment and bureaucracy required to maintain the system. In addition, for gains in economies of scale, they sacrifice a certain amount of flexibility.

ADMINISTERED MARKETING CHANNEL SYSTEMS

In an administered vertical channel system, marketing activities are coordinated through the programs developed by one or a limited number of firms. Fleming Foods, as illustrated at the beginning of this chapter, administers its wholesaler-to-retailer channel for food by helping its retailer customers to perform their marketing tasks.

Marketing institutions in administered systems generally pursue their individual goals and have no formal organizational structure to bind them together. The marketing program, on the other hand, allows these organizations to collaborate informally on the goals they do share. Although the individual channel members are independently owned, they are willing, on an ad hoc basis, to divide the marketing channel tasks. As in conventional channels, commitment is to the individual firm rather than to the channel as a whole. The difference is that administered channels have at least a minimal amount of systemwide orientation among the member firms.

Suppliers have taken the initiative in developing administered marketing channels (e.g., Fleming, Kraft, Corning Glass, Genuine Parts). In addition, many retailers (e.g., Sears, Montgomery Ward, J. C. Penney, and McDonald's) have programmed their channels backward toward their sources of supply.

One of the most innovative approaches to developing administered systems has been the emergence of programmed merchandising agreements. Under this concept, suppliers and retailers formulate specialized merchandising plans to market the supplier's product line.[5] Such programming generally involves the activities listed in Table 9-1 for each brand and for each store included in the agreement. Manufacturing organizations engaged in programmed merchandising

---

TABLE 9.1 Plans and Activities Covered in Programmed Merchandising Agreements

1. Merchandising Goals
   a. Planned sales
   b. Planned initial markup percentage
   c. Planned reductions, including planned markdowns, shortages, and discounts
   d. Planned gross margin
   e. Planned expense ratio (optional)
   f. Planned profit margin (optional)
2. Inventory Plan
   a. Planned rate of inventory turnover
   b. Planned merchandise assortments, including basic or model stock plans
   c. Formalized "never out" lists
   d. Desired mix of promotional versus regular merchandise
3. Merchandise Presentation Plan
   a. Recommended store fixtures
   b. Space allocation plan
   c. Visual merchandising plan
   d. Needed promotional materials, including point-of-purchase displays, consumer literature, and price signs
4. Personal Selling Plan
   a. Recommended sales presentations
   b. Sales training plan
   c. Special incentive arrangements, including "spiffs," salesmen's contests, and related activities
5. Advertising and Sales Promotion Plan
   a. Advertising and sales promotion budget
   b. Media schedule
   c. Copy themes for major campaigns and promotions
   d. Special sales events
6. Responsibilities and Due Dates
   a. Supplier's responsibilities in connection with the plan
   b. Retailer's responsibilities in connection with the plan

---

Source: Bert C. McCammon, Jr., "Perspectives for Distribution Programming," in Louis P. Bucklin (ed.), *Vertical Marketing Systems* (Glenview, Ill.: Scott, Foresman and Company, 1970), pp. 48–49.

[5] McCammon, "Perspectives for Distribution Programming," p. 48.

activities include General Electric (for light bulbs and major appliances), Baum-ritter (for its Ethan Allen furniture line in nonfranchised outlets), Sealy (for its Posturepedic line of mattresses), Villager (for its dress and sportswear lines), Scott (for its lawn care products), and Hanes (for its L'eggs pantyhose).

To develop effective merchandising programs, suppliers and resellers must cooperate to a high degree. This means joint planning, clear and effective communication of intentions, and close coordination of the performance of the marketing flows. Thus, an administered or programmed channel sharply contrasts with a conventional channel, as detailed in Table 9-2.

TABLE 9.2 Comparison of Characteristics of Supplier-Retailer Relationships in a Conventional Channel versus a Programmed System

Characteristics	Conventional Channel	Programmed System
Nature of contacts	Negotiation on an individual-order basis	Advanced joint planning for an extended time period
Information considered	Supplier sales presentation data	Retailer's merchandising data
Supplier participants	Supplier's territorial salesperson	Salesperson and major regional or headquarters executive
Retailer participants	Buyer	Various executives, perhaps top management
Retailer's goals	Sales gain and percent markup	Programmed total profitability
Supplier's goal	Big order on each call	Continuing profitable relationship
Nature of performance evaluation	Event centered; primarily related to sales volume and other short-term performance criteria	Specific performance criteria written into the program

Source: Reprinted from *Marketing News*, published by the American Marketing Association, " 'Distribution Channel Détente' Benefits Suppliers, Retailers, *and* Consumers," by Ronald L. Ernst, March 7, 1980, p. 19.

For suppliers, the key benefits of programming reseller merchandising activities are:[6]

- The development of maximum sales and profit potential without competing for it on a day-to-day basis.
- Continuity of promotion and sales for more economic scheduling of production and distribution activities.
- Improved sales forecasting ability for manufacturing and distribution planning.
- Achievement of a totally coordinated, planned, and controlled marketing approach to reach the consumer.

[6] Ronald L. Ernst, " 'Distribution Channel Détente' Benefits Suppliers, Retailers, *and* Consumers," *Marketing News*, March 7, 1980, p. 19.

- Clearly specified retailer inventory requirements that allow inventory management and control efficiencies.

The central benefits for resellers, including wholesalers and retailers, of participating in programmed merchandising activities are:[7]

- Adequate and timely availability of merchandise.
- Preferential consideration from key resources or suppliers.
- Assortment planning and merchandise-control assistance.
- Clearly specified inventory investment requirements.
- The security of merchandising on a price-maintained basis.
- High levels of vendor service with regard to product quality and general account maintenance.
- Economy and efficiency through shifting functions, such as ordering, to the supplier.

For an in-depth look at how channel members benefit from one supplier's approach to administering its marketing channel, see Exhibit 9-2.

The concept of administering the channel through systemwide programs is also being applied in the logistics field.

Ryder System, Inc., has instituted a program that eliminates several intermediate warehousing operations for its truck-leasing customers. Ryder offers its trucks as rolling warehouses. Newly manufactured goods go first into the manufacturer's warehouse, next are shipped to a retailer's warehouse, and then are shipped once again either to the store or to the retailer's customer. This process often leads to a minimum of six loadings and unloadings into warehouses before the goods reach their final destination. Ryder claims that by using trucks as warehouses, shippers can minimize loading and unloading. This speeds up the shipment cycle, and thus can reduce trucking needs by 20 percent.[8]

CONTRACTUAL MARKETING CHANNEL SYSTEMS

Often organizations desire to formalize their marketing channel relationships by using contractual agreements to coordinate their activities. While virtually every business transaction is covered by some form of contract (either explicit or

---

[7] Ibid.

[8] "Marketing When the Growth Slows," *Business Week*, April 14, 1975, p. 50. Another logistics company that has administered its channels in a unique and profitable way is CAST, a Canadian shipping company. See James O'Shea, "Rival Calls U.S. Shippers Lazy," *Chicago Tribune*, Sect. 5, April 20, 1980, pp. 1, 2.

EXHIBIT 9-2
An Illustration of an Administered Channel:
Norwalk Furniture Corporation

Norwalk Furniture Corporation, based in Norwalk, Ohio, is an upholstery furniture manufacturer that has programmed its channel system. Because of its unique manufacturing facility, Norwalk is one of the few such firms that can guarantee 30-day delivery on all special orders; most furniture makers require delivery times of at least 8 weeks. This rapid delivery time is the centerpiece of Norwalk's total-effort-dealer program.

Total-effort-dealers are required to:

1. Display Norwalk furniture in nine out of ten upholstered furniture room settings.
2. Operate on a special-order basis and not sell floor samples, which would jeopardize future sales.

In turn, Norwalk:

1. Guarantees 30-day delivery.
2. Provides customized advertising materials, catalogs, and extra-large fabric swatches.
3. Conducts an annual factory-authorized sale.
4. Provides inventory financing.
5. Provides an advertising allowance.
6. Conducts sales meetings for floor sales personnel.
7. Provides in-store merchandising assistance.

Because all dealer sales are made on a custom-order basis with 30-day guaranteed delivery, the only inventory the dealer needs to carry is in floor samples. Also, because all sales under the program are special orders, the dealer typically experiences higher gross margins as a result of the reduced risks of carrying poor selling items. Markdowns are minimized, and lower warehousing and handling costs are achieved.

In addition to these benefits, the program has enabled the dealer sales force to achieve higher sales productivity by focusing on one upholstered line. Norwalk also provides promotional materials and in-store merchandising assistance to improve sales performance even further.

Source: Based on an article from *Marketing News*, published by the American Marketing Association, " 'Distribution Channel Détente' Benefits Suppliers, Retailers, *and* Consumers," by Ronald L. Ernst, March 7, 1980, p. 19.

implied), contracts in vertical marketing systems are used to specify, in writing, the functions to be performed by each channel member.

Table 9-3 illustrates the variety of forms contractual channels can take.

TABLE 9.3 Principal Types of Contractual Vertical Marketing Systems

Contractual Systems Involving Forward Integration	Contractual Systems Involving Backward Integration
Wholesaler-sponsored voluntary groups	Retailer-sponsored cooperative groups
Wholesaler-sponsored programmed groups	Retailer/wholesaler-sponsored buying groups
Supplier franchise programs for individual brands and specific departments	Retailer-sponsored promotional groups
Supplier franchise program covering all phases of the licensee's operation	Nonprofit shipping associations
Nonprofit shipping associations	Retailer/wholesaler resident buying offices
Leased department arrangements	Industrial, wholesale, and retail procurement contracts
Producer marketing cooperatives	Producer buying cooperatives

However, these essentially collapse into the three principal forms of contractual integration—wholesaler-sponsored voluntary groups, retailer-sponsored cooperative groups, and franchise systems. The focus here is on these principal forms.

Voluntary and Cooperative Groups

A *wholesaler-sponsored voluntary chain* is a group of independently owned retailers that are banded together by a wholesaler. A retailer joins a voluntary group to achieve the benefits of promoting and buying in larger scale than would be possible if operating independently. Perhaps the best-known wholesaler-sponsored voluntary association is the Independent Grocers Alliance (IGA). In the hardware field, voluntary groups like Pro, Liberty, and Sentry provide their retailers with services similar to those found in the IGA system. Wholesaler-sponsored voluntary chains are used in other merchandise lines as well; for example, Western Auto (automobile accessories) and Ben Franklin (notions and general merchandise).

The *retailer-sponsored cooperative* is also a voluntary association, but here the impetus for banding together comes from the retailers. The retailers organize and democratically operate their own wholesale company. The incentive to form a retail cooperative is exactly the same as that for joining a voluntary group—that is, to achieve the economies-of-scale in promotion and purchasing that are available to larger-scale organizations.

Topco Associates, Inc., is a food buying organization owned cooperatively by a group of supermarket chains and grocery wholesalers located throughout the United States. Topco's central function is to serve its owner-member companies in purchasing, product development, quality control, packaging, and promotion of a wide variety of private-label merchandise sold in supermarkets. Its brands include Top Frost, Gaylord, Elna, and Food Club, and are marketed through such firms as Big Bear Stores in Columbus, Ohio; Dillon Stores in Hutchinson, Kansas; Hinky-Dinky Stores in Omaha, Nebraska; and Fred Meyer, Inc., in Portland, Oregon.

Historically, retailer-sponsored cooperatives, such as Topco, Associated Grocers, and Certified Grocers, have been important in the food industry; they also have become prominent in the hardware business, where they account for about 35 percent of total wholesale sales. Among the better known of the hardware retailer-sponsored cooperatives are Cotter and Company (True Value), Ace Hardware, Hardware Wholesalers, Inc. (HWI), and Our Own Hardware Company.

Except for the ownership difference, wholesaler- and retailer-sponsored contractual systems operate similarly. The members join with the understanding that they will purchase a substantial portion of their merchandise from the group and will standardize retail advertising, identification, and operating procedures to conform with those of the group. Members usually contribute to a common advertising fund and operate stores under a common name. These standardization procedures enable the group to achieve greater market impact and economies of scale.

Voluntary and cooperative groups were initially formed in the 1930s to give smaller firms the same buying power enjoyed by the rapidly growing chain stores. As they evolved, however, voluntaries and cooperatives developed a vast number of marketing programs involving centralized consumer advertising and promotion, store location and layout, training, financing, accounting, and, in some cases, a total package of support services.

Contractual marketing channel systems have experienced phenomenal growth. For example, IGA now operates more stores than A&P, and Super Valu outlets' annual sales are higher than Kroger's. Nationwide, the share of grocery store sales enjoyed by voluntary and cooperative groups combined is equal to that held by corporate chains. One of the reasons for this successful growth is the "clarity of total offer" made possible by the implementation of systemwide marketing programs. Once customers see the store sign, they clearly understand the outlet's marketing orientation, including product, service, and atmosphere.[9] This point is stressed in Exhibit 9-3, which provides additional insight into the workings of the IGA voluntary group.

Generally, the wholesaler-sponsored voluntary groups have been more effective competitors than retailer-sponsored cooperatives. In the voluntary groups, wholesalers use their expertise and market power to provide leadership within the channel. Since in retail cooperatives power is diffused throughout the membership, coordination of the marketing channel functions is more difficult to achieve.

Before we discuss perhaps the most popular form of contractual vertical marketing channel systems—franchising—we should note that farm producer cooperatives have played an important role in distribution in the United States. Farm cooperatives, such as Farmland Industries, Associated Milk Producers, Agway, Sunkist Growers, and Land O'Lakes, act as both customers and suppliers to their members. Farmers sell their output to cooperatives and buy seed,

[9] Bert C. McCammon, Jr., Alton F. Doody, and William R. Davidson, *Emerging Patterns of Distribution* (Columbus, Ohio: Management Horizons, 1969), pp. 5–6.

EXHIBIT 9-3
Independent Grocers Alliance (IGA)

Independent Grocers Alliance (IGA), based in Chicago, is a wholesaler-owned cooperative that operates the nation's largest wholesale-sponsored voluntary chain in food retailing. Of the 33 wholesalers that own the IGA system, the two largest are The Fleming Companies and Wetterau. The basic rationale behind the IGA voluntary is to enable its affiliated, independent retailers to compete more effectively with the large supermarket chains such as Safeway, Kroger, and Albertson's.

For an independent retailer, there are several advantages to joining the IGA voluntary group. First, the IGA group has an established name with a strong consumer franchise, particularly in the Midwest. Thus, IGA's store identification programs and its private-label merchandise provide a new store with a ready-made market presence. In addition, they allow mobile consumers to shop with confidence in a new market area. Second, IGA conducts national advertising to nurture and develop further the overall image of IGA stores. Finally, each store in a local market area contributes a fixed percentage of its sales revenue to a local advertising and promotion fund. The sponsoring wholesaler, in conjunction with the local retailers, develops and administers newspaper, radio, television, and direct-mail advertising for the group. Cooperative advertising enables the local IGA stores to compete more effectively against the chains than they could by advertising on their own.

In addition to these economic advantages, two other characteristics of the IGA voluntary group enhance its ability to compete. First is the cooperation between the IGA retailers and their sponsoring wholesalers. For example, these channel members work together weekly to formulate advertising plans—specifically, to determine the items to be featured, their prices, and other special promotional plans. Second, the food retailers are owners of independent businesses, and therefore may be more highly motivated to succeed than are company-employed managers.

To qualify for the IGA group, retailers must meet certain standards. First, the store must meet minimum square footage size requirements and must be at least a minimum distance from other IGA stores. Second, the retailer must agree to support the local group advertising program, adhere to certain cleanliness standards, and price its merchandise competitively. Finally, the retailer must pay weekly or monthly membership fees to the wholesaler and to the IGA headquarters.

By cooperating, the wholesale sponsors and retail members of the IGA voluntary group are able to compete effectively on a systemwide basis against the vertical marketing systems of the corporate supermarket chains.

Source: Based on personal interviews with Jim Clark and Ann Bornholdt, The Fleming Companies, November, 1985.

agrichemicals, farm equipment, feed, and other goods from them. While some farm coops have vertically integrated both backward and forward within their marketing channels, they are primarily wholesalers of goods and services that administer the channels they control with the approval of the farmers who own them.

✳ FRANCHISE SYSTEMS

Franchise systems are major components of the distribution structure of the United States. In 1985, sales of goods and services by all franchising companies (manufacturing, wholesaling, and retailing) exceeded $500 billion. Approximately 33 percent of all U.S. retail sales flow through franchise and company-owned units in franchise chains. There are roughly one-half million establishments employing over five million people in franchise-related businesses.[10] Because of their growing importance, their makeup, design, and orientation are examined in considerable detail in this section.[11]

Exactly which channel arrangements should be termed franchise systems is not altogether clear. For example, some classification schemes include wholesaler-sponsored voluntary chains as franchise systems. Others include channels in which a retailer or a wholesaler is franchised to sell a product in a specified territory along with other products obtained from other sources. The latter interpretation more accurately describes the franchise method of distribution rather than franchise *systems*. This confusion leads to inaccurate statistics on the number of franchisors and franchisees as well as the sales volume of franchise systems. One of the major sources of confusion is the great variety of franchise agreements (see Table 9-4).

A *franchise system* is defined for our purposes as the licensing of an *entire* business format where one firm (the franchisor) licenses a number of outlets (franchisees) to market a product or service and engage in a business developed by the franchisor, using the latter's trade names, trademarks, service marks, know-how, and methods of doing business. Within legal bounds, the franchisor may sell the products, sell or lease the equipment, and/or sell or lease the premises necessary to the operation. For example, McDonald's insists that all of its units purchase from approved suppliers, provides building and design specifications, provides or helps locate financing for its franchisees, and issues quality standards that each unit must abide by in order to hold its franchise.

The franchisor may occupy any position within the channel. For example, the franchisor might be the manufacturer (e.g., Midas Mufflers), a service specialist (e.g., Kelly Girl), or a retailer franchising other retailers (e.g., Howard Johnson's during its early years of operation).

[10] Data on franchising obtained from U.S. Department of Commerce, Industry, and Trade Administration, *Franchising in the Economy 1983–85* (Washington, D.C.: U.S. Government Printing Office, January 1985).

[11] For additional detail, see Charles L. Vaughn, *Franchising*, 2nd ed. (Lexington, Mass.: Heath Lexington Books, 1979); and Rick Rounsborg and Robert T. Justis, *Basics of Franchising* (Lincoln: International Center for Franchise Studies, University of Nebraska, n.d.).

TABLE 9.4 Type of Franchise Systems

Type	Explanation
Territorial franchise	The franchise granted encompasses several counties or states. The holder of the franchise assumes the responsibility for setting up and training individual franchises within his territory and obtains an "override" on all sales in his territory.
Operating franchise	The individual independent franchisee runs his own franchise. He deals either directly with the parent organization or with the territorial franchise holder.
Mobile franchise	A franchise that dispenses its product from a moving vehicle, which is either owned by the franchisee or leased from the franchisor. Examples are Tastee Freeze and Snap-On Tools.
Distributorship	The franchisee takes title to various types of goods and further distributes them to subfranchisees. The distributor has exclusive coverage of a wide geographical area and acts as a supply house for the franchisees who carry the product.
Co-ownership	The franchisor and franchisee share the investment and profits. Examples are Aunt Jemima's Pancake Houses and Denny's Restaurants.
Co-management	The franchisor controls the major part of the investment. The partner-manager shares profits proportionately. Examples are Travelodge and Holiday Inn in the motel business.
Leasing	The franchisor leases the land, buildings, and equipment to franchisees. These are used in conjunction with other provisions.
Licensing	The franchisor licenses the franchisee to use his trademarks and business techniques. The franchisor either supplies the product or provides franchisees with a list of approved suppliers.
Manufacturing	The franchisor grants a franchise to manufacture its product throught the use of specified materials and techniques. The franchisee distributes the product, utilizing the franchisor's techniques. This method enables a national manufacturer to distribute regionally when distribution costs from central manufacturing facilities are prohibitive. One example is Sealy.
Service	The franchisor describes patterns by which a franchisee supplies a professional service, as exemplified by employment agencies.

Source: Based on Gerald Pintel and Jay Diamond, *Retailing* (Englewood Cliffs, N.J.: Prentice-Hall, 1971), pp. 23–26.

There are four basic types of franchise systems:[12] ✻

1. *The manufacturer-retailer franchise* is exemplified by franchised automobile dealers and franchised service stations.

2. *The manufacturer-wholesaler franchise* is exemplified by Coca-Cola, Pepsi Cola, Royal Crown Cola, and Seven-Up, who sell the soft-drink syrups they manufacture to franchised wholesalers who, in turn, bottle and distribute soft drinks to retailers.

3. *The wholesaler-retailer franchise* is exemplified by Rexall Drug Stores, Sentry Drug Centers, and ComputerLand.

4. *The service sponsor-retailer franchise* is exemplified by Avis, Hertz, and National in the car rental business; McDonald's, Chicken Delight, Kentucky

[12] William P. Hall, "Franchising: New Scope for an Old Technique," *Harvard Business Review*, Vol. 42 (January–February 1964), pp. 60–72.

Fried Chicken, and Taco-Tico in the prepared foods industry; Howard Johnson's and Holiday Inn in the lodging and food industry; Midas and AAMCO in the auto repair business; and Kelly Girl and Manpower in the employment service business.

Franchise systems are represented in almost all business fields and cover a wide variety of goods and services (see Table 9-5 and Exhibit 9-4).[13] Despite this diversity, automobile and petroleum franchise systems dominate this industry,

TABLE 9.5 Examples of Franchise Organizations and the Businesses They Represent

Automotive Accessories & Parts
  Firestone Tire & Rubber
  Goodyear Tire & Rubber
  Western Auto Supply
  White Stores
	Food Operations
	  Bonanza Restaurants
	  Bressler's 33 Flavors
	  Burger King
	  Chi-Chi's
	  Mr. Donut of America
	  Hickory Farms of Ohio

Automotive Repair and Service
  AAMCO Transmissions
  Jiffy Lube International
  Midas International
  Ziebart
	International House of Pancakes
	  McDonald's
	  Orange Julius of America
	  Taco Bell

Auto Rental
  Ajax Rent-A-Car System
  Budget Rent-A-Car System
	Home Furnishings
	  Pier 1 Imports
	  United Consumers Club

Business Aids and Services
  H & R Block
  Muzak
  Telechek Services
	Hotels and Motels
	  Hilton Inns
	  Holiday Inns
	  Ramada Inns
	  Rodeway Inns
	  Travelodge

Clothing and Shoes
  The Athlete's Foot
  Gingiss International
  Knapp Shoes
	Printing and Copying
	  Kwik-Kopy
	  Postal Instant Press
	  Sir Speedy

Computer Stores
  Computerland
  Entré Computer Centers
  MicroAge Computer Stores
	Real Estate
	  Century 21
	  Coldwell Banker
	  ERA Real Estate

Convenience Food Markets
  Southland (7-Eleven Stores)
	Weight Control
	  DietCenter

Employment Agencies
  Bryant Bureau
  Manpower
  Personnel Pool of America
	Nutri-System Weight Loss Centers
	  Physicians Weight Loss Centers

Source: International Franchise Association, *Directory of Membership, 1983*, (Washington, D.C.: International Franchise Association, 1983).

[13] For a more comprehensive listing of the types of businesses in which franchising plays an important role, see U.S. Department of Commerce, International Trade Administration and Minority Business Development Agency, *Franchise Opportunities Handbook* (Washington, D.C.: U.S. Government Printing Office, October 1984).

EXHIBIT 9-4
Thumbnail Sketches of Selected Franchise
Systems

Budget Rent-A-Car

Budget Rent-A-Car has a fleet of 100,000 trucks and automobiles, ranking it third in the vehicle rental industry. Budget, unlike its competitors, is essentially a franchisor. It retains a nucleus of company-owned operations to assist in developing and piloting operating and marketing programs. The company and its licensees provide the same automobile rental service as its major competitors, but generally at lower cost. Budget began its operations in off-airport, downtown, and suburban locations, and remains the leader in those markets. (Note that Budget also operates Sears car rentals.) The company has recently emphasized expanding into airport locations and, by 1983, had in-terminal facilities at about 200 U.S. airports that serve virtually every U.S. commercial air traveler.

Ramada Inns

At the end of 1982, the hotel group of Ramada Inns, Inc., oversaw 571 hotel properties with 94,400 rooms. Although Ramada manages its own properties as well as those of some of its licensees, it is primarily a franchisor—nearly 90 percent of its properties and almost 80 percent of its rooms are franchised. During 1982, the Ramada Inns system realized over $700 million in gross room revenues and earned nearly $300 million in franchise fee and royalty revenues.

AAMCO Transmissions

Started in 1963, AAMCO Transmissions, Inc., the world's largest chain of transmission repair centers, grew to 928 franchised outlets by the end of 1984. AAMCO's chief competitive strengths are: (1) it offers a repair warranty that is honored at all AAMCO shops nationwide; and (2) it has the only chain-owned parts supply network in the industry. In addition, AAMCO has developed a national fleet accounts program that generates over $10 million in annual business for its franchisees.

Mary Moppet's Day Care Schools

In 1983, Mary Moppet's Day Care Schools, Inc., was caring for over 10,000 children in 93 schools throughout 14 states, largely west of the Mississippi. When it began in 1968, Mary Moppet's set as its mission the provision of quality day care for children aged six months to ten years. Accordingly, both company-owned and franchised schools are required to have state day-care operator's licenses and to serve at least one hot meal per day. All schools are open from 6:30 A.M. to 6:30 P.M. five days a week, while some maintain longer hours. Building plans, school equipment, learning programs for children, training programs for staff, and resource materials are the key franchisee services provided by Mary Moppet's.

accounting for about 33 percent of all franchised outlets and nearly 70 percent of total franchise sales.

Modes of Operation[14]

All franchisees are expected to provide a constant market for their franchisor's product or service. This product or service is ideally characterized by its *consistent* quantity and quality and by strong promotion. Through its market- and image-building promotional efforts, the franchisor aims for widespread acceptance from both prospective franchisees and ultimate customers.

Franchisors provide both initial and continuous service to their franchisees. *Initial* services include:

- Market survey and site selection.
- Facility design and layout.
- Lease negotiation advice.
- Financing advice.
- Operating manuals.
- Management training programs.
- Franchisee employee training.

In many cases, the degree of franchisor involvement with franchisees is clearly high; however, the fact that franchisors provide an initial service does not indicate anything about the depth of that service.

Over 95 percent of all franchised outlets are built from the ground up. That is, similar and ongoing businesses did not previously exist on the current franchisee's location. However, the degree of control a franchisor exercises over site location and development varies widely. McDonald's does all locational site analysis and most land acquisition and development. On the other hand, Budget Rent-A-Car merely assigns territories and allows franchisees to build where they please, subject to franchisor review and advice.

Franchisors' *continuous services* can include:

- Field supervision.
- Merchandising and promotional materials.
- Management and employee retraining.
- Quality inspection.

[14] This section is based largely on National Industrial Conference Board, *Franchised Distribution* (New York: National Industrial Conference Board, 1971).

- National advertising.
- Centralized purchasing.
- Market data and guidance.
- Auditing and record keeping.
- Management reports.
- Group insurance plans.

Exhibit 9-5 illustrates the continuous services Ramada Inns provides its franchisees.

Almost all franchisors have a continuous program of field services. Field representatives visit the franchise outlet to aid the franchisee in everyday operation, check the quality of product and service, and monitor performance.

All franchisees are usually required to report monthly or semimonthly on key aspects of their operations, e.g., weekly sales, local advertising, employee turnover, profits, and other financial and marketing information. These systematic reports are intended to facilitate the various financial, operating, and marketing control procedures.

As might be expected, the reaction of franchisees to field services and operating controls is not always positive. Franchisees are independent business owners even though they have signed contractual agreements with franchisors. When conflict over supervision arises within their systems, franchisors have tended to rely on their field representatives to act as channel diplomats. However, these representatives are responsible for serving existing franchisees as well as recruiting new ones. Complaints are often heard that the franchisor pays too little attention to franchisees' management problems, especially when the field representatives have too many conflicting responsibilities.

Another source of friction between franchisors and franchisees is dual distribution. Many franchisors have a number of company-owned outlets, some of which directly compete with franchisee-owned operations. Although franchisors generally try to avoid the problems associated with this form of intrabrand competition, they sometimes find that owning their own outlets is necessary. First, franchisor-owned and -operated units serve as models for the rest of the system and can be used for research and training purposes. Second, such units may accelerate network growth, especially during the initial development period. Third, wholly owned units may be profitable. They also give the franchisor first-hand insight into day-to-day operating problems. Finally, court decisions and legislation may force franchisors to own more and more of their outlets if they wish to maintain strong control over the operations of the system as a whole. Although some people feel that the number of company-owned stores is generally increasing,[15] the move to company-owned operations is significant only in the restaurant field, where the percentage of company-owned outlets rose from 19.4 in 1972 to 29.6 in 1979 to 31.8 in 1985, but now appears to be slowing.

[15] Donald W. Hackett, *Franchising: The State of the Art* (Chicago: American Marketing Association, 1977), p. 41.

EXHIBIT 9-5
Assistance Offered by Ramada Inns to Its
Franchisees

Ramada Inns, Inc., is the third-largest hotel chain in the world, operating under the Ramada Inns, Ramada Hotels, and Ramada Renaissance Hotels banners.

Many of Ramada's hotels are owned and operated by franchisees who pay an initial franchise fee of $20,000 to $50,000, depending on the number of rooms in the hotel facility. Royalty payments are 3 percent of gross room sales, and an additional 3 percent of gross room sales is assessed for specific services, including advertising and promotional programs, management training, and reservation system charges.

In return for its fees, franchisees receive the following services and assistance from Ramada Inns:

- *Worldwide Reservation System*: Including toll-free telephone numbers for travelers, travel agents, and major airlines; data base for generating management reports for each hotel; and tie-ins to an individual hotel's computer system.

- *Marketing Support*: National advertising, regional cooperative advertising programs, local advertising assistance; marketing research support; public relations assistance; creative services for the production of brochures, posters, directories, postcards, stationery, business cards, etc.; and sales support for responding to changing market conditions and new sales opportunities.

- *Management Contract Services*: Total management services for the real estate developer/owner who does not want to manage the hotel personally. Included are strategic planning; financial reporting; sales and marketing; internal audit and control; operational and physical quality control; and personnel selection, training, and supervision.

- *Quality Assurance*: Inspection and grading of each hotel to ensure that quality standards, ranging from maintenance to advertising and food service to accounting, are being met. Assistance in correcting any deficiencies is also offered.

- *System Operations Consulting*: Business advice to franchisees and managers on financial, food and beverage, sales and marketing, housekeeping, and other operations in the hotel.

- *Ramada Management Institute*: Management development for hotel owners, general managers, and department heads.

- *Purchasing Services*: For supplies, operating furnishings, and equipment.

Source: Adapted from franchisee information materials, Ramada Inns, Inc., 1983.

The proportion of company-owned stores for *all* franchising remained virtually stable between 1979 (18.8 percent) and 1985 (18.9 percent).[16]

To illustrate some of the conflicts that exist between franchisors and franchisees, Exhibit 9-6 briefly outlines the experience of Burger King, now a subsidiary of Pillsbury Company.

Sources of Franchisor Revenue

Sources of franchisor revenue and their relative importance are illustrated in Figure 9-1. The various sources include:

1. *Initial franchise fees.* Many franchisors charge an initial fee to new franchisees that ranges from $1,000 to $100,000, with the mode falling between $10,000 and $25,000. The fee covers the franchisor's expenses for site locations, training, setting operating controls, and other initial services, as well as developmental costs in building the system. Initial fees tend to rise as a franchise becomes more successful.

2. *Royalty fees.* Many franchisors charge a royalty fee or commission based on the gross value of a franchisee's sales volume. Five percent of gross sales is the most common royalty agreement in franchising. Some franchisors require a minimum payment of $150 to $200 per month. In certain cases, the royalty rate decreases as sales volume increases, while in others, the royalty fee is a flat rate regardless of the sales volume. Some franchisors collect a royalty on a unit-of-sale basis. For example, motel franchisors charge a fee per room; soft ice cream franchisors charge a fee for each gallon of mix sold to the franchisee; car wash equipment franchisors charge a fee per car washed.

3. *Sales of products.* Some franchisors function as wholesalers by supplying franchisees with raw materials and finished products. Other franchisors manufacture their products, such as Holiday Inns with its furniture and carpeting and Coca-Cola with its soft-drink syrups. In some cases, the franchise company sells the equipment needed by the franchisee. These practices are limited by recent court decisions, however, as was pointed out in Chapter 6.

4. *Rental and lease fees.* The franchise company often leases the building, equipment, and fixtures used in its outlets. Some franchise contracts involve escalator clauses that require franchisees to increase their lease payments as their sales volume increases.

5. *License fees.* The franchisee sometimes is required to pay for the use and display of the franchisor's trademark. The license fee applies especially to industrial franchises, where a local manufacturer is licensed to use a particular patent or process.

[16] U.S. Department of Commerce, Industry, and Trade Administration, *Franchising in the Economy*, pp. 27 and 36. Nonfood retailing franchise systems include general merchandise; wearing apparel; hardware, paints, and floor covering; drugs; electronics; and cosmetic items.

EXHIBIT 9-6

**Conflicts in Franchising: A Case Example—
Burger King in the Late 1970s**

1,489 Burger King restaurants out of a total of 2,726 are operated by franchisees who own the land and buildings themselves, or rent them from someone other than Pillsbury. In contrast, McDonald's owns or leases nearly all of the land and buildings used by its 5,747 restaurants. The advantages of ownership to the franchisor are compelling. The land is an appreciating asset and the building a source of depreciation write-offs. Equally important, however, is the fact that, as the franchisee's landlord, the franchisor has power. McDonald's franchisees, for example, are not allowed to own any other fast-food restaurants, and they have no territorial rights or protection. On the other hand, until relatively recently, Burger King granted exclusive rights to large territories and allowed franchisees to buy land and build as many stores as they liked. A franchisee was free to sell sections of his territory to others if he wanted; he could even diversify into other fast-food businesses.

The consequence of Burger King's early policies has been that some of its franchisees have grown so large that they are very difficult for the franchisor to control. Two of its franchisees—Chart House, Inc., and Horn & Hardart Company—have engaged in all-out battles with Pillsbury over such issues as expansion and diversification into other restaurant businesses. (Chart House owns Cork 'N Cleaver, the Chart House group in California, and over 350 Burger King restaurants. Horn & Hardart operates its famous Automats as well as a number of Arby's restaurants in addition to over 20 Burger King restaurants.)

Burger King has established a far more demanding contract with its franchisees. Franchisees must now agree not to own any other fast-food business and to live within an hour's drive of their Burger King restaurants, which makes it difficult for a franchisee to own more than a dozen restaurants.

Burger King franchisees are interested in their restaurants' profits and losses. Pillsbury is more interested in their sales. (Apart from a one-time franchise fee of $40,000, Pillsbury obtains most of its revenue from the franchisee's sales—3½ percent of sales as royalty; 4 percent for the marketing fund; and, if Pillsbury owns the land and building, an additional 8½ percent as rent. McDonald's levies a franchise fee of $12,500, a royalty of 3 percent, a marketing fee of 3 percent, and rent of 8½ percent.) There is a potential incompatibility of goals in almost all franchise arrangements, including Burger King's, especially when increasing sales push costs so high that the franchisee's profit goes down. For example, many Burger King franchisees originally strongly resisted Pillsbury's desire that they shift to multiple lines, such as McDonald's was using, in existing restaurants. The franchisees believed that the additional cash registers and extra help would cost more than the increased sales would justify.

Source: Lee Smith, "Burger King Puts Down Its Dukes." *Fortune*, June 16, 1980, pp. 90–98 © 1980 Time Inc. All rights reserved. As an epilogue, see "Horn & Hardart Co., Burger King Settle Franchise Dispute," *Wall Street Journal*, November 5, 1980, p. 12.

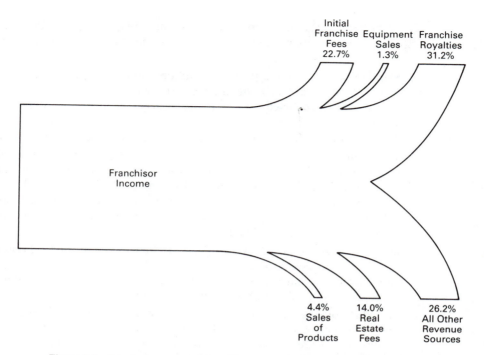

Initial
Franchise Equipment Franchise
Fees   Sales   Royalties
22.7%   1.3%   31.2%

Franchisor
Income

4.4%   14.0%   26.2%
Sales   Real   All Other
of   Estate   Revenue
Products   Fees   Sources

Figure 9-1 Principal sources of franchise company revenue. *Source*: E. Patrick McGuire, *Franchised Distribution* (New York, The Conference Board, 1971), p. 20.

6. *Management fees*. In a few cases, franchisees are charged fees for consulting services received from the franchisor such as management reports and training.

Rationale for Using Franchise Vertical Marketing Systems

As an alternative form of marketing channel organization, franchising offers several advantages to both suppliers and resellers of goods and/or services. However, these advantages must be balanced against the weaknesses of this form of distribution. The following sections explore the pros and cons of franchising from the perspective of the marketing channel.[17]

Advantages of Franchising. Franchising offers the marketing channel the following benefits:

1. Suppliers can expand distribution coverage with little equity investment. Franchisees provide front-end franchise fees to fund expansion after the initial start-up costs have been recovered. In addition, the franchisor's risks are reduced since the expansion funds are provided by the franchisees.

[17] For the specific advantages and disadvantages of franchising for franchisors and franchisees, see Rounsborg and Justis, *Basics of Franchising*, pp. 15–19.

2. Franchisees' royalty payments for national advertising and their contributions toward cooperative advertising reduce the franchisor's promotional costs.

3. Standardized marketing programs and operating procedures enable franchisees to be competitive immediately. If they are successful, these programs provide the franchisee with a ready source of customers demanding the product.

4. Since local franchisees share in the profits of the business, they tend to be more conscientious, motivated, and "bottom line"–oriented than company-paid managers. This profit motive provides franchisees with the incentive to follow the franchisor's operating guidelines and quality control standards. Thus, where monitoring the performance of company-owned outlets is difficult and costly, suppliers use franchising to ensure that the business will be operated according to standards.

5. In many market areas, franchisors attempt to reduce intrabrand competition among franchisees through territorial restrictions. This allows franchisees to concentrate on maintaining the quality of the good or service being sold in order to be more effective in interbrand competition.

6. Franchise businesses generate goodwill for the franchisors in the communities in which they operate. Locally, franchisees are often viewed as successful business people who are as involved in community activities as independent businesses are.

Disadvantages of Franchising. As with any method of organizing the marketing channel, franchising has several weaknesses that must be recognized before it is used. Among them are the following:

1. Not all businesses are amenable to franchising. A successful franchise must have a unique good or service that lends itself to enforceable standards of quality, service, and procedure.

2. Finding potentially successful channel partners may be difficult. Many successful franchise systems are highly selective in their choice of franchisees, while many potential franchisees avoid marginal franchisors.

3. Franchise systems can be more inflexible than either conventional channels, administered channels, voluntary chains, or retail cooperatives. Franchise agreements are long-term contracts, usually ranging from 10 to 25 years. Terminating poor franchisees or selling an outlet in a weak franchise system is often very difficult. In addition, responding to changing market conditions rapidly in large franchise networks is very cumbersome and often proceeds slowly.

4. Control over the marketing functions may be more difficult in franchise systems than in completely vertically integrated systems, since franchisees are independent business people as opposed to company-paid managers.

5. Conflict and distrust among channel partners are often characteristic of franchise systems. The root of these problems is the franchisor's desire for

control over its franchisees versus the franchisees' need for autonomy. Some specific issues of franchisor-franchisee conflict were illustrated in Exhibit 9-6. Other issues include franchisees' honest reporting of gross income (franchisors' royalties are based on this figure), franchisee maintenance of quality control standards (customers may generalize poor quality at any one outlet to the entire franchise system), franchisee acceptance of standardized marketing programs (a consistent systemwide image depends on a unified marketing mix), and the franchisor's honesty and integrity in developing and maintaining strong consumer demand (franchisors' unkept promises drive out those franchisees who are more likely to be successful in other franchise channels).

6. **Franchising is also subject to heavy legal and political influences.** Antitrust legislation limits franchisor practices such as tying arrangements, exclusive territories, and exclusive dealing. In addition, the Federal Trade Commission requires franchisors to file disclosure and registration documents; these requirements attempt to restrict franchisors' use of unfair and unethical practices in signing up franchisees. Moreover, in certain industries (e.g., automobile distribution), legislation prohibits franchisees from being terminated without just cause. Finally, many franchisees have organized into trade associations (e.g., National Automobile Dealers Association, Ford Dealers Alliance) that place political pressure on franchisors.

To judge from the growth in franchising over the past two decades, the balance between the benefits and costs of franchising has tipped in favor of the benefits for many firms.

Clearly, a wide variety of organizations want to control their marketing channels by establishing franchises or some other form of contractual arrangement. The next logical question is: Why don't they go all the way and vertically integrate the relevant marketing flows? The answer to this question is pursued in the next section, where we examine corporate channels.

CORPORATE VERTICAL MARKETING SYSTEMS

Corporate vertical marketing systems exist when channel members at different levels of distribution for a particular product are owned and operated by one organization. Corporate forward integration occurs when manufacturing firms own wholesale and/or retail operations or when wholesalers establish their own retail outlets. For example, Evans Products Company, a manufacturer of plywood, integrated forward when it purchased wholesale lumber distributors to promote its products more aggressively through retail lumber dealers. Evans has used acquisition to integrate vertically, while other firms, such as Tandy Corporation with its Radio Shack stores, have used internal expansion to move closer to their target markets.

Vertical forward integration is undertaken by both suppliers and resellers for at least three major reasons.[18] First, channel firms may achieve greater effectiveness and efficiency by owning the organizations that participate in the physical and ownership flows. Even more important is the control that channel institutions gain over distribution activities by integrating forward toward the target market.

Church's Fried Chicken, Inc., a San Antonio–based restaurant chain, operates 1,120 stores, mainly in the South and Southwest. One reason it is among the most profitable companies in the fast-food industry is the control it wields over its primarily company-owned outlets. Church's has, for the most part, avoided franchising, choosing to maintain meal quality by directly owning and managing the operations side of the business.[19]

Finally, forward vertical integration allows suppliers access to marketing channels that they might otherwise be denied.

Forward vertical integration may be partial, where the manufacturer performs its own wholesaling function and the retail task is undertaken by one or more independently owned and operated establishments. In addition, the wholesaling operation might be manufacturer owned in some markets and independently owned in others. In this situation, known as *dual distribution*, the producer uses multiple channels to reach its target markets.[20]

Anheuser-Busch, the world's largest brewer, markets its line of beers through approximately 960 independent wholesale distributors whose customers are restaurants, bars, supermarkets, convenience stores, liquor stores, and other retail outlets. The brewer also distributes through ten company-owned wholesalers. Thus, Anheuser-Busch engages in partial forward vertical integration as well as dual distribution.

Producers may also completely vertically integrate forward toward the target market by owning and operating their own retail network. Manufacturers such as Singer (sewing machines); Sherwin-Williams (paint and wall coverings); Hart, Schaffner, and Marx (men's suits); Goodyear (tires); Sohio (gasoline); and IBM (office electronics) offer their goods and services through corporate vertical marketing systems.

[18] For a more complete description of the advantages of forward vertical integration, see Michael E. Porter, *Competitive Strategy* (New York: The Free Press, 1980), pp. 302–315.

[19] "Church's: A Fast-Food Recipe That Is Light on Marketing," *Business Week*, February 20, 1978, pp. 110, 112; and "Church's Fried Chicken: Cutting Loose from Its Penny-Pinching Past," *Business Week*, February 27, 1984, p. 72.

[20] For an in-depth discussion of dual distribution, see Mary Jane Sheffet and Debra L. Scammon, "Legal Issues in Dual Distribution Systems," a paper presented at the First Annual Society of Franchising Conference, Omaha, September 1986.

Corporate backward integration occurs when either a retailer or a wholesaler owns its suppliers of marketing channel goods and services. Integrated chain store systems are often viewed as the primary example of corporate backward vertical integration. All chain store organizations have integrated the wholesaling functions, and many of them also own manufacturing facilities.

As with forward corporate systems, backward vertical integration can be either partial or complete. For example, Sears is a major stockholder in the Kellwood Company, its supplier of jeans, other wearing apparel, home furnishings, and camping equipment. Since Sears also buys its jeans from Levi's and Texas Apparel, Sears is partially integrated, although it does not completely own Kellwood. (For a more in-depth look at Sears' rationale for owning portions of some of its suppliers, see Exhibit 9-7.)

Some major wholesalers are engaged in successful backward vertical integration as well.

W. W. Granger, Inc., an electrical distributor with sales of $1 billion and a return on net worth of 16 percent in 1984, operates its own manufacturing facilities and has an aggressive private-brand program.

American Hospital Supply Corporation, with sales of $3.3 billion and return on net worth of 15.2 percent in 1983, is a vertically integrated distributor of health-care products and services. Products that American Hospital Supply makes itself accounted for 46 percent of its 1983 sales.[21]

A number of steel wholesalers, such as Joseph T. Reyerson & Son, Inc., A. M. Castle & Company, and Earle M. Jorgenson Company, have become metal service centers. These firms offer a wide variety of processing services, including slitting, welding, and forming. These service centers now dominate the wholesale segment of the steel market.

Backward vertical integration is undertaken for a variety of reasons.[22] First, by operating its own factories or wholesale operations, a channel institution can assure itself of a continuous supply of consistent-quality merchandise. Second, the physical, information, and transaction flows can be more effectively and efficiently undertaken in vertically integrated channels. Finally, resellers often acquire their sources of supply as a competitive move. For example, by acquiring partial ownership of Intel, a large computer chip manufacturer, IBM has assured that (1) it will not be foreclosed to Intel's products and (2) competition may find it more difficult to enter the market.

[21] "American Hospital Supply: Snaring New Business with Freebies and Bonuses," *Business Week*, April 8, 1985, pp. 88–89.

[22] For a more complete description of the advantages of backward vertical integration, see Porter, *Competitive Strategy*.

EXHIBIT 9-7

A Pioneer of Vertical Marketing Systems:
Sears, Roebuck and Company

In the 1920's, Sears, Roebuck and Co. foresaw the need to integrate mass distribution with mass production to reach its changing target market. The basic idea was to provide growing urban America with better quality goods at lower prices. Key to accomplishing this task was Sears' buying strategy, which emphasized partnership arrangements with efficient and dependable sources of supply. Sears' objective

> was to build stable partnerlike relationships in which both parties would have a significant stake and which would be in the interests of both to strenghten and maintain. This meant that the source as well as Sears would have to be able to count on a reasonable profit. The tremendous volume in which Sears bought was not to be used as a club to beat down the source's prices but a foundation on which the source as well as Sears could build a prosperous business.[1]

Through these channel partnerships, Sears could provide its markets with merchandise of good value.

Sears' channel partnerships are based on three key facets.[2] The first is specification buying, in which Sears provides product designs to its suppliers. Sears then works with its sources "to determine what should be made and when and to find ways of reducing costs at all stages, from the acquisition of materials through manufacturing, distribution, and final delivery to the customer."[3] Second, Sears' buying quantities enables its suppliers to achieve production economies of scale. In fact, Sears takes responsibility for procuring some raw materials because it can achieve greater buying economies than can any individual supplier. Finally, Sears is able to achieve lower costs since it performs most of the marketing functions cheaper than can its suppliers. Thus, once a good is produced, Sears undertakes all of the marketing functions for it to reach the target consumer.

Through its partnership arrangements with its suppliers, Sears is able to achieve the advantages of vertical integration without incurring its disadvantages. By and large, Sears does not vertically integrate, except in special circumstances. Among the reasons leading Sears to vertical integration are: (1) to protect Sears' interests where the source was Sears' sole supplier of a particular item(s); (2) to strengthen the capacity of small, reliable suppliers by injecting them via loans, advance payment for merchandise, or equity investment; and (3) to achieve lower costs through a capital investment on behalf of the supplier.[4] Only in rare cases does Sears have majority ownership interests, and in no case does Sears own a factory outright.

> [M]inority ownership, whether or not it included representation on the source's board, [is] sufficient to protect Sears' interests while simultaneously keeping prime responsibility for satisfactory performance where it belong[s]—in the hands of the manufacturing partner.[5]

Among the companies Sears has a minority interest in are Globe Battery (which makes DieHard batteries), Roper (Kenmore ranges), De-Soto (Easy Living paints), Swift (textiles), Kellwood (jeans), and, of course, Whirlpool (Kenmore dishwashers, clotheswashers, and dryers).

Sears' partnership with Whirlpool is typical of its relationship with its suppliers. The predecessor company made driving rods and other components for steam locomotives. When General Robert E. Wood, then head of Sears, heard that the market for steam locomotives was de-pressed, he proposed that, using an investment from Sears, the company refurbish its entire plant to begin making refrigerators for Sears. Eventu-ally, this company merged with another manufacturer of Sears appliances to evolve into Whirlpool.[6] In 1983, Sears accounted for "... 43% of Whirlpool's $2.7 billion annual sales of dishwashers, dryers, and clothes washers which it sells under its own Kenmore name."[7] The most striking feature of the channel partnership between Sears and Whirlpool is that "[t]he relationship has gone on for 65 years, with no written contract."[8]

Perhaps the marketing channel relationship between Sears and its suppliers is best summarized by James C. Worthy, long-time executive with the firm: "In general, Sears sources felt that they were part of the Sears team; typically, they tended to talk and act as though they were part of Sears, as in attitudinal and operational fact they were."[9]

[1] James C. Worthy, *Shaping an American Institution* (Urbana, IL: University of Illinois Press, 1984), p. 68.

[2] This discussion was drawn from ibid., pp. 69–75.

[3] Ibid., p. 69.

[4] Ibid., p. 77.

[5] Ibid.

[6] Ibid., p. 71.

[7] "Sears' Sizzling New Vitality, "*Time* (August 20, 1984), p. 88.

[8] Ibid.

[9] Worthy, *op. cit.*, p. 79.

DISTINCTIVE ADVANTAGES OF VERTICAL MARKETING SYSTEMS

Unlike conventional channels, vertical marketing systems are made up of channel institutions that recognize their interconnectedness. As a result, they coordinate, through detailed planning and comprehensive programming, how the marketing flows will be performed. The aim is to achieve systemwide efficiency and effectiveness in serving the target market. These systems rigorously control which marketing institutions may or may not participate in the channel. For contractual and corporate systems, specific agreements or ownership assure that channel members remain loyal to the system as a whole; therefore, these channel networks tend to be relatively stable. Decision makers in such systems are professional managers who focus on costs, volume, and investment at *all stages* of the marketing process. In addition, they are generally committed to applying sophisticated marketing concepts rather than more traditional or outmoded business practices.[23]

Unlike many conventional channels, vertical marketing systems seem to capitalize on programmed organization, economies of scale, and economies of standardization at the various levels of distribution. On the other hand, although the absence of long-term planning in independent channels results in higher distribution cost, independent retailers are free to buy from a number of manufacturers and wholesalers to better meet the needs of their markets. Thus, although distribution cost is lower for corporate chains, for example, chain store managers have less flexibility to react to changes in their markets. The franchise operator seems to occupy the middle ground on both the cost and flexibility fronts. While cost advantages favor vertical marketing systems, independent operators seem to have a distinct advantage when it comes to adapting to changing market opportunities.[24] The standardized level of performance achieved within vertical marketing systems, though, is rarely attained in conventional channels. Both industrial and household consumers prefer uniformity in the quality of goods and services they purchase, which gives systems capable of delivering such uniformity a strong competitive advantage.

From a managerial perspective, vertical marketing systems are developed to achieve a degree of control over the cost and quality of the functions performed by various channel members. The strength of such systems lies in their ability to specify channel roles by shifting and allocating the marketing flows among channel members. In theory, the performance of a vertical marketing system can approximate the performance of the "normative channel" in that channel members can be grouped and organized in such a way that no other type of grouping could create greater profits or more consumer satisfaction per dollar of product cost.

Managers within a vertical marketing system recognize the entire channel as the relevant unit of competition. In conventional channels, independent members tend to believe that competitive viability rests solely on actions taken at their individual levels of distribution.

Given all these advantages, "planned vertical marketing systems are rapidly displacing conventional marketing channels as the dominant mode of distribution in the American economy."[25]

Given the competitive strength of vertical marketing systems, members of conventional channels will obviously be forced to use fresh strategies if they are to survive. A few strategies are proposed below. The first three can be imple-

---

[23] This paragraph is based on McCammon, "Perspectives for Distribution Programming," p. 44.

[24] Louis P. Bucklin, "The Economic Base of Franchising," in Thompson (ed.), *Contractual Marketing Systems*, pp. 33–62; Guiltinan, "Changes in Distribution Channels;" and James R. Brown, Robert F. Lusch, and Harold F. Koenig, "Environmental Uncertainty Regarding Inventory Ordering," *International Journal of Physical Distribution and Materials Management*, Vol. 14 (1984), pp. 19–36.

[25] McCammon, "Perspectives for Distribution Programming," p. 43.

mented in the short term, but the fourth requires long-run adjustments.[26] In fact, implementation of the fourth suggestion would begin the development of the channel into a vertical marketing system.

1. *Develop programs to strengthen customers' competitive capabilities.* This alternative would involve manufacturers and wholesalers in such activities as sponsoring centralized accounting and management reporting services, formulating cooperative promotional programs, and co-signing shopping center leases.

2. *Enter new markets.* For example, building supply distributors have initiated cash-and-carry outlets. Steel warehouses have added glass and plastic product lines to their traditional product lines. Industrial distributors have initiated stockless buying plans and blanket order contracts so that they may compete effectively for customers who buy on a direct basis.

3. *Effect economies of operation by developing management information systems.* For example, some middlemen in conventional channels have become involved with their suppliers in electronic data interchange systems to improve their control over inventory.

4. *Determine, through research, which organization in the channel holds enough power in the channel to reorganize the marketing flows.* The potential channel leader may be located on any level of the channel, as we will discuss in Chapter 10.

We conclude our discussion of vertical marketing systems by exploring some of the legal implications of administering marketing channels.

LEGAL ASPECTS OF VERTICAL MARKETING SYSTEMS

As we noted in Chapters 2, 5, and 6, certain marketing channel practices are limited by federal legislation aimed at prohibiting restraint of trade. Some vertical marketing systems use more of these practices than others. For example, functional discounts and quantity discounts are frequently used in conventional channels, while promotional allowances and consignment selling are often employed in administered channels. Exclusive territories, resale restrictions, refusals to deal, exclusive dealing, tying contracts, and full-line forcing are practices common to contractual channels. Because of the questionable legality of many of these activities, some channel institutions have vertically integrated to avoid legal difficulties. This strategy, however, is not a guaranteed method of circumventing legal problems.

Vertical integration through internal expansion seems to be positively sanctioned by the antitrust enforcement agencies so long as it does not lead to monopolization in restraint of trade, a violation of the Sherman Act. On the other hand, the tenaciousness of these agencies in scrutinizing vertical integration by

---

[26] The first three suggested were adapted from McCammon, Doody, and Davidson, *Emerging Patterns of Distribution*, pp. 9–10.

merger depends on the presidential administration's philosophy concerning government intervention in business affairs. As noted in Chapter 2, the laissez-faire policies of the Ford, Carter, and Reagan administrations led to the deregulation of several industries, most notably financial services, transportation, and telecommunications. The Reagan administration carried this policy further by allowing several large vertical and horizontal mergers. Thus, the prevailing political climate directly affects how rigorously federal legislation pertaining to vertical integration by merger will be enforced.

As with franchising, integrating vertically often leads to dual distribution conflicts when sellers become competitors of some of their independently owned resellers. Although dual distribution is not illegal in all circumstances, Congress periodically examines this practice to ensure that small independent marketing intermediaries are not being severely hurt by it.

SUMMARY

Conventional marketing channels consisting of independently owned institutions and agencies frequently suffer from several weaknesses. Chief among them are the absence of a systemwide orientation and inclusive goals. If a locus of power is also absent, the specification of roles and the management of conflict in conventional channels are likely to be difficult. Even when a locus of power is present (as in the marketing channel for motion pictures), there is no guarantee that the channel will perform any better than when power is diffused.

Vertical marketing systems have emerged as significant forms of channel organization and represent, for the most part, sophisticated attempts on the part of management to overcome the inherent weaknesses of conventional channels. Administered vertical marketing systems are those in which marketing activities are coordinated through the use of programs developed by one or a limited number of firms. Improved channel effectiveness is achieved through careful administrative planning and the exercise of power. This approach has been most frequently adopted by suppliers and by carriers. They have used facilities management, modular merchandising, coordinated display, and automatic replenishment programs as well as programmed merchandising agreements to achieve success.

Contractual vertical marketing systems are those in which independent firms at different channel levels integrate their programs on a contractual basis to achieve economies and increased market impact. They include, among other forms of organization, wholesaler-sponsored voluntary groups, retailer-sponsored cooperative groups, and franchise systems. Because of the legal weight behind their agreements, contractual systems tend to be more tightly knit than administered systems.

Corporate vertical marketing systems are those in which channel members on different levels of distribution are owned and operated by one organization. In fact, such systems are synonymous with both forward and backward vertical integration. Forward integration is on the increase, even within franchise systems.

Backward integration has long been typified by corporate chain store systems. There are key trade-offs in instituting any corporate vertical marketing system. For example, the loss of flexibility and investment required may be outweighed by the resulting gain in control over marketing activities in the channel and the increase in operating economies.

The organizational characteristics of conventional and vertical marketing channel systems are summarized in Table 9-6. From a managerial perspective, vertical marketing systems appear to offer distinct advantages over conventional channels. The former use a systemwide approach, are committed to scientific decision making, and foster channel member loyalty and network stability. Economies of scale can be achieved because the marketing functions are routinized. Since decision making can be centralized, some control over the cost and quality of the functions performed by various channel members can be realized. Furthermore, members of vertical marketing systems implicitly acknowledge an important fact—the relevant unit of competition is the marketing channel itself.

DISCUSSION QUESTIONS

1. Explain which type of marketing channel is used for each of the following products and services.
   a. Cincinnati Reds baseball players
   b. Reese's peanut butter cups
   c. H&R Block accounting services
   d. Farmland bacon
   e. Television reruns
   f. Ford automobiles

2. Suggest three ways in which the marketing channels for motion pictures might be improved.

3. Many department stores and discount stores operate leased departments for merchandise such as health and beauty aids (or cosmetics) and shoes. Rather than operating the department itself, the outlet leases the store space to another firm that specializes in retailing this merchandise. Why would a retailer lease its shoe department, for example, instead of operating it itself? Why would a supplier operate leased departments rather than open its own retail facilities? Explain which kind of marketing channel administrative pattern best describes leased departments.

4. The differences between a wholesaler-sponsored voluntary group and a retailer-owned cooperative chain are very subtle. Find examples of each of these contractual channels operating in your town. Carefully explain the differences between the two.

5. Bell's Supermarkets, based in Buffalo, administers a chain of supermarkets throughout western New York. Some of Bell's stores are company owned, while others are franchised. What are the advantages of operating a dual distribution system such as this? What are the disadvantages?

6. Barb's Balloons and Belly Dancers is a "special occasion" greeting service operating out of five locations in a large midwestern metropolitan area. Barb's distinctive competitive advantage is that her service is "wholesome and avoids the sleaziness of

TABLE 9.6 Characteristics of Conventional and Vertical Marketing Channel Systems

Characteristic	Conventional Channel	Type of Vertical Marketing System			
		Administered	Contractual		Corporate
			Voluntary and Cooperative	Franchise	
Systemwide goals	None	Limited and informal	Limited and formal	Extensive and formal	Pervasive and formal
Mechanism for coordination	Bargaining and negotiation	Marketing programs	Contract	Contract	Corporate policy
Locus of decision-making	Individual organization	Informal collaboration	Wholesaler with ratification	Franchisor with ratification	Decentralized/centralized
Channel commitment	Unstable	Minimal	Moderate	Very high	Very high
Opportunities for scale economies	Infrequent	Possible	Good	Very good	Excellent
Flexibility	Very high	High	Moderate	Low	Very low
Investment needed	Very low	Moderate	High	High	Very high

most competitors.'' Barb is considering entering the Indianapolis, Dayton, and Cincinnati markets with her service, and eventually, she would like to expand nationwide. She has a variety of options available to her but is leaning toward franchising her concept. Develop a franchising concept for Barb's Balloons and Belly Dancers. Be sure to include likely sources of income, franchisee assistances, balance between company-owned and franchised outlets, and other points discussed in this chapter.

7. Montgomery Ward describes its supplier investments as ''very minimal'' and says it will consider such relationships ''only as a last resort to meet the company's requirements for satisfying its customer needs.'' In fact, Ward's only major supplier investment is in a paint manufacturer.

   Compare and contrast Ward's philosophy with Sears'. Which would you endorse as an overall corporate policy if you were running a comparable retailing organization (e.g., J. C. Penney)?

8. Several fast-food franchisors have bought out the more successful of their franchisees, thus converting those outlets to company-owned stores. In contrast, automobile manufacturers steadfastly refuse to become involved in the widespread ownership of car dealerships. Discuss the reasons why franchisors in these two industries have such different philosophies of dual distribution.

9. Which of the following products and services would best lend themselves to franchising? Explain.
   a. Custom-made furniture
   b. An automobile body shop
   c. A bookstore
   d. A men's ties and accessories shop
   e. Management consulting services
   f. A women's fashion store

10. Daniels Furniture Company is a manufacturer of a broad line of moderately priced case goods (i.e., nonupholstered furniture such as chests of drawers, wall units, coffee and end tables, and dining room sets). Daniels has hired you to revamp how it administers its marketing channels. Phil Daniels, the company president, has hinted that he would be receptive to setting up a corporate vertical marketing channel system. Which factors would you consider in making your recommendations to Daniels? In your answer, be sure to address Mr. Daniels' hint about corporate channels.

Red Lion Knitwear Channel Design

BACKGROUND OF THE COMPANY

Red Lion Knitwear is an established manufacturer of men's underwear and socks and is currently expanding into sweaters and other knitwear items. The company,

TABLE 9.7 Changes in Retail Department and Variety Stores 1948–1977

	Percent of Sales by Store Group					
	1948	1958	1965	1967	1972	1977
Department Stores						
Single units (individual stores)	37%	14%	8%	6%	3%	1%
2–10 units	21	24	22	15	9	6
11+ units	43	62	70	79	88	93
Total	100	100	100	100	100	100
Variety Stores						
Single units	14	16	16	17	16	16
2–10 units	6	6	4	4	4	4
11+ units	80	78	80	79	81	79
Total	100	100	100	100	100	100

Sources: U.S. Census of Retailing, Distribution, and Business, selected years.
Note: Some totals may differ slightly because of rounding.

located in southeastern United States, has been in business for over 70 years and has established a solid reputation with both the trade (retailers) and consumers in a nationwide market. The demand for its product lines has been essentially stable, although some of the newer knitwear lines have grown with the increased emphasis on casual dress in recent years. The current product line amounts to about 1,200 items, which is not considered excessive within the industry (each item is one size of one particular product).

EXISTING CHANNELS

Red Lion distributes through approximately 300 wholesalers, who then sell to approximately 100,000 retailers. In general, it is unusual for one wholesaler to handle more than 500 accounts in this business; the general attitude in the trade has been that to sell to more than that number stretches the sales force very thin. To sell to fewer than 500 tends to be inefficient; there appear to be some fixed administrative costs which do not vary with the number of accounts.

During Red Lion's 70 years, substantial changes have been taking place in dry goods retailing. The U.S. Census of Retailing summarizes national data on two classes of Red Lion's customers. Red Lion has traditionally sold through wholesalers to both large chains and individual stores. However, the trend of sales has followed the national trend very closely, with an increasing share coming from sales to department store chains, as shown in Table 9-7.

Red Lion's market has shifted towards these chains at a slower pace than the industry as a whole, meaning that a large share of sales still come from these smaller retail accounts.

The differences in serving these two groups of customers are substantial. Small retailers are generally costly to serve. Order quantities tend to be small, requiring individual documentation and involving small shipments with high transportation charges. These stores do not, as a rule, have any kind of systematic stock control which results in erratic order. Small stores tend to be located in smaller communities. From the standpoint of sales representation, they are less productive because of both sales volumes and distance.

Large retailers, and particularly the chains, have lower distribution costs for these same reasons. Shipments are frequently in full truck load quantities. Often large retailers use computerized inventory control so that orders are consistent in frequency and volume, and special conditions can be anticipated. Sales representation can also be efficient because it is usually handled through a single point of contact.

For the moment, the chains continue to buy from wholesalers. However, the wholesalers have begun to report pressure from the department store chain buyers to sell them either private label merchandise or national brands like Red Lion at discounted prices. The chains say they need to meet the rising costs of their own operations and recover the profit margins they had been earning in previous years.

Red Lion's own representatives have occasionally held meetings with some of the department store buyers. As they left these meetings, the representatives felt increasingly convinced that other manufacturers were not only willing to offer private label merchandise, but were prepared to ship directly to the stores without using wholesalers at all.

The large customers are too important to ignore. They appear to control a larger share of the market than ever—about 60 percent. However, there is still a significant volume to be sold at high margins through the traditional channel. Any strategy decision on dealing with large customers will also involve making a decision about the smaller shops. The small shops prefer to have nationally advertised brands in their store as customers recognize the quality image. Even department stores do not wish to go completely to private label, as the manufacturer's label provides a reference point for consumers to compare value and prices.

THE WHOLESALERS

In addition, there is a problem with the 300 wholesalers. Red Lion has dealt with many of these firms since it was founded. Many long-standing personal friendships extend over more than one generation. Red Lion built its business on the strength of these relationships. In a recent speech at a sales meeting, the company president, J. P. Lyon III, went on record about his concerns over the future of these relationships: "We are a major threshold of the wholesaler system. We believe in it and want to make sure that our wholesalers understand there is a place—and a profitable one—for them in any new distribution system."

The wholesalers' efficiency varies widely. Some, actually only a few, are efficient and as progressive and well-managed as the best in the industry. Many others, perhaps even a majority, are traditionally managed, family-owned enterprises that have drifted along for years. These have made improvements only reluctantly.

The real test of Red Lion's relationships with these firms is RL's desire to encourage the establishment of computer-controlled inventory reordering systems at the wholesale level. This has been prompted by too many instances of poor inventory service to Red Lion's retail customers. However, Red Lion products are only a portion, although a significant one, of their total business. Most of these firms do not understand the computer or modern techniques of inventory control, and certainly do not wish to become involved with either unless they can be assured of continuing their association with Red Lion over a long period of time. These wholesalers have traditionally been independent of either manufacturer or retailers, and there is little that Red Lion can do directly to change their operating practice.

STRATEGIC OPTIONS

Red Lion's management is meeting to ponder possible courses of action. The solution is critical to the future of the company. To continue in precisely the same relationship with the wholesalers does not seem to be productive. On the other hand, to abandon them means not only dealing directly with the large stores and chains, but eliminating 40 percent of Red Lion's current sales base. Another alternative, taking away the large retail accounts, would also be equivalent to abandoning them since the large accounts contribute collectively about 60 percent or more at wholesaler revenue. In any event, to continue to deal with the large stores is going to require some kind of change.

The nature of these changes does not focus on the quality of the representation the wholesalers have provided. In fact, there are some valuable relationships between the wholesalers and their customers. The problem is more closely related to the physical distribution of the product line. A traditional function of the wholesaler in the past has been to provide inventory for its customers. With the pressure for direct sales, the wholesalers' failure to maintain control over their inventory is clearly the dominating issue. Another alternative, to sell and ship directly from the factory to retail customers, would be prohibitively expensive, both to maintain a sales force and ship small orders for long distances. Is there a way to keep these wholesalers, provide them with enough volume for them to survive, and yet improve the process of product movement to customers? Or is it necessary to abandon them and turn to a company-owned and -controlled channel? If that happens, what strategy will be necessary to service the smaller accounts?

1. What are the problem areas facing Red Lion?
2. What alternative channels could Red Lion pursue that would meet its requirements for physical distribution?
3. Evaluate these channels from the standpoint of Red Lion and each group of channel members.
4. What channel decision should Red Lion make? For what reasons?

Source: Philip B. Schary, *Logistics Decisions: Text and Cases* (Chicago: The Dryden Press, 1984), pp. 49–52.

Sta-Lube, Inc.

Mr. Laird Stabler, vice-president of marketing of Sta-Lube, a manufacturer of motor oil and other related automotive lubricants and a hand cleaner, was planning his motor oil marketing program for the coming year. A number of changes in distribution and projected usage patterns for motor oil made his task more complex than usual.

THE COMPANY

Sta-Lube Corporation was founded in the 1930s by Mr. Stabler's grandfather, Dr. Laird J. Stabler, Professor of Engineering Chemistry and Dean of the School of Pharmacy at the University of Southern California. Dr. Stabler was a creative chemist who assayed and suggested uses for many minerals native to California. He also developed a number of lubricants from California crude oil as well as new pharmaceuticals and food products.

One product, high performance motor oil formulated with selected additives, was pioneered by Dr. Stabler and became a favorite of automobile racers in the early 1950s. Today, all motor oils contain additives to improve their function. While no longer unique, Sta-Lube motor oil is considered equal or better than the quality of competing brands on the market.

Sta-Lube motor oils are attractively packaged and come in nondetergent, super, multiple viscosity, and competition grades. These motor oils can be purchased in 24-quart cases, 5-gallon cans or 55-gallon barrels. Other items in the Sta-Lube line are greases, automatic transmission fluid, gear oils, a waterless hand cleaner, paint and chemical sundries, and a line of marine products.

In an earlier period, Sta-Lube had sold almost always directly to auto parts stores or "jobbers" as they are known in the trade. By gradually getting warehouse distributors to sell and distribute their products, costs were reduced, market coverage was increased, and profits were improved. However, competition both at the manufacturing and retail level has caused Mr. Stabler to reexamine his marketing program for oil.

The primary market for Sta-Lube Motor Oil was California, with the largest user concentration in the Los Angeles–Long Beach–Orange County major metropolitan area. Last year Sta-Lube sold 100,000 cases of motor oil representing $600,000 in sales.

DISTRIBUTION

Sta-Lube sold through two basic channels of distribution as shown in Exhibit 1. The first channel involved the use of warehouse distributors who in turn sell and

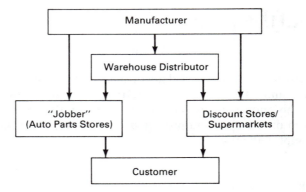

Exhibit 1: Channel structure for motor oil.

distribute to "jobbers" and regular retail outlets. About 85 percent of all motor oil sales were made in this manner. The second channel is a direct one to retail and "jobber" outlets. The remaining 15 percent of sales were distributed in this manner.

Freight on all shipments to the Los Angeles area was prepaid on orders of six cases or more. For orders of less than six cases, a two-dollar handling and shipping charge was made. Deliveries within the major metropolitan areas were by company-owned trucks.

Warehouse Distributors

The greater Los Angeles area had approximately sixty-five warehouse distributors who specialized in selling and distributing automotive supplies. Of this number, thirty-three were currently handling Sta-Lube Motor Oil.

Although warehouse distributors varied in size and products carried, operations tended to be similar. Sales volume for the average warehouse distributor ranged from $70,000 to $605,000 monthly; with the average being $125,000. In order to achieve this volume, warehouse distributors normally carried between seventy-five and ninety different manufacturers' products, and maintained an average inventory balance of $1.0 to 1.5 million. Warehouse distributors sold directly to retail jobbers and employed between five and twelve salesmen. (A sales force of seven can normally accommodate two hundred retail jobbers.)

Virtually every warehouse distributor stocked motor oil. However, sales of motor oil accounted for only 0.3 to 1.0 percent of total monthly sales, or about 200 cases per month. Because of the low volume, warehouse distributors preferred to stock only two or three competing brands. This was done to reduce warehousing space and inventory. Also, because of the low volume, very little sales effort was exerted on jobbers.

The brands that warehouse distributors normally stocked were manufactured by relatively small independent companies such as Sta-Lube. The reason for this was that the larger oil companies (Pennzoil and Valvoline) prefer to sell directly to the retail jobbers at a price below that offered by warehouse distributors. However, Valvoline would sell to warehouse distributors at an additional 20 percent off. Most did not object to manufacturers' selling the same product directly if they did not undercut the warehouse distributors' price and discount schedule. This price normally included a 25 to 40 percent markup, as did most of the products they carried. An exception to this policy was an additional 10 percent given by warehouse distributors to jobbers who ordered in 25-case quantities.

Most warehouse distributors' deliveries to jobbers in the Los Angeles–Orange County metropolitan area were made by company-owned trucks. Deliveries to the outlying perimeter and beyond were contracted to public carriers.

Many of the warehouse distributors had sophisticated levels of operation. Centralized data-processing equipment was widely used for inventory and order processing. In addition, management personnel usually had training in quantitative tools and computer operations.

Most warehouse distributors felt they had excellent working relations with the entire channel (manufacturer-WDs-jobbers).

Auto Parts and Supply Houses (Jobbers)

There are approximately 650 retail jobbers located in the greater Los Angeles area. Of this number, 575 are thought to be currently selling Sta-Lube products; 250 jobbers purchased directly from time to time. Monthly sales volume per jobber ranged from $19,000 to $125,000, depending on store size and location. The average inventory needed to generate this volume ranged from $35,000 to $250,000 and usually consisted of two lines: automotive replacement parts and auto accessory supplies.

Theoretically, sales were made at two levels at different pricing schedules. The first level is the retail (walk-in) customer who often accounted for as much as 40 percent of sales, and was expected to pay the retail price. The second level was the wholesale customer (gas stations, garages, and auto dealers) who accounted for the remaining 60 percent of sales and who was charged according to the discounted wholesale schedule. In reality, a larger portion of sales was discounted as many retail customers were given discounts due to increasing competition from the discount auto stores and auto departments in discount stores now in the market.

Another marginal practice exists in that theoretically to be classified as a jobber, automotive services (lubes, oil changes, brake work, etc.) were not to be offered by them. However, some jobbers were able to perform these services, provided that their wholesale customers did not protest to a point of prohibiting them.

Ordering practices vary considerably among jobbers. In some stores, warehouse distributors' or manufacturers' salesmen made periodic sales calls to write orders. However, in other outlets, salesmen were prohibited from entering the store. This resulted in orders being phoned directly to the manufacturer or the the warehouse distributor. Because of the latter practice, little selling effort can be exerted by the sales force.

Regarding motor oil, each jobber normally carries three to five competing brands. These usually include one brand of re-refined motor oil (inexpensive) and one brand of competition racing oil such as Castrol or Sta-Lube. The volume of motor oil sales per jobber was relatively small, with monthly sales ranging from ten to forty cases. Depending on the price being charged, motor oil sales accounted for approximately 1 to 4 percent of total jobber sales. Because it accounted for only a small percentage of sales, little promotional or selling effort was exerted. An occasional window display was set up or an ad was run in the local paper if motor oil was to be priced as a "leader" for temporary periods.

Products were generally priced so that margins of 30 percent on automotive replacement parts and 40 percent on auto accessories were received. However, the pricing policy on motor oil varied. At one extreme, premium prices were charged (70 cents to $1.25) with the philosophy of having the motor oil on hand if anyone wanted to pay the price. At the other extreme, jobbers priced the motor oil at cost (75 cents to 45 cents) and used it as a "leader." This policy was often supplemented by also discounting complementary products (oil filters, and the like). Normally, this was done to generate store traffic by those jobbers who were more directly competing with the discount outlets. The majority of jobbers fell between these extremes and prices according to the manufacturers' suggested prices (50 cents to $1.00).

The brands that jobbers carried depended a great deal upon the pricing policy they adopted. Those jobbers who sold below premium price or who tried to compete with the discount outlets preferred to purchase directly from the large manufacturers (Pennzoil and Valvoline). The reason for this preference was that the larger manufacturers granted an additional 10 percent discount under the warehouse distributors' prices. This practice then allowed the jobbers to reduce the retail price and better compete for the discount customer.

Finally, jobber operations indicated that management was somewhat less than sophisticated in marketing practices. Emphasis resulting either from personal background or experience tended to be directed more toward the automotive service trade rather than the retail customer.

PRICING AND DISCOUNT SCHEDULES

Sta-Lube's suggested retail pricing schedule is such that jobber prices for equal quality motor oil (90 cents to $1.25 per quart) fall between those quoted by discount outlets (29 cents to 63 cents) and filling stations or auto dealers (70 cents to $1.50). All grades of motor oil fall within these price ranges. In addition, Sta-Lube utilizes a dual-pricing schedule that suggests lower boundaries for discount pricing (72 cents to 99 cents per quart).

PROMOTION

Sta-Lube's primary promotional tool consists of personal selling. At present, the company has two full-time salesmen who sell and promote motor oil products in the greater Los Angeles area. Sta-Lube's salesmen currently have 260 jobber and forty-two warehouse distributor accounts. Jobbers were contacted every three months, while warehouse distributors were contacted between twelve and twenty-four times a year.

Salesmen were compensated by a combination of salary and commission, which in total normally amounted to between $14,000 and $20,000 annually. An additional $4,800 per year was reimbursed for selling expenses.

Other than personal selling, Sta-Lube did a limited amount of promotional work. On occasion, sales meetings were conducted jointly by warehouse distributors and Sta-Lube to discuss the problems and marketing conditions that arose. In addition, salesmen from Sta-Lube would occasionally spend time in the field with warehouse distributor salesmen. This was done primarily to help promote sales to potential jobbers and to resolve the product problems encountered by warehouse distributors. In addition, salesmen were authorized a limited budget for free goods and trade show promotions.

TRENDS IN MOTOR OIL USAGE

Recently, the total market for automotive motor oil was 854 million gallons. Current forecasts indicated that the market would decline at a negative rate of 1.2 percent annually until the middle 1970s. Predictions after 1975 were conflicting, with some sources stating a five-year growth rate of 1.3 percent annually. Other sources felt that forecasts are meaningless until the pollution controversy is settled. This uncertainty stems from the possibility of redesigning or possibly eliminating the internal combustion engine.

The major reason for the projected decrease in the demand for engine oil was that the intervals between oil changes would increase. In turn, this would result in less oil consumed per car, per year, or a decrease in total annual consumption (see Exhibit 2). The increase in oil change intervals was due primarily to advances in automotive engine designs and the increased use of nonleaded gasoline.

Those who forecasted an increase in motor oil consumption in the latter half of the decade based their prediction on the belief that the increased number of automobiles on the road would be large enough to offset the declining yearly consumption per automobile.

Another trend in the marketplace was the increased use of multigrade motor oil. In 1967, multigrade oil accounted for 33 percent of all motor oil sales, whereas 1970 figures showed a 5 percent market share increase, or 38 percent of sales.

With regard to the national home-user market, auto parts and supply houses (jobbers) had substantially outsold the discount outlets. However, discount outlet sales were increasing at a somewhat faster rate than that of jobbers (7.5 percent to 5.0 percent).

In addition to national statistics on motor oil consumption, some data on motor oil change behavior for the Los Angeles area were also available. The data are highlighted in Exhibit 3. Exhibit 4 shows which brands of motor oil were last purchased in the Los Angeles area, based on a *Los Angeles Times* marketing research report.

EXHIBIT 2
Fuel and Oil Consumption

Year	Avg. Miles Per Year[a]	Avg. Gal. Gasoline[a]	Avg. Miles Per Gal.[a]	M/O[b] Ratio	Avg. Qts. Motor Oil[c]
1980	9,600	762	12.6		
1979	9,600	756	12.7		
1978	9,600	750	12.8		
1977	9,600	744	12.9		
1976	9,600	738	13.0	.34	10.00
1975	9,600	733	13.1	.34	10.00
1974	9,600	727	13.2	.34	10.00
1973	9,600	722	13.3	.35	10.00
1972	9,600	716	13.4	.35	10.00
1971	9,600	711	13.5	.35	10.00
1970	9,600	706	13.6	.39	11.0
1969	9,600	701	13.7	.43	12.0
1968	9,627	698	13.8	.47	12.9
1967	9,531	684	13.9	.54	14.7
1966	9,506	679	14.0	.60	16.3
1965	9,387	667	14.1	.63	16.8
1964	9,286	652	14.3	.67	17.5
1963	9,378	652	14.4	.75	19.6
1962	9,441	657	14.4	.79	20.8
1961	9,465	658	14.4	.85	22.4
1960	9,446	661	14.3	.90	23.8

[a]1960–1968 United States Department of Transportation, Bureau of Public Roads, 1969–1980, NPN estimates.

[b]Motor Oil Ratio. The number of gallons of oil sold per 100 gallons of gasoline.

[c]1969–1975 estimated from earlier data.

MARKETING PLANNING

Before working on next year's marketing plan, Mr. Stabler reviewed some cost and service assumptions for direct versus warehouse distributor channels (Exhibit 5). He wondered if the emphasis on wholesale distribution was still valid and what type of selling effort and marketing activities Sta-Lube should be using. He also wondered if he could use the data he had to evaluate several distribution alternatives so as to better develop Sta-Lube's distribution strategy.

This case was prepared by Associate Professor David McConaughy, University of Southern California, as a basis for class discussion.

Source: Roger A. Kerin and Robert A. Peterson, *Strategic Marketing Problems* (Boston: Allyn and Bacon, 1978), pp. 308–316.

EXHIBIT 3

Motor Oil Change Behavior

Where Do You Usually Have The Motor Oil Changed in Your Car?

Place of Motor Oil Change	Total				By Family Income				
	1948	1955	1968	1970	Under $5,000	$5,000– $7,999	$8,000– $9,999	$10,000– $14,999	$15,000 or More
Service station	75%	72%	59%	57%	62%	53%	59%	52%	60%
New car dealer/agency	8	12	15	15	12	13	11	16	22
At home	14	14	23	23	21	29	26	28	15
Other place	3	2	3	3	3	4	3	3	3
Undetermined	—	—	—	2	—	1	1	1	—
Total	100%	100%	100%	100%	100%	100%	100%	100%	100%

Place of Motor Oil Change	By Age, Household Head					By Education, Household Head			
	Under 30	30–39	40–49	50–64	65 or Over	Some H.S. or Less	H.S. Graduate	Some College	College Graduate
Service station	48%	58%	54%	59%	74%	60%	50%	57%	66%
New car dealer/agency	18	15	15	16	11	10	17	16	20
At home	31	23	27	21	11	26	28	23	11
Other place	2	4	2	3	1	2	2	4	3
Undetermined	1	—	2	1	3	2	3	—	—
Total	100%	100%	100%	100%	100%	100%	100%	100%	100%

Where Did You Purchase Motor Oil for the Last "at Home" Change?

Place of Motor Oil Purchase for "At Home" Change	Total	By Family Income		By Age		By Education	
		Less than $10,000	$10,000 or More	Under 40	40 or Over	No College	College
Service stations	16%	17%	17%	15%	20%	17%	19%
Discount stores	43	40	41	38	42	41	38
Auto/tire stores	11	12	9	8	7	9	5
Grocery/drug stores	9	7	9	18	5	10	11
Other stores	10	10	14	10	13	10	16
Undetermined	11	14	10	11	13	13	11
Total	100%	100%	100%	100%	100%	100%	100%

Source: Los Angeles Times Marketing Research Department. Reprinted by permission.

EXHIBIT 4
Motor Oil: Brand Last Purchased

Brand	1971 Percent	1973 Percent
Pennzoil	17.4	20.9
Shell	11.4	10.7
Texaco	10.5	9.7
Standard	7.9	7.0
Mobil	6.3	6.0
Union	5.0	5.5
Arco	4.4	4.3
Valvoline	3.5	4.1
Quaker State	2.9	3.9
Other	9.4	6.6
Undetermined	21.3	21.3

Source: Los Angeles Times Marketing Research Department. Reprinted by permission.

EXHIBIT 5
Data Assumptions for Direct and Warehouse Distributor Distribution

Selling Costs to:	
warehouse distribution	$10.00/hour
jobber	$ 7.00/hour
detailing (salary only)	$ 5.00/hour
Travel cost	.15/mile
Average distance between calls	2 miles
Driving time between calls	.13 hour
Call time	
warehouse distributor call	1 hour/call
high service (jobber)	.5 hour/call
low service (jobber)	.25 hour/call
Freight cost:	
less than truckload	.087 × sales
truckload (20,000 lbs.)	.025 × sales
Order costs	$ 3.00/order
Order frequency	
jobbers	9/year
warehouse distributor	20/year
Estimated sales in southern California market	100,000 cases
Case weight (24 quarts)	50 pounds

Source: *Company Records.*

Benson Ford

Jim Benson was an ambitious young man in his mid-thirties who had risen to a middle management spot in a consumer credit firm specializing in automobile loans. His only business experience was in credit, but what he learned there about the retailing of automobiles made him aware of the opportunities. He decided to try for a franchise. With the help of family members, he was able to scrape together an initial capital of $125 thousand. He hoped this would cover a franchise purchase price and initial working capital. Inventory, he knew, could be carried under a floor plan arrangement. Building rental was estimated at $380/mo.

The only franchise available within his means proved to be a Ford "closed point" (a failed operation) in the rural county seat town of St. Lukes, some 37 miles from the state capitol (population about 100,000) of his southeastern state. The Ford Co., of course, was eager to have this point reopened. Based on a company estimate of 120–150 new vehicles per year, the capital to open the dealership was $115 thousand. The primary local competition was a strong Chevrolet dealer with sales four times the previous Ford Dealer's average of 50/yr. Benson, however, felt he could do much better by drawing trade from the capital area. He was estimating monthly sales of 35 cars and trucks and thought that he could break even with a margin of $500 per vehicle. His first surprise was the rent on the rather shabby building—the only suitable one locally: $1,000 per month. Nevertheless, he committed himself to the purchase, determined to make up the extra cost with added volume through extensive advertising.

At this point, the Ford Zone manager had his first contact with Benson. To the zone manager, it was obvious that Benson's inexperience had led him into some major errors of judgment. From the zone manager's knowledge of the whole area, certain sobering facts were apparent:

- Competition in the nearby metropolitan area and some surrounding towns was very keen, and the dealers in those places well-capitalized (see map, Figure 9-2).
- The gross margin obtained per vehicle in the state capital was only $350, and no more than $375–380 in the small towns around.
- A realistic sales potential for the St. Luke's dealership was 10–15 vehicles per month, and Benson's finances could not support sales of more than 15–20 per month in any case. This kind of volume would put his breakeven at an impossible $1100 per month, if his success hinged on new car sales as the principal source of profit.

The zone manager also could see that in its eagerness to get the dealership reopened, the Ford Company had not discussed 3 important points Benson had overlooked:

- in taking over a closed dealership, he would be starting out with zero volume.

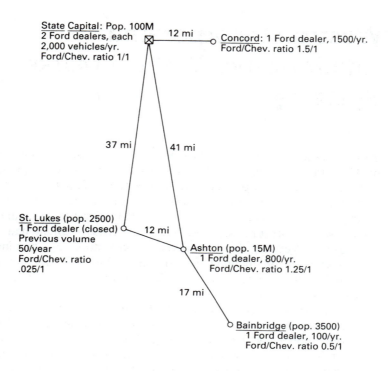

Figure 9-2 Ford and Chevrolet dealerships in St. Lukes & surrounding area.

- the previous dealer had failed because of his poor reputation both as a dealer and for service.
- the local Chevy dealer was an exceptionally able one, and strong in every respect.

At this point, it was clear that Benson had only two alternatives: either (a) drop the dealership immediately and take a loss of around $36,000 needed to pay off the lease and other commitments, or (b) develop a radically different plan for survival, based on the level of finances he had available.

In his discussions with Benson, the zone manager had perceived one ray of hope. Benson seemed to really understand the used car market. This was a valuable asset; a skill many dealers lack. In this market, buyers are not familiar with cost, and the opportunity for substantial profit margins are available.

Whatever plan could be developed, it was clear that any significant advertising in the state capital, other than a nominal yellow pages listing, would be money thrown away. The yellow pages might bring a couple of bargain hunters a year, and he could afford to take a low margin on such sales. Nearly all of his revenue would have to come out of the local trade area.

Source: Chester R. Wasson, *Cases in Policy, Strategy & Marketing Management* (Charlotte, N.C.: ECR Associates, 1983), pp. 64–66.

Westron Incorporated Administered Vertical Marketing Systems

Westron Incorporated had introduced a complete line of power tools during the pre-Christmas season in 1968. These tools were of very high quality and were priced, on the average, eight to ten percent higher than the highest-priced competitive line. The Westron line of products was *demonstrably* superior to other lines—the power tools were virtually vibrationless, and so the finished results were more precise. One television advertisement had, in fact, demonstrated the Westron line's ultrasmooth operation by running a power drill unsupported on an inclined waxed board. The drill did not move—showing, presumably, that the extremely low level of vibration was not sufficient to break the inertia of the drill.

Westron was relatively new to the home power-tool market—indeed, its basic reputation was not in products for final consumers at all. The Westron name was well known and very highly regarded in the realm of industrial markets. Westron had, for over 80 years, manufactured both heavy and light tools for use in industry. These industrial tools were of very high quality and were sold for a premium price. Westron had originally become interested in the home power-tool market when approached by a major general-merchandise chain organization to produce power tools under the name of the chain. Westron had ultimately decided not to produce a line of tools for the private brand, but the management had not dismissed the idea of developing a line of products for home workshops.

When the home power-tool line was finally introduced in 1968, the consumer reaction had not been breathtaking. Dealers had not been easy to find. Many of the stronger dealerships were working under exclusive arrangements with other brands of home power tools. And while promotional support for the new line had been adequate, it was focused *exclusively* on final consumers. The dealers that did take the line often took only part of it; often they wanted only the power drills— the ¼- and ⅜-inch being most popular. The Westron management had wanted full-line "shoppes" to be the dealer norm. These shoppes would display all of the Westron line and provide a demonstration "pit" in which various skills with power tools could be demonstrated and taught. But, in truth, at the end of three years of experience with the product line, very few dealers, even in large metropolitan areas, met this standard.

In the summer of 1971 the Westron management began to develop plans to strengthen the Name Power Tool Division. A complete review of their present power-tool policy showed it to be as summarized in the following list.

1. Dealer margins were set at 35 percent of final selling price. This was thought to be a customary dealer margin in the distribution of hardware.

2. Dealer development included a brochure picturing and describing some of the special uses for Westron power tools.

3. Westron field salespeople were available to dealers—depending on dealer size—at least once every six months. When special problems arose, a Westron representative could be available in a matter of several days.

4. Dealers were encouraged to advertise Westron products. The encouragement took the form of a cooperative advertising program in which Westron would pay fifty percent of the media cost upon receiving satisfactory proof that the ad had been run.

5. A demonstration table, capable of providing a secure mount for all Westron power tools, was provided all Westron dealers. The cost of this table to Westron was almost $50.

6. Dealers were given cash terms of 2/10 net 30—which meant they could deduct a 2 percent cash discount if they paid within 10 days of receipt of a shipment of tools. If they did not wish to pay that quickly, the bill became due at the end of 30 days. In effect, dealers had 30 days in which to generate the money with which to pay their Westron bills.

Several ideas for modifying the present dealer plan had been considered. For example, management had discussed a dealer training program in which one person in each dealership would be appointed a Westron "key man" and trained to demonstrate and sell Westron power tools.

Likewise, the possibility of Westron's leasing departments in some cities had been considered. Under this plan Westron would, in effect, run its own "shoppes"—including staffing, training, and selling. The management of Westron had also developed an interest in something called "vertical marketing systems." These systems included "corporate" systems, "contractual" systems, and "administered" systems. And while the Westron managers were not sure exactly what these systems involved, they had heard that the administered system was best suited to their situation.

Source: Bert Rosenbloom, *Marketing Channels: A Management View*, 3rd ed. (Chicago: The Dryden Press, 1987), pp. 544–545.

DISCUSSION QUESTIONS

1. What specific changes in the Westron dealer plan would you make? Why? Make sure you consider the addition of wholly new features to the plan as well as deletion or modification of present features.

2. What is a vertical marketing system? How do these vertical marketing systems relate to the Westron case? Which basic type of vertical marketing system is probably best for Westron? Why?

10

Using Marketing Channel Power To Lead the Channel

LEARNING OBJECTIVES

Upon completing this chapter, you will be able to:

- *Diagram and discuss the process for coordinating the marketing flows within channels of distribution.*

- *Describe how channel members become dependent upon one another and how this dependence forms the basis for marketing channel power.*

- *List the six bases of marketing channel power and give examples of each.*

- *Discuss the consequences of using the different bases of power to coordinate the activities of the channel.*

- *Explain the various factors affecting the leadership and control process in marketing channels.*

- *Describe the key arguments as to why any marketing institution—be it a manufacturer, wholesaler, retailer, or physical distribution company—could lead a marketing channel.*

- *Understand that who should lead a particular channel depends upon the specific situation.*

The Changing Balance of Power in the Grocery Business ⊁

Consumer-packaged-goods manufacturers, through their tremendous advertising and promotion budgets, have traditionally been able to pull consumers into grocery stores. Because of their strong customer franchise and volumes of market demand information, manufacturers such as Procter and Gamble and H. J. Heinz could get supermarkets to follow their merchandising suggestions and to stock unquestioningly their new products.

In the late 1970s and early 1980s, however, the twin economic terrors of inflation and recession forced a change in the balance of power within this channel. The change centered around weakened loyalty toward both national brands and stores as consumers attempted to reduce the effects of inflation and recession on their food budgets.

To keep their newly cost-conscious consumers from defecting to lower-priced competitors, supermarkets were forced to become more efficient and to lower their prices without sacrificing their already-skimpy margins. For one thing, they began to perform more of the marketing functions themselves and attempted to shift more of their costs back to the manufacturers. Scanning systems, for instance, enabled supermarkets to keep close track of product demand without having to rely on supplier information. Food retailers also became more efficient in stocking and data processing by eliminating all but the top one or two national brands in a product category. In addition, they reduced the number of sizes of the most popular brands they carried. This made scarce shelf space even scarcer for suppliers of the number 3 or 4 brands and gave supermarkets much more clout over these manufacturers.

Supermarkets promoted lower-priced private-label goods more heavily and introduced generic products during this period to take advantage of weakened brand loyalty. This allowed them to put additional pressure on their suppliers. First, because manufacturers of the less popular brands were losing demand, they conceded much higher gross margins to the supermarket chains just to keep their plants operating. Next, many more efficient manufacturers accepted such lower-margin orders because they feared the chains would move their regular private-label business to competitors if they refused.

As a result of the supermarket chains' newly found power, manufacturers changed many aspects of their marketing strategies. For example, they assisted their retailers more with point-of-purchase displays, offered packaging methods more convenient to retailers, prepriced their products, provided increased promotional allowances, and circulated more consumer coupons. In addition, some producers developed budget brands to compete with the private label and generic brands. Procter and Gamble, for example, introduced Banner toilet tissue with a wholesale price about 25 percent lower than its premium Charmin and White Cloud brands. Although they continued to use pull promotional strategies to obtain and maintain shelf space, manufacturers stepped up their push promotional efforts to respond to retailers' demands. Deals and allowances were more frequently offered to supermarkets, as were merchandising and display materials. On the other hand, manufacturers' salespeople called less often on their retail accounts because retailers viewed these sales calls as being less useful than before and because EDI systems made ordering more routinized.

Although the sales of generic brands peaked in 1982, they were still strong in the mid-1980s in some product categories, most notably paper goods, coffee filters, plastic trash bags, and disposable diapers. The more favorable economic climate after 1982 had reduced the attractiveness of private labels and generic brands, thereby restoring some of the manufacturers' original power over their food retailers. However, by the mid-1980s, they had still not regained all their power. Indeed, the economic turmoil of the late 1970s and early 1980s seems to have permanently altered power relationships in the marketing channels for food.

Sources: "Food Chains Pressure Suppliers, Altering Industry Power Balance," *The Wall Street Journal*, August 21, 1980, p. 25; "Manufacturer Relations," *Progressive Grocer*, April 1984, pp. 115ff; "No-Frills Food: New Power for the Supermarkets," *Business Week*, March 23, 1981, pp. 70ff; and "No-Frills Products: An Idea Whose Time Has Gone," *Business Week*, June 17, 1985, pp. 64–65.

To compete effectively and efficiently against other marketing systems, a marketing channel must carefully coordinate its marketing functions and flows. The way in which coordination is achieved is through the use of power within the marketing channel. The food distribution example at the beginning of the chapter illustrates three key points about power within marketing channels. First, any firm within the channel may take responsibility for coordinating and controlling the activities of the channel. Thus, manufacturers, wholesalers, retailers, or facilitators can wield power within any particular channel. Second, the balance of power—or which firm takes primary responsibility for leading the channel—can shift over time. Formerly, consumer packaged-goods manufacturers held most of the power within channels for food, but because supermarkets were better able to respond to changing economic conditions, they were able to grab some of this power away from their suppliers. Finally, a variety of tactics can be used in controlling the marketing activities of other channel members. The supermarkets promoted their private-label and generic-brand products more heavily, putting pressure on their suppliers to grant higher margins, offer larger promotional allowances, and increase the amount of assistance they offered to retailers.

Before we begin to discuss power within marketing channels in detail, it is important to set the context for acquiring and using power. That context is the process for coordinating the activities of individual members of the marketing channel.

COORDINATING THE FLOWS WITHIN MARKETING CHANNELS ✳

The long-run objective of channel management is to produce and deliver the marketing channel services the target market desires, while providing individual channel members with satisfactory returns (e.g., profits, market share, or other rewards) as compensation for their specific contributions. Overall channel performance is determined by channel structure and by individual channel member ✳ behavior. The specific channel designs available to marketing managers were discussed in Chapters 8 and 9. We now turn our attention to the process of coordinating individual channel member behavior within those channel structures.

As noted earlier in the text, a channel organization has to define its target markets and determine the goods and services it must supply to satisfy the needs and wants of those targets. Only then can it decide how best to make those goods and services available for consumption. As indicated in Chapter 8, the *first* step is to determine the level of channel services demanded by the target market. The *second* step involves specifying (1) which marketing tasks must be undertaken to deliver that level of services and (2) which of the available marketing channel institutions can form a delivery system best able to perform those tasks.

Sometimes the available organizations do not adequately perform the required functions for one reason or another. In such cases, it might be necessary to use influence or channel leadership strategies to achieve the desired level of performance; on the other hand, vertical integration of the flows or functions might be the only way to deliver the desired channel services to the target markets. Even if functions and flows are vertically integrated, their performance still must be coordinated to successfully provide the channel services. Therefore, the *third* step in coordinating the channel's activities is to determine exactly which influence or leadership strategies should be used to accomplish the channel's objectives.

The *fourth* step of the coordination process involves managing the conflict that inevitably arises when independent organizations work together. This step is the subject of Chapter 11. The fifth and final step is achieving successful channel performance. Chapter 12 is devoted to evaluating this performance.

Each step in coordinating the activities of the marketing channel is depicted in Figure 10-1 and the first three steps are discussed in detail in the following sections of this chapter.

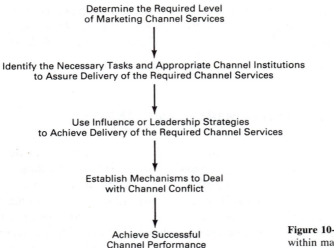

Determine the Required Level
of Marketing Channel Services

Identify the Necessary Tasks and Appropriate Channel Institutions
to Assure Delivery of the Required Channel Services

Use Influence or Leadership Strategies
to Achieve Delivery of the Required Channel Services

Establish Mechanisms to Deal
with Channel Conflict

Achieve Successful
Channel Performance

Figure 10-1 Coordinating activities within marketing channels.

DETERMINING THE REQUIRED LEVEL OF MARKETING CHANNEL SERVICES

As discussed in Chapter 8, a primary consideration in designing a marketing channel is determining the channel services required by the target market. The most significant channel services are (1) lot size, (2) delivery or waiting time, (3) locational convenience, and (4) breadth and depth of product or service assortment. Simply stated, consumers are concerned with how much of the product they are required to buy, how long they must wait for delivery, how far they must travel to get the product, and how many choices they have once they arrive at the store. The relevant list of channel services to consider depends, of course, on the buying situation. For example, the sale of complex products may call for technical assistance, demonstration, and flexible financing, while availability and delivery factors might be more important for more simple products.

Example 1: Cigarettes

Estimating the channel services demanded for any good or service requires an in-depth study of consumer needs and wants. For example, consumers wish to purchase cigarettes in very small lot sizes (one package per purchase, generally), desire immediate delivery of the product once requested, prefer as many outlets as possible from which to purchase, and want the broadest and deepest possible assortment from which to choose. Therefore, channels providing these services are designed to meet these needs. Individual packages of cigarettes are available for purchase from widely placed outlets that offer almost every conceivable type (e.g., filtered or nonfiltered, regular or menthol flavored, soft-pack or box) and brand. Delivery time is instantaneous.

To provide these services, the channel for cigarettes is generally long and complex. It includes manufacturers' distribution centers that ship to tobacco and grocery wholesalers or chain warehouses, which, in turn, ship to individual retail outlets (e.g., stores, vending machines, restaurants). In addition, because of high turnover, the supplies at the retail level must be continually replenished, making the labor costs of maintaining point-of-purchase stocks very high. The end result is that retail prices of cigarettes are extremely high relative to the cost of manufacturing them.

Example 2: Automotive Replacement Parts

The marketing of automotive replacement parts is similar to that for cigarettes. When consumers take their cars to service stations to have worn-out gaskets replaced, they pay a price for those gaskets (excluding the labor charges to install them) that is several times greater than the cost of manufacturing them. The reason for the high price of automotive parts can be traced to the levels of channel services demanded by consumers. Consumers want to have the gaskets replaced as quickly as possible, but service stations do not generally maintain an inventory of gaskets. Mechanics have to call a local automotive parts jobber, who then delivers the part quickly (usually within an hour) to the service station. Furthermore, consumers demand to purchase such parts in small lot sizes (one gasket at a time) but do not want to travel long distances to obtain them. The channel system must, therefore, maintain an enormous, widely available inventory of parts to support the anticipated demands of consumers.

Thus, it is clear why such parts cost what they do and why more and more consumers purchase automotive parts from discount stores and install them themselves. The do-it-yourselfers are willing to forgo some of the service outputs available from the traditional automotive repair channel to achieve a lower cost of car maintenance. (Note that if consumers were to place a higher value on their time, the cost savings might not be as great.)

Example 3: Groceries

In many lines of trade, alternative marketing channel structures have been developed because different market segments require different levels of channel services. For example, some consumers of groceries still demand "full service" and shop at local butcher shops or specialized produce stores. However, most consumers prefer to forgo such service to obtain the lower prices available at supermarkets, even though they must travel by car to reach the supermarkets and generally purchase in larger lot sizes during any one shopping trip. Other consumers are even willing to provide more of their own labor (e.g., bagging their own groceries, remembering the shelf prices of goods). These consumers prefer to shop at warehouse supermarkets where prices are discounted because the channel services are severely limited (e.g., stores are not as conveniently located as supermarkets, assortments are narrower and not as deep, and services such as check cashing and bottle returns are eliminated).

Example 4: Stainless Steel

The need for marketing channels to deliver a variety of channel service combinations can be illustrated in industrial goods marketing as well. If purchasers of stainless steel sheet prefer to buy in large lots, are not concerned about speed of delivery, desire only one or a limited number of grades of sheet, and are willing to transact business over long distances rather than dealing with someone locally, they are likely to get a better price from a direct channel of distribution (e.g., buying directly from the steel mill) than from an indirect one (e.g., through a local wholesale steel service center).

As pointed out in Chapter 8, many factors beyond determining the level of services demanded by target markets influence channel design. However, in the process of coordinating channel activities, knowledge of organizational customer or end-consumer demand for channel services is critical, for once this is known, the specific marketing institutions capable of providing the desired services can be identified.

IDENTIFY THE NECESSARY TASKS IN THE MARKETING CHANNEL

The channel services are provided by organizing the marketing functions and flows—physical possession, ownership, promotion, negotiation, financing, risking, ordering, and payment—in a wide variety of ways. Each channel member participates in at least one flow; however, most are involved in several flows and some participate in all of them. In the cigarette example described above, a large number of channel members must participate in the physical possession and ownership flow in order to provide the lot sizes, locational convenience, and delivery times demanded by consumers. Consequently, almost every channel member carries an inventory. On the other hand, not all cigarette channel members must invest heavily in the promotion flow; manufacturers have assumed almost total responsibility for media advertising. This is not the case in the marketing of consumer durables, where retailers are expected to play a much more significant role in promotion via local advertising and personal selling.

Successful channel management involves assigning the right marketing functions to the right marketing institutions in order to provide the proper mix of channel services desired by the target market. If new car buyers need financing, for example, either the manufacturer (e.g., General Motors Acceptance Corporation), the retailer, or some outside intermediary (e.g., Chase Manhattan Bank or Beneficial Finance) can provide it. Where no channel intermediaries are willing to accept the risk of financing, the car manufacturer may have to assume the flow. However, in many instances, manufacturers and other suppliers prefer to specialize in those flows that they can perform best and to rely on marketing institutions to perform those flows where they have a comparative advantage.

In the marketing of many goods and services, there is an organized network of specialized institutions and agencies. Indeed, channel members choose positions in the channel (e.g., manufacturer, wholesaler, retailer) according to their capacities, interests, goals, expectations, values, and frames of reference. This is particularly true for entrepeneurs.

One independent businessman markets an orange breakfast drink nationally. He holds a patent right on the drink formula and contracts its manufacturing to a contract packer. He has engaged brokers to call on dairies, which he franchises to sell his product via their home delivery routes. This entrepreneur states, "I simply do not like to be involved with that mess of manufacturing. . . . I love to fool around with product development, and promotion is my bag."[1]

Given this tendency toward specialization, channel members must be highly interdependent to deliver all of the channel services the target market desires. For the system to operate effectively, the roles defining which organizations participate in which marketing functions must be clearly defined and understood by all members of the channel. In addition, channel members must perform their assigned tasks properly and cooperate and coordinate with one another to achieve their individual and overall channel goals.

Ideally, the extent to which any channel member participates in the various flows determines that organization's share of the channel's profits. However, such is not always the case. In many lines of trade, standard trade discounts have been established on the basis of what position (e.g., wholesaler, retailer, transportation carrier) an organization occupies within the channel. Although these discounts are frequently called *functional discounts* (see Chapter 6), they are often based on trade tradition rather than on how much a specific institution participates in the flows.

One manufacturer was known to grant large discounts to his distributors on the basis of the warehousing (physical possession) functions they performed. After analyzing the distributors' financial positions, the manufacturer found that they were earning returns on their investments of 50 to 100 percent. While intermediaries are entitled to earn satisfactory returns, these distributors were being excessively compensated. This was particularly apparent when further analysis indicated that the manufacturer, through its arrangements with public warehouses, was undertaking most of the inventory-holding function.

Identifying, assigning, and performing tasks within the channel are the most critical factors in determining whether the appropriate channel services will be delivered, whether high levels of performance will be achieved, and whether

[1] Robert A. Robicheaux and Adel I. El-Ansary, "A General Model for Understanding Channel Member Behavior," *Journal of Retailing*, Vol. 52 (Winter 1975–1976), p. 18.

individual channel members are being adequately compensated. A central task for channel management is to *specify* the appropriate roles for each organization within the system. In conventional channels, these role specifications are often taken for granted, since channel institutions perform their traditional functions. Vertical marketing systems utilize a more explicit approach—social and economic power—to specifying roles and ensuring their performance.

USING INFLUENCE AND LEADERSHIP STRATEGIES TO SPECIFY CHANNEL ROLES

Power in the marketing channel is used for a variety of reasons. Central to the discussion in this chapter is the use of power to specify the appropriate functions for each channel member and to coordinate the performance of those functions among all channel members. Note that Chapter 11 deals with the use of marketing channel power to manage conflict among channel institutions. Before understanding how power can be effectively used within the channel, the key elements of power—dependence and the bases of power—must be grasped.

Dependence—The Foundation of Power

Simply put, *power* is the ability of one channel member to affect the marketing strategy decisions of another organization in the channel.[2] More specifically, one channel member's (A's) power over another (B) can be defined as the change in B's probability of behaving a certain way after A has attempted to influence B. Note that:

1. Power is a characteristic of a relationship. To say that A is powerful is not meaningful, but to say that A (e.g., Sears) is powerful with respect to B (e.g., Michelin) is.
2. A may use a variety of means in attempting to influence B. Among them are coercion, rewards, expertise, identification, legitimacy, and information. These will be discussed below.
3. A may have power over B even though A's attempts at influencing B do not directly result in a change in B's behavior. Attempts at influence may only increase the probability that B will act in the desired manner. Additional efforts may be necessary to change B's behavior.[3]

The power of channel member A over firm B is rooted in the dependence of B upon A. First, marketing institutions are dependent on one another for scarce resources. Suppliers provide highly demanded goods and services that resellers

[2] Much of the following discussion on power is developed from Frederick J. Beier and Louis W. Stern, "Power in the Channel of Distribution," in Louis W. Stern (ed.), *Distribution Channels: Behavioral Dimensions*, (Boston: Houghton Mifflin, 1969), pp. 92–116.

[3] Ibid.

need to satisfy their target market's needs. For example, IBM controls a scarce resource—its highly demanded line of personal computers—that computer dealers wish to carry. Resellers, on the other hand, control suppliers' access to target markets, another scarce resource. Many small manufacturers would like Sears to carry their products because of Sears' vast base of loyal customers, for example. Second, as noted above, marketing organizations rely upon one another to perform specialized marketing functions. Thus, channel members depend upon one another to perform their assigned tasks and to provide scarce resources.

The more A provides resources and performs functions that B needs, the more dependent B becomes upon A, particularly if B cannot obtain those resources or functions from a channel member other than A. The more dependent B is on A, the more power A can wield over B.[4] Many firms actively seek to reduce their dependence on other organizations within the channel. Some attempt to increase others' dependence on them. Exhibit 10-1 illustrates how one firm has tried to alter its dependence on the largest customer for one of its product lines.

Highly valued resources and marketing functions can take many different forms. For example, A may have the ability to offer B generous promotional allowances, highly respected expertise, and timely market information. If B values these resources and functions, B may potentially become dependent on A for them. This would enable A to achieve power over B. These valued resources and functions are often termed *bases of power*, particularly when they are used to create power and dependence relationships and to achieve influence. The following section will discuss these bases of power in more detail.

The Bases of Power

Individual channel members use various types of power to create dependence and to influence the decisions and behavior of other channel members. Exerting power is the mechanism for specifying roles, realigning roles when necessary, and enforcing role performance. As indicated above, a number of bases or types of power may be available to channel members as they attempt to influence one another.[5]

Rewards. Reward power is based on channel member B's belief that channel member A has the ability to provide rewards for him. A's effective use of reward power rests on his having some resource that B values and believes he can obtain by conforming to A's request. Specific rewards used by individual channel members may include the granting of wider margins, the allocation of various types of promotional allowances, and the assignment of exclusive territories.

---

[4] Richard M. Emerson, "Power-Dependence Relations," *American Sociological Review*, Vol. 27 (February 1962), pp. 32–33; Richard P. Bagozzi and Lynn W. Phillips, "Representing Organizational Theories: A Holistic Construal," *Administrative Science Quarterly*, Vol. 27 (September 1982), pp. 459–489; and Gary L. Frazier, "On the Measurement of Interfirm Power in Channels of Distribution," *Journal of Marketing Research*, Vol. 20 (May 1983), pp. 158–166.

[5] John R. P. French and Bertram Raven, "The Bases of Social Power," in Dorwin Cartwright (ed.), *Studies in Social Power*, (Ann Arbor, MI: University of Michigan Press, 1959), pp. 150–167; and Bertram H. Raven and Arie W. Kruglanski, "Conflict and Power," in Paul Swingle (ed.), *The Structure of Conflict*, (New York: Academic Press, 1970), p. 73.

EXHIBIT 10-1
Easco Corporation:
Altering its Dependence upon Sears,
Roebuck & Co.

Being overly dependent upon a single customer or single supplier can leave a marketing channel member at the mercy of other organizations, as one firm found out.

Easco Corp. learned in 1980 that selling as much as 80% of a product line to one customer can be dangerous. That year, Sears, Roebuck & Co. slashed orders for Easco-made Craftsman hand tools by 50%, and the Baltimore company posted its first quarterly loss, even though it continued to operate a thriving aluminum-extrusion business. . . .[a]

"Since then, Easco has tripled the number of hand-tool outlets to nearly 15,000 and has seen Sears' share of its hand-tool sales fall to 66%."[b] The company has also taken other steps to reduce its dependence upon Sears.

Last year, it began a major push to expand the industrial market for small tools by signing up 20 agents to knock at factory doors. Now the company is debating a move into garden tools, which are sold by many of the same stores that display Easco wrenches and screwdrivers.[c]

And, "[i]n late 1983, Easco snared a coveted account: sole supplier of auto repair tools for the National Automotive Parts Assn.'s 6,000 stores."[d] Increasing Sears' dependence upon it is also one of Easco's aims.

At the same time, it will upgrade its Craftsman line in 1985 with new sets of specialty automotive tools for Sears to sell to professionals and advanced do-it-yourselfers. Even if they do as well as he hopes, [Easco President Richard P.] Sullivan predicts the giant retailer will account for only 55% of Easco's hand-tool sales by 1989.[e]

As a result of these efforts, Easco should be able to alter the balance of power in its relationship with its largest customer, Sears.

[a] "Easco Using Profits from Aluminum to Repair Its Tool Business," *Business Week*, (July 2, 1984), p. 90.

[b] ibid.

[c] ibid.

[d] ibid.

[e] ibid.

American Hospital Supply (AHS), a medical supplies wholesaler, rewards its hospital group customers with guaranteed price ceilings for their purchases. To qualify for these price ceilings, hospital groups must link themselves to AHS's order-entry systems and must meet a specified minimum annual volume of purchases (e.g., $2,500).[6] The reward power employed by AHS enables hospital groups to stem the tide of rising health-care costs.

---

[6] "American Hospital Supply's Pricing Promise," *Sales & Marketing Management*, January 14, 1980, p. 24.

Coercion. Coercive power is based on B's expectation that A will punish him if he fails to conform to A's influence attempt. Coercion exists where one firm perceives that another is capable of using negative sanctions or punishments such as reductions in margins, the withdrawal of rewards previously granted (e.g., an exclusive territorial right), and the slowing down of shipments. In fact, coercive power is often viewed as the opposite of reward power. Note, however, that the threat and use of negative sanctions may be seen as "pathological" and may be more damaging over the long run than other power bases that produce more positive side effects.[7] Therefore, coercion should be used only when all other avenues of influence have been traveled.

Coercive power is often employed in situations where there is an extreme imbalance of power within the channel. Such a situation can arise, for example, where very large and well-financed retailers face small, highly dependent manufacturers or vice versa.

- Because of its strong consumer demand, Procter & Gamble, maker of such products as Tide laundry detergent, Jif peanut butter, Duncan Hines cake mixes, Folger's coffee, and Charmin bathroom tissue, has long been able to wield coercive power over its retailers. Unlike its competitors, P&G carefully scrutinizes retailers' performances to make sure that they actually earn the promotional and trade allowances they receive. When a retailer is found not to have undertaken a marketing task he has been compensated for, he must repay the unearned allowances or have his credit cut off altogether.[8]
- Hartz Mountain Corporation controls over 75 percent of the pet supplies market. Some charge that this market share is partially due to the reward and coercive tactics the company used to influence its dealers. In a 1979 Federal Trade Commission consent decree, Hartz Mountain agreed to stop forcing dealers to carry only its products and to stop giving its resellers discounts for not carrying competitive products.[9]

Channel members continually subjected to coercion attempt to counterbalance this power by restructuring dependencies within the channel. For example, Florida citrus growers have formed associations to counteract the coercive activities of processors and grocery chains; franchisees in the fast-food, petroleum, and automotive industries have also banded together to forestall their franchisors' use of coercion. In virtually every instance where some channel members use coercive power continually, resistance to influence and conflict have

[7] Jack J. Kasulis and Robert E. Spekman, "A Framework for the Use of Power," *European Journal of Marketing*, Vol. 14 (1980), pp. 180–191.

[8] "Why P&G Wants a Mellower Image," *Business Week*, June 7, 1982, pp. 60, 64.

[9] "The King of Hartz Mountain Polishes His Image," *Business Week*, July 15, 1985, pp. 124, 126.

resulted. If such a situation cannot be remedied through more judicious management practices or government intervention, the channel will become increasingly unstable and lose is competitive strength.

Expertise. Expert power is based on B's perception that A has special knowledge or skill. Examples of channel members assuming expert roles are widespread. Small retailers, for instance, rely heavily on their wholesale suppliers for expert advice. In the drug, grocery, and hardware trades, merchant wholesalers generally provide retailers with sales promotion assistance and materials, sales training for store employees, advice on getting special displays, counsel on store layout and arrangement, and suggestions about a host of other business functions. In addition, many wholesalers develop management training programs for their retailer customers.

- Under American Hospital Supply's order-entry system for hospital groups discussed above, once a hospital joins AHS's plan, teams of experts arrive to analyze the hospital's inventory needs, brand name preferences, and materials flow. Then an order transmitter linked to a central computer at the company's headquarters is installed. Benefits to the hospital include reduced inventory requirements, improved cash flow, less paperwork, and 24-hour delivery on the great majority of orders.[10]
- Sweda International, Inc., the cash register subsidiary of Litton Industries, Inc., uses 200 independent dealers to market its high-technology products. Because customers generally question the sophistication and responsiveness of independent dealers, Sweda's competitors frown on this policy. Through intensive dealer training, however, Sweda has overcome this concern. For example, an executive of McCrory Corporation, which purchased 2,000 Sweda electronic cash registers for 750 department stores, has been quoted as saying: "We have found in some locations that Sweda's dealers are better than the company's employees."[11]

Nonetheless, expert power is often not a very durable base of power in marketing channels. If after receiving initial advice from A, channel member B learns to operate without A's expert advice, then A's expertise is no longer a base of power. However, manufacturers might retain their expert power by offering to their intermediaries unique, well-planned, multifaceted promotional programs each time they introduce new products.

Where expertise can be readily applied outside the existing channel, marketers have sometimes taken rather drastic action to prevent that application from occurring.

[10] "American Hospital Supply's Pricing Promise," p. 24.

[11] "Sweda: Aggressive Marketing Produces a Spirited Turnaround," *Business Week*, March 31, 1980, p. 101.

- Horn & Hardart Company, one of Burger King Corporation's largest franchisees with 20 outlets in the New York City area, planned to become the Manhattan franchisee for Arby's, a roast beef chain owned by Royal Crown Company. Claiming that Horn & Hardart was in violation of its franchise agreement and would be operating in conflict of interest, Burger King informed Horn & Hardart that it was terminating several of its franchises.[12]

- Similarly, McDonald's contract with its franchisees specifies that McDonald's may take over a restaurant without advance notice for cause if a franchisee discloses confidential McDonald's documents. The contract also forbids franchisees from investing in another restaurant business.[13]

Both Burger King and McDonald's fervently guard the expertise they have developed and have no desire to share it with others.

✳ *Information.* To the extent that B perceives A as providing information not previously available to B, or when A points out consequences of actions B may not have been aware of, A has information power over B. Superficially, information power appears to be very similar to expertise; however, the two bases of power are really quite different. A's information power is based on B's accepting the logic of A's arguments rather than on A's perceived expertise; thus, influence attained through information power is sometimes called *persuasion.*

Marketing channel members, particularly retailers and industrial distributors, obtain information power by virtue of their close contacts with consumers of their suppliers' products. By gathering, interpreting, and transmitting valuable market information, an organization can enhance its power over other members of the channel.

General Foods performed a massive study of materials handling in distribution warehouses. It then made its results and recommendations available to wholesalers through a group of specialists carefully trained to help implement the recommendations. The company also undertook a major study of retail space profitability and then offered supermarket owners the opportunity to learn a new way of space profitability accounting.[14]

[12] "Burger King Sues Firm Controlled by President of Horn & Hardart Co.," *Wall Street Journal,* November 9, 1979, p. 10.

[13] Paul Merrion, "Tougher Pact Riles Big Mac Owners," *Crain's Chicago Business,* Vol. 2 (September 17, 1979), p. 33.

[14] Theodore Levitt, "Marketing Success Through Differentiation—of Anything," *Harvard Business Review,* Vol. 58 (January-February 1980), p. 89.

Identification. Identification and referent power are closely linked.

> The referent power of A over B has its basis in the identification of B with A. By identification, we mean a feeling of oneness of B to A, or a desire for such an identity. . . . If A is an attractive group, B will have a feeling of membership or a desire to join. If B is already closely associated with A, he will want to maintain this relationship.[15]

That referent power exists within many marketing channels is undeniable. This is especially true where wholesalers or retailers pride themselves on carrying certain brands (e.g., Schwinn bicycles and Estée Lauder perfumes) and where manufacturers pride themselves on having their brands carried in certain outlets (e.g., Neiman-Marcus and Bloomingdale's). Thus, the prestige associated with these products and stores enables manufacturers and retailers, respectively, to influence others in the marketing channel. Referent power also exists in channels for industrial products, particularly where suppliers have developed favorable reputations.[16]

✳ *Legitimacy.* Legitimate power stems from B's belief that A "should" or "has a right to" exert influence, and that he (B) has an obligation to accept it. The appearance of legitimate power is most obvious in *intra*organizational relations. That is, because subordinates feel that supervisors have a right to direct their work in a certain manner, they will generally conform to the superior's desires. Such legitimate power is often called *authority*.

Within marketing channels that are not vertically integrated, no formal hierarchy of authority exists; however, individual firms may perceive such a hierarchy. For example, the largest firm could be considered the leader by other channel members. If this is the case, then legitimate power may be available to that firm. It is also often available to manufacturers, particularly in the United States, since one U.S. cultural norm is that producers have the right to dictate how their products are marketed unless they transfer that right to another member of the channel.

Obviously, the legal system allows firms to maintain agreements, such as franchises and other contracts, that confer legitimate power. In addition, patent and trademark laws give owners a certain amount of freedom and justification in supervising the distribution of their products. Another example of legal legitimate power is manufacturers' grants of exclusive dealerships to their dealers.

---

[15] French and Raven, "The Bases of Social Power," p. 161.

[16] Theodore Levitt, *Industrial Purchasing Behavior: A Study of Communications Effects*, (Boston: Division of Research, Graduate School of Business Administration, Harvard University, 1965), pp. 31–32.

EXHIBIT 10-2

**Combining the Bases of Power:
Digital Equipment Corporation's
Commercial Distributor Program**

Digital Equipment Corporation, one of the world's largest computer manufacturers, has instituted a Commercial Distributor Program. This program incorporates a variety of influence strategies, using mainly reward, referent, and expert power bases. It includes the following features:

- A Trade Show Program, which supports distributors' participation in trade shows.
- An Open House Program, which provides assistance in attracting prospects and creating new sales leads for distributors.
- A Product Guide, which contains the latest information on Digital products, prices, configurations, and environmental requirements. Executive Seminars for distributor personnel.
- A Demonstrator Program, which allows distributors to purchase a Digital computer for demonstration and development purposes at a premium discount.
- A Warehouse Program, which assures shipment of certain standard small business systems and computer peripherals within seven working days.
- A Commercial Operations Guide, which contains recommended guidelines for handling customer surveys, detailed specifications, proposals, contracts, acceptance criteria, warranties, and user documentation.
- An Authorized Digital Computer Distributor Logo, which authorized distributors may use on all sales, stationery, sign, collateral, and advertising materials.
- A Cooperative Advertising Program, under which Digital will reimburse 40 percent of approved advertising expenditures to authorized distributors.

Combining the Power Bases

So far, discussion of power bases has treated each separately. In reality, however, they are used in combination. For an illustration of how one manufacturer does this, see Exhibit 10-2.

By using power bases in combination, channel members can achieve synergy in their attempts to influence other firms. For example, identification may enhance expertise and vice versa, and coercion may sometimes be necessary to

TABLE 10.1 Consequences of Using the Bases of Marketing Channel Power

Base of Power	Consequences
Mediated Bases of Power	Consequences of Mediated Power Bases
Coercion	Low cooperation
Reward	High conflict
Legal legitimate	Low predictability of compliance
	High need for monitoring performance
	Short-run response
Nonmediated Power Bases	Consequences of Nonmediated Power Bases
Information	High cooperation
Traditional legitimate (authority)	Low conflict
Expert	High predictability of compliance
Referent	Low need for monitoring performance
	Long-term response

Sources: Developed from Jack J. Kasulis and Robert E. Spekman, "A Framework for the Use of Power," *European Journal of Marketing*, Vol. 14, (1980), pp. 180-191; Jean L. Johnson, Harold F. Koenig, and James R. Brown, "The Bases of Marketing Channel Power: An Exploration and Confirmation of Their Underlying Dimensions," in Robert F. Lusch et al. (eds.), *1985 AMA Educators' Proceedings* (Chicago: American Marketing Association, 1985), pp. 160-165; and Gary L. Frazier and John O. Summers, "Interfirm Influence Strategies and Their Application within Distribution Channels," *Journal of Marketing*, Vol. 48 (Summer 1984), pp. 43–55.

reinforce legitimacy.[17] On the other hand, certain power bases may conflict. For example, a channel member's use of coercive power may undermine any information power that firm might have developed.

Note that the bases of power can be grouped according to whether or not a firm can provide other channel members with "tangible" inducements to perform the desired activities. Through the *mediated power bases* (i.e., coercive, reward, and legal legitimate), "tangible" inducements (i.e., punishments, rewards, and legal contracts, respectively) are used to achieve the desired behaviors. In contrast, the *nonmediated power bases* (information, traditional legitimate or authority, referent, and expert) employ no "tangible" inducements to gain influence.[18]

To use the power bases effectively, channel members must understand the economic, social, and political costs associated with applying the various power bases. As shown in Table 10-1, using the mediated power bases over the long run generally results in low cooperation and high conflict among channel members.

[17] For further discussion of the relationship among the bases of marketing channel power, see George John, "An Empirical Investigation of Some Antecedents of Opportunism in a Marketing Channel, *Journal of Marketing Research*, Vol. 21 (August 1984), pp. 278–289; John F. Gaski, "Interrelations Among a Channel Entity's Power Sources: Impact of the Exercise of Reward and Coercion on Expert, Referent, and Legitimate Power Sources," *Journal of Marketing Research*, Vol. 23 (February 1986), pp. 62–77; and Roy D. Howell, "Covariance Structure Modeling and Measurement Issues: A Note on 'Interrelations Among a Channel Entity's Power Sources'," *Journal of Marketing Research*, Vol. 24 (February 1987), pp. 119–126.

[18] Jean L. Johnson, Harold F. Koenig, and James R. Brown, "The Bases of Marketing Channel Power: An Exploration and Confirmation of Their Underlying Dimensions," in Robert F. Lusch et al. (eds.), *1985 AMA Educators' Proceedings* (Chicago: American Marketing Association, 1985), pp. 160–165.

Because of these consequences, a firm cannot very accurately predict whether influencing other channel members through a mediated power base will result in the desired behavior. Therefore, a channel member must somehow ensure that the desired activities are actually being undertaken before granting rewards or invoking punishments. In spite of these negative consequences, the mediated power bases are particularly effective in getting channel members to perform some behavior in the short term. Using the nonmediated power bases results in the opposite consequences—that is, higher cooperation, lower conflict, less monitoring, and greater predictability. The chief reason compliance is more predictable is that it is based on channel members' norms and values, which are more stable than their reactions to "tangible" inducements. But shaping a channel member's norms and values is a time-consuming process, so influence based on the nonmediated power bases is only effective over the long run.

In addition to the costs of using the power bases to coordinate channel activities and to ensure effective performance, influence attempts are constrained by norms that exist within channel systems. These norms, or "rules" of competition, aid in defining appropriate channel member behavior and can be even more limiting than legal restrictions in some cases.

During periods of short supply in the steel industry, many buyers are willing to pay above "normal" prices for steel. This alternative is less expensive than shutting down production. Because of short supply, steel distributors in the established marketing channels can command higher prices; however, they frequently refrain from doing so. This is because they feel that their customers expect certain restraints from them, even though some of these same customers go outside the legitimate, established channel structure to purchase higher-priced steel from so-called gray market sources. The established distributors refrain from coercing these latter customers via such tactics as boycotts because the norms of market behavior in this channel do not sanction such actions.[19]

When channel leadership is used to shift the flows or functions among institutions within the channel, the marketing channel services desired by the target markets can be delivered more efficiently and effectively. The following section discusses how an organization, through its bases of power and environmental circumstances, can become a channel leader.

A Framework for Channel Leadership and Control

A channel leader is that marketing channel institution that formulates marketing policies for other channel members and therefore controls their marketing decisions. Overall channel performance, as well as individual channel member

[19] Louis Kriesberg, "Occupational Controls Among Steel Distributors," in Louis W. Stern (ed.), *Distribution Channels: Behavioral Dimensions*, (Boston: Houghton Mifflin, 1969), pp. 48–62.

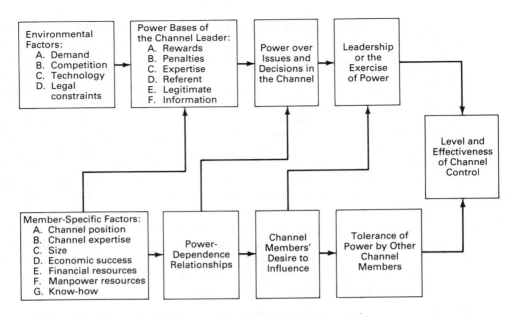

Figure 10-2   A framework for channel leadership and control.
Explanation:

- Power bases accrue to channel members as a result of environmental factors and/or the specific characteristics of the channel member.
- Power is issue–oriented. Power over issues and decisions is a function of the bases of power accumulated by a channel member and his power–dependence relationships vis-à-vis other channel members.
- Leadership, or the exercise of power, can only occur when a channel member has power over issue(s) and desires to exercise his or her power.
- The level and effectiveness of channel control achieved is a function of the quality of leadership, nature and magnitude of power resources deployed, and tolerance of power by other channel members.

Source: Based, in part, on an article from *Journal of Marketing Research*, published by the American Marketing Association, "Channel Environment and Channel Leadership," by Michael Etgar (February 1977) p. 70.

performance, is often determined by the level of control that some firms have over others. Note, however, that the scope of control does not have to be broad for a channel member to successfully influence others. In fact, because of the degree of specialization within most channels, the scope of any channel member's power over others may be limited to only a few of the marketing flows. For example, transportation agencies are not likely to want to influence promotional activities in the channel; many producers feel likewise about financing ultimate consumers' purchases.

The extent to which a channel leader manages the marketing channel hinges on a number of interrelated factors and conditions (see Figure 10-2). A discussion of these factors and their interrelationships follows.

Channel Environment and Channel Leadership. Channel member A's ability to exercise control is determined by the bases of power at its disposal. These power bases are generated by the organization's size, financial strength, economic success, special skills, access to information, and other characteristics. In addition, A's power bases may reflect the nature of the marketing channel's environment (e.g., competition, technology, legal restrictions, state of the economy, demand factors) and its ability to capitalize on these forces. Therefore, the power, and ultimately the control, of a channel leader are determined by the characteristics of both the environment and the organization itself.[20]

Marketing institutions with the necessary power bases can often increase their control over the channel in environments characterized by:

1. Declining rather than growing demand.
2. Unstable demand.
3. The importance of personal selling and high postsales service as marketing channel services.
4. Strong interchannel competition.
5. Diverse environmental elements.
6. Variability in demand.[21]

✴ The Use of Mediated and Nonmediated Power. Before a channel member can successfully attempt to control other channel members, he must possess bases of power. As noted earlier in this section, particular power bases are more effective in some circumstances than in others. For example, the mediated power bases (coercion, reward, and legal legitimate) are more effective in obtaining short-run control than are the nonmediated bases (information, traditional legitimate or authority, expert, and referent). The reason is that the mediated power bases can, within certain legal bounds, (1) be applied on an individual basis and directed toward a specific channel member and (2) be related to specific performance by channel members. Thus, a manufacturer may allocate more of a fast-moving product only to those dealers who also stock the slow-moving items in the line. Because the nonmediated power bases are less flexible and may be unrelated to a channel member's performance of a particular marketing task, they are less likely to be effective in obtaining short-run control.[22] However, as we will see in Chapter 11, the disadvantage of using the mediated bases of power is that they generate conflict among organizations within the channel and may produce unstable long-run channel relationships.

[20] Michael Etgar, "Channel Environment and Channel Leadership," *Journal of Marketing Research*, Vol. 14 (February 1977), pp. 69–76.

[21] Environmental characteristics 1–4 were found by ibid., while characteristics 5 and 6 were uncovered by F. Robert Dwyer and M. Ann Welsh, "Environmental Relationships of the Internal Political Economy of Marketing Channels," *Journal of Marketing Research*, Vol. 22 (November 1985), pp. 397–414.

[22] Michael Etgar, "Selection of an Effective Channel Control Mix," *Journal of Marketing*, Vol. 42 (July 1978), pp. 53–57.

TABLE 10.2 Tolerance for Control in Marketing Channels

B's Expectations for Success if B Controls the Marketing Flow	B's Expectations for Success if A Controls the Marketing Flow	
	High	Low
High	A and B share control	B retains control
Low	B relinquishes control to A	No change in either A's or B's control

Source: Adapted from *Journal of Marketing Research*, published by the American Marketing Association, "A Sociopsychological Explanation for Why Marketing Channel Members Relinquish Control," by Punam Anand and Louis W. Stern, Vol. 22 (November 1985), p. 366.

The organization of the channel also plays a role in the use of the bases of power. For example, manufacturers in conventional channels may rely primarily on product-related means of power, such as width of product selection, promptness of delivery, development and introduction of new products, frequency of delivery, and product expertise. Manufacturers in contractual channels, on the other hand, may rely on retail assistance such as training sales people, store management and layout, and provision of sales leads.[23] Moreover, leaders of vertical marketing systems are generally seen as having more of both the mediated and nonmediated power bases than are leaders in conventional channels. Specifically, leaders in corporate and contractual channels have more legitimate power than those in conventional channels. In addition, conventional channel leaders have less referent power than corporate channel leaders, and less expert power than contractual channel leaders.[24]

Tolerance for Influence. Channel member A's ability to exert leadership over channel member B is partially determined by B's tolerance for A's control over B's marketing activities. The fewer the number of B's alternatives to A and the less B wishes to be independent of A, the more B will tolerate A's control.[25] In addition, B's expectations will shape his tolerance for A's control.[26] As table 10-2 illustrates, if B believes that his success will be higher than A's if he controls a particular marketing flow, he will retain control of that flow. If he believes that success can be achieved if either firm controls the marketing flow, B will share control with A. On the other hand, if B believes that he will not be as successful as A if he controls a specific marketing flow, he will relinquish control to A.

[23] Michael Etgar, "Differences in the Use of Manufacturer Power in Conventional and Contractual Channels," *Journal of Retailing*, Vol. 54 (Winter 1978), p. 59.

[24] James R. Brown and Glenn T. Stoops, "Sources of Marketing Channel Power: Differences Across Channel Types," in Michael G. Harvey and Robert F. Lusch (eds.), *Marketing Channels: Domestic and International Perspectives*, (Norman: Center for Economic and Management Research, School of Business Administration, the University of Oklahoma, 1982), pp. 59–66.

[25] Louis P. Bucklin, "A Theory of Channel Control," *Journal of Marketing*, Vol. 37 (January 1973), pp. 39–47.

[26] Punam Anand and Louis W. Stern, "A Sociopsychological Explanation for Why Marketing Channel Members Relinquish Control," *Journal of Marketing Research*, Vol. 22 (November 1985), pp. 365–376.

Finally, if he believes that neither firm will be successful by controlling that flow, B will maintain the status quo.

Geri Ackerman, owner of Geri Ackerman Ford, is a fiercely independent but highly astute car dealer. For the most part, Geri is willing to accede to Ford's leadership, since she believes that "Ford has a good handle on the car business." Occasionally, however, she refuses to go along with its wishes, particularly when it comes to the mix of cars Ford wants her to carry. "Ford sometimes tries to ram down our throats models that are slow sellers in this market. But I know better than the factory what'll sell and what won't in this market. Sometimes, you've got to let 'em know who's boss," Geri explains, "and not take all of what they want to give you."

Regardless of how tolerant wholesalers and retailers are of producers' attempts to control these issues, producers are constrained by legal restrictions, as we showed in Chapters 5, 6, and 8. Because legal restrictions are based on recent court decisions, a channel leader must keep abreast of those decisions.

The Channel Control Process. A channel leader's ability to achieve channel control and coordination hinges to a large extent on three factors:

1. Whether the channel institutions perceive their marketing channels as a system or are merely concerned with their immediate suppliers and customers. If channel members do not perceive themselves as members of a total system, channel coordination is more difficult.
2. How the members perceive the control process within the channel. Differences in perceptions indicate that channel members are likely to respond differently to similar situations.
3. Which marketing activities are perceived as being controlled by each channel member. Leadership and control are not exercised over a range of issues, but rather over specific issues or marketing channel activities. Unless channel members similarly perceive who controls what, leadership attempts may result in chaos rather than the desired coordination and control.[27]

These factors underscore the importance of a channelwide communication and information system (as discussed in Chapter 7) to broaden the base of common understanding and foster common perceptions among channel members.

Thus far, we have concentrated on factors that influence the process of channel leadership and control. To understand which institutions are most likely to lead the channel, we now turn to a discussion of the leadership abilities of various marketing institutions.

[27] Thomas W. Speh and E. H. Bonfield, "The Control Process in Marketing Channels: An Exploratory Investigation," *Journal of Retailing*, Vol. 54 (Spring 1978), pp. 14–16.

WHO SHOULD LEAD THE MARKETING CHANNEL?

The question of who should lead the channel hinges largely on which organizations hold the balance of power in particular marketing channels. The following sections present some basic generalizations about the abilities of several classes of marketing institutions—manufacturers, wholesalers, retailers, and logistics firms—to lead the channel. However, because each channel system varies widely in structure and administrative pattern, a careful analysis of each situation is necessary to discover the best answer to the question of who should lead the marketing channel.

CHANNEL MANAGEMENT BY MANUFACTURERS

Too often, the manufacturer or producer is automatically assumed to be the channel leader and the intermediaries to be the channel followers. But, as we shall see later, manufacturers have not always been the channel leaders.

Large manufacturers are always potential leaders of channels because of their size and dominance in the markets in which they compete. Their power emanates from their considerable financial resources, which enable them to maintain superior product research and development, cultivate consumer franchises through promotion, maintain continuous flows of market information, offer high margins and support to middlemen, and retain control over their products until ultimate consumers or industrial buyers purchase them.

However, small manufacturers may sometimes control and direct an interorganizational channel network.[28] While limited economic resources hamper their opportunities, a good product offers manufacturers the possibility of developing effective bases of power. The manufacturer with an outstanding product may have, from the perspective of those purchasing it, a "right" to dictate how it should be sold and consumed, an image with which others seek to identify, and probably a greater assumed knowledge about the market for his product than anyone else. Furthermore, those controlling a new product that is desired by many consumers—irrespective of whether they are large or small—can elect to offer or withhold their product from various middlemen.

The manufacturer-directed channel concept is based primarily on the belief that because the manufacturer creates and produces the product and designs the network through which it passes on its way to consumers, he is entitled, on the basis of legitimacy if nothing else, to impose his marketing policies on other channel members and to direct the activities of the channel. Although a number of channels are manufacturer-dominated for just these reasons (especially when the manufacturers have considerable economic power), the question of channel leadership is not as easy to answer as it might seem. Many other factors must be considered before manufacturers are deemed the logical channel managers.

First, manufacturers are not always eager to manage the channel. Their sole concern may simply be with the firms above and below them in the channel. After

---

[28] Robert W. Little, "The Marketing Channel: Who Should Lead This Extracorporate Organization?" *Journal of Marketing*, Vol. 34 (January 1970), p. 34.

all, manufacturers' dealings are usually with their immediate suppliers and customers and not with any of the other resellers of their products. They may not care at all about the problems of other channel members as long as their own needs are satisfied. Manufacturers, it must be noted, are not unique in this respect; similar assertions could be applied to resellers. Furthermore, manufacturers may prefer to concentrate their efforts on product research and development because they have limited marketing management capacity or capability. As was shown in an earlier chapter, this accounts for the heavy reliance on wholesalers in a number of industrial goods industries.

Second, manufacturers may simply not be powerful enough, in relation to other channel members, to impose policies on them. This is particularly true if manufacturers are interested in using large wholesaling and retailing institutions. In general, intermediaries do not have to handle the manufacturer's product if they do not desire to do so, especially if substitutes are readily available. Many resellers face limited display and warehouse space as well as the need for immediate cash flow. In such cases, manufacturers must often curry the favor of middlemen in order to assure that their products are adequately stocked and promoted. Moreover, resellers can often develop in their customers greater loyalty to their outlets than to the products they carry.

In summary, manufacturer dominance of the marketing channel is not an absolute certainty for several reasons. Among these are the manufacturer's own reluctance to lead and the relative strength of middlemen in the channel. On the other hand, *if* manufacturers possess relatively unique products with strong consumer demand (or can provide unique services that enhance the use of products), and *if* resellers are relatively weak (e.g., if they have limited options and limited resources), then manufacturers are likely to assume the channel management role quite easily.

Methods of Manufacturer Dominance

Of the many methods that manufacturers can use to dominate the channel, perhaps the most common is the development of strong end-user attraction or loyalty to their products. This factor is particularly important in the case of products sold through convenience retail outlets, where little or no personal selling assistance is provided and where the locational density of outlets is high.

> If the manufacturer can develop a strong brand image through advertising, the retailer has very little power because (1) the retailer is little able to influence the buying decision of the consumer in the store; (2) a strong manufacturer's brand image creates consumer demand for the product, which assures profits to the retailer from stocking the product and at the same time denies him the credible bargaining counter of refusing to deal in the manufacturer's goods.[29]

[29] Michael E. Porter, "Consumer Behavior, Retailer Power and Market Performance in Consumer Goods Industries," *The Review of Economics and Statistics*, Vol. 56 (November 1974), p. 423.

A manufacturer may also use coercive methods or policies. For example, Procter and Gamble refuses to sell to resellers who only wish to buy P&G products on "deal." Producers can also employ resale restrictions, exclusive dealing, and tying contracts. These methods, when legal, work only if resellers strongly desire to carry a manufacturer's product line. Therefore, they must generally be coupled with significant brand identification, the availability of few comparable product sources, and the opportunity for sizable rewards. Other methods of manufacturer dominance are forward vertical integration and/or the use of contractual agreements.

If manufacturers can amass sufficient expert, referent, and/or legitimate power, they may be able to lead the channel. Manufacturers who gain leadership this way have made a long-term commitment to gathering and disseminating crucial market information as well as to ensuring continual product and managerial innovations, so that other channel members seek to identify with them and believe that they have a right to direct their activities.

Such efforts, with the exception of new-product development, are not necessarily unique to manufacturers. If channel members at other levels choose to undertake them, the mantle of leadership (or the rights of dominance) may fall to them. Thus, in some industries, channels are led by wholesalers and retailers rather than by manufacturers because these intermediaries have done a more effective job of accumulating a significant amount of power within their channel networks.

CHANNEL MANAGEMENT BY WHOLESALERS

Wholesalers' roles in modern marketing channels are greatly reduced from what they once were. During the early stages of economic development in the United States (prior to the mid-1800s), merchant wholesalers were in a natural position to lead the channel because they generally stood between small manufacturers and small retailers. However, during the rapid industrial growth of the late 1800s, large manufacturers and retailers began placing increased pressure on wholesalers. Manufacturers often felt that, given their increased production capacities, they could more effectively market their own goods without using wholesalers. And retailers, as their size increased, were more capable of buying directly from manufacturers, thus obtaining discounts and allowances that normally went to wholesalers.

In general, wholesalers have been able to remain in a dominant channel position only in those industries where the buyers and producers are small in size, large in number, and relatively scattered geographically, and where manufacturers are financially weak and lack marketing expertise.[30] Except in a limited number of fields, these conditions no longer exist in the United States. The fact that wholesalers are still a significant factor in distribution, as was shown in detail

[30] Edwin H. Lewis, "Channel Management by Wholesalers," in Robert L. King (ed.), *Marketing and the New Science of Planning* (Chicago: American Marketing Association, 1968), p. 138.

in an earlier chapter, attests to their success in readjusting to their changing environment, at least to some degree.

Despite this rather gloomy description of the wholesaler's opportunity for channel leadership, there are certain circumstances in which wholesalers do, in fact, engage in strong and effective channel leadership.

One form of channel organization that has been particularly successful for wholesalers in strengthening their leadership positions is the voluntary chain, especially in the marketing of grocery products. As noted in the preceding chapter, wholesalers are clearly the leaders of these contractual vertical marketing systems. Retailers receive the benefits of centralized buying, private brands, the identity of the group, large-scale promotion, and other management aids, while the wholesalers allocate the resources of their respective voluntary systems in such a way as to enhance their overall performance relative to competitive systems.

Besides voluntary groups, wholesalers have also been active in franchising. Wholesaler-franchisors, such as Southland (7-Eleven Stores) and ComputerLand, clearly dominate their channels by exercising strict control over operations at the retail level. Also, because they are rarely tied to brand names, wholesaler-franchisors' purchasing power, combined with their maintaining alternative sources of supply, enables them to influence the marketing activities of their suppliers and thus to specify roles throughout the entire franchise system.

Another method used by wholesalers to achieve dominance has been the development of their own private brands.[31] Wholesalers' private brands appear to be successful mainly in fields where the products are relatively undifferentiated, frequently purchased, and where demand for the product has already been established. However, the fact that the products are relatively undifferentiated forces wholesalers to use price as the primary appeal in selling their brands. In addition, unless wholesalers can develop private brands in each of their key lines, their control will be slight. The development of private brands also requires considerable capital and substantial promotion as well as products of relatively high quality. Therefore, using private brands to achieve channel dominance is obviously not an easy task.

The development of electronic data interchange (EDI) systems may be another means that wholesalers can use to recapture positions of dominance in specific channels. For example:

> In a channel characterized by a loose coalition of independent retailers and wholesalers, where no middleman is particularly dominant, one of the wholesalers may take the lead in developing [EDI systems] thereby "tying" a number of the retailers to him. . . . Positionally, wholesalers are probably best able to assume leadership in the development of [EDI systems] in such channels. It would not be feasible, from an economic perspective, to maintain a great number of parallel (communication) flows, since each data link represents a cost. In any channel with more than two retailers and more than two manufacturers, the number of links can

[31] Ibid., p. 140.

be minimized by employing a wholesaler. With a large number of possible links, the saving can be substantial. . . .

A wholesaler is [also] in an ideal position to help smaller retailers with inventory management, accounts receivable, payroll, and other applications beyond the capabilities of the latter's own equipment. . . . Moreover, with the wholesaler-retailer links established, the wholesaler can readily build on the wholesaler-manufacturer links. With a large exclusive domain of retailers, a wholesaler will be able to exert power over manufacturers. By controlling inventories, maintaining receivables, and helping to prepare the payroll, the wholesaler will further entrench himself in the retailer's operation.[32]

In summary, wholesalers apparently are not qualified to lead channels in many of today's highly developed markets since they dominate channels in only a few industries (e.g., hardware, drugs, motion pictures, liquor, auto accessories and parts, and industrial supplies). The apparent strength of wholesalers lies in their role as builders of assortments, integrators of product lines, and reliable sources of merchandise for their customers. In order simply to hold their present positions, they must maintain their differential advantage in performing this role. Otherwise, they will become increasingly vulnerable and will eventually be bypassed.

CHANNEL MANAGEMENT BY RETAILERS

A significant number of retailers have grown in size to the point where they rival or even dwarf many large manufacturers. These retailers are likely to exert some control over the channels in which they are members.

Large-scale retailers have integrated the wholesaling functions within their channels and a number of them have, as was pointed out in the preceding chapter, integrated backward to the manufacturing level. Similar to large manufacturers, these firms have considerable coercive, reward, and expert power that can be employed in an effort to control channels. First, by virtue of their close proximity to local markets, these retailers have an opportunity to accumulate information power by continually assessing the needs of consumers within their communities. While other members of the channel could perform the same information-generating tasks, they would undoubtedly have to expend more effort in data collection than large retailers, simply because of the latter's locational advantage. Second, large-scale retailers like J. C. Penney, Sears, and K-Mart have ready access to large markets that manufacturers desire to reach. In effect, they are gatekeepers. The larger the markets that they serve, the more important they become to manufacturers, and thus the stronger their potential for leadership. Third, so long as these retailers can maintain alternative sources of supply, manufacturers will tend to be more dependent on them, especially in cases where a generic demand for a given product class has been established.

Interestingly, channel management is not always practiced by large retailers, even though they often have the necessary power to do so. Instead, they

[32] Louis W. Stern and C. Samuel Craig, "Interorganizational Data Systems: The Computer and Distribution," *Journal of Retailing*, Vol. 47 (Summer 1971), pp. 83–85.

frequently seem more concerned with obtaining specific types of concessions than with exerting a strong influence over aspects of new-product development, promotional and inventory policies of the entire channel, and the like.[33] As a result of their self-selected task of serving wide markets, managers of large-scale retail organizations concentrate their efforts on selecting and maintaining stocks and providing and merchandising the services that accompany them.[34] Therefore, two very important functions that might be considered within the domain of channel leaders—product development and demand stimulation—are, to a large extent, left unattended by large retailers. By dint of their closeness to and contact with ultimate consumers, retailers are in the best position of any channel members to discover exactly what the preferences of consumers are. However, they are much too engrossed with the details of their own operations to consider performing these functions on a channelwide basis. Thus, channel leadership frequently falls to manufacturers by default.

Methods of Retailer Dominance

The large retailers have at their disposal a variety of means by which they could dominate their channels. As with manufacturers, the most prominent means is the building of a consumer franchise through advertising, sales promotion, and branding.[35] Stores like Hudson's, Filene's, Bullock's, Sears, Richway, I. Magnin, and Safeway have established a loyal following by assembling an assortment of merchandise appropriate to their target markets, adequately promoting that assortment, and providing ancillary services. In other words, the successful retail operations have achieved positions of power within their markets through effective programming of the retailing mix elements, just as manufacturers have achieved success by combining the various elements of the marketing mix in unique ways.

In addition, many large-scale retailers have developed private-label programs that generate or reinforce strong customer loyalty, enabling them to secure channel control.[36] However, as in wholesaling, retailers' brands are economically feasible only after the market has widely accepted the product.[37] On the other hand, if generic product acceptance already exists, then the large-scale retailer can decide not only to enter the market with its own brand, but also which of the leading brands it will stock. Thus, it will be able to play off one supplier against another in order to achieve various concessions.[38]

[33] Roger A. Dickinson, "Channel Management by Large Retailers," in Robert L. King, *Marketing and the New Science of Planning* (Chicago, American Marketing Association, 1968), p. 128.

[34] Little, "The Marketing Channel," p. 35.

[35] Bruce Mallen, "Conflict and Cooperation in Marketing Channels," in Bruce Mallen (ed.), *The Marketing Channel: A Conceptual Viewpoint* (New York: John Wiley & Sons, 1967), p. 131.

[36] "Caught in a Cross Fire, Brand-Apparel Makers Design Their Defenses," *Wall Street Journal*, January 24, 1984, pp. 1, 12.

[37] Little, "The Marketing Channel," p. 35.

[38] Ibid., p. 36.

When manufacturers fail to develop a strong consumer franchise for their brands, power is clearly weighted in favor of large-scale retailers in many of the channels where they are strong participants. As pointed out above, however, these retailers are not always willing to assume leadership roles, and therefore the task of marshalling the resources of the various channel systems falls to other parties. Channelwide organization may be very difficult under these circumstances, either (1) because the units with the most power are simply not willing to take an active part in specifying roles and coordinating channel tasks, or (2) because these units are powerful enough to wield veto power over others' attempts to reallocate resources throughout the channel.

For example, retailers become very powerful when manufacturers selling through convenience outlets are unable to develop brand images through advertising. In such situations, a manufacturer's ability to achieve product differentiation in the eyes of the consumer is severely limited. Because many outlets must stock the product in order for manufacturers to achieve an efficient density of market coverage, producers become highly dependent on retailers.[39] Furthermore, where retail outlets provide significant sales assistance and the outlets are selectively rather than intensively located, retailers, irrespective of size, will likely be the dominant channel members. In the case of shopping goods, the retailer exerts considerable influence on the purchase decision of the consumer in several ways. First, the retailer controls some of the channel services that the consumer may desire. The reputation, image, physical amenities, and attendant services (e.g., credit, billing, delivery, warranty, repair) of a retail store can sway consumer purchase decisions. Second, the retailer can influence the sale of products sold through nonconvenience outlets by providing sales information.[40] The influence retailers have over consumers can be translated into increased retailer bargaining power over their suppliers.

Small Retailers as Channel Leaders

Collectively, small retailers have been known to exert considerable pressure on channel activities. They have lobbied local, state, and national governments for legislation that restrains competition or provides impediments to change.[41] They have colluded, through trade associations, to prevent marketing activities that they have perceived to be threatening to their survival. Through their legislative and collusive actions, they have sometimes been able to influence marketing strategy throughout the channel (e.g., state and local restrictions on entry, licensing requirements, antipeddler and anti-itinerant vendor ordinances, chain store taxes, evening and Sunday closing laws, advertising restrictions) to soften or curb competitive impacts. Clearly, this form of negative channel leadership is not

[39] Porter, "Consumer Behavior," p. 423.

[40] Ibid., pp. 420–421.

[41] Stanley C. Hollander, "Channel Management by Small Retailers," in Robert L. King, *Marketing and the New Science of Planning* (Chicago: American Marketing Association, 1968), pp. 132–134.

laudatory. In many situations, these impediments have short-lived effects and have failed to effectively restrain many innovations in distribution.

On the other hand, small retailers have attempted to exert positive channel leadership by developing retailer-sponsored cooperatives. The retailer cooperative is an obvious effort to overcome the size and subsequent buying disadvantages faced by individual small retailers. However, as indicated in the preceding chapter, retailer-sponsored cooperatives face some very serious problems. Within them, power is diffused, and therefore there is considerable doubt whether they can provide the tightly knit control needed to compete successfully with corporate and voluntary chains unless like Cotter and Ace in the hardware industry, they give up some of their autonomy and independence to central organizations.

CHANNEL MANAGEMENT BY PHYSICAL DISTRIBUTION AGENCIES

Although not normally considered potential managers of channel relations, common carriers could possibly assume such roles if they were to utilize more effectively the power bases at their disposal. In fact, logistical institutions of all types occupy unique positions in this respect because they have the advantage of being *neutral* relative to many of the channel policies and activities of major concern to manufacturers, wholesalers, and retailers.[42] While the latter channel members may have difficulty in looking beyond their immediate suppliers and customers, logistical institutions can take a broader perspective of channel problems.

Note that channel leadership is possible with regard to each of the marketing flows taken separately or to all of the flows taken together. Thus, it is clear that common carriers can lead the channel with respect to the physical possession flow, but their influence relative to the remaining flows is likely to be minimal. In other words, the scope of a common carrier's power is limited to those activities with which it is directly concerned. Figure 10-3 illustrates the position occupied by common carriers within a generalized channel arrangement and some of the power bases that are available to them. Some specific examples of the reward and expert power bases that could be, and sometimes are, used by common carriers are:[43]

- Reductions in rates charged to shippers. (However, because of competitive reaction, such reductions are likely to have limited impact over the long run.)
- Reductions in the overall cost of transportation by eliminating loss and damage claims, special schedules, and/or minimum weight requirements.

[42] J. L. Heskett, "Costing and Coordinating External and Internal Logistics Activities," in Donald J. Bowersox, Bernard J. LaLonde, and Edward W. Smykay (eds.), *Readings in Physical Distribution Management* (New York: Macmillan, 1969), pp. 81–83.

[43] Frederick J. Beier, "The Role of the Common Carrier in the Channel of Distribution," *Transportation Journal*, Vol. 9 (Winter 1969), pp. 12–21.

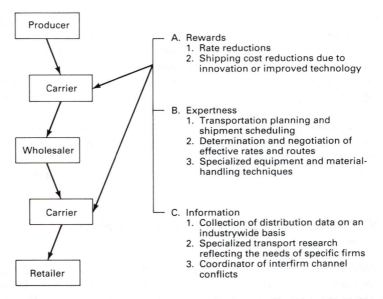

Figure 10-3 Range of common carrier contributions to other channel members.
Source: Adapted from Frederick J. Beir, "The role of the Common Carrier in the Channel of Distribution," *Transportation Journal*, Vol. 9 (Winter 1969), p. 19.

- Providing special arrangements such as rent-a-train services whereby carriers rent specialized equipment designed to serve particular clients. The provision of specialized equipment increases the dependence of shippers on carriers.

- Providing consulting services to shippers whereby staff specialists assigned to a particular industry advise shippers in that industry about rates, routing, and other services. Traditionally, carriers have acted as advisors relative to plant locations in their operating areas.

- Making available part of a carrier's large computing facilities in order to institute a channelwide communication system relative to information about shipments.

- Providing information with regard to the transportation and materials-handling requirements of other channel members. (Carriers can thereby suggest compatible handling systems that would lead to more efficient coordination of the physical and information interface between channel members.)

Similarly, the distribution center may play an important role in channel management if it deploys its expertise and informational resource bases.

> The distribution center manager . . . is familiar with marketing-related objectives and patterns of distribution not only of his customers, but also of his customers' customers and of the carriers and other institutions in the distribution chain. He

knows their needs, wants, aspirations, and operations. As he fulfills these services, the user becomes more dependent upon him and he becomes more powerful.[44]

At this juncture it should be clear that channel control is a dynamic process. As the grocery industry example at the beginning of the chapter illustrates, there are no guarantees that those who control the marketing channel today will continue in command tomorrow. There is no substitute for an analysis of the dynamics of power and its structure in an industry to reach plausible conclusions about who controls the marketing channel.

SO, WHO SHOULD LEAD THE MARKETING CHANNEL? ⚹

Although the question as to which institution or agency should lead the channel has been debated for many years, no single satisfactory answer has emerged. The fact is that the answer depends upon the *specific* situation. The issues involved in each industrial setting must be carefully examined and the scope of each commercial channel member's power with respect to each of the marketing flows must be defined. It may even be necessary to break the flows down into component parts in order to perform an adequate analysis. For example, the flow of physical possession incorporates both transportation and storage of merchandise. One channel member may be able to exert more influence with regard to the first component, while another may have more power with respect to the second. Clearly, the analysis—based on empirical findings—must account for the tolerance levels in the channel for control by each of the members as well as the payoffs that accrue to each as a result of control.[45] Furthermore, the influence of elements in a commercial channel's task environment (e.g., consumers and government) must be considered in determining or constraining the leadership question. It should, however, be clear from the discussion in this chapter that each commercial channel member has at least the potential for leadership with regard to one or more of the marketing flows, because each has amassed or is capable of amassing power of one form or another relative to other channel members. The ultimate answer as to who should lead must, however, be left to an empirical analysis of power and the relevant payoffs from its use on a case-by-case basis.

SUMMARY

The central theme of this chapter is that a high degree of coordination is required within a marketing channel if that channel is to have a long-run impact on the markets that it serves. The basic coordination process involves five key steps:

[44] James A. Constantin, Jack J. Kasulis, and Robert F. Lusch, "The Distribution Center: A Potential Locus of Power," in Robert J. House and James F. Robeson (eds.), *Interfaces, Logistics, Marketing and Production* (Columbus: Transportation and Logistics Research Fund, The Ohio State University and NCDPM, 1976), p. 42.

[45] Adel I. El-Ansary and Robert A. Robicheaux, "A Theory of Channel Control: Revisited," *Journal of Marketing*, Vol. 38 (January 1974), pp. 4–7.

1. Determine channel service levels.
2. Identify the necessary tasks and the marketing institutions needed to perform those tasks.
3. Use power or leadership to ensure that the services are properly delivered.
4. Deal with channel conflict.
5. Achieve successful channel performance.

Steps 1–3 will be briefly summarized below. Steps 4 and 5 will be discussed further in Chapters 11 and 12, respectively.

All marketing effort should begin with an assessment of the needs and wants of end users. Marketing management's task is to develop goods and services that will satisfy the needs and wants of defined market segments. Once relevant markets have been isolated and appropriate products have been developed and tested, how those products will be made available to potential end users must be determined. After the channel services demanded by resellers and consumers are known, a channel can be structured to deliver those services. Important services are lot size, delivery or waiting time, locational convenience or market decentralization, and product variety, among others.

Once marketing managers know the channel services required, they can begin to search for channel partners who are capable of providing those services. Because the services can only be generated by organizing the marketing flows and functions, managers must specify which tasks various channel members should perform.

Power generally must be used in a marketing channel to specify these tasks, ensure that the tasks are complementary, gain cooperation, and achieve satisfactory delivery of the channel services desired by the target market. Power is the ability of one organization to influence the marketing strategy of others in the channel. It is based on dependence; the more highly dependent channel member A is upon channel member B, the more power B has over A. Channel members have several power bases available to them to change others' behavior or to gain continued cooperation. These include rewards, punishments, expertise, identification, legitimacy, and information. Power bases are most potent when used in combination, typically as either mediated or nonmediated power. However, the costs associated with using power bases must be considered in developing an influence or leadership strategy within the marketing channel.

This chapter also focused on factors influencing the leadership and control processes in marketing channels. The channel environment, the use of mediated versus nonmediated power, and channel members' tolerance for influence were some of the factors discussed. How the leadership and control processes fit in with the coordinative process is illustrated in Figure 10-4.

The potential of manufacturers, wholesalers, retailers, and physical distribution agencies to assume the role of channel leaders was also explored. In coming to grips with this issue, a crucial consideration is the amount and kinds of power available to each institution.

The potential channel leadership role of manufacturers appears to hinge on the strength of their products, brands, and services as viewed by their target

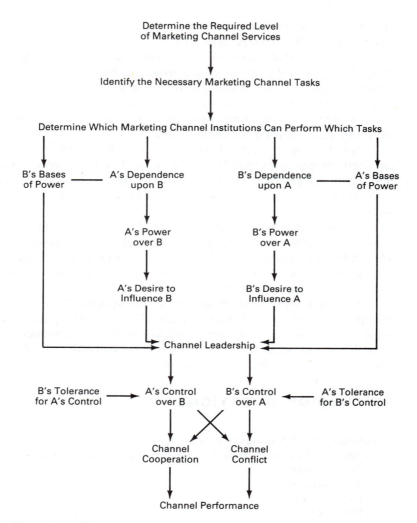

Determine the Required Level
of Marketing Channel Services

↓

Identify the Necessary Marketing Channel Tasks

↓

Determine Which Marketing Channel Institutions Can Perform Which Tasks

B's Bases of Power —— A's Dependence upon B ⟶ A's Power over B ⟶ A's Desire to Influence B ⟶ Channel Leadership

B's Dependence upon A ⟶ B's Power over A ⟶ B's Desire to Influence A ⟶ Channel Leadership —— A's Bases of Power

B's Tolerance for A's Control ⟶ A's Control over B

A's Tolerance for B's Control ⟶ B's Control over A

A's Control over B ⟶ Channel Cooperation / Channel Conflict

B's Control over A ⟶ Channel Cooperation / Channel Conflict

Channel Cooperation ⟶ Channel Performance

Channel Conflict ⟶ Channel Performance

Figure 10-4 Using power to coordinate the activities of marketing channels. *Source*: Adapted from Robert A. Robicheaux and Adel I. El-Ansary, "A General Model for Understanding Channel Member Behavior," *Journal of Retailing*. Vol. 52 (Winter 1975-1976), p. 16.

markets. The traditional belief that manufacturers are the "natural" channel leaders is based on the notion that because they create and produce their products, they are entitled to impose their marketing programs on other channel members and to direct the activities of the channel.

From a historical perspective, wholesalers have been able to lead the channel only in those industries where the buyers and producers are small in size, large in number, and relatively scattered geographically, and where manufacturers are financially weak and lack marketing expertise. Wholesalers have been particularly successful in strengthening their positions by organizing voluntary groups and franchise systems as well as by developing private-label programs and electronic data interchange networks.

The potential of large-scale retailers to lead the channel appears to stem from their close physical proximity to consumers, their ability to provide access to highly demanded target markets, and their maintenance of alternative sources of supply. Their continuous control over display space within their outlets, their development of strong patronage motives, and their use of private-label programs have enhanced their power considerably.

Smaller-scale retailers have collectively been able to lead some of their channels, primarily by restricting the channel power of other marketing institutions through legislation. Also, some smaller-scale retailers have banded together to form cooperatives as a means of enhancing their leadership positions within their channels.

Physical distribution agencies could possibly assume a greater role in channel leadership if they were to utilize their bases of power more effectively. Their influence, however, would generally be limited to activities involved in the physical possession flow, even if they were to become more aggressive within the channels in which participate.

The question of who should lead a channel cannot be answered without an in-depth study of the particular situation. Each and every institution has at least some power relative to the various marketing flows. A channel organization may exert leadership with respect to only one or many of these flows or functions, depending upon that firm's scope of power.

DISCUSSION QUESTIONS

1. For each of the following goods or services, develop what you think is a list of marketing channel services target customers would want delivered by the marketing channel.
   a. Record albums
   b. Motion pictures
   c. Forklift trucks
   d. Health care
   e. Audio equipment
   f. Dental appliances
2. For the channel services you listed for each of the goods or services in Question 1, discuss which marketing flows or functions need to be performed to deliver those channel services. Which marketing channel institutions would be most likely to perform those functions? Discuss.
3. The chapter described power as being determined by dependence. Using the food industry example at the beginning of the chapter, explain how food retailers are dependent on food manufacturers. Be as specific as you can in your answer.
4. Using the food industry example at the beginning of the chapter as a foundation, provide specific illustrations of the bases of power that are available to food retailers. Do the same for manufacturers.
5. Because McDonald's Corporation is an extremely effective marketer, its fast-food franchisees are virtually guaranteed success. What bases of power might McDonald's

wield over its franchisees? Explain. In spite of McDonald's proven success, why might some franchisees be reluctant to bow to McDonald's attempts to influence them? Discuss.

6. Some marketing channels (e.g., those for agricultural products and raw materials) persist and survive without an apparent channel leader. Explain how this can occur. Can such channels survive over the long run? Discuss.

7. In general, which type of institution—manufacturer, wholesaler, or retailer—should lead the marketing channel for the following products? Explain your answer.
   a. Toys
   b. Stainless steel
   c. Office supplies
   d. Heavy-duty trucks
   e. Prescription drugs
   f. Aviation jet fuel

8. Intertype competition or scrambled merchandising characterizes many lines of trade. Health and beauty aids, for example, can be found at department stores, discount stores, drugstores, and supermarkets. Which institution is likely to lead the channel for health and beauty aids—the manufacturer, the wholesaler, or the retailer? Can your conclusion be generalized to other lines of trade where intertype competition is prevalent? Explain.

9. Chapter 2 discussed the increasing polarity in retail trade—in other words, retail outlets should become either "high tech" or "high touch" if they are to survive. What effect does this trend have on who should lead the marketing channel for the following types of goods? Explain your answer.
   a. Automobiles
   b. Photographic film
   c. Books and magazines
   d. Sporting goods
   e. Business apparel (e.g., suits)
   f. Dental care

performance
conflict

11

Using Marketing Channel Power to Manage Conflict

Conflict
conflict resolving
performance measures

LEARNING OBJECTIVES

Upon completing this chapter, you will be able to:

- *Diagram and discuss the key aspects of the process of conflict in marketing channels.*

- *Describe the three chief causes of conflict in marketing channels: goal incompatibility, domain dissensus, and differing perceptions of reality.*

- *Explain how conflict may serve useful purposes within the channel, as well as be damaging. Diagram the relationship between conflict and marketing channel performance.*

- *Discuss the key mechanisms for managing marketing channel conflict: supraorganizational, interpenetration, boundary, and bargaining and negotiation methods.*

- *Explain under which situations the major conflict-management mechanisms are most appropriate.*

- *Describe how the bases of marketing channel power are used to implement the supraorganizational, interpenetration, boundary, and bargaining and negotiation mechanisms of conflict management in marketing channels.*

Conflict in Wholesaler-Retailer Channels: The ComputerLand Experience

The personal computer industry, following the classic sales patterns of the product life cycle, reached its late growth and early maturity stages in the mid-1980s. The heady sales increases of late introduction and early growth protected many suppliers, wholesalers, and retailers from their own inefficiencies and ineffectiveness. As the sales growth rate began to slow down, competition increased and many of these firms could not longer count on large surges in sales to keep them financially healthy. Particularly affected by this industry shakeout were computer retailers.

Franchisees of ComputerLand, the world's largest chain of computer stores with over 800 outlets in 24 countries, were not exempt from the industry's slump. ComputerLand's franchisees paid annual franchise royalty fees ranging anywhere from 5 to 9 percent of total gross sales. Many complained that these fees prevented them from making a profit and that ComputerLand was not providing enough assistance for the fees it required. Some franchisees also charged that ComputerLand failed to follow through on its promise to sell them computers at cost. In addition to these complaints, many franchisees were irritated by ComputerLand's generous executive perquisites (e.g., the corporate jet, high salaries, expensive training programs, and lavish buildings) and by the arrogant manner of the Millards, William (founder, chairman, and chief executive officer) and his daughter Barbara (chief operating officer).

To voice their demands for reduced royalty fees, more company-provided assistance, increased frugality at corporate headquarters, and more responsive management, about 300 ComputerLand franchise store owners engaged their trade group, the International Association of Computer Dealers (IACD), to negotiate with ComputerLand for them. At one point, the negotiations between ComputerLand and its franchisees were so tense that some franchisees talked about leaving the company and the IACD threatened to sue ComputerLand to enforce the company's franchise agreements.

As a result of the conflict between ComputerLand and its franchisees, the Millards resigned management control of the firm, although they retained about 95 percent ownership. By late-1985, new management, promised to lower the franchise fee to 7 percent of the franchisee's gross annual sales and to slightly lower the freight rates it charged the stores for delivering computers and other goods. This reduction would apply to about 375 of chain's stores. The remaining franchisees bought their franchises in the late 1970s and pay lower fees (typically 5 or 6 percent), thus are not under as severe financial pressure as the newer franchisees.

Although ComputerLand made an attempt to respond to the franchisees' concerns, preliminary indications were that these concessions were not enough to appease the unhappy store owners.

Sources: "ComputerLand Says Millards Resign Top Posts in Bid to Mollify Franchisees," *The Wall Street Journal*, September 30, 1985, p. 2; "ComputerLand's Faber Resumes Duty in Move to Allay Franchisee Worries," *The Wall Street Journal*, October 3, 1985, p. 38; "All in the Family: ComputerLand's Chief Is Out," *Time*, October 14, 1985, pp. 65, 68; and "Computerland to Reduce Fees Franchisees Pay," *The Wall Street Journal*, November 4, 1985, p. 17.

As the ComputerLand vignette illustrates, channel members are dependent upon one another for achieving their goals and for performing specialized marketing functions or flows within the channel. In addition, as noted in Chapter 10, channel members depend upon one another to provide scarce resources such as access to target markets and to heavily demanded products. If individual channel member and overall channel system goals are to be achieved, and if the channel functions are to be performed effectively, channel members must cooperate; otherwise, the channel will eventually cease to be competitive. Cooperation within the channel allows channel members to facilitate planning, coordinate information and decision making, and determine a method for rewarding each member according to the functions he performs.

The very reason channel members cooperate, however, is also the reason they conflict. If conflict is not adequately managed, it can rapidly get out of hand and cause the performance of the channel and its members to decline. If, for example, ComputerLand and its franchisees were to allow their conflict to continue, they would become vulnerable to competitive chains that do not have so much internal turmoil.

The effective use of marketing channel power is a critical tool for managing channel conflict. This chapter explores how power is used as a conflict-management device. But before specific conflict management mechanisms are discussed, it is necessary to have an understanding of the nature of conflict, its causes, and consequences.

THE NATURE OF CONFLICT IN MARKETING CHANNELS

In general, channel members recognize their interdependence concerning scarce resources and needed functions. However, if these organizations are independently owned, they strive to retain some independence over their own operations. This strain for autonomy in situations of mutual interdependence causes channel members to have mixed motives. On the one hand, they desire overall channel efficiency and cooperation, and on the other, they want to achieve their own individual goals. Greater interdependence among organizations in the channel generally leads to greater opportunities for firms to interfere with one another's ability to retain their individual goals. This leads to a greater possibility for conflict among channel members.

For conflict to actually occur, channel members must usually first become cognizant of issues (e.g., sizes of gross margins, cooperative advertising allowances, amount and mix of inventory carried) over which disagreements might arise. Disagreements generally occur in marketing channels when channel members do not perform their tasks as expected. Performance may fall short of expectations for a variety of reasons, including situational factors (e.g., a price war in a retailer's trading area), incompatible organizational objectives, lack of clear and open communication flows between channel members, and differences in channel members' anticipations.

After they become aware of the conflict situation, channel members generally personalize the conflict; in other words, the channel organization's management develops hostile feelings (sometimes called *affect*) toward the other channel organization. The firms then decide how to behave toward each other. They may openly oppose each other, passively resist each other's influence attempts, ignore the conflict situation, or strive to resolve their differences. Regardless of the specific form their behavior takes, some outcome results. The outcome may be no resolution, partial resolution, or complete resolution of the conflict issue. When conflict over an issue is very intense, another possible outcome is an organization leaving the channel.[1]

This process of marketing channel conflict is summarized in Figure 11–1. Note that the extent of which channel members become aware of conflictful situations, develop emotional reactions to them, engage in conflictful behavior, and resolve their disagreements depends upon the importance of the issue in conflict, the frequency of disagreements over the issue, and the intensity of those disagreements.[2] Thus, for example, because ComputerLand's franchise royalty fee does not hinder their success as much, profitable and growing franchisees may not experience as much channel conflict over this issue as other franchisees.

Each time channel members conflict over a particular issue they progress through the conflict process. Each progression through the process is termed a "*conflict episode.*" To the extent that a conflict episode is not completely resolved, it becomes the basis for future conflict episodes. Thus, conflict episodes tend to build on each other if they are not adequately managed.[3]

[1] Louis W. Stern and Ronald H. Gorman, "Conflict in Distribution Channels: An Exploration," in Louis W. Stern (ed.), *Distribution Channels: Behavioral Dimensions* (Boston: Houghton-Mifflin, 1969), p. 171.

[2] James R. Brown and Ralph L. Day, "Measures of Manifest Conflict in Marketing Channels," *Journal of Marketing Research*, Vol. 18 (August 1981), p. 264.

[3] Ernest R. Cadotte and Louis W. Stern, "A Process Model of Dyadic Interorganizational Relations in Marketing Channels," in Jagdish N. Sheth (ed.), *Research in Marketing*, Vol. 2 (Greenwich, Conn.: JAI Press, 1979), pp. 127–158.

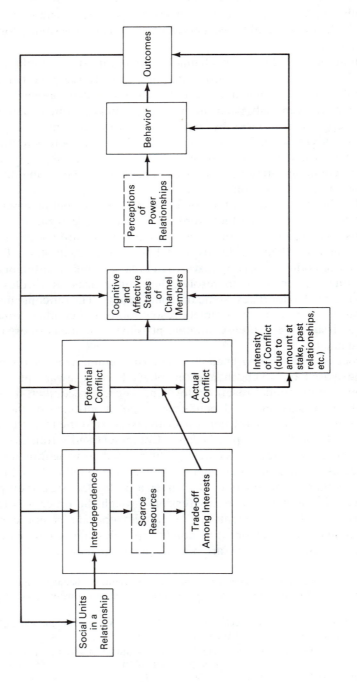

Figure 11-1 The process of conflict in marketing channels. *Source:* Adapted from *1974 Combined Proceedings of the AMA Fall and Spring Conferences*, published by the American Marketing Association, "A Perspective on Conflict and Power in Distribution," by Fuat A. Firat, Alice M. Tybout, and Louis W. Stern. Ronald C. Curan (ed.)

THE CAUSES OF MARKETING CHANNEL CONFLICT

Channel conflict exists when one channel member (say, channel member A) perceives that another channel member(s) (say, channel member B) is engaging in behavior that prevents or impedes A from achieving its goals. It is, in essence, A's frustration brought about by B's interference with A's marketing functions. The amount of conflict in the channel is determined by the degree of incompatibility between A's and B's goals, disagreements over the marketing tasks each is to perform and how these tasks are to be performed, and differences in the ways A and B perceive reality.[4] Furthermore, as A and B become more dependent on each other, relatively minor differences in goals, task definitions, and perceptions are likely to create situations of relatively intense conflict. Thus, franchise systems are likely to experience high degrees of channel conflict.

Goal Incompatibility

Each channel member has a set of goals and objectives, which are often incompatible with those of other channel members.

Among the most common conflict issues facing manufacturers and industrial distributors are (1) how to handle large accounts, (2) required inventory stocking levels for the distributor, (3) the quality of distributor management, (4) overlapping distributor territories, (5) the size of distributor margins, and (6) the philosophical question of whether the distributor's primary obligations and loyalty are to the customer or to the supplier.[5]

Clearly underlying many of these issues are differences in goals, aims, or values among the channel members involved in marketing industrial goods. Suppliers and resellers are at odds over many of these same issues in consumer good channels.[6]

In consumer goods marketing, tens of thousands of small retailers are served by large manufacturers; conflict in these channels often arises over the sales growth versus the profitability goals of these two channel institutions. Large manufacturers tend to be growth-oriented, whereas small retailers are much more interested in maintaining a satisfactory level of profits. Conflict is highly likely

[4] See Louis W. Stern and J. L. Heskett, "Conflict Management in Interorganizational Relations: A Conceptual Framework," in Louis W. Stern (ed.), *Distribution Channels: Behavioral Dimensions* (Boston: Houghton-Mifflin, 1969), pp. 293–294; and Larry J. Rosenberg and Louis W. Stern, "Conflict Measurement in the Distribution Channel," *Journal of Marketing Research*, Vol. 8 (November 1971), pp. 437–442.

[5] Frederick E. Webster, Jr., "The Role of the Industrial Distributor in Marketing Strategy," *Journal of Marketing*, Vol. 40 (July 1976), p. 11.

[6] See, for example, J. Steven Kelly and J. Irwin Peters, "Vertical Conflict: A Comparative Analysis of Franchisees and Distributors," in Barnett A. Greenberg and Danny N. Bellenger (eds.), *Contemporary Marketing Thought* (Chicago: American Marketing Association, 1977), pp. 380–384.

EXHIBIT 11–1
Goal Incompatibility in the Marketing Channel for Beer

The brewing industry is undeniably a major American industry. It manufacturers and markets a specific product. While its marketing procedures vary according to the laws of different states, one of its major retail outlets is the "tavern." The tavern owner is then a "retail dealer"—the end point of the distribution system which places the product in the hands of the ultimate consumer. . . . .

The brewing industry is interested in growing. Individual brewers in the industry are interested in expanding their businesses. One of the ways the brewing industry as a whole can grow is through successful promotion of the use of beer in the home. Consequently "take-out" business in taverns is promoted by all brewers. The obvious avenue of growth for the individual brewery is for more people to drink its particular brand of beer.

However, the tavern owner, as the "retail dealer" of beer, does not necessarily see the above objectives as consistent with his own. He sees the promotion of the use of beer in the home as hurting his own business. He is not interested in having people drink beer at home; he is interested in having them drink beer in his establishment. Regardless of all the "rational" arguments to the contrary, as far as he is concerned, encouraging beer drinking at home means less business for him. Similarly he has little interest in the promotion of any particular brand of beer. He is simply interested in giving his customers what they ask for.

In short, a situation of conflicting interests and misunderstanding exists between the brewer and the tavern owner. The latter generally does not feel that brewers are genuinely interested in his problems. He sees industry "take-home" advertising as undermining his business. He sees the individual brewer as primarily interested in pushing his own brand–something in which the tavern operator is not interested because pushing one brand over another does not really add to *his* overall business.

Source: Reprinted by permission of the *Harvard Business Review*. Excerpt from "Misunderstanding the Retailer" by Warren J. Wittereich (May/June 1962). Copyright © 1962 by the President and Fellows of Harvard College; all rights reserved.

because, in their pursuit of "dynamic" goals (e.g., increased market share and higher returns on investment), large manufacturers will likely adopt innovative marketing programs that conflict with the more traditional orientation of smaller retailers. For an illustration of goal incompatibility in the brewing industry, see Exhibit 11-1.[7]

---

[7] For an empirical examination of goal incompatibility as a cause of marketing channel conflict, see Jehoshua Eliashberg and Donald A. Michie, "Multiple Business Goals Sets as Determinants of Marketing Channel Conflict: An Empirical Study," *Journal of Marketing Research*, Vol. 21 (February 1984), pp. 75–88.

Domain Dissensus

Conflict also arises over how the marketing tasks are allocated within the channel and how the performance of these tasks is evaluated. Indicative of conflict over these issues was the situation facing the marketing channel for Haagen-Dazs ice cream in the mid-1980s.

Haagen-Dazs, a subsidiary of Pillsbury, uses independent distributors to market its super-premium brand of ice cream. Its desire to control those distributors sparked much conflict in the mid-1980s. The chief issues revolved around who should serve large chain store accounts—Haagen-Dazs itself or the independent distributors—and whether or not the distributors could carry competing brands of super-premium ice cream. In addition, Haagen-Dazs claimed the distributors were not aggressive enough in realizing their market potentials.[8]

Conflict may also occur when channel members are assigned tasks they are not capable of fulfilling, when excessive demands are made on channel members, and when channel members feel they are being forced to serve two masters (i.e., their customers and their suppliers) and cannot decide where their prime loyalty should lie. In addition, channel members are likely to stake out their own *domains*—the markets served, the products carried, the functions or duties to be performed, or the technology employed to carry out those functions—and these independent domain definitions often do not conform to the expectations of other channel members.

The outdoor power equipment industry markets lawn mowers, garden tractors, rotary tillers, and snow blowers. Manufacturers, wholesalers, and retailers in this industry disagree over such issues as (1) overlapping territories; (2) where inventories are to be held in the channel; (3) where service facilities are to be located and warranty claims are to be handled; (4) inadequate levels of spare parts at different levels of the channel; (5) inadequate inventory control, especially at the reseller levels; and (6) inadequate financing throughout the channel.

Differing Perceptions of Reality

Differing perceptions of reality are another important cause of conflict since they produce different reactions to the same situation. Thus, channel members may misunderstand one another, develop different strategies for approaching the same situation, and feel mutually frustrated by their differing perceptions of reality.[9] Behaviors stemming from these perceptions are likely to produce conflict.

[8] Based on "Haagen-Dazs Distributors Find Big Profits, but Little Security," *The Wall Street Journal*, November 18, 1985, p. 33.

[9] Michael Etgar, "Sources and Types of Intrachannel Conflict," *Journal of Retailing*, Vol. 55 (Spring 1979), p. 65.

Certain perceptions have traditionally led to poor supplier-retailer relations. For example, retailers perceive that:

- Supplier salespeople oversell without regard to production and delivery capability.
- Supplier salespeople lack an understanding of the retailer's goals and merchandising philosophy.
- Supplier salespeople do not provide adequate in-store services.
- Suppliers do not offer a planned approach to promoting and merchandising products.

On the other hand, suppliers perceive that:

- Retail buyers are preoccupied with "chiseling" the best prices out of suppliers.
- Retail buyers lack decision-making autonomy.
- Retail buyers ignore or move too slowly in accepting promotional deals and other allowances.
- Retail buyers handle too many product lines to be effective product managers and ignore merchandise once an order is placed.
- Retailers refuse to cooperate for fear of being "locked in" to a supplier.[10]

Differing perceptions of reality also cause conflict between manufacturers and distributors of industrial goods. Often, the root cause of these incongruent perceptions, as noted in the ComputerLand and brewing industry illustrations, is incompatible goals and philosophies. Differing perceptions can also be caused by ineffective communications within the marketing channel. The communications noise-reduction techniques described in Chapter 7 can be critical in reducing perceptual differences and subsequent conflict among channel members.

A thorough understanding of conflict is essential to managing marketing channels effectively. The reason is that conflict can have a variety of consequences, most of them undesirable. The following section discusses the chief effects of conflict on marketing channels.

THE CONSEQUENCES OF CONFLICT IN THE MARKETING CHANNEL

As noted earlier in the chapter, a particular conflict episode may result in one of three different outcomes: (1) a complete resolution of the conflict issue, (2) a partial resolution of the conflict issue, or (3) a dissolution of the channel relationship. Regardless of which outcome results, conflict can affect nearly all

[10] Ronald L. Ernst, "Distribution Channel Détente Benefits Suppliers, Retailers, and Consumers," *Marketing News*, March 7, 1980, p. 19.

aspects of the relationship between channel organizations, including channel structure and administrative form, power-dependence relations, and, of course, future conflict episodes. Because all these facets of channel relations are largely influenced by channel performance and channel member satisfaction, how conflict shapes performance and satisfaction will be the focus of the following discussion.

Effect on Marketing Channel Performance

Conflict is generally thought to be counterproductive or *dysfunctional* in that it adversely affects the marketing channel's performance. Conflict can be dysfunctional in several ways. First, channel members may become less cooperative with one another and start to perform for themselves those marketing functions that were formerly provided by other members of the channel. Thus, inefficiencies occur as the conflicting channel members duplicate one another's functions.[11] Retailers embroiled in a conflict episode with their suppliers, for example, may increase their inventories because they anticipate that the suppliers will slow down their store deliveries. Second, channel members may share less information when they distrust one another. As the amount and frequency of channel member interaction decreases, there are fewer opportunities for channel members to develop mutual understanding and identification. In such situations, expert and referent power lose their effectiveness in coordinating channel activities and resolving conflict.[12] Moreover, when vital market information is not shared, channel organizations are unlikely to make optimal decisions. Finally, channel members may devote so much time to resolving their disputes that they have little left over for the routine operation of the channel. As a result, the conflict issue may be resolved, but channel performance will suffer.[13]

Under fair trade laws, which were repealed in 1975, manufacturers could legally dictate the retail prices of their products. In one instance, Lever Brothers had difficulty controlling the prices cut-rate drugstores charged for Pepsodent, then the best-selling brand of toothpaste. Traditional retail druggists were displeased by Lever Brother's lack of success and retaliated by removing Pepsodent from their shelves, thereby forcing consumers to make a specific request for the brand.[14] In the process of getting back at Lever Brothers for not maintaining the retail price on Pepsodent, the druggists hurt themselves by forgoing sales volume and by inconveniencing their customers. As a result of this boycott, the entire channel system for Pepsodent suffered.

---

[11] Stern and Heskett, "Conflict Management," p. 293.

[12] Bertram H. Raven and Arie W. Kruglanski, "Conflict and Power," in Paul Swingle (ed.), *The Structure of Conflict* (New York: Academic Press, 1970), p. 74.

[13] Bert Rosenbloom, "Conflict and Channel Efficiency: Some Conceptual Models for the Decision Maker," *Journal of Marketing*, Vol. 37 (July 1973), p. 28.

[14] Joseph C. Palamountain, Jr., *The Politics of Distribution* (Cambridge, Mass.: Harvard University Press, 1955).

On the other hand, conflict may have *functional* consequences; that is, conflict can positively affect marketing channel performance. This occurs when channel members:

1. Critically review their past actions to find the root cause of the conflict episode and then take steps to rectify things.
2. Engage in more frequent and effective communications among themselves and establish outlets to express their grievances.
3. Agree to a more equitable distribution of system resources such that the *total* marketing channel benefits rather than any one institution within it.
4. Stabilize channel relations by agreeing to standardize methods of resolving conflict.
5. Create a balance of power within the system that restrains the indiscriminant use of power, assures greater equity in resource allocation, and combats complacency in the channel leader.[15]

Exhibit 11-2 illustrates how conflict within marketing channels for new cars resulted in functional consequences for the channel system.

Conflict within marketing channels may be neither functional nor dysfunctional, but *neutral*—that is, have no effect on marketing channel performance. This happens when channel members are so highly interdependent that they have learned not to let their disputes affect the channel's performance.[16]

Marketing channel conflict, then, may have either functional, dysfunctional, or neutral consequences for channel performance. These effects are illustrated in Fig. 11-2. Between C_0 and C_1, conflict is neutral; it has no effect on channel performance. From C_1 to C_2, conflict is functional and performance rises as conflict intensifies, for the reasons discussed above. Beyond C_2 (sometimes called the *threshold*), conflict is dysfunctional, in other words, it causes performance to decline.

Effect on Channel Member Satisfaction

The level of channel member satisfaction is highly related to the extent of conflict within a marketing channel. One channel member's dissatisfaction with how well others are performing their marketing functions often sparks conflict within the entire channel. Indeed, a primary cause of domain dissensus in marketing channels is dissatisfaction with performance.

[15] For an in-depth discussion of each of these points, see Henry Assael, "Constructive Role of Interorganizational Conflict," *Administrative Science Quarterly*, Vol. 14 (December 1969), pp. 576–580.
[16] Rosenbloom, "Conflict and Channel Efficiency," p. 28.

EXHIBIT 11-2

**Functional Consequences of Marketing
Channel Conflict: The General Motors
Experience**

In the mid-1950s, conflict was rampant in General Motors' marketing channels for new automobiles. In fact, the intensity and pervasiveness of dealer dissatisfaction with GM led the U.S. Senate to hold hearings on manufacturer-dealer relations in the automobile industry.

Rather than "digging in its heels," GM, to its credit, reacted to the adverse publicity created by the Senate hearings by liberalizing its relationships with its dealers. Among the specific steps GM took were (1) extending the length of its franchise agreement, (2) increasing allowances for model changes, (3) improving warranty rebates, (4) providing mechanisms for better communication with the manufacturer, (5) withdrawing threats to cancel franchises, and (6) making explicit what its sales expectations were for each dealer.

Even after governmental pressures subsided, GM continued to improve its dealer relations. It granted dealers complete authority for local advertising and gave them greater latitude in ordering new cars, parts, and accessories. GM also undertook a series of policies to strengthen the economic position of its dealers. It encouraged additional dealer investment in facilities and increased the market potential of many dealers by reducing the number of outlets through either relocation, buyouts, or natural business closings of other dealers in their markets. In short, GM adapted the marketing concept with respect to a key target market—its dealers. Although some franchisees (e.g., those relocated or forced to sell out) suffered from GM's enlightened approach to channel relations, the amount of conflict within the channel was drastically reduced and the overwhelming majority of dealers felt that GM's new approach was "for the better."

Source: Reprinted from, "Constructive Role of Interorganizational Conflict," by Henry Assael published in *Administrative Science Quarterly*, Vol. 14 (December 1969), by permission of *Administrative Science Quarterly*.

Recall the ComputerLand illustration at the beginning of the chapter. The franchisees' dissatisfaction with the company occurred because they believed that ComputerLand was not performing its assigned marketing functions as expected. In particular, the franchisees felt that the company was not providing them with assistances commensurate with the franchise fees they were paying. This dissatisfaction, led to conflict within the ComputerLand franchise system.

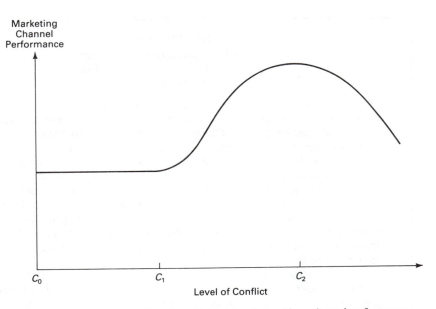

Marketing
Channel
Performance

C_0 C_1 C_2

Level of Conflict

Figure 11-2 Marketing channel conflict and its relationship to channel performance. *Source*: Adapted from *Journal of Marketing*, published by the American Marketing Association, "Conflict and Channel Efficiency: Some Conceptual Models for the Decision Maker," *Journal of Marketing*, by Bert Rosenbloom, Vol. 37 (July 1973), p. 29.

On the other hand, the more satisfied a channel member becomes with the performance of another, the less likely domain dissensus will persist.

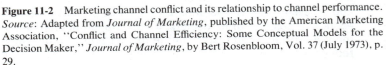

Channel member satisfaction (or lack thereof) can also be a *consequence* of channel conflict.[17] The more satisfied an organization is with the channel relationship, the more likely that it will cooperate with others in the channel.[18]

> By changing its approach to dealer relations in the mid-1950s (see Exhibit 11-2), GM reduced the amount of conflict in the channel and thereby increased dealer satisfaction. As a result, GM's dealers became more cooperative in their channel relations with the manufacturer.

By the same token, the less satisfied an organization is with its channel relationship, the less cooperative it will prove and the more prone it will be to conflict with other members of the channel.

To ensure that conflict does not adversely affect the operation of the distributive system, channel leaders must use their bases of power to manage

[17] Ian Wilkinson, "Power, Conflict, and Satisfaction in Distribution Channels—An Empirical Study," *International Journal of Physical Distribution and Materials Management*, Vol. 11 (1981), p. 24; and Gary L. Frazier, "Interorganizational Exchange Behavior in Marketing Channels: A Broadened Perspective," *Journal of Marketing*, Vol. 47 (Fall 1983), pp. 74–75.

[18] Frazier, "Interorganizational Exchange Behavior, p. 75.

conflict. Conflict management is generally directed toward three objectives.[19] First, it may be necessary to prevent dysfunctional performance and dissatisfaction from occurring (i.e., to restrict conflict to the C_0–C_2 range in Figure 11-2). Second, conflict management may be needed to reduce conflict from dysfunctional levels to functional ones (i.e., to move conflict from beyond C_2 to something less than C_2). Resolving or terminating a conflict episode (i.e., forcing conflict to C_0) is the third objective of conflict management. This last objective is often unattainable. Moreover, since conflict may bring about improvements in channel performance and satisfaction, it may be undesirable in the long run. Partial resolution of a conflict episode (i.e., reducing conflict to less than C_1) may be a more realistic and desirable goal.

In the next section, we discuss specific mechanisms for managing conflict within marketing channels, emphasizing how each of these mechanisms relates to the bases of power discussed in Chapter 10.

EFFECTIVE CONFLICT MANAGEMENT WITHIN MARKETING CHANNELS

A key aspect of marketing channel management is avoiding the negative consequences of marketing channel conflict. In other words, strategies must be developed to keep conflict from becoming dysfunctional and to direct the energies within conflictful situations toward innovative resolutions. For this to happen, channel members must understand the underlying causes of the conflict. But the specific strategy used to manage conflict depends not only on the cause of the conflict but also on the power of the channel member seeking to handle the conflict. The effective use of power, which is required for specifying the tasks within the channel, is also crucial in dealing with the conflicts that inevitably arise among channel members.

Several strategies are available for managing conflict episodes in marketing channels. Each can be tailored to the specific situation and structure of the particular marketing channel. For example, Table 11–1 outlines how these mechanisms might apply to different levels of perceived vertical integration. Each of these conflict-management mechanisms is discussed in the following sections.

Supraorganizational Mechanisms

For supraorganizational conflict-management mechanisms to be effective, channel members must view themselves as highly interdependent. Despite perceived interdependence, channel organizations often have different goals and objectives, or at least attach different levels of importance to similar goals and objectives.[20]

---

[19] James R. Brown, "Methods of Conflict Resolution: Some Empirical Results," in Neil Beckwith et al. (eds.), *1979 Educators' Conference Proceedings* (Chicago: American Marketing Association, 1979), p. 495.

[20] Louis W. Stern, "Potential Conflict Management Mechanisms in Distribution Channels: An Interorganizational Analysis," in Donald N. Thompson (ed.), *Contractual Marketing Systems* (Lexington, Mass.: Heath Lexington Books, 1971), p. 114.

TABLE 11-1 Mechanisms for Managing Marketing Channel Conflict

Degree of Perceived Vertical Interdependence	Basic Conflict-Management Techniques	Specific Conflict-Management Mechanisms
High	Supraorganizational	Superordinate goals
		Arbitration
		Conciliation and mediation
	Interpenetration	Cooptation
		Exchange-of-persons programs
		Trade association membership
		Education and propaganda
	Boundary	Diplomacy
Low	Bargaining and negotiation	Bargaining strategy

Source: Adapted from Louis W. Stern, "Potential Conflict Management Mechanisms in Distribution Channels: An Interorganizational Analysis," in Donald N. Thompson (ed.), *Contractual Marketing Systems* (Lexington, Mass.: Heath Lexington Books, 1971), p. 114.

Thus, supraorganizational methods of dealing with conflict are most prevalent in vertical marketing systems, such as corporate, contractual, and administered channels. Among the key supraorganizational mechanisms are establishing superordinate goals, submitting the disputes to arbitration, and conciliating and mediating the disagreements.

Superordinate Goals. Superordinate goals are those that are shared by channel members involved in conflict. Superordinate goals cannot be achieved by any one organization, but require the concerted effort of the entire channel to be attained. Under this mechanism, effective conflict resolution requires finding a common goal or set of interests on which all channel members can agree. In other words, the traditional legitimate and information power bases are used to develop consistent norms, values, and objectives within the channel. In addition, identification is developed via the expert and referent power bases, so that channel members feel they are integral parts of the overall distribution system.

A superordinate goal can be an explicit desire by channel members to resist a threat to the channel's survival or growth from some outside pressure (e.g., competitive or legal). In such situations, channel members often transfer their intrachannel hostilities to the outside common "enemy." For an illustration of how superordinate goals have been used to combat an outside enemy in the soft-drink industry, see Exhibit 11-3.

Superordinate goals are effective means of managing channel conflict when there are outside pressures, but will intrachannel conflict return once the outside threat has been removed? It is possible that working together to counter the outside threat will cause channel members to gain a greater understanding of one another's goals, methods of operation, and problems in doing business. Perhaps the original conflict issues—those that existed prior to the outside threat—will decay as energies are directed toward the outside threat. But it is also possible that the prior conflict will reemerge, unaffected by the temporary unity achieved under the threat of an outside enemy.

EXHIBIT 11-3

**The Great Soft-Drink Wars: The Importance
of Superordinate Goals**

The great soft-drink wars have been fought for the past decade, with PepsiCo chipping away at Coca-Cola's share of the $30 billion carbonated beverage market. As of early 1986, Pepsi held a 35 percent share of this market compared to Coke's 39 percent.

A keystone of the marketing strategies of both firms is their distribution systems of independent bottlers. These bottler-wholesalers buy syrup from the soft-drink producers, add water to the concentrate, package the beverage, and distribute the product to a variety of retail and institutional customers. Effective bottlers are highly successful in acquiring and maintaining shelf space in supermarkets and fountain placement in restaurants, critical factors in soft-drink marketing. Accordingly, both Pepsi and Coke have upgraded and consolidated their bottling networks and have tried to view them as vertical marketing systems as opposed to conventional channels.

Coke, for example, was widely known for its authoritarian dealings with its bottlers. As long as the baby-boomers were in their prime soft-drink guzzling years, shelf space was plentiful, competitors were not troublesome, and Coke could afford "unhealthy" bottler relations. Bottlers were particularly upset with Coke's insistence that a single advertising and promotional package be used nationwide despite different local market needs and preferences. Beginning in the late-1970s, however, Pepsi's challenge to Coke's preeminence caused Coke to improve its bottler relations. It discontinued its national promotions, began focusing on local market conditions, and started to offer more management assistance to its bottlers. The "external threat"—Pepsi's aggressiveness in attacking Coke's market leadership—forced Coke to view its bottler network as a key element of a vertical marketing system. As a result, it strived to placate its bottlers in order to compete more effectively against Pepsi's vertical marketing system.

Source: Based on "Coke's New Program to Placate Bottlers," *Business Week*, October 12, 1981, p. 48; "Pepsi's Seven-up Deal: Shaking Up the Soft-Drink Wars," *Business Week*, February 3, 1986, p. 31; and Timothy K. Smith and Scott Kilman, "Coke and Pepsi Acquisition Agreements Cause Turmoil at Independent Bottlers," *The Wall Street Journal*, February 24, 1986, p. 14.

Moreover superordinate goals are often not effective in resolving conflict within highly interdependent marketing channels. A key reason for this is that channel members cannot, or will not, agree upon goals. Thus, additional supraorganizational measures are needed to manage channel conflict.

Conciliation and Mediation. Conciliation and mediation refer to the intervention of a third party to settle conflict within marketing channels by persuading conflicting members to (1) continue their negotiations when they have bogged down, (2) consider the mediator's procedural recommendations, or (3) consider the mediator's substantive recommendations. Note that, in practice, conciliation and mediation are synonymous.[21] Effective mediators clarify facts and issues, keep parties in contact with each other, explore possible bases of agreement, encourage parties to agree to specific proposals, and supervise the implementation of agreements. Mediation essentially involves offering the conflicting channel members alternative opportunities or trading moves that they otherwise might not have seen. Furthermore, channel members may be more amenable to resolutions when they are suggested by a mediator.

In industries with a history of distribution conflicts (e.g., the automobile industry), retired judges, professors, and consultants often mediate disputes among channel members. Many trade associations also attempt to mediate channel conflict, but their interests are generally slanted, making them inappropriate for the task. Besides, there are possible antitrust implications of trade associations performing this role.

Arbitration. Arbitration can be either compulsory or voluntary.[22] With compulsory arbitration, channel members are required by law to submit their dispute to a third party whose decision is final and binding. In marketing channels, government regulatory agencies (e.g., the Federal Trade Commission) or the federal court system may settle disputes among channel organizations. Exhibit 11-4 illustrates how compulsory arbitration was used in one fast-food franchise system.

Under voluntary arbitration, the disputing channel members voluntarily agree to submit their conflict to a third party whose decision is considered final and binding.

The Federal Trade Commission, in concert with television set manufacturers, distributors, and dealers, set up 32 industry rules to protect consumers and reduce distributive conflicts. Five distribution conflict areas were arbitrated: (1) tie-in sales; (2) price-fixing; (3) mass shipments used to clog outlets and foreclose competitors; (4) discriminatory billing, and (5) special rebates, bribes, refunds, and discounts.[23]

The whole idea of relying on law and law enforcement (i.e., using legal legitimate power) to manage marketing channel conflict is suspect because permanently legislated solutions are not likely to be equitably applied to future conflicts in different channel contexts. Historically, conflict resolution within the

[21] William H. Miernyk, *The Economics of Labor and Collective Bargaining* (Boston: D. C. Heath, 1965), pp. 271–272.

[22] Robert E. Weigand and Hilda C. Wasson, "Arbitration in the Marketing Channel," *Business Horizons*, October 1974, pp. 39–47.

[23] Robert G. Biedermann and Richard L. Tabak, "The Television Receiver Industry," in Henry Assael (ed.), *The Politics of Distributive Trade Associations: A Study in Conflict Resolution* (Hempstead, N.Y.: Hofstra University, 1967), pp. 280–82.

EXHIBIT 11-4
Arbitration in Resolving Marketing Channel
Conflict: Arthur Treacher's Fish & Chips

Seeing a compatible business that offered growth possibilities, Mrs. Paul's Kitchens, Inc., a Philadelphia-based food processor with annual sales of about $150 million, acquired the Arthur Treacher's Fish & Chips fast-food franchise system in 1979.

By 1981, however, Mrs. Paul's found itself embroiled in conflict with about 90 percent of its 400 Arthur Treacher's franchisees. These franchisees were boycotting Mrs. Paul's by refusing to pay approximately $14 million in outstanding royalty fees. Moreover, many were openly defying a Mrs. Paul's ban on such menu items as Alaskan crab legs, spaghetti, and tacos.

In any channel conflict episode, the underlying cause varies according to which channel member tells the story. The Arthur Treacher franchisees accused Mrs. Paul's of not providing the product and marketing support they were entitled to under the franchise agreement. In addition, they claimed that Mrs. Paul's was not interested in maintaining sources of Icelandic cod—the fish on which Arthur Treacher's built its reputation. Rather, they said Mrs. Paul's merely wanted Arthur Treacher's as an additional retail distribution outlet for its line of frozen fish products. For its part, Mrs. Paul's argued that it only wanted to introduce additional products into the system, not to replace existing ones.

To resolve the dispute, Mrs. Paul's and the dissident Arthur Treacher franchisees took their grievances to court; all in all, there were more than a dozen lawsuits involving over 50 franchisees. Because they did not pay their royalties, Mrs. Paul's charged that the dissident franchisees were illegally using the Arthur Treacher trademark. The franchisees countercharged that the company was in breach of contract for not providing them with adequate marketing and product support.

In the first of the suits to be settled, a federal court judge ruled that 11 franchisees of Arthur Treacher's Fish & Chips illegally used the company's trademark and practiced unfair competition. He ordered them to pay Mrs. Paul's nearly $4 million, primarily in damages, overdue royalties, and lawyers' fees. As a result of this settlement, a number of boycotting franchisees began negotiations with the company to resolve their disputes through other means.

Source: Adapted from Betsy Morris, "To Mrs. Paul's Distress, Its Fish and Chips Unit Verges on Bankruptcy," *The Wall Street Journal*, December 23, 1981, pp. 1, 6; and "Two Arthur Treacher's Franchisees Ordered to Pay Firm Royalties," *The Wall Street Journal*, January 18, 1982, p. 2.

channel has been found to be more satisfactory than "external" or legally imposed resolution.[24]

The supraorganizational conflict-management mechanisms are best suited to

[24] Henry Assael, "The Political Role of Trade Associations in Distributive Conflict Resolution," *Journal of Marketing*, Vol. 32 (April 1968), pp. 21–28.

those marketing channel systems in which manufacturers, distributors, wholesalers, retailers, and other marketing institutions perceive a high degree of interdependence (e.g., corporate channels and contractual systems). For channels with a lesser degree of perceived vertical integration, other mechanisms for managing conflict are more suitable. One particularly useful group is the interpenetration mechanisms.

Interpenetration Mechanisms

The interpenetration methods of conflict management are aimed at "increasing the number of meaningful interactions among channel members and, concomitantly, for reducing conflict within the channel."[25] Increasing the number of contacts channel organizations have with one another develops a sense of identification and common norms and values within the channel. In terms of the discussion in Chapter 10, the interpenetration methods of conflict management employ the non-mediated (i.e., referent, expert, traditional legitimate, and information) bases of power in preventing and reducing marketing channel conflict. The most commonly used interpenetration mechanisms are cooptation, exchange-of-persons programs, joint membership in trade associations, and education and propaganda. Of all these methods, cooptation creates the strongest sense of interdependence among marketing channel organizations.

Cooptation. Cooptation is the process of absorbing new participants into the leadership or policy-determining structure of an organization as a means of reducing threats to its stability or existence.[26]

Some members of the Independent Grocers Alliance (IGA) system have used cooptation successfully for many years. A number of wholesalers within the IGA system have formed retailer advisory councils. These councils generally meet four times a year with the wholesaler and are composed of elected representatives of the retailers served by that wholesaler. At each meeting, the council members discuss a wide variety of merchandising and logistics subjects and raise questions of concern to the retailers they represent. When the council members return to their own stores, they inform their fellow retailers of what happened at the meeting. If a new program was presented, they explain it and recommend either its acceptance or rejection.[27]

Cooptation has many advantages as a conflict-resolution strategy. It may provide a formal structure for sharing routine information, providing assistance, or making requests within the channel. It also permits responsibility to be shared

[25] Stern, "Potential Conflict Management Mechanisms," p. 122.

[26] Philip Selznik, *TVA and the Grass Roots* (Berkeley; University of California Press, 1949), p. 13.

[27] "The Retail Senate," *IGA Grocergram*, Vol. 51, (October 1977), p. 31.

so that a variety of channel members become identified with and committed to the programs developed for a particular product or service. Thus, cooptation is one way in which referent, expert, traditional legitimate, and information power are used to manage conflict within marketing channels.

This conflict-management mechanism has some real dangers, however, especially for the coopting organization. Cooptation can constrain alternative courses of action available to a firm. For example, General Motors is not likely to radically depart from its franchised dealer distribution system as long as it seriously considers its dealer council's advice on such matters. Thus, cooptation places an "outsider" in a position to influence marketing channel policy quite dramatically. Because of this limitation, many organizations view cooptation as an extreme measure. Exchange-of-persons programs overcome this limitation and, at the same time, attempt to create common norms and values as well as identification with the channel system.

Exchange-of-Persons Programs.   Through the process of role reversal, this interpenetration conflict-management mechanism attempts to increase channel members' understanding of one another's roles and difficulties in performing those roles. In an exchange-of-persons program, employees of one or more channel organizations are temporarily employed in other channel member firms.

One of the several steps Levi Strauss has taken in the past few years to ease tensions with its retail customers is an exchange-of-persons program. During 1983, for example, 10 top Levi executives worked on the selling floors of 35 major retail customers to gain an understanding of retailers' operations and problems. When these executives returned to Levi Strauss, they became "account sponsors," fielding questions and complaints and acting as customer advocates within the company.[28]

Participants in exchange-of-persons programs gain a "channel" perspective of their jobs by learning the complexities of another channel member's organization, mission, and activities. In addition, these people become personally and professionally involved in the channel by meeting and associating with others who share their specific tasks, professions, and interests. The deeper understanding of the interconnection among channel members' goals and domains that comes from such exchanges can lead to reduced levels of conflict. Thus, exchange-of-persons programs are particularly effective means of increasing identification among channel members and of developing common norms and values for the channel.

Because of their costs, however, exchange-of-persons programs are not always feasible. Where they are not, joint membership in trade associations can often accomplish a similar objective.

[28] "Levi Strauss; A Touch of Fashion—And a Dash of Humility," *Business Week,* October 24, 1983, p. 88.

Joint Membership in Trade Associations. In many cases, having manufacturers belong to intermediaries' trade associations, or having intermediaries belong to manufacturers trade organizations, is extremely beneficial in managing conflict situations. In the U.S. television receiver industry,

> the lack of communications in the channel of distribution was one of the major dealer complaints. Another was the lack of product knowledge and the lack of understanding of the dealers' problems on the part of the distributor sales[force]. The approach used to correct the lack of communications was to invite the manufacturers to become members of the National Appliance and Radio TV Dealers Association (NARDA). Twelve of the major manufacturers are now members, and representatives of these and other companies now attend NARDA conventions. Manufacturers' relations meetings are a regular convention feature. Executives of manufacturing organizations are regular speakers at NARDA training seminars and at the regular convention.[29]

Another example of trade association cooperation that resulted in an innovative and effective solution is the Universal Product Code (see Chapter 7 for a more complete discussion of the UPC). The UPC was developed by a joint committee of the food manufacturers' trade association (Grocery Manufacturers of America) and a food retailers' association (Food Marketing Institute).

The key benefit of using this method of managing conflict is that channel members, through sharing a common, worthwhile task, more effectively coordinate their activities and become less hostile toward each other. A disadvantage is that sporadic interaction among channel members at trade association–sponsored events is not sufficient to resolve day-to-day disagreements and long-term incompatibility over goals. Perhaps a more effective way to handle day-to-day disagreements is to prevent them from occurring in the first place. A continual program of education and propaganda within the channel is expressly designed for that purpose.

Education and Propaganda. Basically, this mechanism uses information and educational activities to manage conflict within marketing channels. Some of the aims of such activities are:

1. To enhance knowledge and understanding.
2. To cultivate goodwill among channel members, gain prestige, and perhaps to undermine the goodwill and prestige of a competitor or competitive channel.
3. To shape attitudes among the personnel of another firm, to influence its management to follow or not to follow a certain course of action.

Using these mechanisms to change the values or norms of channel members is one way to contain conflict. Many manufacturers and wholesalers, for example, have tried to educate certain retailers to think of profitability in terms of return-on-investment rather than gross profit margins; this use of expert and information power is aimed at changing these retailers' norms and values as well

[29] Biedermann and Tabak, "The Television Received Industry," p. 287.

as their retail operating methods. All other things being equal, educational programs are most effective when information is presented as part of the ordinary action of the channel (e.g., on-the-job training)—that is, when channel members interact directly with one another in the performance of a common task rather than when information is offered in trade publications or a general program. An approach that falls somewhere between the on-the-job and the general information approaches might be the establishment of libraries or training schools or both by channel members, either individually or collectively.

Perhaps interpenetration can best be accomplished through the process of *uncertainty absorption* by one channel member for others in the system. Recall from Chapter 7 that this process takes place when inferences are drawn from a body of evidence and the inferences, instead of the evidence itself, are then communicated.[30] The problem is to reduce uncertainty to the point where meaningful predictions are possible, leading to the achievement of at least a relatively uniform perception of the environment in which channel members operate.

As noted in Exhibit 11-2, the automobile industry has experienced considerable conflict within its marketing channels. Both Ford and General Motors develop statistical averages on sales volume, profit margins, and operating data useful for comparisons by dealers and area sales managers. These data provide the dealers with norms to strive for in altering their sales policies. Once their actions are based on a more complete understanding of their markets, the dealers, with the support of the area sales managers, may ''negotiate'' their ''environment'' in a more realistic and calculated manner.

Using the nonmediated bases of power (i.e., referent, expert, traditional legitimate, and information) is one way in which channel members can reduce or absorb uncertainty.[31] Since higher degrees of uncertainty are associated with higher levels of channel conflict,[32] absorbing uncertainty is an effective mechanism for lowering conflict within marketing channels.

Although the interpenetration methods are often effective means of preventing and managing conflict, they implicitly assume that channel institutions perceive a high degree of interdependence. Thus, they are most effective in corporate and contractual vertical marketing systems. For less vertically integrated systems, such as administered and conventional channels, other conflict-

[30] See James G. March and Herbert A. Simon, *Organizations* (New York: John Wiley & Sons, 1958), p. 165.

[31] Harold F. Koenig, Terrence T. Kroeten, and James R. Brown, ''The Bases of Power: Their Effect upon Retailers' Perceptions of Uncertainty,'' in Russell W. Belk et al. (eds.), *1984 AMA Educators' Proceedings* (Chicago: American Marketing Association, 1984), pp. 266–270.

[32] James R. Brown, Robert F. Lusch, and Harold F. Koenig, ''Environmental Uncertainty Regarding Inventory Ordering,'' *International Journal of Physical Distribution and Materials Management*, Vol. 14, 3 (1984), pp. 19–36.

management mechanisms are more appropriate. These include the boundary and bargaining and negotiations methods of conflict resolution.

Boundary Mechanisms—Diplomacy

In an analogy with international relations, *channel diplomacy* is the method by which channel relations are conducted, adjusted, and managed by personnel operating at the boundaries of channel member organizations.[33] The functions of channel "diplomats" or boundary personnel include defining and shaping channel policies, conducting negotiations with their counterparts in other channel organizations, and conveying information within the channel.

Boundary personnel are used widely in marketing channels. For example;

- Business management specialists counsel dealers in the automobile industry.
- Factory specialists aid electrical equipment distributors.
- Company liaisons represent and interpret food manufacturers' policies to the company's wholesale and retail customers.

These channel diplomats represent the "front line" in preventing and reducing channel conflict.

Boundary personnel often use all of the power bases—rewards, coercion, legal contracts, identification, expertise, authority, and information—in performing their functions. Note that boundary personnel not only have the organizational power bases of their employers, they also have their personal bases of power to manage conflict within the channel. In fact, the personal bases of power can sometimes be more effective than the organizational ones in handling channel conflict.[34]

Either because of insensitivity, personal goals, organizational pressures, or other reasons, however, channel diplomats may invoke the wrong base of power at the wrong time, consequently sparking conflict within the channel. Thus, boundary people not only manage channel conflict, but are sometimes the cause of it.

Boundary mechanisms, of course, vary in sophistication according to the administrative pattern of the channel. The more vertically integrated channels use boundary mechanisms to develop superordinate goals and to engage in arbitration and mediation and conciliation. Diplomacy is employed in less integrated chan-

---

[33] An organization's boundary personnel are those people who, as part of their jobs, are in direct contact with employees of other organizations. For example, a supplier's salespeople, physical distribution personnel, accounts receivable staff, and even top management frequently interact with a buyer's boundary personnel to consummate transactions and to ensure that the marketing functions are being properly executed by other channel members. A buyer's boundary personnel might include the purchasing staff, physical distribution personnel (particularly receiving), accounts payable staff, and also, perhaps, top management.

[34] Gary L. Frazier, "On the Measurement of Interfirm Power in Channels of Distribution," *Journal of Marketing Research*, Vol. 20 (May 1983), pp. 158–166.

nels to implement the interpenetration methods of conflict management. Boundary mechanisms are used to coordinate the activities of the channel organizations as well as to manage conflict.

One last technique for managing conflict within the marketing channel—bargaining and negotiation—can also be used regardless of the administrative form of the channel.

Bargaining and Negotiation Mechanisms

No matter which conflict-management strategy is adopted, resolution is always the result of bargaining. Bargaining is the making of commitments, offering of rewards, or threatening of punishments among channel members. Thus, bargaining relies heavily on the mediated bases of power to resolve channel conflict. For bargaining to be a successful conflict-management mechanism, there must be mutual respect and trust. In addition, compromise is a prerequisite to successful bargaining, for negotiations are possible only if each side is prepared to give up something to gain some of its objectives. In other words, the conflicting parties must be ready to accept a compromise rather than to seek a final resolution of all their differences. The difficulty with compromises, of course, is that they may not resolve the basic problem, which then continues as a source of tension.

On many separate occasions, steel manufacturers and distributors have reached compromise solutions over the size of functional discounts granted to distributors in the channels for stainless steel. The basic problem—competing effectively against imported steel—still provides the foundation for continuing disagreement over pricing policies in the channel. Neither side to the bargain has been satisfied with the outcome.

Bargaining and negotiation are most useful in resolving disagreements over domains. This mechanism is not likely to settle differences in goals, values, or norms. Another context in which bargaining and negotiation is useful is when the means for resolving channel conflict are being decided on. Exhibit 11-5 illustrates this conflict-management mechanism in the channel for soft drinks.

As Table 11-1 illustrates, not all conflict-management mechanisms are appropriate for all administrative patterns of marketing channels. Effective conflict resolution depends upon selecting the technique that is best suited to the degree of vertical interdependence channel members perceive. In addition, some of the conflict-management mechanisms discussed in this chapter more effectively alleviate some causes of conflict, while others are better at handling other causes. The bases of power underlying these conflict-management mechanisms also must be used with care. The nonmediated bases of power are best suited for reducing

EXHIBIT 11-5
Bargaining and Negotiation in Resolving Marketing Channel Conflict: Coca-Cola Bottling Company of New York

As noted in Exhibit 11-3, Coca-Cola, like most soft-drink manufacturers, markets its beverages through franchised bottlers. These bottlers are independent wholesalers who buy syrup concentrate from Coke, add water to it, package the product, and distribute the soft drinks to a variety of retail and institutional establishments.

For 59 years, Coke's franchise agreement with its bottlers called for it to sell its syrup at a fixed price of $0.88 per gallon plus the price of sugar; the price of sugar was allowed to fluctuate according to a set formula based on the commodity price of sugar. In the late 1970s, however, Coke wanted to amend its franchise contract, analysts thought, to increase marketing spending. The new ceiling price for syrup would be $1.675 per gallon, to be adjusted for changes in the consumer price index as well as for changes in the market price of sugar.

About half of Coke's 566 U.S. bottlers—largely the smaller ones—signed the amended franchise agreement. The larger ones—including Coca-Cola Bottling Company of New York, the nation's biggest soft-drink bottler—refused to sign because they thought the new price for syrup was too high.

After bargaining and negotiation, Coca-Cola Bottling Company of New York agreed to a new price of $1.095 and a more favorable method of figuring the price of sugar. (These terms were to apply to all other bottlers, whether or not they had signed the $1.675/gallon agreement. Other large bottlers, however, still balked at signing the agreement. One issue was who should arbitrate disputes between Coke and individual bottlers over any new price ceiling changes. One large southeastern bottler felt that Coke had too much control over the composition of the arbitration committee. Thus, bargaining and negotiation are used to solve both disagreements over domains and disagreements over how conflicts are to be resolved.

Source: Based on Bill Abrams and John Koten, "New York Coke Agrees to Amend Franchise Accord," *The Wall Street Journal*, April 19, 1979, p. 7.

---

conflict levels, while the mediated power bases (i.e., reward, coercion, and legal legitimate), if used improperly, may spark conflict rather than contain it.[35]

Regardless of which mechanism is used, the ultimate goal of conflict management is to enhance the performance of the marketing channel. Exactly what is meant by marketing channel performance is the topic of the next chapter.

---

[35] See John F. Gaski, "The Theory of Power and Conflict in Channels of Distribution," *Journal of Marketing*, Vol. 48 (Summer 1984), pp. 9–29.

SUMMARY

Although the vast majority of marketing channel relationships are cooperative, some are quite conflictful. Indeed, the consequences of conflict within a channel are sometimes so grave that managing conflict among member organizations is one of the most significant facets of marketing channel management.

Conflict in the marketing channel is typically viewed as a process comprising the underlying conditions, perceptions of conflict, feelings of conflict, overt conflictful behavior, and the outcomes of conflict. Marketing channel conflict stems from three basic roots: (1) incompatibility among channel member goals; (2) domain dissensus among channel members (i.e., disagreements over the markets served, the products carried, the functions performed, or the technology employed to perform those functions); and (3) differing perceptions of reality among channel members.

Regardless of its cause, conflict within a marketing channel has three basic outcomes. First, the conflict may be completely resolved. Second, it may be partially resolved. Finally, if conflict is too extensive, it may lead to a dissolution of channel relationships.

Conflict within the channel is related to channel performance and channel member satisfaction in three possible ways. First, marketing channel conflict can be dysfunctional; that is, it can cause channel performance and channel member satisfaction to decline. When this occurs, the "vicious cycle" of conflict–poor performance–dissatisfaction–conflict must be broken as soon as possible to prevent crippling of the channel. The second possible consequence of conflict within the channel is its functional or positive effects. In other words, conflict may actually cause channel performance to improve and member organizations to be more satisfied with the channel relationship. That conflict has both functional and dysfunctional consequences implies that there is a threshold below which conflict is functional and above which it is dysfunctional. The third possible consequence is that conflict can be neutral—that is, have no effect on channel performance and channel member satisfaction.

Several conflict-management mechanisms are available to the channel leader to prevent conflict from becoming dysfunctional or to reduce dysfunctional conflict to functional levels. In essence, each of these mechanisms is a way of using the bases of power to handle channel conflict. The major conflict-management mechanisms are establishing superordinate goals, using arbitration or conciliation and mediation, attempting cooptation, implementing exchange-of-persons programs, joining other channel members' trade associations, developing education and propaganda programs, employing channel diplomacy, and engaging in bargaining and negotiation strategies. Each of these mechanisms varies in effectiveness, depending on the cause of conflict and the administrative pattern that characterizes the channel.

Because conflict does exist in marketing channels and has potential dysfunctional consequences, channel leaders must know how to manage rationally. If they do not, the channel will probably fail to compete effectively against those vertical marketing systems that have learned to manage their disputes successfully.

DISCUSSION QUESTIONS

1. Recall the ComputerLand illustration at the beginning of the chapter. Use Figure 11-1 to explain the process of marketing channel conflict between ComputerLand and its franchisees.
2. Discuss which of the three major causes of marketing channel conflict sparked the dispute between ComputerLand and its franchisees.
3. Explain which of the conflict-management mechanisms discussed in this chapter would be most appropriate for resolving or lessening the amount of conflict between ComputerLand and its franchisees.
4. Recall the Arthur Treacher's Fish & Chips illustration of Exhibit 11-4. Discuss the probable dysfunctional consequences of the conflict between Mrs. Paul's and its Arthur Treacher's franchisees. Explain what is likely functional consequences of this conflict might be.
5. Recalling the Haagen-Dasz example, state which of the various mechanisms discussed in this chapter would be most appropriate for managing conflict between Haagen-Dasz and its independent distributors and explain why.
6. Some observers argue that conflict may be neutral or that it causes performance to be either functional or dysfunctional. Others counterargue that it is performance (or lack thereof) that drives conflict within the channel. With which position do you agree: Does conflict cause performance or does performance cause conflict? Explain.
7. Schedule an interview with a boundary person employed by a channel organization with which you are familiar. In your interview, determine how that boundary person handles conflict with his or her counterpart in other channel organizations. In particular, try to ascertain (1) the most commonly encountered channel disputes, (2) the causes of those disputes, (3) the conflict-management mechanisms used to handle those disputes, and (4) the relative importance of the boundary person's organizational bases of power and his or her personal bases of power in handling those disputes.
8. Choose an industry that you find interesting. From trade journals in the library, determine the major conflict issues among channel members in that industry. What do you think are the underlying causes of those conflict issues? Explain.
9. Chapter 10 argued that conflict was a consequence of using the wrong bases of power, in a particular situation, to coordinate channel members' marketing activities. This chapter, on the other hand, has argued that the bases of power are central in managing conflict. Which is it: Does using the bases of power cause conflict, or does the existence of conflict stimulate the use of the power bases to manage that conflict? Explain your answer.

12

Evaluating Marketing Channel Performance

LEARNING OBJECTIVES

Upon completing this chapter, you will be able to:

- *List the four key dimensions of marketing channel performance.*
- *Diagram and discuss the five key steps in evaluating total channel effectiveness.*
- *Explain what is meant by the channel system equity dimension of marketing channel performance.*
- *Discuss how productivity is measured in the distributive trades.*
- *Compare productivity growth in the distributive trades with that of other sectors of the economy.*
- *Explain the factors that influence levels of productivity within marketing channels.*
- *Discuss ways in which understanding channel productivity can be used to manage distribution systems as well as individual marketing institutions.*

- *Outline a procedure for determining the costs of using specific marketing channels.*

- *List the key components of the strategic profit model.*

- *Compute the strategic profit model ratios for distributive institutions.*

- *Discuss two important variants of the strategic profit model and describe their key weaknesses.*

- *Compute direct product profit for a merchandise item and suggest strategies for improving the profitability of that product.*

- *List many other quantitative and qualitative measures of marketing channel performance.*

- *Describe several key factors that influence the performance of marketing channels.*

Evaluating Retail Marketing Channels: Exxon's Approach

Exxon Company, U.S.A., is a vertically integrated refiner and marketer of petroleum products in the United States. As part of its marketing activities, Exxon operates thousands of gasoline service stations.

Many of these stations are company-leased retail stores, with Exxon owning the land, building, and equipment. An independent dealer then signs a three-year dealer lease and supply agreement with Exxon. Exxon supplies gasoline and tires, batteries, and accessories (TBA), and the dealer agrees to (1) pay a fixed monthly rent to Exxon, (2) purchase products from Exxon distributors, and (3) maintain certain quality standards—primarily to do with cleanliness and safety—set forth by Exxon.

To evaluate the performance of these company-leased stations, Exxon uses target return-on-investment measures of profitability. When a station consistently yields low returns on investment despite favorable market conditions and solid company support, it becomes part of the "swing store" program.

The "swing store" program is an in-depth evaluation of marginal service stations that hover between success and failure. Through this program, Exxon hopes to identify problems and "swing" these stores into the successful category.

For stations in the swing store program, Exxon compares the store's actual monthly gasoline sales with company forecasts. These forecasts are based on a traffic count at the corner of the site, the number of automobile registrations within 1½ miles of the site, the number of other competitors nearby, the average market price or competitors' price in the vicinity, the number of regional shopping centers in the area, and whether there are any other traffic generators in the area.

In addition, the Exxon Retail Store Evaluation Form is used. This form employs over 100 individual items designed to measure subjectively five key dimensions of dealer quality: (1) store appearance, (2) personnel appearance, (3) product merchandising, (4) selling and service capability, and (5) other aspects of station management.

These two aspects of the swing store program—comparing actual with forecasted sales volume and assessing dealer quality—are designed to answer two key questions: (1) Has Exxon made a poor individual investment and/or is it the quality of the dealer that stands in the way of higher store income levels? (2) What can Exxon do to improve the situation? Therefore, the swing store program is designed to identify the causes of low retail store performance and to point out methods of improving that performance.

Source: Based on Stephen W. McDaniel, "Exxon Company, U.S.A.: 'Swing Store Program,'" In Richard T. Hise and Stephen W. McDaniel (eds.), *Cases in Marketing Strategy* (Columbus, Ohio: Charles E. Merrill, 1984), pp. 535–544.

In the preceding chapters, we examined the various institutions that form marketing channels. We also looked at the factors that influence how these institutions link up with one another to make up a channel structure. The channel management process is not complete without an evaluation of the performance of these institutions and the channel structures they constitute.

As the Exxon example illustrates, the performance of marketing institutions as well as distribution channel systems can be assessed along many different dimensions. Exxon evaluates its retail stores along quantitative profitability criteria as well as along qualitative dealer quality criteria. In addition to this purely business-oriented perspective, marketing channel performance can be evaluated from a societal viewpoint.

By combining both perspectives, we get four key dimensions along which the performance of marketing channel structures and institutions can be evaluated: (1) system effectiveness, (2) system equity in serving various markets, (3) system productivity, and (4) system profitability (see Figure 12-1). We will review the historical performance of some key channel institutions (e.g., wholesalers and retailers) as well as present a number of alternative managerial and channel audit mechanisms that can be used in monitoring channel performance.

CHANNEL SYSTEM EFFECTIVENESS

Recall from Chapter 1 the marketing flows or functions of physical possession, ownership, promotion, negotiation, financing, risking, market information, ordering, and payment. These functions are organized by institutions and agencies making up commercial marketing channels so that goods and services are provided in the desired quantities (lot size) when needed (delivery time). These goods and services are made available at a number of different locations (market decentralization or locational convenience), where they are displayed and generally combined with complementary and substitutable items (assortment depth and breadth) according to the target market's desires. Therefore, the "output" of a particular channel of

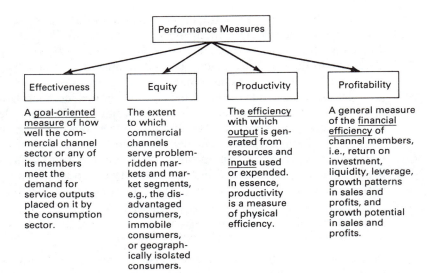

Figure 12-1 Performance measurement in marketing channels.

distribution may be viewed as lot size, delivery time, locational convenience, and assortment breadth.[1] Household consumers and organizational users are key actors in distribution channels because they participate directly in the marketing flows. However, the less they participate in the flows, the more work that must be done by commercial channel members in providing the ''output.'' Consequently, the final price of goods and services to these buyers will be higher. If they were willing to absorb more of the marketing task (e.g., increase the amount of search and selection devoted to purchasing), the prices they pay could probably be reduced. Thus, marketing channel system performance must be assessed from a ''total channel'' perspective, including commercial channel institutions and their target markets.

As Figure 12-2 indicates, evaluating total channel system effectiveness begins with assessing which marketing channel services the target market needs and wants the commercial channel to provide. Because buyer's tastes and preferences change, up-to-date marketing research studies are needed for this assessment.

One general trend is for consumers to buy in larger lot sizes.[2] This enables retailers to buy in larger lots, which, in turn, reduces the need for wholesaler services. This translates into lower distributive costs, since commercial channel services are reduced and, consequently, lower prices to consumers are possible.

---

[1] This model and discussion of system output draws heavily from Louis P. Bucklin, ''Marketing Channels and Structures: A Macro View,'' in Boris W. Becker and Helmut Becker (eds.), *American Marketing Association Combined Conference Proceedings* (Chicago: American Marketing Association, 1973), pp. 32–35.

[2] David Schwartzman, *The Decline of Service in Retail Trade* (Pullman: Washington State University, Bureau of Economic and Business Research, 1971).

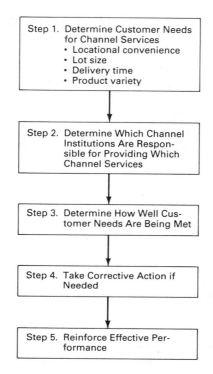

Step 1. Determine Customer Needs
for Channel Services
• Locational convenience
• Lot size
• Delivery time
• Product variety

Step 2. Determine Which Channel
Institutions Are Respon-
sible for Providing Which
Channel Services

Step 3. Determine How Well Customer Needs Are Being Met

Step 4. Take Corrective Action if
Needed

Step 5. Reinforce Effective Performance

Figure 12-2 Evaluating total channel effectiveness.

Note that this is a *general* trend, as are others noted in Chapter 2, and does not necessarily apply to all market segments. Only marketing research studies of the target market, not the market in general, are useful in determining buyers' tastes and preferences for marketing channel services.

The second step in evaluating marketing channel system effectiveness is to determine which channel institutions are responsible for providing which marketing channel services. Although this step is accomplished in designing the marketing channel structure and administrative pattern (the topics of Chapters 8 and 9, respectively), channel members do not always perform the functions they are assigned nor do they always perform them adequately.

The manufacturer-dealer channel for new automobiles has been designed to provide warranty, maintenance, and repair service for those cars once they have been sold. Increasingly, however, automobiles are serviced at places other than new-car dealerships.[3] Such outlets include gasoline stations, independent garages, tire dealers, and specialty car-care retailers. Obviously, these institutions in the channel for automobile service must be considered in evaluating channel system performance.

---

[3] Mel S. Moyer and Neil M. Whitmore, "An Appraisal of the Marketing Channels for Automobiles," *Journal of Marketing*, Vol. 40 (July 1976), pp. 35–40.

Information about which channel members are performing which functions can be obtained from the boundary person's sales, service, and buying reports; these reports may be either formal (e.g., sales call reports) or informal (e.g., a casual observation passed on to the boundary person's superiors). Of course, this information may also be gathered from market research studies.

The third step in assessing the effectiveness of the total marketing channel system is to determine how well the target market's needs and wants for channel services are being met. Specifically, this step involves conducting marketing research studies to determine how well each channel institution provides the target market with its desired channel services. (Exhibit 12-1 illustrates such a survey for automobile warranty, maintenance, and repair service.)

In practice, the marketing research information required for Steps 1 and 3 is gathered in a single study. Not only can this information be obtained for channel institutions in general (e.g., all specialty steel service centers), it can also be gathered for specific channel members (e.g., Joseph Ryerson, Inc.).

Taking any needed corrective action to ensure that the channel services desired by the target market are being adequately delivered is the fourth step in the evaluation process. Corrective action can take at least three different forms. First, it may involve clarifying the tasks to be undertaken by marketing organizations within the channel. Often the required levels of performance are either taken for granted or are ignored by members of the channel. The judicious use of channel power is sometimes necessary to reinforce expectations and requirements for performing each of the marketing flows and functions. Second, the use of power may be required to respecify which institutions perform which channel tasks. This is particularly true when channel institutions have evolved into performing more functions (e.g., J. C. Penney upgrading its merchandise line by carrying more national brands) or undertaking fewer functions (e.g., Arco eliminating its consumer gasoline credit card). The third and most drastic corrective action in improving marketing channel system effectiveness is eliminating those channel members who chronically fail to provide the target market with the channel services it desires. Because this action requires a modification of the existing channel structure and because it may bring about costly litigation, eliminating channel members is a last resort in attempting to improve the effectiveness of the marketing channel system.

Evaluating the effectiveness of the marketing channel system and its individual channel members is no easy task; however, with much planning and the proper information, it can be done successfully. Evaluating how well marketing channels equitably serve disadvantaged consumers is also very difficult, but is a topic that channel managers should address.

CHANNEL SYSTEM EQUITY

Given the sheer number of wholesaling and retailing institutions in the United States, it is hard to imagine that pockets of the population do not have access to goods and services at reasonable prices. Yet, this is indeed the case for many of

One method used to evaluate the effectiveness of marketing channels is marketing research. The following poll gives some insights as to how consumers view the performance of the marketing channel for automobile warranty and repair service.

The question asked was:

People go to different places to get basic service for their cars—gas stations, auto dealers, independent garages, tire dealers, and specialty shops like Sears and Midas. In the following categories, who do you think does the best job?[a]

The responses were:[b]

	Quality of Service	Value for the Money	Being Honest	Caring about Customers
Gas Stations	7%	10%	9%	9%
Auto Dealerships	32%	21%	25%	9%
Garages	28%	31%	32%	32%
Tire Dealers	10%	7%	7%	10%
Specialty Retailers	15%	19%	13%	12%
None	3%	2%	6%	2%
Not Sure	5%	10%	8%	6%

These findings were based upon a

[t]elephone survey of 631 adults in households that have bought a new car within the past five years. The poll was conducted May 16–20 [1986] by Louis Harris & Associates Inc. for *Business Week*. Overall results should be accurate to within five percentage points.[c]

[a] "BW/Harris Poll: Dealerships Should Be Small—and More Reliable," *Business Week*, (June 2, 1986), p. 66.

[b] ibid.

[c] ibid.

---

the poor in the United States, especially those living in urban ghettos or rural communities. Some merchants, through their pricing and credit practices, discriminate against minority groups.[4] However, the primary reason for the absence of broad assortments of reasonably priced merchandise and services is more related to the structure of trade in these areas than to deliberate racial or

[4] See, for example, David Caplovitz, *The Poor Pay More* (New York: The Free Press, 1963); Frederick D. Sturdivant (ed.), *The Ghetto Marketplace* (New York: The Free Press, 1969); and Alan R. Andreason, *The Disadvantaged Consumer* (New York: The Free Press, 1975).

socioeconomic bias. For example, a lack of competition is often responsible for the marketing channel system serving these markets inequitably.

Food chain prices have been found to be similar in both ghetto and suburban locations within a given trading area. However, whether the quality of meat and fresh produce differs between these locations is a subject of controversy.[5] The absence of competition in the ghetto and rural areas, as well as their inhabitants' limited mobility, prohibits these consumers from obtaining the benefits available to suburbanites in the same general trading area.

Although it is true that many stores serving the economically disadvantaged charge high prices and extend credit at excessive rates, their profitability is very low. This indicates that their costs of doing business are extremely high.[6] Table 12-1 lists some of the reasons for this. One reason for these high costs is that ghetto retailers perform more of the marketing functions of their customers than suburban retailers do. For example, because they lack transportation, ghetto consumers typically shop at stores close to their homes and buy in small lot sizes. In addition, ghetto merchants offering credit face higher bad-debt risks than their suburban counterparts; in other words, ghetto retailers participate more heavily in the risking flow.

Food chains, department stores, and regional shopping centers, among others, are reluctant to enter the ghetto and poor rural areas because of high occupancy costs, high crime rates, and/or residents' lack of discretionary income to support new, large-scale retail ventures. Because fewer stores are committing to these areas, consumers remain truly disadvantaged relative to those who live near more affluent shopping areas. As long as this situation continues, there will be great inequity in the distribution system. What is needed is greater interorganizational coordination among government agencies, retail chain organizations, wholesalers, manufacturers, and various facilitating agencies (e.g., insurance and credit firms) so that channel organizations will be stimulated to enter these markets. Further, elevating the incomes and increasing the mobility of disadvantaged consumers is obviously necessary if they are to be served equitably by the distribution system.

Without doubt, effectiveness and equity are important pieces in the marketing channel performance mosaic. The total picture of channel performance cannot

[5] Donald E. Sexton, Jr., "Do Blacks Pay More?" *Journal of Marketing Research*, Vol. 8 (November 1971), pp. 420–426; Charles S. Goodman, "Do the Poor Pay More?" *Journal of Marketing*, Vol. 32 (January 1968), pp. 18–24; and Donald F. Dixon and Daniel J. McLaughlin, Jr., "Low-Income Consumers and the Issue of Exploitation: A Study of Chain Supermarkets," *Social Science Quarterly*, Vol. 51 (September 1970), pp. 320–328.

[6] *Economic Report on Installment Credit and Retail Sales Practices of District of Colombia Retailers* (Washington, D.C.: Federal Trade Commission, 1968), p. 18; and Frederick C. Klein, "Black Businessmen Running Ghetto Store Can Be a Survival Test," *Wall Street Journal*, January 31, 1977, pp. 1, 13.

TABLE 12-1 Reasons Cited by Retailers as Barriers to Successful Ghetto Distribution

1. Higher risk of store damage from vandalism, leading to higher insurance premiums.
2. Low sales per square footage of space.
3. Low inventory turnover.
4. Exploitive image: "If something goes wrong in the neighborhood, someone would always find an excuse to blame us."
6. Higher credit losses due to bad checks.
7. Higher costs of logistics such as material handling and transportation due to, among other things, poor location and smaller lots.
8. Higher personnel costs since "they must be given an incentive to work in a ghetto location."

Source: Reprinted from *New Marketing For Social and Economic Progress and Marketing's Contribution to the Firm and Society*, published by the American Marketing Association (Chicago: American Marketing Association Combined Proceedings, 1974), "Inequality in the Ghetto Distribution Structure and Opportunity Equalization for the Ghetto Dweller," by Igbal Mather and Subbash Jain, Ronald C. Curhan (ed.), p. 280.

be seen, however, until the productivity and profitability pieces are put into place. The next section examines channel productivity from the perspective of the entire channel and from the viewpoint of the individual channel member.

CHANNEL SYSTEM PRODUCTIVITY

Productivity is a measure of how efficiently an organization (e.g., retail store, retail chain, industrial distributor, manufacturer, facilitating agency, entire marketing channel) uses resources such as land, labor, and capital to generate outputs such as sales volume, gross margins, and value added. Obviously, marketing channels that employ their resources more efficiently are better able to compete on a price basis than less efficient channels. For this reason, an understanding of the concept of productivity is critical to developing successful marketing channel systems. The following sections discuss productivity in the distributive trades, how it is measured, what correlates with high levels of productivity in wholesaling and retailing, and specific managerial uses of productivity information. Knowledge of the general concept of productivity and its measurement is the first step in comprehending this important dimension of marketing channel performance.

Measuring Productivity in the Distributive Trades[7]

A channel member's productivity is typically measured as the ratio of that firm's output to the resources used to produce that output:

$$\text{Productivity} = \frac{\text{Amount of output}}{\text{Amount of input}}.$$

In calculating this ratio for marketing institutions, a firm's sales volume is often used as the output variable, with the amount of labor as the input variable.

[7] For the most part, this section is based on the concepts presented in Louis P. Bucklin, *Productivity in Marketing* (Chicago: America Marketing Association, 1978), pp. 15–43.

The ABC Electrical Supply Company, a wholesaler serving electrical contractors in the Rocky Mountain states, employs an average of 50 people annually. Each person typically works 47 weeks per year (excluding vacations, holidays, sick leave, and personal time) and puts in an average of 45 hours per week (including overtime). Last year, ABC's labor productivity reached $75.65 sales per labor hour on $8 million of annual sales.

Note that productivity is ideally a measure of physical efficiency (e.g., the number of automobiles rolling off GM's Oklahoma City assembly plant per each hour of labor needed to run that plant). For marketing institutions, however, physical measures of efficiency are hard to derive.

One difficulty is measuring the output of marketing channel institutions. First, channel intermediaries primarily add the economic utilities of place, time, and possession to the form utility largely created by manufacturers, and the amount of these marketing channel services is not as easily measured as the tangible products produced by manufacturers. Second, the quantity and quality of output produced or services rendered by marketing institutions are not homogeneous from transaction to transaction.

On a recent shopping trip, Karen Miller bought $20 worth of groceries and required the supermarket's carryout services to transport them from the store to her car. Among her purchases were one dozen apples and 24-ounce loaf of whole wheat Rainbow bread costing $1.

Two weeks later at that same store, Ellen Smythe also spent $20 on groceries, but had to carry her own bags to her car since the store had dropped its carryout service. Ellen also bought a 24-ounce loaf of just-baked whole wheat bread; however, she bought hers from the store's bakery and had it sliced to her specification. Ellen's bread cost $1.45. In addition, Ellen purchased one dozen oranges.

Clearly, the supermarket's output was different in these two cases. Although she did not pay extra for it, Karen received carryout service, while Ellen did not. On the other hand, Ellen, by paying extra, received fresher bread sliced exactly the way she wanted it.

Thus, another problem is how to combine these different outputs into a single, meaningful measure of marketing channel output.

The common solution to these problems is to use a channel member's dollar sales volume as the measure of that firm's output. Such a measure, corrected for changes in the general price level (i.e., inflation or deflation), enables heterogeneous outputs to be combined into a single output measure. From a physical output perspective, a partial measure of the supermarket's output might be two loaves of bread. This view ignores the difference in channel services received by the two shoppers. If a sales volume measure is used, the additional 45 cents Ellen paid for her loaf of bread very roughly reflects the additional output (i.e., more freshness, custom slicing) she received from the supermarket. Dollar sales volume measures of marketing channel output also allow the sales of different physical products (e.g., apples and oranges) to be combined.

This solution is not without its weaknesses. First, sales volume measures do not separate the output of individual channel members from that of other firms preceding them in the marketing channel. To take the supermarket example again, the $1 Karen paid for her loaf of bread includes the supermarket's compensation for the channel services it performed as well as the Rainbow Bakery's compensation for the services it undertook. Although this measure of output is acceptable for examining the entire marketing channel's productivity, it is less appropriate for measuring the supermarket's productivity. In other words, sales volume measures of output do not reflect an individual channel member's unique *value added* to the goods and services it sells. Second, sales volume measures do not adjust for the quality of output. Recall that Karen received carryout service, while Ellen did not; in other words, the quality of the supermarket's output had declined over the two-week period, yet the output of both transactions was recorded as $20. Unless they are reflected in output price changes, changes in output quality are not incorporated into sales volume measures of output—nor into physical output measures, for that matter.

Another difficulty in assessing the physical efficiency of marketing channels is measuring the resource inputs, particularly when "total-factor" measures of productivity are used. *Total-factor productivity measures* assess the efficiency with which a firm or marketing channel employs all of its input resources. For example, the input measure used in computing an electronics wholesaler's total-factor productivity would include the amount of labor, the amount of capital (e.g., inventory investment, equipment usage, warehouse usage), and the amount of services purchased from other organizations (e.g., energy, insurance, advertising). The key problem in creating such a total-factor input measure is deciding how to combine the various quantities of inputs. Although there are ways of handling this problem, they are beyond the scope of this text; therefore, we will concentrate on "single-factor" measures of productivity.[8]

Single-factor productivity measures assess the productivity of only one input resource. Examples of single-factor productivity measures are sales per employee, sales per labor-hour, sales per square feet of selling space, sales per store, sales per cubic feet of warehouse space, and ton-miles per truck. Compared to other industries, the distributive trades are quite labor-intensive; indeed, persons engaged in wholesaling and retailing represent 22 percent of the U.S. labor force.[9] Because of this, most published productivity statistics report labor

---

[8] For a more in-depth discussion of total-factor productivity measurement in retailing, see Brian T. Ratchford and James R. Brown, "A Study of Productivity Changes in Food Retailing," *Marketing Science*, Vol. 4 (Fall 1985), pp. 292–311.

[9] Philip Van Ness, *Productivity in Wholesale Distribution* (Washington, D.C.: Distribution Research and Education Foundation, 1980), p. 1.

TABLE 12-2   Percent Change in Output per Hour of All Persons by Major Sector

Economic Sector	% Change 1970–1975	% Change 1976–1981
Farming	18.4	28.0
Mining	−16.4	−24.9
Manufacturing	17.9	7.2
Transportation	12.1	−3.7
Communications	34.5	20.5
Electric, gas, and sanitary services	16.6	−6.0
Distributive trades	11.2	4.4

Source: *Productivity and the Economy: A Chartbook*, U.S. Department of Labor, Bureau of Labor Statistics, June 1983, Chart 5, p. 65.

productivity—a single-factor measure. Accordingly, the discussion in the following sections focuses primarily on labor productivity.

Productivity in the Distributive Trades

In addition to reflecting productivity per labor-hour, most productivity figures are presented as average annual percentage rates of change. This makes it much easier to compare the productivity of a single firm over time, different sectors of the economy, and different marketing channel institutions. How efficiently the distributive trades utilize labor is compared with other industries in Table 12-2.

During the 1970–1981 period, retailers took several steps to improve their productivity. Among these steps were computerizing their operations, encouraging increased transaction size, and reducing the level of the services they provided with each transaction by shifting functions forward to their consumers or backward to their suppliers. During this same period, wholesalers took similar measures; they also computerized their operations, as well as modernized their warehouses, upgraded their materials-handling technology, and trained their employees to work more efficiently. Despite these efforts, the distributive trades achieved the lowest growth of any economic sector experiencing productivity gains during this period.

There are a number of possible explanations for the lagging productivity in wholesaling and retailing. First, the distributive trades, as already noted, are labor-intensive. The amount of labor used in this sector increased at a substantially faster rate than in other sectors of the economy.[10] Second, the distributive trades are more dependent than manufacturing on growth in sales volume to improve productivity.[11] This means that the likelihood of persistent low growth in constant-dollar retail sales,[12] accompanied by higher growth in labor-hours, guarantees lower gains in productivity. Finally, the distributive trades face a

[10] Ibid., p. 5.

[11] Louis P. Bucklin, "Growth and Productivity Change in Retailing," in Ronald W. Stampfl and Elizabeth C. Hirschman (eds.), *Theory in Retailing: Traditional and Nontraditional Sources* (Chicago: American Marketing Association, 1981), p. 22.

[12] Ibid., p. 21.

Line of Retail Trade	1979	1980	1981	1982	1983	1984	Average Annual % Change 1979–1984
Retail food stores	97.3	99.7	96.8	95.2	96.9	95.9	−0.5
Franchised car dealers	94.6	99.5	96.6	97.4	106.2	106.1	2.2
Gasoline stations	106.9	104.3	105.8	110.7	118.5	119.0	2.8
Apparel stores	114.4	120.1	127.1	130.9	138.1	146.4	4.9
Men's & boys' clothing stores	108.2	106.4	115.6	115.7	120.2	127.0	3.4
Women's ready-to-wear stores	120.7	125.5	139.0	158.2	169.0	184.1	9.4
Family clothing stores	107.7	122.6	131.4	139.6	149.3	155.0	7.3
Shoe stores	112.2	109.3	113.0	108.9	109.9	116.3	0.5
Eating & drinking establishments	99.1	99.2	96.5	95.9	96.4	94.4	−1.0
Drug stores	103.1	106.0	106.2	106.1	107.9	109.8	1.1
Commercial banking	99.3	92.7	90.5	93.2	102.7	—	0.7
Hotels & Motels	102.4	98.6	96.2	94.5	95.5	102.9	−0.3
Laundry services	97.6	90.7	88.2	90.4	90.3	93.3	−0.6
Beauty & barber shops	107.4	102.9	109.2	108.3	114.1	104.5	0.5
Beauty shops	108.0	106.2	114.7	113.1	120.0	111.7	1.5

[a] 1977 = 100.

Source: Arthur S. Herman, "Productivity Continued to Increase in Many Industries During 1984," *Monthly Labor Review*, March 1986, pp. 14–15.

number of constraints in adopting new technology that enhances labor productivity. In supermarket retailing during the 1970s, for example, these constraints included the diversion of capital investment from labor-saving to energy-saving equipment, consumer and labor resistance to new technologies, the high cost of capital, and the necessity for complex cooperation within the food industry to develop improved technologies beyond the UPC.[13]

Growth in the labor productivity of the distributive trades in general is sluggish when compared with other sectors of the economy. These overall productivity growth figures, however, mask important trends occurring within the distribution sector. For example, Table 12-3 illustrates changes in labor productivity in selected sectors of retailing between 1979 and 1984. The greatest productivity gains occurred in apparel retailing of all kinds, and were probably due to the increasing use of self-service in these lines of trade. Offsetting these gains was the decline of labor productivity in other lines of trade, including food retailing, eating and drinking establishments, lodging, and laundry services. Until more dramatic changes in technology occur, labor productivity in these lines of trade is likely to remain stagnant.

Following general productivity trends in the distributive trades helps channel management to understand how efficiently it can expect its channels to operate. For channel managers to act upon this information, however, they must understand what factors affect productivity within marketing channels.

[13] Louis P. Bucklin, "Technological Change and Store Operations: The Supermarket Case," *Journal of Retailing*, Vol. 56 (Spring 1980), p. 13.

Correlates of Productivity in Marketing Channels

A number of factors affect the productivity of marketing channels and the specific institutions that constitute them. As shown in Figure 12-3, these factors include environmental conditions, marketing channel structure, and channel member marketing policies. The distribution system for food dramatically illustrates how these factors affect productivity in marketing channels.

Several *environmental factors* have been found to improve productivity in food retailing, for example. Among them are: (1) higher wage rates, which attracts better-quality employees; (2) higher population growth rates, which implies more modern and efficient retail facilities; (3) greater competitiveness in food store retailing as evidenced by a greater number of "mom and pop" food stores per household; (4) higher household incomes, which lead to greater transaction sizes and more purchases of expensive merchandise; (5) smaller household sizes; and

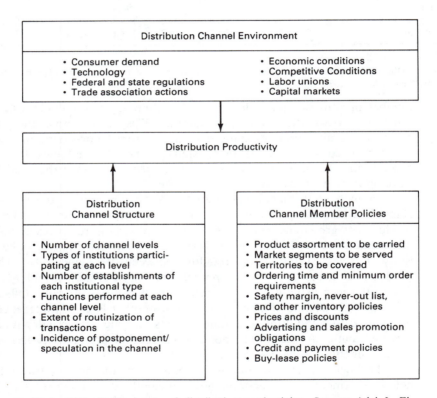

Figure 12-3 Determinants of distribution productivity. *Source*: Adel I. El-Ansary, "Distribution Productivity in the United States: Analysis and Frameworks," in *Distribution Channels*, Proceedings of the 8th International Research Seminar in Marketing (Aix-en-Provence, France: Institut d'administration des Entreprises, Université d'Aix-Marseille, 1981), p. 12.

(6) more private transportation and lower congestion, both of which cause greater competition among geographically dispersed food retailers.[14]

Distribution channel member policies can affect food store productivity. For instance, higher capital-to-labor ratios were found to be linked to increased productivity in food stores.[15]

Changes in *distribution channel structure*, resulting from functional shifting have also led to improved productivity in the marketing channels for meat:

> The cutting of meat, for example, is being moved from the store [back to the meat processing plant] and the role of the butcher shifted to display and customer relations. With higher labor costs for skilled meat personnel, savings are possible because of the improved opportunities for automation in cutting, packaging, and handling equipment for meat in high volumes.[16]

Understanding these influences upon marketing channel productivity is the first step toward improving the efficiency with which goods and services are made available to household and organizational target markets. But improving channel efficiency is only one way in which productivity information can be used to manage marketing channels. The following section explores some of the other ways in detail.

Using Productivity Information to Manage Marketing Channels[17]

Productivity information is critical in managing effective marketing channels. Channel managers can use productivity data to their advantage in (1) evaluating competitive positions, (2) developing ways of improving productivity, (3) providing standards for motivating and rewarding marketing channel personnel, (4) forecasting future labor and capital needs, and (5) determining marketing channel structure.

Evaluating Competitive Positions. Productivity measures can provide insightful information on how efficiently other marketing channels use their scarce resources. Channel management, for example, might compare its productivity with industry averages published by the Bureau of Labor Statistics such as those used in Tables 12-2 and 12-3. Obviously, if the channel is less productive than its competitors, it uses its input resources less efficiently, and is therefore less able to

---

[14] Charles A. Ingene, "Labor Productivity in Retailing," *Journal of Marketing*, Vol. 46 (Fall 1982), pp. 75–90; and Charles A. Ingene, "Labor Productivity in Retailing: What Do We Know and How Do We Know It?" *Journal of Marketing*, Vol. 49 (Fall 1985), pp. 99–106.

[15] Ibid.

[16] Louis P. Bucklin, "Supermarket Technology and the Traditional Department Store," in Ronald W. Stampfl and Elizabeth Hirschman (eds.), *Competitive Structure in Retail Markets: The Department Store Perspective* (Chicago: American Marketing Association, 1980), pp. 17–18.

[17] This section is based on Louis P. Bucklin, "Research in Productivity Measurement for Marketing Decisions," in Jagdish N. Sheth (ed.), *Research in Marketing*, Vol. 1 (Greenwich, Conn.: JAI Press, 1978), pp. 6–19.

compete with them on price basis. These comparisons might also be made over time to see if the channel's productivity is improving, decreasing, or holding steady with respect to competitive marketing channels.

Developing Ways of Improving Productivity. By examining the productivity of its operations, channel management can pinpoint areas for improvement. Perhaps labor practices (e.g., workforce quality, job enrichment and restructuring, employee turnover) can be enhanced. Maybe management practices (e.g., organizational structure, labor relations, administrative procedures) should be revamped. Perhaps the type of capital, as well as the amount and timing of its usage, should be altered.

Consider the hypothetical case of Dealin' Dan's Autorama (Table 12-4).[18] Part A of Table 12-4 shows three important streams of data for a 13-year span: labor-hours used, capital employed, and output produced. Labor-hours reflect the amount of time management and workers have actually put into their jobs. Note that the number of labor-hours takes account of vacation time, reduced work-weeks, and the greater use of part-time personnel. Capital employed reflects the money resources employed by the firm: among other things, land, buildings, and, most importantly for distributive institutions, inventories. To control for inflation, all capital input figures are adjusted to base period values. The level of output is measured in terms of the number of automobiles sold; however, ideally, this measure should be adjusted for the size of automobile and the range of accessories sold per car.[19] To compare the labor and capital inputs and the sales output across the period, index numbers with 1974 as the base year were created. The productivity indexes were then computed as the ratio of the output index to the relevant input index.

Part B of Table 12-4 shows the sales and major expense information for Dealin' Dan's Autorama for the same 13-year period. Note that the profits for 1986 are lower than those for 1976, 1980, and 1982. Dealin' Dan might well believe that his manufacturer's channel policies are creating undue competitive pressure on him. As we saw in Chapter 11, he might reasonably be expected to complain to his factory rep the first chance he got.

A review of the productivity indices, however, offers Dealin' Dan an alternative explanation. Labor productivity, while growing at an average rate of more than 3 percent per year, has been relatively flat since 1980. Moreover, capital productivity growth has averaged only slightly better than 1 percent annually over the 13-year period, and *has actually declined* since 1980. The conclusion is that over the entire period—and especially since 1980—labor productivity gains have been heavily dependent on increased use of capital. Dealin' Dan appears, therefore, to have developed little real technological improvement since at least 1976, and perhaps earlier.

By keeping productivity records, Dealin' Dan has accumulated evidence

[18] The Dealin' Dan example is adapted from ibid., pp. 6–8.

[19] For an exposition of this adjustment procedure, see Brian T. Ratchford, "A Simple Technique for Measuring Differences in Product Quality," in Thomas V. Greer (ed.), *1973 Combined Proceedings* (Chicago: American Marketing Association, 1974), pp. 356–359.

TABLE 12-4 Productivity and Profitability Measures for Dealin' Dan's Autorama

(A) Productivity Measures

	Labor Input		Capital Input		Sales Output		Productivity Indexes	
Year	Hours	Index	($000)	Index	Units	Index	Labor	Capital
1974	10000	1.00	200	1.00	500	1.00	1.00	1.00
1976	12400	1.24	250	1.25	800	1.60	1.29	1.28
1978	10500	1.05	255	1.28	425	0.85	0.81	0.67
1980	13500	1.35	280	1.40	950	1.90	1.41	1.36
1982	14000	1.40	320	1.60	975	1.95	1.39	1.22
1984	12500	1.25	323	1.62	825	1.65	1.32	1.02
1986	14000	1.40	355	1.78	1050	2.10	1.50	1.18

(B) Profitability and Expense Data

Year	Sales ($000)	Gross Margin ($000)	Gross Margin (% Sales)	Labor Costs ($000)	Interest Expense ($000)	Other Expenses ($000)	Profits ($000)	Profits (% Sales)
1974	750.0	105.0	14.0	40.0	5.0	40.0	20.0	2.7
1976	1280.0	181.8	14.2	52.3	7.0	70.8	51.7	4.0
1978	743.8	81.8	11.0	50.4	8.0	54.8	−31.4	−4.2
1980	1682.5	222.0	13.2	75.6	12.0	74.5	59.9	3.6
1982	1974.4	256.7	13.0	95.2	15.0	91.4	55.1	2.8
1984	1980.0	207.9	10.5	97.6	17.0	92.4	0.9	.0
1986	2625.0	354.4	13.5	134.4	20.0	155.0	45.0	1.7

Source: Adapted from Louis P. Bucklin, "Research in Productivity Measurement for Marketing Decisions," in Jagdish N. Sheth (ed.), *Research in Marketing*, Vol. 1 (Greenwich, Conn.: JAI Press, 1978), p. 7.

that the efficiency with which he has used his resources to produce higher sales has changed very little during the 13 years of operations. At the same time, however, he has added substantial quantities of new capital. Dealin' Dan would be wise to study current developments in dealerships to update his technology so that his productivity and profitability can both increase.

Providing Standards for Motivating and Rewarding Marketing Channel Personnel. Productivity information may be used to measure the performance of marketing channel personnel in a variety of ways. For example, store managers can be evaluated on the basis of the productivity of their retail outlets as measured by sales per square foot or sales per labor-hour. Moreover, such productivity-based measures as sales calls per day, orders per sales call, and dollar or unit sales per order can be used to evaluate the performance of a channel institution's sales force.[20]

To the extent that these productivity measures are related to the marketing organization's goals or the goals of the overall channel, they can be used to motivate and reward marketing channel personnel. Store managers' base compensation and/or bonuses can readily be tied to improving or maintaining their stores' productivity performance, for example.

[20] See Eugene M. Johnson, David L. Kurtz, and Eberhard E. Scheuing, *Sales Management: Concepts, Practices, and Cases* (New York: McGraw-Hill, 1986), pp. 441–443.

Forecasting Future Labor and Capital Needs. A strong advantage of tracking historical productivity within a channel organization, or within the channel as a whole, is that such information can be used to forecast future resource needs. Consider how DeWitt Food Wholesalers, Inc., has used such information to forecast its labor needs over the next five years.

DeWitt Food Wholesalers, Inc., has experienced a steady increase in labor productivity of 3 percent annually over the past few years. All indications are that this trend will continue for the next seven to ten years. DeWitt has also projected that its sales output will increase 8 percent annually over the next five years. To achieve this rate of sales growth, given the trend in labor productivity, DeWitt determined that it should increase its labor input by about 270 percent annually over the next five years.

Similarly, if a channel member anticipates that its suppliers will raise their prices, historical productivity information can be used to pinpoint areas where productivity increases are necessary. Productivity increases in these areas will enable the firm to avoid raising its prices to its customers dramatically.

Determining Marketing Channel Structure. Adapting marketing channel structure and developing new marketing institutions are two ways in which channel managers can improve channel productivity. Productivity improvements in the commercial channel occur as the distribution chain bypasses inefficient channel members and shifts certain marketing functions to the target market. One new marketing institution that enabled channel productivity to increase by adapting marketing channel structure and by shifting marketing functions to the buyer is wholesale price clubs (see Exhibit 12-2).

Just as the productivity of the commercial channel affects channel structure, so does the productivity of the total channel (including the buyer) influence channel structure.[21] As noted in Chapters 3 and 8, the extent to which new channel institutions and structures evolve depends upon a host of other factors. Among them are the productivity of the individual marketing organizations, the productivity of the target market, gross margins available at each level of the channel, and the prices of labor, capital, and other input resources.

As is readily apparent from the Dealin' Dan example of Table 12-4, productivity (for both the individual channel member and the channel system) is closely related to profitability. The next section discusses profitability, the final dimension of marketing channel performance.

[21] For a further elaboration of the linkage between functional shifting and productivity in retailing, see Charles A. Ingene, "Productivity and Functional Shifting in Spatial Retailing: Private and Social Perspectives," *Journal of Retailing*, Vol. 60 (Fall 1984), pp. 15–36.

EXHIBIT 12-2

Warehouse Clubs:
High Performance Through Shifting
Marketing Channel Functions

"The[se] stores are drafty when the weather is cold and stuffy when it is hot. Customers have to find dollies and grappling hooks and then wrestle refrigerators, desks, and other heavy items to the checkout line themselves. There are no home deliveries. Credit cards are not accepted, and shoppers even pay a membership fee for the privilege of spending their money. But no one seems to mind."[a]

The primary market for the stores described above—warehouse clubs—is small business owners who, because of their size, cannot easily buy from wholesalers. A secondary target are consumers, specifically those with a history of paying their bills such as credit union members and government employees.

If the assortments are limited and service is minimal, what explains the growing success of these retail outlets? "These huge stores offer rock-bottom prices on everything from dishwashers and stoves to canned goods and TV dinners. These cash-and-carry clubs are open to members only, offer no amenities, and do little advertising, but they typically sell merchandise at 20% to 40% below supermarket and discount-store prices."[b]

In addition to shifting more of the marketing channel functions onto their customers, warehouse clubs are able to offer such low prices because of their tremendous efficiency. For example, their inventory turnover is several times greater than other retailers. This high turnover enables warehouse clubs to sell their merchandise before they have to pay for it. In addition, store buyers concentrate their purchases with those suppliers offering substantial deals on their products.

[a] "Boom Times in a Bargain-Hunter's Paradise," *Business Week*, (March 11, 1985), p. 116.
[b] ibid.

CHANNEL SYSTEM PROFITABILITY

Just as productivity within the marketing channel can be viewed in many different ways, so can profitability. In the following sections, we present several different techniques for evaluating marketing channel profitability: (1) distribution cost analysis, (2) the strategic profit model associated financial ratios, and (3) direct product profit. Each of these techniques views profitability from a slightly different perspective.

Distribution Cost Analysis

Distribution cost analysis is a tool that can help channel members determine the profitability of the channels in which they currently participate. It can also suggest whether alterations and modifications in those channels are needed. Generally, a distribution cost analysis is undertaken by a manufacturer or the original supplier of a particular good or service. The reason is that these channel members tend to have the greatest vested interest in the performance of that good or service throughout the whole channel. The benefits of this analysis can be far-reaching, as the following examples illustrate.

One manufacturer allocated marketing costs to four existing channels of distribution. On the basis of the results, an entire channel was eliminated and a number of small customers in another channel were discontinued. In addition, marketing efforts were increased on the remaining profitable channels. In one year, net profits doubled from approximately $150,000 to $300,000.

Another manufacturer found through a distribution cost analysis that two-thirds of all customers sold direct were responsible for losses ranging from 26 to 86 percent of sales. By transferring unprofitable small accounts to wholesalers, the company has achieved a 40 to 50 percent net reduction in marketing costs and a 25 percent increase in the percentage of net profits.[22]

Thus, there appears to be considerable opportunity to reduce costs and increase profits through analyses of relative costs by channels.

A distribution cost analysis involves three major steps. First, the accounting data typically available to a firm on its profit and loss statement must be reorganized and reclassified into marketing function or flow categories.[23] Second, the functional costs must be allocated to each of the marketing channels used by the firm. Finally, a profit and loss statement for each channel must be prepared. Following the distribution cost analysis and any additional analysis, decisions about modifying the channel can be made.

To see how a distribution cost analysis works, consider the case of Harrison Manufacturing company, a hypothetical producer of plastic towel racks, dish drains, soap dishes, and other kitchen and bathroom accessories. Harrison's overall profit and loss statement appears in Table 12-5. Assume that the expenses listed in the table are limited to those associated with the marketing flows of physical possession (storage and delivery), promotion (personal selling, advertising, sales promotion, and publicity), and ordering and payment (billing and collecting).

---

[22] These examples were drawn from Charles H. Sevin, *How Manufacturers Reduce Their Distribution Costs*, Economic Series No. 72, U.S. Department of Commerce (Washington, D.C.: U.S. Government Printing Office, 1948), p. 4.

[23] The discussion of distribution cost analysis here is based largely on Martin Zober, *Marketing Management* (New York: John Wiley & Sons, 1964), pp. 241–267; and Philip Kotler, *Marketing Management: Analysis, Planning, and Control*, 5th ed. (Englewood Cliffs, N.J. Prentice-Hall, 1984), pp. 754–759.

Sales		$35,000
Cost of goods sold		20,000
Gross margin		15,000
Expenses		
Salaries	$ 3,000	
Advertising	2,500	
Trucking	500	
Rent	3,500	
Insurance	1,400	
Supplies	1,000	
	11,900	
Net profit		$ 3,100

Deriving Functional Costs. The first step in distribution cost analysis is to show how each of the natural expense items shown in Table 12-5 was incurred through Harrison's participation in each of the flows. A hypothetical breakdown is presented in Table 12-6. For example, most of the salaries went to salespeople and the rest went to an advertising manager, a sales promotion manager, a traffic manager, and an accountant, along with various support personnel in each area.

The simplistic example used belies the difficulty involved in splitting natural expenses into functional cost groups. Generally, careful study is required, along with considerable research, before the costs can be allocated equitably. Also, it has been assumed that all of the natural expenses listed in Table 12-5 were directly allocable into functional (flow) groupings. Clearly, this is an oversimplification because many of the expenses incurred by a firm do not relate directly to the performance of marketing functions.

Allocating Functional Costs to Marketing Channels. The second step in distribution cost analysis is to determine how much of each activity has gone into serving the various channels used by the firm. This step calls for allocating the

TABLE 12-6 Functional (Flow) Expense Breakdown (in thousands of dollars)

Natural Expenses	Total	Physical Possession		Promotion			Ordering and Payment
		Storage	Delivery	Personal Selling	Advertising	Sales Promotion	Billing and Collecting
Salaries	$ 3,000	$ 150	$ 100	$2,000	$ 500	$ 200	$ 50
Advertising	2,500				1,500	1,000	
Trucking	500		500				
Rent	3,500	2,500	50	500	200	100	150
Insurance	1,400	1,000	350				50
Supplies	1,000		500	100	150	150	100
Total	$11,900	$3,650	$1,500	$2,600	$2,350	$1,450	$350

TABLE 12-7 Allocating Functional Group Costs to Marketing Channels

Function (Flow) Group	Physical Possession		Promotion			Ordering and Payment
	Storage	Delivery	Personal Selling	Advertising	Sales Promotion	Billing and Collecting
Allocation Bases	Floor Space Occupied in Own Warehouse (000 cu ft)	Number of Shipping Units (000 cases)	Number of Sales Calls (000)	Cost of Advertising Space (000)	Cost of Promotions (000)	Number of Orders (000)
Channel Types						
Department stores	200	500	5	$ 150	$ 100	1
Discount houses	450	1000	20	700	400	5
Supermarket chains	350	800	30	650	500	4
Total	1000	2300	55	$1500	$1000	10
Functional group Cost (000)	$3650	$1500	$2600	$2350	$1450	$350
Number of units	1000	2300	55	$1500	1000	10
Average cost	$ 3.65	$ .65	$ 47	1.57×	1.45×	$ 35

various costs associated with each functional (flow) category to each channel. Assume that Harrison Manufacturing Company sells directly to department stores, discount stores, and supermarket chains. The results of allocating functional costs to each of these three channels appear in Table 12-7. Thus, it costs Harrison $3.65 per cubic foot of warehouse space to store the merchandise it markets, $.65 to deliver each case of its merchandise to its retail customers, $47.00 for every sales call made to each of the stores in the various retail chains, and $35.00 for billing and collecting per order. The advertising and sales promotion figures (1.57X and 1.45X, respectively) are multipliers that must be applied to each advertising and sales promotion dollar expended by Harrison in each channel. Note that each multiplier also included the cost of the support (e.g., personnel, rent, and supplies) that has been allotted to each of these functional areas.

Developing P&L Statements for Each Channel. The third and final step in distribution cost analysis is the preparation of a profit and loss statement for each channel. In Table 12-8, cost of goods sold has been allocated to each channel in proportion to the revenues that the channel delivers to Harrison. The expense figures are derived from the information in Table 12-7. Clearly, Harrison's distribution cost analysis indicates that all channels are returning a net profit;[24] however, the return from serving supermarket chains is very low relative to the return from the other two channels. In addition, the return from the

[24] Actually, the net profit figures of Table 12-8 represent contributions to profit, since not all cost figures (e.g., interest, corporate overhead) have been included in this hypothetical example.

TABLE 12-8 Profit and Loss Statement for Harrison's Channels (in thousands of dollars)

	Department Stores	Discount Houses	Supermarket Chains	Total
Sales	$7,500	$15,500	$12,000	$35,000
Cost of goods sold	4,400	8,800	6,800	20,000
Gross margin	3,100	6,700	5,200	15,000
Expenses				
Storage ($3.65 per cu ft)	$ 730	$ 1,643	$ 1,277	$ 3,650
Delivery ($0.65 per case)	325	650	525	1,500
Personal selling ($47 per call)	245	940	1,414	2,600
Advertising (1.57 x)	235	1,095	1,020	2,350
Sales promotion (1.45 x)	145	580	725	1,450
Billing and collecting ($35 per order)	35	175	140	350
Total expenses	$1,715	$ 5,083	$ 5,102	$11,900
Net profit (or loss)	$1,385	$ 1,617	$ 98	$ 3,100
Profit-to-sales ratio	18.5%	10.4%	0.8%	8.9%

department store channel is surprisingly high. Thus, Harrison might consider increasing its business to department stores and/or deemphasizing sales to supermarket chains.

The results of a distribution cost analysis *do not by themselves* provide enough information to change marketing channel structure. Rather, before any such decisions are made, management must answer the following kinds of questions:[25]

- To what extent do buyers buy on the basis of the type of retail outlet versus the brand? Would they seek out the brand in those channels that are to be emphasized?
- What are the trends with respect to the importance of these three channels?
- Have company marketing strategies directed at the three channels been optimal?

In isolation, a distribution cost analysis can only indicate symptoms. Additional analysis might be needed to uncover the true problems facing a marketing channel. For example, a product line analysis might uncover an interaction between the type of channel and product profitability. Moreover, an understanding of channel members' perceptions of marketing programs can shed additional light on any channel problems that may be occurring. Some additional procedures for evaluating channel profitability, which will be discussed in the next sections, can also be useful for illuminating problems within marketing channels.

The effects of modifying marketing channel structure on other aspects of the organization must also be considered. For example, eliminating the supermarket channel will most likely lead to a drop in demand. With declining demand, there

[25] Kotler, *Marketing Management*, p. 757.

are fewer units against which fixed costs can be allocated; moreover, production economies may be lost. As a result, production costs per unit will increase. The temptation may be to increase prices in order to preserve unit profits, but increases should not be undertaken unless sales forecasts show they will not lead to a further decline in sales volume.

Aside from the decision-making dilemma, considerable controversy surrounds the allocation methods used in distribution cost analysis.[26] This controversy involves whether to allocate all costs or only direct or traceable costs. In our example, we followed the latter approach by allocating only those costs that are directly traceable to each marketing channel. Thus, the net profit figures reported in Table 12-8 are more correctly termed *contribution-to-profit* figures. This allocation procedure is reasonable for marketing channel problems since allocating indirect, nontraceable costs, which are common to alternate channels (e.g., general management salaries, taxes, interest, and other types of overhead), is extremely difficult.

Distribution cost analysis for the most part deals with profitability in terms of sales revenues and costs. Although these are important facets of a marketing channel's or a channel member's profitability, they are by no means the only ones. Other aspects of profitability are (1) return on investment, (2) liquidity or the ability of the firm to meet its financial liabilities, (3) capital structure or leverage ratio, (4) growth pattern of sales and profits, and (5) growth potential of sales and profits.[27] Managers can evaluate nearly all of these additional aspects of channel profitability by using the strategic profit model.

Strategic Profit Model

The strategic profit model (see Figure 12-4) explores the interrelationship among various financial ratios. The key components of the strategic profit model are briefly discussed below.

Net Profits/Net Sales (Net Profit Margin). This ratio indicates management's ability to recover its costs—including the cost of merchandise or services, the expenses of operating the business (including depreciation), and the cost of borrowed funds—from sales revenues generated during a given time period. The ratio also points out management's ability to compensate the owners for providing their capital at a risk. In short, net profit margin essentially expresses the cost/price effectiveness of a business.

Although the net profit margin demonstrates how well the firm is performing, given a particular level of sales, it does not show how well the firm is using its resources. For this reason, the net profits/net sales ratio should also be considered in connection with the turnover of inventory and accounts receivable. Rapid turnover of inventory and receivables may be a result of reduced sales prices and

[26] John J. Wheatley, "The Allocation Controversy in Marketing Cost Analysis," in Stanley J. Shapiro and V. H. Kirpalani (eds.), *Marketing Effectiveness: Insights from Accounting and Finance*, (Boston: Allyn and Bacon, 1984), pp. 34–43.

[27] Robert F. Lusch and James M. Kenderdine, "Financial and Strategic Trends of Chain Store Retailers: 1974–1975," *Review of Regional Economics and Business*, April 1977, pp. 11–17.

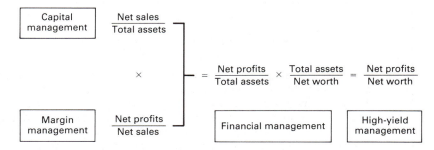

Figure 12-4 The straight profit model (SPM). *Source*: Bert C. McCammon, Jr., "Perspective for Distribution Programming," in Louis P. Bucklin (ed.), *Vertical Marketing Systems*. ©1970 by Scott, Foresman and Company. Reprinted by permission of the publisher.

relatively high rates of cash discounts. Unless costs are reduced in such situations, the smaller sales income will result in lower net profit. A low net profit may also be the result of excessive selling and general administrative expenses.

Net Sales/Total Assets (Asset Turnover). The ratio of net sales to total assets is a measure of how well management is using its capital and may show whether the firm has overinvested in assets. This applies especially to inventory and receivables in the case of wholesalers and retailers. The ratio, sometimes referred to as the *turnover ratio*, roughly indicates the size of asset commitment required to generate a given level of sales. Conversely, the turnover ratio shows the approximate sales that can be generated for each dollar of investment.

Net Profits/Total Assets (Return on Assets). Neither the net profit margin (i.e., net profits/net sales) nor the turnover ratio (i.e., net sales/total assets) by itself is an adequate measure of operating efficiency. The net profit margin ignores the efficiency with which assets are used, whereas the turnover ratio ignores the profitability of sales. The return on assets (ROA) ratio resolves these shortcomings. A firm can improve its ROA if it can increase the turnover on existing assets, profit margin, or both.

If Wholesaler A has an asset turnover of 4.0 times and a net profit margin of 3 percent, its return on assets is 12 percent. Wholesaler B also earns a 12 percent return on assets while realizing an 8 percent net profit margin on an asset turnover of 1.5 times. Thus, the two firms use two different operating styles to arrive at the same return on assets. Wholesaler A has followed a relatively lower-margin, higher-turnover strategy, while Wholesaler B has taken the relatively higher-margin, lower-turnover course.

Total Assets/Net Worth (Leverage Ratio). This ratio indicates how much a firm relies upon borrowed funds for both short- and long-term purposes. The

EXHIBIT 12-3
W. W. Grainger, Inc.: An Illustration of the Strategic Profit Model

W. W. Grainger, Inc., based in Skokie, Illinois, is a nationwide distributor of electric motors, fans, blowers, air compressors, pumps, and other products. It purchases more than 12,500 products from some 700 manufacturers and distributes them through a network of nearly 200 branches located throughout the United States. These products are marketed to other distributors, dealers, contractors, service shops, industrial and commercial maintenance departments, and original equipment manufacturers. More than 60 percent of the items it distributes carry Grainger's private labels, which are well-known and well-respected by its target markets.

Grainger's strategic profit model ratios were calculated from its financial statements for 1984 and 1985. Comparisons were then made between the two years and with averages reported for the industry (viz., SIC 5063—electrical apparatus and equipment wholesalers).

SPM Ratio	W. W. Grainger 1985	W. W. Grainger 1984	1985 Key Business Ratios Upper Quartile	Median	Lower Quartile	Mean
Profit margin	0.062	0.065	0.07	0.03	0.01	0.04
Net sales/total assets	1.521	1.619	3.70	2.78	1.92	2.63
ROA	0.094	0.105	0.12	0.06	0.03	0.11
Total assets/net worth	1.386	1.409	1.40	1.97	3.13	2.07
ROI	0.131	0.148	0.28	0.14	0.07	0.24

Compared to 1984, Grainger's ROI dipped slightly because of small declines in each of the SPM ratios between 1984 and 1985.

When compared to the industry, Grainger appears to follow a high-price, low-turnover strategy. Its profit margins fall into the upper quartile of the 2,435 establishments used in calculating the industry ratios. On the other hand, its asset turnover is in the lower quartile of these wholesalers. Grainger's orientation is undoubtedly one of emphasizing a high degree of service rather than price to its target markets.

Grainger's leverage ratio is in the upper quartile of the reporting electrical apparatus and equipment wholesalers. This means that Grainger is relatively more equity financed than its competitors are, on average. With an ROI of about 13 percent, Grainger falls in the median return on investment profitability category.

As is obvious from the industry ratios, electrical equipment wholesalers can and do follow a variety of marketing strategies to achieve moderate to high return on investment. Grainger's strategic choices are merely illustrative of these strategies.

Source: W. W. Grainger, Inc., *1984 Annual Report and Form 10-K*; *Standard & Poor's NYSE Stock Reports*, Vol. 53 (June 18, 1986), p. 1039; *Industry Norms and Key Business Ratios* (Murray Hill, N.J.: Dun & Bradstreet, 1985), p. 130.

lower the ratio, the more the firm is financially supported by owners' equity as opposed to debt capital. A low ratio indicates a high degree of solvency as well as management's desire to rely on ownership or equity capital for financing the organization. In addition, it points out that management is probably highly conservative and risk-averse. On the other hand, management has more control over paying returns on invested capital in this situation, since dividends are paid at the discretion of the directors and capital does not have to be repaid.

In general, equity capital is more costly than debt capital. If the firm retains an excessive amount of ownership capital relative to debt capital, it may be forgoing opportunities to trade on its equity (i.e., *leveraging* its equity). Leveraging occurs when capital is borrowed at relatively low interest rates and is invested to earn greater rates of return. Consequently, aggressive management often relies heavily on debt capital.

Net Profits/Net Worth (Return on Investment). The main interest of the owners of an enterprise will be the returns that management achieves on their behalf. An effective measure of the return on owners' investment (ROI) is the relationship of net profit to net worth, sometimes called *owners' equity, shareholders' equity*, or *paid-in capital*. A low ROI ratio may indicate that the business is not very successful because of (1) inefficient and ineffective production, distribution, financial, or general management; (2) unfavorable general business conditions; or (3) overinvestment in assets. A high ROI may be the result of efficient management throughout the company, favorable business conditions, or effective leveraging (i.e., trading on the company's equity).

The strategic profit model has four important managerial purposes:

1. The model specifies that a firm's principal financial objective is to earn an adequate or target rate of return on net worth.
2. The model identifies the three "profit paths" available to an enterprise. That is, a firm with an inadequate return on investment can improve its performance by increasing its asset turnover, boosting its profit margin, or leveraging its operations more highly.
3. The model dramatizes the principal areas of decision making within the firm, namely, capital management, margin management, and financial management. Furthermore, firms interrelating their capital, margin, and financial plans are engaging in high-yield management.
4. The model provides a useful perspective for appraising the financial strategies used by different organizations to achieve target rates of return on net worth.[28]

How the strategic profit model might be used to evaluate the performance of a marketing channel firm is illustrated in Exhibit 12-3.

As noted above, analyzing the strategic profit model ratios assists managers in understanding the key determinants of their organization's profitability. It is

[28] Bert C. McCammon, Jr., "Perspectives for Distribution in Programming," in Louis P. Bucklin (ed.), *Vertical Marketing Systems*, (Glenview, IL: Scott, Foresman, 1970), p. 38.

EXHIBIT 12-4
Correlates of Profit Performance in Retailing

A limited amount of research has identified several factors that are associated with high levels of profit performance in retailing. In these studies, profitability has been defined as return on assets.

For drugstores and variety stores, higher levels of inventory turnover were associated with higher returns on assets. In addition, economies of scale in some lines of trade enabled those retailers to realize higher ROAs. Higher returns on assets were found for furniture stores and supermarkets that more productively utilized their store space, as measured by sales per square foot.[a]

Retail supermarket chains that earned returns on assets also experienced:

- higher market shares
- higher sales growth rates
- higher liquidity (i.e., a higher ratio of current assets to current liabilities),
- lower sales per square foot.[b]

[a]Bert C. McCammon, Jr. and Albert D. Bates, "Reseller Strategies and the Financial Performance of the Firm," in *Strategy + Structure = Performance*, Hans B. Thorelli (ed.), (Bloomington, IN: Indiana University Press, 1977), pp. 151–153.
[b]J. Joseph Cronin, Jr. and Stephen J. Skinner, "Marketing Outcomes, Financial Conditions, and Retail Profit Performance," *Journal of Retailing*, 60 (Winter 1984), 9–22.

---

also important for channel managers to grasp other factors that can enhance the profitability of their organizations and that of the channel as a whole. Exhibit 12-4 describes some of those other factors that researchers have found to affect profitability in retailing.

The strategic profit model has spawned a couple of other ratios retailers can use to evaluate the profitability of their operations. These are gross margin return on inventory and gross margin return on selling space.

Gross Margin Return on Inventory (GMROI).[29] This ratio allows retailers to evaluate how well their investments in merchandise inventory produce gross profits. The two key components of GMROI are the gross margin ratio[30] and the inventory turnover rate (see Figure 12-5A). As with the strategic profit model, the gross margin ratio indicates the ability of sales revenue to cover the costs of doing business. The ability of retailers to produce sales revenue from their investment in inventory is the inventory turnover ratio; note that this ratio is analogous to the asset turnover ratio of the strategic profit model.

[29] For further discussion, see Daniel J. Sweeney, "Improving the Profitability of Retail Merchandising Decisions," *Journal of Marketing*, Vol. 37 (January 1973), pp. 60–68.

[30] See Chapter 6 for precisely what is meant by gross margin.

A. Gross Margin Return on Inventory (GMROI)

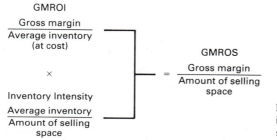

$$\underset{\substack{\text{Gross margin}}}{\underbrace{\dfrac{\text{Gross Margin}}{\text{Net sales}}}} \times \underset{\substack{\text{Inventory Turnover}}}{\underbrace{\dfrac{\text{Net sales}}{\substack{\text{Average inventory}\\ \text{(at cost)}}}}} = \underset{\substack{\text{GMROI}}}{\underbrace{\dfrac{\text{Gross margin}}{\substack{\text{Average inventory}\\ \text{(at cost)}}}}}$$

B. Gross Margin Return on Selling Space (GMROS)

GMROI
$$\dfrac{\text{Gross margin}}{\substack{\text{Average inventory}\\ \text{(at cost)}}}$$

×

Inventory Intensity
$$\dfrac{\text{Average inventory}}{\substack{\text{Amount of selling}\\ \text{space}}}$$

GMROS
$$= \dfrac{\text{Gross margin}}{\substack{\text{Amount of selling}\\ \text{space}}}$$

Figure 12-5 Gross margin return on inventory (GMROI) and on selling space (GMROS).

All too often retailers equate high gross margins with high net profits and, accordingly, high returns on investments with high gross margins. GMROI shows that this is not necessarily the case; high inventory turnover with low profit margins can also generate high net profits, as the following example illustrates:[31]

Item	Gross Margin	×	Inventory Turnover	=	GMROI
A	50%		3		150%
B	30%		5		150%
C	25%		6		150%

For many product categories, price competition precludes raising gross margin. By improving inventory turnover in such instances, the returns on inventory investment can be boosted. On the other hand, a retailer might "knowingly lower its gross margin in an effort to produce a higher sales to inventory ratio and a higher GMROI."[32]

A critical weakness of the GMROI ratio is that it overlooks how profitably retailers utilize another of their scarce resources—selling space.[33] To overcome this difficulty, another ratio has been developed—gross margin return on selling space.

Gross Margin Return on Selling Space (GMROS).   As can be seen from Figure 12-5B, GMROS is also the product of two component ratios, in this case, GMROI and inventory intensity. GMROS enables retailers to evaluate both the return on

[31] From Albert D. Bates, *Retailing and Its Environment* (New York: D. Van Nostrand Company, 1979), p. 155.

[32] Ibid., p. 156.

[33] Robert F. Lusch, "Two Critical Determinants of Retail Profitability and Productivity," *Zale Retailing Issues Letter*, Vol. 2 (April 1986), p. 1.

their merchandise inventory investment and how intensively retail space is used to carry that inventory. As the following example illustrates, a merchandise item can overcome a lower GMROI with a higher inventory intensity:

Item	GMROI	×	Inventory Intensity	=	GMROS
A	180%		$20		$36
B	150%		$24		$36

Measures such as GMROI and GMROS are used for several reasons. First, they are helpful in deciding which merchandise items to add or delete. Second, their underlying components indicate what merchandising strategies might be used to improve the profitability of selected merchandise lines. Finally, retailers who use such profitability measures can pressure their suppliers to perform more of the marketing functions.

There are several channel services that retailers who use more sophisticated methods of evaluating their profitability can extract from their suppliers. First, they can demand adequate margins. Second, they can often force suppliers to promote their items extensively to generate the unit sales volume required to achieve high levels of inventory turnover. Third, these retailers can push their suppliers to improve their delivery times, thus reducing the need for shelf space and inventory investment. Finally, they can also press their suppliers to increase the amount of inventory per square foot of selling space that can be carried at any one time. By obtaining such additional channel services, retailers can improve their profitability.

GMROI and GMROS suffer from two key weaknesses, however.[34] First, they focus on short-term as opposed to long-term profitability. Hence, retail managers who use these two ratios might choose investments that promise high short-run payoffs over investments that offer greater profit in the long run. The second weakness of these ratios is that they do not reflect the true financial investment in merchandise inventory. More specifically, investments in accounts receivable and funds borrowed via accounts payable should be included in computing inventory investment. In addition, the costs of carrying inventory (i.e., capital costs; space costs; costs of inventory obsolescence, damage, or pilferage; insurance costs; and taxes) are not included in the components of GMROI or GMROS. Obviously, these ratios should reflect this important facet of merchandise inventory investment.

Despite these weaknesses, GMROI and, to a lesser extent, GMROS are still widely used to measure the profit performance of retail establishments. Another concept—direct product profit—is becoming an important tool for evaluating product performance in retailing, particularly in the supermarket industry.

[34] For a fuller discussion, see Michael Levy and Charles A. Ingene, "Residual Income Analysis: A Method of Inventory Investment Allocation and Evaluation," *Journal of Marketing*, Vol. 48 (Summer 1984), pp. 93–104.

Direct Product Profit

Direct product profit (DPP) is a method of evaluating the profitability of the products a channel member carries. From detailed accounting data, individual profit and loss statements are created for each product by:

- adjusting gross margin for each item to reflect deals, allowances, cash discounts, etc.
- identifying and measuring costs that are directly attributable to marketing that product (e.g., labor, space, inventory, transportation)[35] and deducting them from the adjusted gross margin.

DPP information provides retailers with a more accurate measure as to how much each individual product contributes to their overall profit than do traditional measures of performance such as gross margin, GMROI, and GMROS. DPP focuses only on direct costs associated with the operating or merchandising activities undertaken for each product; fixed expenses (e.g., indirect labor, headquarters overhead) are excluded. Thus, DPP strikes a practical balance between net profit, which is relatively meaningless for individual products, and gross profit which ignores discounts and allowances as well as direct operating costs.

DPP for two different dry grocery products are illustrated in Table 12-9. It shows that the "true" contributions of two different items can vary substantially. It also shows that gross margin can be a misleading indicator of actual performance.

> In fact, . . . products with a high gross margin may actually contribute less to the bottom line than those with a lower margin.[36]

By following one or more of the options listed in Table 12-10, manufacturers can improve the DPP of products such as Item B in Table 12-9.

Their slim earnings mandate that food distributors boost their productivity and lower their costs. DPP analysis can help distributors reduce their expenses by forcing them to learn in detail how much their warehouse and storage functions—receiving, moving to storage, paperwork, selecting, checking, loading, and space usage—actually do cost. For small items, shelving and checkout costs must be closely examined; for large items, conserving shelf space is a must.[37] Knowledge of DPP can be especially helpful in improving space management.

Although the concept was first developed in the early 1960s by McKinsey

---

[35] "Insight Report: Direct Product Profitability in Perspective," *Competitive Edge* (a publication of Willard Bishop Consulting Economists, Ltd.), Vol. 5 (September 1984), p. 1.

[36] *CPDA News* (December 1985–June 1986), pp. 14–15.

[37] *The Economics of Food Distributors*, McKinsey General Foods Study (New York: General Foods Corporation, 1963), pp. 37–38.

TABLE 12-9 Direct Product Profit for Two Different Dry Grocery Products

	Item A	Item B
Sales revenues	100.0%	100.0%
− Cost of goods	79.5	76.5
Gross margin	20.5	23.5
+ cash payment discounts	1.6	0.0
+ Deals/allowances	2.0	1.2
+ Forward-buy profits (net)	1.3	0.0
+ Back-haul revenues	0.8	0.0
Adjusted gross margin	26.2	24.7
Warehouse costs		
− Labor	1.1	1.6
− Space	1.0	1.2
Transportation costs		
− Labor/equipment	1.2	1.5
Store costs		
− Stocking labor	2.6	2.9
− Checkout labor	1.7	1.9
− Space (energy, occupancy)	2.2	2.7
Headquarters costs		
− Inventory carrying	0.7	0.4
Total direct product costs	10.5	12.2
Direct product profit	15.7	12.5
− Fixed costs (allocated)	10.5	10.5
Net profit	5.2	2.0

Source: "Insight Report: Direct Product Profitability in Perspective," *Competitive Edge* (a publication of Willard Bishop Consulting Economists, Ltd.), Vol. 5 (September 1984), p. 2.

TABLE 12-10 Manufacturers' Options to Improve the DPP of Their Items

- Consolidation of retail product sizes
- Streamlining package configurations
- Better utilization of case cube
- Back-haul (customer pick-up) programs
- Drop shipments to stores
- Product line reductions
- Case-pack modularity
- Consolidated shipping programs
- Customized "mixed" pallet ordering
- Smaller case packs for slow movers
- Prebuilt display modules

and Company for General Foods Corporation,[38] the explosion of computerization and modern-day scanning systems have made it a reality.[39] In fact, the Food Marketing Institute (FMI) has embraced the DPP concept and is coordinating

[38] Ibid.
[39] *CPDA News*, pp. 14–15.

industry efforts to develop a unified DPP model so that its use can be more widespread.[40] Three chief benefits of doing this are:[41]

1. Knowledge of DPP can help to identify high-cost products or activities that can be improved through manufacturer-distributor cooperation. Such activities include standardizing package and case sizes, designing product containers, and developing better delivery methods.

2. By supplementing market research information on product movements and shelf facings, distributors and manufacturers can use DPP data to develop store shelving plans, test store display methods and locations, and study the profitability of specific product categories.

3. Understanding DPP can materially affect a manufacturer's sales strategies and programs. By learning more about distributors' costs and how they behave, manufacturers should be able to shape their promotional activities to win greater acceptance by wholesalers and retailers.

OTHER MEASURES OF MARKETING CHANNEL PERFORMANCE

Up to this point, we have discussed four basic dimensions of marketing channel performance—effectiveness, equity, efficiency, and profitability. There are host of other variables that are meaningful in evaluating performance in distribution.

From a macro perspective, the innovativeness and adaptiveness of marketing channels and channel institutions are important facets of channel performance. This is particularly true with respect to changes in technology. The reason is that by adopting new technology, distributive channels and their member organizations can improve their productivity and profitability. In addition to innovativeness and adaptiveness, the effect of various distributive practices on energy consumption, unemployment rates, and the quality of the environment should be assessed.

From a micro perspective, an evaluation of the number of stockouts, obsolete inventories, damaged shipments, and markdowns over time, among other operating variables, will indicate specific ways to enhance profitability and productivity. Table 12-11 lists some of the quantitative measures of micro performance, while Table 12-12 lists some of the qualitative indicants of this aspect of marketing channel performance.

Unfortunately, aggregate measures for these macro and micro performance variables are generally unavailable or are restricted to narrow lines of trade. Therefore, channel managers must generally rely primarily on the kind of qualitative information (system output, cost, efficiency, profitability, and equity) described earlier in the chapter to judge the overall performance of the distributive trades.

Nonetheless, a landmark study by the Council of Logistics Management (formerly the National Council for Physical Distribution Management) provides comprehensive lists of productivity measures of physical distribution activities (e.g., transportation, warehousing, order processing, and inventory manage-

[40] *CPDA News*, p. 15.
[41] *The Economics of Food Distributors*, pp. 34–35.

TABLE 12-11 Quantitative Measures of Channel Performance

1. Total distribution cost per unit
2. Transportation cost per unit
3. Warehousing cost per unit
4. Production cost per unit
5. Costs associated with avoiding stockouts
6. Percent of stockout units
7. Percent of obsolete inventories
8. Percent of bad debts
9. Customer service level by product, by market segment
10. Accuracy of sales forecasts
11. Number of errors in order filling
12. Number of new markets entered
13. Percent sales volume in new markets entered
14. Percent of markdown volume
15. Number and percent of discontinued channel intermediaries (distribution turnover)
16. Number and percent of new distributors
17. Percent of damaged merchandise
18. Percent of astray shipments
19. Size of orders
20. Ability to keep up with new technology—data transmission
21. Percent of shipments—less than truckload (LTL) versus
                            truckload (TL)
                        —less than carload (LCL-used with rail
                            shipments) versus carload (CL)
22. Energy costs
23. Number of customer complaints

Source: Adel I. El-Ansary, "A Model for Evaluating Channel Performance," unpublished paper, Louisiana State University, 1975 pp. 10–11, reported in Douglas M. Lambert, *The Distribution Channel Decision* (New York: National Association of Accountants, 1978), p. 40.

ment).[42] Although this study does not actually analyze productivity in physical distribution, it does offer a framework for doing so, thus paving the way for future studies to undertake this task.[43]

AUDITING MARKETING CHANNEL PERFORMANCE

One approach to auditing the performance of the marketing channel system is the channel environment, structure, and policy audit.[44] The basic framework for conducting this audit appears in Figure 12-6. The basic assumption underlying this

[42] Kearney Management Consultants, *Measuring Productivity in Physical Distribution* (Chicago: National Council for Physical Distribution Management, 1978).

[43] The extent to which many of the proposed measures are utilized by a cross-section of channel members in a number of industries can be found in Douglas M. Lambert, *The Distribution Channel Decision* (New York: National Association of Accountants, 1978), pp. 82–86.

[44] Another method for auditing marketing channel performance is the matrix analysis of marketing flows developed in Louis W. Stern and Jay W. Brown, "Distribution Channels: A Social Systems Approach," in Louis W. Stern (ed.), *Distribution Channels: Behavioral Dimensions*, (Boston: Houghton Mifflin, 1969), pp. 8–12. For an application of matrix analysis to the pharmaceutical industry, see Mickey C. Smith, Kenneth B. Roberts, and Darego Maclayton, "The Pharmaceutical Industry I: Distribution Channels and Relationships," *M M & M Journal*, January 1976, pp. 32–34.

TABLE 12-12 Qualitative Measures of Channel Performance

1. Degree of channel coordination
2. Degree of cooperation
3. Degree of conflict
4. Degree of domain consensus (role prescription and variation)
5. Recognition of superordinate goals
6. Degree of development of channel leadership
7. Degree of functional duplication
8. Degree of commitment to channel
9. Degree of power locus development
10. Degree of flexibility in functional shiftability
11. Availability of information about:
    a. Physical inventory
    b. Product characteristics
    c. Pricing structure
    d. Promotional data
       i) personal selling assistance
       ii) advertising
       iii) point of purchase displays
       iv) special promotions
    e. Market conditions
    f. Services available
    g. Organizational changes
12. Assimilation of new technology
13. Innovation in distribution generated within the channel
14. Extent of intrabrand competition
15. Extent of routinization of channel tasks
16. Extent of use of optimal inventory standards
17. Relations with trade associations
18. Relations with consumer groups

Source: Adel I. El-Ansary, "A Model for Evaluating Channel Performance," unpublished paper, Louisiana State University, 1975, pp. 10–11, reported in Douglas M. Lambert, *The Distribution Channel Decision* (New York: National Association of Accountants, 1978), p. 41.

approach is that the performance of a channel system is contingent on several factors. First, as noted in Chapter 2, the market environment facing individual channel members has a definite impact on their performance. Second, the structure, behavior, and performance of marketing institutions within the channel influence the performance of individual channel members. Third, the marketing strategy adopted by the channel affects an individual channel member's performance. Finally, the performance of each channel member determines the performance of the marketing channel as a whole. Since these factors are all dynamic, a periodic audit of channel environment, structure, and policy is necessary to ensure that each channel member is performing the marketing flows and functions according to expectations.

SUMMARY

To manage marketing channels effectively, the performance of the individual channel institutions as well as that of the channel system itself must be evaluated. Channel evaluation is necessary to ensure that the channel is progressing toward

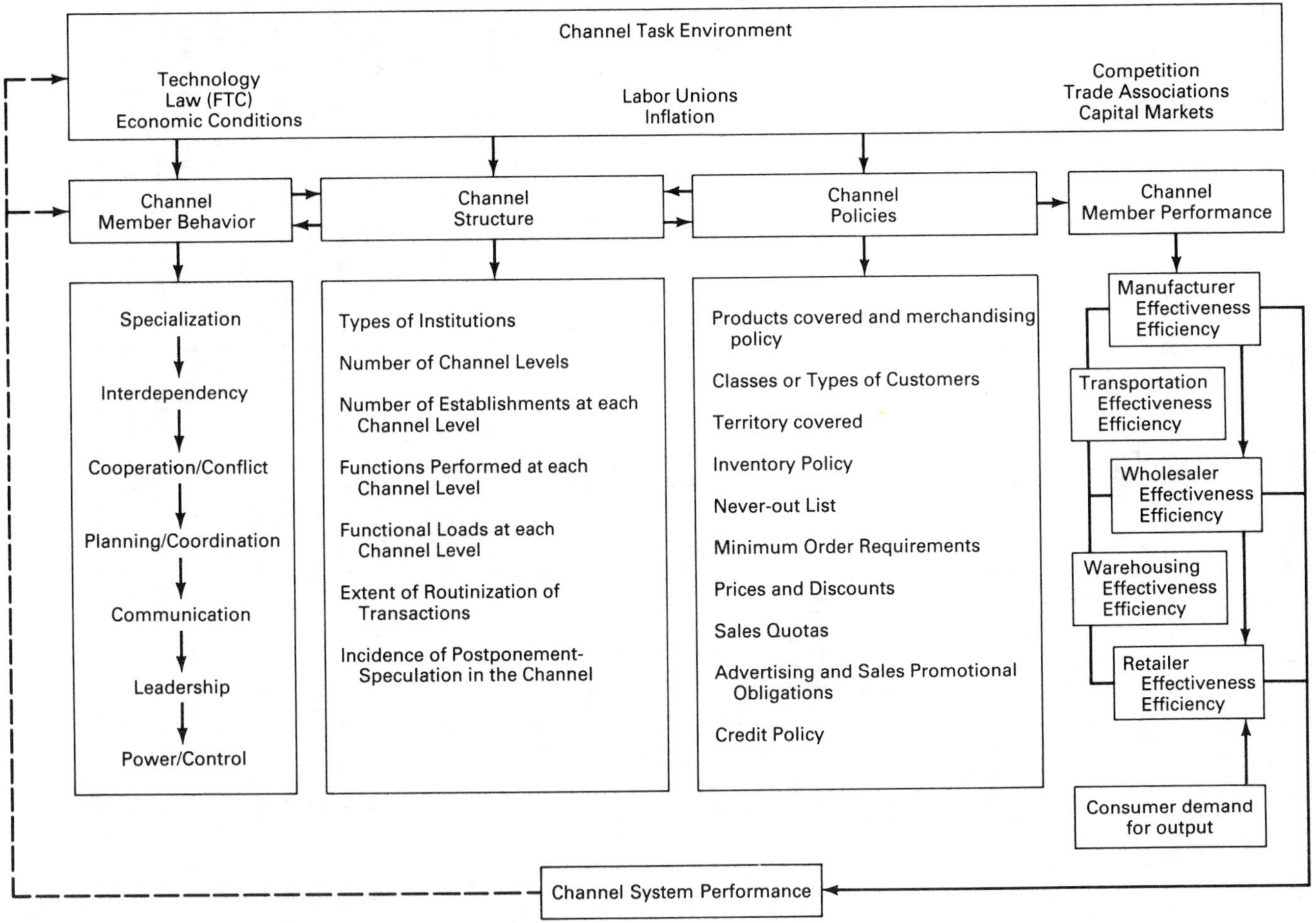
Channel Task Environment
Technology
Law (FTC)
Economic Conditions
Labor Unions
Inflation
Competition
Trade Associations
Capital Markets
Channel Member Behavior
Channel Structure
Channel Policies
Channel Member Performance
Specialization
Interdependency
Cooperation/Conflict
Planning/Coordination
Communication
Leadership
Power/Control
Types of Institutions
Number of Channel Levels
Number of Establishments at each Channel Level
Functions Performed at each Channel Level
Functional Loads at each Channel Level
Extent of Routinization of Transactions
Incidence of Postponement-Speculation in the Channel
Products covered and merchandising policy
Classes or Types of Customers
Territory covered
Inventory Policy
Never-out List
Minimum Order Requirements
Prices and Discounts
Sales Quotas
Advertising and Sales Promotional Obligations
Credit Policy
Manufacturer Effectiveness Efficiency
Transportation Effectiveness Efficiency
Wholesaler Effectiveness Efficiency
Warehousing Effectiveness Efficiency
Retailer Effectiveness Efficiency
Consumer demand for output
Channel System Performance

Figure 12-6 An environmental framework for channel system performance. *Source*: Adel I. El-Ansary, "Perspectives on Channel System Performance," in Robert F. Lusch and Paul H. Zinzer (eds.), *Contemporary Issues in Marketing Channels* (Norman, Okla.: The University of Oklahoma Printing Services, 1979), p. 51.

its goals and objectives, or, if not, to suggest alternative courses of action. This chapter discussed the four chief dimensions of evaluating marketing channel performance: channel effectiveness, equity, productivity, and profitability.

Channel effectiveness refers to how well the marketing institutions within the channel deliver the channel services desired by the target market. The importance of having timely market information to assess channel effectiveness adequately was underscored.

How well marketing institutions serve disadvantaged markets such as ghetto and rural markets is the essence of *channel system equity*. The inability of consumers within these markets to perform some of the marketing functions for themselves is one reason that marketing channel systems so often fail to equitably serve them. Another reason is that since channel members cannot perform many channel services for these markets economically, they tend not to perform them at all. Serving disadvantaged markets equitably remains a critical challenge for marketing channel systems.

Channel productivity refers to the efficiency with which the channel as a whole or individual channel members utilize their scarce resources in generating marketing channel services. Since distribution is so labor-intensive, the most commonly used indicator of channel productivity is sales per labor-hour. The productivity of marketing channel institutions has grown at a slower rate than the productivity of other sectors of the economy. Still, productivity growth is fairly high in certain lines of retail trade. Productivity in marketing channels can be affected by several factors, among them the channel environment, channel structure, and channel procedures and policies. Understanding the concept of distribution productivity enables marketing channels to be more effectively managed. For example, assessing channel productivity is important in (1) evaluating competitive positions, (2) developing ways of improving channel efficiency, (3) providing standards for motivating and rewarding marketing channel personnel, (4) forecasting future labor and capital needs, and (5) suggesting changes in marketing channel structure.

Channel profitability measures how effectively and efficiently channel management utilizes its financial resources. A variety of techniques useful in assessing channel member profitability as well as channel system profitability were presented. The first, distribution cost analysis, enables managers to assess the profitability of each marketing channel it uses. A second technique, the strategic profit model (SPM) and its variants, evaluates channel profitability from different perspectives. Specifically, the SPM and similar ratios examine profitability in terms of return on sales, return on assets, and return on investments. And third, direct product profit enables channel members to evaluate the revenues and costs associated with each individual item of merchandise. All three of these methods for evaluating channel profitability are used to assess individual channel members, specific marketing channel structures, and particular marketing programs within specific channel structures. These assessments should indicate any changes that need to be made within the marketing channel.

Several aspects of channel performance other than effectiveness, equity, efficiency, and profitability were also presented. Among these were a variety of quantitative and qualitative measures of performance.

Finally, the chapter offered a structure for auditing channel performance that outlines the key factors affecting the performance of individual marketing institutions as well as of the channel as a whole. Among these key factors are the channel environment, channel member behavior, channel structure, channel policies, and individual channel member performance. Only after its performance has been audited can channel managers be assured that the channel is operating effectively, equitably, efficiently, and profitably.

DISCUSSION QUESTIONS

1. Using the procedure outlined in Figure 12-2 and any other resources at your disposal (e.g., library, personal acquaintances in the industry), evaluate the effectiveness of the marketing channel systems for each of the following products:
   a. Agrichemicals
   b. Packaged foods
   c. Lubricating oils
   d. Amateur photography equipment
   e. Long-distance phone service
   f. Heavy construction equipment

2. As noted in the chapter, various market segments may be disadvantaged for economic reasons or for locational reasons. Select a disadvantaged market segment with which you are reasonably familiar. For each of the following products, discuss whether that market is being equitably served by the marketing channel system as a whole.
   a. Packaged foods
   b. Household appliances
   c. Medical services
   d. Mass transportation services
   e. Books and periodicals
   f. Telecommunication services

3. Susie's SuperSales and Jack's JustRite Foods, two supermarkets competing in the same geographic area, use different measures of productivity to evaluate the efficiency of their stores. Susie's uses dollar sales per employee and dollar sales per square foot, while Jack's uses transactions per employee and transactions per square foot. Which of these stores is more accurately measuring its productivity? Explain. Discuss some better ways for Susie's and Jack's to measure productivity.

4. For each of the following types of "retail stores," suggest ways in which marketing channel structure might be changed to improve productivity.
   a. Full-service restaurants
   b. Colleges and universities
   c. Building supply stores
   d. Automobile dealerships
   e. Movie theaters
   f. Supermarkets

5. Fragrant Floral Wholesalers wants to assess the productivity of its operations. Flora Fragrant, owner of the firm, doesn't know where to begin but believes that this an important managerial task. Outline a procedure for helping Ms. Fragrant assess the productivity of her company.

6. Select two wholesaling or retailing companies that directly compete with each other and whose stock is publicly traded. From their annual reports (or other sources available in most university business libraries), compute the strategic profit model ratios for the past two years.
   a. For each company, discuss the trends in the ratios over the two years.
   b. From the ratios, discuss the apparent differences in managerial strategies between the two companies.

c. Discuss how both companies' ratios compare with the industry average ratios. (These are also available in most university business libraries.)

7. Atlantic Seaboard Food Wholesalers, Inc., markets through three principal retail channels. First, Atlantic administers the well-known Prime Choice voluntary group of retail food stores. Many of the retailers operating under the Prime Choice banner do business at a single location only; Atlantic calls this group of retailers the *single stores group*. Other Prime Choice food retailers operate a number of stores in a given geographic market. This *multiple stores group* accounts for the largest portion of Atlantic's sales. Atlantic's final group of retailer customers, the *independents*, does not do business under the Prime Choice banner. Rather, these retailers operate under their own names, but buy national brands and non–Prime Choice private-label merchandise from Atlantic.

From the basic information provided below, conduct a distribution cost analysis for Atlantic Seaboard Food Wholesalers, Inc. Discuss any changes in marketing channel strategy that this analysis suggests.

		Functional Expense Breakdowns					
		Physical Possession		Promotion			Ordering & Payment
Income Statement—1987 ($000)		Storage	Delivery	Selling	Advertising	Sales Promotion	Billing & Collecting
Sales	$60,000						
Costs of goods sold	$36,000						
Gross margin	$24,000						
Expenses							
Salaries	$ 9,000	$2,000	$2,000	$4,000	$ 400	$ 500	$100
Advertising	$ 1,000				$ 900	$ 100	
Trucking	$ 4,000		$4,000				
Rent	$ 6,000	$5,600	$ 100	$ 50	$ 50	$ 100	$100
Insurance	$ 2,000	$1,100	$ 830	$ 5	$ 5	$ 10	$ 50
Supplies	$ 1,000	$ 100	$ 200	$ 100	$ 100	$ 400	$100
Total	$23,000	$8,800	$7,130	$4,155	$1,455	$1,110	$350
Net profit	$ 1,000						

			Functional Cost Allocation					
Marketing channel	Sales (000)	Gross Margin (000)	Storage- 000 cu. ft	# Cases Shipped	# Sales Calls	Advertising	Sales Promotion	# Orders (000)
Single stores	$15,000	$ 9,356	322	1305	12.8	$ 389	$307	1.75
Multiple stores	$24,000	$14,564	648	2625	18.8	$ 350	$230	2.00
Independents	$21,000	$12,080	790	3200	8.3	$ 463	$365	1.25
Total	$60,000	$36,000	1760	7130	39.9	$1,202	$902	5.00

8. A recent income statement for Atlantic Seaboard Food Wholesalers, Inc., is given in Question 7. Note that Atlantic's earnings were based on fixed assets of $12 million and net worth of $5 million. Calculate the strategic profit model ratios for Atlantic Seaboard Food Wholesalers, Inc. Assuming the following industry averages, compare Atlantic's performance to that of the general grocery wholesaling industry: (1) net profit margin

= 2.0 percent; (2) asset turnover = 4.5 times; (3) return on assets = 9.0 percent; (4) leverage ratio = 2.11 times; and (5) return on investment = 19.0 percent.

9. It has been determined that Atlantic's average inventory during the year amounted to $12 million and that the company devoted 250,000 square feet of its available space to storing inventory. From this information, as well as the data, about Atlantic given in Questions 7 and 8 compute the gross margin on inventory investment (GMROI) and the gross margin on selling space (GMROS) for Atlantic. Suggest ways in which the company might improve its GMROI and GMROS.

10. Ralph's Men's Shop carries hundreds of items for the well-dressed male. Ralph's management has heard that the supermarket industry is adopting a concept known as Direct Product Profit (DPP). Ralph's management thought that DPP might be useful for their business, particularly for their high fashion items.

Ralph's carries four high fashion lines of clothing—Nehru jackets, leisure suits, disco clothes, and Miami Vice jackets. The following table details the relevant performance information for each of these product lines in Ralph's Men's Shop.

	Nehru Jackets	Leisure Suits	Disco Suits	Miami Vice Jackets
Costs				
Cost of Goods Sold	$20.00	$25.00	$ 45.00	$ 60.00
Unload, Price Mark, Shelve	2.00	2.00	2.00	2.00
Space Costs	15.00	15.00	25.00	10.00
Capital Costs	3.50	4.00	5.00	1.88
Obsolescence Cost	0.60	0.75	1.35	1.80
Insurance and Taxes	1.00	1.25	2.25	3.00
Price	$30.00	$30.00	$ 45.00	$120.00
Inventory Turnover	0.5	0.5	0.3	3.0
Cubic Feet of Space	45.0	60.0	105.0	300.0

a. Calculate the gross margin percentage, GMROI, GMROS, and DPP for each of the four product lines.

b. Based on these calculations, what are your recommendations for Ralph's Men's Shop with respect to these four product lines? Explain your answer carefully.

11. Using the environmental framework for auditing marketing channel performance (Figure 12-6), evaluate the performance of the marketing channels for one of the following products:

a. Subcompact automobiles
b. Farm equipment
c. Computer chips
d. Premium ice cream
e. Coal
f. Carbide grinding wheels

Ace Brokerage Company

John Kline is concerned about his recent conversation with Bob Morreaux, vice president of marketing and distribution of the Morreaux Sugar Company. Kline is president of the Ace Brokerage Company, a large food broker located in Steel

City, Alabama. During their conversation, Morreaux told Kline that his firm wanted Kline to put more emphasis on developing an institutional trade for sugar. In the past, he had done an excellent job of developing the retail grocery market for Morreaux. As a matter of fact, almost 70 percent of all sugar purchased in Steel City area supermarkets is Morreaux brand. However, the rapid growth in away-from-home eating had caused Morreaux's sales to level off in the Steel City area. Ace Brokerage had concentrated its efforts on supermarkets in Steel City and had never attempted to obtain institutional distribution for the principals it represented. Kline wondered if he should consider hiring new personnel to begin developing the institutional business in response to the request by Morreaux.

BACKGROUND

Steel City is a unique market area for the supermarket industry, particularly food processors and manufacturers, since over 80 percent of all retail grocery sales are made through locally owned chains or local cooperatives. Although the metropolitan area contains over 600,000 people, only one national chain has more than four outlets and that chain captures only about 10 percent of total retail volume. In contrast, Table 12.13 presents data concerning the major local chains and

TABLE 12.13   Major Supermarket Outlets in Steel City

Firm name	Type	Number of stores	Approximate market share (Percent)
Freedom Grocers	Local chain	3	13
Bear Stores	Local chain	18	22
Southern Supermarkets	Cooperative	18	18
Bigg's Super Stores	Cooperative	16	16

cooperatives in Steel City. Thus, food processors depend upon Steel City food brokers to present their lines to supermarket buyers since they cannot rely on their contacts with the national supermarket chains to obtain penetration in the market.

There are more than twenty food brokers in the Steel City area. Ace Brokerage is one of the three largest, with brokerage commissions of approximately $500,000 per year. Ace represents twenty-five noncompeting grocery and household supply manufacturers. Although Ace's contracts with its principals (suppliers) specify commission rates varying from 1 to 5 percent, average commissions are slightly less than 3 percent. Thus, Ace accounts for about $18 million in sales for its principals.

To earn the commissions, Ace performs several services for the principals as well as for the supermarket buyers. Ace representatives visit buyers periodically to present new products, take orders, and inform them of possible market changes. In this capacity, the firm acts much as the manufacturer's own sales force might. Ace also employs ten field personnel who visit individual stores to help with counting stock, replenishing shelf stock, delivering manufacturer point-of-purchase displays, and attempting to make sure that Ace principals are receiving adequate support in the stores. Ace also maintains a small warehouse with some inventory (provided on consignment by the principals) to meet any emergency needs of its customers.

Although Ace represents twenty-five principals, Morreaux Sugar Company is one of the largest. Over $80,000 of Ace's brokerage commissions come from Morreaux. The other major account for Ace is a large tuna and canned fish processor which, like Morreaux, has a 70 percent market share in Steel City and generates about $80,000 per year brokerage fee for Ace. The remainder of Ace's revenues is spread over the other principals, with yearly commissions ranging from less than $1,000 to $35,000.

Kline believes that his firm has an excellent reputation with supermarket buyers due to the quality of service offered by his firm as well as the principals represented by Ace. As one example of Kline's emphasis on quality products and service, he had recently withdrawn from a brokerage agreement with a processor of fruits and pie fillings due to some indications of quality control problems in the processor's plant. Two supermarket buyers had asked Kline to remove a few cases of the product from their shelves and arrange reshipment and credit due to poor quality. Although both buyers indicated that they would reorder from the same manufacturer (specifying different canning dates from those of the off-quality goods), Kline felt that quality problems caused his field personnel too much trouble and might, in the long run, damage the reputation of Ace Brokerage. Even though this principal had paid brokerage commissions of over $30,000 to Ace in the previous year, Kline terminated his relationship with the processor and found another fruit packer desiring representation in the Steel City market. While the lost revenues have not been totally replaced by the new principal, Kline is satisfied that his firm has been able to generate commissions of $12,000 from a principal who is new to the Steel City market.

Kline admits that his lack of concern over the lost commission may be partially due to the fact that Ace Brokerage Company will report a net profit of $85,000 for the year. As owner of 60 percent of the shares in the firm (the remainder is held by three other employees), he seems satisfied with his salary as president and the dividends paid from the firm's earnings.

ACE-MORREAUX RELATIONSHIP

Ace Brokerage Company has represented the Morreaux Sugar Company in the Steel City market for four years. Prior to this arrangement, Morreaux utilized the services of Underwood Brokers, Inc., whereas Ace represented Provincial Sugar. Underwood Brokers is another of the three largest firms in Steel City. Four years ago, Morreaux was unhappy with the performance of Underwood, as their brand had only one-third of the total market at that time. Bob Morreaux felt that stronger effort by the broker would result in higher market share. Underwood was unwilling to devote more effort to Morreaux and expressed the belief that sugar was such a competitive commodity that a market share of more than 30 to 35 percent was unreasonable. At that same time, John Kline and Ace Brokerage had become disenchanted with Provincial Sugar because of that firm's refusal to commit more money to advertising and promotion in Steel City. Kline felt he could increase Provincial's penetration considerably greater than its 25 percent market share with more promotional effort by the firm. It was under these conditions that Kline and Morreaux met and decided that the two firms seemed compatible in their goals. In effect, a swap was arranged, with Morreaux being represented by Ace and Provincial handled by Underwood. Morreaux is very pleased that he was correct about the potential to increase market share in the retail grocery business. On the other hand, he knows that Provincial Sugar still has 20 percent of the retail market for sugar and that Underwood Brokers has actively solicited wholesale distributors in the institutional field to carry the Provincial brand. As a result, Provincial controls about 30 percent of the institutional sugar sales. Morreaux, on the other hand, obtains very little of this business since it has no active representation in the field.

PRIMARY CONCERNS OF MORREAUX SUGAR COMPANY

Morreaux is concerned about the failure of Ace Brokerage Company to solicit wholesale institutional distribution for several reasons. Obviously, the lost sales potential is a major concern. Although the institutional food business is not as large as the retail grocery field in sales volume, it still represents a major opportunity for food processors and manufacturers. The growth of the away-from-home eating market is a particular concern to everyone in the food industry. Morreaux had read reports which estimate that approximately one-third of all meals consumed in the United States during 1975 were consumed away from home. He is particularly interested in projections estimating that, by the mid-1980s, one-half of all meals will be consumed away from home.

The growth of the institutional business may explain Morreaux's second concern, which is the leveling off of sales in the Steel City area. With a 70 percent share of a market which expects little real growth, he believes it will be very difficult to increase sales substantially unless alternative forms of distribution are developed. Incremental gains to be realized from capuring further market share points would, in his opinion, be outweighed by the costs involved.

Morreaux is also concerned because he has recently concluded meetings with several major restaurant, fast-food, and institutional feeding companies, all of which have outlets in the Steel City area. Some of these firms wanted to sign contracts with Morreaux which would specify that Morreaux Sugar be used in their outlets. In return, Morreaux would package the sugar in individual serving envelopes imprinted with messages specified by the customers. Morreaux's major problem lies in promising distribution capability to these companies. While two of the feeding institutions maintain their own distribution centers in Steel City and could be supplied directly, the other utilize Steel City wholesalers and would need to have the product available from at least one of them.

Morreaux believes he could find time himself to call on a distributor in Steel City and find the means to fulfill these contracts. Most distributors would be willing to handle the product, since its sale is essentially guaranteed by the contract and because it would immediately give the distributor a means to develop sales of other products to the outlets. However, Morreaux knows that this action would not solve the basic problem of Ace's failure to cultivate the institutional market.

ALTERNATIVES

Both Ace Brokerage Company and Morreaux Sugar Company have several possible solutions to their problem. Kline may simply refuse to open an institutional sales division and wait to see the reaction of Morreaux to this decision. He knows that if he makes this decision, Morreaux can do one of two things. First, Morreaux may decide to forgo the lost opportunity in the institutional field and be satisfied with the retail grocery trade. Second, Morreaux may cancel its relationship with Ace and look for a broker with capability in both retail and institutional sales. Kline hopes that since the other large brokers already have principals for sugar, Morreaux will be afraid to cancel their agreement since dealing with a small brokerage firm would be somewhat risky for Morreaux. Of course, Morreaux could also find a broker to handle its products for the institutional business only. Kline is afraid that if Morreaux took this course and other principals followed, a fourth large brokerage firm might emerge in the Steel City market. Still, Kline knows that developing an institutional division would require addition of at least two new staff members and would create a new set of customers and problems with which he would have to deal. He also knows that Morreaux has to be concerned about Ace's reaction to any of Morreaux Sugar Company's decisions since, after all, Ace has been largely responsible for Morreaux's market dominance in Steel City.

QUESTIONS

1. How would you assess the relative power positions of these two firms? What power bases can each draw upon? Be specific. In your opinion, who has the power advantage?
2. In reference to the alternatives discussed in the text, how might the conflict between these two firms be resolved?
3. If you were John Kline, what would you do? Why?
4. If you were Bob Morreaux, what would you do? Why?

Source: Donald J. Bowersox, M. Bixby Cooper, Douglas M. Lambert, and Donald A. Taylor, *Management in Marketing Channels* (New York, McGraw-Hill, 1980), pp. 122–126.

The Touch of Nature Company

BACKGROUND

The Touch of Nature Company was started by Linda Miller and Debbie Johnson in 1971. They started the company to capitalize on the growing natural foods industry.

The Touch of Nature Company has experienced tremendous success in the short period it has been in existence. Sales volume has increased each year. In fact, last year's sales volume exceeded $6 million. Sales are projected to double within three years.

PRODUCT LINE

Initially, Touch of Nature depended on a line of candy bars. The candy bars were given the brand name of Nature's Finest. They were made from ingredients to appeal to the health-minded consumer. For example, honey was substituted for sugar, and carob was used instead of chocolate. A variety of candy bars were produced. The different types included plain carob, carob and almond, carob and peanuts, and carob and coconut.

DISTRIBUTION

Initially, the sole channel of distribution consisted of utilizing wholesalers to reach health food stores. It would not have been feasible for Touch of Nature to distribute directly to the health food stores because the sales made in each store would not be large enough to cover the expenses of a sales representative.

In 1980 Touch of Nature expanded their distribution channels. They began marketing their product lines in grocery stores. They used wholesalers for the smaller grocery stores, but used sales representatives for the larger grocery stores. By 1982 there were eleven sales representatives, each assigned to a designated territory.

In 1983 Linda Miller analyzed recent sales figures to determine if their products were doing well in the grocery stores. She was satisfied when she discovered that 10 percent of the company's sales were to grocery stores.

CHANNEL CONFLICT

The health food store operators were becoming increasingly unhappy about Touch of Nature's natural candies and cookies being sold in supermarkets. They felt that Touch of Nature was being disloyal to them. The following letter from a health food store owner reflects many of their feelings.

Dear Ms. Miller and Ms. Johnson:

I have been carrying your products since 1971. When the public had not even heard of Nature's Finest, I prominently displayed your entire product line on my shelves and personally recommended them to my customers.

How do you think I felt when I saw your products in a grocery store? (At a lower price yet!) After everything I've done for your products, I feel that I deserve better treatment.

At a recent convention for health food store owners, I discussed this situation with other store operators. They shared my sentiments.

In conclusion, I am considering dropping the Nature's Finest product line from my product mix.

Very truly yours,

Margaret Hein

QUESTIONS

1. Identify possible alternatives to reduce the conflict in Touch of Nature's channels of distribution.
2. Evaluate the pros and cons of the most promising alternatives.
3. Select the best alternative for reducing channel conflict and justify your choice.

Source: Reprinted by permission of PWS-Kent Publishing Company, a division of Wadsworth, Inc. Meyers and Lusch, *Study Guide: Principles of Marketing*, Boston: Kent Publishing Company, 1987, pp. 138–139. © by Wadsworth, Inc.

Laramie Oil Company: Retail Gasoline Division

In April 1980 George Thomas, vice president in charge of domestic automotive gasoline distribution for the Laramie Oil Company, was considering what action he should take with regard to the company's 12,400 franchised and lessee-operated service stations. A number of developments that indicated discontent among franchisees and lessees had recently occurred. Although he was unsure as to what extent these developments indicated real widespread discontent, Mr. Thomas was wondering what might be causing it, and what action he should take at the present time, and in the long run.

COMPANY BACKGROUND

The Laramie Oil Company was a fully integrated petroleum company with operations in 21 countries. In 1979 domestic sales were $8.79 billion, and net income was $823.4 million. The Laramie product line included automotive gasoline, aviation fuels, distillates, lubricants, and assorted agricultural and industrial chemicals. Sales of automotive gasoline and related products accounted for 52 percent of revenues earned and 64 percent of net profit.

Both the international and domestic American Head Offices were situated in New York City. As distribution vice president, George Thomas had responsibility for the overall maintenance of a strong network of retail outlets. This responsibility involved the setting of policies concerning lease terms, the selection of dealers, the training of dealers, the motivation of dealers, the dismissal of dealers, and any other factors involving the maintenance of dealer morale and overall effectiveness. Mr. Thomas only had responsibility for the company's Laramie brand stations. Laramie Oil also operated about 50 discount outlets and expected to open more in the near future. These outlets operated under a different brand name.

George Thomas described his objective as distribution vice president as follows:

> We've done a great deal of research to determine why gasoline purchasers use one brand of gasoline or another. In almost every instance, the consumer's perception of the gasoline retail outlet was a very significant determinant in brand selection. It appears that we're halfway to first base if we can keep our outlets modern and clean, plus provide the service that the consumer desires. By service, I mean more than just good, fast, competent pump island work. Service includes having outlets open when consumers need them, and making sure that outlets handle our national promotions. There is nothing more irritating to a customer who expects to receive a glass or coupon than to find that the station that he happens to be in isn't participating in the national promotion. That is one of the best ways to lose customers for good.
>
> Our whole retail distribution policy is directed toward providing a consistent type of physical outlet and service from one end of the country to the other. That's how gasoline is sold.

IMPLEMENTATION OF DISTRIBUTION POLICIES

George Thomas's control over the implementation of his department's policies was quite indirect. A general manager in each of five geographical divisions had responsibility for all marketing activities in his division, including retail distribution. Each division had a distribution manager whose responsibilities included the day-to-day implementation of corporate policies in regard to service station

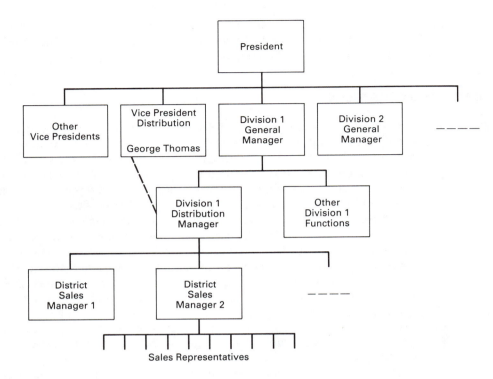

EXHIBIT 1 Partial Organization Chart.

operations. The division distribution manager reported directly to the division general manager. The corporate and divisional distribution managers did, however, maintain informal contact with each other. Each divisional distribution manager had a number of district sales managers reporting directly to him. Direct contact with service station operators was maintained by company sales representatives, each of whom reported to a district sales manager. The sales representative was the final link in the chain of implementation between George Thomas's office and the service station operator. (See Exhibit 1 for a partial organization chart.)

TYPES OF SERVICE STATIONS

Laramie Oil Company distributed its automotive products through three types of service stations:

1. *Company operated.* These stations were owned or leased by Laramie Oil who hired the service station personnel to operate them on a straight salary basis. Laramie controlled the retail price and all other aspects of all products sold through these stations. About 100 of Laramie's 12,400 stations were operated in this manner.

2. *Franchised dealers.* The station site and all physical facilities of franchised dealer operations were owned by the dealers themselves. Laramie did, however, provide financing, so that an individual dealer could commence operation by putting up as little as $2,000. The company, or local financial institutions, held mortgages on the land and physical facilities. About 500 outlets were in this category.

3. *Lessee operated.* Lessee operators were dealers who leased their service station from Laramie Oil. The stations, in these cases, continued to be owned by Laramie Oil. The lessee purchased petroleum products from Laramie but was free to set his own operating policies as related to such things as hours, prices, and brands of accessories carried. The lessee's cost price of gasoline was based on a "tank wagon price" which included all taxes and delivery charges to the lessee's station. Typical lessee operators were charged per gallon, as shown in the accompanying table.

Transport price (except tax)	$0.660
Plus: State and federal taxes	0.450
Transport price (including tax)	1.110
Plus: Jobber margin	0.085
Tank wagon price	1.195
Plus: Rent paid to Laramie	0.055
Lessee's margin	0.070
Retail price	$1.320

The cost price of gasoline to franchised dealers closely approximated the lessee cost arrangement, except that rent charges were not included. For most franchisees, interest charges on their mortgages tended to make up this cost difference.

A CLOSER LOOK AT TWO LARAMIE LESSEE DEALERS

1. Jerry Williamson's Laramie service station, Dearborn, Michigan. Jerry Williamson's service station was located at one of the main intersections in the Detroit suburb of Dearborn. His customers were drawn mainly from local residents and commuters who drove through Dearborn on their way to and from their work in Detroit. Williamson was a class A automobile mechanic who had worked for a Ford dealership for eight years before becoming a Laramie dealer in 1964. He had put up $9,500 of his own money to obtain the right to be the Laramie lessee for his Dearborn location. Most of the $9,500 had been used to finance product inventories and tools, while some had been used to physically upgrade the station.

Williamson did a large automobile repair business. Over the years he had built up an excellent reputation among the residents of Dearborn for providing competent and reliable repair service. As a result of this business and his good

EXHIBIT 2
Percentage Profit Statements for Jerry Williamson's and Fred Shaw's Service Stations for 1979

	Jerry Williamson	Fred Shaw
Sales	100.00%	100.00%
Cost of goods sold	75.36	75.24
Gross profit	24.64	24.76
Expenses:		
Labor for outside work	0.46	0.29
Supplies	0.75	0.79
Wages (excluding owner)	8.38	8.69
Repairs and maintenance	0.34	0.24
Advertising	0.79	0.93
Delivery	0.41	0.42
Bad debts	0.02	0.02
Administrative	0.38	0.35
Miscellaneous	0.96	0.72
Rent	2.60	2.00
Insurance	0.47	0.46
Utilities	0.96	1.00
Taxes	0.74	0.66
Interest	0.10	0.11
Depreciation	0.60	0.65
Total expenses	17.96	17.33
Net profit	6.68%	7.43%
Inventory turnover × 1 year	17.26	12.88

location for attracting gasoline customers, he did an annual sales volume of slightly over $494,000. His profit statement for 1979 is presented in Exhibit 2.

Williamson took great pride in the fact that he had been able to build a very successful business operation. He thought of himself as being a part of the community as he took part in community work through his memberships in the Lion's Club, and the Chamber of Commerce. In the latter organization he had risen to the position of vice president, and was looking forward to being president at some time.

When he was asked if there were any negative aspects to being a Laramie dealer, Williamson replied as follows:

> Well . . . not really; it's tough to complain a lot when you're making $33,000 a year. The only thing I really have to complain about is that Laramie pressures me to buy most of my repair parts and accessories from their own supply company or from company-approved jobbers. I think I could get slightly better margins from other jobbers, as the company takes a percentage rake-off from the approved jobbers. However, it's really a small complaint when you consider all the pluses that Laramie gives. Overall, I'm extremely pleased.

2. Fred Shaw's Laramie service station, Detroit, Michigan. Fred Shaw's service station was located in an industrial section of Detroit, with most of his customers being people who worked in the plants in the surrounding area. Prior to becoming the lessee of his current station, Shaw had worked as an employee in a suburban Laramie station. He had always wanted to be in business for himself, and whenever he heard that a station was available, he would approach the sales representative involved to see if he could obtain the station. Most of the stations had required too much capital, but finally he was able to obtain his current station by putting up $8,500 for the required inventories.

Although managing his station required long hours for Shaw, he preferred it to a very great extent over working for another dealer. It was in a very real sense to him the fulfillment of his dream of being his own boss.

Due to the nature of the surrounding environment, Shaw's station was quiet most of the day except when the shifts changed and then it was extremely busy. This constant changing from feast to famine made proper staffing extremely difficult, and required long hours to cover all shift changes.

Shaw's station was not as productive in either gasoline sales or repair service as was Jerry Williamson's. As a result, his 1979 sales volume was just under $95,000. Exhibit 2 presents his 1979 profit statement.

Hank Homes was the Laramie sales representative in Shaw's district, and on one of his weekly visits recently he asked to Fred to take part in a special Bicentennial china giveaway promotion. Part of the conversation between the two men went as follows:

HANK. This looks to me to be one of the best promotions the company has ever put together. They're going to put about $2.5 million in advertising behind it. You should draw a pile of customers.

FRED. Come on, Hank. The type of customer who buys from my outlet isn't interested in bone china. It may be fine for other outlets, but I don't want in on this one. Besides, since the gasoline shortage of '73 and '74, I can't believe anyone wants to start these rotten giveaways again.

HANK. I disagree, Fred. I'm sure you'd do well with it. Why don't you let me sign you up. I think you'd be pleased with the results. We pretested this in Denver and it went well. Think about it for a few minutes while we discuss a few other things. It looks to me as if your station could use a new coat of paint this spring. If we let it go any longer, it will chase customers away.

FRED. I don't think I can afford to put out for the paint right now, Hank. You know what a problem I'm having making ends meet here.

HANK. Well, maybe I can help you out on that score. If I work on them at the regional office, they might let me absorb part or even all of the expense for you. . . . Think about the china promotion, Fred, and I'll drop back tomorrow.

FRANCHISEE AND LESSEE DISCONTENT

The following dealer comments were taken from meetings of several Laramie retail dealer associations in various part of the United States. Laramie retail dealer associations were groups of Laramie dealers who had gotten together on their own for such purposes as: the discussion of mutual problems, the collective purchasing of products from independent suppliers, and the undertaking of various social activities. Not all Laramie dealers belonged to associations and the strength and activity level of the associations varied greatly.

LESSEE 1. The company claims that we can set our own prices, but that damn sales rep comes into my place and tells me I can't sell at more than a four-cent markup. I can hardly scrape from one week to the next at that rate. . . . I know for sure he'll drop my lease if I don't set these prices. Our dealer association has had economists do studies that showed that on the average it takes a gross profit margin of nine cents a gallon to operate profitably. Margins today run from about three cents to eight cents with the average at about five and a half cents. That's just not enough.

LESSEE 2. What really bugs me is those stupid premium offers I have to put up with. They advertise them like mad on TV, so I have to carry them or the customers start screaming. . . .I don't get any more business with them—all my competitors are running some premium too—all they do is add to my costs. It's really frustrating. I thought the oil crisis had finished these things. I guess I was wrong.

LESSEE 3. I couldn't be more satisfied. I make a really good living. If some of you guys stopped complaining and started working, you could do the same.

LESSEE 4. You know I'd really like to close my place down at night . . . the only reason I'm open nights is 'cause the sales rep said he wouldn't renew my lease if I didn't keep his hours—imagine that, I've worked for Laramie for 15 years as a dealer and they'd drop me just like that. I can't afford to lose my station but I'm losing money by staying open.

LESSEE 5. What's really got me worried is that they are going to turn my station into a company-owned and -operated outlet. Where would I be then?

LESSEE 6. The company is more interested in their gallonage than our profits, and those one-sided leases let them dictate what we'll charge and what products we'll sell. They also use the lease to ride herd on our prices.

LESSEE 7. I had hoped that the Supreme Court rulings prohibiting forcing their TBA (tires, batteries, and accessories) brands on us would have helped; however, all it's done is to make their methods more subtle.

FRANCHISEE 1. I thought when I put up my bucks I was going to be in business for myself—fat chance—that sales rep is in my place all the time suggesting what hours to work, how to work, what price to set . . . If I object, he starts talking about revoking my franchise. I know the Laramie name draws customer but some of his suggestions are unreasonable.

FRANCHISEE 2. This business of them running their own discount stations in competition with me has really got me bugged, too.

COMMENTS OF SALES REPRESENTATIVES (SR)

The following comments were taken from individual interviews with selected sales representatives:

SR 1. Sure, I set hours and prices and procedures; if I didn't, some of those dolts would be out of business tomorrow.

SR 2. To get the volume out of my territory that the district manager demands, I have to pressure the dealers. Talking about the lease is always effective. However, I've never actually threatened any of my dealers with the loss of the lease.

SR 3. If you're honest and friendly with your dealers and show them what they will gain from following what you suggest, then you don't have to threaten them to get cooperation.

SR 4. You can bet your life I'm out pushing our TBA line to dealers. That right hasn't been taken away from us. However, that doesn't mean we're going to club them over the head if they don't.

COMMENTS BY GEORGE THOMAS

(Made before a congressional committee.)

It isn't our policy to require dealers to maintain company directed hours or prices. The whole idea is that the dealer has the right to establish his own hours and prices.

I'd fire any sales representative found pressuring dealers on matters like prices or hours or contests.

It seems to me that what we have here is a situation completely analogous to the normal arrangement between the landlord and tenant. We have up to $200,000 invested in large stations, and if the dealers are mismanaging them we have a right and a duty to protect our investment.

DEVELOPMENTS IN 1980

A number of developments that concerned George Thomas took place in 1980.

1. A group of dealers in Chicago filed a suit against Laramie, alleging that Laramie violated the Sherman Act by using short-term leases to intimidate the dealers into following suggested retail prices. No decision had been handed down yet by the court.

2. A Laramie Marketing Research Staff report indicated that the turnover rate among Laramie dealers had increased significantly in the last few years. This problem of dealer turnover was common throughout the oil industry. Estimates indicated that approximately one third of all service stations in the

United States change management every year. The Laramie turnover rate was below the national average, but was still very high. This high turnover was considered to be a very serious problem by George Thomas. Also disturbing was the fact that a significant number of long-service Laramie dealers had left to join cut-rate chains who guaranteed station managers at least $1,500 income per month.

3. The Automotive Retail Trade Association had requested the Federal Trade Commission (FTC) to charge the seven major oil companies (including Laramie) with misrepresentation, breach of contract, and promotion of price wars. The writ alleged misrepresentation of "exclusive" franchise agreements and breach of contract because the oil companies have opened "off-brand" stations near franchise service stations. The association charged that the off-brand stations sell at prices lower than the wholesale prices charged to the franchise dealers. The association wants an injunction to stop oil companies from creating subsidiary stations in direct competition with franchised dealers.

The writ also criticized the oil companies for nondisclosure of fees or profits received by oil companies from firms which supply automobile products to the service stations. The association wanted to know this information since service station lessees are requested to buy the accessories only from designated dealers.

Finally the writ criticized promotional gimmicks and giveaways as a financial burden to operators and alleged that oil companies "demanded" cooperation and participation under threat of nonrenewal of leases.

4. The Central States Automotive Retailers Association presented a brief to the governors of six states asking for legislation to prohibit gimmicks and giveaways connected with gasoline selling. The association alleged that an end to giveaways could reduce the selling price of gasoline by one or two cents a gallon. The brief also asked that oil companies be required to sell gasoline at one price to all customers. At present the wholesale price varies from customer to customer, with the highest being charged to leased gas stations.

5. Laramie had recently closed many marginal stations as a result of gasoline shortages in 1979. A group of dealers dispossessed in this process had brought suit against Laramie charging violations of their franchise agreement and conspiracy to restrain trade.

Mr. Thomas reflected on these developments and wondered what alternative courses of action were available to him, and what action he should take both in the short run and in the long run. He also wondered what factors had caused the current problems.

Source: Written by Thomas C. Kinnear and C. Merle Crawford, The University of Michigan. Reprinted with permission.

Bob Clayton's Sports Centers

Bob Clayton's Sports Centers is a chain of five sporting goods stores headquartered in Hanover, Texas, a city with a population of just under 100,000. The main, flagship store is located in downtown Hanover, and four smaller stores have been opened in nearby towns over the years. All stores are supplied on a direct shipment basis by merchandise suppliers.

Mr. Robert Clayton founded the firm in 1952 upon graduation from college. Although he had little retailing experience, Mr. Clayton had been an all-American football player in college and earned a degree in business administration. Since he was a local sports hero, he had little trouble financing his first store in his hometown.

The company grew steadily throughout the 1950s, and the opening of four other stores during the 1960s boosted sales rapidly. During the 1960s, Mr. Clayton made some important decisions. First, he incorporated the business and began to use stock ownership as an inducement to attract and retain qualified management personnel. Also, he made a major thrust into the team sports and educational markets.

EXHIBIT 1
Five Year Performance History for Bob Clayton's Sports Centers
(Thousands of Dollars)

Year	Net Sales	Gross Margin		After-Tax Net Profit	
		$	% of Sales	$	% of Sales
1978	$3,601	$1,235	34.3%	$84	2.3%
1979	3,890	1,225	31.5	79	2.0
1980	4,173	1,317	31.5	74	1.8
1981	4,325	1,341	31.0	66	1.5
1982	4,096	1,221	29.8	55	1.3

Strategic profit model for Bob Clayton's sports centers.

The firm has always stressed "quality merchandise and customer service." To support this image, the company offers repair service for most of the products it sells; provides auxiliary services, such as stringing tennis rackets and drilling bowling balls; and has an extremely liberal merchandise return policy.

MANAGEMENT

Mr. Clayton functions as president and chief executive officer of the company, but is also heavily engaged in the buying end of the business. He feels that the supplier relationships he has built up over the years require his continued involvement to

EXHIBIT 2
Income Statement for
Bob Clayton's Sports Centers,
1982

Item	Amount	Percent of Sales
Net Sales	$4,096,247	100.0%
Cost of Goods Sold	2,874,751	70.2
Gross Margin	1,221,496	29.8
Operating Expenses		
Owners' salaries	40,000	1.0
Other payroll	638,211	15.6
Fringe benefits	73,425	1.8
Rent	120,000	2.9
Utilities	75,935	1.9
Advertising	65,210	1.6
Other expenses	121,991	2.9
Total expenses	1,134,772	27.7
Net Profit Before Taxes	86,724	2.1
Income Taxes	31,899	.8
Net Profit	$ 54,825	1.3%

EXHIBIT 3
Balance Sheet for
Bob Clayton's Sports Centers,
December 31, 1982

Item	Amount	Percent of Total Assets
Cash	$ 15,612	.5%
Accounts receivable	248,926	9.0
Inventory	1,646,014	59.5
Other current assets	343,711	12.5
Total current assets	2,254,263	81.5
Physical facilities and equipment	510,726	18.5
Total assets	$2,764,989	100.0%
Accounts payable	563,240	20.4%
Short-term notes payable	250,000	9.0
Other current liabilities	263,421	9.5
Total current liabilities	1,076,661	38.9
Long-term notes payable	437,106	15.8
Total liabilities	1,513,767	54.7
Net worth	1,251,222	45.3
Total liabilities and net worth	$2,764,989	100.0%

```
                        EXHIBIT 4
            Merchandising Performance by Product
            Category for Bob Clayton's Sports Centers,
                        1982 ($000)
```

Product Line	Net Sales	Gross Margin	Inventory
Baseball and softball equipment	$ 124	$ 34	$ 34
Basketball equipment	105	29	30
Camping equipment	274	78	89
Exercise equipment	302	88	92
Firearms and hunting equipment	534	180	188
Fishing tackle	250	85	109
Golf equipment	259	78	88
Tennis equipment	236	86	141
Bicycles and supplies	561	185	175
Outboard marine motors	298	112	234
Team and institutional sales	699	145	115
Other products	454	121	351
Total	$4,096	$1,221	$1,646

assure the best buying deals possible. Although buying groups (retail companies making joint purchases to take advantage of quantity discounts and freight economies) exist in the sporting goods industry, the company has not joined one since Mr. Clayton believes it is not necessary.

All store managers report directly to Robert Clayton. He tries to visit every store at least once a week to make sure things are going smoothly. Store personnel are chosen carefully by the store managers. Mr. Clayton insists that all store sales personnel have a well-rounded knowledge of sports. He believes that this knowledge, combined with on-the-job training, produces the high level of customer service that his customers have come to rely on.

RECENT DEVELOPMENTS

Profits continued to be adequate during the 1960s and early 1970s. However, in 1976, profits began declining and have been "flat" for the last several years. Mr. Clayton is worried that something is wrong with the company's performance. Although sales continued to increase with the exception of the recessionary year of 1975, net profit as a percent of sales has taken a nosedive.

Mr. Clayton believes part of the problem has been increased competition. In the early 1970s, three discount department stores, two catalog showrooms, and two Oshman's stores opened in the market area. (Oshman's is a large chain of sporting goods stores located throughout the Sun Belt.) In order to meet this competition, Sports Centers had to reduce prices on its low-end products and

EXHIBIT 5

**The Hanover Guardian Sporting Goods
Consumer Survey**

Relative Importance of Store Attributes When Shopping for Sporting Goods
[Scale of 5 (very important) to 1 (very unimportant)]

	Average Ranking
Low Prices	4.2
High Quality of Merchandise	4.1
Convenience	3.8
Knowledgeable Sales Clerks	3.8
Hours of Operation	3.4
Delivery	2.2

Ranking of Stores by Attributes
[Scale of 5 (store ranks very high) to 1 (store ranks very low)]

Price		Quality	
Wal Mart	4.5	Oshman's	4.2
H. J. Wilson (catalog showroom)	4.1	Sports Centers	4.1
K-Mart	4.1	Sears	3.9
Sears	3.6	Dillard's	3.7
Oshman's	3.5	H. J. Wilson	3.0
Dillard's (department store)	3.1	Wal Mart	2.9
Sports Centers	2.9	K-Mart	2.2

Convenience		Customer Service	
Sears	3.9	Sports Centers	4.5
Dillard's	3.5	Dillard's	4.3
Sports Centers	3.4	Sears	4.1
Oshman's	3.3	Oshman's	4.1
Wal Mart	3.3	H. J. Wilson	2.9
H. J. Wilson	3.2	Wal Mart	2.4
K-Mart	3.2	K-Mart	2.2

promote more heavily. This seemed to keep volume up, but last year the local Sears store completely remodeled and expanded its sporting goods department and was beginning to have an impact on the sales volume of high-end products. Mr. Clayton had added outboard marine motors as a new product line to help boost gross margin.

Robert Clayton believes his stores are well merchandised. The merchandise is of high quality and the shelves are generally well stocked. He is proud of the fact that consumers rarely complain about an item being out of stock.

Mr. Clayton is also wondering whether his customers are changing. He frequently makes statements like, "People don't care about quality anymore—all they look for is the lowest price."

In January of 1983, Mr. Clayton decided to take stock of where he was. Despite reasonable sales for 1982 given the recession, profits were far from adequate. Determined to change things, Mr. Clayton took the weekend off, gathered up some key financial information, and headed for the family cabin on Bear Lake to plan the future. As he was leaving the store on Friday afternoon,

EXHIBIT 6 Composite Results for Sporting Goods Stores, 1982	Percent of Net Sales
Net Sales	100.0%
Cost of Goods Sold	66.8
Gross Margin	33.2
Operating Expenses:	
Payroll	16.3%
Occupancy	3.4
Advertising	2.2
Insurance	1.0
Depreciation	.9
Other	4.7
Total Operating Expenses	28.5
Operating Profit	4.7%
Other (Income) Expense	.7
Profit Before Tax	4.0
Income Taxes	1.2
Net Profit	2.8%
Net Profit Margin	2.8%
Asset Turnover	1.9
Return on Assets	5.3%
Financial Leverage	1.8
Return on Net Worth	9.6%
Sales to Inventory	3.6
Inventory Turnover (Cost of Goods Sold ÷ Inventory)	2.4
Current Ratio	1.9
Quick Ratio	1.1
Total Debt to Net Worth	.8

Matt Jacobson, the space salesman for the *Hanover Guardian*, dropped by with a new consumer survey. Mr. Clayton wasn't sure it would help, but he decided to take it along.

QUESTIONS

1. How good is the company's financial performance? Use any analytical techniques that you feel are appropriate.
2. What specific problems does the company face? How are these problems holding down the level of profitability?

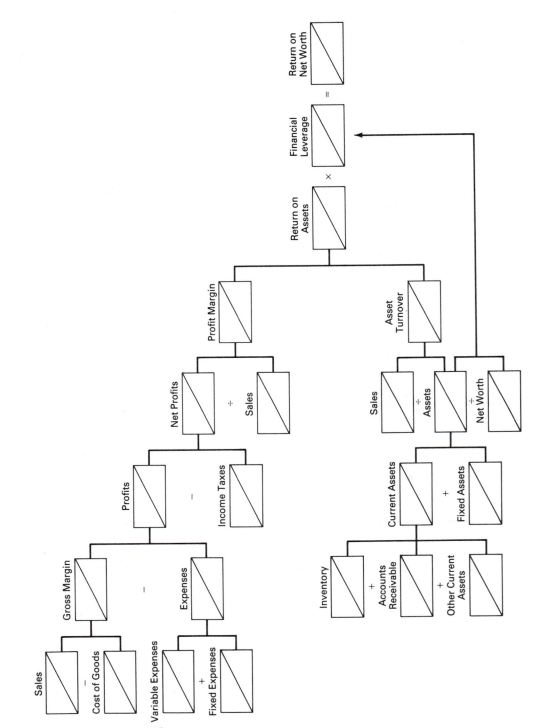

EXHIBIT 7 Strategic profit model for Bob Clayton's sports centers.

3. Develop a financial plan for 1983.

4. Identify the specific actions that are necessary to support the financial plan.

Source: Albert D. Bates, Profit Planning Group Boulder, Colo. Prepared for the Strategic Planning and Retail Management Faculty of Management Studies, University of Toronto.

Exxon Company, U.S.A.: "Swing Store Program"

Brian Walters,[1] Regional Market Development Manager for Exxon Co., U.S.A., has just returned from a trip to Alpha district, the largest district in his region. For the past two weeks he has been evaluating Exxon retail automotive stores in the district. He must sort through the mass of data he has collected and make some recommendations to solve the problem he has been investigating.

The problem came to his attention last month, when the latest report from Exxon's Market Investment Program Group (which keeps close tabs on the profitability of each of Exxon's 23,000 retail stores) indicated that 41 of the 300 stores in Alpha district were consistently yielding an unsatisfactory return on investment—despite favorable market conditions and solid company support of marketing efforts in the district. Walters decided an in-depth evaluation of each of these forty-one stores was needed; he would give the matter his personal attention. The program was known as the "swing store program" because the stores investigated were hovering between success and failure. Exxon hoped it could identify problems and "swing" some of these stores into the successful category rather than shutting them down. Walters described the swing store program and what he hoped to discover from it:

> Here is the problem: We have $15 million invested in these stores. They are not yielding us a satisfactory return on investment. Our current monthly rent collected does not come close to our market value rent. We, of course, have two relationships with our dealers: landlord/tenant and supplier/customer. Our target is to have the current monthly rent at or close to the market value rent, and to sell monthly motor fuels at each store at or close to IMOD projection.[2] Therefore the major questions we are asking are: 1) have we made poor individual investments, and/or is the quality of the dealer at each location such as to retard the store income potential? 2) what can we do about it?

[1] All names have been changed.

[2] IMOD Projection: A quantitative estimate of sales based on the computerized "investment model" (IMOD). See further explanation in section on sales performance.

ALPHA DISTRICT RETAIL STORES

Alpha District includes one of the top five metropolitan areas in the United States. Because of its size, the district is divided into three areas. Heading up the retail store operations in each district is a field sales manager; each field sales manager is responsible for about 100 retail stores.

Alpha District is a relatively new geographic market for Exxon. The company has marketed products in the area for only the past fifteen years. However, due to its rapid population growth, the company has been trying to establish a stronger foothold. Exxon would like to see the present 300 retail stores in Alpha District increased by 50 percent over the next five or ten years.

Virtually all Exxon retail stores in Alpha district are company-leased stations; the company owns the grounds and facilities, but leases all of the property to an independent businessman—the Exxon dealer. The dealer signs a three-year dealer lease agreement and a supply agreement with Exxon. Exxon agrees to supply gasoline and other automotive products, and the dealer agrees to pay a fixed monthly rent to Exxon, purchase the products from Exxon distributors, and maintain certain quality standards set forth by Exxon. These dealer quality standards concern primarily cleanliness and safety. The leadership agreement gives Exxon the right to terminate the relationship if the dealer does not maintain the standard. As a rule, Exxon generally waits until the lease period is up before terminating a dealer. But, explained Walters, "Even then it is very difficult to terminate a dealer who has been with you for a while, even three years. We find it better to work with the dealer and help him correct the problems he is having, rather than just get rid of him."

Sales Performance

Walters looked first at the 1981 figures showing monthly sales performance for each of the stores (see Exhibit 1). He then compared these with the IMOD projections he had previously calculated for each store. The IMOD projection is a monthly motor gasoline volume projection of the amount of fuel each store is expected to sell, based on Exxon's investment in that store. Several different variables are included in the computer model used to calculate this figure: traffic count at the corner of the site; the number of automobile registrations within one-and-a-half miles of the site; the number of other competitors nearby; the average market price or competitors' price in the vicinity; the number of regional shopping centers in the area; and whether there are any other traffic generators in the area. Since the IMOD projection indicates sales potential, it is typically higher than the actual sales volume figures. For example, for all 300 stores of Alpha district, the IMOD is approximately 80 (i.e., an average of 80,000 gallons of gasoline per month), while the actual sales volume is closer to 45. Since Alpha District is still a relatively new market for Exxon, this ratio of actual to projected is less than for the U.S. as a whole. Nationwide, actual sales volume averages 80 percent of IMOD projections. Walters is particularly concerned about those retail stores having a smaller-than-average actual to projected sales ratio.

EXHIBIT 1 Exxon retail automotive stores average monthly sales performance—1981

	Store #	Gasoline		After-market	
		Actual Sales Volume (,000 gallons per month)	IMOD Projected Sales Volume (,000 gallons per month)	After-market Actual Sales Volume ($,000 per month)	After-market Projected Sales Volume ($,000 per month)
AREA 1	1	44	58	4.9	10.8
	2	31	69	2.9	12.6
	3	15	74	1.0	5.8
	4	32	57	5.1	12.0
	5	28	95	15.7	21.7
	6	38	80	0	13.5
	7	41	69	13.2	17.3
	8	31	71	8.0	13.0
	9	16	53	5.1	9.9
	10	36	71	5.7	5.2
	11	39	76	7.2	13.8
AREA 2	12	41	114	4.1	15.1
	13	29	102	4.2	15.3
	14	30	52	1.9	24.6
	15	32	60	18.9	23.3
	16	30	68	4.4	14.2
	17	26	81	6.0	19.1
	18	25	69	5.4	18.2
	19	30	71	9.8	17.7
	20	30	70	8.0	13.7
	21	30	53	8.2	14.5
	22	29	65	12.8	14.4
	23	46	70	6.4	14.4
	24	30	50	2.8	19.7
	25	20	78	4.1	15.6
	26	27	75	7.9	16.1
	27	30	80	8.6	11.3
AREA 3	28	40	74	6.2	5.9
	29	31	36	5.8	13.8
	30	50	83	10.1	19.2
	31	35	69	8.4	12.9
	32	30	60	9.3	19.0
	33	23	102	4.2	19.1
	34	21	117	4.0	19.1
	35	45	69	7.2	19.4
	36	37	81	7.7	30.4
	37	33	77	4.3	36.4
	38	35	115	28.8	51.2
	39	46	88	9.0	19.4
	40	30	74	13.7	33.6
	41	32	88	13.9	20.9

Along with data on monthly motor gasoline volume, Walters also has figures showing the after-market actual sales volume and after-market projected sales volume. After-market sales are store sales of all products and services excluding gasoline: TBA items (tires, batteries, and accessories), as well as automotive repair and service. This information is also provided in Exhibit 1.

Dealer Quality

The second part of the swing store program was more time-consuming. He decided to visit each problem store over two weeks and formally evaluate each one. Before the evaluation, Walters informed each dealer that he would be visiting

---

EXHIBIT 2 Items included in Exxon retail automotive store evaluation

I. Store Appearance

Outside

1. Grounds well kept. (No junk cars, motors, etc.)
2. Drive swept clean.
3. Perimeter curbing neat and clean.
4. Islands neat and clean.
5. Pumps and pump glass clean.
6. Pump glass not broken/out.
7. Vending machines/oil cabinet clean/painted.
8. Exterior walls clean and free of dirt.
9. All exterior windows clean.
10. Islands and ramps not closed/blocked.
11. Rear of store is neat, clean, uncluttered.
12. Landscaping neat.
13. Exterior signing ok/lights working.

Inside

14. Floor swept clean. (Bays/sales room)
15. All walls clean.
16. Sales room ceiling clean.
17. Shelf displays clean/neat.
18. Sales room/kiosk neat/orderly/clean.
19. Equipment/tools/inventory neat, orderly.

Restrooms

20. Walkway clean.
21. Floor clean.
22. Walls and ceiling clean.
23. Ventilation fresh.
24. All equipment in working order.
25. Mirror clean.
26. Commode/urinal clean.
27. Wash basin clean.
28. Waste basket available.
29. Lights working.
30. Hand soap available.
31. Towels available.
32. Toilet tissue available.

II. Personnel Appearance/Service

First Impression

1. Prompt attention.
2. "Good Morning" or appropriate greeting.

Sales Service

3. Asked for order and/or fill up.
4. Cleaned windshield (street island).
5. Cleaned rear window (street island).
6. Under the hood sales inspection (customer permitting) street island.
7. Cashier/customer salesman settled the purchase in a courteous manner.
8. All personnel in approved uniform.
9. All personnel neat and clean.

III. Product Merchandising

1. Motor fuel price sign prominent and attractive.
2. Enough motor oil displayed.
3. Motor oil displayed prominently and attractively.
4. Enough tires displayed at island (area permitting).
5. Enough tires displayed in front bays.
6. Enough tires displayed in front of sales room (area permitting).
7. Tires displayed attractively.
8. Tires are price merchandised.
9. Batteries displayed prominently and attractively.
10. Enough batteries displayed.
11. Impulse items displayed outside at island or store front.
12. Accessories/coolant well displayed in bay and sales room.
13. Window displays fresh, current and attractive (zoning permitting).
14. Prices indicated on Value Center advertising.
15. Other seasonal Value Center ads current and attractive.

EXHIBIT 2   (continued)

16. Vaccum and vending machines working and attractive.
17. Store merchandised for Self Service sales/express service (if has Self Service/express sales).

IV. Selling/Service Capability

Tires

1. Adequate coverage of fast moving sizes.
2. Adequate coverage by line (radial, belted, conventional).
3. Adequate tire selling skills by retailer/employees.
4. Retailer has planned system for selling tires (price cards, codes, etc. that customer salesmen understand and use).
5. Mogas customers solicited for tire sales or service at island.
6. Tires checked while car is being serviced.
7. Tire changer.
8. Spin or bubble balancer.
9. Air wrenches.
10. Wheel alignment.

Batteries

11. Adequate coverage of fast moving sizes.
12. Adequate coverage by line.
13. Adequate battery selling skills by retailer/employees.
14. Retailer has a planned system for selling batteries (price cards, codes, etc. which customer salesmen understand and use).
15. Hydrometer.
16. Battery charger.
17. Battery tester used.
18. Battery tester used while car is being serviced.

Accessories/Impulse Items

19. Adequate accessory/impulse item inventory level.
20. Coverage of fast moving lines and sizes.
21. Customer salesmen/cashier solicit accessory/impulse item/motor oil sales.

Motor Oil

22. Adequate motor oil inventory.
23. Employees trained to sell add oil and oil change at the island.

Services

24. Tune up.
25. Brake service.
26. Air conditioning service.
27. Road service.
28. Pick-up and delivery service.
29. State inspection/license.
30. "Customer Reminder" system in use.
31. Of services performed, has proper equipment to produce work quality of other top notch service centers in the market.

V. Retailer Evaluation

1. Spends enough time meeting people on the front.
2. Adequate product knowledge.
3. Work/car wash quality equal to top notch service centers car washes in the market.
4. Customer complaints within an acceptable level.
5. Employees are punctual and dependable.
6. Discipline evident among employees.
7. Sends qualified employees to special classes teaching automotive repair.
8. Trains driveway salesmen in proper island service procedures.
9. Runs reference checks on prospective employees.
10. Uses a work order system.
11. Does business records on a daily basis (or supervises the completion of them).
12. Storeroom locked.
13. Full-shelf inventory program.
14. Shift leaders responsible for stock and cash control.
15. Prompt in payment of bills to Exxon.
16. Consistently have higher profit/salary than profit demand.
17. Adequate working cash. (Dealers only-automatic credit for salary stores.)
18. Sets sales and profit objectives.
19. Receives monthly P/L statements (Dealers only).
20. Adequate compensation program.
21. Offers wages and benefits needed to attract qualified technician.
22. Offers wages and benefits needed to attract qualified driveway salesmen.
23. Has motivation and desire to achieve sales potential at the location.

Alpha district over the next two weeks to talk with the dealer and check on different aspects of the store. Each dealer knew he was coming and had time to prepare.

The evaluation form Walters used was the standard Exxon Retail Store Evaluation Form, which is divided into five sections: store appearance, personnel appearance, product merchandising, selling and service capability, and retailer or dealer evaluation. For each individual item, he gave a score of between *0* and whatever the item's weight factor was. As a general rule, each item was rated either *satisfactory*, in which case the weight factor score was given, or *unsatisfactory*, in which case a score of *0* was given. Walters spent from one to three hours at each retail store talking with the dealer about the operation, observing the activities at the store, and checking all relevant aspects of the business.

This case was prepared by Stephen W. McDaniel, Assistant Professor of Marketing, Texas A&M University, as a basis for class discussion rather than to illustrate either effective or ineffective marketing management.

Source: Richard T. Hise and Stephen W. McDaniel, *Cases in Marketing Strategy* (Columbus, Ohio: Charles E. Merrill, 1984), pp. 535–545.

Store appearance evaluation form — weight factors and scores by area.

		Area 1											Area 2																Area 3													
Weight Factors		1	2	3	4	5	6	7	8	9	10	11	12	13	14	15	16	17	18	19	20	21	22	23	24	25	26	27	28	29	30	31	32	33	34	35	36	37	38	39	40	41
Store Appearance																																										
A. Outside																																										
1. Grounds	8	8	8	8	8	8	8	0	0	8	0	8	0	0	8	0	8	8	8	0	0	0	0	0	8	8	0	0	8	0	0	8	0	0	0	0	8	8	0	0	0	8
2. Driveway	3	0	0	0	0	3	3	0	0	3	0	3	0	0	0	0	3	3	3	0	0	0	0	0	3	3	0	0	0	0	0	0	0	0	0	3	3	3	0	0	0
3. Curbing	3	3	0	3	3	3	3	3	3	3	3	3	0	3	3	3	3	0	0	3	0	0	0	3	3	3	0	3	3	2	3	3	3	3	3	3	3	0	0	0	0
4. Islands clean	8	0	8	0	8	0	8	0	0	0	8	0	8	8	8	0	8	8	8	8	8	0	0	8	8	8	0	0	0	3	8	8	8	8	8	8	0	8	8	8	0
5. Pumps	4	0	0	0	0	0	0	0	0	4	4	0	0	0	0	4	0	0	0	0	0	0	0	0	0	0	0	0	4	4	4	0	4	0	0	0	4	0	0	0	0
6. Pump glass	3	3	3	3	3	3	3	3	3	3	3	3	3	0	0	0	3	0	0	3	3	3	3	3	0	0	3	3	3	3	0	0	3	3	3	0	0	0	3	3	0
7. Vending machine	3	0	0	3	3	3	0	0	0	3	0	3	0	3	0	3	3	0	0	0	0	0	0	0	0	0	0	3	3	0	3	0	3	3	0	3	3	3	3	3	3
8. Walls	2	2	2	2	2	3	2	0	0	0	2	2	2	2	2	2	0	2	2	0	2	2	0	2	0	2	2	0	0	0	0	2	2	0	0	0	0	2	2	2	2
9. Windows	3	2	2	2	2	3	2	3	0	3	3	3	3	2	3	3	0	0	2	2	2	3	3	3	3	3	0	2	2	3	3	2	3	3	3	3	3	3	3	3	2
10. Island open	8	8	8	8	8	8	8	0	0	8	8	8	8	8	0	0	8	8	8	0	0	8	8	8	0	8	8	8	8	8	8	8	8	0	0	0	0	8	8	8	8
11. Rear	3	0	0	0	3	3	0	0	0	0	3	3	3	0	3	0	0	3	0	0	0	0	0	0	0	0	0	0	0	0	3	0	0	0	0	0	0	0	3	0	0
12. Landscaping	7	0	0	0	7	0	0	7	7	0	0	0	0	0	0	0	0	0	7	7	0	7	7	0	7	0	0	0	7	7	7	7	0	7	7	7	7	0	0	0	0
13. Signs/Lights	7	0	7	7	0	7	0	7	7	7	7	7	0	7	7	7	7	7	7	7	7	7	7	7	0	7	7	7	0	7	7	7	7	7	7	7	7	0	0	0	0
B. Inside																																										
14. Floors	2	0	0	0	2	2	2	0	0	2	2	0	0	2	0	0	0	2	0	2	0	0	2	0	2	0	0	0	0	0	2	0	0	0	0	0	2	2	0	0	0
15. Walls	2	0	0	2	2	2	2	0	0	0	0	0	0	2	0	0	0	0	0	0	2	0	0	2	2	0	0	2	0	0	0	2	2	2	2	0	0	0	2	2	0
16. Ceilings	2	2	2	2	0	2	2	0	0	2	2	2	0	0	2	2	0	2	0	0	2	2	0	0	0	0	2	0	2	2	0	0	2	0	0	0	0	0	2	2	2
17. Shelf display	2	0	2	0	2	2	2	0	0	2	0	0	2	0	0	2	0	2	2	0	2	2	2	2	2	0	0	2	0	2	2	2	2	2	0	2	0	0	0	2	2
18. Salesroom	2	0	0	0	2	2	0	0	0	2	0	0	0	0	0	2	0	2	2	2	0	2	2	0	0	2	2	0	0	2	0	0	2	0	0	0	2	0	0	2	0
19. Equipment/tools	2	2	2	2	2	2	2	0	0	2	2	0	0	0	0	0	0	0	2	2	0	2	2	2	0	0	2	2	2	0	2	2	0	2	2	0	2	0	0	0	0
C. Restrooms																																										
20. Walkways	2	2	2	2	2	2	2	0	0	2	2	2	2	2	2	2	2	2	2	2	0	2	2	2	2	2	2	2	2	2	0	2	2	2	2	2	2	2	0	2	2
21. Floor	2	2	0	0	0	0	2	0	0	2	2	2	0	0	0	0	0	2	0	0	0	2	0	0	0	2	0	0	0	2	0	2	0	2	0	0	2	2	0	0	0
22. Walls/ceilings	2	2	2	2	0	0	2	0	0	2	2	2	0	2	2	2	2	2	2	2	2	2	2	2	0	0	2	0	2	2	0	2	2	0	2	2	0	2	2	2	2
23. Ventilation	2	2	2	0	2	0	2	0	0	2	2	0	0	2	0	0	0	0	0	0	2	0	2	2	0	0	0	0	2	2	2	0	2	2	0	2	2	0	2	2	2
24. Equipment	2	2	2	2	2	2	2	2	0	2	2	2	2	2	2	2	2	2	2	2	2	0	2	2	2	2	2	0	2	2	2	2	2	2	2	2	2	2	2	2	2
25. Mirror	2	0	0	0	2	0	0	0	0	2	0	0	0	2	2	2	0	2	2	2	0	2	2	2	2	2	2	0	0	0	2	0	2	2	2	2	2	2	0	0	0
26. Commode/urinal	2	0	0	0	0	0	2	0	0	2	2	2	0	2	0	0	0	0	0	0	2	0	2	2	0	0	0	0	2	0	0	0	2	2	2	2	2	2	0	0	0
27. Wash basin	2	0	0	0	0	0	0	0	0	2	2	2	0	2	2	2	2	2	2	2	2	0	2	2	2	2	2	0	2	2	2	2	2	2	2	2	2	2	2	2	2
28. Waste basket	2	2	2	2	0	2	2	0	0	2	2	2	0	0	0	0	0	0	0	0	0	2	0	0	0	2	0	0	2	0	0	0	0	2	0	2	2	2	2	2	2
29. Lights	2	2	2	2	2	2	0	2	0	2	2	2	2	2	2	2	2	2	2	2	2	2	2	2	2	0	0	2	2	0	2	0	2	2	0	2	2	2	2	2	2
30. Soap	2	0	0	0	0	2	0	0	0	2	2	2	2	2	2	0	0	0	2	2	2	2	0	0	0	2	0	0	2	0	0	0	0	2	0	0	2	2	0	0	0
31. Towels	2	2	2	2	2	0	2	2	2	2	2	2	2	2	2	2	2	2	2	2	2	2	2	2	2	2	2	0	0	2	2	2	2	2	2	2	2	2	2	2	2
32. Toilet tissue	2	2	2	2	2	2	0	2	0	2	2	2	0	2	2	2	0	2	2	2	2	2	2	0	2	2	2	2	2	2	2	2	2	2	2	2	2	2	2	2	2
Appearance Score	100	21	58	58	82	75	63	38	15	80	85	82	26	63	63	44	50	51	76	73	65	66	47	48	13	75	38	41	55	33	67	43	54	61	53	59	54	87	43	34	30	36

Page 450

IV. Selling/Serv. Capability	Weight	Area 1											Area 2																Area 3													
		1	2	3	4	5	6	7	8	9	10	11	12	13	14	15	16	17	18	19	20	21	22	23	24	25	26	27	28	29	30	31	32	33	34	35	36	37	38	39	40	41
A. Tires																																										
1. Fast moving sizes	5	0	0	5	0	5	5	5	0	5	5	5	0	0	5	5	0	0	0	5	0	0	5	5	5	0	0	0	5	0	5	0	0	0	0	0	0	0	0	0	5	5
2. Coverage by line	5	0	0	5	5	0	5	5	0	0	0	5	0	5	0	0	0	0	0	5	5	0	0	0	0	0	0	0	0	5	0	5	0	0	0	5	0	0	5	5	5	5
3. Tire selling skills	10	0	0	0	10	5	10	0	10	10	0	0	0	10	10	0	0	0	0	0	0	0	10	0	0	0	0	0	10	10	10	0	10	0	0	0	10	0	10	10	10	0
4. Planned sales sys.	5	0	0	0	0	0	5	0	0	5	5	0	0	0	0	0	0	0	0	0	0	0	0	0	0	0	0	0	0	0	5	0	0	0	0	0	5	5	0	0	0	0
5. Suggestion selling	2	0	0	0	0	0	5	2	0	5	0	0	0	0	0	0	0	0	0	0	0	0	0	0	0	0	0	0	0	0	2	0	0	0	0	0	0	0	0	0	0	0
6. Tires checked	2	2	2	2	2	2	2	2	2	2	2	2	2	2	2	2	2	2	0	2	2	2	2	2	2	2	2	0	2	2	2	2	2	2	2	2	2	2	2	2	2	2
7. Tire Changer	2	2	2	2	2	2	2	2	2	2	2	2	2	2	2	2	2	2	2	2	2	2	2	2	2	2	2	2	2	2	2	2	2	2	2	2	2	2	2	2	2	2
8. Balancer	2	2	2	2	2	2	2	2	2	2	2	2	2	2	2	2	2	2	2	2	2	2	2	2	2	2	2	2	2	2	2	2	2	2	2	2	2	2	2	2	2	2
9. Air Wrenches	2	2	2	2	2	2	2	2	0	2	2	2	2	2	2	2	2	2	2	2	2	2	2	2	2	0	2	2	2	2	2	2	2	2	2	2	2	2	2	2	2	2
10. Wheel alignment	2	0	0	0	0	0	0	0	0	2	2	2	0	0	0	0	0	2	2	0	0	0	0	0	0	0	0	0	0	0	0	0	0	0	0	2	2	2	2	0	0	0
B. Batteries																																										
11. Fast moving sizes	5	0	0	0	0	5	5	5	0	5	5	5	0	0	5	5	0	0	0	5	0	0	5	5	5	0	0	0	5	5	5	5	5	5	5	0	5	5	5	0	5	5
12. Coverage by line	5	0	0	5	0	5	5	5	0	0	0	5	0	5	5	5	0	0	0	5	5	0	5	5	0	0	0	0	5	5	5	5	5	5	5	0	5	5	5	0	5	5
13. Batt. selling skills	6	0	0	0	0	6	6	6	0	6	6	6	0	0	6	6	0	0	0	6	0	0	0	0	0	0	0	0	0	6	6	6	6	6	6	0	6	6	6	0	6	0
14. Planned sales sys.	4	0	0	0	0	4	4	4	0	4	4	4	0	2	0	0	0	0	0	0	4	0	0	0	0	0	0	0	0	4	4	4	0	0	0	0	4	4	4	0	4	0
15. Hydrometer	2	2	2	2	2	2	2	2	2	2	2	2	2	2	2	2	2	2	2	2	2	2	2	2	2	2	2	2	2	2	2	2	2	2	2	2	2	2	2	2	2	2
16. Battery charger	2	2	2	2	2	2	2	2	2	2	2	2	2	2	2	2	2	2	2	2	2	2	2	2	2	2	2	2	2	2	2	2	2	2	2	2	2	2	2	2	2	2
17. Battery tester	2	2	2	2	2	2	2	2	2	2	2	2	2	2	2	2	2	2	2	2	2	2	2	2	2	2	2	2	2	2	2	2	2	2	2	2	2	2	2	2	2	2
18. Battert tester used	2	2	2	2	2	2	2	2	0	2	2	2	2	2	2	2	2	2	2	2	2	2	2	2	2	2	2	2	2	2	2	2	2	2	2	2	2	2	2	2	2	2
C. Acc./Impulse Items																																										
19. Adequate supply	2	2	2	2	2	0	2	2	2	2	2	2	0	0	0	0	0	0	0	2	2	2	2	2	2	2	2	2	0	0	0	2	0	0	2	0	2	2	2	0	2	2
20. Fast moving items	4	4	4	4	4	4	4	4	4	4	4	4	4	2	4	4	4	4	4	4	4	4	4	4	4	2	4	0	2	0	4	4	4	4	4	4	4	4	4	2	2	0
21. Suggestion selling	2	0	0	0	0	0	0	2	0	2	2	2	2	2	0	0	2	2	2	2	0	2	2	0	2	4	4	0	0	0	2	2	0	2	2	0	0	2	2	0	0	0
D. Motor oil																																										
22. Adequate supply	4	4	4	4	4	4	4	4	0	4	4	4	4	4	4	4	4	4	4	4	2	4	4	4	4	4	4	4	4	4	4	4	4	4	4	4	4	4	4	4	4	4
23. Employee competence	4	4	4	4	4	4	4	4	0	4	4	4	4	4	4	4	4	4	4	4	4	4	4	4	4	4	4	4	4	4	4	4	4	0	4	4	4	4	4	4	4	4
E. Service																																										
24. Tune-up	2	2	2	2	2	2	2	2	2	2	2	2	2	2	2	2	2	2	2	2	2	2	2	2	2	2	2	2	2	2	2	2	2	2	2	2	2	2	2	2	2	2
25. Brake service	2	2	2	2	2	2	2	2	2	2	2	2	2	2	2	2	2	2	2	2	2	2	2	2	2	2	2	2	2	2	2	2	2	2	2	2	2	2	2	2	2	2
26. Air cond. service	2	2	2	2	2	2	2	2	2	2	2	2	2	2	2	2	2	2	2	2	2	2	2	2	2	2	2	2	0	2	2	2	0	2	2	2	2	2	2	2	2	2
27. Road service	2	2	2	2	2	2	2	2	2	2	2	2	2	2	2	2	2	2	2	2	2	2	2	2	2	2	2	2	2	2	2	2	2	2	2	2	2	2	2	2	2	2
28. Pick-up and delivery	2	0	0	0	0	0	0	0	0	2	2	2	0	0	0	0	0	0	0	0	2	2	0	0	0	0	0	0	0	0	2	0	0	0	0	0	2	2	2	0	0	0
29. State inspect./lic.	2	2	2	2	2	2	2	0	2	2	2	2	0	0	0	0	2	2	2	0	0	2	2	0	2	0	0	0	0	0	0	0	0	0	0	2	2	2	2	0	0	0
30. "Customer reminder"	2	0	0	0	0	0	0	0	0	0	0	0	0	0	0	0	0	0	0	0	0	0	0	0	0	0	0	0	0	0	0	0	0	0	0	0	0	0	0	0	0	0
31. Proper equipment	5	5	5	5	5	5	5	5	5	5	5	5	0	0	5	5	0	0	5	5	5	5	5	5	5	0	0	0	0	5	5	5	5	5	5	0	5	5	5	5	5	5
Service Capability Score	100	50	40	65	58	75	90	81	30	88	88	71	40	46	67	85	42	36	56	90	47	71	70	53	57	34	38	40	47	33	96	53	69	74	50	58	63	81	91	53	90	63

Factors	Weight	1	2	3	4	5	6	7	8	9	10	11	12	13	14	15	16	17	18	19	20	21	22	23	24	25	26	27	28	29	30	31	32	33	34	35	36	37	38	39	40	41
I. Personnel Appearance/Service																																										
A. First Impression																																										
1. Attention	10	10	10	10	10	10	10	10	0	10	10	10	10	10	10	10	10	0	10	10	10	10	0	0	0	0	10	10	10	0	10	10	10	10	10	10	10	10	10	10	10	10
2. Greetings	10	10	10	10	10	10	10	10	10	10	10	10	0	10	10	10	10	10	10	10	10	10	10	10	0	10	10	10	10	10	10	10	10	10	10	10	10	10	10	10	10	10
B. Sales/Service																																										
3. Orderfill up	10	0	10	10	10	10	10	10	0	10	10	10	0	0	10	10	10	10	10	10	10	10	10	10	0	0	10	10	10	10	10	10	10	10	10	10	10	10	10	0	10	10
4. Windshield	10	10	10	10	10	10	10	10	10	10	10	10	10	10	10	10	10	10	10	10	10	10	10	10	10	10	10	10	10	10	10	10	10	10	10	10	10	10	10	0	10	10
5. Rear window	10	0	0	0	10	0	0	0	0	10	10	10	15	10	0	10	10	10	10	10	10	10	10	10	10	10	10	10	0	10	10	10	10	10	10	10	10	10	10	10	0	0
6. Hood Inspection	15	15	15	15	15	15	15	0	0	15	15	15	15	15	15	15	15	15	15	15	15	15	15	15	15	15	15	15	15	15	15	15	15	15	15	15	15	15	15	15	15	15
7. Transaction	15	15	15	15	15	15	15	15	0	15	15	15	15	15	15	15	15	15	15	15	15	15	15	15	15	15	15	15	15	15	15	15	15	15	15	15	15	15	15	15	15	15
8. Approved uniforms	15	0	0	0	0	15	0	0	15	15	15	15	0	0	15	0	0	0	0	0	0	0	0	0	0	0	0	0	0	0	0	15	0	15	0	0	0	0	0	15	0	0
9. Personnel appearance	10	10	10	10	10	10	10	10	0	10	10	10	0	10	10	10	10	10	10	10	10	0	10	10	10	10	10	10	0	0	10	10	10	10	0	10	10	0	0	10	0	0
Personnel Score	100	65	75	85	100	90	75	85	25	100	100	100	25	50	70	85	85	60	95	85	100	75	65	45	55	35	75	65	55	45	75	90	85	100	75	65	85	85	80	75	65	65
II. Product Merchandising																																										
1. Price sign	15	0	15	0	0	0	0	0	0	15	15	15	0	15	15	15	0	15	15	15	15	15	15	0	15	15	10	15	15	15	15	5	15	0	15	10	10	10	0	0	0	0
2. Oil display	3	0	0	0	0	0	5	0	0	3	3	3	0	3	3	3	3	3	3	3	3	3	0	3	3	3	0	3	3	3	3	0	0	0	0	0	0	3	5	2	3
3. Oil display attractiveness	3	0	0	0	0	0	5	0	0	3	3	3	0	0	0	0	0	0	0	0	3	0	0	0	3	0	0	0	3	5	3	0	0	0	0	0	3	3	0	3	0
4. Tires at island	6	0	0	6	0	6	0	0	0	6	6	6	0	0	0	0	0	0	0	0	0	0	0	0	0	6	0	0	3	3	5	0	0	0	0	0	3	3	0	0	3	0
5. Tires at bay	6	0	0	6	0	6	0	0	0	6	6	6	0	6	6	6	6	6	0	0	0	6	6	6	0	0	0	0	0	3	0	0	0	0	6	0	0	0	0	0	0	0
6. Tires in sales room	6	0	6	0	0	6	0	0	0	6	6	6	6	0	0	6	0	6	0	0	0	0	0	0	6	0	6	0	0	6	6	6	6	0	6	6	0	0	0	0	6	0
7. Tires display attractiveness	10	0	0	0	0	0	0	0	0	10	0	0	0	0	0	0	0	0	0	0	0	10	0	0	0	0	0	0	0	0	0	0	0	0	0	0	0	0	0	0	0	0
8. Tires price display	6	0	0	0	0	0	0	0	0	0	10	10	0	0	0	0	0	0	0	0	0	0	0	0	0	0	0	0	0	0	6	6	6	0	6	6	0	0	0	0	6	0
9. Batteries display attract.	3	0	0	0	0	0	0	3	0	0	3	0	3	0	0	0	3	0	3	3	3	0	0	0	3	0	0	0	3	0	0	0	3	0	0	0	3	0	0	0	0	0
10. Batteries display	3	0	0	0	0	0	0	3	0	0	0	0	0	3	3	0	0	3	3	0	3	0	3	3	3	0	3	3	3	0	0	3	3	3	0	0	0	3	3	0	0	0
11. Impulse items display	6	0	0	6	0	0	0	0	0	0	6	6	0	0	0	0	6	6	0	0	0	6	0	0	0	0	0	0	6	0	0	0	6	0	0	0	0	6	0	0	0	0
12. Accessories display	6	0	6	0	0	6	0	0	0	0	6	6	6	6	6	6	6	6	6	6	6	6	6	6	6	6	0	0	6	0	0	0	0	0	0	0	0	6	0	0	0	0
13. Window display	6	0	0	6	0	0	0	0	0	0	6	0	0	6	6	6	0	0	0	6	6	0	0	0	6	6	6	0	6	0	0	6	6	6	0	0	0	0	0	0	0	6
14. Value center adv.	6	0	0	0	0	0	6	6	0	6	6	6	6	6	6	6	6	6	6	6	6	6	6	6	6	6	6	6	0	0	0	0	6	0	0	0	0	0	0	0	0	6
15. V.C. ads. current	6	0	0	6	0	6	6	3	0	0	3	0	6	6	6	6	6	6	6	6	6	0	6	6	6	0	0	0	0	6	6	6	6	6	6	0	0	0	0	0	6	6
16. Machines Working	3	3	3	3	3	3	3	3	0	3	3	3	3	3	3	3	3	3	3	3	3	3	3	3	3	3	3	3	3	3	3	6	6	3	3	3	3	3	3	3	3	3
17. Self service/express	6	6	6	6	6	6	6	6	6	6	6	6	6	6	6	6	6	6	6	6	6	6	6	6	6	6	6	6	6	6	6	6	6	6	6	6	6	6	6	6	6	6
Merchandise Score	100	6	24	21	9	43	37	21	6	36	92	60	9	42	45	39	15	49	33	36	33	42	61	18	50	30	16	24	39	30	68	23	48	15	30	43	25	37	33	30	17	38

Area 1 | Area 2 | Area 3

Weight Factors		1	2	3	4	5	6	7	8	9	10	11	12	13	14	15	16	17	18	19	20	21	22	23	24	25	26	27	28	29	30	31	32	33	34	35	36	37	38	39	40	41
V. Retailer Evaluation																																											
1. Meets people	5	0	5	5	5	5	5	5	0	5	5	5	0	0	0	0	0	5	5	5	5	5	5	0	0	5	5	5	0	5	0	0	0	5	0	5	0	0	0	0	0	0
2. Product knowledge	5	0	0	0	5	5	5	5	5	5	0	5	0	0	5	5	5	5	5	5	5	5	5	5	5	5	0	5	5	5	5	5	5	5	0	5	5	5	5	5	5	5
3. Carwash quality	5	0	0	0	5	5	5	5	0	5	5	5	0	5	0	5	5	5	5	5	5	5	5	5	5	0	0	5	0	5	5	5	5	5	5	5	5	5	5	5	5	5
4. Customer complaints	2	5	5	5	0	2	2	2	5	5	5	2	0	0	2	2	2	2	2	5	2	2	2	2	2	0	5	2	2	2	2	2	2	2	2	2	2	2	2	2	2	2
5. Employees dependable	2	2	2	2	2	2	2	2	0	2	2	2	2	2	2	2	2	2	0	2	2	2	0	2	2	0	2	2	0	0	2	2	2	2	2	2	2	2	2	0	2
6. Discipline	2	0	5	5	2	2	5	5	0	5	2	0	0	5	0	0	0	0	2	5	0	0	5	0	0	0	5	0	0	2	2	2	5	2	2	0	2	2	2	2	0
7. Auto repair class	2	0	2	2	2	2	2	2	2	2	2	2	2	2	2	2	2	2	2	2	2	2	2	2	2	0	0	2	2	2	2	2	5	2	2	2	2	2	2	2	5
8. Trains salesman	2	2	2	2	2	2	2	2	0	2	2	2	5	5	5	5	5	5	5	5	5	5	5	5	5	5	5	5	5	5	5	5	5	5	5	5	5	5	5	5	5
9. Empl. reference checks	2	2	2	2	2	2	2	2	0	2	2	2	0	2	2	0	0	0	0	0	0	0	0	0	0	0	0	0	0	0	0	0	2	0	0	0	0	0	0	0	0
10. Work order system	5	5	5	5	5	5	5	5	5	5	5	5	2	2	2	2	2	2	2	2	2	2	2	2	2	2	2	2	2	2	2	2	2	2	2	2	2	2	2	2	2
11. Business records	2	2	5	0	0	0	0	0	0	0	0	2	2	0	2	0	0	0	0	0	0	0	0	0	0	0	0	0	0	0	0	0	0	0	0	0	0	0	0	0	0
12. Storeroom locked	2	0	0	0	0	0	0	0	0	0	0	0	0	0	0	0	0	0	0	2	0	0	0	0	0	0	0	2	2	2	2	2	2	2	2	2	2	2	2	2	2
13. Inventory program	2	2	2	2	2	2	2	2	2	2	2	2	2	2	2	2	2	2	2	2	2	2	2	2	2	2	2	2	2	2	2	2	2	2	2	2	2	2	2	2	2
14. Shift leaders resp.	2	2	2	2	2	2	2	2	2	2	2	2	0	0	0	0	5	5	5	5	5	5	5	5	0	0	5	5	5	5	5	5	0	0	5	5	5	5	5	5	5
15. Payment of bills	5	5	0	0	0	5	5	5	0	5	0	0	5	0	0	5	5	5	0	0	0	0	0	0	5	5	0	0	0	5	5	5	0	5	5	5	0	5	5	5	5
16. Profits/salary	5	5	0	0	5	5	5	5	0	5	0	5	5	5	5	5	5	5	5	0	0	0	0	0	0	0	0	5	0	0	0	0	0	0	0	0	0	0	0	0	0
17. Working cash	5	0	0	7	0	0	0	0	0	7	7	0	5	0	0	5	5	0	0	0	0	0	7	0	0	0	0	0	5	0	5	5	5	5	5	0	0	0	0	0	0
18. Sales and profit obj.	5	5	5	5	5	5	5	5	5	5	5	5	5	5	5	5	5	5	5	5	5	5	5	5	5	0	5	5	5	5	5	5	5	5	5	5	5	5	5	5	5
19. P/L Statement	5	10	10	10	10	10	10	10	0	10	10	5	10	10	10	10	0	0	10	10	10	10	10	0	10	0	0	0	0	10	10	10	10	10	10	10	10	10	10	10	10
20. Compensation programs	10	10	10	10	10	10	10	10	0	10	10	5	10	10	10	10	0	0	10	10	10	10	10	0	10	0	0	0	0	10	10	10	10	10	10	10	10	10	10	10	10
21. Qualified technician	5	0	5	0	5	5	5	5	5	5	5	5	5	5	5	5	0	0	5	5	5	5	5	0	0	0	0	5	0	5	5	5	5	5	5	5	5	5	5	5	5
22. Qualified salesman	5	5	5	0	0	5	5	5	5	5	5	5	0	5	5	5	0	0	0	5	5	5	5	0	5	0	5	0	0	5	5	5	5	5	5	5	5	5	5	5	0
23. Motivation and desire	10	10	10	10	0	0	10	10	0	5	10	10	0	0	0	0	0	0	0	0	0	0	0	0	0	0	0	0	0	0	10	0	10	10	0	10	0	0	0	0	0
Retailer Score		62	52	69	64	89	87	96	12	91	81	81	43	49	48	74	44	42	67	78	79	59	57	39	57	19	38	51	27	41	71	77	59	81	52	55	74	74	74	60	52	69
Overall Evaluation Score		204	249	288	303	377	347	331	78	395	446	384	143	250	274	333	231	266	324	354	325	294	301	162	300	156	208	201	223	182	377	286	315	331	260	268	313	358	316	257	254	271

PART V MARKETING CHANNELS IN OTHER CONTEXTS

13

Marketing Channel Management in Other Contexts

LEARNING OBJECTIVES

Upon completing this chapter, you will be able to:

- *Discuss the importance of international marketing channels to the U.S. economy.*

- *Explain the importance of the U.S. market to foreign marketers.*

- *Compare and contrast the four key methods of entering international markets and provide examples of each.*

- *List important criteria used in determining which of the four methods of international expansion a marketer should use.*

- *Diagram several alternative marketing channel structures for entering foreign markets.*

- *Describe several wholesaling institutions that are unique to international trade.*

- *Outline the advantages and disadvantages of including foreign intermediaries in international marketing channels.*

- *Discuss what is meant by counter trade and explain why it is a growing aspect of international trade.*

- *List some of the major problems for firms wishing to expand into international markets.*

- *Point out the unique characteristics of services marketing and how they affect the channel structure for delivering those services.*

- *Explain the key differences between goods retailing and services retailing.*

- *Describe marketing channels for health-care services as well as for lodging services.*

- *Discuss the major marketing channel issues in recycling usable waste materials.*

- *Compare and contrast marketing channels for new products with those for used goods.*

Up to this point, the primary focus of the text has been on marketing channels for new products in domestic markets. However, much marketing activity takes place in other contexts. For example, managing distributive systems in the international arena is becoming an important facet of global competitive activity. Furthermore, as the United States moves away from an industrial-based economy toward a service-based one, understanding how to structure and manage channels for services is becoming critical for many organizations. Finally, effectively managing marketing channels for used products, including recyclable materials, is imperative in an environment of limited resources. This chapter focuses on these three additional and important contexts of marketing channels: international channels, channels for services, and channels for used products and materials. The illustration in Exhibit 13-1 opens the discussion of international marketing channels.

INTERNATIONAL MARKETING CHANNELS

Except for the smallest marketers of goods and services, modern channel institutions must recognize and deal with the international marketplace in one form or another. As international car makers have discovered (Exhibit 13-1), the opportunities to be gained from trading with foreign countries, serving foreign consumers, or offering assortments composed of merchandise selected from the world's production are simply too great to ignore.

In this section of the chapter, we introduce the international context of marketing channels. We begin with a discussion of the importance of international trade to the U.S. economy. Then we examine the marketing channels available to organizations that wish to tap foreign markets. We also discuss some of the difficult problems associated with trying to use them and describe possible alternatives for overcoming these problems.

Note, however, that generalizations about international marketing channels are difficult to make because of the vast environmental differences from country to country. (See Figure 13-1 for a depiction of the similarities as well as the differences among marketing channel structures for several countries.) Thus, for example, automobile manufacturers wishing to tap the Japanese market must understand the subtle nuances of that country's distributive system if they are to be successful. BMW's "rebellion" from the traditional way of distributing

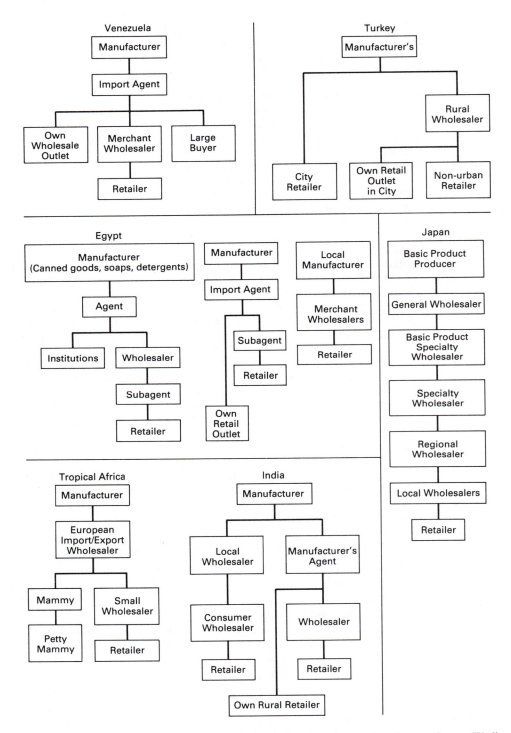

Figure 13-1 Marketing Channels in selected countries. *Source*: George Wadinambiaratchi, ''Channels of Distribution in Developing Economics,'' *The Business Quarterly*, Vol. 30 (Winter 1965), pp. 74–82.

TABLE 13-1 The 25 Largest U.S. Multinationals

Company	Foreign Revenue (millions)	Total Revenue (millions)	Foreign as % of Total	Foreign Operating Profit (millions)	Total Operating Profit (millions)	Foreign as % of Total
Exxon	$69,386	$97,173	71.4%	$2,208	$4,343	50.8%
Mobil	37,778	60,969	62.0	880	1,380	63.8
Texaco	31,118	46,986	66.2	833	1,281	65.0
Standard Oil Calif.	16,957	34,362	49.3	404	1,377	29.3
Phibro-Salomon	16,600	26,703	62.2	218	337	64.7
Ford Motor Company	16,526	37,067	44.6	460	−658	P/D
IBM	15,336	34,364	44.6	1,646	4,409	37.3
General Motors	14,376	60,026	23.9	−107	963	D/P
Gulf Oil	11,513	28,427	40.5	300	900	33.3
E I du Pont de Nemours	11,057	33,223	33.3	488	1,491	32.7
Citicorp	10,865	17,814	61.0	448	723	62.0
ITT	9,824	21,922	44.8	851	1,194	71.3
BankAmerica	8,051	14,955	53.8	253	389	65.0
Chase Manhattan	6,207	10,171	61.0	215	307	70.0
Dow Chemical	5,544	10,618	52.2	143	356	40.2
General Electric	5,490	27,192	20.2	395	1,817	21.7
Sun Co.	4,901	15,739	31.1	54	706	7.7
Standard Oil Indiana	4,862	28,389	17.1	618	1,826	33.8
Occidental Petroleum	4,715	18,527	25.4	345	548	63.0
Safeway Stores	4,380	17,633	24.8	84	160	52.5
J. P. Morgan	4,268	6,885	62.0	283	394	71.8
Eastman Kodak	4,181	10,815	38.7	302	1,860	16.2
Manufacturers Hanover	3,929	7,640	51.4	147	295	49.8
Procter & Gamble	3,737	11,994	31.2	88	777	11.3
Xerox	3,630	8,456	42.9	151	424	35.6

Source: Forbes, July 4, 1983, p. 114. © Forbes Inc., 1987.

imported automobiles will succeed only if it accurately factors into its marketing strategy the unique environmental influences of the Japanese market.

The Importance of International Trade to the U.S. Economy

U.S. involvement in the international marketplace is becoming more and more complex as dramatic changes take place in the economy. Basic conditions such as the strong dollar, sluggish growth abroad, and debt problems among the lesser developed countries (LDCs) have generated trade deficits over the last several years and are expected to influence U.S. trade well into the 1990s.[1]

U.S. companies are becoming increasingly involved in and reliant on international business. Over the past 30 years, they increased their investment in foreign affiliates from about $25 billion to over $200 billion.[2] Table 13-1 provides

[1] Business America, "U.S. Trade Outlook" (U.S. Department of Commerce, ITA), Vol. 9, No. 6, March 17, 1986, p. 3.

[2] Philip R. Cateora, *International Marketing*, 5th ed. (Homewood, Ill.: Richard D. Irwin, 1983) p. 3.

data on the largest U.S. multinationals and the importance of their foreign operations to their total performance. These firms have taken several approaches to become involved in foreign trade.

Expanding into International Markets: A Marketing Channel View

The perspective taken here is basically that of a U.S. manufacturer considering expanding abroad. There are only four basic routes to this kind of expansion (though there are numerous possible variations). These are exportation, licensing, joint ventures, and direct investment.

Exportation. The simplest form of expansion is for a company to export its products to other nations where a demand for those products exists. Exportation can be achieved directly through the use of foreign distributors or agents, or by establishing overseas marketing subsidiaries. Alternatively, a firm can export its goods by using trading companies, domestic export management companies, or piggybacking.

Piggybacking is an arrangement whereby one manufacturer uses another manufacturer's overseas distribution channels to sell its products.[3] A firm that uses piggybacking benefits from another firm's existing distributing system, established contacts, and developed knowledge of the foreign market.[4] In addition, piggybacking supplements existing marketing efforts by providing coverage in markets where a manufacturer is not currently represented.[5] For the established international marketer, piggybacking provides additional revenue through exports for firms whose export potential is too small to justify greater investment in international distribution channels.

Singer Sewing Machine Company distributes products closely allied to its own, such as facrics, patterns, notions, and thread.[6]

Sony, the Japanese electronics firm, sells U.S. and European products in Japan. Through Sony International Housewares, it distributes for Whirlpool, Schick, Regal Ware, Heath, and other U.S. firms.[7]

Colgate Palmolive Company buys razors and blades from the Wilkinson Sword Company in Britain and distributes them in the United States, Puerto Rico, Canada, and Scandinavia. Henkel Company of Germany uses Colgate to distribute Pritt Glue Stick.

Borg-Warner markets Hamilton Beach Company's small appliances, McGraw Edison Company's Toastmaster products, and In-Sink

[3] Vern Terpstra, *International Marketing*, 3rd ed. (Hinsdale, Ill.: Dryden Press, 1983) p. 330.

[4] Ruel Kahler, *International Marketing*, 5th ed. (Cincinnati, Ohio: South Western Publishing Co., 1983), p. 172.

[5] Ibid.

[6] Cateora, *International Marketing*, p. 593.

[7] Kahler, *International Marketing*, p. 172.

Erator Company's garbage disposals through established channels in Europe.[8]

The chief advantage of exportation to foreign markets is that it involves minimal investment; thus, failure will not usually affect the overall activities of the firm. The primary disadvantage of relying mainly on export agencies is that the company will have little control over the marketing of its products.

Licensing. In this form of expansion, the company forges a contractual agreement with a foreign organization to manufacture and/or sell its products abroad. The usual understanding in licensing agreements is that a certain percentage of the profits will be divided between each of the parties.[9] In addition, the "home" company is generally expected to furnish technical assistance to the foreign firm.

The main advantages of licensing are the low investment required by the home company and the assurance that at least some marketing activities will be undertaken for the firm's products. However, as in the case of simple exportation, there may be little real control over the licensee's operation. Moreover, the licensee might eventually acquire the technical expertise of the home firm, thereby altering the balance of dependence between these two channel members. Thus, power may rapidly shift to the foreign firm.

Joint Ventures. Joint ventures represent a more involved route to international expansion. With a joint venture, two or more firms collaborate on an investment in manufacturing and/or distributive systems to reach foreign markets and share in the risk of the expansionary effort. If the joint venture is forged with a foreign firm, the home firm obviously gains the commitment of the foreign firm to share its skills and its market access. Again, there are problems of control, but they appear to be less substantial than in situations where there is no mutual investment.

Joint ventures enable U.S. companies to penetrate difficult markets such as Japan.

Baxter Travenol Laboratories, Inc., of Deerfield, Illinois, a leading manufacturer of medical-care products, has a successful joint venture with Sumitomo Chemical Company. Sales of the joint venture

[8] Terpstra, *International Marketing*, p. 332.

[9] In consumer goods marketing, soft-drink companies (PepsiCo, Coca-Cola) have long been engaged in international franchising. More recently, fast-food firms (e.g., McDonald's) have expanded, using licensing arrangements. See "Europe: Wolfish Hunger for U.S. Fast Foods," *Business Week*, October 21, 1972, p. 34.

are reported as increasing at a faster rate than the parent firm's 23 percent annual growth rate.[10]

Sears Roebuck & Company has a joint venture with Seibu Stores, Inc., in Japan. The venture operates 80 stores, and significant annual sales increases are reported in applicances and apparel.[11]

Kentucky Fried Chicken Japan is a joint venture between KFC, Inc., and Mitsubishi Corporation. KFC opened its first ten restaurants in 1970 and has dramatically expanded since then.[12]

Similarly, Japanese companies cracked the U.S. market via joint ventures such as the one formed between General Motors and Toyota to produce and market the Chevrolet Nova in the U.S.

Direct Investment.   If the home company wishes to achieve a high degree of control over the marketing of its products abroad, it will probably follow this fourth basic expansionary route. A direct investment occurs when a firm establishes a wholly owned subsidiary in a foreign country. Companies that choose this route must commit themselves to learning the mores and nuances of each foreign market they enter.

One disadvantage of direct investment is that the dollar amount of the investment, both in terms of capital expenditure and management time, is likely to be substantial. Another is the risk of expropriation and nationalization, particularly in politically unstable countries.[13]

Still, direct investment is often attractive because foreign trade restrictions frequently make it difficult or impossible for a U.S. company to compete in a foreign market without having a plant or subsidiary located abroad. In addition:

> An overvalued dollar made it cheap to acquire assets abroad. It also made it unattractive to convert foreign earnings back into dollars and thus tended to encourage reinvestment of profits abroad. In the late 1950's and the early 1960's, the profitability of investment simply was higher abroad than in the U.S.[14]

Thus, by 1983, U.S. direct investment abroad reached $226.12 billion compared with $135 billion of foreign direct investment in the United States. The United States is the largest investor abroad, with approximately 50 percent of

---

[10] Mike Thorp, "Drive to Bolster Dollar by Increasing Exports Encounters Obstacles," *Wall Street Journal*, September 20, 1978, p. 20.

[11] Ibid.

[12] Mike Thorp, "Marketing in Japan Takes Twisty Turns, Foreign Firms Find," *Wall Street Journal*, March 9, 1977, p. 19.

[13] For data on some of the political difficulties encountered in direct investment, see "Multinationals Find the Going Rougher," *Business Week*, July 14, 1975, pp. 64–69.

[14] Robert Solomon, quoted in Lindley H. Clark, Jr., "Global Crossroads: Multinational Firms Under Fire All Over, Face a Changed Future," *Wall Street Journal*, December 3, 1975, p. 21.

total direct investment. That investment has been much more concentrated in the developed than in the developing countries.[15]

In recent years, direct investment in the United States has been increasing. As a matter of fact, foreign direct investment in the United States doubled between 1978 and 1982.[16] There are several reasons for this increase: (1) the depreciation of the American dollar relative to other currencies; (b) lower prices for land, energy, transportation, and work space; (c) political stability; and (d) the large size and potential of the U.S. market.[17]

As illustrated in Table 13-2, Americans consume products and services provided by many foreign firms with direct investments in the United States. Examples of some of the most commonly used products and services are Peter Paul candy bars, Pepsodent toothpaste, Hardee's hamburgers, and A&P groceries.

In selecting among foreign market entry methods, decision criteria related to the firm, its industry, the foreign market, and the entry method have to be established. Key decision criteria, along with how well each international expansion option performs on each criterion, are summarized in Figure 13-2.

Designing International Distribution Strategy

Regardless of the expansionary route followed, the international marketer will be faced with the problem of designing and implementing a distribution strategy. The channel system for international marketing, especially for those firms not undertaking direct investment, almost always involves two channel segments, one domestic and the other foreign, as shown in Figure 13-3.

Compared to marketing channels within one's home country, the international marketing channel is longer. This is because it generally involves using a large number of intermediaries, which play a major role in smoothing the flow of products from domestic production to foreign consumption. Because of the idiosyncrasies of international intermediaries, the environments in which they operate, and the lack of control over their operations, managing international marketing channels is extremely complex.

In designing international distribution channels and in developing distribution strategy, international marketers focus on goals which are similar to those employed in domestic channels, including:

1. Achieving adequate market coverage.
2. Maintaining control over how goods are marketed within the channel.
3. Holding distribution costs to reasonable levels.
4. Ensuring the continuity of channel relationships and, consequently, continuous presence in the markets.

[15] Donald Ball and Wendell McCulloch, Jr., *International Business*, 2nd ed. (Plano, Tex.: Business Publications, Inc., 1985) p. 32.

[16] Martin C. Schnitzer, Marilyn L. Liebrenz, and Konrad W. Kublin, *International Business* (Cincinnati: South Western, 1985), p. 404.

[17] Ibid.

TABLE 13-2 The 15 Largest Foreign Investments in the United States

	Foreign Investor	Country	U.S. Company	Industry	Revenue ($ million)	Assets ($ million)
1.	Seagram Co. Ltd	Canada	Joseph Seagrams (100%)	Spirits and wines	$ 1,480	$ 4,780
			E. I. duPont (21%)	Chemicals	35,173	24,432
2.	Anglo-American Corporation	South Africa	Phibro-Salomon (21%)	Metal trading and metals	36,653	43,694
			Engelhard (29%) & others		32,417	
3.	Royal Dutch Shell	Netherlands	Shell Oil (69%)	Energy, metals	20,978	22,169
		Great Britain	Billiton Metals (100%) and others			
4.	British Petroleum	Great Britain	Standard Oil Ohio (53%)	Energy	11,599	16,362
			B P North America (100%)		N.A.	N.A.
5.	Mitsui & Company	Japan	Alumax (50%)	Aluminum	1,510	1,512
			Mitsui & Co. USA (100%)	General trading	8,055E	2,046
6.	B.A.T.	Great Britain	BATUS (100%)	Paper, tobacco, retailing	9,545	3,903
					5,524	
			Hardee's Food (100%)	Fast food	807	364
			People's Drug Stores (96%)	Drugstores	791	229
7.	Flick Group	Germany	W. R. Grace (28%)	Multicompany	7,122	5,035
8.	Tenglemann Group	Germany	Great A & P Tea (51%)	Supermarkets	6,219	1,200
					5,222	
9.	Renault	France	American Motors (46%)	Automotive	3,272	1,724
			Mack Truck (46%)		1,212	973
10.	Brascan, Ltd.	Canada	Scott Paper (24%)	Paper products	2,465	2,252
			Noranda, Inc. (100%)	Aluminum	1,023	N.A.
			MacMillan Bloedel (100%)	Forest products	763	N.A.
11.	Philips	Netherlands	North American Philips (59%)	Electronics	4,251	2,252
					3,800	
			Signetics (100%)	Semiconductors	450	N.A.
12.	General Occidentale	France	Grand Union (100%)	Supermarkets	3,519	765

Source: Forbes, July 2, 1984, pp. 117–18. © Forbes, Inc., 1984

TABLE 13-2 (continued)

	Foreign Investor	Country	U.S. Company	Industry	Revenue ($ million)	Assets ($ million)
13.	Volkswagen	Germany	Volkswagen of America (100%)	Automotive	2,992	N.A.
			Royal Business Machines (100%)	Office equipment	500E	N.A.
					3,492	
14.	Bayer	Germany	Mobay Chemical	Chemicals	3,445	2,700E
			Miles (100%)	Health care		
			Agfa-Gervaert (100%) and others	Photography		
15.	Mitsubishi	Japan	Mitsubishi Int'l Co.	Trading company	3,165	N.A.

Notes: E—Estimated
N.A.—Not Available

Source: "The 100 Largest Foreign Investments in the U.S.," *Forbes,* July 2, 1984, pp. 117–118.

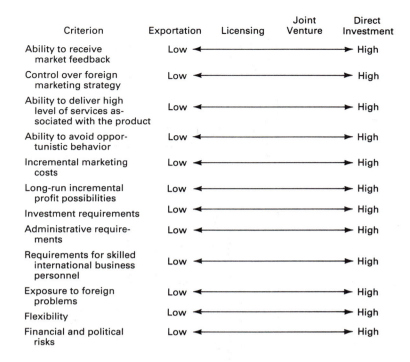

Criterion	Exportation	Licensing	Joint Venture	Direct Investment
Ability to receive market feedback	Low ◄———————————————► High			
Control over foreign marketing strategy	Low ◄———————————————► High			
Ability to deliver high level of services associated with the product	Low ◄———————————————► High			
Ability to avoid opportunistic behavior	Low ◄———————————————► High			
Incremental marketing costs	Low ◄———————————————► High			
Long-run incremental profit possibilities	Low ◄———————————————► High			
Investment requirements	Low ◄———————————————► High			
Administrative requirements	Low ◄———————————————► High			
Requirements for skilled international business personnel	Low ◄———————————————► High			
Exposure to foreign problems	Low ◄———————————————► High			
Flexibility	Low ◄———————————————► High			
Financial and political risks	Low ◄———————————————► High			

Figure 13-2 Ability of international market expansion options to satisfy decision criteria for entering foreign markets. *Source*: Based on Vern Terpstra, *International Marketing*, 3rd ed. (Hinsdale, Ill.: Dryden Press, 1983), pp. 312–320; and Erin Anderson and Anne T. Coughlan, "International Market Entry and Expansion via Independent or Integrated Channels of Distribution," *Journal of Marketing*, Vol. 51, (January 1987), pp. 71–82.

5. Achieving marketing goals expressed in terms of volume, market share, margin requirements, and return on investments.

Most international marketers will find these goals difficult to achieve because of the idiosyncrasies of international channel intermediaries. The next section discusses wholesale and retail intermediaries that operate in international marketing channels.

International Marketing Channels: Institutions and Structure

Figure 13-3 provides some idea of the international channel alternatives available to a domestic producer. Domestic intermediaries are located in the producer's home country and provide marketing services from the domestic base. Because these institutions are closer to the manufacturer, they are convenient to use, but because they are removed from the foreign markets, they may not be able to

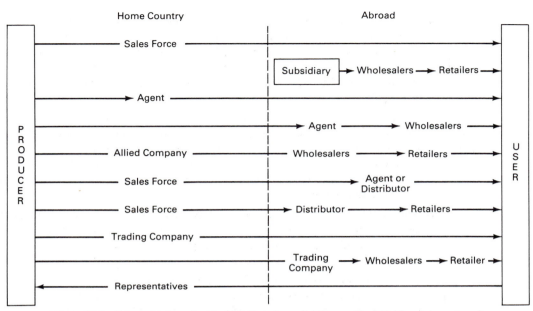

Figure 13-3 Selected international marketing channels. *Source*: Ruel Kahler, *International Marketing*, 5th ed. (Cincinnati, Ohio: Southwestern Publishing Company, 1983), p. 165.

provide the kind of market information and representation available from foreign-based wholesale and retail institutions.[18]

The basic retail and wholesale institutions involved in international marketing channels are similar to the domestic ones described in Chapters 3 and 4, respectively. There are some important differences, however, and they are discussed in the following sections. Also addressed are issues in structuring international marketing channels and problems of control over those channels.

Wholesalers.[19] Several types of wholesale institutions are unique to international trade:

- *EMC (Export Management Companies).* These are agent wholesalers who generally serve a number of principals, (each of which has a relatively small international volume) and act as the international marketing department for the firms they represent. The main functions performed by EMCs are contact with foreign customers and negotiations for sales. Since they usually do business under a principal's name (e.g., they use the principal's letterhead), foreign customers seldom know that they are not dealing directly with the export department of the principal. EMCs operate mainly on commission but may also receive fees.

[18] Cateora, *International Marketing*, p. 581.

[19] The discussion in this section is based largely on the excellent descriptions provided in ibid., pp. 582–585, 598.

- *MEA (Manufacturer's Export Agents)*. These agent wholesalers are similar to EMCs, except that they do not serve as the producer's export department (i.e., they only have a short-term relationship), cover only one or two markets, and operate on a straight commission basis. Another difference is that MEAs do business in their own names rather than in the name of their principals.

- *Comprador or Del Credere Agents*. These agent wholesalers function in Far Eastern countries and have historically been particularly important in trade with China. They are essentially general managers who represent foreign merchants in their operations in a given Oriental country. Compradors are used because of their intimate knowledge of the obscure and enigmatic customs and languages of the importing country.

- *Norazi*. These agent wholesalers specialize in shady or difficult transactions, such as those involving contraband materials (e.g., radioactive products, war matériel), black market currency operations, untaxed liquor, and narcotics.

- *Trading Companies*. These merchant wholesalers perform the traditional functions associated with merchant wholesaling. In addition, trading companies gather market information, develop and implement marketing plans, handle and warehouse merchandise, finance distributors and retailers, seek out and develop new sources of supply and demand, and provide political accessibility and acceptability for their clients. By no means are trading companies new marketing institutions. Such well-known firms as the British Hudson Bay Company and East India Company, the Japanese Mitsubishi Corporation and Mitsui and Company, the French United Africa Company, and the Saudi Arabian Jomaih Zahid are long-established international trading companies.

- *Combination Retailer-Wholesaler*. Many foreign retailers frequently engage directly in importing for both retailing and wholesaling purposes. Because the combination retailer-wholesaler is more important in foreign countries than in the United States, many of the larger retailers in a given city wholesale their goods to local shops and dealers.

Except for these unique international agent and merchant wholesalers, foreign wholesalers generally perform the same functions that wholesalers do in the United States. And as with U.S. wholesaling, the functions performed and marketing flows participated in may vary from situation to situation and are generally subject to negotiation. We should also note that wholesalers play a crucial role in economic development in the LDCs. They handle imports as well as the products of small domestic manufacturers; they also finance the flow of goods between the producers and retailers.

Several trends have been developing in wholesaling that have important implications for international marketers. One worldwide trend is the move toward greater vertical integration from the wholesale or retail level back to the manufacturer.[20] Marketers who have depended on a wholesaler to handle their products often find the channel blocked by wholesalers handling their own custom-manufactured products.

Another development is the emergence of wholesaler-sponsored voluntary chains, resident buying offices, and buying pools.[21] As in the United States, these chains have been formed to counteract the increasing clout of the vertically integrated channels.

Retailing. Retailing in many aspects is a localized activity, deeply influenced by prevailing social and cultural norms as well as by government controls. Any institutional framework in a country is a function of its environment. Thus, as a country becomes more economically developed, retailing is generally performed by larger and larger units.[22] In the United States, as noted in Chapter 3, food retailing is dominated by larger supermarkets. However, this is not necessarily true of the rest of the world.

In Europe, supermarkets are progressing, but over 80 percent of the food trade is still in the hands of small merchants with modest stores. In India, food is still mainly sold through thousands of individual tradesmen squatting in open markets, hawking their goods from door to door, or selling from tiny hole-in-the-wall shops.[23]

Just as the size of retail establishments varies with economic development, so does the level of service that retailers provide to both manufacturers and consumers. Thus, large retail houses generally carry inventory, render financial help, display and promote merchandise, and furnish market information. Smaller retailers tend to depend on the manufacturer or wholesaler to provide these functions.

Dealing directly with smaller retailers is usually difficult for an international marketer. Thus, in nations where retailing in a mom-and-pop business, wholesalers are vitally important. By the same token, new ideas and innovations can only be successfully introduced at the retail level in countries that have large retail houses.[24] Japanese *depatos* are one such retail institution in which innovations and new ideas are welcome (see Exhibit 13-2).

International Marketing Channel Structure and Control. Once a firm decides to expand internationally, it must decide whether or not to deal with the home

[20] Ibid., p. 624.

[21] Ibid.

[22] John Fayerweather, *International Marketing*, 2nd ed. (Englewood Cliffs, N.J.: Prentice-Hall, 1970), p. 61. See also Johan Arndt, "Temporal Lags in Comparative Retailing," *Journal of Marketing*, Vol. 36 (October 1972), pp. 40–45.

[23] Fayerweather, *International Marketing*, p. 62.

[24] Subhash Jain, *International Marketing Management* (Boston: Kent Publishing Co., 1984), p. 442.

EXHIBIT 13-2

New Ideas in Retailing: Japanese Depatos

All major Japanese department stores—or *depatos*, as they are conveniently called in westernized Japanese—emphasize variety, service, and quality. Within a single store, customers can find fancy foods, pet shops, restaurants, Kimonos and fabrics, beauty salons, travel and concert ticket agencies, and florists. In addition, a variety of services are provided for customers. These range from ordering a car, to courses in flower arranging or tea ceremony, or even to securing a loan.

Moreover, Japanese department stores are designed as places for the entire family to visit. They offer rooftop playgrounds, in-store baby-sitting services, and free parking. These *depatos* are organized according to the "trickle-down" theory of market; they lure the entire family to the top-floor exhibition area, and then let them slowly make their way down through the floors, with each area appealing to a certain family member.

Source: Based on "Inside a Japanese Department Store," *World* (Peat Marwick), No. 4, 1983 pp. 40–43.

country agents or merchant wholesalers. The alternative is to deal directly with the intermediaries located in foreign markets.

The advantages of working directly with foreign-based intermediaries are that they (1) provide time and place utility by purchasing and holding the goods at a location relatively convenient to customers, (2) provide credit service, (3) assume the risk of price fluctuations, (4) give varying degrees of sales service, and thus (5) bring the manufacturer closer to markets and shorten its channel.

The disadvantages of this type of arrangement are that merchant wholesalers and retailers (1) select their own selling prices; (2) may have little manufacturer loyalty because they handle large amounts of goods, and are more likely to favor high-profit, high-turnover items; and (3) may be difficult to control. For these reasons, relying heavily on foreign intermediaries to promote and sell a product aggressively is unwise. As with all intermediaries, effectiveness depends on the selection of the middlemen and on the amount of control the manufacturer is willing to exert.[25]

Foreign intermediaries are not significantly different, in terms of the functions they perform, from U.S. wholesalers and retailers. However, because most countries do not have strict antitrust laws like ours, U.S.-based producers may exercise greater coercive, reward, and legitimate power over their foreign intermediaries. Moreover, relationships with suppliers are frequently formalized through tight franchise or ownership arrangements that might be legally challenged in the United States.[26]

Even so, control over the activities and operations of international market-

[25] Cateora, *International Marketing*, pp. 596–597.

[26] See "Using Foreign Distributors Without Fearing Antitrust," *Business Abroad*, March 8, 1965, p. 28.

ing channels is generally more difficult to accomplish than it is within the United States. Although channel institutions perform the same basic functions, wholesaling and retailing patterns in foreign markets are not as well developed as they are in the United States. In many countries, a few huge distributors and many tiny intermediaries predominate. This means that suppliers seeking to tap international markets must either give over control to economically and often politically powerful distributors or develop their own systems. For example:

> In Israel, there are some 1,500 wholesalers, most of whom are small. Contrast these with Hamashbir Hamerkazi, a giant wholesaler who handles all kinds of products and has full or partial ownership in 12 major industrial firms. In the early 1960's they reportedly handled approximately 1/5th of all the wholesaling volume of that country.[27]

International Marketing Channels for Counter Trade

Barter, or counter trade, is one of the most rapidly growing elements of world trade, particularly between Eastern and Western bloc countries.[28] Defined, *counter trade* is any business arrangement in which payment is made by means other than cash for goods.[29] The share of counter trade in East-West trade agreements grew from 28 percent during 1976 to 50 percent in 1984. Private trade experts have estimated that nearly one-third of all world trade, or more than $700 billion, is on a counter trade basis.[30]

One of the largest barter deals made to date involved a 20-year, $20 billion agreement between Occidental Petroleum Corporation and the Soviet Union. Occidental agreed to ship super-phosphoric acid to the Soviets in exchange for ammonia urea and potash.[31]

Counter trade has increased for several reasons: (1) the financial problems of developing economies that limit these countries' credit, (2) cash shortages because of large debt-servicing payments, (3) the strength of the dollar versus the inconvertibility of other currencies, (4) poor marketing channels and marketing expertise, and (5) import restrictions to limit the amount of foreign exchange being drained.[32]

Although counter trade allows an exchange to take place, the arrangements are complicated and take a long time to negotiate. In addition, problems arise over

[27] Cateora, *International Marketing*, p. 623.

[28] V. H. Kirpalani, *International Marketing* (New York: Random House Business Division, 1984), p. 493.

[29] Martha B. Mast, "Some Business Are Turning to Barter in Trading," *Feedstuffs*, July 30, 1984, pp. 5, 53–54.

[30] Ibid.

[31] Cateora, *International Marketing*, p. 598

[32] Mast, "Business Turning to Barter," pp. 53–54.

(1) the quality and types of goods offered, (2) the values of the goods, and (3) the financial strain placed on the company because its capital is tied up longer than for a normal transaction. For these reasons, most U.S. companies avoid barter transactions.

Nevertheless, understanding marketing channels involved in counter trade is important because of the special nature of counter trade, the problems associated with these transactions, and their growing importance in world trade, particularly with the Eastern bloc countries.

Special channel arrangements have been developed to handle counter trade. The following are illustrative of these arrangements:

- The selling responsibility of the goods in the barter agreement may be turned over to specialists known as barter houses, switch traders, intermerchants, or trading houses. Also, Japanese trading companies engage in nonmoney trading. These specialists are located in London, Vienna, Zurich, Munich, and Hamburg, and trade in virtually anything.
- Some multinational corporations have established in-house counter trade units. An example is Northrop's offset program. When Northrop sells aircraft to many countries, part of the payment is received as the transaction is concluded. The balance is paid when the offset program has successfully sold goods and services of the country that bought the aircraft to third-party countries.
- Some multinationals look to other multinationals to help sell the products they acquire in counter trade. For example, when Pullman-Kellogg agreed to receive fertilizer in payment for designing and building a plant in Nigeria, it turned to International Mineral and Chemicals and Transcontinental Fertilizers to market the Nigerian fertilizers.[33]
- The product received may be sold through the company's regular marketing channels. Exhibit 13-3 presents a well-known illustration of this special counter trade channel arrangement.

Obviously, the last two channel alternatives are the shortest and easiest. However, they are the exception rather than the rule in counter trade.

Problems in Establishing and Managing International Marketing Channels

The final section dealing with the context of international marketing channels is a recap of the major problems firms encounter when they expand into foreign markets. The objective is not to discourage managers from developing international markets for their products, but to warn them of some of the major obstacles they face in doing so.

Careful planning is crucial if a company is to obtain the lucrative benefits possible from serving foreign markets. Only with a knowledge of likely problem areas can such planning be undertaken. Six such problems—the availability of

[33] Robert E. Weigand, "Barter and Buy-Backs—Problems for the Marketing Channels," in Richard P. Bagozzi et al. (eds.), *Marketing in the 1980s: Changes and Challenges* (Chicago: American Marketing Association, 1980), p. 257.

EXHIBIT 13-3

**U.S. Marketing Channels for Stolichnaya
Vodka: Counter Trade Arrangements
in Action**

An interesting marketing channel arrangement for counter trade is the one that occurred when the Soviet Union agreed to allow PepsiCo to market Pepsi in the U.S.S.R. Under the terms of the agreement, PepsiCo would ship its syrup from the United Kingdom, bottle it in the U.S.S.R., and sell it in small quantities. In compensation, PepsiCo agreed to take back Soviet products.

Stolichnaya vodka had never sold well in the United States, partly because it competed with American vodka and with vodka coming from countries that enjoyed most-favored nation treatment. Still, PepsiCo took Stolichnaya instead of cash and agreed that the amount of Pepsi Cola that would be bottled in the U.S.S.R. would depend upon the amount of Soviet vodka sales in the United States. Fortunately for PepsiCo, the vodka fit neatly into one of Pepsi's channels. It became part of the product line of Monsieur Henri, a subsidiary of PepsiCo that imports and distributes liquor and wines for the American market.

Source: Adapted from *Marketing in the 1980's: Changes and Challenges*, published by the American Marketing Association (Chicago: 1980), "Barter and Buy Backs—Problems for the Marketing Channels," by Robert E. Weigand, Richard P. Bagozzi (ed.), p. 257.

---

intermediaries, barriers in choosing channels, differences in promotional emphasis, status quo orientations, motivating intermediaries, and maintaining control—are briefly discussed below.

Intermediary Availability. It is not always an easy task to find out which intermediaries are available to handle a company's merchandise, and even after potential channel partners are identified, it is sometimes hard to determine if they are adequately qualified. The importance of careful selection of foreign channel organizations cannot be overemphasized. The reason is that the home company may not easily dissolve relationships with incompetent intermediaries; these firms may be protected by law. For example, in Norway, a manufacturer often cannot change agents without proof of negligence.

Barriers in Choosing Channels. The international marketer may be constrained in choosing a channel by a variety of barriers in the foreign market. These barriers include (1) host country trade practices concerning how particular products may be distributed, (2) governmental policies about private versus state-controlled markets, and (3) cultural conditions that may rule out using a particular type of channel.[34] In addition, access to markets may be blocked by

[34] Jain, *International Marketing Management*, p. 431.

existing financial and other tie-in arrangements among domestic channel institutions. Such arrangements are not often available to foreign producers.

In Japan, manufacturers are one of the primary sources of financial assistance to the wholesalers and retailers with whom they deal.[35] Such assistance solidifies trade relations within that country. That solidarity, plus the fact that Japanase society is relatively cohesive, means that foreign producers may have difficulty in breaking into an established channel system.

Differences in Promotional Emphasis.   More than likely, a larger proportion of a company's advertising budget will have to be devoted to trade promotion in a foreign country than in the United States. The reason is that there are so many small intermediaries that must be reached.[36]

Status Quo Orientation.   Intermediaries in less developed countries are distinctly less venturesome than those in more advanced ones; therefore, they are less willing to accept the risk of adopting new products as well as new methods of doing business. Because such firms are often mom-and-pop operations, they many times prefer to limit the scope of their business, simply to maintain personal control over it. Accordingly, companies seeking to enter such markets must assume a greater burden of developing demand than they would in the United States.

Motivating Intermediaries.   Motivating intermediaries in foreign markets can be a formidable task. To many, marketing simply means sitting on a product and waiting for the customer to come and buy it. The "carrot and stick" philosophy of motivating agents and distributors in the United States, Canada, and Europe often fails in others parts of the world.

Maintaining Control.   Maintaining some semblance of control over the distribution system may be absolutely necessary if the international marketer is to achieve any success in foreign markets. This may be difficult to do, since, as we have noted, distribution through intermediaries in foreign locales always entails compromise. The trade-off is the loss of control over foreign marketing operations in order to gain the benefits of relatively low cost market representation.[37] Manufacturers/exporters must compare their goals with those of the foreign distributor and decide whether or not the trade-off is acceptable.

Exhibit 13-4 illustrates the problems that happened when Levi Strauss

---

[35] Robert E. Weigand, "Aspects of Retail Pricing in Japan," in Louis W. Boone and James C. Johnson (eds.), *Marketing Channels* (Morristown, N.J.: General Learning Press, 1973), p. 320.

[36] Don T. Dunn, Jr. "Agents and Distributors in the Middle East," *Business Horizons* (October 1979), p. 74.

[37] Jain, *International Marketing Management*, p. 436.

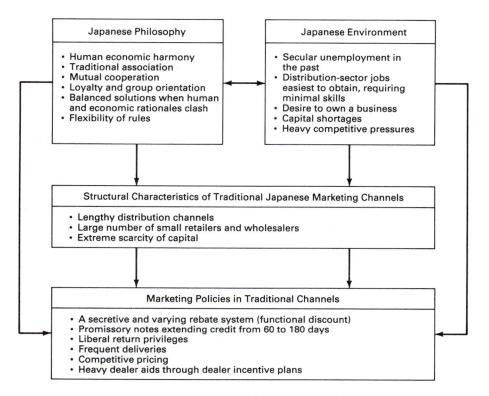

Figure 13-4 The anatomy of the traditional Japanese marketing channel. *Source*: Based upon analysis presented in M. Shimaguchi, "Japanese Distribution Channels: Traditions, Customs, and Evolution," working paper, Keio University, Tokyo, Japan, undated; M. Shimaguchi and Larry Rosenberg, "Demystifying Japanese Distribution," *Columbia Journal of World Business*, Spring 1979, pp. 32–41; and M. Shimaguchi and William Lazar, "Japanese Distribution Channels: Invisible Barriers to Market Entry," *MSU Business Topics*, Winter 1979, pp. 49–62.

attempted to expand in to international markets in a big way. As the exhibit makes abundantly clear, it is crucial to develop functioning and meaningful information systems. In fact, this facet of international marketing may be the most arduous problem, given the current state of foreign distribution and the power held by the middlemen in those markets.

Problems in establishing and managing international marketing channels can be more readily understood and effectively dealt with when marketers develop a better understanding of the traditions, customs, and evolution of the marketing channels in the countries in which they operate. Figure 13-4 provides a summary analysis of the Japanese philosophy and environment and their impact on the structure and policies of the traditional Japanese marketing channel. This figure underscores our parting comment on international marketing channels: Environmental and cultural sensitivity is a must for successfully dealing with marketing channel arrangements in international marketing.

EXHIBIT 13-4
Problems in International Wholesale
Distribution: Levi Strauss' Experience

Perhaps one of the most fascinating examples of the problem of achieving effective wholesale distribution abroad is the story of Levi Strauss' efforts to gain a large market share for its clothing products (jeans, pants, and shirts) in Europe in the late 1960s and early 1970s. According to a *Fortune* report on its problems, Levi Strauss made "a fast grab for the European market without sufficient control on inventory and distribution." This experience cost the company at least $12 million and left it with a deficit of over $7 million in the fourth quarter of 1973. Some of the relevant facts of the debacle are detailed below.

Because demand in Europe was far outrunning supply, management saw no pressing need for inventory controls. In 1970, Levi Strauss Europe (L.S.E.)'s inventory turned over seven times (about four is normal for apparel), and the main warehouse in Antwerp had to be fully replenished an incredible 19 times. Independent distributors were buying L.S.E.'s merchandise without any careful planning as to future demand. Learning that a shipment was arriving, distributors would send trucks to Antwerp and buy anything they saw.

To improve Levi's distribution within Europe as quickly as possible, L.S.E. acquired the firms that had been its national distributors in ten countries and turned them into sale subsidiaries. The company chose to do this rather than bring in Levi Strauss salespeople, who were experienced in domestic apparel markets but unfamiliar with marketing in Europe. Close relationships between manufacturers and retailers are vital in the apparel business, and management believed that L.S.E.'s distributors and their salespeople would provide that tie, enabling the company to keep attuned to changes in each national market. However, meshing the acquired firms with L.S.E. proved to be unexpectedly difficult. Their presidents were long-established in their own countries and resisted changing their methods of doing business. In Britain, one former owner resisted proposals for warehouse consolidation and other managerial changes so strongly that the company shifted him into another job.

In keeping with well-established Levi Strauss policy, each national manager retained full autonomy and profit responsibility. At first, L.S.E. received only quarterly balance sheets—outdated information. Moreover, each new subsidiary operated differently, with its own accounting and inventory-control systems. Only in Switzerland was the operation computerized, but its system did not fit with L.S.E.'s. Furthermore, several of the firms did not have accurate information about their inventories. Their reports were often so lacking in details (about sizes and styles, for example) as to be meaningless.

Almost three quarters of the pants the company sold in Europe were imported from plants located outside the continent. Once the goods did reach Europe, L.S.E. could not keep track of where they were. Moreover, the ever-increasing volume of pants overwhelmed the efforts of clerks to keep adequate records of the movements. As a result, warehouse workers often did not know where to find goods stacked in the bins. Incredible as it seems, if a retailer returned a shipment, L.S.E.'s warehouse had no means of reentering the goods into inventory.

On top of all this, fashion changes sweeping Europe compounded what was already a major catastrophe in the making. Further evidence of L.S.E.'s lack of control was found when one distributor who had not been acquired requested a particular style, which L.S.E. declined to produce. Rather than accepting L.S.E.'s decision, the distributor flew to Hong Kong and ordered two million pairs of the style he wanted directly from the Levi Strauss manufacturing subsidiary there.

Although one might argue that even with the lack of control, L.S.E. was able to accomplish its objective because it eventually captured the largest share of the European market for jeans, there can be little doubt that the European experience was a traumatic experience that the corporation would not like to repeat. The European wholesalers were, to a very large extent, the root cause of L.S.E.'s major problems, and even vertical integration was ineffective in securing needed control over their operations. One lesson is, therefore, abundantly clear—if adequate distribution and effective channel management were so difficult for a sophisticated U.S. manufacturer and marketer to secure in a developed, highly industrialized market like Europe, it is likely to be even more difficult to secure in less developed economies. In international marketing channels, nothing can be taken for granted.

As we noted at the beginning of the chapter, the international context is one of several in which marketing channels operate. Another important context is marketing channels for services, which are a very large and increasing proportion of the gross national product of the United States.[38]

MARKETING CHANNELS FOR SERVICES

Among the characteristics distinguishing goods from services, none is more important for marketing channel strategy than the fact that services are intangible. Intangibility means that (1) services cannot be stored or transported and (2) they cannot be produced in one location and then shipped to another for resale.[39]

A critical task of service marketing, therefore, is to make services widely available so that organizational and household buyers can easily acquire them. To do this, service marketers must focus on marketing channel strategies and tactics, which involve decisions about the number and types of ''retail'' outlets to employ, the kinds of ''intermediaries'' to use, and the types of facilitating agencies needed.

[38] James L. Heskett, *Managing in the Service Economy* (Boston, Mass.: Harvard Business School Press, 1986).

[39] Gregory D. Upah, ''Mass Marketing in Service Retailing: A Review and Synthesis of Major Methods,'' *Journal of Retailing*, Vol. 56 (Fall 1980), pp. 60–61.

TABLE 13-3 Potential Management Problems Associated with the Retailing of Services

Services as Compared with Goods	Managerial Changes Needed for Services Retailing
Measuring Performance	
Capital expenditures vary widely for different services	Return on net worth may not be the most important measurement of the value of a service to the retailer
Little or no inventories are required to offer services	Turnover, mark-down controls, and other goods-related controls are not appropriate
Higher labor costs	Profit after labor costs replaces the gross margin of goods retailing
Some services support the sale of goods	Sales-supporting services should be evaluated differently from revenue-producing services
Cost accounting is more important	Job-specific records will be required to assess the profitability of each sale
Store Organization	
More specialized supervision	Separate management for service areas will be required
More specific search for service employees	Nontraditional sources for identification of employees must be used
Lower employee turnover	Frequent salary and performance reviews must be carried out
Higher pay for skilled craftspeople than for merchandising personnel	Pay levels will need to be adjusted upward over periods of longevity for service employees
Service Production	
More involvement in manufacturing of the service	Production skills will need to be obtained by supervisors
More emphasis on quality control	Supervisors must be able to assess the quality of a service performed for a customer
More need to monitor consumer satisfaction	Need for research with prior customers to measure their satisfaction with the service
More need to refine scheduling of employees	Maximizing the service employees' time requires matching consumer purchasing to ability to produce the service
Quality must be consistent among all outlets	Standards for consistency of the service must be established and continually evaluated; central training may be required for craftworkers in multiple branch operations
Pricing	
Services vary in cost; therefore, pricing is more difficult	Prices may be quoted within a range instead of an exact figure before the purchase
More difficulty in price competition or promotion based upon price	Services should be promoted on the basis of criteria other than price
Sales Promotion	
Value is more difficult for consumers to determine	Consumers need to be convinced of value through personal selling

TABLE 13-3 (continued)

Services as Compared with Goods	Managerial Changes Needed for Services Retailing
Difficult to display within store	In-store signing or a service center is required to notify customers of services availability
Visual presentation is more important	Before-and-after photographs may be possible with some services
	Testimonials may be possible with other services
Cross-selling with goods is important	A quota or bonus for goods salespersons who suggest services will lead to increased service selling
More difficult to advertise in catalogs	Conditions for the sale and away-from-the-store performance must be specified
Complaints	
More difficult to return a service	Policies must be established on adjusting the service purchased with a dissatisfied customer
A customer is more sensitive about services involving the person	Specific guarantees and policies about adjustments must be established; new types of insurance must be added to cover liabilities
Controls	
Greater opportunity to steal customers	Employee assurance of loyalty must be established
	Protection of store loyalty must be obtained

Source: J. Patrick Kelly and William R. George, "Strategic Management Issues for the Retailing of Services," *Journal of Retailing*, Vol. 58 (Summer 1982), pp. 40–42.

For nonprofit organizations, this task is compounded by the fact that two separate distribution systems must be established, one dealing with resource *allocation* and the other with resource *attraction*. In any case, whether a service is provided by a for-profit or not-for-profit organization, a major issue is the availability of something intangible.

In many service industries (e.g., banking and travel), service "wholesalers" and "retailers" can be readily identified. The basic principles of channel management discussed throughout this text apply to the marketing of service in these industries. In other situations, where production and sale take place simultaneously (e.g., dentistry, restaurants, barber shops), there are very few purely "vertical" (multilevel) marketing channel problems. Here, special attention must be on location issues, because such services are valuable to endusers largely to the extent that they provide time and place utilities. Since location decisions for services are very similar to retail location decisions, the discussion in Chapter 3 on that topic will not be repeated here.

Although the retailing of goods and the retailing of services are similar in many ways, they are not identical. In fact, a failure to recognize the distinctions between them can give rise to a number of management problems. These distinctions and their managerial implications are summarized in Table 13-3.

The following sections explain the basic elements of marketing channels for

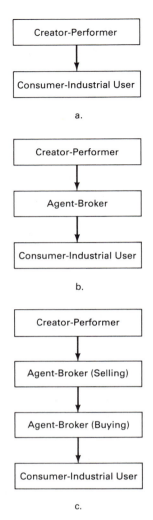

Figure 13-5 Dominant channel configurations in the service sector. *Source*: John M. Rathmell, *Martketing in the Service Sector* (Cambridge, Mass.: Winthrop Publishers, 1974), p. 110.

services. These elements include service channel institutions and structure as well as the behavior of institutions within those channels. Then, to give the reader a better appreciation for how the principles of marketing channel management discussed in the previous 12 chapters apply to channels for services, two in-depth examples are presented. These illustrate marketing channels for health care and for lodging.

Marketing Channel Institutions and Structures in the Services Sector

The dominant channel structures in the service sector are depicted in Figure 13-5.[40] Intermediaries in the form of agents or brokers appear in particular service industries.

[40] John M. Rathmell, *Marketing in the Service Sector* (Cambridge, Mass.: Winthrop Publishers, 1974), pp. 109–110.

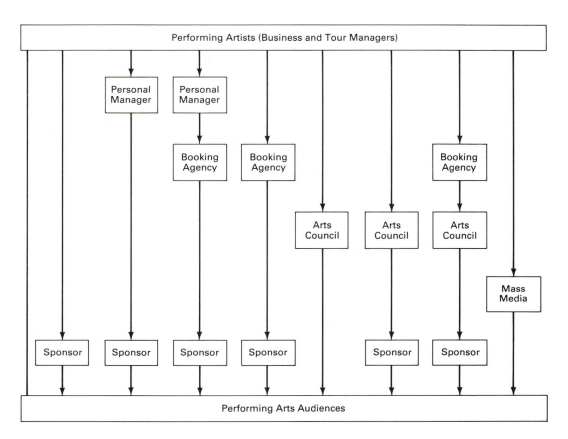

Figure 13-6 The marketing channels for the performing arts. *Source*: John R. Nevin, "An Empirical Analysis of Marketing Channels for the Performing Arts," in Michael P. Mokwa, William M. Dawson, and E. Arthur Prieve (eds.), *Marketing the Arts* (New York: Praeger Publishers, 1980), p. 204.

These intermediaries bring together service performers and consumers. They may represent the performer, the consumer, or both. For example, sports agents represent professional athletes wishing to sell their services to major league teams. Stock brokers represent corporations, investment firms, individual investors, and others who have financial securities for sale. Figure 13-6 illustrates a number of alternative marketing channels, both direct and indirect, for the performing arts.

Because the marketing channel tasks they perform vary so widely from channel to channel, it is difficult to typify the functions of the various agents and brokers in service channels. However, service agents and brokers are, like their counterparts in other contexts, clearly involved primarily with flows of promotion and negotiation. For automobile repair and restaurants, for example, merchant wholesalers play an important role in providing the basic supplies needed for those services to be performed. The actual service, however, originates at the retail level. Franchising is extremely important in the marketing of a wide variety of services, such as automobile rentals, carpet cleaning, dry cleaning, temporary

---

EXHIBIT 13-5

**Conflict in Marketing Channels for Air
Travel Services**

In early 1980, Pan Am was considering a proposed plan to sell large blocks of tickets on scheduled flights at wholesale prices to contractors or intermediaries who would assume the risk and responsibility for pricing and marketing the tickets as they saw fit. Travel agents spoke out in opposition to the plan because they felt that it positioned them in direct competition with their own supplier, the airline. They also pointed out that the already bewildering fare structure could be further muddied by the diversity of prices offered by contractors (i.e., the wholesalers). Moreover, travel agents feared that the plan would allow nontravel-related merchants to retail airline tickets at their wholesale cost as a promotional tool for their basic line of merchandise.

Traditionally, airlines paid a fixed-rate commission of 7 percent for point-to-point domestic ticket sales. In return for creating conditions that made the travel agency profitable, airlines have always been able to write the rules governing agency competition. A Civil Aeronautics Board rule that became effective in May 1980 abolished the fixed-rate commission and ordered carriers to propose new plans for compensating travel agents. Board officials indicated that their intent was to promote retail price competition and encourage new alternative retail outlets.

United Airlines was the first airline to respond with a proposal to pay a flat $8.50 per ticket. Travel agencies reacted by diverting traffic to other airlines that offer higher commissions. United suffered a 14 percent sales drop in one month. Finally, United withdrew the plan and offered an alternate sliding scale plan that paid travel agents from $7.50 to $37.50, depending on distance flown. Other airlines offered different plans. For example, Eastern proposed a commission ranging from 8 to 11 percent, Frontier Airline's plan called for 10 to 11 percent, and American Airline's plan was so complex that most agents said they could not understand it.

Source: Josh Levine, "Pan Am Seeks Ticket Wholesaling," *Advertising Age*, January 23, 1980, pp. 1 and 84; "The Fracas over Who Will Sell Airline Tickets," *Business Week*, April 28, 1980, p. 107; "United Air to Pay Travel Agents Flat Fee, Replaced Commissions Based on Fares," *Wall Street Journal*, February 5, 1980, p. 5; and "United Air, Responding to Complaints, Alters Travel Agent Compensation Plan," *Wall Street Journal*, February 19, 1980, p. 8.

---

office help, and motels. In fact, any *standardized* service is an appropriate candidate for franchising.[41]

Behavior in Marketing Channels for Services

Marketing channels for services, like those for goals, often resist change. This is especially true if the channel comprises small, entrepreneurial firms. But these

[41] Ibid., p. 111.

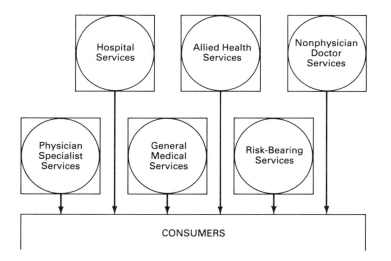

Figure 13-7 The flat nonintegrated structure for the delivery of health–care services. *Source*: Louis P. Bucklin and James M. Carman, "Vertical Market Structure Theory and the Health Care Delivery System", in Jagdish N. Sheth and Peter L. Wright (eds.), *Martketing Analysis for Societal Problems* (Urbana, Ill.: University of Illinois Bureau of Economic and Business Research, 1974), p. 23.

individual firms must "pull together" if the channel is to compete successfully against other vertical marketing systems. Effective marketing channel management uses power to implement change within the channel. Sometimes, as we noted in Chapter 11, this use of power results in conflict among channel members. Exhibit 13-5 describes how changing relationships in the distribution channel for air travel sparked channel conflict.

Applying Channel Concepts to Services: Two Examples

Health-Care Services.[42] Three different market structures for the delivery of health-care services may be isolated, although a number of others also exist. The first, called the *flat, nonintegrated structure* (see Figure 13-7), represents the present private practice, fee-for-service system. In this channel structure, every hospital, each physician, and all other health-care providers sell directly to consumers. The organizations involved in this system undertake no effort to coordinate their activities; any coordination that does take place comes from consumer market pressures.[43]

The second is the *vertically integrated structure*, where the activities of all providers are coordinated by a comprehensive health-care institution. Such an

[42] The discussion of health-care services is drawn from the excellent and innovative essay by Louis P. Bucklin and James M. Carman, "Vertical Market Structure Theory and Health Care Delivery System," in Jagdish N. Sheth and Peter L. Wright (eds.), *Marketing Analis for Societal Problems* (Urbana: University of Illinois Bureau of Economic and Business Research, 1974), pp. 7–39.

[43] Ibid., p. 23.

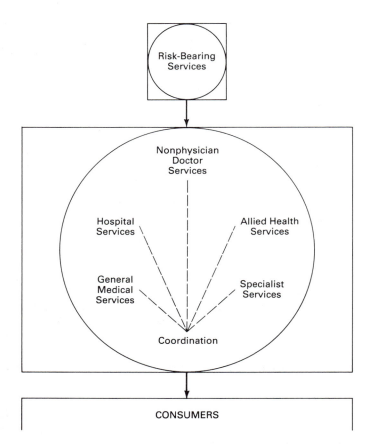

Figure 13-8 The vertically integrated structure for the delivery of health–care services. *Source*: Louis P. Bucklin and James M. Carman, "Vertical Market Structure Theory and the Health Care Delivery System," in Jagdish N. Sheth and Peter L. Wright (eds.), *Marketing Analysis for Societal Problems* (Urbana: University of Illinois Bureau of Economic and Business Research, 1974), p. 25.

institution (e.g., Kaiser Permanente) provides for all potential patient health needs within a single establishment.[44] Although this channel structure varies somewhat, Figure 13-8 is representative of a major form of these so-called health maintenance organizations (HMOs). Functions are coordinated through an internal control mechanism. Consumers pay an annual or monthly lump-sum fee, regardless of how much health care they receive. Moreover, each consumer belongs to only one HMO.

The third type of arrangement, the *long, vertical nonintegrated structure*

[44] Ibid., p. 24. Kaiser employs 5,200 physicians. For a discussion of the changing face of health care in the United States, see Ann B. Fisher, "The New Game in Health Care: Who Will Profit?" *Fortune*, March 4, 1985, pp. 138–143; "The Big Business of Medicine," *Newsweek*, October 31, 1983, pp. 62–74; and "Rx: Competition," *Business Week*, February 8, 1982, pp. 58–64.

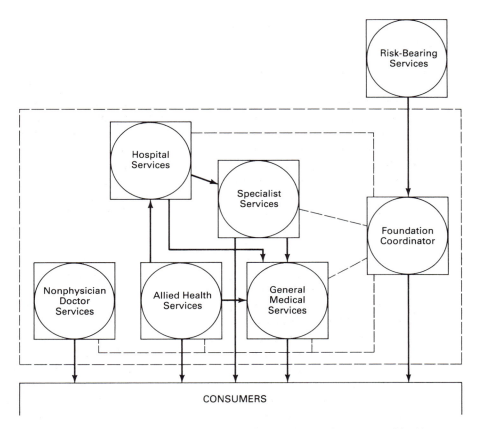

Figure 13-9 The long, vertical, nonintegrated structure for the delivery of health–care services. *Source*: Louis P. Bucklin and James M. Carman, ''Vertical Market Structure Theory and the Health Care Delivery System,'' in Jagdish N. Sheth and Peter L. Wright (eds.), *Marketing Analysis for Societal Problems* (Urbana: University of Illinois Bureau of Economic and Business Research, 1974), p. 28.

(see Figure 13-9), is characterized by the presence of multiple modes of coordination. In these health-care channels:

> [G]eneral financial support and insurance services are provided through a nonprofit foundation for a complete health package. Individual providers would similarly belong to the foundation which would reimburse the former on a fee-for-service basis. The foundation would develop its own techniques, such as peer review, to control the use of providers and their charges for service. All consumers within a given area, such as a county, would be members of the foundation.[45]

As in the vertically integrated structure, consumers make an annual lump-sum payment, only in the long, vertical nonintegrated structure, their payment goes to the foundation.

[45] Bucklin and Carmen, ''Vertical Market Structure Theory,'' pp. 26–27.

As we noted in Chapter 8, the channel structure used largely depends upon the specific services consumers demand. The structure of health-care channels is also determined by the cost of providing those channel services. Some general observations are as follows:[46]

1. The consumer search for information and the need for seller promotion appear to be greatest in the flat, nonintegrated structure (e.g., the traditional health-care channel). The least seller promotion and consumer search cost are provided by the vertically integrated structure.

2. The flat, nonintegrated structure is the one that is likely to adapt best to consumer needs in terms of providing facilitating services, such as transportation (e.g., ambulance services), risk-bearing services (i.e., health insurance), and third-party payment systems (e.g., Medicare). It is also the one that gives consumers the greatest opportunity to select that particular health service they perceive as best suiting their needs.

3. The flat, nonintegrated structure is likely to be the one that incurs the greatest waste of resources, is least efficient, and provides the greatest degree of discrimination among consumer groups. Although wealthy consumers may be able to cope handily with the system, impoverished consumers may literally fail to survive it.

4. The vertically integrated system (HMO) is likely to result in better use of existing health-care resources and to be more efficient. It also provides the basis for evenhanded care for all people.[47] On the other hand, HMOs most likely must minimally adjust their standardized facilitating services to be more responsive to consumer needs. Without competition, local communities may have difficulty wielding control over the health care provided by these channels. As with all vertically integrated channels, bureaucratic rigidities tend to set in over time. Consumers have the least choice of specific providers in these health-care channels.

5. The vertically nonintegrated structures are a middle ground, with characteristics of both the flat, nonintegrated structure and the vertically integrated structure. Consumer choice opportunities are improved over HMOs, but the possibility for some discrimination in resource use also appears likely. Vertically nonintegrated systems also provide maximum opportunity for new types of structures to develop; hence, they stimulate innovation in health-care delivery. An example of extreme innovation in health-care marketing channels is presented in Exhibit 13-6.

Each structure varies in terms of the extent to which power may be used to coordinate channel activities and to manage any conflict that may arise. Note the

[46] Ibid., pp. 29 and 35.

[47] Some evidence indicates that HMOs have a positive competitive impact on health care, in that they provide service at lower cost. See, for example, "FTC Staff Report Says HMOs Have Competitive Impact," *FTC News Summary*, August 1977, p. 1; "HMO's Can Hold Down Health Care Costs," *Wall Street Journal*, August 5, 1977, p. 5; and "Unhealthy Costs of Health Care," *Business Week*, September 4, 1978, pp. 58–68.

EXHIBIT 13-6

**National Medical Enterprises, Inc.:
A Vertically Integrated Channel for Health
Care Services**

National Medical Enterprises, Inc. (NME), the nation's second-largest (after Humana, Inc.) health-care services company, is testing what amounts to an enormous shopping mall for health care on a 40-acre campus in Delray Beach, Florida.

The complex includes: (1) Delray Community Hospital, a 211-bed general acute-care hospital; (2) Hillhaven Convalescent Center of Delray, a 120-bed skilled-care nursing home; (3) the Fair Oaks Hospital of Boca/Delray, a 72-bed psychiatric hospital that specializes in substance abuse; and (4) a 60-bed rehabilitation hospital to treat victims of spinal cord injuries and stroke. Also nearby is a shopping center, on company-owned land, containing everything from a health-food store to a pharmacy, to a bank, as well as three medical buildings containing condominium offices sold to physicians by NME.

NME claims that it saves money on operating costs by having neighboring facilities that can pool purchasing dollars and even share medical facilities. The proximity also improves medical care because doctors find it easy to check up on a nursing patient as long as they are at the neighboring hospital. Physician convenience promotes cross-referrals that boost NME's business.

Source: Michael L. Millenson, "Health Care's 1-Stop Shopping," *Chicago Tribune*, Sect. 7, February 9, 1986, p. 3.

---

parallel between the health-care channel structures described here and the patterns for administering channels (i.e., conventional, administered, contractual, and corporate channels) described in Chapter 9. Thus, the concepts developed for understanding the structure and behavior of marketing channels for tangible products can be used to improve health-care delivery systems.[48]

/ *Lodging Services*.[49] In general, hotels throughout the world tend to be small; for example, over 40 percent of the hotels and motels in the United States are too small to have even one paid employee. Nonetheless, there is an increasing amount of economic concentration in the lodging industry. This concentration has occurred partly because of the development of interorganizational communication systems, franchised networks, and corporate vertical marketing systems. Thus,

[48] For further discussion of this point, see Louis W. Stern and Frederick D. Sturdivant, "Discussion," in Jagdish N. Sheth and Peter L. Wright (eds.), *Marketing Analysis for Societal Problems* (Urbana: University of Illinois Bureau of Economic and Business Research, 1974), pp. 39–41; and Donald E. L. Johnson, "University Hospitals Will Anchor Vertical Systems," *Modern Health Care*, December 1979, pp. 50–54.

[49] The discussion of lodging services is drawn from William H. Kaven, "Channels of Distribution in the Hotel Industry" in John M. Rathmell, *Marketing in the Service Sector* (Cambridge, Mass.: Winthrop Publishers, 1974), pp. 114–121.

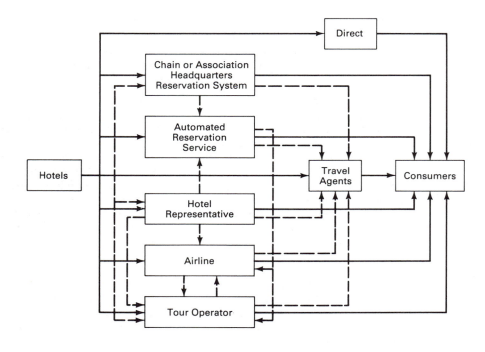

- - - - - Indicates Alternative Channels

Figure 13-10 Marketing Channels for lodging services. *Source*: William H. Kaven, "Channels of Distribution in the Hotel Industry," in John M. Rathmell (ed.), *Marketing in the Service Sector* (Cambridge, Mass.: Winthrop Publishers, 1974), p. 118. Reprinted by permission of the publisher.

marketing channels associated with the lodging industry (hotels, motels, motor inns, tourist courts, etc.) are becoming rather more complex and sophisticated.

The complexity of the channels of distribution in the lodging industry can be seen in Figure 13-10. Direct channels of distribution between hotels, motels, and other lodging operations and their customers are mainly concerned with the sales function. That is, an individual hotel's salespeople concentrate on:

1. Maintaining sales contact with channel intermediaries such as tour operators, travel agents, representatives, and transportation companies.
2. Maintaining sales contact with community firms and organizations in an attempt to obtain lodging and function business.
3. Following the leads furnished by other sources.[50]

Indirect channels, however, are more significant than direct channels to lodging establishments. Intermediaries in indirect channels include travel agents,

[50] Ibid., p. 116.

hotel representatives, tour operators, space brokers, airlines, and centralized reservation and sales operations of franchised or chain hotels.

- *Travel agents* may contract for rooms on a customer's behalf, but they more frequently deal through other intermediaries who hold blocks of rooms or otherwise act as agents for the hotels.
- *Hotel representatives* act as sales and reservation agents for a number of noncompeting hotels such as resorts.
- *Automated reservation services* such as American Express Space Bank maintain, for a fee, in their computers an inventory of available hotel rooms from around the world so that travel agents can buy rooms for their customers.
- *Airlines*, chiefly for overseas destinations, also maintain an inventory of available rooms to accommodate customers and travel agents who prefer to make complete arrangements for both flight and room reservations with a single phone call.
- *Centralized reservation and sales operations* of associated, franchised, or chain hotels/motels work as information clearinghouses. They offer room availability information to potential customers and promote, sell, and accept reservations for space.[51]

As hotel and motel operators have become more dependent upon these intermediaries, the lodging "wholesalers" have gained power in channels for lodging service. These intermediaries can maintain a wide number of alternatives and are able to mediate considerable rewards for lodging providers. In reaction to these changing power relationships, many hotel and motel owners, as well as several organizations closely connected to the industry such as airlines, have formed vertical marketing systems. Either through contractual or ownership arrangements, these systems permit central control over all channel flows, especially those associated with information processing.

The move to vertical marketing arrangements like those forged by Holiday Inns has been motivated by other reasons as well. Such arrangements permit greater economies of scale in promotion, purchasing, and operations. In addition, vertical marketing systems can achieve increased speed and economy in the flow of information. Through improved information technology (e.g., toll-free nationwide hotel reservation numbers), lodging providers have also become closer to their customers at the time they are making purchase decisions. Most importantly, effectively managed vertical systems project to their target markets the image of being national or regional companies of high standards with whom customers can deal with confidence. Exhibit 13-7 illustrates how one firm has used vertical marketing arrangements to improve its effectiveness and efficiency.

As the health-care industry and lodging industry examples show the basic principles of marketing channel management that have been discussed throughout the text are clearly applicable to the delivery of services. They are also relevant

[51] Ibid., pp. 116–117.

> **EXHIBIT 13-7**
> **Vertical Marketing Systems in the Lodging**
> **Industry: The Marriott Corporation**
>
> One of the outstanding practitioners in the lodging industry is the Marriott Corporation. Marriott, which claims its business is to manage hotels and not to own them, has been more aggressive than its rivals in selling hotels to investors and operating them under the Marriott name. This vertical arrangement has paid off handsomely for the company.
>
> Typically, Marriott puts up its money to build a hotel and then sells it to a group of investors—an insurance company, a limited partnership, or a real estate investment trust—that get the tax breaks and some of the hotel's cash flow. Marriott then manages the property in return for about 5 percent of the hotel's revenues and 20 percent of its operating profits. In 1985, about 43,000 of Marriott's 61,000 rooms operated under this arrangement, more than its rivals. (Roughly 10,000 rooms were franchised to others and 7,900 were owned by Marriott outright.)
>
> Its management system uses as its foundation a multivolume *Book of Knowledge* that contains tens of thousands of instructions. Marriott relies on it to institutionalize friendliness and consistency. The idea is for customers to find the same pleasurable experience in every one of Marriott's hotels. Because of its system, Marriott has been the most successful lodging operation in the United States over the last decade.
>
> *Source*: Leslie Wayne, "Marriott States Out New Territory," *New York Times*, Sect. 3, September 22, 1985, p. 1; David Elsner "No Room for Error at Marriott," *Chicago Tribune*, Sect. 7, February 2, 1986, p. 1; and "Bill Marriott's Grand Design for Growth: Upscale and Down in the Lodging Market," *Business Week*, October 1, 1984, pp. 60–61.

to extended marketing channels, those distributive arrangements that dispose of previously used products.

MARKETING CHANNELS FOR PREVIOUSLY USED MATERIALS AND PRODUCTS

A major national and international public policy challenge is how to husband the world's scarce resources. Part of that challenge relates to the disposition of products once original users no longer derive utility from them.[52] If ways can be found to increase the utility of previously used products, scarce resources will be spared.

Marketing channels can play an important role in extending the useful life of many products. The subject of this section of the chapter is how to apply marketing channels to increase the utility of previously used materials (i.e., recyclable materials such as paper, aluminum, and glass) and used durable goods.

[52] For a more in-depth discussion of product disposition, see Jacob Jacoby, Carol K. Berning, and Thomas F. Dietvorst, "What About Disposition?," *Journal of Marketing*, Vol. 41 (April 1977), pp. 22–28.

Marketing Channels for Recycling Used Materials [53]

As we saw in Chapter 8, one very basic problem facing marketing channels management is to design channel structures that can perform the marketing functions effectively, efficiently, equitably, and profitably. Recycling used materials is a classic illustration of this problem.

> Buyers currently pay low prices for used materials (bottles, cans, paper, etc.). On the other hand, the costs of collecting these goods, sorting them, and transporting them to recycling plants is quite high. Because of the price-cost structure of this market, the recycling industry relies heavily on civic and community groups, who use volunteer help in the collection process. Normal business costs are usually absent when these groups handle the collection because labor and vehicles are generally donated. However, one of the problems in relying on these groups is that their efforts are generally sporadic, at best. Furthermore, the waste problem is growing faster than the membership of ecology-minded groups.

Thus, current marketing channels for recyclable materials do not appear to be very effective, very efficient, very equitable, or very profitable. To understand better how this can be overcome, a closer look at channels for recyclable materials is needed.

For these materials, traditional channel concepts must be reversed because, in the case of soft drinks especially, the consumer is the *producer* of the waste materials (e.g., bottles and cans) that are to be recycled. Thus, the consumer becomes the first to link in the recycling channel of distribution rather than the last. The recycling of waste materials is essentially a ''reverse distribution'' process. [54]

The contrast between forward and reverse channels is illustrated in Figure 13-11 and Table 13-4. The reverse-direction channel returns reusable waste products from consumer to producer.

> Conceptually, reverse distribution is identical to the traditional channel of distribution. The consumer has a product to sell, and in essence, he assumes the same position as a manufacturer selling a new product. The consumer's (seller's) role is to distribute his waste materials to the market that demands his product. [55]

However, most consumers do not consider themselves to be producers of waste materials. Therefore, they are not really concerned with planning marketing

[53] The discussion of marketing channels for recycling services is drawn primarily from an unpublished term paper by Sam B. Dunbar, Jr., ''The Recycling of Waste Products: Effects on Distribution Channels and Marketing.''

[54] William G. Zikmund and William J. Stanton, ''Recycling Solid Wastes: A Channels-of-Distribution Problem,'' *Journal of Marketing*, Vol. 35 (July 1971), pp. 34–35.

[55] Ibid., p. 35.

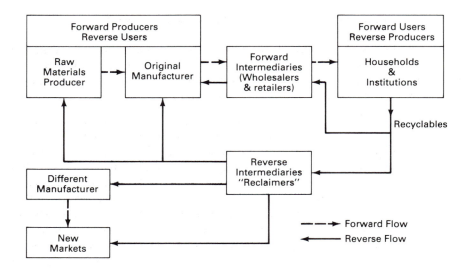

Figure 13-11 Forward and reverse channels of distribution. *Source*: Joseph Guiltinan and Nonyelu Nwokoye, "Reverse Channels for Recycling: An Analysis of Alternatives and Public Policy Implications," in Ronald C. Curhan (ed.), 1974 *Combined Proceedings* (Chicago: American Marketing Association, 1975), p. 341.

TABLE 13-4 Forward versus Reverse Channels: Some Key Distinctions

Forward Channels	Reverse Channels
Products:	
High unit value	Low unit value
Highly differentiated	Little or no differentiation
Much product innovation	Little or no innovation
Few producers	Many originators
Markets:	
Routinized transactions established	Routinized transactions not established
Many final users	Few final users
Varied customer demands	Standardized demands
Supply often less than or equal to demand	Supply typically greater than demand
Large assortment discrepancy	Small assortment discrepancy
Key Functions:	
Assorting	Sorting
Allocation	Accumulation
Heavy promotional effort	Low promotional effort
Speculative inventories	Few speculative inventories
Packaging	Collection

Source: Reprinted from *1974 Combined Proceedings*, published by the American Marketing Association (Chicago, 1975), "Reverse Channels for Recycling: An Analysis of Alternatives and Public Policy Implications," Ronald C. Curhan (ed.), by Joseph Guiltinan and Nonyelu Nwokoye, p. 342.

strategies for their products—reusable wastes. When producers are unaware of or indifferent to the fact that they indeed *are* producers, the problem becomes acute. If effective reverse channels of distribution are to be realized the ultimate consumers must be motivated to start the reverse flow.

In addition, channel members must cooperate to a much greater degree in reversing the physical flow than they presently do. Coordination among reverse channel members is essential if the sorting, storage, payment, and other functions are to be performed successfully.[56] Absent legislation mandating recycling efforts (or taxing noncompliers) and without profit incentives, getting intermediaries to participate more heavily in reverse channels may depend on appealing to their higher sense of social responsibility.

Should commercial interest in recycling pick up, several new types of recycling intermediaries are likely to grow in importance. One of these is the *reclamation or recycling center*. The reclamation center is really a modernized junk yard placed in a convenient location for the customer. These centers pay an equitable amount for their waste goods and do the initial processing of the waste materials.

Aluminum producers, can makers, and beverage distributors have set up more than 2,000 recycling centers across the U.S.A. Some producers even send trucks to neighborhoods to pick up cans.[57]

In addition to recycling centers, *central processing warehouses* can be developed by existing intermediaries in traditional channels. At these warehouses, recyclable products are stored and limited processing operations on waste material can be performed.

Aluminum can producers are equipping beverage distributors with can flattners, shredders, compactors, and truck trailers to encourage them to accept empties for recycling.[58]

Transportation cost is a major barrier to such recycling efforts, however. Other possibilities are such reverse channels as *manufacturer-controlled recycling centers, joint-venture resource recovery centers*, and *secondary dealers*.[59]

[56] James H. Barnes, Jr., "Recycling: A Problem in Reverse Logistics," *Journal of Macromarketing*, Vol. 2 (Fall 1982), pp. 31–37.

[57] "Recycling Ease Gives Aluminum an Edge over Steel in Beverage-Can Market Battle," *Wall Street Journal*, January 2, 1980, p. 28.

[58] Ibid.

[59] For a discussion of these latter channels, see Joseph Guiltinan and Nonyelu Nwokoye, "Reverse Channels for Recycling: An Analysis of Alternatives and Public Policy Implications," in Ronald C. Curhan (ed.), *1974 Combined Proceedings* (Chicago: American Marketing Association, 1975), pp. 343–344; and Zikmund and Stanton, "Recycling Solid Wastes," p. 38.

The development of reverse channels of distribution has been influenced by federal, state, and local legislation directed at all phases of protecting the environment.

Reverse channels have received considerable impetus in states that have enacted "bottle bills" banning nonreturnable drink containers. Oregon, Vermont, Michigan, Massachusetts, South Dakota, and several other states now have such recycling laws. The Oregon Minimum Deposit Act is the most comprehensive recycling law. It requires retailers and distributors to accept and pay refunds on all empty cans and bottles of the kind, size, and brands sold by them.

As more states, counties, and localities enact recycling laws, reverse distribution channels will become a permanent part of the distribution structure in the United States.[60]

Extended Channels of Distribution for Used Durable Goods

Extended channels are those marketing channels in which used durable goods are remanufactured, repaired, or resold.[61] As with forward marketing channels for new products extended marketing channels may be characterized according to their administrative patterns (see Chapter 9). Thus, extended marketing channels may be centrally coordinated to a greater or lesser degree.

Used furniture, musical instruments, sporting goods, bicycles, minor electrical appliances, typewriters, and child-related durables are marketed through *personal channels*.[62] Most of these goods are sold directly to other households through classified ads, outdoor advertising, personal contacts and garage sales. Unwanted used goods are also donated directly to other households or to charitable institutions, such as Goodwill Industries and the Salvation Army. These organizations then act as intermediaries in extended channels.[63]

These personal channels are considered conventional marketing channels since there is little coordination among channel members. Some people who sell or

[60] Peter M. Ginter and Jack M. Starling, "Reverse Distribution Channels for Recycling," *California Management Review*, Spring 1978, pp. 77 and 78.

[61] Norman Kangun, James R. Brown, and Russell Laczniak, "Formalizing Extended Channels of Distribution for Used Durable Goods—Some Suggestions," paper presented at the 1986 Macromarketing Conference, Boulder, Colo., August, 1986, p. 2.

[62] Dean S. Roussos, "Acquisition and Discarding of Used Household Durable Goods," unpublished working paper, Youngstown State University, 1975.

[63] Kangun et al., "Formalizing Extended Channels of Distribution," pp. 14–15.

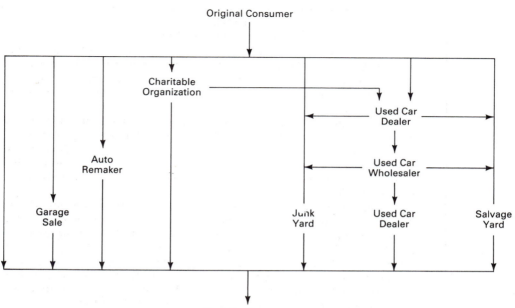

Figure 13-12 A simplified marketing channel structure for used automobiles. *Source*: Adapted from Norman Kangun, James R. Brown and Russell Laczniak, "Formalizing Extended Channels of Distribution for Used Durable Goods—Some Suggestions," paper presented at the 1986 Macromarketing Conference, Boulder, Colo., August 1986, p. 23.

donate used items are not likely to care what happens to them. These channels have very little, if any, marketing programming.

On the other hand, some extended channels are vertically integrated. As Exhibit 13-8 illustrates, the marketing channel for used Boeing commercial airliners is a more organized one.

Perhaps applying the basic aspects of marketing channel management to extended channels can be best understood from an in-depth example. The following section discusses marketing channels for used cars.

Extended Marketing Channels for Automobiles [64]

As illustrated in Figure 13-12, used cars are marketed through a variety of extended channel structures. Extended channels may be short, sometimes called *direct*; for example, when the original consumer sells directly to the used car buyer. They may also be long, or *indirect*, for example, when new car dealers sell their trade-ins through automobile wholesalers to used car dealers.

Used car buyers are less willing to devote as much time and effort to shopping as are buyers of new cars. Consequently, the distribution intensity of used car channels is more intensive than that for new ones.

[64] This section is largely based on ibid., pp. 12–13.

EXHIBIT 13-8
The Market for Used Commercial Aircraft[a]

Prior to the early 1980s, airlines routinely sold used aircraft to one another. Buying used equipment was one way an airline could quickly add to its capacity in order to respond to increasing demand. Selling used planes enabled an airline to rid itself of obsolete planes or to eliminate excess capacity.

In the early 1980s, the market for used commercial airliners rapidly expanded. In 1983, industry analysts estimated that there were over 500 transactions involving hundreds of used aircraft that year.[b] Boeing also estimated in 1983 that of the 400 or so airlines flying planes around the world, only 16 percent bought them new, compared with 65 percent just five years prior.[c]

One reason for the increased interest in these jets was the glut of used aircraft. Because orders for new planes were down in the early 1980s, the airlines pushed commercial aircraft manufacturers like Boeing and McDonnell Douglas to accept trade-ins as part of their new plane purchases. Thus, major aircraft manufacturers reluctantly entered the used airplane business, competing against such brokers as the Arizona-based Evergreen Air Center and International Lease Finance Corporation of Los Angeles.

Naturally, the aircraft makers preferred not to have to deal with used planes. First of all, used aircraft affected the market for new jets, although airplane producers hoped that buyers would eventually trade up to new jets. Second, manufacturers really didn't like to pay for storing used aircraft. McDonnell Douglas avoided this by allowing airlines to continue to fly their trade-ins while it tried to find buyers for those planes. Finally, aircraft makers worried that they might get stuck with hangars full of unsalable jets, particularly as those planes became increasingly obsolete.

Meanwhile, the airlines' demand for used jets increased. Fuel costs leveled off at the same time that interest rates rose, so flying used aircraft became an economical alternative to operating a shiny new fleet, in spite of their lower fuel efficiency. And with proper maintenance, these used jets could be operated just as safely as the new ones.[d]

The demand for used planes was also stimulated by deregulation in the commercial airline industry.[e] Deregulation spawned many new carriers, some of which decided to operate as low-cost airlines. To pull off this strategy, these firms greatly needed cheaper aircraft, and used jets provided a perfect solution. For example, the now defunct People Express started in 1981 by buying, at $3.7 million apiece, 17 Boeing 737s formerly owned by Lufthansa. People Express saved over $8 million per plane by shunning new aircraft.

[a] Unless otherwise noted, this exhibit is based upon Roy J. Harris, Jr. and Norman Thorpe, "Commercial-Jet Makers Are Trying to Cut Big Stockpile of Used Planes," *Wall Street Journal*, July 18, 1983.

[b] "The Hot Martket in Used Jets," *Newsweek*, December 5, 1983, p. 90.

[c] ibid.

[d] ibid.

[e] This paragraph is based upon ibid.

EXHIBIT 13-9

**An Important Link in Extended Marketing
Channels: Remanufacturers**

David R. Leggett (founder of Automotive Import Recycling, Inc., an Allentown, Pa.-based remanufacturer of import cars, like Volvos and BMWs) "buys up old cars wherever he can find them. And many of his customers bring in their tired automobiles for remanufacturing. Each car is completely disassembled, and every part is carefully inspected. Broken parts are either repaired or replaced with new ones. Then the car is reassembled, the body painted, and new interior upholstery installed. After a final test drive, the car is given a new warranty: one year or 12,000 miles. For all that, his cars sell for as little as $9,000 each, less than half the price of a new model."[a]

Remanufacturing, such as that done by Leggett's firm, lengthens the economic life of durable goods. Thus, remanufacturing is becoming an important method of saving energy and materials.

[a] "A Growing Love Affair with the Scrap Heap," *Business Week*, (April 29, 1985), p. 69.

A new type of intermediary in extended marketing channels for automobiles, the automobile remanufacturer, is emerging. Not only do these intermediaries add the usual economic utilities of time, place, and possession, they also improve the physical form of the product (see Exhibit 13-9).

Many different administrative patterns are found in the distribution of used automobiles. Since most original consumers and used car intermediaries do not view themselves as parts of a coordinated marketing channel, most channels for used cars are conventional ones.

Corporate, contractual, and administered channels are all used to market used cars, as well.

The car rental companies Avis and Hertz own large fleets of late-model automobiles. They also operate their own used car lots to dispose of their used vehicles before they are no longer rentable. These lots are in large, concentrated markets where used car purchases are made often enough to justify them economically, where reconditioning can be performed in-house, and where fleet owners can maintain their quality images by retaining control over how their used cars aremarketed. Thus, Avis and Hertz operate *corporate, extended marketing channels.*

Franchise systems such as Triex (see Exhibit 13-10) also develop and perpetuate a quality image. By using national or regional advertising campaigns or by capitalizing on positive word-of-mouth, these

---

EXHIBIT 13-10

**Franchising in Extended Channels for
Automobiles: Triex**

Triexcellence, Inc. " . . . franchises used car departments of dealer-ships under the Triex brand name."[a]

Triex dealers take used vehicles from private owners on consign-ment and attempt to sell them as though they owned them outright.

Auto owners sign a listing agreement with a franchised dealer—the way homeowners list their homes for sale with real estate brokers—and the dealer tries to sell the car to a buyer at an agreed-upon price. . . . In merchandising, the listing method is similar to the consign-ment method. The seller retains ownership of the car until the dealer makes the sale.[b]

In other words, the dealers associated with this network act as agents for the private owners.

Sellers benefit from this service because the dealer performs many of the marketing functions for them. Indeed, "[t]he dealer who receives a negotiable fee for his efforts, sells the listed cars just as he sells his own—by taking them on his lot, preparing them mechanically, handling the advertising and demostrating, negotiating with the buyer and providing, if necessary, the financing or insurance."[c]

Belonging to this network benefits dealers in several ways. First, they do not take the risk of owning these used vehicles. They also have access to quality used cars, since the cars are better screened than they are at used car auctions. (Used car auctions is the chief form of wholesal-ing used automobiles.) Because of the higher quality, dealers are able to realize gross higher sales. The national listing also benefits dealers, enabling them to turn their used car inventory over much more rapidly. In addition, "Triex provides its dealers with business plans, sales training, service development and bonding against fraudulent actions, as well as the traditional franchising trappings of uniform signs, marketing pro-grams and local and national advertising."[d]

[a] Leonard Sloane, "Franchiser Seeking An Improved Image for Used Car Sales," *The New York Times*, Section IV, (January 6, 1983), p. 4.

[b] ibid.

[c] ibid.

[d] ibid.

---

firms can realize economies of scale. In addition, since they handle larger quantities of used cars than the corner used car lot, they are able to use economically computerized information systems to locate specific models of used cars. Without large quantities, such systems would not be feasible.

One disadvantage of corporate and franchise channels is the amount of investment they require. Owning and operating a wholesale or retail business takes both financial capital and expertise. Franchisors must bear the costs of developing and promoting the franchise system, while franchisees must invest franchise fees, pay periodic royalties, and so forth. Another disadvantage is that because of the standardized nature of their marketing programs, such channels are sometimes unresponsive to the needs of local markets.

Administered, extended marketing channels fall somewhere between conventional channels and the contractual and corporate ones. In administered channels, a minimal amount of control can be gained, while the large investment required of contractual and corporate channels can be avoided.

Ford Motor Company operates an administered channel for the used fleet of automobiles it handles. By simply coordinating auctions of these cars, Ford can avoid the problems of both the contractual and corporate channels for used automobiles.

As we saw with international channels, channels for services, and channels for usuable waste materials, the basic principles for managing marketing channels developed earlier in the text can also be applied to extended channels of distribution. A variety of other contexts for examining marketing channel structure and behavior exist. Many of these channels trade in contraband, such as gambling, prostitution, drugs, and arms. Again, the same principles we have examined apply to these underground distributive systems.

SUMMARY

The basic tenets of marketing channel management presented in the first twelve chapters of the text were largely developed in the context of new, tangible goods. The objective of this chapter was to illustrate that these same basic principles apply to other contexts. The key contexts addressed in this chapter were channels for international trade, channels for services, and channels for previously used goods and materials.

Because of the importance of international trade to the U.S. economy as a whole and to individual marketers in particular, we discussed marketing channels in the international arena. Among the primary issues addressed were methods of entering international markets, international marketing channel institutions, international marketing channels for counter trade, and problems with entering international markets.

Four key methods of expanding into international markets were presented. *Exportation*, the simple exporting of a firm's products, requires the least investment, entails the least amount of risk, but provides the least amount of control over how the company's products are marketed. The second method, *licensing*, grants foreign intermediaries the contractual rights to market a firm's products or the rights to its production technology. Compared to exportation, licensing involves a bit more investment, a bit more risk, and a bit more control over foreign marketing strategy. The third method occurs when two or more firms share the investment, the risks, and the control in entering foreign markets. Such an arrangement is called a *joint venture*. In general, joint ventures require heavier investments, entail more risks, but allow for more control than either exportation or licensing. *Direct investment* requires the greatest financial commitment and risk handling of the four international expansion methods. It also gives international marketers the most control over how their products are sold.

A number of wholesale institutions unique to international channels were introduced. Among them were export management companies (EMCs), manufacturers' export agents (MEAs), compradors, norazis, trading companies, and combination retailer-wholesaler companies. Two key trends in international wholesaling were also noted: (1) increasing backward vertical integration and (2) the emergence of contractual arrangements between wholesalers and retailers.

The growing importance of barter or counter trade in international marketing was discussed, as were some of its inherent problems. Examples of channel arrangements for counter trade were also presented.

Among the chief distribution problems facing marketers attempting international trade are: (1) finding competent intermediaries to handle their products, (2) overcoming governmental and cultural barriers in selecting marketing channels, (3) shifting their promotional emphasis from pull to push, (4) living with the status quo orientation of many foreign wholesalers and retailers, (5) motivating intermediaries, and (6) maintaining control over how their products are marketed. Many of these problems can be alleviated by a thorough understanding of the environment and culture of foreign markets.

The marketing of services is another important context of marketing channels. The intangibility of services means that they cannot be stored or transported; thus, location is an important element of channel structure. While for-profit service organizations deal solely with resource allocation, not-for-profit service providers face the additional task of resource attraction. As with channels for goods, wholesalers and retailers are found in service channels. These marketing channels also employ administrative patterns similar to those used in goods channels. Conventional, administered, contractual, and corporate channel arrangements were illustrated in the marketing channels for health care and lodging.

The final context of marketing channels discussed in this chapter was the distribution of previously used materials and products. *Reverse marketing channels* funnel recyclable materials such as aluminum cans, paper, and bottles to manufacturers, which convert these goods into usable forms. The key challenges facing reverse channels are, first, getting waste producers (i.e., households and institutions) to see that they must initiate the physical flow, and next, improving the profit incentives to encourage greater participation in these channels. Used durable products are disposed of through *extended marketing channels*. Not-for-profit organizations such as Goodwill Industries and St. Vincent de Paul Societies are important intermediaries in extended channels for use merchandise. Large corporations like Boeing and McDonnell Douglas also participate in extended marketing channels. Both reverse channels and extended channels play important roles in protecting the world's scarce resources.

The key message of this chapter was that the same principles that guide the structure and management of domestic marketing channels for new products can also be applied to other contexts.

DISCUSSION QUESTIONS

1. The importance of the environment in designing marketing channels was discussed extensively in Chapter 2. One of the environmental elements stressed in that chapter was household resources, which impact the demand for marketing channel services. From library resources, determine the degree to which important household resources (e.g., automobile ownership, home ownership) are held in the United States and in Sweden for any given year. Discuss how those household resources have affected the structure of retailing in those two countries differently.

2. For each of the following products, describe the methods of international expansion used by foreign companies to enter the U.S. market.
   a. Renault Alliance
   b. Broccoli
   c. French wines
   d. Aprica baby strollers
   e. Yugo automobiles
   f. Lowenbräu beer

3. The chapter discussed several problems U.S. firms face in entering foreign markets. What problems might foreign firms encounter in expanding into the U.S. market?

4. For each of the marketing channel flows introduced in Chapter 1, diagram the marketing channel structure for rock concerts. Discuss why some of these flows take place in longer channels than others. Explain which administrative pattern—conventional, administered, contractual, or corporate—you believe characterizes this channel.

5. Higher education is an important service near and dear to all our hearts. Diagram the marketing channel structure for your university's educational services. Evaluate the effectiveness of this channel structure. (Hint: You might wish to reread the section on marketing channel effectiveness in Chapter 12.)

6. What are some feasible ways in which producers and potential intermediaries of reusable waste materials can be persuaded to participate more heavily in reverse channels of distribution? Be specific in your suggestions.

7. Describe the extended marketing channels for each of the following products in terms of their structure and administrative patterns.
   a. Homes
   b. Pleasure boats
   c. Machine tools
   d. Mainframe computers
   e. Office equipment
   f. Farm equipment

8. Exhibit 13-8 discusses extended marketing channels for used commercial aircraft. Using that exhibit, diagram the marketing channel structure for used airliners. Discuss the reasons for the channel lengths you uncovered. (Hint: You might want to refresh your understanding of marketing channel structure by reviewing Chapter 8.) Also explain how intensively you believe these used jets are distributed.

9. To free Americans taken hostage in Lebanon, the Reagan administration became involved in a rather complex and, to say the least, controversial, arms deal with Iran in 1986. As noted at the end of the chapter, the international weapons trade is yet another

context for studying marketing. Dig through the news accounts of this arms deal and construct the marketing channel structures for each of the following channel flows: (1) physical possession of both the arms and the hostages, (2) ownership of the arms, (3) financing, (4) negotiation, (5) information, (6) payment, and (7) risking.

Levi Strauss: Developing a New Market in Japan

Levi Strauss produces high quality blue jeans, denim pants, and slacks and shirts for men, women and children. The firm is located in San Francisco and exports its goods to various countries in Western Europe and Japan. Since international operations were begun in 1960, foreign sales have grown from $8 million to over $130 million. In 1968 Levi Strauss decided to market its product in Japan.

The company's most important product is the rugged, tight-fitting blue jean which dates back to the Californias gold rush days. The blue jeans were first sold to miners who needed durable clothing in their work. Levi Strauss's patent on the denim fabric expired in 1908, but the company has still remained dominant in this market.

A marketing research study found that young people under 30 in Japan would be a receptive market for Levi Strauss. The executive team at Levi Strauss determined that Japanese youth were quite fashion oriented and that their company name would be considered a status symbol. Consequently, the company's marketing program was directed to satisfy youthful preferences. Blue jeans were branded "Miss Levi" for the girls market. Corduroy slacks were manufactured in a variety of colors and styles and distributed through wholesalers.

Levi Strauss decided to market its products through traditional Japanese channels of distribution. Products were shipped to Japanese importers, who in turn resold the goods to twenty large wholesaling firms. These companies dispatched Levi Strauss products to local wholesalers. The local wholesaler sold these products to large department stores. Each wholesaler also carried other brands of jeans since there were about approximately 100 brands of jeans distributed in Japan. Figure 13-13 shows the many levels of the distribution system. Levi Strauss found that one of the wholesalers was not only distributing Levi Strauss products but was distributing his own brand as well to department stores.

Sales for Levi Strauss products were low but remained steady throughout 1969. Low sales were attributed to handling costs and the resulting high prices for Levi pants. Studies and investigations convinced the company that despite the

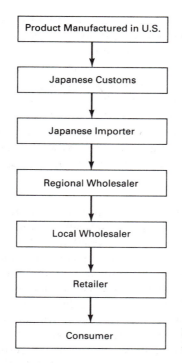

Figure 13-13 Marketing channels in Japan.

lengthy distribution channels, headway was made in establishing brand recognition. As a result, the company increased its shipments of goods to Japan.

In the 1970's, however, Levi Strauss began to reevaluate existing channels of distribution. Sales in Japan had declined over $860,000 annually. The company found that the cost of Levi products was often 100 percent higher than its manufacturing cost because of all of the middlemen handling the items. For example, it was estimated that approximately 42 percent of Japanese wholesalers' sales were to other wholesalers compared to 19 percent in the United States. The wholesalers often favored local brands, and retail display efforts for Levi trousers were minimal.

Three teams of executives were given the responsibility for investigating the situation and formulating definite proposals. The first team of executives submitted the following report.

1. Although the company is facing many trials and tribulations in a foreign economy, it is essential that we continue to work within the Japanese marketing structure. Any variance from this policy will only serve to cause ill-will and undermine our position in the market.

2. The country is beginning to liberalize its business regulations in view of more efficient marketing techniques. Traditional distribution methods will soon be outmoded and the system will become more viable.

3. In the short run, perhaps six months to a year, sales may grow slowly but the company can build its reputation, advertise its product and promote good

will. The company will gain approval from the government as well as from consumers. This will enhance brand recognition and sales, once the traditional channels of distribution give way.

4. Effective communication with wholesalers can break down existing and potential marketing barriers. The company's product should be explained, objectives should be established, and mutual interests explored. Their business style should be discerned and accepted.

5. Rising incomes and improved standards of living have given rise to a consumption oriented middle class. New purchasing habits are resulting in greater demands for consumer items, including western-style clothing and ready-made apparel.

The second team of executives did not share the first team's hope that the existing distribution channels in Japan would become outmoded in a short period of time. The second team recommended that the company continue with the present marketing channels, but investigate either building a plant in Japan or establishing relationships with a Japanese clothing manufacturer. These executives believed that the import fees would be eliminated, and perhaps once the Company was established in Japan, the firm could deal directly with regional wholesalers and in some cases with local wholesalers. It was hoped that an alliance with a Japanese firm would give Levi Strauss a more desired image with wholesalers and department stores as well as the consumer.

The third team of executives disagreed with the first two teams in their report. This team was not in favor of working through the complex Japanese distribution system. This executive team emphasized that Levi jeans and slacks could be sold much more efficiently through distribution systems that were established by the company. Their long-range objective was direct distribution to retailers. It was maintained that the number of middlemen could be reduced and competitive promotional tactics as well as competitive prices could be implemented. This executive team cited Coca Cola as an example of a firm that successfully created their own distribution network in Japan even though it faced much opposition initially. Moreover, it was believed that once Japanese distribution channels were bypassed, demand for blue jeans would increase as a result of Levi's selling methods. The executives maintained that the Levi Strauss name was as well known as the Coco-Cola name. The third executive team cited that the complexity of the Japanese distribution network was too costly and too inefficient to continue to market Levi Stauss products.

QUESTIONS

1. Evaluate the recommendation of the first executive team to retain the present system of distribution. What problems might be encountered?

2. Evaluate the recommendation of the second executive team. What problems might be encountered?

3. Evaluate the recommendation of the third executive team. What problems might be encountered?

4. What distribution pattern do you recommend for Levi Strauss and Company? Why?

Source: Ronald D. Michman and Stanley D. Sibley, *Marketing Channels and Strategies*, 2nd ed. (Columbus, Ohio: Grid Publishing, 1980), pp. 569–572.

Index

Abrams, B., 380
Accounts receivable wholesalers' management of, 121–22
Adams, K.A., 108
Administered marketing channel systems, 274–77, 302, 378
Administrative patterns, 238, 269–319, 493–96
  case studies of, 303–19
  conventional channels, 271, 272–74, 302
  vertical channel systems, 271, 274–300, 302
Advertising, 87–89, 164, 166–69
Agents, service, 476–77
Agent wholesalers, 103–4, 106, 108
Aging of U.S. population, 29–31
Air transportation, 159–60
Alderson, W., 7, 98
Alexander, R.S., 111
Allowances, 190–91, 195
Allvine, F.C., 202
Alpert, M.I., 193
Anand, P., 340
Anderson, E., 464
Andreason, A.R., 389
Applebaum, W., 77
Arbeit, S.P., 52
Arbitration, 372–74
Arndt, J., 467
Assael, H., 367, 374
Asset management, 121–23
Assets, return on, 407
Asset turnover, 407
Assortments, creating, 10
Assortments, discrepancy of, 98
Atlas, J., 38
Atmosphere, store, 70
Attitudes, consumer, 36–37

Auction companies, 104
Auditing channel performance, 416–17
Authority, 334
Automobiles, extended marketing channels for, 493–96

"Baby boom" generation, 29–31
Bagozzi, R.P., 471
Baker, S., 209
Ball, D., 461
Ballou, R.H., 142, 143, 151
Bargaining mechanisms, 379
Barnes, J.H., Jr., 490
Barriers in choosing foreign channels, 471–72
Barter, 469–70, 471
Bass, S.J., 47, 48, 51
Bates, A.D., 37, 47, 48, 51, 55, 57, 58, 89, 90, 92, 410, 411, 443
Becker, R.J., 259
Beckman, T.N., 63, 66
Beier, F.J., 328, 349, 350
Bernhardt, K.L., 163
Berning, C.K., 488–89
Berry, L.L., 31–33
Biedermann, R.G., 372, 376
Blackwell, R.D., 37, 38, 42
Blattberg, R.C., 34, 35
Bonfield, E.H., 341
Bornholdt, A., 270, 281
Boundary mechanisms, 378–79
Bowersox, D.J., 142, 148, 152, 158, 426
Branches, manufacturers' sales, 104–5, 106
Brands, 83–84, 119, 184–85, 345, 347
Breaking bulk, 10
Brion, J.M., 261
Brokerage allowances, 195

Brokers, 104, 108, 476–77
Brown, J.R., 254, 264, 298, 336, 340, 359, 369,
    377, 393, 492, 493
Brown, J.W., 416
Bucklin, L.P., 65, 74, 115, 116, 238, 239, 249,
    298, 340, 386, 391, 394, 395, 397–99,
    477, 479, 483–85
Buesing, T., 34, 35
Burnett, S.C., 179
Bursk, E.C., 130
Business user, wholesaler's service to, 111–13
Byrne, H.S., 142

Cadotte, E.R., 359
Capital, forecasting future needs, 400
Capital costs, 57
Caplovitz, D., 389
Captive distributors, 104–5
Cardozo, R.N., 111
Cardwell, J.J., 246
Carman, J.M., 477, 479, 483–85
Carrington, T., 39
Cash-and-carry wholesalers, 101
Cash discounts, 189–90
Cateora, P.R., 457, 458, 467–69
Celler-Kefauver Act (1950), 54
Centralized exchange, 8
Checklist methods, 253–56
Clark, J., 270, 281
Clayton Antitrust Act (1914), 54
Coercive power, 331–32
Cohen, S.B., 77
Commercial subsystem, 17
Commission merchants, 104
Communication overload, 206, 207
Communication systems, 201–35
    cast studies on, 221–35
    electronic data interchange systems, 215–20,
        345–46
    elements of, 203–5
    noise, 205–15
Competition, 19–21, 146–47, 191–92, 389, 397–
    98
Competitive environment, 44–52
Comprador agents, 466
Conciliation, 371–72
Conflict, marketing channel:
    causes of, 361–64
    channel power to manage, 356–82
    consequences of, 364–69
    effective management of, 369–80
    interdependence and, 358–59
    nature of, 358–60

Consignment selling, 258
Constantin, J.A., 351
Construction costs, 58
Consumer attitudes, 36, 37
Consumer expectations of retailers, 69, 70–73
Consumer goods wholesalers, 114–17
Consumer life styles, 36–38
Consumer subsystem, 17
Contracts, typing, 187
Contractual marketing channel systems, 277–
    82, 302
Control:
    channel member desire for, 246
    framework for channel, 337–41
    international marketing and, 467–69, 472–73
    process, 341
    tolerance for, 340–41
Convenience stores, 74, 75
Conventional marketing channel, 271, 272–74
Cooper, M.B., 426
Cooperative advertising, 166–69
Cooperatives, 102, 279–80
Cooptation, 374–75
Coordination of flows within marketing chan-
    nels, 323–24
Corey, E.R., 212
Corporate vertical marketing systems, 293–97
Corstjens, M., 259
Costs:
    capital, 57
    construction, 58
    distribution cost analysis, 401–6
    retail, 71–72
    ultimate cost concept, 112
Cost-service orientation, 143
Coughlan, A.T., 464
Counter trade, 469–70, 471
Coupon promotions, consumer, 170–71
Courtney, P.L., 111
Coverage, channel, 243–46
Cox, R., 14, 202, 205
Craig, C.S., 346
Cravens, D.W., 30
Crawford, C.M., 436
Creaming approach, 80–83
Cronin, J.J., Jr., 410
Cross, J.S., 111
Cultural environment, 35–38
Customers as channel participants, 16–17
Customer service, 142, 143
    standards, 144–48

Dale, A.D., 157
Dalrymple, D.J., 77, 84

Darlin, D., 455
Davidson, W.R., 27, 47, 48, 51–53, 55, 63, 66, 69, 70, 78, 85, 280, 299
Day, R.L., 359
Decentralized exchange, 8
Decision models, structure, 259–61
Deflation, 56
Del Credere agents, 466
Demographic environment, 29–34
Department stores, 65
Depatos, 468
Dependence, 328–29, 330
Deregulation, 55
Dhalla, N.K., 180
Diamond, J., 283
Dickinson, R.A., 347
Dietvorst, T.F., 488–89
Diplomacy, channel, 378–79
Direct investment, 460–61
Direct product profit (DPP), 413–15
Discount houses, 67
Discounts, 189–90, 327
Discrepancy of assortments, 98
Displays, 90, 164–65
Distortion, 205–6
Distribution centers, 149–50, 151, 350–51
Distribution cost analysis, 401–6
Distribution saturation, 244–46
Distributive trades, productivity in, 391–95
Distributor chains, 118–19
Dixon, D.F., 390
Dixon, J., 151
Doebler, P., 116
Domain dissensus, 363
Doody, A.F., 27, 280, 299
Dower, J.B., 151
Doyle, P., 259
Drop shippers, 101
Dual distribution, 172, 287, 294
Dunbar, S.B., Jr., 489
Dunn, D.T., Jr., 472
Durable goods, used, 492–93
Dwyer, F.R., 339

Economic environment, 55–58
Economic order quantity (EOQ) formula, 153–55
Economy, importance of international trade to U.S., 457–58
Education, conflict management using, 376–77
Education, increasing levels of, 33
Effectiveness, evaluating, 385–88
Efficiency in market exchange, 7–10

El-Ansary, A.I., 46, 259, 327, 351, 353, 396, 416–18
Electronic data interchange (EDI) systems, 215–20, 345–46
Electronic shopping, 27–28
Eliashberg, J., 362
EMC (Export Management Companies), 465
Emerson, R.M., 329
Engel, J.F., 37, 163, 169–72
Environment, 26–61, 418
    changing consumer resources, 34–35
    channel leadership and, 339
    competitive, 44–52
    demographic, 29–34
    economic, 55–58
    legal and political, 52–55
    marketing channel structure and, 257–58
    productivity and, 396–97
    social and cultural, 35–38
    task, 17–19
    technological, 38–44
Eovaldi, T.L., 186, 187, 194, 195, 258
Equity, evaluating, 388–91
Ernst, R.L., 276–78, 364
Etgar, M., 32, 34, 272, 338–40, 363
Ethnic composition of U.S., 33
Evaluating channel performance, 383–452
    auditing, 416–17
    case studies of, 422–52
    effectiveness, 385–88
    environment framework for, 418
    equity, 388–91
    productivity, 391–401
    profitability, 401–15
Evaluation process models, 259
Evans, R.H., 144
Exchange, efficiency in market, 7–10
Exchange-of-persons programs, 375
Exclusive dealing, 186
Exclusive territories, 257–58
Expectations, consumer, 69, 70–73
Expert power, 332–33, 349–50
Exportation, 458–59

Farris, P.W., 190, 191
Fayerweather, J., 467
Federal laws, 53, 54
Feedback mechanisms, 210–11
Few, K.S., 202, 205
Financial industry, 55
Financial ratios, 406–12
Firat, F.A., 360
Flat, nonintegrated structure, 477, 481
Flows in marketing channels, 14–15
    coordination of, 323–24

Forecasting, 157, 400
Foreign investments in U.S., 462–63. *See also*
    International marketing channels
Franchise systems, 282–93, 345, 495, 497
Frazier, G.L., 336, 368, 378
Free-form corporations, growth of, 45, 46
Freight forwarders, 160
French, J.R.P., 329, 334
Friedman, W.F., 150
FTC Act (1914), 54
FTC Trade Practice Rules, 54
Fuller, D.A., 36
Full-function wholesalers, 99–101
Full-line forcing, 187
Functional costs, 403–4
Functional discounts, 327
Functional spin-off, theory of, 251–53
Functions in marketing channels, 12–14

Garreau, J., 33
Gaski, J.F., 336, 380
Gee, M., 74
George, W.R., 479
Ghetto distribution, 390, 391
Ginter, P.M., 492
Gist, R.R., 83, 84
Goal incompatibility, 361–62
Goals, superordinate, 370–71
Goodman, C.S., 390
Gorman, R.H., 359
Grabner, J.R., Jr., 205–7
Greene, R., 44
Greer, T.V., 225
Grether, E.T., 14
Greyser, S.A., 130, 166–68
Grimshaw, G., 132
Grocery retailing institutions, 86
Gross, W., 203, 206, 209
Gross margin return on inventory (GMROI),
    410–11, 412
Gross margin return on selling space
    (GMROS), 411–12
Guiltinan, J.P., 46, 272, 490–92
Gulledge, L., 165

Hackett, D.W., 287
Hacklander, E.H., 74
Haefner, J.E., 111
Hall, W.P., 283
Hamilton, R.N., 210, 211
Hannaford, W.J., 113
Harrigan, K.R., 182, 183

Harris, R.J., Jr., 494
Health-care services, 477–84, 486
Herman, A.S., 395
Heskett, J.L., 142, 160, 250, 349, 361, 365,
    473
Hierarchy of effects model, 168–69
Higby, M.A., 259
Hill, R.M., 100, 109, 111, 112
Hills, G.E., 30
Hirschman, E.C., 44, 52
Hise, R.T., 448
Hollander, S.C., 47, 348
Hours, retail, 70
Household, changing American, 31–32
House-to-house selling, 68
Howell, R.D., 336
Huff, D.L., 77
Hutchinson, W.M., Jr., 146

Identification, power based on, 334
Incompatibility, goal, 361–62
Independent markets, 21
Industrial distributors, 117–20
Inflation, 56
Information:
    needs, predetermining, 214
    power based on, 333
    productivity, 397–401
    from retailers, expectations of, 72
Ingene, C.A., 45, 397, 400, 401, 412, 414
Institutional life cycles, 47–51
Integrated marketing strategy, 141–42
Integration, vertical, 182–83, 477
    growth of, 45, 46
Intensity, channel, 172
Intensity of distribution, 179–82, 243
Interbrand and intrabrand competition, 191–92
Interdependency, 17–19, 358–59
Intermediaries, 7, 9, 472
    foreign-based, 468–69, 471
    promotional activities of, 163–66, 171–72
    in service sector, 476
International marketing channels, 454–73
    for counter trade, 469–70, 471
    designing distribution strategy, 461–64
    expanding into international markets, 458–
      61
    institutions and structure, 464–69
    problems in establishing and managing, 470–
      75
Interpenetration methods of conflict manage-
    ment, 374–78
Intertype competition, 45

Inventory:
  decisions, 153–58
  GMROI, 410–11, 412
  kanban system, 197
  wholesalers' management of, 122–23
Investment, direct, 460–61
Investment, return on, 409–10

Jacoby, J., 488–89
Jain, A.K., 77
Jain, S., 391, 467, 472
Japanese marketing channel, 476
Jenkins, C.H., 149
John, G., 336
Johnson, D.E.L., 484
Johnson, E.M., 399
Johnson, J.C., 144, 213
Johnson, J.L., 336
Joint membership in trade associations, 376
Joint ventures, 459–60
Just-in-time supply systems, 197
Justis, R.T., 282, 291

Kahler, R., 458, 465
Kanban inventory systems, 197
Kangun, N., 492, 493
Kasulis, J.J., 331, 336, 351
Kaufmann, P.J., 216–18, 220
Kaven, W.H., 484, 485, 487
Kelly, J.P., 479
Kelly, J.S., 361
Kenderdine, J.M., 115, 123, 406
Kerin, R.A., 129, 132, 312
Kilman, S., 371
Kinnear, T.C., 163, 169, 170, 436
Kirpalani, V.H., 469
Kitler, P., 184
Klein, F.C., 390
Koenig, H.F., 298, 336, 377
Koepp, S., 39
Koten, J., 380
Kotler, P., 15, 28, 29, 70, 127, 179, 235, 245, 262, 402, 405
Krasnoff, B., 43
Kriesberg, L., 337
Kroeten, T.T., 377
Kruglanski, A.W., 365
Kublin, K.W., 461
Kurglanski, A.W., 329
Kurtz, D.L., 399

Labor, forecasting future needs for, 400
Labor productivity, 58, 395

Labor unions, 53–54
Laczniak, R., 492, 493
LaLonde, B.J., 145
Lambert, D.M., 142, 143, 159, 160, 263, 416, 426
Language, specialized, 211
Laws, federal, 53, 54
Layout, store, 78, 81, 82
Lazar, W., 476
Leadership, 342–51
  framework for channel, 337–41
  by manufacturers, 342–44
  by physical distribution agencies, 349–51
  by retailers, 346–49
  by wholesalers, 344–46
Legal aspects:
  of pricing, 194–95
  of product strategy, 186–87
  of promotional strategies, 172–73
  of vertical marketing systems, 299–300
Legal environment, 52–55
Legitimate power, 334
Lehmann, D.R., 144
Leverage ratio, 407–9
Levine, J., 482
Levitt, T., 333, 334
Levy, M., 259, 412, 414
Lewis, E.H., 344, 345
Licensing, 459
Liebrenz, M.L., 461
Life cycle, institutional, 47–51
Life cycle, product, 178–83
Life styles, consumer, 36–38, 40–41
Lilien, G.L., 245
Limited-function wholesalers, 101–3
List prices, 189
Little, R.W., 342, 347
Location, 70, 74–78, 80, 151–53
Locational convenience, 239–40
Lodging services, channels for, 484–88
Long, vertical nonintegrated structure, 479–80, 483, 484
Lopata, R.S., 97, 104, 112, 122, 123
Lot size, 240
Lusch, R.F., 5, 82, 87, 88, 298, 351, 377, 406, 411

McCammon, B.C., Jr., 45, 115, 123, 258, 259, 271, 275, 280, 298, 299, 407, 409, 410
McCarthy, E.J., 101–3
McCulloch, W., Jr., 461
McDaniel, S.W., 385, 448
McLaughlin, D.J., Jr., 390
Maclayton, D., 416

McNair, M.P., 52, 65
McVey, P., 21
Magee, J.F., 142
Mahajan, V., 77
Mail-order houses, 68
Mail-order wholesalers, 102
Makens, J.C., 71, 75
Makridakis, S., 157
Maldistribution, problem of, 160–61
Mallen, B.E., 251, 347
Manufacturers:
   channel management by, 342–44
   promotional activities, 166–71
   selection of wholesaler, 110
Manufacturers' agents, 103–4
March, J.G., 214, 377
Margin decisions, 84–85
Margin management, 121
Marketing channels:
   competition and management of, 19–21
   composition of, 12–17
   defined, 5
   as network of systems, 17–19
   structures, 3–12
Marketing mix, 196–98
   retail, 69, 73–93
   See also Physical distribution management;
      Pricing strategy; Product strategy; Pro-
      motion strategy management
Marquardt, R.A., 71, 75
Mason, J.B., 49, 74, 78, 81, 85
Mast, M.B., 469
Mather, I., 391
May, E.G., 52, 65
Mayer, M.L., 49, 74, 78, 81, 85
MEA (Manufacturer's Export Agents), 466
Media for retail advertising, 88, 89
Mediation, 371–72
Merchandise, retail, 70–71
Merchandise availability, 58
Merchandising agreements, programmed, 275–
   77
Merchandising decisions, 78–84
Merchand wholesalers, 99–103, 106, 107–8
Merrion, P., 333
Michie, D.A., 362
Michman, R.D., 55, 247, 503
Miernyk, W.H., 372
Millenson, M.L., 486
Missionary selling, 169–70
Mitchell, A., 36, 38, 39, 41
Mitchell, D., 150
Monroe, K.B., 71, 188, 190
Moore, J.R., 108
Morris, B., 373

Motion pictures, channels for, 273–74
Moyer, M.S., 387
Multinational corporations, 457, 470

Naisbitt, J., 32
Negotiation mechanisms, 379
Nelson, R., 79
Net profits/net sales (net profit margin), 406–7
Net profits/net worth (return on investment),
   409–10
Net profits/total assets (return on assets), 407
Net sales/total assets (asset turnover), 407
Nevin, J.R., 481
Noise, communication, 205–15
Nonstores retailing, 64, 67–68
Norazi, 466
Nwokoye, N., 490–92

Objectives, establishing, 241–42
Off-price retailer, 87
Omission, 205
O'Neal, C.R., 197
O'Neill, R.E., 82
Oresman, S.B., 160, 161
Organizational rigidity, 259
O'Shaughnessy, J., 144
O'Shea, J., 277
Ownership, channel, 248
Oxenfeldt, A.R., 192–94

Palamountain, J.C., Jr., 365
Parsons, L.J., 84
Partners, choosing channel, 261–65
Patronage motives, customer, 244, 245
Peacock, P., 34, 35
Perceptions of reality, differing, 208–9, 363–64
Performance:
   conflict and effect on, 365–66
   controls, customer service, 147–48
   quantitative and qualitative measures of
      channel, 416, 417
   See also Evaluating channel performance
Perreault, W.D., Jr., 101–3, 147
Person, M., 150
Personal channels, 492–93
Personal computer retailing, 80
Personal interaction, customer expectations
   of, 72
Personal selling, 89–90, 164
Peters, J.I., 361

Peterson, R.A., 129, 132, 312
Physical distribution management, 142–62
  channel management by agencies, 349–51
  concept, 142, 143–44
  customer service standards, 144–48
  inventory decisions, 153–58
  problem of "maldistribution," 160–61
  transportation decisions, 158–60
  warehousing decisions, 148–53
Piggybacking, 458
Pintel, G., 283
Pipeline carriers, 159
Polarization in retailing, 49–52
Political environment, 52–55
Population, U.S., 29–33
Porter, M.E., 294, 295, 343, 348
Postponement-speculation, principle of, 249–51
Power, channel, 320–55
  bases of, 329–37, 339–40, 349–50
  coordinating flows within channels, 323–24
  dependence as foundation of, 328–29, 330
  determining required level of services, 324–26
  identifying necessary tasks in channel, 326–28
  leadership, 342–51
  to manage conflict, 356–82
  strategies to specify channel roles, 328–41
Premiums, consumer, 90–91
Price, retail, 71–72
Price discrimination, 195
Pricing strategy, 177–78, 188–96
Private-label brands, 83–84, 119, 184, 345, 347
Private warehousing, 149–50
Producer cooperatives, 102
Product allowances, 191
Product demonstration, 91
Productivity, evaluating, 58, 391–401
Product life cycle, 178–83
Product positioning, 184–86
Product strategy, 178–88
Product variety, 240
Profitability, evaluating, 401–15
Profitable wholesale marketing strategy, 120–23
Profit and loss statement, preparation of, 404–6
Programmed merchandising agreements, 275–77
Promotional allowances, 190–91
Promotion strategy management, 147, 162–73
Propaganda, 376–77
Publicity, 91
Public warehousing, 148–49, 150

Purwar, P.C., 264
Push vs. pull promotion, 162–63
Putka, G., 30

Quantity discounts, 191
Quelch, J.A., 190, 191
Queuing, 213

Rack jobbers, 102–3
Rail transportation, 158–59
Rangan, V.K., 259
Ratchford, B.T., 393, 398
Rathmell, J.M., 476, 477, 480
Ratios, financial, 406–12
Raven, B.H., 329, 334, 365
Recession, 57
Recycling used materials, 489–96
Redundancy, 213–14
Referent power, 334
Refusals to deal, 187, 258
Remanufacturers, 496
Reordering decisions, 153–57
Resale price maintenance, 194–95
Resale restrictions, 258
Research, marketing, 388
Reseller solidarity, 258–59
Resources, changing consumer, 34–35
Retail cooperatives, 102
Retailers, 62–95
  alternative ways of classifying, 66
  channel management by, 346–49
  customer expectations of, 69, 70–73
  differing perceptions of reality, 364
  marketing mix of, 69, 73–93
  marketing strategy, 68–69
  productivity, 394–95
  segmenting retail markets, 73
  selection of suppliers by, 112, 264
  wholesalers' service to, 109–11
Retailer-sponsored cooperative, 279–80
Retailing:
  correlates of profit performance in, 410
  international, 467
  life-style, 38
  polarization in, 49–52
  of services, potential management problems in, 478–79
  structure of, 63–68
Retail life cycle, 47–51
Return on assets, 407
Return on investment, 409–10
Revenue, franchisor, 289–91

"Reverse distribution" process, 489–92
Reward power, 329–30, 349–50
Roberts, K.B., 416
Robicheaux, R.A., 327, 351, 353
Robinson-Patman Act (1936), 54, 172
Roe, R.G., 71, 75
Roles, blurring of male and female, 36, 37
Roles specifications, 327–41
Rosenberg, L.F., 205–7
Rosenberg, L.J., 44, 52, 361
Rosenbloom, B., 232, 254, 319, 365, 366
Rosson, P., 266
Rounsborg, R., 282, 291
Roussos, D.S., 492
Routinization of transactions, 11
Russ, F.A., 147

Sales promotion, 90–91
Samples, 164–65
Satisfaction, conflict and channel member, 366–69
Scammon, D.L., 194, 294
Schary, P.B., 306
Scheidt, M.A., 113
Scheuing, E.E., 399
Schnitzer, M.C., 461
Schuttle, T.F., 202, 205
Schwartzman, D., 386
Scrambling, 83
Scudder, C.D., 160, 161
Search process, facilitating, 11–12
Seasonal discounts, 191
Secrecy, 206–7
Segmenting retail markets, 73
Selective distribution, 243–44
Selling:
    consignment, 258
    house-to-house, 68
    missionary, 169–70
    personal, 89–90, 164
    systems, 112–13
Selling agents, 104
Selznik, P., 374
Sen, S.K., 34, 35
Sequencing, 213
Service, technical and warranty, 186
Service bureau, third-party, 218–20
Services:
    customer needs for channel, 238–41
    determining required level of, 324–26
    intangibility of, 473
    marketing channels for, 473–88
    retail, 72, 91–92
    sales of, 64
    of wholesaler, 98–99

Service wholesalers, 99–101
Sevin, C.H., 402
Sexton, D.E., Jr., 390
Shapiro, B.P., 5, 6, 12, 20
Shapiro, R.D., 142, 250
Sheffet, M.J., 194, 294
Sherman Antitrust Act (1890), 54
Shimaguchi, M., 476
Shopping centers, planned, 67
Shopping store, 75
Shycon, H., 144, 147
Sibley, S.D., 503
Simon, H.A., 214, 377
Single-factor productivity measures, 393–94
Siskel, G., 274
Site location analysis, retail, 77–78, 79
Skinner, S.J., 410
Sloane, L., 496
Smallwood, J.E., 47
Smith, L., 290
Smith, M.C., 416
Smith, T.K., 371
Smykay, E.W., 157
Social environment, 35–38
Solomon, R., 460
Spaldin, L.A., 87
Specialization, channel member, 15–16
Specialized languages, 211
Specialty stores, 65–67, 75
Speculation strategy, 249–51
Speh, T.W., 341
Spekman, R.E., 331, 336
Sprague, C.R., 144, 147
Stampfl, R.W., 53, 55, 69, 70, 78, 85
Standards:
    customer service, 144–48
    to motivate and reward personnel, 399
Stanton, W.J., 489, 490, 492
Starling, J.M., 492
Status quo orientation, foreign, 472
Stephenson, P.R., 113, 121
Stern, L.W., 46, 186, 187, 194, 195, 207, 216–18, 220, 258, 259, 328, 340, 346, 359–61, 365, 369, 370, 374, 416, 483
Stigler, G.J., 252
Stix, G., 208, 216, 218
Stock, J.R., 142, 143, 159, 160
Stockouts, controlling, 157–58
Stolle, J.F., 146
Stoops, G.T., 340
Storage in transit, 150–51
Store(s):
    atmosphere, 70
    displays, 90, 164–65
    layout, 78, 81, 82

location, 74–78, 80
positioning, 185–86
sales of retail, 64
See also Retailers
Strategic profit model, 406–12
Strategy:
    integrated marketing, 141–42
    international distribution, 461–64
    pricing, 177–78, 188–96
    product, 178–88
    promotion, 147, 162–73
    retail marketing, 68–69
    setting channel, 242–48
    of wholesalers, 120–23
    See also Consumer expectations of retailers; Marketing mix
Structure and design, channel, 3–12, 236–68
    choosing channel partners, 261–65
    determining, 400
    establishing objectives, 241–42
    for health-care services, 477–84
    impediments to, 257–59
    international marketing channels, 464–69
    of retailing, 63–68
    selecting appropriate, 248–61
    in services sector, 476–77
    setting strategy, 242–48
    understanding customer's needs for services, 238–41
    of wholesaling, 105–8
Sturdivant, F.D., 483
Summers, J.O., 336
Sunbelt, movement to, 32–33
Supermarkets, 67, 82, 321–23
Superordinate goals, 370–71
Suppliers:
    differing perceptions of reality, 364
    selection by retailers, 112, 264
    wholesalers as channel partners for, 109
Support, channel, 192–93, 246–48
Supraorganizational conflict-management mechanisms, 369–74
Swan, J.E., 113
Sweeney, D.J., 53, 55, 69, 70, 78, 85, 410
Systems competition, 45, 46
Systems purchasing, 113
Systems selling, 112–13

Tabak, R.L., 372, 376
Talarzyk, W.W., 38, 39, 42, 43, 63, 66, 229
Target markets, reaching, 38–44
Task environment, 17–19
Tasks, identifying necessary, 326–28

Tauber, E.M., 72
Taylor, D.A., 426
Technical service, 186
Technological changes, 27–28
Technological environment, 38–44
Technology, communication, 211–12
Terpstra, V., 458, 459, 464
Territories, exclusive, 257–58
Third-party service bureau, 218–20
Thompson, D.L., 77
Thorelli, H.B., 179
Thorp, M., 460
Thorpe, N., 494
Time, increasing poverty of, 32, 33–34
Timing in communications, poor, 207–8
Timing of retail advertising, 88–89
Tolerance for influence, 340–41
Total assets/net worth (leverage ratio), 407–9
Total-factor productivity measures, 393
Trade associations, joint membership in, 376
Trade discounts, 190
Trading area measurement and evaluation, 76–77
Trading companies, 466
Transactions, routinization of, 11
Transportation decisions, 158–60
Trawick, I.F., 113
Trombetta, W.L., 258
Truck carriers, 159
Truck wholesalers, 101–2
Turnover decisions, 84–85
Turnover ratio, 407
Tybout, A.M., 360
Tying contracts, 187

Ultimate cost concept, 112
Uncertainty absorption, 214, 377
United States:
    foreign investments in, 462–63
    population, 29–33
Universal product code (UPC), 211
Upah, G.D., 473
Urbany, J.E., 39
Used materials and products, channels for previously, 488–96

Vaile, R.S., 14
VALS (values and life styles), 37–41
Value, retail price and, 71–72
Value added, 393
Van Breda, M., 259
Vanderwicken, P., 475

Van Ness, P., 393, 394
Varadarajan, P.R., 171
Vaughn, C.L., 282
Vending machines, automatic, 67
Vendor relations, 92–93
Vertical channel systems, 271, 274–300, 302,
    487–88
  administered, 274–77, 278, 302
  contractual, 277–82, 302
  corporation, 293–300, 302
  distinctive advantages of, 297–99
  franchise systems, 282–93, 302
  growth of, 45, 46, 271, 487–88
  legal aspects of, 299–300
Vertical integration, 182–83, 477
Videotex services, 27, 38–39
Voluntary arbitration, 472
Voluntary chain, 279, 280, 345

Wadinambiaratchi, G., 456
Wagon jobbers, 101–2
Waiting time, 240
Warehousing decisions, 148–53
Warranty service, 186
Warren, R.L., 271
Warshaw, M.R., 163, 169, 170, 188
Wasson, C.R., 217
Wasson, H.C., 372
Water transportation, 159
Wayne, L., 488
Webster, F.E., Jr., 109, 117–19, 123, 361
Weigand, R.E., 21, 372, 470–72
Welsh, M.A., 339
Wheatley, J.J., 406

Wheelwright, S., 157
Whitmore, N.M., 387
Wholesalers, 96–139
  case studies of, 125–39
  channel management by, 123, 344–46
  international, 465–67
  productivity, 394–95
  rationale for emergence of modern, 98–99
  selecting and using, 108–20
  strategic management, 120–23
  structure of, 105–8
  types of, 99–105, 114–17
  wholesaling defined, 97
Wholesaler-sponsored voluntary chain, 279,
    280, 345
Widing, R.E., II, 43
Wikström, S., 28
Wilkinson, I., 368
Williamson, O.E., 257
Wittereich, W.J., 362
Wood, D.F., 144
Woodruff, R.B., 30
Workforce, composition of U.S., 33
Worthy, J.C., 297

Yalch, R., 127
Young, R.F., 166–68
Yuspeh, S., 180

Zikmund, W.G., 489, 490, 492
Zinszer, P.H., 145, 205